STRATEGIC MANAGEMENT

HARVARD BUSINESS REVIEW EXECUTIVE BOOK SERIES

Executive Success: Making It in Management

Survival Strategies for American Industry

Managing Effectively in the World Marketplace

Strategic Management

Financial Management

Catching up with the Computer Revolution

Marketing Management

Using Logical Techniques for Making Better Decisions

STRATEGIC MANAGEMENT

RICHARD G. HAMERMESH
Editor

JOHN WILEY & SONS, INC.

New York • Chichester • Brisbane • Toronto • Singapore

Library of Congress Cataloging in Publication Data:

Main entry under title:

Strategic management.

  (Harvard business review executive book series)
  Includes indexes.
    1. Management—Addresses, essays, lectures.
2. Corporate planning—Addresses, essays, lectures.
I. Hamermesh, Richard G.

HD31.S696389   1983   658.4'012   83-1336

Printed in the United States of America

10 9 8 7 6 5

Foreword

For sixty years the *Harvard Business Review* has been the farthest reaching executive program of the Harvard Business School. It is devoted to the continuing education of executives and aspiring managers primarily in business organizations, but also in not-for-profit institutions, in government, and in the professions. Through its publishing partners, reprints, and translation programs, it finds an audience in many languages in most countries in the world, occasionally penetrating even the barrier between East and West.

The *Harvard Business Review* draws on the talents of the most creative people in modern business and in management education. About half its content comes from practicing managers, the rest from professional people and university researchers. Everything *HBR* publishes has something to do with the skills, attitudes, and knowledge essential to the competent and ethical practice of management.

Strategic Management consist of 33 articles dealing with the problems and opportunities of conceiving and implementing corporate strategy. Neither abstruse nor superficial, the articles chosen for this volume are intended to be usefully analytical, challenging, and carefully prescriptive. Every well-informed businessperson can follow the exposition in its path away from the obvious and into the territory of independent thought. I hope that readers can adapt these ideas to their own unique situations and thus make their professional careers more productive.

KENNETH R. ANDREWS, Editor
Harvard Business Review

Contents

STRATEGIC MANAGEMENT

Introduction

RICHARD G. HAMERMESH

The collection of articles in this volume represents twenty-five years of contributions that the *Harvard Business Review* has made to the study of strategic management. It is not surprising that some of the best articles to appear in *HBR* have dealt with this important subject. Indeed, eight of the thirty-three articles in this volume received the McKinsey Award for the best article in *HBR* during their year of publication.

The purpose of this introduction, however, is not to praise the contents of the volume. Rather it is to place the field of strategic management in historical perspective, to explain the organization and content of the articles, and to speculate on future developments in the field. The reason for this approach is that the current popularity of strategic management (and of the word "strategy") has made it easy to lose perspective on both the history and substance of the ideas that have led to its widespread acceptance.

Strategic management had its genesis in the concept of corporate strategy that was developed in the early 1960s by a group of faculty members at the Harvard Business School. They taught the Business Policy course, which dealt with the tasks and responsibilities of the general manager. Although Policy had been a required course since 1911, it had resisted precise conceptualization. A breakthrough came as the Harvard academics began to collect detailed case studies on several companies within the same industry. Faced with data on many companies operating in the same industry, the researchers had to develop a way of understanding why some companies with very different approaches to their industry could succeed and why others that followed similar approaches were not equally successful. The concept of strategy provided an explanation.

Writings on the concept of strategy in this context were first published in 1964 and had three major propositions:[1]

1 Strategy was defined as "the pattern of objectives, purposes, or goals and major policies and plans for achieving those goals, stated

in such a way as to define what business the company is in or is to be in and the kind of company it is or is to be.''

2　Strategy entails two equally important and interrelated tasks: strategy formulation and strategy implementation.

3　The formulation of strategy requires the general manager to create a fit among:

    a.　The opportunities in the external industry environment,

    b.　The strengths and weaknesses of the firm,

    c.　The personal values of the key implementers, and

    d.　The broader societal expectations of the firm.

As illustrated in Figure 1, the concept of how to formulate a strategy is both succinct and powerful. It is succinct in the sense that it concentrates attention on the four major areas listed in proposition 3. It is powerful in that it helps to explain some of the anomalies that were suggested by the industry case studies. For example, companies can succeed with different strategies in the same industry by pursuing different opportunities (niches) within the industry that uniquely match their own internal strengths and weaknesses and the talents of their key managers. Conversely, a firm with a similar (but ''me too'') strategy would not be as successful if its strategy were not as consistent with the skills and resources of the firm. In the home appliance industry, for example, General Electric and Design and Manufacture are both very successful, even though General Electric's approach has been to produce a full line of high-quality branded products, whereas Design and Manufacture has produced a narrow line of private-label products. Westinghouse followed a strategy similar to GE, but lacked GE's skills and resources. Eventually, consistently low returns prompted Westinghouse to exit this business.[2]

The power of the concept of strategy did not go unnoticed by other academics or within industry. The 1960s witnessed the first round of explo-

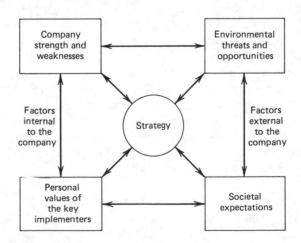

sive growth in long-range planning. By the 1970s long-range planning was renamed and reconceptualized as strategic planning. Soon, a number of consulting companies were formed that specialized in this activity.

In academia, Alfred D. Chandler's historical studies of the development of the modern corporation revealed important links between a company's strategy and organization structure.[3] Chandler's work not only inspired important subsequent research, but also underscored the important interrelationship between strategy formulation and implementation.

From these rather humble beginnings have come a wealth of research and ideas that has changed the way top managers think about and approach their task. Today strategic management is thought of as a way of managing a company whereby the overall strategy and purposes of the firm dominate decision-making at all levels and in all functions of the company. No longer is it sufficient for the chief executive alone to have a sense of where the company is headed. Strategy must be communicated with sufficient clarity so that it can dominate action throughout the organization.

The remarkable growth and acceptance of the strategic management concept can be attributed to its origins in the field of business policy and in the concept of corporate strategy. Strategic management is not concerned solely with advanced techniques of strategic analysis, nor is it limited to the mechanics of formal planning systems. At its best, strategic management is concerned with the role of top management in creating purposeful organizations and in formulating and implementing major goals and objectives.

It is this view of strategic management that has guided the organization and selection of articles for this volume. The five major sections—basic concepts, formulating successful strategies, strategic planning, implementing strategy, and the role of top management—reflect the breadth of the field. The articles themselves reflect the depth with which these topics are explored and their practical significance. It is this combination of the broad scope of the field, the important concepts and findings that patient researchers have added, and the orientation toward the practical problems of top managers that explains the impact and acceptance of the strategic management concept.

Contents

The five sections of this volume not only provide a way of organizing the articles, but also define the broad scope of the field. Within each section, some of the articles develop broad concepts and frameworks, whereas others present specific findings. We now turn to the contents of the articles and their relationship to each other.

Corporate Strategy: Basic Concepts

Despite the current profusion of writings about strategic management, it is important not to lose sight of the basic concepts that serve as the foundation of the field. In "The Big Power of Little Ideas," for example, Peter Drucker reminds us that successful strategies are built around simple ideas that enable a company to better serve a specific and narrow market. Business strategists do not have to be clairvoyant with regard to the future of our society or economy, but they do have to understand their own industry and be willing to welcome new ideas that change the workings and growth of their business. The importance of basic ideas to the development of strategy is the topic of Melvin Anshen's "The Management of Ideas."

While strategy begins with a basic concept or idea of how to compete in an industry, it is then necessary to translate the concept into specific business decisions. In "Key Options in Market Selection and Product Planning," Raymond Corey discusses four of these choices: what market to serve, what form the product should take, what the product should do for the user, and which customer group will find the product most important. Whereas Corey highlights basic choices that managers face in developing their strategies, Michael Porter provides a powerful framework for performing the analysis that enables one to make these choices. In "How Competitive Forces Shape Strategy," Porter argues that it is the threat of new entrants, the bargaining power of customers, the threat of substitute products, the power of suppliers, and the rivalry among current competitors that determine the degree of competition in an industry. "Knowledge of these underlying sources of competitive pressure provides the groundwork for a strategic agenda of action."[4]

The final two articles of this section deal with both the basic ideas and specific analyses and choices that are the cornerstones of successful strategies. Peter Drucker's "Managing for Business Effectiveness" highlights the managerial actions that lead to purposeful management. And in "How to Evaluate Corporate Strategy," Seymour Tilles suggests six questions that can serve as criteria for evaluating a strategy. Tilles' criteria emphasize that strategy should be bold and innovative, yet consistent with the resources and skills of the firm.

Formulating Successful Strategies

The first set of articles emphasizes the broad scope and basic concepts of strategic management. The articles in the second section report specific findings that have both increased our knowledge of strategy and enabled managers to formulate strategies that have a higher likelihood of succeeding in the marketplace. In general, the researchers were able to develop their findings because they were willing to focus on a specific set of strategic problems. Thus we find articles suggesting strategies for firms that compete in low-growth industries, companies that have small market shares, companies that compete in hostile environments, companies that compete globally, and small companies. The degree of specificity that the authors achieve in each of these articles is testimony to the progress being made in the study of strategy.

The two other articles in this section, "Market Share—A Key to Profitability," by Robert Buzzell, Bradley Gale, and Ralph Sultan, and "Pyrrhic Victories in Fights for Market Share," by William Fruhan, Jr., deal with the role of market share in strategy. Based on a study of 620 business units, the authors of "Market Share—A Key to Profitability" conclude that "on the average, a difference of 10 percentage points in market share is accompanied by a difference of about 5 points in pretax ROI."[5] Armed with this finding, the authors argue that establishing market share objectives is a basic strategic issue for management. In his counterpiece, William Fruhan, Jr., considers three situations in which the pursuit of market share led to lower performance. The disagreement over the significance of market share, which is highlighted in these two articles and which is referred to in the other articles of this section as well, has been a major bone of contention in the field of strategic management. As the articles demonstrate, however, it is an unfortunate disagreement. Market share or market share objectives cannot replace a well-developed corporate strategy. It is sound strategy that produces high financial returns and, in some cases, large market share as well. The relationship simply doesn't hold when it is reversed.

Strategic Planning

The acceptance of the concept of strategy and the specific findings about the content of successful strategies have led many companies to develop formal planning procedures that facilitate the formulation of effective strategies. The task is a difficult one, since the mere formalization of long-range planning can often be enough to squash the creativity and boldness that is so vital to strategy formulation. The *Harvard Business Review* articles on strategic planning have all recognized this problem and offer ways of dealing with it. None of the articles contains the standard lists of "do's and don't's" and "how-to-do-it" checklists that seem to have great appeal to staff planners but little relevance to general managers.

Richard Vancil and Peter Lorange, in "Strategic Planning in Diversified Companies," offer a thorough description of the two major dimensions of a formal planning effort. Vancil and Lorange describe how planning is both a multilevel and a longitudinal process. Successful strategic planning requires attention to both of these dimensions.

The next four articles offer practical advice for making planning work. John Shank, Edward Niblock, and William Sandalls, Jr., the authors of "Balance 'Creativity' and 'Practicality' in Formal Planning," for example, identify three categories of features that can be manipulated to influence the extent to which planning encourages either creativity and entrepreneurship or realism and practicality. Robert Linneman and John Kennell, the authors of "Shirt-Sleeve Approach to Long-Range Plans," examine the problem of developing flexible plans and strategies. Their "shirt-sleeve" process is especially relevant for smaller companies that lack a planning staff.

Myles Mace, in "The President and Corporate Planning," and Norman Berg, in "Strategic Planning in Conglomerate Companies," discuss the essential role of the chief executive in the planning process and the importance of allocating resources in a way that is consistent with strategic intentions. Berg's article also presents a thoughtful discussion of planning as a social and economic process.

As companies have gained more experience with strategic planning, they have been able to shift their attention away from the technicalities of the planning process to the substantive issues facing them. In "Strategic Management for Competitive Advantage," the authors discuss four phases through which a company is likely to progress as it gains greater competence and experience in strategic planning. The fourth phase, strategic management, is discussed in considerable detail. Philippe Haspeslagh's "Portfolio Planning: Uses and Limits" continues the discussion of strategic management. Since 1970, nearly 45% of the *Fortune "500"* have introduced portfolio planning to their strategic planning processes. Haspeslagh's article provides considerable data and reflections on their experiences.

Implementing Strategy

The articles in the first three sections deal with different aspects of *formulating* strategy. The articles in this section focus on the equally important task of *implementing* strategy. Just being able to conceive bold new strategies is not enough. The general manager must also be able to translate his or her strategic vision into concrete steps that "get things done." Yet despite the widespread recognition of the critical importance of implementation, many writings on strategy tend to overlook the topic. As reflected in the articles in this section, strategy implementation has not been overlooked in the pages of the *Harvard Business Review*. Rather the topic has been addressed often and sensibly.

The first two articles spell out the major task of implementing strategy that is to create a fit between the company's strategic goals and all of the activities of the organization. John Hobbs and Donald Heany, in "Coupling Strategy to Operating Plans," discuss the importance of adopting functional policies in marketing, manufacturing, engineering, and finance that reinforce and are consistent with the corporate strategy. Hobbs and Heany point out that general managers cannot simply assume that the announcement of a new strategy will be enough to ensure that functional policies reflect the strategy, since the basic character of the functions often leads to ingrained behaviors that are not easily changed. In "Beyond Theory Y," John Morse and Jay Lorsch discuss the need for developing management systems and processes that are consistent with strategy. In particular, the authors address the importance of creating a fit among the task or strategy of the company, its organization structure and climate, and the type of people who work for the company and are assigned to key positions.

One of the most powerful sources of influence at the disposal of the general manager is the incentive compensation structure. Yet all too often incentives are not linked to the goals of the firm and reflect short-term, rather than strategic, performance. In "Tailor Incentive Compensation to Strategy,'' Malcolm Salter discusses how the key aspects of incentive compensation can be employed so that they have a positive impact on a firm's strategy.

The development of corporate strategy inevitably leads to the need to develop new lines of business and to discard old businesses and products. Yet it is much easier to discuss business development and liquidation in theory than to put either into practice. The authors of "Phasing Out Weak Products" (Philip Kotler) and "Better Management of Corporate Development" (Richard Vancil), however, are able to address both of these topics in very practical terms. A six-step control system is offered to facilitate the recognition and disposition of weak products, and an ingenious approach to planning and control systems is suggested as a way to focus more attention on internally generated growth.

As Hugo Uyterhoeven points out in "General Managers in the Middle," the growth and diversity of many corporations have provided for an increasing number of middle-level general managers. These general managers play a particularly important role in the implementation of strategy. Yet, as Uyterhoeven emphasizes, these jobs are particularly demanding and require the skills to meet the needs of superiors, subordinates, and peers. Rosabeth Kanter, in "The Middle Manager as Innovator," continues the discussion of middle managers and shows how they can become a very positive force in the development of their corporations.

The Role of Top Management

No treatment of strategic management would be complete without recognition of the essential role of top management. Effective strategies are neither formulated nor implemented in a vacuum. It is only with strong leadership that organizations are able to deal with their futures in a proactive manner.

The articles in this section all speak of the need for top management leadership in the strategic management of companies. Reflecting the strengths of *HBR*, three of the articles were selected as McKinsey Award Winners for the best article contributed in their year of publication. Our lead article, and a McKinsey winner, is Abraham Zaleznik's "Managers and Leaders: Are They Different?" After developing a useful distinction between managers (administrators) and leaders, Zaleznik raises the crucial issue of whether today's large organizations foster the development of leaders. If they don't, or if a way cannot be found to combine the skills of managers and leaders, our industrial society is in for considerable turmoil.

The authors of "The Manager's Job: Folklore and Fact" (Henry Mintzberg) and "Good Managers Don't Make Policy Decisions" (H. Edward Wrapp) are concerned with the real world environment and work of top managers. Both authors go beyond clichés to explore the ways in which top managers actually provide leadership and direction to their organizations. Their conclusions seem to repudiate the "organized and rational" behavior that is typically attributed to top managers.

In the oldest article in our collection, George Albert Smith, Jr., poses thirteen "Questions the Business Leader Should Ask Himself." Smith's article predates virtually all of the "advances" in the field of strategic management. Yet the questions he raises are still relevant and serve to remind us that strategic management is essentially a simple concept requiring managers to see their environments, their organizations, and themselves as they are, not as they wish they were, and to manage their enterprises with integrity and a sense of purpose.

Our final two articles are more contemporary and raise the issues of how well top managers are answering Smith's questions and if the practice of strategic management is nearly as widespread as its publicity. In "Directors' Responsibility for Corporate Strategy," Kenneth Andrews argues persuasively for greater board of directors involvement in the formulation and ratification of strategy. His proposition bears repeating:

> A responsible and effective board should require of its management a unique and durable corporate strategy, review it periodically for its validity, use it as a reference point for all other board decisions, and share with management the risks associated with its adoption.[6]

Perhaps because so few boards have played the role Andrews suggests, we have arrived at the point where many are questioning the validity of American management principles. In their widely quoted and award-winning article, "Managing Our Way to Economic Decline," Robert Hayes and William Abernathy contend that modern management techniques, among them corporate portfolio management, are responsible for the deteriorating competitive positions of many American companies. Though their diagnosis is new (or was at the time it was first published), their solution is not. Rather it is consistent with other articles in this volume. It bears repeating:

> The key to long-term success—even survival—in business is what it has always been: to invest, to innovate, to lead, and to create value where none existed before. Such determination, such striving to excel requires leaders . . .[7]

A Prospective

This review of the articles in this volume has highlighted the scope of strategic management and the contributions the *Harvard Business Review* has made to its development. And while it is important to reflect on past developments, it is also worthwhile (but more difficult) to speculate as to the future of the field.

Two scenarios seem likely. Each shares the common element that in the future it is unlikely that strategic management will enjoy the same level of popularity that it does today. In the first scenario, those managers who have adopted the language of strategic management, but not its substance, will soon find themselves frustrated by its demands. As the popularity of strategic management wanes, the field could well head in the direction of other academic disciplines. A cadre of researchers will pursue more and more specialized aspects of the field and will communicate with each other at their professional conferences and in their academic journals. In time, branches of the field will be formally established, and eventually strategic management will dissolve into its separate specialties. In this scenario the combination of frustrated managers and specialized academics will lead to a rapid decline in the practice of strategic management.

In the second scenario, the declining trendiness of strategic management will not dissuade practitioners from finding new ways to apply and implement strategic management concepts or researchers from pursuing the full breadth and complexity of the field. Currently, the greatest needs are for work on the role of top management and on implementing strategy. But as emphasis is placed on these areas, there will be a need for additional research on formulating strategy and strategic planning. And new basic concepts and frameworks will be eagerly embraced by practitioners. In other words, there will be creative tension among the aspects of strategic management that will help to move the entire field forward in a way that captures and relates to the full complexity of the general manager's job.

Which of these scenarios will come to pass cannot be predicted with any certainty. What is more certain is that if the second scenario dominates, articles reporting the health of, and the advances in, strategic management will be appearing in future issues of the *Harvard Business Review*.

Notes

1. Edmund P. Learned, C. R. Christensen, K. R. Andrews, and W. D. Guth, *Business Policy—Text and Cases* (Homewood, Ill.: Richard D. Irwin, 1965).

2. See "Note on the Major Home Appliance Industry" in C. Roland Christensen, K. R. Andrews, and J. L. Bower, *Business Policy—Text and Cases* (Homewood, Ill.: Richard D. Irwin, 1973).

3. Alfred D. Chandler, Jr., *Strategy and Structure* (Cambridge: The M.I.T. Press, 1962).

4. Michael E. Porter, "How Competitive Forces Shape Strategy," *Harvard Business Review*, March–April 1982, p. 138.

5. Robert D. Buzzell, B. T. Gale, and R. G. M. Sultan, "Market Share—A Key to Profitability," *Harvard Business Review*, January–February 1975, p. 97.

6. Kenneth R. Andrews, "Directors' Responsibility for Corporate Strategy," *Harvard Business Review*, November–December 1980, p. 30.

7. Robert H. Hayes, and William J. Abernathy, "Managing Our Way to Economic Decline," *Harvard Business Review*, July–August 1980, p. 77.

PART ONE
CORPORATE STRATEGY: BASIC CONCEPTS

AN OVERVIEW

The field of strategic management is grounded in a number of basic concepts which have both strengthened and supported the subsequent development of the field. The six articles in this section present these basic concepts with unusual clarity and insight. These concepts can be divided into two groups: those that require managers to think broadly and futuristically and those that require managers to define their strategies precisely.

Peter Drucker's "The Big Power of Little Ideas" and Melvin Anshen's "The Management of Ideas" focus managers' attention on change and the future. Drucker writes:

> But the future always does come, sooner or later. And it is always different. Even the mightiest company will be in trouble if it does not work toward the future. It will lose distinction and leadership. All that will be left is big company overhead. It will neither control nor understand what is happening.
>
> By not daring to take the risk of making the new happen, management takes, by default, the greater risk of being surprised by what will happen. This is a risk that even the largest and richest company cannot afford to take. And it is a risk that even the smallest company need take.

To deal with the eventuality of change, both Drucker and Anshen recommend that managers proactively exploit the inevitable and shape their futures.

Whereas Drucker advocates pursuing "small ideas" that are consistent with future trends, Anshen's prescriptions are more specific. He calls for attention to technological change, social change, political change, and organizational change.

In contrast to Drucker and Anshen, the concepts introduced by E. Raymond Corey and Michael E. Porter in "Key Options in Market Selection and Product Planning" and "How Competitive Forces Shape Strategy" require managers to define their strategies precisely and in detail. Corey, for example, discusses at length the importance of defining precisely what markets to serve, what types and range of products to offer, what function the product should serve for the customer, and what customer group will most benefit from the product. Corey uses the example of Crown Cork and Seal to illustrate the detail with which each of these areas can be addressed. Michael Porter's prizewinning article is equally specific. Porter calls for careful and detailed analysis of five forces which shape strategy as a prerequisite to the formulation of strategy.

The final articles in this section, Drucker's "Managing for Business Effectiveness" and Tilles' "How to Evaluate Corporate Strategy," introduce concepts that require managers to think both broadly and specifically. Drucker, for example, asks managers first to analyze their future prospects and then to make specific resource allocation decisions that are consistent with the analysis. Tilles also strikes a balance between specificity and forward thinking. For example, he asks managers to question whether their strategies are consistent with trends in the environment, but then to consider if the company has enough and appropriate resources to take advantage of its opportunities.

Taken together, then, the six articles provide an overview of the basic concepts underlying the field of strategic management. Equally important, the articles highlight both the dilemmas and difficulties that thinking strategically pose.

1

The Big Power of Little Ideas

PETER F. DRUCKER

No artist ever sat down and deliberately wrote a masterpiece, Somerset Maugham once pointed out; if he produces a work of art, it is strictly by chance. But if the business entrepreneur succeeds, it is not by chance, says Peter F. Drucker; it is because the small idea his business grew from not only met the needs of the future, but shaped the future as well. All great achievements start with small ideas.

☐   Is long-range planning for the big company only?

☐   Does LRP mean predicting what the future will hold and adapting company actions to the anticipated trends?

Many executives, judging by their actions, would answer *yes* to both these questions. But they are wrong. The correct answer to both is a resounding *no!*

The future cannot be known. The only thing certain about it is that it will be different from, rather than a continuation of, today. But the future is as yet unborn, unformed, undetermined. It can be shaped by purposeful action. And the one thing that can effectively motivate such action is an idea—an idea of a different economy, a different technology, or a different market exploited by a different business.

But ideas always start small. That is why long-range planning is not just for the large company. That is why the small business may actually have an advantage in attempting to shape the future today.

Author's Note. This article is adapted from my book, *Managing for Results: Economic Tasks and Risk-Taking Decisions.*

The new, the different, when judged in dollars, always looks so small and insignificant that it tends to be dwarfed by the sheer volume of the existing business in the large company. The few million dollars in sales which a new idea may produce in the next few years, even if wildly successful, look so puny compared to the hundreds of millions the existing businesses of the large company produce that these dollars are sometimes disregarded.

And yet the new requires a great deal of effort. So much so that the small company is often far more willing to tackle the job. This is why there is good reason for the large company to organize special long-range planning effort; otherwise it may never get around to anything but today's work.

But, of course, the small company that does a good job of shaping the future today will not remain a "small business" very long. Every successful large business in existence was once—and often quite recently, as in the case of IBM or Xerox—a small business based on an idea of what the future should be.

This "idea," however, has to be an entrepreneurial one—with potential and capacity for producing wealth—expressed in a going, working, producing business, and effective through business actions and business behavior. Underlying the entrepreneurial idea is always the question: "What major change in economy, market, or knowledge would enable our company to conduct business the way we really would *like* to do it, the way we would really obtain the best economic results?" The dominant question should not be: "What should future society look like?" This is the question of the social reformer, the revolutionary, or the philosopher—not the entrepreneur.

Because this seems so limited, so self-centered an approach, historians have tended to overlook it. They have tended to be oblivious of the impact of the innovating business person. The *great* philosophical idea has had, of course, much more profound effects. But, on the other hand, very few philosophical ideas have had any effect at all. And while each business idea is much more limited, larger proportions of them are effective. As a result, innovating business people as a group have had a good deal more impact on society than historians realize.

The very fact that theirs are not "big ideas"—ones which encompass all of society or all of knowledge, but "little ideas" which affect just one narrow area—makes the ideas of the entrepreneur much more viable. The people who possess such ideas may be wrong about everything else in the future economy or society. But what does it matter so long as they are approximately right in respect to their own, narrow business focus? All that they need to be successful is just *one* small, specific development. It is true that a few—a very few—big philosophical ideas do become footnotes in history books; however, a great many small entrepreneurial ideas become stock market listings.

Let us turn to history for some little ideas that have led to large results. First, let us note some ideas from which whole industries grew. (Afterward we will look at some ideas from which great corporations have sprung.)

Commercial Banking

The entrepreneurial innovation that has had the greatest impact was that which converted the theoretical proposition of the French social philosopher, Claude Henri Saint Simon, into a bank a century ago. Saint Simon had started with the concept of the entrepreneur as developed earlier by his compatriot, the economist J. B. Say, to develop a philosophical system around the creative role of capital.

Saint Simon's idea become effective through a banking business: the famous Crédit Mobilier which his disciples, the brothers Pereire, founded in Paris during the middle of the nineteenth century. The Crédit Mobilier was to be the conscious developer of industry through the direction of the liquid resources of the community. It came to be the prototype for the entire banking system of the then "underdeveloped" continent of Europe of the Pereires' days—beginning with France, The Netherlands, and Belgium. The Pereires' imitators then founded the business banks of Germany, Switzerland, Austria, Scandinavia, and Italy, which became the main agents for the industrial development of these countries.

After our Civil War the idea crossed the Atlantic. The U.S. bankers who developed U.S. industry—from Jay Cooke and the American Crédit Mobilier, which financed the transcontinental railroad, to J. P. Morgan— were all imitators of the Pereires, whether they knew it or not. So were the Japanese Zaibatsu—the great banker-industrialists who built the foundations for the economy of modern Japan.

The most faithful disciple of the Pereires, however, has been Soviet Russia. The idea of planning through controlled allocation of capital has been taken directly from the Pereires. There is nothing of this in Marx, above all no planning. All the Soviets actually did was to substitute the state for the individual banker. This was actually a step taken by an Austrian, Rudolf Hilferding, who started out in Vienna as a banker in the business bank tradition and ended as the leading theoretician of German democratic socialism. Hilferding's book, *Finance Capital* (1910), was acknowledged by Lenin to have been the source of his planning and industrialization concepts.

Every single "development bank" started today in an underdeveloped country is still a direct descendant of the original Crédit Mobilier. But the point about the Crédit Mobilier is not that it has had tremendous worldwide impact. The point is that the Pereires started a business—a bank with the intention of making money.

Chemical Industry

By all odds, the modern chemical industry should have arisen in England. In the mid-nineteenth century, England, with its highly developed textile industry, was the major market for chemicals. It also was the home of the scientific leaders of the time—Michael Faraday and Charles Darwin.

The modern chemical industry did actually start with an English discovery: Perkin's discovery of aniline dyes in 1856. Yet 20 years after Perkin's discovery (around 1875), leadership in the new industry had clearly passed to Germany. German businessmen contributed the entrepreneurial idea that was lacking in England: the results of scientific inquiry, organic chemistry in this case, can be directly converted into marketable applications.

Modern Merchandising

The most powerful private business in history was probably managed by the Japanese House of Mitsui, which before its dissolution after World War II was estimated by American occupation authorities to have employed one million people throughout the world. Its origin was the world's first department store, developed in Tokyo during the mid-seventeenth century by an early Mitsui.

The entrepreneurial idea underlying this business was that of the merchant as a principal of economic life, not as a mere middleman. This meant fixed prices to the customer. And it also meant that the Mitsuis no longer acted as agents in dealing with craftsmen and manufacturers. They would buy for their own account and give orders for standardized merchandise to be made according to their specifications. In overseas trade the merchant had acted as a principal all along. However, by 1650 overseas trade had been suppressed in Japan, and the Mitsuis promptly took the overseas-trade concepts and built a domestic merchant-business on them.

Mass Distribution

Great imagination is not necessary to make an entrepreneurial idea successful. All that may be needed is systematic work which will make effective in the future something that has already occurred. Typically, for instance, new developments in the economy and market will run well ahead of distribution. Organizing the distribution, however, may make the change effective—and thereby create a true growth business.

A Canadian, Willard Garfield Weston, saw, for instance, that while the English housewives had come, by the end of World War II, to demand packaged, sliced bread, there was no adequate distribution system to supply them with what they wanted to buy where they wanted to buy it. Because of this small idea one of the largest food-marketing companies in Great Britain was established in a few years.

Today similar distribution opportunities may exist in this country as a result of our massive shift to being a society and economy of "knowledge workers"—that is, people with a high degree of formal education who apply knowledge to work, rather than manual skill or brawn. Education itself is perhaps our biggest and fastest growing market—not only schools and colleges, but also industry with its myriad of training programs, the government, and the armed services.

The office supply market—which delivers whatever the knowledge worker needs to be productive, from paper clips to office reproduction equipment and giant computers—is therefore a major growth market. But while this industry and education are each becoming a true mass market, neither has mass distribution yet. The business that organizes distribution in either market today may well be the Sears, Roebuck of tomorrow.

Discount Chains

The rise of the discount house began in the late 1940s with the application of an idea developed by Sears, Roebuck and Co. almost 20 years earlier. Sears, Roebuck became our leading appliance seller in the 1930s when it began to use a sample of each appliance on the store floor solely to demonstrate the merchandise. The appliance purchased by the customer was delivered straight from the warehouse—which realized savings in costs of uncrating, recrating, and shipping of up to 20% of retail price. Sears, Roebuck made no secret of this; yet there were few imitators of this idea. After World War II there was one small Chicago appliance merchant who adapted the idea to other makers' products. Today Saul Polk is credited with creating the first and largest and one of the most profitable discount chains in existence.

Little ideas have frequently been the seeds from which giant corporations have grown. Here are a few instances.

IBM

Thomas J. Watson, Jr., who founded and built IBM, did not see the coming development of business technology. But he had the idea of data processing as a unifying concept on which to build a business. IBM was, for a long time, fairly small and confined itself to such mundane work as keeping accounting ledgers and time records. But it was ready to jump when the technology came in—from totally unrelated wartime work—which made data processing by electronic computers actually possible.

While Watson built a small and unspectacular business during the 1920s by designing, selling, and installing punch-card equipment, the logical positivists (e.g., Perry Bridgman in the United States, Rudolph Carnap in Austria) talked and wrote on the systematic methodology of "quantification" and "universal measurements." It is most unlikely that they ever heard of the young, struggling IBM company, and certain that they did not connect their ideas with it. Yet it was Watson's IBM and not their philosophical ideas which became operational when the new technology emerged during World War II.

Sears, Roebuck

The men who built Sears, Roebuck and Co.—Richard Sears, Julius Rosenwald, Albert Loeb, and finally General Robert E. Wood—had active social concerns and lively social imaginations. But not one of them thought of remaking the economy. I doubt that even the idea of a *mass market*—as opposed to the traditional *class market*—occurred to them until long after 1930. From its early beginning, the founders of Sears, Roebuck had the idea that the poor person's money could be made to have the same purchasing power as the rich person's.

But this was not a particularly new idea. Social reformers and economists had bandied it around for decades. The cooperative movement in Europe grew mainly out of it. Sears, Roebuck was, however, the first business in the United States built on this idea. It started with the question: "What would make the farmer a customer for a retail business?" The answer was simple: "He needs to be sure of getting goods of the same dependable quality as do city people but at a low price." In 1900 or even 1920 this was an idea of considerable audacity.

Bata

The basic entrepreneurial idea may be merely an imitation of something that works well in another country or in another industry. For example, when Tomas Bata, the Slovakian shoemaker, returned to Europe from the United States after World War I, he had the idea that everybody in Czechoslovakia and the Balkans could have shoes to wear as did everybody in the United States. "The peasant goes barefoot," he is reported to have said, "not because he is too poor, but because there are no shoes." What was needed to make this vision of a shod peasant come true was someone supplying him with cheap, standardized, but well-designed and durable footwear as was done in the United States.

On the basis of this analogy with America, Bata began without capital in a rented shack and in a few years built pre-Nazi Europe's largest shoe business and one of Europe's most successful companies. Yet to apply U.S. mass-production methods to European consumer goods was hardly a very original idea in the 1920s when Henry Ford and his assembly line were all the rage in Europe. The only original thing was willingness to act on the idea.

To make the future happen requires work rather than "genius." The person with a creative imagination will have more imaginative ideas, to be sure. But whether the more imaginative ideas will actually turn out to be more successful is by no means certain.

Creativity, which looms so large in present discussions of innovation, is not the real problem. There are usually more ideas in any organization, including businesses, than can possibly be put to use.[1] Ask any company—including seemingly moribund ones—this question: "What in our economy, or our society, or our state of knowledge would give our business its greatest opportunity if only we could make it happen?'' Dozens of responses will burst from management's lips. As a rule we are not lacking *ideas*—not even good, serviceable ideas. What is lacking is management's *willingness to welcome ideas*, in fact, solicit them, rather than just products or processes. Products and processes, after all, are only the vehicles through which the ideas become effective. The specific future products and processes often cannot even be imagined.

For example, when Du Pont started the work on polymer chemistry out of which nylon eventually evolved, it did not know that man-made fibers would be the end product. Du Pont acted on the assumption that any gain in our ability to manipulate the structure of large, organic molecules—a scientific skill at that time in its infancy—would lead to commercially important results of some kind. It was only after six or seven years of research work that man-made fibers first appeared as a possible major result area.

Indeed, as the IBM experience shows, the specific products and processes that make an idea truly successful often come out of entirely different and unrelated work.

But there must always be a willingness to think in terms of the general rather than the specific, in terms of a business, the contributions it makes, the satisfactions it supplies, the market and economy it serves. This is the entrepreneurial point of view. And it is accessible to the average business person.

Also, the manager must have the courage to commit resources—and in particular first-rate people—to work on making the future happen. The staffs for this work should be small. But they should contain the very best people available; otherwise, nothing will happen.

The business person needs a touchstone of validity and practicality for entrepreneurial, future-making ideas. Indeed, the reason some businesses fail to innovate is not that they shy away from ideas. It is that they engage in hopelessly romantic ones—at great cost in personnel and money. An idea must meet rigorous tests of practicality if it is to be capable of making a business successful in the future.

It must first have operational validity. Can we take action on this idea? Or can we only talk about it? Can we really do something right away to bring about the kind of future we desire? Sears, Roebuck, with its idea of bringing the market to the isolated U.S. farmer, could show immediate results. In contrast, Du Pont with its idea of polymer chemistry could only organize research work on a very small scale. It could only underwrite the research of one first-rate man. But both companies could *do* something right away.

To be able to spend money on research is not enough. It must be research directed toward the realization of the idea. The knowledge sought may be general—as was that of Du Pont's project. But it must be reasonably clear, at least, that, if available, the knowledge gained will be applicable to operations.

The idea must have economic validity. If it could be put to work immediately, it would have to be able to produce economic results. We may not be able to do *all* that we would like to see done—not for a long time, and perhaps never. But if we could do something right away, the resulting products, processes, or services would find a customer, a market, an end use, and would be capable of being sold profitably. In short, they should satisfy a want and need.

Finally, the idea must meet the test of personal commitment. Do we really believe in the idea? Do we really want to be that kind of people, do that kind of work, run that kind of business?

To make the future demands courage. It demands work. But it also demands faith. To commit oneself to the expedient is simply not practical. It will not suffice for the trials ahead. For no such idea is foolproof—nor should it be.

The one idea about the future that *must* fail is the apparently sure thing, the riskless idea, which is believed to be incapable of failure. The ideas on which tomorrow's business is to be built *must* be uncertain; no one can really say, as yet, what they will look like if and when they become reality. They *must* be risky; they have a probability of success, of course, but also a probability of failure. If they are not both uncertain and risky, they are simply not practical ideas for the future.

Conclusion

It is not absolutely necessary for every business to search for the idea that will make the future, and to start work on its realization. Indeed, a good many managements do not even make their present business effective—and yet their company somehow survives for a while. Big business, in particular, seem able to coast a long time on the courage, work, and vision of earlier executives before they erode and run down.

But the future always does come, sooner or later. And it is always different. Even the mightiest company will be in trouble if it does not work toward the future. It will lose distinction and leadership. All that will be left is big-company overhead. It will neither control nor understand what is happening.

By not daring to take the risk of making the new happen, management takes, by default, the greater risk of being surprised by what will happen. This is a risk that even the largest and richest company cannot afford to take. And it is a risk that not even the smallest company need take.

Note

1.   See Theodore Levitt, "Creativity Is Not Enough," *HBR*, May–June 1963, p. 72.

2
Key Options in Market Selection and Product Planning

E. RAYMOND COREY

In practice, marketing strategy for an industrial company is far more subtle and sophisticated than it is often made out to be. Instead of being the one-dimensional task often portrayed, it involves two dimensions. There is a horizontal dimension—what segments of the end-use market should the company serve? And there is a vertical dimension—on what level of the manufacturing process should the company concentrate? Along each of these dimensions management has a series of important options. In deciding on them, management should take into account corporate strengths and weaknesses, market opportunities, relations with customers and suppliers, the meaning of the product to the users, and other considerations. These options are illustrated in this article by the experiences of Crown Cork & Seal, Aluminum Company of America, and other companies.

In 1957 when John F. Connelly was elected president of Crown Cork & Seal Company, the company was on the verge of bankruptcy. A loss of $600,000 was reported in the first quarter of that year, a $2.5 million loan was being called by Bankers Trust, and an additional $4.5 million in short-term notes was due by the end of 1957. Only seven years later Crown Cork enjoyed a higher return on sales than its two largest competitors, as Exhibit 1 shows, and forces had been set in motion that led to rising sales volume and profitability throughout the 1960s and early 1970s.[1]

The main secret of the company's success—and Connelly's—was an understanding of marketing strategy. I believe the approach used by Crown Cork & Seal may prove valuable to other companies as well. But before abstracting and generalizing the concepts involved, let us look in more detail at the situation Connelly had to contend with.

Exhibit 1.   Sales and Return on Sales (After Taxes) for Three Companies

Year	Net Sales (in Millions)			Return on Sales (After Taxes)		
	Crown Cork & Seal	Continental Can	American Can	Crown Cork & Seal	Continental Can	American Can
1964	$218	$1,198	$1,292	5.1%	4.1%	3.8%
1965	256	1,234	1,337	5.7	4.8	4.9
1966	280	1,339	1,449	6.0	5.3	5.2
1967	301	1,398	1,522	6.3	5.6	5.0
1968	337	1,508	1,636	6.2	5.5	4.8
1969	371	1,780	1,724	6.2	5.2	3.7
1970	414	2,037	1,838	6.2	4.6	3.6
1971	448	2,082	1,897	6.3	3.6	2.6
1972	489	2,193	2,016	6.4	3.7	2.7
1973	572	2,540	2,182	6.0	3.8	3.0
1974	766	3,087	2,658	5.2	3.9	3.6

Source: Annual reports of the three companies.

Crown Cork & Seal was (and is) a major producer of metal cans, crowns (bottle caps), closures (screw caps and bottle lids), and filling machinery for beer and soft drink cans. With sales of $115 million in 1956, the company competed in an industry dominated by two giants, American Can (with sales of $772 million in 1956) and Continental Can (with sales of $1,010 million in that year).

The industry was and still is characterized by a high degree of technological change; glass, aluminum, fiberfoil, and the plastics have competed with tinplate to serve the packaging needs of more than 135 different industries. New and revolutionary concepts in packaging have emerged with developments such as the aerosol containers and the "pop-top" metal can. To compete in this industry companies must make large capital investments in can-making lines. In addition, the major can producers have found it necessary to invest large amounts in research and development.

A "fact of life" in the industry is the ever-present threat of self-manufacture by large users. For example, one of the largest manufacturers of cans in the United States is a user company, Campbell Soup. Another fact is the high cost of materials as a percentage of total manufacturing cost. When John Connelly assumed the presidency of Crown Cork, approximately 65% of the price to users of tinplate cans went to the tinplate producers. Thus value added by manufacture was only one-third of the value of shipments of metal cans.

Pressed on one side by rising material and labor costs, on another side by the threat of new low-cost materials, and on a third side by large, powerful customers and the threat of self-manufacture, companies in the metal container business have had to put up with typically low profit margins and prices.

The major manufacturers have responded to these conditions, first, by investing heavily in research on packaging materials, container design, and can manufacturing and using equipment. Second, they have diversified within the packaging field to provide a wide range of paper, plastics, glass, and aluminum as well as tinplate containers to a broad range of customers. Third, they have offered increased customer service in such areas as market studies, product planning, materials handling, and production layout and design.

Unique Strategy

John Connelly's strategic response in 1957 was significantly different from that of his giant competitors. He elected to concentrate on two product/market segments. One was metal cans for such "hard-to-hold" products as beer and soft drinks, and the second was the emerging aerosol container market. Both markets were growing rapidly. Both called for high skills in container design and manufacturing, thus reducing the threat of self-manufacture. In both market segments it was likely that metal would be the dominant material—and Crown Cork had particularly high skills in metal forming and fabrication. In the canned beverage market, Crown Cork had a particular advantage, since its machinery division supplied 60% of all the filling equipment used by soft drink manufacturers and 90% of the filling equipment used in the brewing industry.

In spite of the fact that Crown Cork had captured 50% of the huge motor oil can business when it introduced the first aluminum one-quart can in 1958, its management decided *not* to continue to compete aggressively in this market. Fiberfoil was rapidly emerging as the dominant packaging material for motor oil containers, and management felt that the cost economics of the paper can would give the paper companies a significant advantage. Moreover, there was a high risk of self-manufacture of such cans because the technology was simple, the product was standardized, and the oil companies required large quantities of these containers.

Connelly's decision to stay essentially with metal containers, based on a judgment that long-run requirements in the beer, soft drink, and aerosol markets would favor metal, allowed him to conserve considerably on R&D expenses and to focus these efforts sharply.

Connelly did commit major capital investments to plant improvement and relocation. In particular, he embarked on a program of moving plants to places where there were large concentrations of customers in his chosen markets. He designed his plants to serve the full range of customer needs, including prompt delivery.

The new strategy paid off. By 1974, Crown Cork had increased its sales to $766 million (see Exhibit 1). Consolidated net income was over $39 million in 1974, and earnings per share had grown from $0.01 (corrected for stock splits) in 1957 to $2.20 in 1974. As the exhibit indicates, Crown Cork outperformed its two larger competitors both in sales growth and in return on sales in the 1964–1974 period.

During this time American Can and Continental Can diversified widely. The former moved strongly into such customer items as Dixie cups and Butterick dress patterns, as well as chemicals, printing, and biomedical items. The latter company stressed forest products in its diversification moves, operating woodlands and mills for making building products and corrugated containers. Continental Can also added such diversified items as cellulose casings for meats and soy protein products. But Crown Cork continued to build its strength in the beer and aerosol container markets. In 1973, for example, it invested $40 million in new plants, of which $27 million was for drawn and ironed steel can capacity in the United States.

The success of Crown Cork after 1956 can be attributed to a wide range of actions, including a changed organization structure, a modified control system, constant emphasis on overhead reduction and top management leadership. At the heart of its success, however, are the choices management made with regard to markets and products. These choices might be divided into four categories. I shall describe these categories next, then return to Crown Cork.

Key Concepts

In problems of market selection and product planning, it is important to keep four key ideas in mind.

1.   What Markets Should Be Served?

The most important decisions in planning marketing strategy are those related to the choice of a market or markets to serve. All else follows. Choice of market is a choice of the customer and of the competitive, technical, political, and social environments in which one elects to compete. It is not an easily reversed decision; having made the choice, the company develops skills and resources around the markets it has elected to serve. It builds a set of relationships with customers that are at once a major source of strength and a major commitment. The commitment carries with it the responsibility to serve customers well, to stay in the technical and product-development race, and to grow in pace with growing market demand.

Such choices are not made in a vacuum. They are influenced by the company's background; by its marketing, manufacturing, and technical strengths; by the fabric of its relations with existing customers, the scientific community, and competitors; and by other considerations.

2. What Form Should the Product Take?

Products are planned and designed to serve markets. Marketing strategies should not be developed for products but for *markets*—the product is a variable, not a given, in the strategy. In theory, at least, market selection comes first, and the choice of product form follows. An aluminum manufacturer, for example, might elect to serve the residential housing market by supplying aluminum siding, shingles, gutters, and downspouts. Alternatively, it could supply aluminum sheet stock and coil to independent fabricators of these building components. Another option, conceivably, would be to make and sell certain types of housing, such as mobile homes.

The *market*, in this case, might be broadly defined as residential housing. The *product options* are semifabricated materials, building components, and end products. Other product choices may be whether to make a full line or narrow line in any given product area; whether to offer high, medium, or low quality; and whether to have a full range of sizes or to work across only part of the range.

3. What Should the Product Do for the User?

The "product" is what the product *does;* it is the total package of benefits customers receive when they buy. This includes the functional utility of the goods, the product service that manufacturers provide, the technical assistance they may give their customers, and the assurance that the product will be delivered when and where it is needed and in the desired quantities. Another benefit might be the seller's brand name and reputation; these may help buyers in their promotional activities.

Another benefit that the customer may gain has to do with the range of relationships, technical and personal, that may develop among people in the selling and buying organizations. Particularly in industrial marketing, such relationships are normally part of the "package of benefits" that the purchaser is likely to buy.

My point is that the product should not be conceived of narrowly in terms of its primary function. Even if it is nondifferentiable, in the most narrow sense, the supplier may differentiate it from competitive offerings through special service, distribution, or brand image.

4. For Whom Is the Product Most Important?

The product, in this broader sense, will have different meaning to different customers. It is strategically advantageous for a supplier to concentrate on those prospective customer groups that will value the product the most. If, for example, technical service is an important part of what the seller provides, a promising market may be smaller companies that have no research and development facilities of their own. Larger, technically sophisticated customers with extensive in-house research skills may place little or no value on that aspect of the product offering. Also, of course, a product generally commands the highest prices among the customers for whom it has the greatest utility.

Making Product/Market Choices

One observation that should emerge from this discussion is that product planning and market selection are integrally related. Decisions in these two areas cannot be made independently. Accordingly, I shall use the term *product/market* to describe the choices and strategies that management is concerned with.

Strategic choices with regard to product/market strategy may be made along two dimensions, *horizontal* and *vertical*. On each dimension there are choices to be made with regard to customer subgroups, that is, the specific customers that the company will seek to cultivate. These types of choices might be differentiated as follows:

☐ Horizontally, industrial markets can be segmented in terms of end-use application. A manufacturer of air conditioning systems, for example, will distinguish among such market segments as residential tract builders, small "stick" builders, and commercial contractors.

☐ On the other hand, vertical product/market choices have to do with the market level at which the supplier sells. For instance, the aluminum producer serving the residential housing market may have a choice whether to sell raw materials, semifabricated materials, components, or end products.

☐ Customer subgroup choices relate to the selection of particular types of customers within a horizontal or vertical market segment. Generally, customer subgroups may be distinguished in terms of buyer-behavior characteristics. For instance, government agencies typically make their purchases differently than private companies do. Large companies typically have more sophisticated buying organizations and procurement processes than do small ones. Some companies tend to be innovative and are among the first to try new products, while others exhibit "follower" characteristics.

Now let us consider the horizontal and vertical dimensions of strategy in turn.

Horizontal Product/Market Selection

Market selection, as noted earlier, is influenced considerably by manufacturers' assessments of their own strengths and weaknesses. They may count their product design, possibly protected by patents, as an important asset. They may start with a technical innovation and seek the market segments and product forms that would give them a competitive advantage over products performing similar functions. They may perceive their established position and reputation with existing customers as their critical strength. They may regard their size, financial strength, and production resources as their strong suit. Limitations in any of these areas must be counted as weaknesses.

Over and against this assessment of strengths and weaknesses should be posited a list of feasible product/market opportunities, with an evaluation of buying behavior, market needs, and the competitive environment for each one. Market selection is then a matter of electing those product/market opportunities where the company has a meaningful edge and where its weaknesses will not be critical deterrents to success.

Crown Cork's Decision Analyzed

At Crown Cork & Seal, for example, management elected to concentrate on markets for aerosol cans and metal containers for beer and soft drinks. It did not commit itself to the large and growing markets for such applications as frozen citrus juices and motor oil. One might have matched corporate strengths and limitations against market needs and opportunities as follows:

Corporate Strengths

☐ Technical capability in the design, manufacture, and use of *metal* containers for "hard-to-hold" applications

☐ Good working relationships with major suppliers of metals

☐ A major position as a supplier of filling equipment for soft drink and beer cans

Corporate Limitations

☐ Much smaller market share than the two major companies in the industry

☐ Limited financial resources for supporting research and development

☐ Outmoded manufacturing plants not located near concentrations of potential customers

Market Needs, Opportunities, and Risks

Beer, soft drink, and aerosol containers:

☐ High growth rate

☐ Need for high-strength containers (probably metal)

☐ Technical maturity of metal cans and relatively low needs for R&D (aerosol tops and pull-tops)

☐ Low risk of self-manufacture by user companies

☐   High service needs for delivery, for layout and operation of can-filling lines, and for lithographing container surfaces

☐   Customer desire for at least two sources of supply

Motor oil cans:

☐   Large market potential

☐   Rapid changes in packaging materials mean greater risk of self-manufacture by user companies and relatively low value added in fiberfoil containers

Having assessed the company's strengths and limitations against known market opportunities, Crown Cork's management made clear choices—and with considerable success. There was and is, of course, some risk attached to a dependency on a narrow market base. Crown Cork may be vulnerable to new materials or new forms of packaging for applications in which its metal cans are now used. But these risks seem a fair trade-off for the advantages of the strategy.

Diversifying into New Markets

In the situation where an industrial company is diversifying into new markets, four considerations are very important. They can be stated in the form of questions for managers to ask:

1   Does the market have high growth potential?
2   Is the market currently dominated by large and powerful competitors, or is it still possible to claim a large market share? Companies with large market shares generally enjoy higher returns on investment than their competitors with lower market shares. The competitor with the largest market share often enjoys a low unit cost position in manufacturing and marketing. He may be able to support the largest R&D effort. He may, in addition, be able to exercise some price leadership. In a study of a widely diversified sample of approximately 620 businesses in 57 different companies, undertaken by the Marketing Science Institute, it was demonstrated that businesses with large market shares had much higher returns on investment than those businesses with relatively low market shares.[2]
3   Is the market easy or difficult for competitors to enter? Relative ease of entry depends on how high the required investments are in manufacturing plants, in R&D, and in field sales and service facilities. In many industries—basic chemicals, heavy electrical equipment, steel, aluminum, pharmaceuticals, aircraft, synthetic fibers, paper, and office equipment, among others—large investments in all three types of facilities are generally needed.
     More important, a certain "critical mass" is needed for a

producer to be efficient. To achieve low unit manufacturing costs, very large plants are needed. The "critical mass" concept is also relevant in such areas as R&D and field sales and service.

To support and justify such investments there may have to be the prospect of a significant market share. Yet the level of demand may support only a handful of suppliers—say, three to eight. Such considerations would make it difficult for new competitors to enter a market, thus providing a measure of protection for those who can afford the high stakes required.

4 How high is the value added by manufacture, or, conversely, how low is the ratio of the cost of materials and purchased parts to the selling price? Low value added tends to make the product/market opportunity less attractive. Manufacturers are vulnerable to rising costs of materials and equipment—costs that they may not be able to pass on to their customers in the form of higher prices. If, on the other hand, the value added is high relative to the selling price, manufacturers control a large portion of their costs and may usefully pursue cost-reduction programs to gain a competitive edge. Equally important, they probably have opportunities to develop unique skills through which they may differentiate their product from those of competitors, thus achieving a market advantage.

Product/Market Positioning

Very often, selecting markets is a matter of identifying potential applications for some new product, possibly one that comes from a research laboratory. The problem then is one of product/market positioning.

After accurately defining the product's performance characteristics, management should determine what applications maximize its advantages and minimize its disadvantages. For instance, a plastic that has high tensile strength, dimensional stability, heat resistance, and machinability but poor electrical properties (e.g., not fire-retardant) might be very useful for making certain appliance parts but not for making electrical components.

Engineers and marketers often seem to get carried away with new technical innovations and to be insufficiently objective in defining that "window" in the range of competing products where the innovation has its real place. Failing to establish a niche based on unique performance advantages, the strategists turn, usually unprofitably, to fighting for the market survival of the product on a price basis.

Product-Line Proliferation

The extension of a product line to provide a range of sizes, models, or specifications, each designed for some particular market segment and end use, is a key competitive weapon in the fight for market share. For example, a synthetic fiber like Du Pont's nylon may be purchased in more than a thousand different "put-ups." Each fiber is tailored for use in a different end product, such as women's hosiery, parachutes, or nylon-reinforced rubber tires. Often, too, product-line proliferation comes through providing a range of optional equipment to meet the individual preferences of users.

Product-line growth may take the form of developing larger and larger units as technology permits and market needs grow—steam turbines for power plants, jet engines for aircraft, and so on. For the technical leader this kind of proliferation may be immensely useful as a means of achieving overall market leadership, preserving a dominant market share, and increasing profits.[3]

In still other cases, product-line proliferation may be forced by competitors. When this happens, the manufacturer who is defending his market position may be faced with a Hobson's choice: suffer a sharp drop in market share or add products to match competitive offerings and suffer a loss in profits. For example, with the rapid growth of markets for minicomputers, small computer manufacturers are threatening the large, integrated companies at one end of the product range. The logical response for the latter has been to develop and aggressively promote small computers, even though they may be less profitable to sell than the large machines.

Vertical Product/Market Selection

At what stage of manufacture should a company market its products? At issue here are management's willingness and ability to invest in the required manufacturing and marketing resources at different levels. The resource requirement varies considerably from one stage to another. In addition, of cource, the market "environments" vary greatly from stage to stage along with customer characteristics. To illustrate:

Shortly after World War II, the Aluminum Company of America (Alcoa) undertook the market introduction of an aluminum bearing for use in large diesel engines. The bearing was made from a special aluminum alloy called Alloy 750. Performance tests indicated that bearings made from Alloy 750 were superior to conventional bearings in that they resisted corrosion better. Also, they dissipated heat more rapidly, minimizing the possibility of a bearing freezing on a crankshaft in the event of insufficient lubrication. Moreover, it was claimed that solid aluminum bearings would outwear conventional bearings many times over. Yet they cost much less to make than conventional bearings.

Alcoa managers had three options with regard to market level. (1) They could supply Alloy 750 to bearing manufacturers, (2) they could supply castings to bearing manufacturers and/or diesel engine builders, or (3) they could make and sell finished bearings to diesel engine builders and, as replacement parts, to diesel engine users.

Initially, an effort was made to supply castings. One reason was the importance of assuring product quality. Alloy 750 required special foundry techniques. If Alcoa did the casting, it could considerably minimize the risk of product failure due to poor casting quality. In addition, by making bearing castings rather than supplying aluminum ingot to foundries, Alcoa could realize higher sales and profit margins.

The company's field representatives worked with large diesel engine builders to generate interest in aluminum bearings. The representatives then referred these companies to bearing manufacturers as sources of supply for finished aluminum bearings. This approach was relatively unsuccessful because bearing manufacturers promoted their own conventional bearings, thus negating Alcoa's efforts to build a market for the new aluminum bearings. After ten years, annual sales of aluminum castings were only a small fraction of the potential that Alcoa managers had envisaged. The question that comes to mind, of course, is why Alcoa chose this particular marketing option.

Analyzing the Market-Level Choice

Let us put ourselves in the position of Alcoa's management when it was choosing its market. What were the pros and cons of the different market levels?

First, let us begin with the question of customer receptivity:

□ Diesel engine *users* could realize significant advantages from having long-life, troublefree bearings. Not only might there be a saving in the cost of replacement bearings, but there could also be significant savings in downtime for engine maintenance.

□ Diesel engine *builders* might realize some advantage in designing engines with Alloy 750 bearings if this feature could be given promotional significance in selling diesel engines. On the other hand, some diesel engine builders might be reluctant to experiment with new components, especially if they were advised against it by their regular bearing suppliers, the recognized experts in the field.

□ Bearing *manufacturers* would have strong disincentives for adopting aluminum bearings. Such a move would make their facilities for producing conventional bearings obsolete. It would also sacrifice their position as manufacturers of proprietary products, with little or nothing by way of product differentiation to support claims to their respective market shares. Finally, aluminum bearings made from castings would mean less value added by manufacture.

In short, a compelling consideration is what market segment will benefit the most from adopting the product. In this case, diesel engine users would seem to have the most to gain.

What about the product quality question? Particularly in the early stages of market development, control of end-product quality is critically important. Poor quality and misapplications of the product can easily kill its potential. If Alcoa elected to make bearing castings, it could control one element of quality. If it chose to make finished bearings, it could assure itself of complete quality control. Moreover, it could become involved in direct working relationships with engine builders on diesel engine matters having to do with the use of aluminum bearings; this would mean opportunities to promote aluminum bearings through the company's technical service.

These three considerations—market receptivity to the product concept, ability to control end-product quality, and product promotability—argue for choosing a position in the finished bearings market. The major disadvantage would be the high cost of holding such a market position. It would probably be desirable to build a sales force at least as large as those of the major bearing manufacturers. It might be necessary to make and sell a full line of different types of bearings to support such a sales force and to serve the full range of customer needs. The prospective payoff from such commitments would have to be weighed against the anticipated gains and costs of other strategies.

To market bearing castings to the ten or so bearing manufacturers was undoubtedly the least-cost, lowest-commitment option. In the long run, however, it was not likely to yield optimal results as measured in terms of sales volume and profits.

By making this choice, Alcoa's management indicated that it was unwilling, in view of other opportunities it might have had to increase sales of aluminum, to make the necessary resource commitments to manufacture and sell finished bearings. While it thus reduced its risk, it was less successful than it had hoped in developing a market for aluminum bearings.

The Alcoa case does not mean that a position at the end-product level is always to be preferred. It may be desirable to take a position as a materials or components producer because barriers to entry may be greater at the early stages in the manufacturing process, while profit margins may fall short at the end-product market level because of intensive competition among large numbers of sellers.

In addition, the product innovation may be less beneficial to end users than to prospective buyers at intermediate stages in the production process. One medium-sized chemical company, for example, undertook to develop a market for a siliceous mineral that could be used as a filler in making tiles, paints, and some plastic products. As a filler for tiles—and this was by far the largest potential use—the mineral could be used by the tile manufacturers to reduce production costs significantly.

By contrast, the product had no benefits either structural or aesthetic for tile contractors, builders, or home owners. The product benefits all related to cost savings in tile manufacture, not to use. This was an important consideration in management's decision to function as a materials supplier rather than as a producer of ceramic tiles.

Questions for Managers to Ask

It is largely in connection with *vertical* product/market selection that management should remember that the product is a variable in marketing strategy. At what market level is the product concept most meaningful? Does it have the greatest value to end users (as in the case of the aluminum bearing), or is it most meaningful to end-product manufacturers (as in the case of the filler material)? Everything else being equal, industrial marketers should elect to sell the product at that market level where the product concept has the greatest meaning and in the form that that market can use.

As suggested earlier, the choice of product form (material, component, or end product) is influenced by the importance of controlling product quality and application. This is an especially important matter in developing markets for new products. The relevant questions to ask are these:

☐ Is there a possibility that market development may be aborted by poor product quality or by product misuse?

☐ At what points in the manufacturing chain do quality risks exist?

☐ Can the company minimize those risks by taking responsibility itself for that step in the manufacturing process?

Not infrequently, these considerations seem to dictate taking a product/market position at or close to the end-product level. But other reasons may favor the choice of some earlier stage. For instance, management may, for one of the following reasons, elect to serve as a supplier of materials or components:

☐ It is unwilling to commit itself to the extensive marketing and manufacturing investments that are required to compete in the end-product market. Alternative product/market opportunities may offer potentially higher returns on the funds available for investment.

☐ There may be higher profits and a more protected market position available if the company functions as a supplier of materials or components. The high plant and technical investments needed to enter the industry at these stages may seem prohibitive to would-be competitors.

☐ The company has traditionally taken a position as a marketer of materials or components to producers of end products and does not want to change its image. Executives may be concerned that if they start making end products, they will be perceived as competing with their customers.

If considerations such as the foregoing dictate taking a position at some early market level in the manufacturing chain, while the product concept is most meaningful at the end-product level, then another strategic option becomes attractive. The industrial marketer may manufacture and sell at the early level, but promote and seek to control quality at or near the end-product stage.

For example, when Dow Chemical was developing a market for polystyrene plastic, it worked with plastic molders in the design of the products made from Dow's polystyrene. If these products met Dow's design criteria, the molders were authorized to mark them with a Dow label. Dow then advertised approved products to retailers and to consumers. Thus, although the company chose to be a supplier of materials, it was also active in quality control and product promotion at the retail level.

This was what is called an industrial marketing "pull" strategy. It sought to put pressure on Dow's immediate customers, the plastic molders, to use Dow's polystyrene by creating demand at the end-user level. It can be a sound strategy indeed, but *only* if there are significant advantages for end-users in the product concept.

Notes

1. For this and other facts on the company, see "Crown Cork and Seal Company and the Metal Container Industry," a Harvard Business School case study (ICCH No. 6–373–077), and the company's 1974 annual report.

2. See Sidney Schoeffler, Robert D. Buzzell, and Donald F. Heany, "Impact of Strategic Planning on Profit Performance," *HBR*, March–April 1974, p. 137.

3. See Ralph G. M. Sultan, *Competition or Collusion: Economic and Legal Issues of Pricing in the Electrical Equipment Industry* (Boston, Division of Research, Harvard Business School, 1974), for a detailed study of how General Electric has retained its long-term dominance in the market for turbine generators.

③
How Competitive Forces Shape Strategy

MICHAEL E. PORTER

The nature and degree of competition in an industry hinge on five forces: the threat of new entrants, the bargaining power of customers, the bargaining power of suppliers, the threat of substitute products or services (where applicable), and the jockeying among current contestants. To establish a strategic agenda for dealing with these contending currents and to grow despite them, a company must understand how they work in its industry and how they affect the company in its particular situation. The author details how these forces operate and suggests ways of adjusting to them, and, where possible, of taking advantage of them.

The essence of strategy formulation is coping with competition. Yet it is easy to view competition too narrowly and too pessimistically. While one sometimes hears executives complaining to the contrary, intense competition in an industry is neither coincidence nor bad luck.

Moreover, in the fight for market share, competition is not manifested only in the other players. Rather, competition in an industry is rooted in its underlying economics, and competitive forces exist that go well beyond the established combatants in a particular industry. Customers, suppliers, potential entrants and substitute products are all competitors that may be more or less prominent or active depending on the industry.

The state of competition in an industry depends on five basic forces, which are diagrammed in Exhibit 1. The collective strength of these forces determines the ultimate profit potential of an industry. It ranges from *intense* in industries like tires, metal cans, and steel, where no company earns spectacular returns on investment, to *mild* in industries like oil field services and equipment, soft drinks, and toiletries, where there is room for quite high returns.

Exhibit 1.   Forces Governing Competition in an Industry

In the economists' "perfectly competitive" industry, jockeying for position is unbridled and entry to the industry very easy. This kind of industry structure, of course, offers the worst prospect for long-run profitability. The weaker the forces collectively, however, the greater the opportunity for superior performance.

Whatever their collective strength, the corporate strategist's goal is to find a position in the industry where his or her company can best defend itself against these forces or can influence them in its favor. The collective strength of the forces may be painfully apparent to all the antagonists; but to cope with them, the strategist must delve below the surface and analyze the sources of each. For example, what makes the industry vulnerable to entry? What determines the bargaining power of suppliers?

Knowledge of these underlying sources of competitive pressure provides the groundwork for a strategic agenda of action. They highlight the critical strengths and weaknesses of the company, animate the positioning of the company in its industry, clarify the areas where strategic changes may yield the greatest payoff, and highlight the places where industry trends promise to hold the greatest significance as either opportunities or threats. Understanding these sources also proves to be of help in considering areas for diversification.

Contending Forces

The strongest competitive force or forces determine the profitability of an industry and so are of greatest importance in strategy formulation. For example, even a company with a strong position in an industry unthreatened by potential entrants will earn low returns if it faces a superior or a lower-cost substitute product—as the leading manufacturers of vacuum tubes and coffee percolators have learned to their sorrow. In such a situation, coping with the substitute product becomes the number one strategic priority.

Different forces take on prominence, of course, in shaping competition in each industry. In the ocean-going tanker industry the key force is probably the buyers(the major oil companies), while in tires it is powerful OEM buyers coupled with tough competitors. In the steel industry the key forces are foreign competitors and substitute materials.

Every industry has an underlying structure, or a set of fundamental economic and technical characteristics, that gives rise to these competitive forces. The strategist, wanting to position his or her company to cope best with its industry environment or to influence that environment in the company's favor, must learn what makes the environment tick.

This view of competition pertains equally to industries dealing in services and to those selling products. To avoid monotony in this article, I refer to both products and services as "products." The same general principles apply to all types of business.

A few characteristics are critical to the strength of each competitive force. I shall discuss them in this section.

Threat of Entry

New entrants to an industry bring new capacity, the desire to gain market share, and often substantial resources. Companies diversifying through acquisition into the industry from other markets often leverage their resources to cause a shake-up, as Philip Morris did with Miller beer.

The seriousness of the threat of entry depends on the barriers present and on the reaction from existing competitors that the entrant can expect. If barriers to entry are high and a newcomer can expect sharp retaliation from the entrenched competitors, obviously he will not pose a serious threat of entering.

There are six major sources of barriers to entry:

1. *Economies of scale.* These economies deter entry by forcing the aspirant either to come in on a large scale or to accept a cost disadvantage. Scale economies in production, research, marketing, and service are probably the key barriers to entry in the mainframe computer industry, as Xerox and GE sadly discovered. Economies of scale can also act as hurdles in distribution, utilization of the sales force, financing, and nearly any other part of a business.

2. *Product differentiation.* Brand identification creates a barrier by forcing entrants to spend heavily to overcome customer loyalty. Advertising, customer service, being first in the industry, and product differences are among the factors fostering brand identification. It is perhaps the most important entry barrier in soft drinks, over-the-counter drugs, cosmetics, investment banking, and public accounting. To create high fences around their businesses, brewers couple brand identification with economies of scale in production, distribution, and marketing.

3. *Capital requirements.* The need to invest large financial resources in order to compete creates a barrier to entry, particularly if the capital is required for unrecoverable expenditures in up-front advertising or R&D. Capital is necessary not only for fixed facilities but also for customer credit, inventories, and absorbing start-up losses. While major corporations have the financial resources to invade almost any industry, the huge capital requirements in certain fields, such as computer manufacturing and mineral extraction, limit the pool of likely entrants.

4. *Cost disadvantages independent of size.* Entrenched companies may have cost advantages not available to potential rivals, no matter what their size and attainable economies of scale. These advantages can stem from the effects of the learning curve (and of its first cousin, the experience curve), proprietary technology, access to the best raw materials sources, assets purchased at preinflation prices, government subsidies, or favorable locations. Sometimes cost advantages are legally enforceable, as they are through patents. (For an analysis of the much-discussed experience curve as a barrier to entry, see the appendix.

5. *Access to distribution channels* The new person on the block must, of course, secure distribution of his or her product or service. A new food product, for example, must displace others from the supermarket shelf via price breaks, promotions, intense selling efforts, or some other means. The more limited the wholesale or retail channels are and the more that existing competitors have these tied up, obviously the tougher that entry into the industry will be. Sometimes this barrier is so high that, to surmount it, a new contestant must create its own distribution channels, as Timex did in the watch industry in the 1950s.

6. *Government policy.* The government can limit or even foreclose entry to industries with such controls as license requirements and limits on access to raw materials. Regulated industries like trucking, liquor retailing, and freight forwarding are noticeable examples; more subtle government restrictions operate in fields like ski-area development and coal mining. The government also can play a major indirect role by affecting entry barriers through controls such as air and water pollution standards and safety regulations.

The potential rival's expectations about the reaction of existing competitors also will influence its decision on whether to enter. The company is likely to have second thoughts if incumbents have previously lashed out at new entrants or if:

☐ The incumbents possess substantial resources to fight back, including excess cash and unused borrowing power, productive capacity, or clout with distribution channels and customers.

☐ The incumbents seem likely to cut prices because of a desire to keep market shares or because of industrywide excess capacity.

☐ Industry growth is slow, affecting its ability to absorb the new arrival and probably causing the financial performance of all the parties involved to decline.

Changing Conditions.   From a strategic standpoint there are two important additional points to note about the threat of entry.

First, it changes, of course, as these conditions change. The expiration of Polaroid's basic patents on instant photography, for instance, greatly reduced its absolute cost entry barrier built by proprietary technology. It is not surprising that Kodak plunged into the market. Product differentiation in printing has all but disappeared. Conversely, in the auto industry economies of scale increased enormously with post-World War II automation and vertical integration—virtually stopping successful new entry.

Second, strategic decisions involving a large segment of an industry can have a major impact on the conditions determining the threat of entry. For example, the actions of many U.S. wine producers in the 1960s to step up product introductions, raise advertising levels, and expand distribution nationally surely strengthened the entry roadblocks by raising economies of scale and making access to distribution channels more difficult. Similarly, decisions by members of the recreational vehicle industry to vertically integrate in order to lower costs have greatly increased the economies of scale and raised the capital cost barriers.

Powerful Suppliers and Buyers

Suppliers can exert bargaining power on participants in an industry by raising prices or reducing the quality of purchased goods and services. Powerful suppliers can thereby squeeze profitability out of an industry unable to recover cost increases in its own prices. By raising their prices, soft drink concentrate producers have contributed to the erosion of profitability of bottling companies because the bottlers, facing intense competition from powdered mixes, fruit drinks, and other beverages, have limited freedom to raise *their* prices accordingly. Customers likewise can force down prices, demand higher quality or more service, and play competitors off against each other—all at the expense of industry profits.

The power of each important supplier or buyer group depends on a

number of characteristics of its market situation and on the relative importance of its sales or purchases to the industry compared with its overall
business.

A *supplier* group is powerful if:

☐ It is dominated by a few companies and is more concentrated than
the industry it sells to.

☐ Its product is unique or at least differentiated, or if it has built up
switching costs. Switching costs are fixed costs buyers face in changing
suppliers. These arise because, among other things, a buyer's product
specifications tie it to particular suppliers, it has invested heavily in
specialized ancillary equipment or in learning how to operate a supplier's equipment (as in computer software), or its production lines are
connected to the supplier's manufacturing facilities (as in some manufacture of beverage containers).

☐ It is not obliged to contend with other products for sale to the
industry. For instance, the competition between the steel companies
and the aluminum companies to sell to the can industry checks the
power of each supplier.

☐ It poses a credible threat of integrating forward into the industry's
business. This provides a check against the industry's ability to improve
the terms on which it purchases.

☐ The industry is not an important customer of the supplier group.
If the industry *is* an important customer, suppliers' fortunes will be
closely tied to the industry, and they will want to protect the industry
through reasonable pricing and assistance in activities like R&D and
lobbying.

A *buyer* group is powerful if:

☐ It is concentrated or purchases in large volumes. Large-volume
buyers are particularly potent forces if heavy fixed costs characterize
the industry—as they do in metal containers, corn refining, and bulk
chemicals, for example—which raise the stakes to keep capacity filled.

☐ The products it purchases from the industry are standard or undifferentiated. The buyers, sure that they can always find alternative
suppliers, may play one company against another, as they do in aluminum extrusion.

☐ The products it purchases from the industry form a component of
its product and represent a significant fraction of its cost. The buyers
are likely to shop for a favorable price and purchase selectively. Where
the product sold by the industry in question is a small fraction of buyers'
costs, buyers are usually much less price sensitive.

☐ It earns low profits, which create great incentive to lower its purchasing costs. Highly profitable buyers, however, are generally less price sensitive (that is, of course, if the item does not represent a large fraction of their costs).

☐ The industry's product is unimportant to the quality of the buyers' products or services. Where the quality of the buyers' products is very much affected by the industry's product, buyers are generally less price sensitive. Industries in which this situation obtains include oil field equipment, where a malfunction can lead to large losses, and enclosures for electronic medical and test instruments, where the quality of the enclosure can influence the user's impression about the quality of the equipment inside.

☐ The industry's product does not save the buyer money. Where the industry's product or service can pay for itself many times over, buyers are rarely price sensitive; rather, they are interested in quality. This is true in services like investment banking and public accounting, where errors in judgment can be costly and embarrassing, and in businesses like the logging of oil wells, where an accurate survey can save thousands of dollars in drilling costs.

☐ The buyers pose a credible threat of integrating backward to make the industry's product. The Big Three auto producers and major buyers of cars have often used the threat of self-manufacture as a bargaining lever. But sometimes an industry engenders a threat to buyers that its members may integrate forward.

Most of these sources of buyer power can be attributed to consumers as a group as well as to industrial and commercial buyers; only a modification of the frame of reference is necessary. Consumers tend to be more price sensitive if they are purchasing products that are undifferentiated, expensive relative to their incomes, and of a sort where quality is not particularly important.

The buying power of retailers is determined by the same rules, with one important addition. Retailers can gain significant bargaining power over manufacturers when they can influence consumers' purchasing decisions, as they do in audio components, jewelry, appliances, sporting goods, and other goods

Strategic Action. A company's choice of suppliers to buy from or buyer groups to sell to should be viewed as a crucial strategic decision. A company can improve its strategic posture by finding suppliers or buyers who possess the least power to influence it adversely.

Most common is the situation of a company being able to choose whom it will sell to—in other words, buyer selection. Rarely do all the buyer groups a company sells to enjoy equal power. Even if a company sells to a single industry, segments usually exist within that industry that exercise less power (and that are therefore less price sensitive) than others. For example, the replacement market for most products is less price sensitive than the overall market.

As a rule, a company can sell to powerful buyers and still come away with above-average profitability only if it is a low-cost producer in its industry or if its product enjoys some unusual, if not unique, features. In supplying large customers with electric motors, Emerson Electric earns high returns because its low-cost position permits the company to meet or undercut competitors' prices.

If the company lacks a low-cost position or a unique product, selling to everyone is self-defeating because the more sales it achieves, the more vulnerable it becomes. The company may have to muster the courage to turn away business and sell only to less potent customers.

Buyer selection has been a key to the success of National Can and Crown Cork & Seal. They focus on the segments of the can industry where they can create product differentiation, minimize the threat of backward integration, and otherwise mitigate the awesome power of their customers. Of course, some industries do not enjoy the luxury of selecting "good" buyers.

As the factors creating supplier and buyer power change with time or as a result of a company's strategic decisions, naturally the power of these groups rises or declines. In the ready-to-wear clothing industry, as the buyers (department stores and clothing stores) have become more concentrated and control has passed to large chains, the industry has come under increasing pressure and suffered falling margins. The industry has been unable to differentiate its product or engender switching costs that lock in its buyers enough to neutralize these trends.

Substitute Products

By placing a ceiling on prices it can charge, substitute products or services limit the potential of an industry. Unless it can upgrade the quality of the product or differentiate it somehow (as via marketing), the industry will suffer in earnings and possibly in growth.

Manifestly, the more attractive the price-performance trade-off offered by substitute products, the firmer the lid placed on the industry's profit potential. Sugar producers confronted with the large-scale commercialization of high-fructose corn syrup, a sugar substitute, are learning this lesson today.

Substitutes not only limit profits in normal times; they also reduce the bonanza an industry can reap in boom times. In 1978 the producers of fiberglass insulation enjoyed unprecedented demand as a result of high energy costs and severe winter weather. But the industry's ability to raise prices was tempered by the plethora of insulation substitutes, including cellulose, rock wool, and styrofoam. These substitutes are bound to become an even stronger force once the current round of plant additions by fiberglass insulation producers has boosted capacity enough to meet demand (and then some).

Substitute products that deserve the most attention strategically are those that (a) are subject to trends improving their price-performance trade-off with the industry's product, or (b) are produced by industries earning high profits. Substitutes often come rapidly into play if some development increases competition in their industries and causes price reduction or performance improvement.

Jockeying for Position

Rivalry among existing competitors takes the familiar form of jockeying for position—using tactics like price competition, product introduction, and advertising slugfests. Intense rivalry is related to the presence of a number of factors:

☐ Competitors are numerous or are roughly equal in size and power. In many U.S. industries in recent years foreign contenders, of course, have become part of the competitive picture.

☐ Industry growth is slow, precipitating fights for market share that involve expansion-minded members.

☐ The product or service lacks differentiation or switching costs, which lock in buyers and protect one combatant from raids on its customers by another.

☐ Fixed costs are high or the product is perishable, creating strong temptation to cut prices. Many basic materials businesses, like paper and aluminum, suffer from this problem when demand slackens.

☐ Capacity is normally augmented in large increments. Such additions, as in the chlorine and vinyl chloride businesses, disrupt the industry's supply-demand balance and often lead to periods of overcapacity and price cutting.

☐ Exit barriers are high. Exit barriers, like very specialized assets or management's loyalty to a particular business, keep companies competing even though they may be earning low or even negative returns on investment. Excess capacity remains functioning, and the profitability of the healthy competitors suffers as the sick ones hang on.[1] If the entire industry suffers from overcapacity, it may seek government help—particularly if foreign competition is present.

☐ The rivals are diverse in strategies, origins, and "personalities." They have different ideas about how to compete and continually run head-on into each other in the process.

As an industry matures, its growth rate changes, resulting in declining profits and (often) a shakeout. In the booming recreational vehicle industry of the early 1970s, nearly every producer did well; but slow growth since then has eliminated the high returns, except for the strongest members, not to mention many of the weaker companies. The same profit story has been played out in industry after industry—snowmobiles, aerosol packaging, and sports equipment are just a few examples.

An acquisition can introduce a very different personality to an industry, as has been the case with Black & Decker's takeover of McCullough, the producer of chain saws. Technological innovation can boost the level of fixed costs in the production process, as it did in the shift from batch to continuous-line photo finishing in the 1960s.

While a company must live with many of these factors—because they are built into industry economics—it may have some latitude for improving matters through strategic shifts. For example, it may try to raise buyers' switching costs or increase product differentiation. A focus on selling efforts in the fastest growing segments of the industry or on market areas with the lowest fixed costs can reduce the impact of industry rivalry. If it is feasible, a company can try to avoid confrontation with competitors having high exit barriers and can thus sidestep involvement in bitter price cutting.

Formulation of Strategy

Once corporate strategists have assessed the forces affecting competition in their industry and the underlying causes, they can identify their company's strengths and weaknesses. The crucial strengths and weaknesses from a strategic standpoint are the company's posture vis-à-vis the underlying causes of each force. Where does it stand against substitutes? Against the sources of entry barriers?

Then the strategist can devise a plan of action that may include (1) positioning the company so that its capabilities provide the best defense against the competitive force; and/or (2) influencing the balance of the forces through strategic moves, thereby improving the company's position; and/or (3) anticipating shifts in the factors underlying the forces and responding to them, with the hope of exploiting change by choosing a strategy appropriate for the new competitive balance before opponents recognize it. I shall consider each strategic approach in turn.

Positioning the Company

The first approach takes the structure of the industry as given and matches the company's strengths and weaknesses to it. Strategy can be viewed as building defenses against the competitive forces or as finding positions in the industry where the forces are weakest.

Knowledge of the company's capabilities and of the causes of the competitive forces will highlight the areas where the company should confront competition and where avoid it. If the company is a low-cost producer, it may choose to confront powerful buyers while it takes care to sell them only products not vulnerable to competition from substitutes.

The success of Dr Pepper in the soft drink industry illustrates the coupling of realistic knowledge of corporate strengths with sound industry analysis to yield a superior strategy. Coca-Cola and Pepsi-Cola dominate Dr Pepper's industry, where many small concentrate producers compete for a piece of the action. Dr Pepper chose a strategy of avoiding the largest selling drink segment, maintaining a narrow flavor line, forgoing the development of a captive bottler network, and marketing heavily. The company positioned itself so as to be least vulnerable to its competitive forces while it exploited its small size.

In the $11.5 billion soft drink industry, barriers to entry in the form of brand identification, large-scale marketing, and access to a bottler network are enormous. Rather than accept the formidable costs and scale economies in having its own bottler network—that is, following the lead of the Big Two and of Seven-Up—Dr Pepper took advantage of the different flavor of its drink to "piggyback" on Coke and Pepsi bottlers who wanted a full line to sell to customers. Dr Pepper coped with the power of these buyers through extraordinary service and other efforts to distinguish its treatment of them from that of Coke and Pepsi.

Many small companies in the soft drink business offer cola drinks that thrust them into head-to-head competition against the majors. Dr Pepper, however, maximized product differentiation by maintaining a narrow line of beverages built around an unusual flavor.

Finally, Dr Pepper met Coke and Pepsi with an advertising onslaught emphasizing the alleged uniqueness of its single flavor. This campaign built strong brand identification and great customer loyalty. Helping its efforts was the fact that Dr Pepper's formula involved lower raw materials cost, which gave the company an absolute cost advantage over its major competitors.

There are no economies of scale in soft drink concentrate production, so Dr Pepper could prosper despite its small share of the business (6%). Thus Dr Pepper confronted competition in marketing but avoided it in product line and in distribution. This artful positioning combined with good implementation has led to an enviable record in earnings and in the stock market.

Influencing the Balance

When dealing with the forces that drive industry competition, a company can devise a strategy that takes the offensive. This posture is designed to do more than merely cope with the forces themselves; it is meant to alter their causes.

Innovations in marketing can raise brand identification or otherwise differentiate the product. Capital investments in large-scale facilities or vertical integration affect entry barriers. The balance of forces is partly a result of external factors and partly in the company's control.

Exploiting Industry Change

Industry evolution is important strategically because evolution, of course, brings with it changes in the sources of competition I have identified. In the familiar product life-cycle pattern, for example, growth rates change, product differentiation is said to decline as the business becomes more mature, and the companies tend to integrate vertically.

These trends are not so important in themselves; what is critical is whether they affect the sources of competition. Consider vertical integration. In the maturing minicomputer industry, extensive vertical integration, both in manufacturing and in software development, is taking place. This very significant trend is greatly raising economies of scale as well as the amount of capital necessary to compete in the industry. This in turn is raising barriers to entry and may drive some smaller competitors out of the industry once growth levels off.

Obviously, the trends carrying the highest priority from a strategic standpoint are those that affect the most important sources of competition in the industry and those that elevate new causes to the forefront. In contract aerosol packaging, for example, the trend toward less product differentiation is now dominant. It has increased buyers' power, lowered the barriers to entry, and intensified competition.

The framework for analyzing competition that I have described can also be used to predict the eventual profitability of an industry. In long-range planning the task is to examine each competitive force, forecast the magnitude of each underlying cause, and then construct a composite picture of the likely profit potential of the industry.

The outcome of such an exercise may differ a great deal from the existing industry structure. Today, for example, the solar heating business is populated by dozens and perhaps hundreds of companies, none with a major market position. Entry is easy, and competitors are battling to establish solar heating as a superior substitute for conventional methods.

The potential of this industry will depend largely on the shape of future barriers to entry, the improvement of the industry's position relative to substitutes, the ultimate intensity of competition, and the power captured by buyers and suppliers. These characteristics will in turn be influenced by such factors as the establishment of brand identities, significant economies of scale or experience curves in equipment manufacture wrought by technological change, the ultimate capital costs to compete, and the extent of overhead in production facilities.

The framework for analyzing industry competition has direct benefits in setting diversification strategy. It provides a road map for answering the extremely difficult question inherent in diversification decision: "What is the potential of this business?" Combining the framework with judgment in its application, a company may be able to spot an industry with a good future before this good future is reflected in the prices of acquisition candidates

Multifaceted Rivalry

Corporate managers have directed a great deal of attention to defining their businesses as a crucial step in strategy formulation. Theodore Levitt, in his classic 1960 article in *HBR*, argued strongly for avoiding the myopia of narrow, product-oriented industry definition.[2] Numerous other authorities have also stressed the need to look beyond product to function in defining a business, beyond national boundaries to potential international competition, and beyond the ranks of one's competitors today to those that may become competitors tomorrow. As a result of these urgings, the proper definition of a company's industry or industries has become an endlessly debated subject.

One motive behind this debate is the desire to exploit new markets. Another, perhaps more important motive is the fear of overlooking latent sources of competition that someday may threaten the industry. Many managers concentrate so single-mindedly on their direct antagonists in the fight for market share that they fail to realize that they are also competing with their customers and their suppliers for bargaining power. Meanwhile, they also neglect to keep a wary eye out for new entrants to the contest or fail to recognize the subtle threat of substitute products.

The key to growth—even survival—is to stake out a position that is less vulnerable to attack from head-to-head opponents, whether established or new, and less vulnerable to erosion from the direction of buyers, suppliers, and substitute goods. Establishing such a position can take many forms— solidifying relationships with favorable customers, differentiating the product either substantively or psychologically through marketing, integrating forward or backward, establishing technological leadership.

Notes

1. For a more complete discussion of exit barriers and their implications for strategy, see my article, "Please Note Location of Nearest Exit," *California Management Review*, Winter 1976, p. 21.

2. Theodore Levitt, "Marketing Myopia," reprinted as an *HBR* Classic, September–October 1975, p. 26.

Appendix: The Experience Curve as an Entry Barrier

In recent years, the experience curve has become widely discussed as a key element of industry structure. According to this concept, unit costs in many manufacturing industries (some dogmatic adherents say in *all* manufacturing industries) as well as in some service industries decline with "experience," or a particular company's cumulative volume of production. (The experience curve, which encompasses many factors, is a broader concept than the better known learning curve, which refers to the efficiency achieved over a period of time by workers through much repetition.)

The causes of the decline in unit costs are a combination of elements, including economies of scale, the learning curve for labor, and capital-labor substitution. The cost decline creates a barrier to entry because new competitors with no "experience" face higher costs than established ones, particularly the producer with the largest market share, and have difficulty catching up with the entrenched competitors.

Adherents of the experience curve concept stress the importance of achieving market leadership to maximize this barrier to entry, and they recommend aggressive action to achieve it, such as price cutting in anticipation of falling costs in order to build volume. For the combatant that cannot achieve a healthy market share, the prescription is usually, "Get out."

Is the experience curve an entry barrier on which strategies should be built? The answer is: not in every industry. In fact, in some industries, building a strategy on the experience curve can be potentially disastrous. That costs decline with experience in some industries is not news to corporate executives. The significance of the experience curve for strategy depends on what factors are causing the decline.

If costs are falling because a growing company can reap economies of scale through more efficient, automated facilities and vertical integration, then the cumulative volume of production is unimportant to its relative cost position. Here the lowest cost producer is the one with the largest, most efficient facilities.

A new entrant may well be more efficient than the more experienced competitors; if it has built the newest plant, it will face no disadvantage in having to catch up. The strategic prescription, "You must have the largest, most efficient plant," is a lot different from, "You must produce the greatest cumulative output of the item to get your costs down."

Whether a drop in costs with cumulative (not absolute) volume erects an entry barrier also depends on the sources of the decline. If costs go down because of technical advances known generally in the industry or because of the development of improved equipment that can be copied or purchased from equipment suppliers, the experience curve is no entry barrier at all— in fact, new or less experienced competitors may actually enjoy a cost *advantage* over the leaders. Free of the legacy of heavy past investments, the newcomer or less experienced competitor can purchase or copy the newest and lowest cost equipment and technology.

If, however, experience can be kept proprietary, the leaders will maintain a cost advantage. But new entrants may require less experience to reduce their costs than the leaders needed. All this suggests that the experience curve can be a shaky entry barrier on which to build a strategy.

While space does not permit a complete treatment here, I want to mention a few other crucial elements in determining the appropriateness of a strategy built on the entry barrier provided by the experience curve:

☐ The height of the barrier depends on how important costs are to competition compared with other areas like marketing, selling, and innovation.

☐ The barrier can be nullified by product or process innovations leading to a substantially new technology and thereby creating an entirely new experience curve.* New entrants can leapfrog the industry leaders and alight on the new experience curve, to which those leaders may be poorly positioned to jump.

☐ If more than one strong company is building its strategy on the experience curve, the consequences can be nearly fatal. By the time only one rival is left pursuing such a strategy, industry growth may have stopped and the prospects of reaping the spoils of victory long since evaporated.

*For an example drawn from the history of the automobile industry, see William J. Abernathy and Kenneth Wayne, "The Limits of the Learning Curve," *HBR*, September-October 1974, p. 109.

4
The Management of Ideas

MELVIN ANSHEN

Current advances in management science stress improved analytical and administrative tools. But these alone will not be enough for survival in the future, because they are geared primarily to improve the efficiency of present operations. The new business leaders will be those who can stretch their minds beyond the management of physical resources. They will have the capacity to conceptualize broad new philosophies of business, and translate their vision into operations. To the traditional skills of managing people, material, machines, and money, they will add a challenging new skill—management of ideas.

A profound change in the main task of top management is emerging as a result of the accelerating dynamics of technologies, markets, information systems, and social expectations of business performance. If this projection is correct, the threat of obsolescence of managers will pass swiftly from today's conversational shocker to tomorrow's operating reality. Executives best prepared to survive this challenge may turn out to be those equipped to think like philosophers—a type of intellectual skill not ordinarily developed in business schools or by the common work experiences of middle management.

The roots of this radical transformation of the general management job can be identified in recent business history:

☐ *Resources.* Up to about the last two decades the main task of top management could fairly be described as the efficient administration of physical resources. The focus was essentially short-range and unifunctional, and the dominant decision criteria were economic. The highest demonstration of management skill was the successful manipulation of revenues and costs in the production and distribution of materials, machines, and products.

□ *People.* Beginning in the 1930s this concern with managing physical things was enlarged by a growing interest in managing people. This was enlargement, rather than change, because the ultimate goal of effective people management was still effective thing management, with top executives extending their grasp over resources by means of their ability to organize and motivate people. The focus of management attention remained within short-term horizons and unifunctional activity.

□ *Money.* After World War II, in a business environment marked by rapid growth in corporate size, product and market diversification, accelerated technological development, and shortened product life cycles, the principal task of top management evolved from concentration on physical and human resources to a major concern with money. This shift was accompanied by an extension of planning horizons and a transition from a unifunctional to a multifunctional view of a company's activities.

In contrast to physical resources, money is inherently neutral; to be used it must be transformed into physical and human resources. Money also is flexible through time, that is, capable of expansion and contraction, as well as of rapid shifts in the forms, risks, and costs of financial instruments. These characteristics of neutrality and flexibility encouraged a broader management view that encompassed many functions within a company as well as longer term planning horizons.

□ *Ideas.* We are now beginning to sense that a focus on managing money, although broader than the earlier focus on physical and human resources, still fosters a dangerous sort of tunnel vision. The world of management is in a revolutionary phase. Within the company, racing technologies destroy both their own foundations and inter-technological boundaries. Outside the company, the environment is moving faster (in market evolution and consumer behavior), exploding in geographic scope (from nation to world), and reflecting the demands and constraints of a new society in which the traditional role of private business and traditional criteria of management performance are challenged by new concepts and standards.

At the same time, new analytical techniques, largely quantitative and computer-based, are presenting a management opportunity that is unique in at least two important ways. First, they provide an administrative capability without parallel in breadth, depth, and speed. Second, for their full and efficient utilization they press management to establish a unified command over the totality of a business, including the dynamic interface of external environment and internal activities. These changes are defining a novel view of management itself as a universally applicable resource, readily transferred from one business to another, from one industry to another, from one technology to another, from one country to another.

In this emerging management world, what will be the main task of management, common to top-level administrators in all types and sizes of companies? I suggest a combination of spatial and temporal intellectual vision, with the ability to transform vision into operating results through the flexible administration of physical, human, and financial resources in any environment. This might be described as applied conceptualization—or, more simply, as the management of ideas.

Central Focus for Ideas

Skill in generating and manipulating ideas is precisely the skill of the great philosophers—the ability to universalize from here and now to everywhere and always. If it is true that top executives in the years ahead are going to be tested above all by their ability to manage ideas, then they are going to have to understand what it means to think like philosophers and develop skill in doing it. This has implications for management education, training, and selection, especially at the higher levels of administration. It also carries a substantial threat of obsolescence for managers now holding broad responsibilities whose talent, education, and experience have not equipped them to use their intellects in this manner.

The implications are not limited to the purely intellectual demands placed on general managers. They also extend to corporate purpose, organization, and function. A business devoted to the identification of central ideas and the formulation of strategies for moving swiftly from ideas to operations will differ in structure and activity from a business primarily concerned with management of money, or of physical and human resources.

Management of ideas is a broader concept than either management by objectives or long-range planning. The use of objectives and planning are techniques equally relevant for any major management task, whether it be a focus on physical resources or money, or a principal concern with ideas.

Management of ideas also goes beyond the concept of strategy. Just as there are alternative strategies for attaining an objective, so there are alternative strategies for executing an idea that defines the central purpose of a business. Focusing on the management of ideas contributes to more realistic planning, more appropriate objectives, more relevant strategies.

Ideas for Technology
One example of how an idea may be viewed as the central focus for management attention can be found in industries characterized by advanced, dynamic technologies.

Soft Answers. In this arena, it is attractively easy to frame a soft answer to the hard question of how to organize resources for maximum effectiveness. A typical soft answer:

> In our fast-moving technological environment, the big winners will be those companies with large investments in research and development, because out of R&D come the new products that capture markets and generate high return on investment. Therefore we should invest every available dollar in R&D.

The inadequacy of this operating design is suggested by the common management complaint in these industries that it is difficult to establish rational control over investment in and performance of R&D, difficult to measure payback on R&D investment, and difficult to concentrate research efforts on projects with high potential payoffs.

Hard Answers. However, there are a few companies in high-technology industries in which such complaints rarely arise. These are the companies whose top managers have done the thinking that develops hard, rather than soft, answers. They have observed that a commitment to R&D without a specific central concept for total organization effort is a clumsy, even a meaningless, commitment. But by resolute probing, they have found an opportunity for defining a core idea around which total company effort can be designed. This opportunity can be described in terms of three specific idea options:

1 To mobilize all of a company's resources around the concept of becoming a creative technological leader—the first in the industry to discover, develop, and market new products at the leading edge of moving technology.
2 To organize resources around the central idea of becoming an early imitator and adapter of the successful innovations of the industry's creative leader.
3 To become a low-price mass producer of established products, sacrificing the high margins (and high risks) of innovation for the high volume (and limited risks) of low-price imitation.

Each of these options carries specific implications for the kind of investment in product and market research, as well as for organization structure, information network, scale of activity and risk, and many other aspects of a company's physical, personal, and financial resources. In short, out of each of these idea options can be derived a total scheme for operating a business. This total scheme will be uniquely determined by the central idea and will represent the top management choice among alternative strategies for executing the idea throughout the business.

Ideas for Conglomerates

Another example can be found among diversified or conglomerate companies. Here, too, there have been many soft answers, framed around a generalized acquisition drive. Economic pressures have revealed the inadequacies of this course. In contrast, some managements have exploited opportunities to select as a base for a total enterprise commitment a central idea from several identified options:

1   A structure of unrelated or accidentally related companies anchored to a central core of unusual management competence, both general and functional, available to strengthen the performance of each satellite company.
2   A designed diversification aimed at exploiting complementary technologies, production resources, or market systems.
3   A diversification aimed at balancing high-risk and low-risk ventures, fluctuating and stable industries, and cyclical and seasonal variations.

As with the high-technology idea options, each of the diversification models carries specific implications for every element in a business and for the goals and strategies by which the elements are activated.

Other Examples

Still other examples of central ideas may be cited briefly:

☐   A shift in the definition of a business from one concerned with the sale of a product to one concerned with the delivery of a complete system of customer values—as an airlines' marketing of packaged vacations, computer manufacturers' marketing of systems to solve customers' information problems, and consumer hard-good companies' marketing of assured lifetime performance of products.

☐   The discovery, almost the invention, of new industries—such as environmental hygiene and control, education as a lifespan need, and the profit-oriented performance of traditional public services such as urban redevelopment or even urban creation.

☐   The abandonment of accepted notions of industry boundaries—as in the transformation of a steel company into a materials company or of a petroleum company into an energy company.

☐   The evolution of "scrambled merchandising" in retail stores which focus on a pattern of consumer needs and buying habits rather than on historic product categories such as groceries or drug products.

Each of these ideas is the energized core of a unique design for a business. The exploitation of each idea requires a comprehensive intellectual grasp of the totality of a business viewed as an interacting system that includes both internal resources and functions and external distribution systems and markets. From such a comprehensive vision will issue a flow of strategic options for products, services, costs, prices, technology, organization structures, responsibilities, information networks, and motivations for all levels of management.

New Ways of Thinking

Thinking in terms of such ideas, from initial concept through full implementation, is a difficult intellectual task. It is no assignment for second-rate minds, or even for first-rate but narrowly oriented minds. Moreover, it demands the special intellectual ability to visualize the translation of ideas and strategies into controlled operating systems responsive to dynamic change.

The need for these unusual talents is the inevitable outcome of radically new conditions within and outside the corporation. The critical new condition is an acceleration in the rate of change of such magnitude that change itself becomes the central object of management attention. Up to now, with rare exceptions, the administration of change has been handled as a supplement to the administration of established ongoing activities. In this context, the future evolves from the present at a controllable pace, and it is reasonable for managers to concentrate mainly on targets of efficiency and to treat adapting to market challenges as a subsidiary element within a larger administrative responsibility.

Only a few companies have been in a position to report to stockholders such dramatic news as that "50% of our sales in the past year and 75% of our profits were generated by products that we did not handle five years ago." When many companies report such news, or make equally startling observations about short-term penetration of new markets or new technologies (whether from internal development or acquisitions), the fact of change moves to the center of the stage and all else is peripheral.

Preparing for Change

At this point, it becomes more important to make correct decisions about the direction, timing, and implementation of change than to attain a high level of efficiency in administering steady-state operations. However, few business organizations have been designed to give primary support to this unfamiliar ordering of goals. In most companies the values, organization, responsibility, control systems, information networks, and performance standards are not well adapted to this requirement.

Most companies, including many with reputations for being well managed, are organized primarily to administer yesterday's ideas. Investments and operations are measured by efficient performance, with relatively short-term targets for achievement, and a primary focus on taut administration of existing resources and markets. This was an appropriate corporate design concept when the rate of changes within and outside the company was slow.

The weakness of such organizations is revealed, however, whenever a new opportunity or a forced adaptation is sensed by a single department. Rapid exploitation of new markets usually increases production costs, and is therefore resisted by managers whose performance will be adversely affected in any shift in ongoing efficient activities. Less common, but equally possible, is resistance from the marketing people to innovation in production technology with its risk of cost, quality, and delivery uncertainties.

But even this view is simplistic. For in spite of the current touted commitment to a marketing orientation in management, the performance record in many companies suggests that leadership by the marketing function frequently generates little more than better adaption of existing products to better defined existing markets. This may be a move in the right direction in the short run. But it is not good enough in a period when new technology may erode established market positions or capture untouched markets "overnight."

Inherent in the concept of core ideas for top management is a total business orientation, rather than a market-oriented administration (or a technology-oriented or any "other-oriented" administration). A total business orientation views the company as a system of physical, financial, and human resources in dynamic interaction with a changing environment. It views swift response to opportunities and problems as more important for long-run success than efficient control of current operations. It values the future above the present. Such an orientation has revolutionary implications for many management designs and tasks.

New Organizational Patterns

Consider, as one example, the way companies assign authority and responsibility. Whatever the shape of a company's organization tree, it shares certain characteristics with all organization structures. First among these, and most visible because it is specifically charted, is some type of cluster design that gathers together a prescribed set of related activities. The design may focus on patterns of functions, products, geography, or projects. Whatever the pattern, the task performance is substantially influenced by the prescription of the pattern itself, and the pressures of the perceived reward criteria.

With one exception (the project cluster), all of these cluster patterns inevitably develop a built-in resource and emotional investment in the continuance of the established design. Since there are no defined time limits for the exercise of responsibility within the cluster, the accumulating managerial bias must be toward preservation of existing activities and status.

In such an environment, it would be extraordinary if radical change claimed a dominant share of management attention. Thus we see the common practice of establishing a long-range planning function at a single, usually remote, location in the organization tree, with the resulting problems of working through informal channels to bring ideas about the future into contact with current operations.

In these structures, radical change is painful. It is viewed as disruptive and costly by managers committed to the present and appraised by their administration of the present. In their constrained sighting they are right. They resist change because it is in their perceived economic interest to resist and because change threatens their status and their intellectual and emotional commitments.

This may go a long way toward explaining why so many of the major conceptual innovations—the great new ideas—are introduced and initially exploited by companies other than the corporate giants. (It should be noted, however, that this conclusion has nothing to do with the development and application of technological progress which is one of the prime accomplishments of large research-oriented companies.)

The single organization pattern that is free from this built-in bias is the project cluster. While there may be difficult administrative problems associated with project-oriented structures, they offer the important advantages of tailor-made design to fit unique tasks, flexible resource commitments, defined termination points, and an absence of enduring commitment that encourages resistance to radical innovation.

The project pattern suggests important clues for the characteristics of an organization structure focused on the management of ideas in a dynamic environment. One principal requirement will be unconstrained adaptability to new tasks, with easy transitions across technological, product, and market boundaries. Another will be performance measurement and motivation that give substantial encouragement to future-oriented management thinking. A third will be an ability to bring multifunctional considerations quickly to bear on opportunities that appear initially in the field of vision of a single function.

All of these requirements suggest a fluid concept of organization structure marked by short-lived, specific-assignment clusters, flexibility in job definitions, and a high degree of vertical and horizontal teamwork. Thus *both* middle and top management must accept and adjust to this fluid concept. This means critical demands on both the quality of managers' intellectual resources and the ways in which managers are motivated to use these resources. None of these demands can be met by fiat. They call for the creation of a new way of life for which many executives are ill-prepared by education and experience.

Information Revolution

A further example of revolutionary change in administrative design can be found in the area of information generation and use.

A few words about computers are in order at the outset. The history of computer applications in the 17 years since their introduction to the business market reveals two distinct stages in management concepts of their potential.

1 Initially, most managers viewed computers as electronic clerks. The primary use of computers was therefore in familiar tasks.

2 Recently, a second stage of management thinking can be discerned. This has been marked by a superficial popularization of the concept of the integrated information system which calls on the storage, retrieval, and manipulative capability of large computers to bring the total information requirements of a business within an integrated decision network. (This does not imply a computerized decision system, but simply an organized information system, computer-based, to assist comprehensive human decision-making.)

While the notion of the integrated information systems has been widely described and explored in technical and management journals, several probes of management practice suggest that few companies have made a sustained attempt to operate in this way, and few managers have any real grasp of what the concept means in either theoretical or operating terms. There is, to be sure, a growing number of fractional, single-function information systems, such as those linking production, inventory, and procurement activities. And there is a growing disposition to talk about comprehensive management information systems. But the operational application is a long way from the discussion, with many unresolved conceptual and technical problems in between.

It would be a gross misconception to view this gap as the familiar one between software and hardware. The primary task ahead is not to develop programs that will utilize the capabilities of the machines. Rather it is to develop management concepts that define integrated systems. It will then be possible to describe the principal data requirements to make such systems operational, including clear delineation of relationships among the components of a dynamic system responsive to external and internal feedback. The next step will be the design of computer programs to store and manipulate data for management needs.

At present, most top managers have yet to approach even the initial stage of developing basic concepts. The skeptic may be inclined to say: "But this can't be true! Managers are running companies, and this means that they are running systems, with whatever crude tools, including the human brain, they may have at hand." To which the appropriate reply is:

True enough, managers are running companies. But examination of the typical management decision process reveals that what is happening is in no sense total system analysis. Problems are usually fractionated within the total company system—partly to reduce them to a size and order of simplicity that are manageable with available analytical tools, and partly to follow familiar routines and utilize familiar rules of thumb.

What is defined here is not a technical requirement, but an intellectual requirement. This is essentially a command of logical design. The basic design building blocks are:

1 Identification of critical areas of initiating change that generate ef fects in one or several operating areas.
2 Rough measures of the magnitude of the primary cause-effect relationships.
3 Identification of the principal feedbacks.
4 Rough measures of these feedbacks.

For purposes of concept formulation and testing, the degree of precision ordinarily required is modest because this is not primarily a quantitative exercise. One does not need numbers to design a business system. In fact, the truth is quite the reverse. One first needs a concept of a system in order to identify the kinds of numbers needed to work the system.

Furthermore, it is unlikely that any comprehensive business system can be completely quantified in the sense of converting all decision inputs into a set of manipulable numbers. The objective is limited and practical. It is simply to use both quantitative and qualitative analysis to extend management's decision horizon to the total business viewed as a dynamic system, and thereby to improve the quality of decisions. The improvement will be reflected in the ability to make decisions that are broadly consistent with the basic concept of the business, sensitive to impacts and feedbacks throughout the business, and rapidly and flexibly adaptive to changing conditions within and outside the company.

Focus on the Future

Another example of the impact of revolutionary change is the need for upgrading management's ability to forecast the shape of things to come. During the last 20 years economic forecasting has made the transition from favorite parlor game of professional economists to favorite reading matter of professional managers. The prognostications of accredited economic forecasters are a mandatory item on every trade association agenda, while discussions of the economic outlook clog the pages of management magazines.

But economic change is only one of several environmental areas important to managers. Three other areas are equally significant: technological change, social change, and political change. Few companies and few individual managers have addressed themselves in a serious and organized way to the problems of forecasting trends in these areas. Yet changes in the years ahead, coming more rapidly than ever before, will be loaded with opportunities for the forewarned, and with threats for those who have not cast their minds forward and formulated offensive and defensive strategies.

The requirement is for more than a freshened interest in the future.

The evolution of economic forecasting to its present significant role in management planning resulted from the invention of sophisticated tools of analysis. One cannot predict economic trends with a useful level of confidence until the significant economic variables have been identified and their interacting dynamics at least roughly measured. Forecasting of technological, social, and political changes (including both trends and rates of movement) will require a comparable intellectual achievement. Large rewards will be realized by organizations that can anticipate developments in these areas with enough confidence to incorporate their forecasts in strategic planning.

Technological Forecasting

In the area of technology an essential conceptual adaptation must be to extend management thinking beyond the base to which it is commonly tied, that is, the view that improvements will be regularly generated from developments in the technologies that have been their historical foundation. This is an understandable but limiting and risky framework for forecasting.

Analysis of recent technological advances clearly identifies two related phenomena of great importance to management. One is the application of "foreign" technologies in process and product areas where they have played no significant prior role. The other is the erosion, often the disappearance, of traditional industry and product boundaries. Together, they lay down a requirement that technological forecasting be treated broadly.

It will not be safe for a manager to project the shape of technological changes by extrapolating trends in existing applications. Some of the most significant developments affecting both production and marketing are likely to be spawned within technologies that are not currently applicable in the manager's industry and company.

Technological forecasting of this breadth and sophistication will not progress far without the development of a new kind of professional expertise, comparable to that of professional economists. It will be a prime responsibility of enlightened managers to encourage qualified scientists and engineers to address themselves to the assignment, and to build their own ability to communicate with and guide this new corps of professionals.

In addition, just as the sophisticated manager needs the skill to translate economic forecasts into signals of opportunity and threat for his company's future operations, so will he need a parallel skill to translate technological forecasts into meaningful guides for business strategies. This task cannot safely be left to the technicians. There should be little need to emphasize this warning to managers who have grasped, often after painful experience, the need to guide the work of computer specialists to assure that they mobilize information specifically relevant for management control and decision.

A prime ingredient in translating technological projections into business applications will be a thorough understanding of the difference between technical feasibility and economic feasibility. Technology determines what can be done. Economics determines what will be done. Managers must be familiar with this distinction. Many of today's naive forecasters of the technological outlook who are writing in the popular press certainly are not.

Social Forecasting

Forecasting of social trends covers such topics as changing social structure (including racial and ethnic components), evolution of living patterns and related spending patterns, and shifting values and priorities (for example, between work and leisure, between risk assumption and security).

The full implications of the opportunities presented by recent social trends have been grasped by few companies. For instance, managers of a number of financial institutions reveal a persistent preoccupation with superficial economic phenomena of consumers' saving and investment patterns, rather than a probing analysis of the financial service needs of a society marked by widespread affluence, multiple options in discretionary spending, confidence in long-range income security, and rising concern about permanent inflation.

A well-known example of the powerful application of social (appropriately combined with economic) forecasting is the course pursued by Sears, Roebuck and Co. since World War II. The dramatic divergence of this company's performance from that of its direct competitor, Montgomery Ward & Company, Inc., needs no description for a management audience. But the important contribution made by a projection of fundamental social changes and the translation of that forecast into market opportunities deserves to be noted.

Sears made an aggressive exploitation of social perspective through a core institutional idea. The results have been as spectacular as was the comparable grasp of a new business opportunity evoked by socioeconomic change evidenced in the implementation of a core management idea by General Motors under Alfred P. Sloan's direction in the 1920s.

The extension of management's conceptual competence in the area of social dynamics calls for knowledge and perceptiveness that have not been required hitherto. As in the field of technology, managers will be dealing with professional specialists whose work must be directed and interpreted. Competence in doing this will build the confidence to use social projections in designing business strategies that open the way to radical innovations in organization and operations.

Political Forecasting

The principal business element in political forecasting is the shifting boundary between the private and public sectors of the economy. Until recently, the prevailing management view of this area was a superficial conclusion that a transfer of activities was occurring from the private to the public sector, directly by intervention or indirectly by control.

Current developments are beginning to suggest that this is a naive judgment. Movement in the opposite direction can also be discerned, for example, in education, research, and construction. New, mixed public-private enterprise forms, such as Comsat, are being invented. More developments of this sort may be anticipated. Moreover, changes in the domain of private enterprise, in pure or mixed form, are not totally a result of decisions taken within government. Business initiative can open the door to private expansion, particularly where the public performance has been lethargic, unimaginative, or grossly inefficient.

The pejorative descriptive phrase, "socialization of American society," indiscriminately applied to developments in such diverse fields as health, insurance, transportation, housing, or even protection of consumer interests, has a dangerous potential for stultifying thinking about the central issues. A more open view might recognize that an industrialized, urbanized, high-technology society, in which a dramatically visible gap appears between the actual and the potential quality of life, is a society ripe for changes in traditional public-private relationships.

The changes may move in either direction: toward public invasion of the private sector or toward private invasion of the public sector. The direction and rate of these changes will be powerfully influenced by managers who can deal confidently with new ideas in areas where businessmen have seldom allowed their minds to be engaged. The political environment, there can be little doubt, will be redesigned. But those who believe that environment is created by forces outside their control will not be in an intellectual position to particpate in the redesign. An environment will be imposed on them which, however reluctantly, they will be compelled to accept.

On the positive side, a rising interest and skill in forecasting political relationships will identify opportunities for private enterprise to invent new environmental concepts. Formulating these concepts, and relating them to profitable resource investment, will require an intellectual adventure in the world of ideas such as few managers have so far experienced. Part of the process will surely be fresh definitions of the words "private" and "public," which, as applied to business and government activities, have been largely emptied of meaning by emotional abuse.

As in forecasting social change, it is not easy to perceive shifts in the private-public balance, or potential for inducing shifts by initiatives from the private sector. We lack even the professional discipline to generate the knowledge and develop a reliable analytical base for management thinking. Traditional political science is oriented toward the problems of governing men and the performance of institutions for public legislation and administration. The new issues are closer to those implied by the classic term, "political economy," and involve concepts of social design on the grand scale.

Philosopher-Executive

The emerging dominance of ideas as a central concern for top management raises critical questions about the education, selection, and development of candidates for high-level assignments in the years ahead. Neither business school education nor in-company experience is presently structured to emphasize the manager-as-philosopher concept. Rather, the principal thrust in school and company environments is toward new analytic techniques, both quantitative and qualitative, and their application in rational decision-making and control.

There is good reason to doubt that students in professional schools are at a stage of their intellectual development where they would benefit from a major emphasis on the role of central ideas in top management responsibilities. Moreover, the relevant technical input to their education is so important and growing so rapidly that any sharp curtailment would constrain their ability to handle management tasks in junior executive positions.

The education of middle-level managers is another matter, however. There are opportunities at this stage to expose selected high-potential executives to the significance of core ideas in the design of long-range corporate strategies and in the adaptation of organization and resources to their implementation. The opportunities arise in planned job experiences and management education programs, both in-house and university. Imaginative action at this level will produce two important benefits. One is the preparation of a cadre of potential top executives for the broad new responsibilities that the future business environment will thrust on them. The other is a new selection criterion for top-level positions, based on specific performance in mid-career assignments where the ability to think conceptually and to relate ideas to applied management can be tested.

Today's development programs give principal emphasis to new techniques for analysis and control in functional areas, and to strategic planning of resource utilization at the general management level. It would be desirable to curtail the technical content to some degree and introduce material on dynamic environmental change (markets, technologies, social, political), on the role and manipulation of ideas, and on the impact of change on corporate strategy.

A related effort to enrich idea-management experience on the job and test executives' abilities would require more opportunities below the top management level for assignments that require imaginative projection, assessment of the total environmental outlook, and relevant strategic decision. Corporations which move in this direction will fortify their management ability to cope powerfully and speedily with a radically new business world.

5

Managing for Business Effectiveness

PETER F. DRUCKER

Effective management requires precise analysis, rigorous allocation of resources, and timely decision making. The author explains how each of these requirements can be met and how greater attention can be placed on tomorrow's opportunities rather than today's problems. This article won the McKinsey Award for the best *Harvard Business Review* article published in 1963.

What is the first duty—and the continuing responsibility—of the business manager? *To strive for the best possible economic results from the resources currently employed or available*. Everything else managers may be expected to do, or may want to do, rests on sound economic performance and profitable results over the next few years. Even such lofty management tasks as assessing corporate social responsibilities and cultural opportunities are not exempt from this presupposition. And certainly not exempt, by and large, are the individual manager's *own rewards*—money and position.

Accordingly, all business executives spend much, if not all, of their time on the problems of short-run economic performance. They concern themselves with costs and pricing, with scheduling and selling, with quality control and customer service, with purchasing and training. Furthermore, the vast array of tools and techniques available to the modern manager deal to a great extent with managing *today's* business for today's and tomorrow's economic performance. This is the subject matter of 90 out of any 100 books in the business library, and (conservatively) of 90 out of any 100 reports and studies produced within businesses.

No Time for Clichés

Despite all this attention, few managers I know are greatly impressed with their own performance in this work. They want to know how to organize for the task; how to tell the important from the time-wasting, the potentially effective from the merely frustrating. Despite the flood of data and reports threatening to inundate managers today, they get only the vaguest generalities. Such banalities as "low costs" or "high profit margins" are bandied about as answers to the question: What *really* determines economic performance and results in this particular business that I work for?

Even in the boom times of a "seller's market," managing for economic performance tends to be a source of constant frustration. And as soon as times return to normal and markets become competitive again, managing for economic performance tends to generate such confusion, pressure, and anxiety that the decisions made are most unlikely to be the right ones, even for short-run results, let alone for the company's future.[1]

What we need are not more or better tools—we have already many more than any single business (let alone any single manager) can use. What we need are simple concepts—some crude rules of thumb—that will help organize the job by answering:

- ☐ Just what is the manager's job?
- ☐ What is the major problem in it?
- ☐ What is the principle for defining this problem and analyzing it?

Misplaced Emphasis

I do not propose to give here a full-blown "science of management economics," if only because I have none to give. Even less do I intend to present a magic formula, a "checklist" or "procedure" which will do the job for the manager. For his job is *work*—very hard, demanding, risk-taking work. And while there is plenty of laborsaving machinery around, no one has yet invented a "work-saving" machine, let alone a "think-saving" one.

But I do claim that we know how to organize the job of managing for economic effectiveness and how to do it with both direction and results. The answers to the three key questions above are known, and have been known for such a long time that they should not surprise anyone.

1. *What is the manager's job?* It is to direct the resources and the efforts of the business toward opportunities for economically significant results. This sounds trite—and it is. But every analysis of actual allocation of resources and efforts in business that I have ever seen or made showed clearly that *the bulk of time, work, attention, and money first goes to "problems" rather than to opportunities, and, secondly, to areas where even extraordinarily successful performance will have minimal impact on results.*

2. *What is the major problem?* It is fundamentally the confusion between effectiveness and efficiency that stands between doing the right things and doing things right. *There is surely nothing quite so usless as doing with great efficiency what should not be done at all.* Yet our tools—especially our accounting concepts and data—all focus on efficiency. What we need

is (1) a way to identify the areas of effectiveness (of possible significant results), and (2) a method for concentrating on them.

3. *What is the principle?* That, too, is well-known—at least as a general proposition. Business enterprise is not a phenomenon of nature but one of society. In a social situation, however, events are not distributed according to the "normal distribution" of a natural universe (that is, they are not distributed according to the U-shaped Gaussian curve). *In a social situation a very small number of events—10% to 20% at most—account for 90% of all results, whereas the great majority of events account for 10% or less of the results.*

This is true in the marketplace. A handful of customers out of many thousands produce the bulk of the orders; a handful of products out of hundreds of items in the line produce the bulk of the volume; and so on. This is true of markets, end uses, and distributive channels. It is equally true of sales efforts: a few salesmen, out of several hundred, always produce two-thirds or more of all new business. It is true in the plant: a handful of production runs account for most of the tonnage. It is true of research: a few men in the laboratory produce all the important innovations, as a rule.

It also holds true for practically all personnel "problems": the great bulk of the grievances always comes from a few places or from one group of employees (for example, from the older, unmarried women or from the clean-up men on the night shift), as does the great bulk of absenteeism, of turnover, of suggestions under a suggestion system, and of accidents. As studies at the New York Telephone Company have shown, this is true even in respect to employee sickness.

Revenue $ versus Cost $

The importance that this simple statement about "normal distribution" has for managing a business has been grasped by all too few businessmen. It means, first: *while 90% of the results are being produced by the first 10% of events, 90% of the costs are being increased by the remaining and result-less 90% of events.*

In other words, costs, too, are a "social phenomenon." If we put it into mathematical language, we see that the "normal distribution curve" of business events is a hyperbola with the results plotted along the plus half, and the costs along the minus half of the curve. Thus, results and costs stand in inverse relationship to each other.

And now, translated back into common language, *economic results are, by and large, directly proportionate to revenue, while costs are directly proportionate to number of transactions.* The only exceptions to this are the purchased materials and parts that go directly into the final product. For example:

☐   To get a $50,000 order costs no more, as a rule, than to get a $500 order; certainly it does not cost 100 times as much.

☐   To design a new product that does not sell is as expensive as to design a "winner."

☐   It costs just as much to do the paper work for a small order as for a large one—the same order entry, production order, scheduling, billing, collecting, and so on.

☐   It even costs just as much, as a rule, to actually make the product, to package it, and to transport it for a small order as for a large one. Even labor is a "fixed" cost today over any period of time in most manufacturing industries (and in all services) rather than a cost fluctuating with volume. Only purchased materials and parts are truly "variable" costs.

Furthermore, there is the implication that *"normally," revenues and efforts will allocate themselves to the 90% of events that produce practically no results.* They will allocate themselves according to the *number of events* rather than according to results. In fact, the most expensive and potentially most productive resources (i.e., highly trained people) will misallocate themselves the worst. For the pressure exerted by the bulk of transactions is fortified by the person's pride in doing the difficult—whether productive or not.

This has been proved by every single study made; it is, in other words, supported both by principle and by concrete experience. Let me give some examples:

A large engineering company prided itself on the high quality and reputation of its technical service group, which contained several hundred expensive men. The men were indeed first-rate. But analysis of their allocation showed clearly that they, while working hard, contributed little. Most of them worked on the "interesting" problems—especially those of the very small customers—problems which, even if solved, produced little, if any, business. The automobile industry is the company's major customer and accounts for almost one-third of all purchases. But few technical service people within anyone's memory had even set foot in the engineering department or the plant of an automobile company. "General Motors and Ford don't need us; they have their own people," was their reaction.

Similarly, in many companies salespeople are misallocated. The largest group of salespeople (and especially the most effective ones) are usually put on the products that are "hard to sell," either because they are "yesterday's products," or because they are "also rans" which managerial vanity desperately is trying to make into "winners." Tomorrow's important products very rarely get the sales effort required. And the product that has sensational success in the market—and which, therefore, ought to be pushed all-out—

tends to be slighted. "It is doing all right without extra effort, after all," is the common conclusion.

Research departments, design staffs, market development efforts, even advertising efforts have been shown to be allocated the same way in lots of companies—by transaction rather than by results, by what is difficult rather than by what is productive, by yesterday's problems rather than by today's and tomorrow's opportunities!

Unaccountable Accounting

"Revenue money" and "cost money," to put it dramatically, are not automatically the same "money stream." Revenue produces the wherewithal for the costs, of course. But unless management constantly seeks to direct these costs into revenue-producing activities, they will tend to allocate themselves *by drift* into "nothing-producing" activities.

One major reason why managers do not, as a rule, understand this fact is their mistaken identification of *accounting* data and analysis with *economic* data and business analysis.[2] The accountant has to allocate to all products those costs that are not actually and physically tied to a particular unit of production. Today, one way or another, the great bulk of the costs—the 60% to 70% that are not purchased materials and parts—are, consequently, allocated, rather than truly "direct," costs.

Now the only way the accountant can allocate costs is in a way that is proportionate to volume rather than proportionate to the number of transactions. Thus, $1 million in volume produced in one order—or in one product—carries the same cost as $1 million in volume produced by 1 million individual orders or by 50 different production runs.

Similarly, the accountant is concerned with the cost per unit of output rather than with the costs of a product. His or her focus is on profit margin rather than on profit stream—which is, of course, profit margin multiplied by turnover. Finally, the accountant does not classify costs by the economic activity to which they pertain. Instead, he or she classifies by organizational or geographic locus (e.g., "manufacturing" or "plant"), or by legal—or legalistic—categories (e.g., "payroll").

I am well aware of the work done on these and related problems of accounting theory and practice. Indeed, I owe whatever understanding of accounting I have to this work and to the accountants engaged in it. But it will be years before the results of this work will penetrate accounting practice, let alone change the way businessmen use or misuse accounting data.

Rifle Approach

More important than the reasons *why* we have not drawn the right conclusions is: What *are* the right conclusions? What line of action will produce the best possible economic results and performance from the resources available to a business? Let us begin by setting some guidelines:

1 Economic results require that managers concentrate their efforts on the smallest number of products, product lines, services, customers, markets, distribution channels, end uses, and so on which will produce the largest amount of revenue. Managers must minimize the attention devoted to products which produce primarily costs, because their volume is too small or too splintered.

2 Economic results require also that staff efforts be concentrated on the very few activities that are capable of producing truly significant business results—with as little staff work and staff effort as possible spent on the others.

3 Effective cost control requires a similar concentration of work and efforts on those very few areas where improvement in cost performance will have significant impact on business performance and results—that is, on those areas where a relatively *minor* increase in efficiency will produce a *major* increase in economic effectiveness.

4 Managers must allocate resources, especially *high-grade human resources,* to activities which provide opportunities for high economic results.

Unpardonable Profligacy

No wonder so many businesses did poorly the moment the "seller's market" was over. The wonder, rather, is that they did not do worse. For most businesses—those abroad as well as those in this country—operate in direct opposition to every one of the four well-known rules I have just spelled out.

Instead of product concentration we have product clutter. Remember how it used to be fashionable to attack industry, especially U.S. industry, for its "deadening standardization"? Then, a few years ago, it became fashionable to attack industry for its "planned obsolescence." If only there *were* any validity to either of these charges!

Most businesses—today's large U.S. corporations are perhaps the worst offenders—pride themselves on being willing and able to supply *any* "specialty," to satisfy *any* demand for variety, even to stimulate such demands in the first place. And any number of businesses boast that they never, of their own free will, abandon a product. As a result, most large companies typically end up with thousands of items in their product line—and all too frequently fewer than 20 really "sell." However, these 20 items or less have to contribute revenues to carry the costs of the 9,999 nonsellers.

Indeed, the basic problem of U.S. competitive strength in the world economy today may well be product clutter. If properly costed, the main lines in most of our industries will prove to be fully competitive, despite our high wage rates and our high tax burden. But we fritter away our competitive advantage in the volume products by subsidizing an enormous array of "specialties," of which only a few recover their true cost. This, at least, is what I have found in such industries as steel and aluminum. And in electronics the competitive advantage of the Japanese portable transistor radio rests on little more than the Japanese concentration on a few models in this one line—as against the uncontrolled plethora of barely differentiated models in the U.S. manufacturers' lines.

We are similarly profligate in this country with respect to staff activities. Our motto seems to be, "Let's do a little bit of everything"—personnel research, advanced engineering, customer analysis, international economics, operations research, public relations, and so on. As a result, we build enormous staffs, and yet do not concentrate enough effort in any one area to get very far. Nor do we know what to do to remedy the situation. The common way to control costs is still the one everybody knows to be ineffectual if not destructive: the "across-the-board-cut" by 15%. We have not really made a serious attempt to manage resources and pinpoint our efforts. Things are left to drift along.

Three Giant Steps

Criticizing is easy; anyone can find fault. Readers have every right to say, at this point, "Just how can we go about doing a better job of managing?" Even if I had all the answers—and I do not—an article would not be long enough for me to offer a satisfactory reply. This would require a book; and even then every company would *still* have to work out the methods best suited to its own affairs.

So, if readers will bear with me, I will present a series of steps—sketched out only in the lightest of strokes—that I have found to be highly effective in actual business situations, at least as first approaches. Specifically:

Step 1. Analysis. Here managers have to know the facts. They need to identify:

☐ The opportunities and true costs of products.
☐ The potential contributions of different staff activities.
☐ The economically significant cost centers.

Step 2. Allocation. Here managers have to allocate resources according to results anticipated. For this, they need to know:

☐ How resources are allocated now.
☐ How resources should be allocated in the future to support activities of greatest opportunity.
☐ What steps are necessary to get from what *is* to what *ought to be*.

Step 3. Decision. The manager must be prepared to take the most painful step of all—that of deciding on those products, staff activities, or cost areas that breed clutter rather than bring opportunity and results. Naturally, productive resources of any magnitude or potential should never be allocated to these. But which should be abandoned altogether? Which should be maintained at a minimum effort? Which could be changed into major opportunities, and what would it cost to make such a change?

Analyzing the Facts

In the analysis stage, the first job is to take an unsentimental look at the product line. All the standard questions should be asked about each product: its volume, market standing, market outlook, and so on. There is, however, one new key question: What does the product contribute? What does a comparison of its revenue with its true costs show?

In this analysis, revenue should be defined as total sales dollars less costs of purchased materials and supplies. And true costs should be estimated on the basis of this (most probable) assumption—that the real cost of a product is the proportion of the total cost of the business that corresponds to the ratio between the number of transactions (orders, production runs, service calls, and the like) needed to obtain the product's revenue and total number of similar transactions in the business—less, again, materials and parts costs. Since this is cumbersome, let me give a concrete example:

A company had annual revenues of $68 million, after taking out costs of materials and parts purchased. Total costs of the business—materials and parts excepted—were $56 million.

Product A showed revenues of $12 million a year. It required, however, 24% of the total number of transactions—measured in this case by invoices. Its true costs were, therefore, calculated to be $13.5 million a year, which meant a negative contribution, in sharp contrast to the "official" profit margin of almost 12% that the accounting figures showed. (This, by the way, is typical for "yesterday's product," which has either lost the main customers or can be held in the market only by uneconomic efforts.)

Product B, by contrast, despite an "unsatisfactory" profit margin of only 3%, showed a net revenue contribution of almost $4 million—the largest single contribution to profit. It went in sizable orders to a small number—about 50—of substantial customers.

As the example shows, this analysis looks at *all the products* of a business rather than at one at a time. This by itself is unusual and rarely done.

While the product breakdown is normally the most important and most revealing analysis, customers, markets, distribution channels, and end uses all need to be analyzed similarly in respect to their persent and their anticipated contributions.

Staff Contribution

The questions to be asked in this analysis call for managerial judgment rather than for economic data. Here is a list of queries I have found useful:

☐ In what areas would excellence really have an extraordinary impact on the economic results of our business, to the point where it might transform the economic performance of the entire business?

☐ In what areas would poor performance threaten to damage economic performance, greatly or at least significantly?

☐ In what areas would it make little difference whether we perform excellently or poorly?

☐ What results have been attained by the work done in the area? How do these compare with the results promised or expected?

☐ What results can realistically be expected for the future—and how far ahead is the future?

Cost Centers

The object here is to isolate those areas of the business where a concentration of cost control efforts will pay off. Rather than describe methods by which this analysis can be carried out, I would like to show the results of an actual study made by a substantial manufacturer of nationally distributed consumer goods (see Exhibit 1). For convenience, the figures for the various cost centers are given in absolute terms, but each is an approximation. In the actual study, the summary of "total costs," for example, ranged from 90% to 94%, while other figures had ranges somewhat less extreme.

The only innovation as to methods used by the manufacturer is that "cost" is defined (as it must be when one talks about economics) as what the customer spends on the product. In other words, this analysis looks at the entire economic process as one cost stream, and ignores the accountant's restriction that only those costs which are incurred *within* the legal entity of the business should be considered.

As to results, the important conclusions in this particular example are obvious: where most businesses concentrate their cost control efforts—that is, on manufacturing—there is not much to be gained except by a real "breakthrough," such as a radically different process. The potentially most productive cost centers either lie *outside* the business, especially in distribution, and require very different treatment from the usual routine of "cost reduction," or they are areas that management rarely even "sees," such as the cost of money.

What Ought to Be

The next practical step is that of analyzing how resources are *now* being allocated to product lines, to staff support activities, and to cost centers.

Exhibit 1. The Consumer's Dollar—Where It Goes

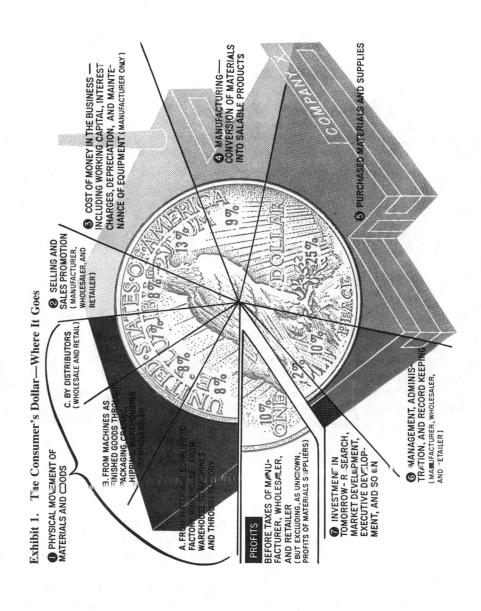

1 PHYSICAL MOVEMENT OF
MATERIALS AND GOODS

2 SELLING AND
SALES PROMOTION
(MANUFACTURER,
WHOLESALER, AND
RETAILER)

3 COST OF MONEY IN THE BUSINESS —
INCLUDING WORKING CAPITAL, INTEREST
CHARGES, DEPRECIATION, AND MAINTE-
NANCE OF EQUIPMENT (MANUFACTURER ONLY)

4 MANUFACTURING —
CONVERSION OF MATERIALS
INTO SALABLE PRODUCTS

5 PURCHASED MATERIALS AND SUPPLIES

C. BY DISTRIBUTORS
(WHOLESALE AND RETAIL)

B. FROM MACHINES AS
FINISHED GOODS THROUGH
PACKAGING, CRATING,
SHIPPING, AND WAREHOUSING
TO WHOLESALER

A. FROM MATERIALS SUPPLIER TO
FACTORY WAREHOUSE, FROM
WAREHOUSE TO MACHINES
AND THROUGH FACTORY

PROFITS

BEFORE TAXES OF MANU-
FACTURER, WHOLESALER,
AND RETAILER
(BUT EXCLUDING, AS UNKNOWN,
PROFITS OF MATERIALS SUPPLIERS)

7 INVESTMENT IN
TOMORROW—R SEARCH,
MARKET DEVELOPMENT,
EXECUTIVE DEVELOP-
MENT, AND SO ON

6 MANAGEMENT, ADMINIS-
TRATION, AND RECORD KEEPING
(MANUFACTURER, WHOLESALER,
AND RETAILER)

COMPANY X

9%

13%

8%

8%

25%

2%

10%

11%

10%

73

The analysis must, of course, be qualitative as well as quantitative. For numbers do not by themselves give the answers to questions like these:

☐ "Are advertising and promotion dollars going to the right products?"

☐ "Are capital equipment allocations in accord with realistic expectations for future demands that will be placed on the company?"

☐ "Is the company's allocation schedule supporting the best people and their activities?"

☐ "Are these good people deployed full-time on important jobs, or are they spread over so many assignments that they cannot do any one job properly?"

Answers to questions of this sort are often unpleasant, and the remedies they cry out for unpleasant to contemplate. Moving from the allocation stage to the decision stage, consequently, often takes courage.

Priority Decisions

There is only one rule that applies here. Specifically:

> The areas of greatest potential for opportunity and results are to be given the fullest resource support—in quantity and quality—before the next promising area gets anything.

Perhaps the area where the toughest and most risky decisions have to be made is that involving products, for the choices are seldom clear-cut and simple. For instance, products will often tend to group themselves into five groups—two with high-contribution potential, three with low- or minus-contribution potential, one in-between. What is fairly typical is a breakdown such as this:

☐ *Tomorrow's breadwinners.* New products or today's breadwinners modified and improved (rarely today's breadwinners unchanged).

☐ *Today's breadwinners.* The innovations of yesterday.

☐ *Products capable of becoming net contributors if something drastic is done.* For example, converting a good many buyers of "special" variations of limited utility into customers for a new, massive "regular" line. (This is the in-between category.)

☐ *Yesterday's breadwinners.* Typically products with high volume, but badly fragmented into "specials," small orders, and the like, and requiring such massive support as to eat up all they earn, and plenty more. Yet this is—next to the category following—the product class to which the largest and best resources are usually allocated. ("Defensive research" is a common example.)

☐ *The "also rans."* Typically the high hopes of yesterday that, while they did not work out well, nevertheless did not become outright failures. These are always minus contributors, and practically never become successes no matter how much is poured into them. Yet there is usually far too much managerial and technical ego involved in them to drop them.

☐ *The failures.* These rarely are a real problem as they tend to liquidate themselves.

This ranking suggests the line that decisions ought to follow. To begin with, the first category should be supplied the necessary resources—and usually a little more than seems necessary. Next, today's breadwinners ought to receive support. By then even a company rich in talent will have to begin to ration. Of the products capable of becoming major contributors, only those should be supported which have either the greatest probability of being reformed, successfully, or would make an *extraordinary* contribution if the reform were accomplished.

And from this point on there are just no high-potential resources available, as a rule—not even in the biggest, best-managed, and most profitable business. The lower half of the third group and groups four, five, and six either have to produce without any resources and efforts or should be allowed to die. "Yesterday's breadwinner," for instance, often makes a respectable "milch cow" with high yields for a few more years. To expect more and to plow dollars into artificial respiration when the product finally begins to fade is just plain foolish.

The "also rans," who after four or five years of trial and hard work are still runts in the product litter and far below their original expectation, should always be abandoned. There is no greater drain on a business than the product that "almost made it." This is especially true if everyone in the company is convinced that, by quality, by design, or by the cost and difficulty of making it (that is what engineers usually mean when they say "quality"), the pet product is "entitled" to success.

This is part of the last and most crucial "how to do it" requirement. the courage to go through with logical decisions despite all pleas to give this or that product another chance, and despite all such specious alibis as the accountant's "it absorbs overhead" or the sales manager's "we need a full product line." (Of course, these are not always unfounded alibis, but the burden of proof of every alibi rests with those that plead it.) It would be nice if I did, but unfortunately I know of no procedure or checklist for managerial courage.

Conclusion

What I have sketched out in this article is the manager's real work. As such it requires that he or she attack the problem of increasing business effectiveness systematically—with a plan of action, with a method of analysis, and with an understanding of the tools needed.

And while the job to be done may look different in every individual company, one basic truth will always be present: every product and every activity of a business begins to obsolesce as soon as it is started. Every product, every operation, and every activity in a business should, therefore, be put on trial for its life every two or three years. Each should be considered the way we consider a proposal to go into a *new* product, a new operation or activity—complete with budget, capital appropriations request, and so on. One question should be asked of each: "If we were not in this already, would we now go into it?" And if the answer is "no," the next question should be: "How do we get out and how fast?"

The end products of the manager's work are decisions and actions, rather than knowledge and insight. The crucial decision is the allocation of efforts. And no matter how painful, one rule should be adhered to: *in allocating resources, especially human resources of high potential, the needs of those areas which offer great promise must first be satisfied to the fullest extent possible*. If this means that there are no truly productive resources left for a lot of things it would be nice, but not vital, to have or to do, then it is better—much better—to abandon these uses, and not to fritter away high-potential resources or attempt to get results with low-potential ones. This calls for painful decisions, and risky ones. But that, after all, is what managers are paid for.

Notes

1. This was brought out clearly by J. Roger Morrison and Richard F. Neuschel, "The Second Squeeze on Profits," *HBR*, July–August 1962, p. 49; see also "Different Dollars," by Louis E. Newman and Sidney Brunell, in the same issue, p. 74.

2. See Morrison and Neuschel, op. cit.; and John Dearden, "Profit-Planning Accounting for Small Firms," *HBR*, March–April 1963, p. 66.

6

How to Evaluate Corporate Strategy

SEYMOUR TILLES

Strategy can be thought of as a set of goals and major policies. Yet how can a manager evaluate or compare strategies? Seymour Tilles argues that a sound strategy must describe how goals will be achieved and how six criteria will be met: internal consistency, consistency with the environment, appropriateness in light of available resources, satisfactory level of risk, reasonable time horizon, and workability.

No good military officer would undertake even a small-scale attack on a limited objective without a clear concept of his strategy. No seasoned politician would undertake a campaign for a major office without an equally clear concept of his or her strategy. In the field of business management, however, we frequently find people deploying resources on a large scale without any clear notion of what their strategy is. And yet a company's strategy is a vital ingredient in determining its future. A valid strategy will yield growth, profit, or whatever other objectives the managers have established. An inappropriate strategy not only will fail to yield benefits, but also may result in disaster.

In this chapter I will try to demonstrate the truth of these contentions by examining the experiences of a number of companies. I shall discuss what strategy is, how it can be evaluated, and how, by evaluating its strategy, a management can do much to assure the future of the enterprise.

Decisive Impact

The influence of strategy can be seen in every age and in every area of industry. Here are some examples:

From the time it was started in 1911 as the Computing-Tabulating-

Recording Co., International Business Machines Corporation has demonstrated the significance of a soundly conceived strategy. Seeing itself in the data-system business at a time when most manufacturers were still preoccupied with individual pieces of equipment, IBM developed a set of policies which resulted in its dominating the office equipment industry.

By contrast, Packard in the 1930s was to the automobile industry everything that IBM is today to the office machine industry. In 1937, it sold over 109,000 cars, compared with about 11,000 for Cadillac. By 1954 it had disappeared as an independent producer.

Strategy is, of course, not the only factor determining a company's success or failure. The competence of its managerial leadership is significant as well. Luck can be a factor, too (although often what people call good luck is really the product of good strategy). But a valid strategy can gain extraordinary results for the company whose general level of competence is only average. And, conversely, the most inspiring leaders who are locked into an inappropriate strategy will have to exert their full competence and energy merely in order to keep from losing ground.

When Hannibal inflicted the humiliating defeat on the Roman army at Cannae in 216 B.C., he led a ragged band against soldiers who were in possession of superior arms, better training, and competent "noncoms." His strategy, however, was so superior that all of those advantages proved to be relatively insignificant. Similarly, when Jacob Borowsky made Lestoil the hottest selling detergent in New England some years ago, he was performing a similar feat—relying on strategy to battle competition with superior resources.

Strategy is important not only for aspiring Davids who need an offensive device to combat corporate Goliaths, it is significant also for the large organization faced with a wide range of choice in domestic and international operations. For instance, the following corporations are all in the midst of strategic changes, the implications of which are worldwide in scope:

☐ Massey-Ferguson, Ltd., with 26 factories located around the world, and vying for leadership in the farm-equipment industry.

☐ General Electric Company and Westinghouse Electric Corporation, the giant producers of electrical equipment who are recasting their competitive policies.

☐ Singer Sewing Machine Company, trying to make its vast assets yield a greater return.

Dynamic Concept

A strategy is a set of goals and major policies. The definition is as simple as that. But while the notion of a strategy is extremely easy to grasp, working out an agreed-upon statement for a given company can be a fundamental contribution to the organization's future success.

In order to develop such a statement, managers must be able to identify precisely what is meant by a goal and what is meant by a major policy. Otherwise, the process of strategy determination may degenerate into what it so often becomes—the solemn recording of platitudes, uselss for either the clarification of direction or the achievement of consensus.

Identifying Goals

Corporate goals are an indication of what the company as a whole is trying to *achieve* and to *become*. Both parts—the achieving and the becoming—are important for a full understanding of what a company hopes to attain. For example:

☐ Under the leadership of Alfred Sloan, General Motors achieved a considerable degree of external success; this was accomplished because Sloan worked out a pattern for the kind of company he wanted it to be internally.

☐ Similarly, the remarkable record of Du Pont in the twentieth century and the growth of Sears, Roebuck under Julius Rosenwald were as much a tribute to their modified structure as to their external strategy.[1]

Achieving. In order to state what a company expects to achieve, it is important to state what it hopes to do with respect to its environment. For instance:

Ernest Breech, chairman of the board of the Ford Motor Company, said that the strategy formulated by his company in 1946 was based on a desire "to hold our own in what we foresaw would be a rich but hotly competitive market."[2] The view of the environment implicit in this statement is unmistakable: an expanding overall demand, increasing competition, and emphasis on market share as a measure of performance against competitors.

Clearly, a statement of what a company hopes to achieve may be much more varied and complex than can be contained in a single sentence. This will be especially true for those managers who are sophisticated enough to perceive that a company operates in more external "systems" than the market. The firm is part not only of a market but also of an industry, the community, the economy, and other systems. In each case there are unique relationships to observe (e.g., with competitors, municipal leaders, Congress, and so on). A more complete discussion of this point is contained in a previous *HBR* article.[3]

Becoming. If you ask young men and women what they want to accomplish by the time they are 40, the answers you get fall into two distinct categories. There are those—the great majority—who respond in terms of what they want to *have*. This is especially true of graduate students of business administration. There are some, however, who will answer in terms of the kind of people they hope to *be*. These are the only ones who have a clear idea of where they are going.

The same is true of companies. For far too many companies, what little thinking goes on about the future is done primarily in money terms. There is nothing wrong with financial planning. Most companies should do more of it. But there is a basic fallacy in confusing a financial plan with thinking about the kind of company you want yours to become. It is like saying, "When I'm 40, I'm going to be *rich*." It leaves too many basic questions unanswered. Rich in what way? Rich doing what?

The other major fallacy in stating what you want to become is to say it only in terms of a product. The number of companies that have gotten themselves into trouble by falling in love with a particular product is distressingly great.[4] Perhaps the saddest examples are those giants of American industry who defined their future in terms of continuing to be the major suppliers of steam locomotives to the nation's railroads. In fact, these companies were so wedded to this concept of their future that they formed a cartel in order to keep General Motors out of the steam locomotive business. When the diesel locomotive proved its superiority to steam, these companies all but disappeared.

The lesson of these experiences is that a key element of setting goals is the ability to see them in terms of more than a single dimension. Both money and product policy are part of a statement of objectives; but it is essential that these be viewed as the concrete expressions of a more abstract set of goals—the satisfaction of the needs of significant groups which cooperate to ensure the company's continued existence.

Who are these groups? There are many—customers, managers, employees, stockholders, to mention just the major ones. The key to corporate success is the company's ability to identify the important needs of each of these groups, to establish some balance among them, and to work out a set of operating policies which permits their satisfaction. This set of policies, as a pattern, identifies what the company is trying to be.

The Growth Fad

Many managers have a view of their company's future which is strikingly analogous to the child's view of himself. When asked what they want their companies to become over the next few years, they reply, "bigger."

There are a great many rationalizations for this preoccupation with growth. Probably the one most frequently voiced is that which says, "You have to grow or die." What must be appreciated, however, is that "bigger" for a company has enormous implications for management. It involves a different way of life, and one which many managers may not be suited for— either in terms of temperament or skills.

Moreover, whether for a large company or a small one, "bigger," by itself, may not make economic sense. Companies which are highly profitable at their present size may grow into bankruptcy very easily; witness the case of Grayson-Robinson Stores, Inc., a chain of retail stores. Starting out as a small but profitable chain, it grew rapidly into receivership. Conversely, a company which is not now profitable may more successfully seek its survival in cost reduction than in sales growth. Chrysler is a striking example of this approach.

There is, in the United States, a business philosophy which reflects the frontier heritage of the country. It is one which places a high value on growth, in physical terms. Managers whose corporate sales are not increasing, the number of whose subordinates is not growing, whose plants are not expanding, feel that they are not successful. But there is a dangerous trap in this kind of thinking. More of the same is not necessarily progress. In addition, few managers are capable of running units several times larger than the ones they now head. The great danger of wholehearted consumer acceptance or an astute program of corporate acquisition is that it frequently propels managers into situations that are beyond their present competence. Such cases—and they are legion—emphasize that in stating corporate objectives, bigger is not always better. A dramatic example is that of the Ampex Corporation:

From 1950 to 1960, Ampex's annual sales went from less than $1,000,000 to more than $73,000,000. Its earnings went from $115,000 to nearly $4,000,000. The following year, the company reported a decline in sales to $70,000,000 and a net loss of $3,900,000. The *Wall Street Journal* reported: "As one source close to the company put it, Ampex's former management was 'intelligent and well-educated, but simply lacked the experience necessary to control' the company's rapid development."[5]

Role of Policy

A policy says something about *how* goals will be attained. It is what statisticians would call a "decision-rule," and what systems engineers would call a "standing plan." It tells people what they should and should not do in order to contribute to the achievement of corporate goals.

A policy should be more than just a platitude. It should be a helpful guide to making strategy explicit, and providing direction to subordinates. Consequently, the more definite it is, the more helpful it can be. "We will provide our stockholders with a fair return," is a policy no one could possibly disagree with—or be helped by. What *is* a fair return? This is the type of question that must be answered before the company's intentions become clear.

The job of management is not merely the preparation of valid policies for a standard set of activities; it is the much more challenging one of first deciding what activities are so strategically significant that explicit decision-rules in that area are mandatory. No standard set of policies can be considered major for all companies. Each company is a unique situation. It must decide for itself which aspects of corporate life are most relevant to its own aspirations and work out policy statements for them. For example, advertising may be insignificant to a company which provides research services to the Defense Department, but critical to a firm trying to mass-merchandise luxury goods.

It is difficult to generalize about which policies are major, even within a particular industry, because a number of extraordinarily sussessful companies appear to violate all the rules. To illustrate:

☐   In the candy industry it would seem safe to generalize that advertising should be a major policy area. However, the Hershey Company, which is so successful that its name is practically the generic term for the product, has persistently followed a policy of no advertising.

☐   Similarly, in the field of high-fidelity components, one would expect that dealer relations would be a critical policy area. But Acoustics Research, Inc., has built an enviable record of sales growth and of profitability by relying entirely on consumer pull.

Need To Be Explicit

The first thing to be said about corporate strategy is that having one is a step forward. Any strategy, once made explicit, can quickly be evaluated and improved. But if no attempt is ever made to commit it to paper, there is always the danger that the strategy is either incomplete or misunderstood.

Many successful companies are not aware of the strategy that underlies their success. It is quite possible for a company to achieve initial success without real awareness of its causes. However, it is much more difficult to successfully *branch out into new ventures* without a precise appreciation of their strategic significance. This is why many established companies fail miserably when they attempt a program of corporate acquisition, product diversification, or market expansion. One illustration of this is cited by Myles L. Mace and George G. Montgomery in their recent study of corporate acquisitions:

A basic resin company . . . bought a plastic boat manufacturer because this seemed to present a controlled market for a portion of the resin it produced. It soon found that the boat business was considerably different from the manufacture and sale of basic chemicals. After a short but unpleasant experience in manufacturing and trying to market what was essentially a consumer's item, the management concluded that its experience and abilities lay essentially in industrial rather than consumer-type products.[6]

Another reason for making strategy explicit is the assistance it provides for delegation and for coordination. To an ever-increasing extent, management is a team activity, whereby groups of executives contribute to corporate success. Making strategy explicit makes it far easier for executives to appreciate what the overall goals are, and what their own contribution to them must be.

Making an Evaluation

Is your strategy right for you? There are six criteria on which to base an answer:

1 Internal consistency.
2 Consistency with the environment.
3 Appropriateness in the light of available resources.
4 Satisfactory degree of risk.
5 Appropriate time horizon.
6 Workability.

If all of these criteria are met, you have a strategy that is right for you. This is as much as can be asked. There is no such thing as a good strategy in any absolute, objective sense. In the remainder of this article I shall discuss the criteria in some detail.

1. *Is the strategy internally consistent?* Internal consistency refers to the cumulative impact of individual policies on corporate goals. In a well-worked-out strategy, each policy fits into an integrated pattern. It should be judged not only in terms of itself, but also in terms of how it relates to other policies which the company has established and to the goals it is pursuing.

In a dynamic company consistency can never be taken for granted. For example:

Many family-owned organizations pursue a pair of policies which soon become inconsistent: rapid expansion and retention of exclusive family control of the firm. If they are successful in expanding, the need for additional financing soon raises major problems concerning the extent to which exclusive family control can be maintained.

While this pair of policies is especially prevalent among smaller firms, it is by no means limited to them. The Ford Motor Company after World War II and The New York Times today are examples of quite large, family-controlled organizations that have had to reconcile the two conflicting aims.

The criterion of internal consistency is an especially important one for evaluating strategies because if identifies those areas where strategic choices will eventually have to be made. An inconsistent strategy does *not* necessarily mean that the company is currently in difficulty. But it does mean that unless management keeps its eye on a particular area of operation, it may well find itself forced to make a choice without enough time either to search for or to prepare attractive alternatives.

2. *Is the strategy consistent with the environment?* A firm which has a certain product policy, price policy, or advertising policy is saying that it has chosen to relate itself to its customers—actual and potential—in a certain way. Similarly, its policies with respect to government contracts, collective bargaining, foreign investment, and so forth are expressions of relationship with other groups and forces. Hence an important test of strategy is whether the chosen policies are consistent with the environment—whether they really make sense with respect to what is going on outside.

Consistency with the environment has both a static and a dynamic aspect. In a static sense, it implies judging the efficacy of policies with respect to the environment as it exists *now*. In a dynamic sense, it means judging the efficacy of policies with respect to the environment *as it appears to be changing*. One purpose of a viable strategy is to ensure the long-run success of an organization. Since the environment of a company is constantly changing, ensuring success over the long run means that management must constantly be assessing the degree to which policies previously established are consistent with the environment as it exists now; and whether current policies take into account the environment as it will be in the future. In one sense, therefore, establishing a strategy is like aiming at a moving target: you have to be concerned not only with present position but also with the speed and direction of movement.

Failure to have a strategy consistent with the environment can be costly to the organization. Ford's sad experience with the Edsel is by now a textbook example of such failure. Certainly, had Ford pushed the Falcon at the time when it was pushing the Edsel, and with the same resources, it would have a far stronger position in the world automobile market today.

Illustrations of strategies that have not been consistent with the environment are easy to find by using hindsight. *But the reason that such examples are plentiful is not that foresight is difficult to apply.* It is because even today few companies are seriously engaged in analyzing environmental trends and using this intelligence as a basis for managing their own futures.

3. *Is the strategy appropriate in view of the available resources?* Resources are those things that a company *is* or *has* and that help it to achieve its corporate objectives. Included are money, competence, and facilities; but these by no means complete the list. In companies selling consumer goods, for example, the major resource may be the name of the product. In any case, there are two basic issues which management must decide in relating strategy and resources. These are:

☐   What are our critical resources?
☐   Is the proposed strategy appropriate for available resources?

Let us look now at what is meant by a "critical resource" and at how the criterion of resource utilization can be used as a basis for evaluating strategy.

Critical Resources

The essential strategic attribute of resources is that they represent action potential. Taken together, a company's resources represent its capacity to respond to threats and opportunities that may be perceived in the environment. In other words, resources are the bundle of chips that the company has to play with in the serious game of business.

From an action-potential point of view, a resource may be critical in two senses: (1) as the factor limiting the achievement of corporate goals; and (2) as that which the company will exploit as the basis for its strategy. Thus, critical resources are both what the company has most of and what it has least of.

The three resources most frequently identified as critical are money, competence, and physical facilities. Let us look at the strategic significance of each.

Money.   Money is a particularly valuable resource because it provides the greatest flexibility of response to events as they arise. It may be considered the "safest" resource, in that safety may be equated with the freedom to choose from among the widest variety of future alternatives. Companies that wish to reduce their short-run risk will therefore attempt to accumulate the greatest reservoir of funds they can.

However, it is important to remember that while the accumulation of funds may offer short-run security, it may place the company at a serious competitive disadvantage with respect to other companies which are following a higher-risk course.

The classical illustration of this kind of outcome is the strategy pursued by Montgomery Ward under the late Sewell Avery. As reported in *Fortune:*

> While Sears confidently bet on a new and expanding America, Avery developed an *idée fixe* that postwar inflation would end in a crash no less serious than that of 1929. Following this idea, he opened no new stores but rather piled up cash to the ceiling in preparation for an economic debacle that never came. In these years, Ward's balance sheet gave a somewhat misleading picture of its prospects. Net earnings remained respectably high, and were generally higher than those of Sears as a percentage of sales. In 1946, earnings after taxes were $52 million. They rose to $74 million in 1950, and then declined to $35 million in 1954. Meanwhile, however, sales remained static, and in Avery's administration profits and liquidity were maintained at the expense of growth. In 1954, Ward had $327 million in cash and securities, $147 million in receivables, and $216 million in inventory, giving it a total current-asset position of $690 million and net worth of $639 million. It was liquid, all right, but it was also the shell of a once great company.[7]

Competence. Organizations survive because they are good at doing those things which are necessary to keep them alive. However, the degree of competence of a given organization is by no means uniform across the broad range of skills necessary to stay in business. Some companies are particularly good at marketing, others especially good at engineering, still others depend primarily on their financial sophistication. Philip Selznick refers to that which a company is particularly good at as its "distinctive competence."[8]

In determining a strategy, management must carefully appraise its own skill profile in order to determine where its strengths and weaknesses lie. It must then adopt a strategy which makes the greatest use of its strengths. To illustrate:

The competence of *The New York Times* lies primarily in giving extensive and insightful coverage of events—the ability to report "all the news that's fit to print." It is neither highly profitable (earning only 1.5% of revenues in 1960—far less than, say, the *Wall Street Journal*), nor aggressively sold. Its decision to publish a West Coast and an international edition is a gamble that the strength of its "distinctive competence" will make it accepted even outside of New York.

Because of a declining demand for soft coal, many producers of soft coal are diversifying into other fields. All of them, however, are remaining true to some central skill that they have developed over the years. For instance:

☐ Consolidation Coal is moving from simply the mining of soft coal to the mining *and transportation* of soft coal. It is planning with Texas Eastern Transmission Corporation to build a $100 million pipeline that would carry a mixture of powdered coal and water from West Virginia to the East Coast.

☐ North American Coal Company, on the other hand, is moving toward becoming a chemical company. It recently joined with Strategic Materials Corporation to perfect a process for extracting aluminum sulfate from the mine shale that North American produces in its coal-running operations.

James L. Hamilton, president of the Island Creek Coal Co., has summed up the concept of distinctive competence in a colorful way:

"We are a career company dedicated to coal, and we have some very definite ideas about growth and expansion within the industry. We're not thinking of buying a cotton mill and starting to make shirts."[9]

Physical Facilities. Physical facilities are the resource whose strategic influence is perhaps most frequently misunderstood. Managers seem to be divided among those, usually technical persons, who are enamored of physical facilities as the tangible symbol of the corporate entity; and those, usually financial persons, who view physical facilities as an undesirable but necessary freezing of part of the company's funds. The latter group is dominant. In many companies, return on investment has emerged as virtually the sole criterion for deciding whether or not a particular facility should be acquired.

Actually, this is putting the cart before the horse. Physical facilities have significance primarily in relationship to overall corporate strategy. It is, therefore, only in relationship to *other* aspects of corporate strategy that the acquisition or disposition of physical facilities can be determined. The total investment required and the projected return on it have a place in this determination—but only as an indication of the financial implications of a particular strategic decision and not as an exclusive criterion for its own sake.

Any appraisal of a company's physical facilities as a strategic resource must consider the relationship of the company to its environment. Facilities have no intrinsic value for their own sake. Their value to the company is either in their location relative to markets, to sources of labor, or to materials; or in their efficiency relative to existing or impending competitive installations. Thus, the essential considerations in any decision regarding physical facilities are a projection of changes likely to occur in the environment and a prediction about what the company's responses to these are likely to be.

Here are two examples of the necessity for relating an evaluation of facilities to environmental changes:

Following the end of World War II, all domestic producers of typewriters in the United States invested heavily in plant facilities in this country. They hypothesized a rapid increase of sales throughout the world. This indeed took place, but it was shortlived. The rise of vigorous overseas competitors, especially Olivetti and Olympia, went hand in hand with a booming overseas market. At home, IBM's electric typewriter took more and more of the domestic market. Squeezed between these two pressures, the rest of the U.S. typewriter industry found itself with a great deal of excess capacity following the Korean conflict. Excess capacity is today still a major problem in this field.

The steady decline in the number of farms in the United States and the emergence of vigorous overseas competition have forced most domestic full-line manufacturers of farm equipment to sharply curtail total plant area. For example, in less than four years, International Harvester eliminated more than a third of its capacity (as measured in square feet of plant space) for the production of farm machinery.

The close relationship between physical facilities and environmental trends emphasizes one of the most significant attributes of fixed assets—their temporal utility. Accounting practice recognizes this in its treatment of depreciation allowances. But even when the tax laws permit generous write-offs, they should not be used as the sole basis for setting the time period over which the investment must be justified. Environmental considerations may reveal that a different time horizon is more relevant for strategy determination. To illustrate again:

As Armstrong Cork Company moved away from natural cork to synthetic materials during the early 1950s, management considered buying facilities for the production of its raw materials—particularly polyvinyl chloride. However, before doing so, it surveyed the chemical industry and concluded that producers were overbuilding. It therefore decided not to invest in facilities for the manufacture of this material. The projections were valid; since 1956 polyvinyl chloride has dropped 50% in price.

A strategic approach to facilities may not only change the time horizon; it may also change the whole basis of asset valuation:

Recently a substantial portion of Loew's theaters was acquired by the Tisch brothers, owners and operators of a number of successful hotels, including the Americana in Florida.[10] As long as the assets of Loew's theaters were viewed only as places for the projection of films, its theaters, however conservatively valued, seemed to be not much of a bargain. But to a keen appraiser of hotel properties the theater sites, on rather expensive real estate in downtown city areas, had considerable appeal. Whether this appraisal will be borne out is as yet unknown. At any rate, the stock, which was originally pruchased at $14 (with a book value of $22), was selling at $23 in October 1962.

Achieving the Right Balance

One of the most difficult issues in strategy determination is that of achieving a balance between strategic goals and available resources. This requires a set of necessarily empirical, but critical, estimates of the total resources required to achieve particular objectives, the rate at which they will have to be committed, and the likelihood that they will be available. The most common errors are either to fail to make these estimates at all or to be excessively optimistic about them.

One example of the unfortunate results of being wrong on these estimates is the case of Royal McBee and the computer market:

In January 1956 Royal McBee and the General Precision Equipment Corporation formed a jointly owned company—the Royal Precision Corporation—to enter the market for electronic data-processing equipment. This joint operation was a logical pooling of complementary talents. General Precision had a great deal of experience in developing and producing computers. Its Librascope Division had been selling them to the government for years. However, it lacked a commercial distribution system. Royal McBee, on the other hand, had a great deal of experience in marketing data-processing equipment, but lacked the technical competence to develop and produce a computer.

The joint venture was eminently successful, and within a short time the Royal Precision LPG-30 was the leader in the small-computer field. However, the very success of the computer venture caused Royal McBee some serious problems. The success of the Royal Precision subsidiary demanded that the partners put more and more money into it. This was no problem for General Precision, but it became an ever more serious problem for Royal McBee, which found itself in an increasingly critical cash bind. In March 1962 it sold its interest in Royal Precision to General Precision for $5 million—a price which represented a reported $6.9 million loss on the investment. Concluding that it simply did not have sufficient resources to stay with the new venture, it decided to return to its traditional strengths: typewriters and simple data-processing systems.

Another place where optimistic estimates of resources frequently cause problems is in small businesses. Surveys of the causes of small-business failure reveal that a most frequent cause of bankruptcy is inadequate resources to weather either the early period of establishment or unforeseen downturns in business conditions.

It is apparent from the preceding discussion that a critical strategic decision involves deciding: (1) how much of the company's resources to commit to opportunities currently perceived, and (2) how much to keep uncommitted as a reserve against the appearance of unanticipated demands. This decision is closely related to two other criteria for the evaluation of strategy: risk and timing. I shall now discuss these.

4. *Does the strategy involve an acceptable degree of risk?* Strategy and resources, taken together, determine the degree of risk which the company is undertaking. This is a critical managerial choice. For example, when the old Underwood Corporation decided to enter the computer field, it was making what might have been an extremely astute strategic choice. However, the fact that it ran out of money before it could accomplish anything in that field turned its pursuit of opportunity into the prelude to disaster. This is not to say that the strategy was "bad." However, the course of action pursued *was* a high-risk strategy. Had it been successful, the payoff would have been lush. The fact that it was a stupendous failure instead does not mean that it was senseless to take the gamble.

Each company must decide for itself how much risk it wants to live with. In attempting to assess the degree of risk associated with a particular strategy, management may use a variety of techniques. For example, mathematicians have developed an elegant set of techniques for choosing among a variety of strategies where you are willing to estimate the payoffs and the probabilities associated with them. However, our concern here is not with these quantitative aspects but with the identification of some qualitative factors which may serve as a rough basis for evaluating the degree of risk inherent in a strategy. These factors are:

1 The amount of resources (on which the strategy is based) whose continued existence or value is not assured.
2 The length of the time periods to which resources are committed.
3 The proportion of resources committed to a single venture.

The greater these quantities, the greater degree of risk that is involved.

Uncertain Term of Existence

Since a strategy is based on resources, any resource which may disappear before the payoff has been obtained may constitute a danger to the organization. Resources may disappear for various reasons. For example, they may lose their value. This frequently happens to such resources as physical facilities and product features. Again, they may be accidentally destroyed. The most vulnerable resource here is competence. The possible crash of the company plane or the blip on the president's electrocardiogram is what makes many organizations essentially speculative ventures. In fact, one of the critical attributes of highly centralized organizations is that the more centralized they are, the more speculative they are. The disappearance of the top executive, or the disruption of communication with him or her may wreak havoc at subordinate levels.

However, for many companies, the possibility that critical resources may lose their value stems not so much from internal developments as from shifts in the environment. Take specialized production know-how, for example. It has value only because of demand for the product by customers—and customers may change their minds. This is cause for acute concern among the increasing number of companies whose futures depend so heavily on their ability to participate in defense contracts. A familiar case is the plight of the airframe industry following World War II. Some of the companies succeeded in making the shift from aircraft to missiles, but this has only resulted in their being faced with the same problem on a larger scale.

Duration of Commitment

Financial analysts often look at the ratio of fixed assets to current assets in order to assess the extent to which resources are committed to long-term programs. This may or may not give a satisfactory answer. How important are the assets? When will they be paid for?

The reason for the risk increasing as the time for payoff increases is, of course, the inherent uncertainty in any venture. Resources committed over long time spans make the company vulnerable to changes in the environment. Since the difficulty of predicting such changes increases as the time span increases, long-term projects are basically more risky than are short ones. This is especially true of companies whose environments are unstable. And today, either because of technological, political, or economic shifts, most companies are decidedly in the category of those that face major upheaval in their corporate environments. The company building its future around technological equipment, the company selling primarily to the government, the company investing in underdeveloped nations, the company selling to the Common Market, the company with a plant in the South—all these have this prospect in common.

The harsh dilemma of modern management is that the time span of decision is increasing at the same time as the corporate environment is becoming increasingly unstable. It is this dilemma which places such a premium on the manager's sensitivity to external trends today. Much has been written about his role as a commander and administrator. But it is no less important that he be a *strategist*.

Size of the Stakes

The more of its resources a company commits to a particular strategy, the more pronounced the consequences. If the strategy is successful, the payoff will be great—both to managers and investors. If the strategy fails, the consequences will be dire—both to managers and investors. Thus, a critical decision for the executive group is: What proportion of available resources should be committed to a particular course of action?

This decision may be handled in a variety of ways. For example, faced with a project that requires more of its resources than it is willing to commit, a company either may choose to refrain from undertaking the project or, alternatively, may seek to reduce the total resources required by undertaking a joint venture or by going the route of merger or acquisition in order to broaden the resource base.

The amount of resources management stands ready to commit is of particular significance where there is some likelihood that larger competitors, having greater resources, may choose to enter the company's field. Thus, those companies which entered the small-computer field in the past few years are now faced with the penetration into this area of the data-processing giants. (Both IBM and Remington Rand have recently introduced new small computers.)

I do not mean to imply that the "best" strategy is the one with the least risk. High payoffs are frequently associated with high-risk strategies. Moreover, it is a frequent but dangerous assumption to think that inaction, or lack of change, is a low-risk strategy. Failure to exploit its resources to the fullest may well be the riskiest strategy of all that an organization may pursue, as Montgomery Ward and other companies have amply demonstrated.

5. *Does the strategy have an appropriate time horizon?* A significant part of every strategy is the time horizon on which it is based. A viable strategy not only reveals what goals are to be accomplished; it says something about *when* the aims are to be achieved.

Goals, like resources, have time-based utility. A new product developed, a plant put on stream, a degree of market penetration, become significant strategic objectives only if accomplished by a certain time. Delay may deprive them of all strategic significance. A perfect example of this in the military sphere is the Sinai campaign of 1956. The strategic objective of the Israelis was not only to conquer the entire Sinai peninsula; it also was to do it in seven days. By contrast, the lethargic movement of the British troops made the operation a futile one for both England and France.

In choosing an appropriate time horizon, we must pay careful attention to the goals being pursued, and to the particular organization involved. Goals must be established far enough in advance to allow the organization to adjust to them. Organizations, like ships, cannot be "spun on a dime." Consequently, the larger the organization, the further its strategic time horizon must extend, since its adjustment time is longer. It is no mere managerial whim that the major contributions to long-range planning have emerged from the larger organizations—especially those large organizations such as Lockheed, North American Aviation, and RCA that traditionally have had to deal with highly unstable environments.

The observation that large corporations plan far ahead while small ones can get away without doing so has frequently been made. However, the significance of planning for the small but growing company has frequently been overlooked. As a company gets bigger, it must not only change the way it operates; it must also steadily push ahead its time horizon—and this is a difficult thing to do. Managers who have built successful enterprises by their skill at "putting out fires" or wheeler-dealers whose firms have grown by a quick succession of financial coups are seldom able to make the transition to the long look ahead.

In many cases, even if the executive were inclined to take a longer range view of events, the formal reward system seriously militates against doing so. In most companies the system of management rewards is closely related to currently reported profits. Where this is the case, executives may understandably be so preoccupied with reporting a profit year by year that they fail to spend as much time as they should in managing the company's long-term future. But if we seriously accept the thesis that the essence of managerial responsibility is the extended time lapse between decision and result, currently reported profits are hardly a reasonable basis on which to compensate top executives. Such a basis simply serves to shorten the time horizon with which the executive is concerned.

The importance of an extended time horizon derives not only from the fact that an organization changes slowly and needs time to work through basic modifications in its strategy; it derives also from the fact that there is a considerable advantage in a certain consistency of strategy maintained over long periods of time. The great danger to companies which do not carefully formulate strategies well in advance is that they are prone to fling themselves toward chaos by drastic changes in policy—and in personnel—

at frequent intervals. A parade of presidents is a clear indication of a board that has not really decided what its strategy should be. It is a common harbinger of serious corporate difficulty as well.

The time horizon is also important because of its impact on the selection of policies. The greater the time horizon, the greater the range in choice of tactics. If, for instance, the goals desired must be achieved in a relatively short time, steps like acquisition and merger may become virtually mandatory. An interesting illustration is the decision of National Cash Register to enter the market for electronic data-processing equipment. As reported in *Forbes:*

> Once committed to EDP, NCR wasted no time. To buy talent and experience in 1953 it acquired Computer Research Corp. of Hawthorne, California. . . . For speed's sake, the manufacture of the 304's central units was turned over to GE. . . .NCR's research and development outlays also began curving steeply upwards.[11]

6. *Is the strategy workable?*   At first glance, it would seem that the simplest way to evaluate a corporate strategy is the completely pragmatic one of asking: Does it work? However, further reflection should reveal that if we try to answer that question, we are immediately faced with a quest for criteria. What is the evidence of a strategy "working"?

Quantitative indices of performance are a good start, but they really measure the influence of two critical factors combined: the strategy selected and the skill with which it is being executed. Faced with the failure to achieve anticipated results, both of these influences must be critically examined. One interesting illustration of this is a recent survey of the Chrysler Corporation after it suffered a period of serious loss:

> In 1959, during one of the frequent reorganizations at Chrysler Corp., aimed at halting the company's slide, a management consultant concluded: "The only thing wrong with Chrysler is people. The corporation needs some good top executives."[12]

By contrast, when Olivetti acquired the Underwood Corporation it was able to reduce the cost of producing typewriters by one-third. And it did it without changing any of the top people in the production group. However, it did introduce a drastically revised set of policies.

If a strategy cannot be evaluated by results alone, there are some other indications that may be used to assess its contribution to corporate progress:

☐ The degree of consensus which exists among executives concerning corporate goals and policies.

☐ The extent to which major areas of managerial choice are identified in advance, while there is still time to explore a variety of alternatives.

☐ The extent to which resource requirements are discovered well before the last minute, necessitating neither crash programs of cost reduction nor the elimination of planned programs. The widespread popularity of the meat-axe approach to cost reduction is a clear indication of the frequent failure of corporate strategic planning.

Conclusion

The modern organization must deploy expensive and complex resources in the pursuit of transitory opportunities. The time required to develop resources is so extended, and the time-scale of opportunities is so brief and fleeting, that a company which has not carefully delineated and appraised its strategy is adrift in white water.

In short, while a set of goals and major policies that meets the criteria listed above does not guarantee success, it can be of considerable value in giving management both the time and the room to maneuver.

Notes

1. For an interesting discussion of this relationship, see A. D. Chandler, Jr., *Strategy and Structure* (Cambridge, Massachusetts Institute of Technology Press, 1962), pp. 1–17.

2. See Edward C. Bursk and Dan H. Fenn, Jr., *Planning the Future Strategy of Your Business* (New York, McGraw-Hill Book Company, 1956), p. 8.

3. Seymour Tilles, "The Manager's Job—A Systems Approach," *HBR*, January–February 1963, p. 73.

4. See Theodore Levitt, "Marketing Myopia," *HBR*, July–August 1960, p. 45.

5. "R for Ampex: Drastic Changes Help Solve Big Headache of Fast Corporate Growth," *Wall Street Journal*, September 17, 1962, p. 1.

6. *Management Problems of Corporate Acquisitions* (Boston, Division of Research, Harvard Business School, 1962), p. 60.

7. "Montgomery Ward: Prosperity Is Still Around the Corner," *Fortune*, November 1960, p. 140.

8. *Leadership in Administration* (Evanston, Ill., Row, Peterson & Company, 1957), p. 42.

9. *Wall Street Journal*, September 11, 1962, p. 30.

10. See "The Tisches Eye Their Next $65 Million," *Fortune*, January 1960, p. 140.

11. "NCR and the Computer Sweepstakes," *Forbes*, October 15, 1962, p. 21.

12. "How Chrysler Hopes to Rebound," *Business Week*, October 6, 1962, p. 45.

PART TWO
FORMULATING SUCCESSFUL STRATEGIES

AN OVERVIEW

While the field of strategic management has its roots in some basic and broad concepts, much of the current publicity and popularity of the field has been caused by specific findings that have helped managers formulate successful strategies. The articles in this section present useful suggestions for formulating strategy in a wide variety of situations. Perhaps because of their specificity, they have been among the most frequently reprinted of recent *Harvard Business Review* articles.

The authors of "Market Share—A Key to Profitability" present what has now become a central part of current thinking in strategic management. Based on a statistical study of 620 business units, the authors conclude that higher market share is associated with higher levels of return on investment. The authors explore the underlying causes of this relationship and its implications for strategy formulation.

Some other implications of the market share/ROI relationship are dealt with in the next two articles. In "Pyrrhic Victories in Fights for Market Share," William E. Fruhan demonstrates that it makes no sense for a company to pursue market share leadership if it lacks the financial resources to win or if it will not be in a viable position should its market-share drive be thwarted, or if regulatory authorities won't permit the company to achieve its objective. The authors of "Strategies for Low Market-Share Businesses" offer strategy prescriptions for companies that don't have the luxury of large market shares. The authors encourage these companies to think small and to compete in narrowly defined market segments.

With the slowdown in economic growth since 1973, companies have had to formulate strategies for a slower growing and more hostile environment. "How to Compete in Stagnent Industries" and "Survival Strategies in a Hostile Environment" deal with this difficult set of conditions and offer similar advice. Both articles conclude that fewer companies will survive under these conditions and that the successful firms will be those that achieve either a low-cost or quality-differentiated position in their markets.

Another major trend in recent years has been toward the globalization of many of the markets for many goods and services. In "Global Industries: New Rules for the Competitive Game," the authors argue that competing globally is essentially different from competing as a domestic supplier for the domestic market only. They then explore some of the different types of logic that need to be applied to become a successful global competitor.

The final article of this section, "Management Strategies for Small Companies," offers practical strategy advice for smaller companies. In light of the fact that small companies have provided most of the new jobs in our economy, it is essential that the field of strategic management continue to address the problems and issues confronting these businesses.

7
Market Share
A Key to Profitability

ROBERT D. BUZZELL, BRADLEY T. GALE, and
RALPH G.M. SULTAN

Earlier work by the authors (March–April 1974 issue of the *Harvard Business Review*) established a link between strategic planning and profit performance; here, with additional data, the authors come up with a positive correlation between market share and return on investment (ROI). The authors discuss why market share is profitable, listing economies of scale, market power, and quality of management as possible explanations; then, using the profit impact of market strategies (PIMS) data base, they show how market share is related to ROI. Specifically, as market share increases, a business is likely to have a higher profit margin, a declining purchases-to-sales ratio, a decline in marketing costs as a percentage of sales, higher quality, and higher priced products. Data also indicate that the advantages of large market share are greatest for businesses selling products that are purchased infrequently by a fragmented customer group. The authors also analyze the strategic implications of the market-share/ROI relationship. They conclude by advising companies to analyze their own positions in order to achieve the best balance of costs and benefits of the different strategies.

It is now widely recognized that one of the main determinants of business profitability is market share. Under most circumstances, enterprises that have achieved a high share of the markets they serve are considerably more profitable than their smaller-share rivals. This connection between market share and profitability has been recognized by corporate executives and

Authors' Note. We wish to acknowledge the contributions of our associates in the PIMS project to the results reported in this article. Sidney Schoeffler, Donald F. Heany, and James Conlin made valuable suggestions, and Paula Nichols carried out numerous analyses very efficiently and cheerfully. The authors are, of course, solely responsible for any errors or misinterpretations that remain.

consultants, and it is clearly demonstrated in the results of a project undertaken by the Marketing Science Institute on the profit impact of market
strategies (PIMS). The PIMS project, on which we have been working since
late 1971,[1] is aimed at identifying and measuring the major determinants of
return on investment (ROI) in individual businesses. Phase II of the PIMS
project, completed in late 1973, reveals 37 key profit influences, of which
one of the most important is market share.

There is no doubt that market share and return on investment are
strongly related. Exhibit 1 shows average pretax ROI figures for groups of
businesses in the PIMS project that have successively increasing shares of
their markets. (For an explanation of how businesses, markets, and ROI
results are defined and measured in the PIMS project, see the Appendix.)
On the average, a difference of 10 percentage points in market share is
accompanied by a difference of about 5 points in pretax ROI.

While the PIMS data base is the most extensive and detailed source
of information on the profit/market-share relationship, there is additional
confirming evidence of its existence. For instance, companies enjoying strong
competitive positions in their primary product markets tend to be highly
profitable. Consider, for example, such major companies as IBM, Gillette,
Eastman Kodak, and Xerox, as well as smaller, more specialized corporations like Dr. Scholl (foot care products) and Hartz Mountain (pet foods and
accessories).

Granted that high rates of return usually accompany high market share,
it is useful to explore the relationship further. Why is market share profitable?
What are the observed differences between low- and high-share businesses?
Does the notion vary from industry to industry? And what does the profit-
ability/market-share relationship imply for strategic planning? In this article
we shall attempt to provide partial answers to these questions by presenting
evidence on the nature, importance, and implications of the links between
market share and profit performance.

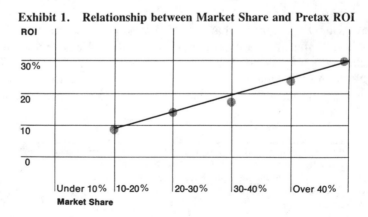

Exhibit 1. Relationship between Market Share and Pretax ROI

Why Market Share Is Profitable

The data shown in Exhibit 1 demonstrate the differences in ROI between high- and low-market-share businesses. This convincing evidence of the relationship itself, however, does not tell us why there is a link between market share and profitability. There are at least three possible explanations:

☐ *Economies of scale.* The most obvious rationale for the high rate of return enjoyed by large-share businesses is that they have achieved economies of scale in procurement, manufacturing, marketing, and other cost components. A business with a 40% share of a given market is simply twice as big as one with 20% of the same market, and it will attain, to a much greater degree, more efficient methods of operation within a particular type of technology. Closely related to this explanation is the so-called experience curve phenomenon widely publicized by the Boston Consulting Group.[2] According to BCG, total unit costs of producing and distributing a product tend to decline by a more or less constant percentage with each doubling of a company's cumulative output. Since, in a given time period, businesses with large market shares generally also have larger cumulative sales than their smaller competitors, they would be expected to have lower costs and correspondingly higher profits.

☐ *Market power.* Many economists, especially among those involved in antitrust work, believe that economies of scale are of relatively little importance in most industries. These economists argue that if large-scale businesses earn higher profits than their smaller competitors, it is a result of their greater market power: their size permits them to bargain more effectively, "administer" prices, and, in the end, realize significantly higher prices for a particular product.[3]

☐ *Quality of management.* The simplest of all explanations for the market-share/profitability relationship is that both share and ROI reflect a common underlying factor: the quality of management. Good managers (including, perhaps, lucky ones!) are successful in achieving high shares of their respective markets; they are also skillful in controlling costs, getting maximum productivity from employees, and so on. Moreover, once a business achieves a leadership position—possibly by developing a new field—it is much easier for it to retain its lead than for others to catch up.

These explanations of why the market-share/profitability relationship exists are not mutually exclusive. To some degree, a large-share business may benefit from all three kinds of relative advantages. It is important, however, to understand from the available information how much of the increased profitability that accompanies high market share comes from each of these or other sources.

How Market Share Relates to ROI

Analysis of the PIMS data base sheds some light on the reasons for the observed relationship between market share and ROI. Businesses with different market-share levels are compared as to financial and operating ratios and measures of relative prices and product quality in Exhibit 2. In examining these figures, remember that the PIMS sample of businesses includes a wide variety of products and industries. Consequently, when we compare businesses with market shares under 10%, say, with those having shares over 40%, we are not observing differences in costs and profits within a single industry. Each subgroup contains a diversity of industries, types of products, kinds of customers, and so on.

Differences Between High- and Low-Share Businesses

The data in Exhibit 2 reveal four important differences between high-share businesses and those with smaller shares. The samples used are sufficiently large and balanced to ensure that the differences between them are associated

Exhibit 2. Relationships of Market Share to Key Financial and Operating Ratios for Overall PIMS Sample of Businesses

Financial and Operating Ratios	Market Share				
	Under 10%	10%–20%	20%–30%	30%–40%	Over 40%
Captial structure					
Investment/sales	68.66	67.74	61.08	64.66	63.98
Receivables/sales	15.52	14.08	13.96	15.18	14.48
Inventory/sales	9.30	8.97	8.68	8.68	8.16
Operating results					
Pretax profit/sales	-0.16	3.42	4.84	7.60	13.16
Purchases/sales	45.40	39.90	39.40	32.60	33.00
Manufacturing/sales	29.64	32.61	32.11	32.95	31.76
Marketing/sales	10.60	9.88	9.06	10.45	8.57
R&D/sales	2.60	2.40	2.83	3.18	3.55
Capacity/utilization	74.70	77.10	78.10	75.40	78.00
Product quality: average of percents superior minus inferior	14.50	20.40	20.40	20.10	43.00
Relative price[a]	2.72	2.73	2.65	2.66	2.39
Number of businesses	156	179	105	67	87

[a]Average value on 5-point scale:
5 = 10% or more lower than leading competitors' average;
3 = within 3% of competition;
1 = 10% or more higher than competition.

primarily with variations in market share, and not with other factors. These differences are:

1. *As market share rises, turnover on investment rises only somewhat, but profit margin on sales increases sharply.* ROI is, of course, dependent on both the rate of net profit on sales and the amount of investment required to support a given volume of sales. Exhibit 2 reveals that the ratio of investment to sales declines only slightly, and irregularly, with increased market share. The data show too that capacity utilization is not systematically related to market share.

On the surface then, higher investment turnover does not appear to be a major factor contributing to higher rates of return. However, this observation is subject to some qualification. Our analysis of the PIMS data base shows that investment intensity (investment relative to sales) tends to vary directly with a business's degree of vertical integration.

(The degree of vertical integration is measured as the ratio of the total value added by the business to its sales. Both the numerator and denominator of the ratio are adjusted by subtracting the pretax income and adding the PIMS average ROI, multiplied by the investment.)

Vertical integration thus has a strong negative relation to the ratio of purchases to sales. Since high market-share businesses are on the average somewhat more vertically integrated than those with smaller shares, it is likely that investment turnover increases somewhat more with market share than the figures in Exhibit 2 suggest. In other words, as shown in Exhibit 3, for a given degree of vertical integration, the investment-to-sales ratio declines significantly, even though overall averages do not.

Nevertheless, Exhibit 2 shows that the major reason for the ROI/market-share relationship is the dramatic difference in pretax profit margins on sales. Businesses with market shares under 10% had average pretax losses of 0.16%. The average ROI for businesses with under 10% market share was about 9%. Obviously, no individual business can have a negative profit-to-sales ratio and still earn a positive ROI. The apparent inconsistency between the averages reflects the fact that some businesses in the sample incurred losses that were very high in relation to sales but that were much smaller

Exhibit 3.   Effect of Vertical Integration on Investment/Sales Ratio

Vertical Integration	Market Share				
	Under 10%	10%–20%	20%–30%	30%–40%	Over 40%
Low	65	61	46	58	55
High	77	76	75	70	69

in relation to investment. In the PIMS sample, the average return on sales exhibits a strong, smooth, upward trend as market share increases.

Why do profit margins on sales increase so sharply with market share? To answer this, it is necessary to look in more detail at differences in prices and operating expenses.

2. *The biggest single difference in costs, as related to market share, is in the purchases-to-sales ratio.* As shown in Exhibit 2, for large-share businesses—those with shares over 40%—purchases represent only 33% of sales, compared with 45% for businesses with shares under 10%.

How can we explain the decline in the ratio of purchases to sales as share goes up? One possibility, as mentioned earlier, is that high-share businesses tend to be more vertically integrated—they "make" rather than "buy," and often they own their own distribution facilities. The decline in the purchases-to-sales ratio is quite a bit less (see Exhibit 4) if we control for the level of vertical integration. A low purchases-to-sales ratio goes hand in hand with a high level of vertical integration.

Other things being equal, a greater extent of vertical integration ought to result in a rising level of manufacturing costs. (For the nonmanufacturing businesses in the PIMS sample, "manufacturing" was defined as the primary value-creating activity of the business. For example, processing transactions is the equivalent of manufacturing in a bank.) But the data in Exhibit 2 show little or no connection between manufacturing expense, as a percentage of sales, and market share. This could be because, despite the increase in vertical integration, costs are offset by increased efficiency.

This explanation is probably valid for some of the businesses in the sample, but we believe that, in the majority of cases, the decline in costs of purchased materials also reflects a combination of economies of scale in buying and, perhaps, bargining power in dealing with suppliers. Economies of scale in procurement arise from lower costs of manufacturing, marketing, and distributing when suppliers sell in large quantities. For very large-scale buyers, custom-designed components and special formulations of materials that are purchased on long-term contracts may offer "order of magnitude" economies.

Still another possible explanation of the declining purchases-to-sales ratio for large-share businesses might be that they charge higher prices, thus

Exhibit 4. Purchase-to-Sales Ratio Corrected for Vertical Integration

Vertical Integration	Market Share				
	Under 10%	10%–20%	20%–30%	30%–40%	Over 40%
Low	54	51	53	52	46
High	32	27	29	24	23

increasing the base on which the percentage is figured. This does not, however, appear to be the case.

In Exhibit 2 we give measures of price relative to competition for each group of businesses that indicate otherwise. Because of the great difficulty of computing meaningful relative price-index numbers, the measure we used here is rather crude. We asked the PIMS participants to indicate on a five-point scale whether their prices were "about the same" as major competitors, "somewhat" higher or lower, or "substantially" higher or lower for each business. The average values of this scale measure are virtually identical for each market-share group, except for those with shares over 40%.

Despite the similarity of relative prices for the first four share groups, the purchases-to-sales ratios decline in a regular, substantial fashion as share increases. In light of this, we do not believe that the decline in purchase costs is a reflection of higher price levels imposed by "market power."

3. *As market share increases, there is some tendency for marketing costs, as a percentage of sales, to decline.* The difference in marketing costs between the smallest and largest market-share groups amounts on the average to about 2% of sales. We believe that this reflects true scale economies, including the spreading of fixed marketing costs and the ability of large-share businesses to utilize more efficient media and marketing methods. In the case of industrial products, large scale permits manufacturers to use their own sales force rather than commissioned agents and, at some point, to utilize specialized sales forces for specific product lines or markets. For consumer goods, large-scale businesses may derive an important cost advantage from their ability to utilize the most efficient mass-advertising media.

In addition, leading brands of consumer products appear to benefit to some extent from a "bandwagon effect" that results from the brand's greater visibility in retail stores or greater support from retail store sales personnel. For example, Anheuser-Busch has for some time enjoyed lower advertising costs per case of beer than its smaller rivals—just as the advertising expense per car of General Motors is significantly lower than that of other competing auto manufacturers.

4. *Market leaders develop unique competitive strategies and have higher prices for their higher-quality products than do smaller-share businesses.* The figures in Exhibit 2 do not show smooth, continuous relationships between market share and the various components of price, cost, and investment. Indeed, it appears that one pattern operates as share increases up to 40%, but a somewhat different pattern above that figure.

Particularly, there are substantial differences in relative price and product quality between market leaders and the rest of the sample. Market leaders obtain higher prices than do businesses with smaller market shares. A principal reason for this may be that market leaders also tend to produce and sell significantly higher-quality products and services than those of their lower-share competitors.

We measured quality as follows: We asked the participating companies to judge for each business the proportions of total sales comprised of products and services that were "superior," "equivalent," and "inferior" to those of leading competitors. The figures shown in Exhibit 2 are averages of the differences between the superior quality and the inferior quality percentages.

The measures we used for relative price and relative quality are not, of course, directly comparable. Thus it is impossible to determine which is greater—the price premiums earned by market leaders, or the differential in the quality of their products. But it is clear that the combination of significantly higher prices and quality represents a unique competitive position for market leaders.

Market leaders, in contrast to their smaller competitors, spend significantly higher amounts on research and developemnt, relative to sales. As shown in Exhibit 2, the average ratio of R&D to sales for the highest-share group of businesses was 3.55%—nearly 40% greater than the ratio for the under-10% share group. This, combined with the quality advantage enjoyed by market leaders, suggests that they typically pursue a strategy of product leadership. Certainly this is consistent with what is known about innovative leaders such as Eastman Kodak, IBM, and Procter & Gamble.

Given that market leaders have a high market share and thus the profitability that goes with it, it is natural to question whether the share and profitability ratio shifts from industry to industry. In other words, do businesses in some kinds of industries need a higher share than others to be profitable?

Variations Among Industries

While our analyses of the PIMS data base clearly demonstrate a strong general relationship between ROI and market share, they also indicate that the importance of share varies considerably from one type of industry or market situation to another. Two of the more striking variations are summarized in Exhibit 4. These figures show that:

1. *Market share is more important for infrequently purchased products than for frequently purchased ones.*   For infrequently purchased products, the ROI of the average market leader is about 28 percentage points greater than the ROI of the average small-share business. For frequently purchased products (those typically bought at least once a month), the correspondingly ROI differential is approximately 10 points.

Why? Infrequently purchased products tend to be durable, higher unit-cost items such as capital goods, equipment, and consumer durables, which are often complex and difficult for buyers to evaluate. Since there is a bigger risk inherent in a wrong choice, the purchaser is often willing to pay a premium for assured quality.

Frequently purchased products are generally low unit-value items such as foods or industrial supplies. The risk in buying from a lesser-known, small-share supplier is lower in most cases, so a purchaser can feel free to shop around.

2. *Market share is more important to businesses when buyers are "fragmented" rather than concentrated.* As Exhibit 5 shows, when buyers are fragmented (i.e., no small group of consumers accounts for a significant proportion of total sales), the ROI differential is 27 percentage points for the average market leader. However, when buyers are concentrated, the leaders' average advantage in ROI is reduced to only 19 percentage points greater than that of the average small-share business.

A likely explanation for this is that when buyers are fragmented, they cannot bargain for the unit cost advantage that concentrated buyers receive, thus allowing higher profits for the large-share business. Obviously, then, the ROI differential is smaller when buyers are somewhat concentrated. In this case, powerful buyers tend to bargain away some of the seller's cost differential by holding out for low prices.

Clearly, the strategic implications of the market-share/profitability relationship vary according to the circumstances of the individual business. But there is no doubt that the relationship can be translated into dynamic strategies for all companies trying to set market goals.

What the ROI/Market-Share Link Means for Strategy

Because market share is so strongly related to profitability, a basic strategic issue for top management is to establish market-share objectives. These objectives have much to do with the rate of return that can reasonably be budgeted in the short and long run, as well as the capital requirements and cash flow of a business.

Setting Market-Share Goals

What market-share goals are feasible, or even desirable, obviously depends on many things, including the strength of competitors, the resources available to support a strategy, and the willingness of management to forgo present earnings for future results. At the risk of oversimplification, we can classify market-share strategies into three rather broad groups:

1 Building strategies are based on active efforts to increase market share by means of new product introductions, added marketing programs, and so on.

2 Holding strategies are aimed at maintaining the existing level of market share.

3 Harvesting strategies are designed to achieve high short-term earnings and cash flow by permitting market share to decline.

Exhibit 5. Industry Variations in the Share/ROI Relationship

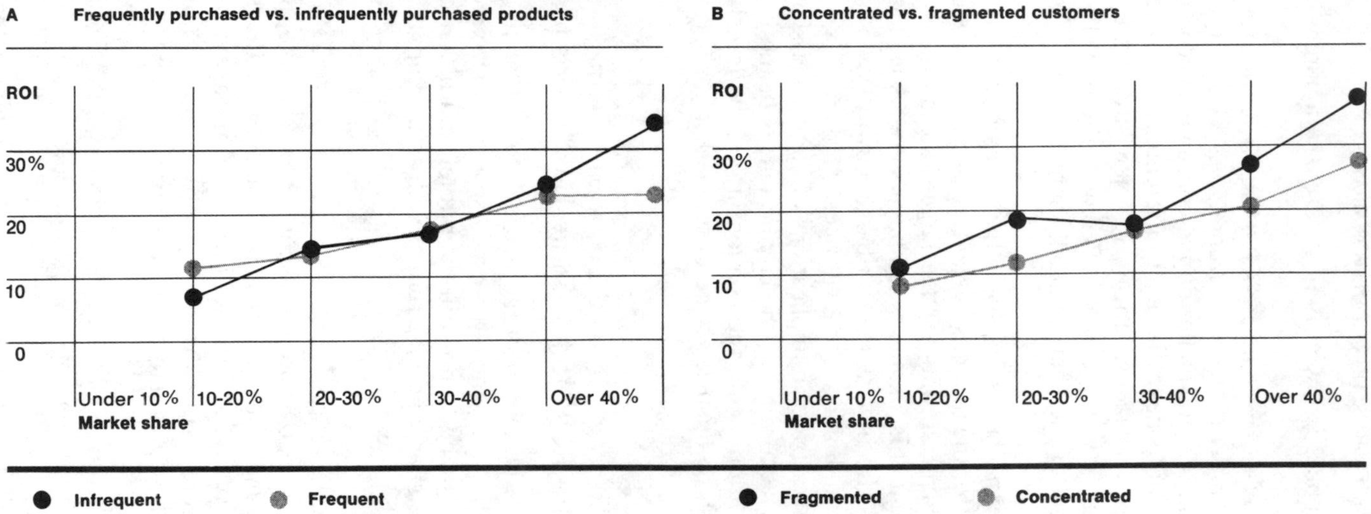
A Frequently purchased vs. infrequently purchased products
ROI
30%
20
10
0
Under 10%
10-20%
20-30%
30-40%
Over 40%
Market share
B Concentrated vs. fragmented customers
ROI
30%
20
10
0
Under 10%
10-20%
20-30%
30-40%
Over 40%
Market share
Infrequent
Frequent
Fragmented
Concentrated

When does each of these market-share strategies seem most appropriate? How should each be implemented? The experiences documented in the PIMS data base provide some clues.

Building Strategies. The data presented in Exhibit 1 imply that, in many cases, even a marginally acceptable rate of return can be earned only by attaining some minimum level of market share. If the market share of a business falls below this minimum, its strategic choices usually boil down to two: increase share or withdraw. Of course there are exceptions to this rule.

But we are convinced that in most markets there is a minimum share that is required for viability. RCA and General Electric apparently concluded that they were below this minimum in the computer business, and they pulled out. Similarly, Motorola, with an estimated 6% to 7% share of U.S. TV-set sales, and a rumored loss of $20 million in the period from 1970 to 1973, announced its intention early in 1974 to sell the business to Matsushita.

On the other hand, when share is not so low as to dictate withdrawal, but is still not high enough to yield satisfactory returns, managers can consider aggressive share-building strategies. They should recognize, however, that (a) big increases in share are seldom achieved quickly; and (b) expanding share is almost always expensive in the short run.

Among the 600 businesses in the PIMS sample, only about 20% enjoyed market share gains of 2 points or more from 1970 to 1972. As might be expected, successful building strategies were most common among relatively new businesses. Of those that have begun operations since 1965, over 40% achieved share increases of 2 points or more—compared with only 17% of the businesses established before 1950.

Generally speaking, businesses that are building share pay a short-run penalty for doing so. Exhibit 6 compares ROI results for businesses with

Exhibit 6. How ROI Is Affected by Market-Share Changes

Market Share 1970	Building: up 2 points or more	Holding: less than 2 points up or down	Harvesting: down 2 points or more
	Market-Share Strategies		
	Average ROI, 1970-1972		
Under 10%	7.5%	10.4%	10.0%
10%–20%	13.3	12.6	14.5
20%–30%	20.5	21.6	9.5
30%–40%	24.1	24.6	7.3
40% or over	29.6	31.9	32.6

different beginning market shares and for businesses with decreasing, steady, and increasing shares over the period 1970 to 1972. Generally, the businesses that were "building" (i.e., had share increases of at least 2 points) had ROI results of 1 to 2 points lower than those that maintained more or less steady ("holding") positions. The short-term cost of building was greatest for small-share businesses, but even for market leaders, ROI was significantly lower when share was rising than it was when share was stable.

Schick's campaign to build sales of the "Flexamatic" electric shaver during 1972 and 1973 dramatically illustrates the cost of increasing market share. In late 1972 Schick introduced the Flexamatic by means of a controversial national advertising campaign in which direct performance comparisons were made with its leading competitors. Trade sources have estimated that Schick spent $4.5 million in 1972 and $5.2 million in 1973 on advertising, whereas the company's advertising expenditures in 1970 and 1971 had been under $1 million annually.

In one sense the effort was successful: by late 1972 Schick's market share had doubled from 8% to 16%. But the impact on company profits was drastic. Schick's operating losses for the fiscal year ending February 28, 1974 amounted to $14.5 million on sales of $93.8 million, and it appears that although it was not the only cause, the high promotional cost of the Flexamatic campaign was a major contributing factor. Only time can tell whether Schick's short-term losses will prove to be justified by increased future cash flows.

The Schick example is, no doubt, an extreme one. Nevertheless, a realistic assessment of any share-building strategy should take into account the strong likelihood that a significant price will have to be paid—at least in the short run. Depending on how great the gains are and how long it takes to achieve them, this cost may or may not be offset by the longer-term gains.

In chapter 8, "Pyrrhic Victories in Fights For Market Share," William Fruhan demonstrates a positive relation between market share and rate of return for automobile manufacturers and for retail food chains. Yet he also cites examples of disasters stemming from overambition in the market-share dimension from the computer industry, the retail food business, and the airline companies.

The main thrust of Fruhan's article is to encourage business strategists to consider certain questions before launching an aggressive market-share expansion strategy: (1) Does the company have the necessary financial resources? (2) Will the company find itself in a viable position if its drive for expanded market share is thwarted before it reaches its market-share targets? (3) Will regulatory authorities permit the company to achieve its objective with the strategy it has chosen to follow? Negative responses to these questions would obviously indicate that a company should forgo market-share expansion until the right conditions are created.

It is fairly safe for us to say, therefore, that whenever the market position of a business is reasonably satisfactory, or when further building of share seems excessively costly, managers ought to follow holding strategies.

Holding Strategies.   By definition, a holding strategy is designed to preserve the status quo. For established businesses in relatively mature markets—which is to say, for the majority of businesses in advanced economies—holding is undoubtedly the most common strategic goal with respect to market share.

A key question for businesses that are pursuing holding strategies is, "What is the most profitable way to maintain market position?" The answer to this question depends on many things, including the possibilities and costs of significant technological change and the strength and alertness of competitors. Because competitive conditions vary so much, few reliable generalizations can be made about profit-maximizing methods of maintaining market share.

Nevertheless, our analyses of the PIMS data base do suggest some broad relationships between ROI and competitive behavior. For example, our data indicate that large-share businesses usually earn higher rates of return when they charge premium prices. (Recall that this pricing policy is usually accompanied by premium quality.) Also, ROI is usually greater for large-share businesses when they spend more than their major competitors, in relation to sales, on sales force effort, advertising, and promotion, and research and development.

For small-share businesses, however, the most profitable holding strategy is just the opposite: on the average, ROI is highest for these businesses when their prices are somewhat below the average of leading competitors and when their rates of spending on marketing and R&D are relatively low.

Harvesting Strategies.   Opposed to a share-building strategy is one of "harvesting"—deliberately permitting share to fall so that higher short-run earnings and cash flow may be secured. Harvesting is more often a matter of necessity than of strategic choice. Cash may be urgently needed to support another activity—dividends, for example, or management's earnings record. Whatever the motivation, corporate management sometimes does elect to "sell off" part of a market-share position.

The experience of the businesses in the PIMS data pool, summarized in Exhibit 6, indicates that only large-share businesses are generally able to harvest successfully. Market leaders enjoyed rates of return about three quarters of a point higher when they allowed market share to decline than when they maintained it over the period 1970–1972. For the other groups of businesses shown in Exhibit 6, differences in ROI between "holding" and "harvesting" are irregular. Of course, these comparisons also reflect the influence of factors other than strategic choice. Market share was lost by many businesses because of intensified competition, rising costs, or other changes which hurt both their profitability and their competitive positions.

For this reason, it is impossible to derive a true measure of the profitability of harvesting. Nevertheless, the PIMS data support our contention that, under proper conditions, current profits can be increased by allowing share to slide.

When does harvesting make sense, assuming it is a matter of choice? A reduction in share typically affects profits in a way directly opposite to that of building: ROI is increased in the short run but reduced in the longer term. Here again, a trade-off must be made. The net balance will depend on management's assessment of the direction and timing of future developments such as technological changes, as well as on its preference for immediate rather than deferred profits.

Balancing Costs and Benefits

Evidence from the PIMS study strongly supports the proposition that market share is positively related to the rate of return on investment earned by a business. Recognition of this relationship will affect how managers decide whether to make or buy to decrease purchasing costs, whether to advertise in certain media, or whether to alter the price or quality of a product. Also, recognizing that emphasis on market share varies considerably among industries and types of market situations, decisions concerning product and customer are likely to be influenced. For instance, a small competitor selling frequently purchased, differentiated consumer products can achieve satisfactory results with a small share of the market. Under other conditions, it would be virtually impossible to earn satisfactory profits with a small share (e.g., infrequently purchased products sold to large, powerful buyers).

Finally, choices among the three basic market-share strategies also involve a careful analysis of the importance of market share in a given situation. Beyond this, strategic choice requires a balancing of short-term and long-term costs and benefits. Neither the PIMS study nor any other empirical research can lead to a "formula" for these strategic choices. But we hope that the findings presented here will at least provide some useful insights into the probable consequences of managers' choices.

Notes

1. See the earlier article on Phases I and II of the project by Sidney Schoeffler, Robert D. Buzzell, and Donald F. Heany, "Impact of Strategic Planning on Profit Performance," *HBR*, March–April 1974.

2. Boston Consulting Group, Inc., *Perspectives on Experience* (Boston, 1968 and 1970).

3. This general argument has been made in numerous books, articles, and speeches dealing with antitrust economics; see, for example, Joe S. Bain, *Industrial Organization*, 2nd edition (New York, John Wiley & Sons, 1968), especially chapter 6.

Appendix: The PIMS Data Base

The data on which this article is based come from the unique pool of operating experience assembled in the PIMS project at the Marketing Science Institute. During 1973, 57 major North American corporations supplied financial and other information on 620 individual "businesses" for the three-year period 1970–1972.

Each business is a division, product line, or other profit center within its parent company selling a distinct set of *products* or *services* to an identifiable group or groups of *customers,* in competition with a well-defined set of competitors. Examples of businesses include manufacturers of TV sets; man-made fibers; and nondestructive industrial testing apparatus.

Data were compiled for individual businesses by means of special allocations of existing company data and, for some items, judgmental estimates supplied by operating managers of the companies.

For each business, the companies also provided estimates of the total sales in the market served by the business. Markets were defined, for purposes of the PIMS study, in much narrower terms than the "industries" for which sales and other figures are published by the Bureau of the Census. Thus the data used to measure market size and growth rates cover only the specific products or services, customer types, and geographic areas in which each business actually operates.

The *market share* of each business is simply its dollar sales in a given time period, expressed as a percentage of the total market sales volume. The figures shown are average market shares for the three-year period 1970–1972. (The average market share for the businesses in the PIMS sample was 22.1%.)

Return on investment was measured by relating *pretax operating profits* to the *sum of equity and long-term debt.* Operating income in a business is after deduction of allocated corporate overhead costs, but *prior* to any capital charges assigned by corporate offices. As in the case of market-share data, the ROI figures shown in Exhibits 1, 5, and 6 are averages for 1970–1972.

As explained in the earlier *HBR* article, the focus of the PIMS project has been primarily on ROI because this is the performance measure most often used in strategic planning. We recognize, however, that ROI results are often not entirely comparable between businesses. When the plant and equipment used in a business have been almost fully depreciated, for example, its ROI will be inflated. Also, ROI results are affected by patents, trade secrets, and other proprietary aspects of the products or methods of operation employed in a business. These and other differences among businesses should naturally be kept in mind in evaluating the reasons for variations in ROI performance.

⑧
Pyrrhic Victories in Fights for Market Share

WILLIAM E. FRUHAN, JR.

Business in the United States has a way of growing compulsively; companies tend to want "in" where a lively market is concerned, and once they are in, they want first place. There are times, as the author shows, when a little self-restraint is an admirable thing. When a company can be sure that moving into a new area or moving up the ladder is going to cost it its lifeblood; when a company can see the hand of government writing restrictive legislation on the wall; when a company must race an established competitor to exhaustion just to get a foothold in a new market—these are times when management should put the ceiling of realism on its ambitions. The author cites examples of disasters stemming from overambition of this kind, from the computer industry, the food business, and the airline companies.

In many U.S. industries, profitability is closely linked to market share. ROI statistics demonstrate this characteristic quite clearly for automobile manufacturing, for example, as Exhibit 1 illustrates.

Since profits can jump impressively in many industries as a company's position in the market-share pecking order advances, market-share battles are often waged with energy; but unfortunately, in spite of the tremendous stakes involved, companies tend to launch their campaigns for building market share without much foresight.

Specifically, they tend to ignore three basic questions:

☐ *Question 1.* Does the company have the financial resources necessary to win—and then support—the level of sales implied by its market-share target; or, if it does not have these resources, can it acquire them at acceptable cost?

☐ *Question 2.* Will the company find itself in a viable position if its drive for an expanded market share should be thwarted—by antitrust action, say–before it has reached its market-share target?

☐ *Question 3.* Will regulatory authorities permit the company to achieve its objective with *the strategy it has chosen to follow?*

To demonstrate the importance of these questions to expansion strategies, let me review the experiences of a number of companies, operating in quite separate industries, that fought, by-and-large disastrously, to increase their market shares.

Main-Frame Computers

Recently, two companies opted out of the main-frame computer manufacturing industry. Prior to their exit from the business, both of these companies had committed themselves to increasing their market shares:

☐ According to press reports during September 1970, General Electric's studies indicated that it had to have a 15% market share if the company were to become competitive in the industry.[1]

☐ About the same time, RCA concluded that it needed a 10% share to become competitive; and the company committed itself, publicly, to meeting that goal by the mid-1970s.[2]

Modest as they might first appear, these market-share objectives represented a more than threefold advance from these companies' 1969 industry standings, which are given in Exhibit 2. Further, both companies planned to meet these objectives solely through internal growth. Both probably felt that antitrust regulations ruled out a strategy for expansion through acquisition of other domestic computer manufacturers, and hence decided to seek their expanded shares through internal means.[3]

A strategy of internal growth in the computer industry, however, demands a major financial commitment. Since a large fraction of manufacturers' output is marketed via leases, operations are capital-intensive. For example, in 1969 IBM required a capital base of about $5.9 billion to support shipment estimated at $4.95 billion, as indicated in Exhibit 2. These figures suggest that, given a stable market share, $1 in annual shipments requires the support of about $1.20 of firm capital in this industry.

Exhibit 1.   Return on Equity for Automobile Manufacturers, Ranked by Market Share

Company	Market-share rank	1960	1962	1964	1966	1968	1970
General Motors	1	16.9%	21.3%	23.5%	21.2%	18.2%	6.1%
Ford	2	15.6	14.6	12.9	13.3	13.0	9.4
Chrysler	3	4.6	8.8	20.4	11.4	14.1	−0.3

Exhibit 2.   Competitors' Standings in the 1969 Main-Frame Computer Market (dollar figures in millions)

Company	Sales Value of Computers Shipped	Market Share	Total Corporate Capital[a] 1969	Total Corporate Revenue 1969	Percent of Total Revenues from Computers
IBM	$4,950	69.0%	$5,906	$7,197	83%
Sperry Rand	400	5.6	977	1,710	36
Honeywell	340	4.7	956	1,281	27
Burroughs	305	4.3	907	759	36
GE	290	4.0	3,554	8,448	3
Control Data	255	3.6	984	1,084	53
RCA	230	3.2	1,875	3,222	7
NCR	195	2.7	1,104	1,255	16
Xerox	75	1.1	1,099	1,483	8
Others	130	1.8	—	—	—
Industry total for year 1969	$ 7,170	100.0%			
Projections of industry shipments 1970	$ 7,720				
1971	8,940				
1972	10,300				
1973	11,800				
1974	13,400				

Source: International Data Publishing Co., annual reports, and author's estimates.
[a]Includes short-term loans, long-term debt, and shareholders' equity.

This degree of capital intensity, coupled with the absolute size of the computer industry and the speed with which RCA (and presumably GE, too) wished to reach its market-share objectives, leads to one inescapable conclusion: the market-share aspirations of GE and RCA required a capital commitment quite out of proportion to their capital-generating ability.

Exhibit 3 shows this clearly. The combined retained earnings and the additions to debt capital which the earnings retentions of GE and RCA might have supported at their debt/equity ratios in the late 1960s were insufficient to meet the future capital needs arising solely from the *computer divisions* of these diversified companies. Yet, in 1969, the computer divisions' revenues accounted for less than 10% of total corporate revenues in the two companies.

The implications are clear. The debt/equity ratios of GE and RCA (already high by IBM standards) would have had to be raised sharply, or equity securities would have had to be sold (at low P/E ratios by IBM

Exhibit 3. Severe Capital Intensity In The Main-Frame Computer Industry
(dollar figures in millions)

A. All-Industry Figures

Year	Projected Industry Computer Shipments	Industry Capital/ Shipments Ratio	Total Capital Required by Industry
1969	$ 7,170	1.2	$ 8,600
1970	7,720	1.2	9,270
1971	8,940	1.2	10,710
1972	10,300	1.2	12,350
1973	11,800	1.2	14,200
1974	13,400	1.2	16,100

B. RCA Projected Goals

Year	Share of Market Projection	Total Capital Required	New Capital Required
1969	3.2%	$ 276	—
1970	4.0	371	$ 95
1971	5.0	536	165
1972	6.3	778	242
1973	8.0	1,135	357
1974	10.0	1,610	475

C. GE Projected Goals

Year	Share of Market Projection	Total Capital Required	New Capital Required
1969	4.0%	$ 344	—
1970	5.2	482	$138
1971	6.8	730	248
1972	8.9	1,100	370
1973	11.5	1,635	535
1974	15.0	2,420	785

D. Capital Generation

	RCA—1969	GE—1968
Profit after taxes	$151	$357
Dividends	68	235
Earnings retentions	$ 83	$122

Exhibit 3. (*Continued*)
D. Capital Generation

	RCA—1969	GE—1968
Debt/equity ratio[a]	×.45	×.27
Debt potential at D/E ratio	37	33
Total capital generation potential	$120	$155

[a]Includes long-term debt only; in the case of RCA, does not include debt of the Hertz Corporation.

standards) before these companies could have come close to achieving their market-share objectives. Exhibit 4 gives the statistics for the competing companies.

As *this* exhibit implies, the prospects for GE and RCA were not always quite this dim. Back in 1955, both companies had sufficient corporate resources (in terms of total profit or cash flow) to challenge IBM. By 1961, however, this ability, even for GE, was somewhat questionable. By the mid-1960s, and certainly after the IBM System 360 became a demonstrated success, the contest was over. IBM had so far outdistanced its nearest competitors, and its markets had grown to enormous size so rapidly, that the simple passage of time was raising market-entry barriers to insurmountable heights.

All that remained were the acknowledgments—which finally came in 1970 and 1971—that neither GE nor RCA could marshal the resources necessary to achieve, without domestic acquisitions, even a marginal market share in the computer industry at acceptable cost. Had they asked my Question 1 somewhat earlier than 1970, both GE and RCA might have greatly reduced their losses in the computer business.

Retail Groceries

The retail grocery trade is a second industry in which the fight for market share is well worth examining.

In food retailing, the Federal Trade Commission has found a high correlation between the *profit contribution* of chain stores in a given geographic market area—usually a city or metropolitan area—and the *market share* achieved by those chain stores in the same market area. (Exhibit 5 demonstrates the strength of this correlation.) Indeed, in reference to one company operating in this industry, the FTC's chief economist has stated, "I have never seen a closer relationship between the market dominance of a firm in an individual market, or group of markets, and its profitability. . . ."[4]

Exhibit 4.   Financial Statistics for Major Computer Manufacturers, 1955–1969

Company	1955	1957	1959	1961	1963	1965	1967	1969
A. Debt/Equity Ratio								
Burroughs	33%	70%	62%	61%	65%	56%	48%	58%
Control Data	—	—	0	0	103	78	163	39
GE	0	25	19	14	11	17	31	27
Honeywell	18	28	24	28	35	42	65	77
IBM	102	60	50	36	27	15	13	10
NCR	50	59	24	41	51	38	69	61
RCA	97	85	76	52	48	43	50	45
Sperry Rand	—	65	60	62	70	58	31	36
Xerox	38	23	28	59	64	72	52	35
B. Average P/E Ratio								
Burroughs	13.1%	24.0%	22.4%	21.3%	24.5%	15.7%	32.4%	43.1%
Control Data	—	—	32.6	95.3	49.9	55.1	53.3	43.2
GE	22.3	21.9	25.8	25.5	26.7	27.1	24.5	28.4
Honeywell	19.2	29.8	30.6	42.2	23.3	26.3	29.6	32.7
IBM	22.7	31.0	42.0	54.9	34.6	35.8	43.5	40.4
NCR	14.3	17.7	23.0	27.0	27.6	22.8	26.3	32.1
RCA	14.3	13.3	23.6	29.8	20.5	22.2	23.5	17.8
Sperry Rand	13.7	22.0	18.7	32.6	18.3	14.4	23.7	18.6
Xerox	30.6	27.4	45.8	78.5	43.8	54.7	62.3	45.7
C. Profit After Taxes (in millions of dollars)								
Burroughs	$ 12	$ 10	$ 11	$ 11	$ 9	$ 18	$ 35	$ 55
Control Data	—	—	—	1	3	8	8	52
GE	201	248	280	242	271	355	361	278
Honeywell	19	21	29	25	35	38	42	63
IBM	73	111	176	253	363	477	652	934
NCR	18	23	22	30	22	29	35	44
RCA	48	39	40	36	66	101	110	131
Sperry Rand	46	28	37	24	27	32	64	81
Xerox	1	1	2	5	23	62	100	161

Source: Annual reports; *Moody's Industrial Manual*, 1970; *Value Line Investment Survey.*

Stated another way, the profitability of an individual company in grocery retailing depends not so much on its total industry market share but, rather, on its weighted-average market share in the various city-market areas in which it participates. This relationship between profitability and city-market share suggests that a growth-minded retail company planning to expand its market position rapidly faces a strategic dilemma: Should it gain

Exhibit 5. Market Shares Charted against Store Contribution to Corporate Profit, by Groups of Cities (1958)

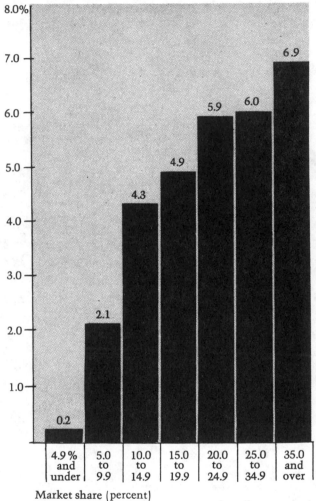

Average contribution
to corporate profit
(percent of sales)

Market share (percent)

toehold positions in a large number of city-market areas (via acquisitions, for example), and then build its share in each city from this limited base later? Or should it devote its resources to building a dominant position in one-city market area at a time?

Many large chains operating in the industry faced precisely this dilemma between 1948 and 1958, a period when the retail food industry was consolidating itself rapidly through mergers. (Exhibit 6 shows the trend

Exhibit 6.   Percentage Distribution of Food Store Sales, by Type of Retailer, for
1948, 1954, and 1958

Type of Retailer	Percent of Food Store Sales		
	1948	1954	1958
Top 20 chains	24.0%	30.1%	34.0%
Other chains	5.2	6.7	9.8
Cooperative members[a]	7.7	12.7	18.8
Voluntary members[a]	4.6	10.0	12.0
Unaffiliated independents	58.5	40.5	25.4
Total	100.0%	100.0%	100.0%

[a]Arrangements between wholesalers and independents have assumed two basic forms: the
retailer-owned cooperative food wholesaler and the wholesaler-sponsored voluntary retail group.
Groups of independents so affiliated with a particular wholesaler commonly are referred to as
voluntary or cooperative groups or chains.

toward consolidation in those years.) In that decade, the most active acquirer
in the field, National Tea, opted for the "toehold" strategy on a nationwide
basis, as did many of its competitors. These companies found themselves
spread quite thin in numerous markets just at the critical moment in 1958,
when (a) the last of the large-store independents were disappearing via merger
into competitive chain operations, and (b) the FTC was taking decisive action
to halt the consolidation movement by blocking future mergers in this industry.

In short, these companies found themselves in disadvantaged competitive positions and without usable strategies. The detrimental effect on
ROI, in the case of National Tea, is clear from the figures in Exhibit 7. What
National Tea and many of the others in the group had failed to do was
adequately test their strategies against my Questions 2 and 3: they had failed
to consider their positions, should they have to shelve their strategies midway

Exhibit 7.   ROI and Acquisition Activity of Three Retail Grocery Companies

Company	Share of U.S. Food Store Sales in Countries Where Company Operates, 1958	ROI				Number of Stores Acquired, 1949–1958	Share of U.S. Food Store Sales, 1958
		1955	1960	1965	1970		
Winn-Dixie	17.2%	17.7%	19.8%	20.6%	18.3%	306	1.3%
A&P	12.6	10.5	12.1	8.8	7.4	0	9.7
National Tea	8.6	9.5	9.1	8.4	5.5	485	1.6

to their goals, and they had failed to prepare themselves for restrictive government regulation.

In contrast, Winn-Dixie—the second most active acquirer in the retail grocery field—appears to have tested its strategies well, judging by the figures given in Exhibit 7. And, in fact, in planning its acquisitions in the 1948–1958 period, Winn-Dixie drove for market depth in a limited geographic area, namely, the Southeast. The company continues to reap the benefits of this bit of foresight in strategy formulation even today. Clearly, there can be an enormous profit payoff in keeping a relatively modest exposure to adverse regulatory responses which might be expected to occur in the middle of a share expansion drive.

Air Transport

My third and final example of a heroic but less-than-successful fight for market share is taken from the air transportation industry.

In this field, consumer buying habits and basic industry economics seem to have entered into a conspiracy to make market-share duels look like very attractive investment opportunities. In making plans, first of all, many air travelers initially contact the air carrier that they believe has the most daily flights to their destination city, which is a natural thing to do. But because of this customer trait, the frequency of a carrier's flight departures in relation to those of its competitors often becomes the crucial factor determining the carrier's share of the passenger traffic in a particular city-pair market. Just as a relatively larger allocation of shelf space in a supermarket might help a cereal manufacturer gain an edge over his competitors, so an added round-trip flight each day between Boston and Chicago might help an airline boost its share of the passenger traffic moving between these cities.

In air travel, the relationship between product availability and market share is especially dramatic. In a city-pair market served by only two air carriers, for example, a carrier with 70% of the "daily flight frequencies" might attract 80% of the passenger traffic (see Exhibit 8).

Equally, the carrier with only 30% of the flights in this situation might get only 20% of the traffic. This relationship between frequency share and market share is, of course, moderated by differences in carrier promotion and quality of service; but it seems to hold true where competitors can be distinguished only by service frequency.

Now, what are the economics in this situation? Since most flights operate at a loss unless passengers occupy at least 40% of the seats available, the minority carriers on many routes operate at a significant loss. In the example I just mentioned, where one carrier has 70% of the capacity and 80% of the business, and his competitor has only 30% of the capacity and 20% of the business, the competitor is almost certain to lose money on his operation. The dominant carrier, on the other hand, often achieves the very

Exhibit 8. Market Share and Capacity Share on a Two-Carrier Route

Market: passengers flown

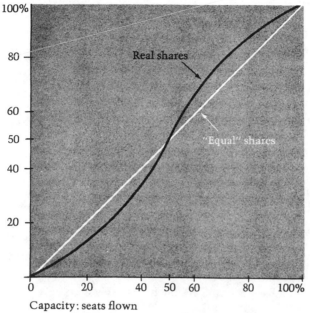

Capacity: seats flown

substantial profits implied by relatively high load factors. (Exhibit 9 presents the details of this situation.)

Thus, in the long run, the air carrier with sufficient financial resources to purchase the extra aircraft and fly the extra flight frequencies necessary to achieve a dominant capacity share in particular city-pair markets is almost bound to come out ahead.

If my analysis is correct, one might expect the history of the airline industry to reflect (a) chronic capacity competition, (b) poor profitability, and (c) frequent failures among the smaller carriers, as the larger carriers

Exhibit 9. Hypothetical Market Shares of Two Carriers Competing in a City-Pair Market

Carrier	Seats Flown per Year	Share of Seats on Route	Share of Market	Total Passengers Flown	Passenger Load Factor
Dominant	70,000	70%	80%	44,000	62.8%[a]
Minority	30,000	30	20	11,000	36.7%[a]
Total	100,000			55,000	

[a]Overall passenger load factor on route—55%.

build their market shares by overwhelming smaller rivals via capacity competition.

While one does indeed find the first two characteristics, a closer look at the record (see Exhibits 10 and 11) illustrates the market shares of the largest carriers shrinking over the past 15 years and the highest level of profitability among the smallest carriers. Frequent failures among the smaller carriers have just not taken place—quite the reverse. Hence, on this point, either my analysis has led us down a blind alley, or something must have intervened in the competitive environment to neatly reverse the anticipated and the actual outcomes. The "something" is, of course, the Civil Aeronautics Board (CAB). This government regulatory body has become, in practice, an allocator of market shares and relative profitability for the domestic trunk air carriers.

Regulatory Inversion

The CAB has been able to accomplish this rather remarkable inversion of free market results for two principal reasons. First, it has the power to grant or withhold licenses permitting air carriers to fly in various markets. Second,

Exhibit 10. Average Market Shares for the 11 Domestic Trunk Air Carriers (Domestic Operations), 1954–1970

Airlines	1954	1958	1962	1966	1970
Big 4					
American	23.7%	22.3%	20.5%	19.0%	17.4%
Eastern	16.9	17.1	12.3	12.6	13.0[a]
Trans World	16.0	14.8	13.7	14.1	12.8
United	20.2	20.9	24.5[b]	21.9	23.7[a]
Little 7					
Braniff	3.7%	4.2%	3.8%	3.8%	3.8%
Continental	1.3	1.9	3.1	4.0	4.6
Delta	5.1	6.1	8.3	9.3	10.1
National	4.1	4.0	4.2	4.8	3.9
Northeast	1.0	1.6	2.4	1.6	2.1
Northwest	5.0	4.5	4.1	5.1	4.7
Western	2.7	2.7	3.3	3.7	3.9
Total for Big 4	76.8%	75.0%	70.9%	67.7%	66.9%
Total for Little 7	23.2	25.0	29.1	32.3	33.1

[a]Data for 1970 show a rising market share for two of the Big 4 carriers. This was due to strikes at National and Northwest which temporarily but significantly reduced their market shares during the year.

[b]Includes Capital Airlines, which merged into United in 1961 and which accounted for 5.6% of domestic trunk revenues in 1960.

Exhibit 11.   ROI for the 11 Domestic Trunk Air Carriers, 1954–1970

Airlines	1954	1958	1962	1966	1970
Big 4					
American	15.6%	12.4%	5.7%	20.2%	− 7.8%
Eastern	13.1	6.3	− 16.7	7.4	− 1.1
Trans World	18.7	2.7	− 20.2	7.4	− 33.9
United	10.8	11.2	1.9	8.8	− 7.2
Little 7					
Braniff	28.4%	10.5%	11.4%	33.0%	− 10.1%
Continental	11.3	− 1.7	6.9	31.7	3.9
Delta	15.7	9.9	26.5	37.2	16.1
National	10.7	4.5	24.5	22.6	− 4.9
Northeast	3.0	—	—	0	—
Northwest	9.7	8.4	6.4	20.2	8.7
Western	13.1	7.3	11.7	23.3	− 3.4
Big 4	14.0%	8.9%	− 3.2%	11.5%	− 11.0%
Little 7	13.4	4.5	12.6	27.3	5.2
Industry	13.9	7.7	1.3	17.2	− 4.5

it can control the number of participants in any given city-pair market. This power is significant because the number of carriers competing in a city-pair market has a very heavy impact on that market's profit potential. So pronounced is the impact of competition, in fact, that one carrier's monopoly routes, although they generated less than 10% of its revenue, supported the fraction of its traffic—more than 50%—which was carried at a loss.

Thus the CAB exercises tremendous profit control over the individual carrier. By making the largest new-route awards to smaller carriers, it can, over a long period of time, regulate a carrier's market share of the total industry traffic.

How has the CAB used this great regulatory power? Exhibits 10 and 11 show that since the carriers were removed from government subsidy in the mid-1950s, the air-carrier market shares have slowly been leveling out. Even at that early date, the CAB may well have looked at the air transportation industry in the context of my Question 1 and come to the conclusion that, without its intervention, small carriers would simply be unable to withstand market-share battles waged by bigger rivals with greater financial resources.

Hence, to avoid capacity duels that might end in small-carrier bankruptcy, and to offset the advantages large carriers have in raising expansion capital, the CAB has tended to give the small carriers a dramatic edge in relative profitability.

Exhibits 10 and 11 point out a meaningful contrast between the growth and profit opportunities of the smallest large carrier (Eastern) and the largest small carrier (Delta). The essence of this contrast was exquisitely penned by Paul H. Frankel 24 years ago, in his study of the petroleum industry:

> There is no more enthusiastic satellite than the biggest operator outside the ring—But the more successful he becomes the greater his danger of cutting off the branch upon which he is sitting. For, beyond a certain point . . . he is faced with . . . joining the inner circle himself. Thus, while the position of the biggest "outsider" is the most desirable, the lot of the smallest "insider" is the most uncomfortable.[5]

The game rules for profitability apply very differently to companies on the two sides of the regulatory fence; and companies which plan to climb that fence had better recognize the fact explicitly.

Further, the intent of the CAB's regulations is to maintain the number of competitors for market share, both large and small; and its resulting regulations may have created, in effect, a no-win market environment for the Big Four carriers.

Unfortunately, this no-win environment does not seem to have muted the willingness of the Big Four carriers to wage wasteful and expensive capacity wars. Indeed, these firms seem quite unwilling to address the implications of Question 3—their need to devise more creative and effective strategies for gaining larger shares.

Word of Warning

Most companies have committed themselves to fight for larger market shares. I contend that companies often make this commitment before they have adequately considered my three basic questions:

1 Are company financial resources adequate?
2 If the fight is stopped short for any reason, will the company's position be competitively viable?
3 Will government regulators permit the company to follow the strategy it has chosen?

In computer manufacturing, GE and RCA both pursued dramatic increases in their market shares long after the evidence indicated that their goals were financially impossible. In choosing an internal-growth rather than an acquisitions strategy, these companies showed they had considered the antitrust aspects of Question 3, but they were quite late in acknowledging the relevance of Question 1.

In grocery retailing, National Tea and many of its competitors evidently neglected Questions 2 and 3. As a result, halfway to their market-share goals, they were trapped in competitively disadvantaged positions. Winn-Dixie's strategy dealt more successfully with Questions 2 and 3, and this company remains a consistent leader in terms of industry profitability.

Finally, in the air transport industry, the CAB has structured a no-win environment for the larger carriers. These companies are simply not permitted to build their market shares through the traditional avenue of internal expansion. For their part, the larger carriers have yet to identify a market-share expansion strategy that recognizes my Question 3—the *feasibility* question—as the capacity wars and eroded profits of recent years demonstrate; yet their taste for doing battle with losing strategies seems undeterred.

Here, as in all the examples I have cited earlier, the cost of ignoring or failing to gather evidence relating to the three questions I posed initially has been frightfully high.

I could continue to add examples, but let me recommend some points for thought instead:

☐ Are you operating in an industry where extremely heavy financial resources are required?

☐ Are you in an industry where an expansion strategy might be cut off abruptly by a regulatory agency?

☐ Are you in an industry where some agency is even now planning some new regulatory hurdles?

If the answer to any of those questions is *yes*, and if yours is the kind of company that fights for market share, reassess your battle plan.

Notes

1. "Honeywell Tries to Make Its Merger Work," *Business Week*, September 26, 1970, p. 93.

2. Gene Smith, "RCA Profits Topple, Kodak Sets Mark," *The New York Times*, October 15, 1970.

3. Allan T. Demaree, "G.E.'s Costly Ventures Into Futures," *Fortune*, October 1970, p. 158.

4. U.S. Federal Trade Commission, *In the Matter of National Tea Co., Findings as to the Facts, Conclusions, and Order*, Docket #7453, March 4, 1966, p. 57.

5. *Essentials of Petroleum* (London, Chapman & Hall, Ltd., 1946), p. 86.

9
Strategies for Low Market-Share Businesses

RICHARD G. HAMERMESH, M. JACK ANDERSON, JR.,
and J. ELIZABETH HARRIS

What do the Burroughs Corporation, Crown Cork & Seal Co., Inc., and the Union Camp Corporation have in common? Although none of them enjoys a dominant market share, all three earn quite respectable returns on their equity, have healthy profit margins, and continue to maintain strong sales growth year after year. In this article, the authors identify and analyze four characteristics that help explain their success: they compete only in areas where their particular strengths are most highly valued, make efficient use of limited research and development budgets, eschew growth for growth's sake, and have leaders who are willing to question conventional wisdom.

During the past several years, a great deal of research on profitability and market share has uncovered a positive correlation between the two. One study shows that "on the average, a difference of ten percentage points in market share is accompanied by a difference of about five points in pretax ROI."[1] Although in general market share and return on investment do go hand in hand, many of the inferences that both managers and consultants have been drawing from this finding are erroneous and misleading.

One of the most dangerous inferences drawn from this generality is that a low market-share business faces only two strategic options: fight to increase its share or withdraw from the industry. These prescriptions completely overlook the fact that, in many industries, companies having a low market share consistently outperform their larger rivals and show very little inclination to either expand their share or withdraw from the fight. Perhaps the best example of this situation is the steel industry, where producers such as Armco Steel, Inland Steel, and Kaiser Steel have consistently earned a higher return on equity than their much larger competitors, United States Steel and Bethlehem Steel.

Often, planning systems that are based on this generality also have serious flaws. Most of these systems place a business in one of four categories, according to its market share and the industry's growth rate.[2] Depending on the category a business falls in, a strategy is automatically prescribed. Low market-share businesses in low-growth industries should be divested; high market-share businesses in low-growth industries should be "milked" or "harvested" for cash; high market-share businesses in high-growth industries should maintain their growth; and low market-share businesses in high-growth industries should increase their market share.

Although each classification system has its own nuances, all such systems share the same shortcoming: they define strategy at such a high level of abstraction that it becomes meaningless. A successful business strategy must be specific, precise, and far-ranging. It should state the markets in which a business will compete, the products that will be sold, their performance and price characteristics, the way in which they will be produced and distributed, and the method of financing. By taking the attention of corporation executives away from these essential details and instead focusing their attention on abstractions, many planning systems do a great disservice.

Finally, such sweeping generalities offer little consolation to those businesses that, for one reason or another, find themselves in a poor market position. Since only one competitor enjoys the highest share of any given market, most businesses must face the disadvantage of not having the highest market share. They must devise a specific strategy that will lead to the best possible performance, regardless of their position.

During the past several months, we have been studying businesses that have outperformed other much larger companies in their industries. We have identified four important characteristics that most of these successful businesses share. In this article, we shall discuss these characteristics.

Indications of Performance

Although there are numerous ways to define successful performance and low market share, we have chosen two straightforward definitions. Low market share is less than half the industry leader's share, and successful companies are those whose five-year average return on equity surpasses the industry median. Applying these criteria to the over 900 businesses in 30 major industries listed in *Forbes Annual Report on American Industry* revealed numerous successful low share businesses. From a list of these companies, we chose three—Burroughs Corporation, Crown Cork & Seal Co., Inc., and Union Camp Corporation—for close study. These three companies have surpassed not only their industries' average return on equity but have actually led their industries in several important performance categories.

Consider Burroughs. During the mid-1960s, many analysts predicted that the corporation, with its narrow line of computers, aging accounting machines, and market share of less than 3%, would soon withdraw from the main-frame computer market. Today, Burroughs competes more effectively with IBM than does any other computer company. Its market share is still dwarfed by that of IBM, but during the past five years, its sales and earnings per share have grown faster than IBM's. And although Burroughs's net profit margin and return on equity trail IBM's, they exceed those of NCR, Sperry Rand, Honeywell, and Control Data by a substantial margin.

It is significant that results by line of business, which are reported in 10-K statements and which distinguish businesses such as Control Data's finance and insurance lines and Honeywell's controls line, also indicate that on a return-on-sales basis, Burroughs's computer line greatly outdistances that of all its rivals except IBM. (See Exhibit 1 for detailed comparisons of the financial positions of main-frame computer manufacturers.)

Crown Cork & Seal is another successful low share company. In fact, as Exhibit 2 shows, its financial performance over the past decade has consistently been the highest of the major metal can manufacturers. Yet Crown Cork & Seal has not always enjoyed such success. In early 1957, the company was near bankruptcy, and with sales of $115 million in 1956, it had to compete with American Can (1956 sales of $772 million) and Continental Can (1956 sales of $1 billion).

Today, Crown Cork & Seal is still much smaller than its two giant rivals, but with profits of $46 million (15.8% return on equity), the prospect of bankruptcy has long since passed. Although Crown Cork & Seal's com-

Exhibit 1. Comparative Performance of Major Main-Frame Computer Manufacturers Through 1976

Company	Total Sales (in millions of dollars)	Net Profit Margin	Return on Equity (five-year average)	Annual Sales Growth (five-year average)	Earnings per Share Growth (five-year average)
IBM	$16,304	14.7%	20.5%	12.8%	14.1%
Burroughs	1,871	9.9	14.3	14.5	17.1
Sperry Rand	3,203	4.8	13.1	11.1	12.9
NCR	2,312	5.0	11.8	9.6	46.0
Honeywell	2,495	4.5	9.7	8.5	5.1
Control Data	1,331	2.5	4.7	12.4	−0.1

Source: Annual reports of the above companies and *Forbes*, January 9, 1978.

Exhibit 2.   Comparative Performance of Major Metal Can Manufacturers Through 1976

Company	Net Sales (in millions of dollars)	Net Profit Margin	Return on Equity (five-year average)	Annual Sales Growth (five-year average)	Earnings per Share Growth (five-year average)
Crown Cork & Seal	$ 910	5.1%	16.2%	14.7%	14.5%
Continental	3,458	3.8	14.1	10.5	14.3
National Can	917	2.5	12.2	16.5	5.9
American Can	3,143	3.3	12.0	9.2	16.9

Source: Annual reports of the above companies and *Forbes,* January 9, 1978.

petitors have all diversified, an analysis of 10-K statements for 1976 shows that the pretax returns on sales of their metal packaging businesses were all below 6%; Crown Cork & Seal's pretax return on sales was nearly 10%.[3]

Our third company, Union Camp, competes in the extremely competitive, highly fragmented forest products industry. Over 3,000 companies have major product lines in this industry, and it has been highly volatile and plagued with overcapacity, depressed prices, pollution control problems, and high construction costs.

Despite these problems, Union Camp's earnings per share have increased by almost 27% annually over the past five years, and average return on equity has been over 20%. As the ninth largest company in its industry, Union Camp competes with such giants as International Paper and Weyerhaeuser, which are three and a half and two and a half times larger than Union Camp. As shown in Exhibit 3, Union Camp's weak market position

Exhibit 3.   Comparative Performance of Major Forest Products Companies Through 1976

Company	Sales (in millions of dollars)	Net Profit Margin	Return on Equity (five-year average)	Annual Sales Growth (five-year average)	Earnings per Share Growth (five-year average)
Union Camp	$1,003	11.1%	21.7%	13.6%	24.9%
Weyerhaeuser	2,868	10.2	19.5	15.4	18.1
Mead	1,599	5.6	17.4	7.5	31.7
International Paper	3,540	6.0	16.2	11.0	21.5
Boise Cascade	1,932	5.2	12.0	1.2	Not applicable

Source: Annual reports of the above companies and *Forbes,* January 9, 1978.

has not prevented the company from outperforming its larger competitors. Comparisons of the pretax return on 1976 sales of the paper and paperboard portions of these companies show that Union Camp leads the pack with a 28% return. The next highest rate was posted by Boise Cascade's paper operations.

Elements of Strategy

Except for their low market-share positions and exceptional performances, Burroughs, Crown Cork & Seal, and Union Camp seem to have little in common. Certainly their competitive environments are extremely different. Computer main-frames constitute a highly technological, rapidly growing industry that is dominated by one company. The metal container industry is extremely mature and, with only four major competitors, is a classic oligopoly. The forest products industry is also mature, but it is very fragmented.

Given these rather substantial differences in industry settings, are there any common strategies that these three successful low share companies have implemented to yield profits? Our research suggests four characteristics that these companies share: they carefully segment their markets, they use research and development funds efficiently, they think small, and their chief executives' influence is pervasive.

Segment, Segment, Segment

First, to be successful, most businesses must compete in a limited number of segments within their industry, and they must choose these segments carefully. Thinking in broader terms than only the range of products offered and the types of customers served, most successful companies define market segments in unique and creative ways. For example, besides products and customers, a market can also be segmented by level of customer service, stage of production, price performance characteristics, credit arrangements with customers, location of plants, characteristics of manufacturing equipment, channels of distribution, and financial policies.

The point is an important one. To be successful, a low share company must compete in the segments where its own strengths will be most highly valued and where its large competitors will be most unlikely to compete. Whether that strength is in the type and range of products offered, the method by which the product is produced, the cost and speed of distribution, or the credit and service arrangements is irrelevant. The important thing is that management spend its time identifying and exploiting unique segments rather than making broad assaults on entire industries.

Aerosol and Beverage Cans. Although the metal container industry sells to numerous industries and faces competition from glass, aluminum, fiberfoil, and plastic containers, Crown Cork & Seal has elected to concentrate on two product segments: (1) metal cans for hard-to-hold products such as beer and soft drinks and (2) aerosol cans. In an industry where transportation costs represent a large proportion of total costs, Crown Cork & Seal has built small single-product plants close to its customers instead of large and possibly more efficient multiproduct plants located at some distance from its customers.

The two market segments Crown Cork & Seal serves have both grown more rapidly than the total industry, but they also require expert skills in container design and manufacturing. The company has a particular advantage over competitors in the soft drink and brewing industries because it is the largest supplier of filling equipment to these companies. Thus Crown Cork & Seal has segmented its market by products, customers, customer service, and plant location. It is significant that the company sells to growth segments in which it has special expertise.

Four Large Paper Mills.   In the forest products industry, Union Camp has had to overcome the disadvantages of having a relatively small timberland holding—only 1.6 million acres—in contrast to International Paper's 23.7 million acres and Weyerhaeuser's 16.7 million acres. Although this difference makes Union Camp's raw material prices higher, the company has achieved consistently lower operating costs than its large rivals. Since the location of plants is important, Union Camp, like Crown Cork & Seal, operates only four very large mills, strategically situated in deep water ports close to both Union Camp's southern timberlands and its eastern customers.

For example, at its Franklin, Virginia plant, Union Camp operates the largest fine-paper machine in the world. As a low-cost producer of paper products, this corporation produces large volumes of only a limited number of paper products, and in bleached paper, Union Camp is not fully integrated. Instead, it sells most of its output to end-product converting companies. By selling to a rather small number of paper converters, the corporation has established a superior service record.

Thus Union Camp has segmented its market by stage of production, manufacturing policies, prices, products, customers, and services.

Three Distinct Computer Lines.   Unlike Union Camp and Crown Cork & Seal, which do not offer complete lines in their industries, Burroughs offers a full line of computers. But in developing its full product line, the corporation has taken advantage of historical ties to the financial community, where it has been a major supplier of accounting machines for decades. Today, Burroughs possesses an 18% share of the banking segment, almost three times its overall market share.

In designing its large computers, the B5000 series, Burroughs has emphasized ease and flexibility of programming at the expense of efficient use of main memory. This form of segmentation has been justified by the tenfold decrease in memory costs since 1964, while talented programmers have become both scarce and expensive.

In medium-size computers, Burroughs has chosen to imitate IBM's design and to compete on price. The company has reportedly underbid IBM by considerable amounts on some large government contracts. In the small-computer market, Burroughs has continued to upgrade its electronic accounting machines and has given them the capability to serve as either terminals to a larger computer or as free-standing accounting machines.

Thus, although Burroughs offers a full line of main-frame computers, within each line it has segmented the market to capitalize on its particular skills and resources.

That Crown Cork & Seal, Union Camp, and Burroughs have had to compete in unique market segments in order to attain their success should not be surprising. But what these three companies reveal is that the opportunities to segment an industry are enormous and extend to every facet of a business. When a business segments its markets in unique and creative ways, it can far surpass the performance of its larger competitors. The marketing vice president of one high market-share business once commented:

> For years, we have been unable to understand why our profits have been mediocre despite our strong market position. The expert planners at corporate staff have been of little help. About a year ago, we decided to do a detailed study of our industry. We found that, although we had the highest market share, in all of the important and more profitable market segments, we were taking a beating. We were leading the pack, however, in the unappealing segments of the markets.

Use R&D Efficiently

Although low market-share companies can improve their performance by pursuing narrow market segments, their larger rivals still seem to have a tremendous advantage, because of their size, in research and development. Our research suggests that smaller companies seldom win R&D battles but that they can channel their R&D spending into areas that are the most likely ones to produce the greatest benefits for them.

Lower Process Costs.   At both Crown Cork & Seal and Union Camp, for example, R&D is focused on process improvements aimed at lowering costs. A Crown Cork & Seal executive has noted:

> We are not truly pioneers. Our philosophy is not to spend a great deal of money for basic research. However, we do have tremendous skills in die forming and metal fabrication, and we can move to adapt to the customer's needs faster than anyone else in the industry.[4]

Alexander Calder, Jr., Union Camp's chairman, has adopted a similar R&D strategy:

> We are known to be very strong in process and in the manufacturing of industrial products. . . . We do little basic research like Du Pont. But

we are good at improving processes, developing improved and some new products, and helping to build new manufacturing capabilities.[5]

Another R&D strategy Union Camp and Crown Cork & Seal have developed is to work closely or jointly with their largest customers on major developments. For example, Crown Cork worked closely with large breweries in the development of the drawn-and-ironed cans for the beverage industry. As a result, the company beat all three of its major competitors in equipment conversion for the introduction of this new product.

Concentrate on Innovations. For Burroughs, the problem of developing an R&D strategy is much more difficult and crucial than for the other two companies because of the rapid changes and high technology in the computer industry. Although Burroughs spends 6% of its sales on R&D compared with IBM's 7.5%, in dollar terms the difference is staggering—$112 million versus $1.2 billion. To compensate, Burroughs runs an extremely efficient R&D operation and concentrates on truly innovative products. And because of its low share position, these products are able to attract enough new customers to more than offset the trading up by Burroughs's existing customers.

IBM, on the other hand, has paced its innovations because, whenever it introduces a new system, a significant amount of its leased equipment is exchanged for the new system. As a result, Burroughs is recognized as one of the technological leaders in the computer industry.

Burroughs also runs an extremely efficient R&D operation. Its chairman, Ray Macdonald, spends a great deal of time at his R&D center and exerts tremendous pressure on his engineers.

Think Small

Another characteristic of successful low market-share companies is that they are content to remain small.[6] Most of them emphasize profits rather than sales growth or market share, and specialization rather than diversification.

Limit Growth. Macdonald limits Burroughs's growth in the rapidly growing computer industry to 15% per year because he maintains that fast growth does not allow for the proper training of people and the development of a management structure. And in an industry where giants such as General Electric and RCA have faltered because they have found the pursuit of market share to be too costly, Burroughs has been consistently profitable despite only slow and modest gains in market share. Macdonald notes:

> There are two theories of growth in this industry. One is ours, where you plan to grow at a sustainable and affordable rate and put market share low on the list of objectives. Then there are others who thought that this rate was inadequate and took risky measures to increase their growth and market share. They were moths around a candle on that one.[7]

Union Camp and Crown Cork & Seal have also emphasized profits rather than size. At Crown Cork & Seal, management decided not to continue to compete in the oil can market even though the company had a 50% share of this segment. Despite the loss of sales, management decided that it had other more profitable opportunities and that new materials such as fiberfoil provided too great a threat in the motor oil can business.

During the 1973–1975 recession, Union Camp's management resisted customer pressure to produce a broad line of white papers. To Union Camp, the extra sales could not be justified by the added production costs.

Diversify Cautiously.   Unlike many of their larger competitors, most successful low market-share companies are not diversified. For example, both Continental Can and American Can have diversified widely, while Crown Cork & Seal has continued to concentrate on making metal cans. When successful low market-share companies do diversify, they tend to enter closely related areas. For example, Union Camp has diversified into wood-based chemicals and retail distribution of building materials. Union Camp's vice chairman, Samuel Kinney, Jr., explained another element of Union Camp's diversification strategy:

> You must have someone in the parent organization who really under-
> stands the [new] business before it gets heavy. Other paper companies
> have had troubles along these lines. They had these MBAs who, I am
> sure, were intelligent. But once they failed, there wasn't a damn thing
> anyone could do back at headquarters. They didn't know the business,
> and they were completely out on a limb.[8]

Ubiquitous Chief Executive

The final characteristic of these companies we found striking is the pervasive influence of the chief executive. John Connelly of Crown Cork & Seal, Alexander Calder of Union Camp, and Ray Macdonald of Burroughs have all been described as extremely strong-willed individuals who are involved in almost all aspects of company operations.

To a large extent, it is understandable that leaders of low market-share companies are dynamic, tough people who see obstacles as challenges and enjoy competing in unorthodox ways. It may simply take a strong-willed leader to convince and inspire an organization to "beat the odds."

This is not to imply that the chief executives of large share companies are not also strong-willed, dynamic, and tough. But most often these executives work with teams of other senior managers and limit their responsibilities to a few key areas. In successful low share companies, the influence of the chief executive often extends beyond formulating and communicating an ingenious strategy to actually having a deep involvement in the daily activities of the business.

At Union Camp, for example, Calder still retains responsibility for sales and marketing. Macdonald of Burroughs is deeply involved in both the development and the marketing of new products.

Of course, the pervasive influence of the chief executive in low market-share business makes the problem of management succession an extremely difficult one. Connelly, now 72, has yet to retire or to pick a successor. While Macdonald retired in December 1977, he has retained the position of executive committee chairman, and analysts are already questioning Burroughs's prospects without him. Though reports differ about what the actual situations are, only Union Camp's Calder seems to have been able to delegate significant responsibilities and to practice a more participatory style of leadership than the others have.

Alternative to Growth

Although this article has an optimistic tone, we must acknowledge that there are some serious obstacles a low market-share business must overcome. These usually include small research budgets, few economies of scale in manufacturing, little opportunity to distribute products directly, little public and customer recognition, and difficulties in attracting capital and ambitious employees. Moreover, previous research indicates that, on the average, the return on investment of low share businesses is significantly less than that of businesses with high market shares.

We have made no attempt to refute these research findings or to deny the obstacles facing low share businesses. But we have sought to demonstrate that many of the inferences being drawn from these findings are simplistic and misleading. Simply put, not all low share businesses are "dogs."

Rather, we have found that a small market share is not necessarily a handicap; it can be a significant advantage that enables a company to compete in ways that are unavailable to its larger rivals. We believe that these findings are significant.

For the independent low share company, these findings represent an alternative to bankruptcy and the high costs and risks associated with efforts to increase market share

To the large diversified company, the findings suggest that formal planning systems must go beyond simply placing each division in one of several categories. Categorization schemes can provide a useful conceptual handle for top executives, but the best planning systems are those which encourage and enable a division to seek the best fit between the opportunities in the competitive environment and the particular skills, strengths, and resources each division possesses.

In sum, our findings indicate that, in a division or in an independent company, management's first objective should be to earn the maximum return on invested capital rather than to achieve the highest possible market share.

Notes

1. Robert D. Buzzell, Bradley T. Gale, and Ralph G.M. Sultan, "Market Share—A Key to Profitability," *HBR*, January–February 1975, p. 97.

2. See *Perspectives on Experience* (Boston, Boston Consulting Group, Inc., 1968 and 1970) for a description of a typical classification system.

3. For a more comprehensive description of Crown Cork & Seal, see E. Raymond Corey, "Key Options in Market Selection and Product Planning," *HBR*, September-October 1975, p. 119.

4. "Crown Cork & Seal and the Metal Container Industry," Harvard Business School case study, ICCH No. 6–373–077 (Boston; Intercollegiate Case Clearinghouse, 1973), p. 30.

5. "Union Camp Corporation," Harvard Business School case study, ICCH No. 9–372–198 (Boston, Intercollegiate Case Clearinghouse, 1972), p. 6.

6. For an excellent discussion of the risks of attempting to build market share, see William E. Fruhan, Jr., "Pyrrhic Victories in Fights for Market Share," *HBR*, September-October 1972, p. 100 (Chapter 8 in this text).

7. "How Ray Macdonald's Growth Theory Created IBM's Toughest Competition," *Fortune*, January 1977, p. 98.

8. "New Growth at Union Camp," *Dun's Review*, March 1975, p. 43.

Appendix: Implications for Diversified Companies

While low market-share divisions of large diversified companies face many of the problems we have encountered in our research, it is important to note that their status creates additional problems as well as some opportunities.

An obvious advantage is that many of the more established diversified companies maintain large, centralized research and development centers. One successful division we studied had few funds itself for new product development. But when a competitor developed a product that was based on a new technology, those at corporate headquarters had their R&D center imitate the development in accordance with a one-time request from the division.

On the negative side, most large companies place great emphasis on growth and reward those division managers whose units grow the fastest. This philosophy runs counter to the needs of many divisions to segment and think small. Many large companies also use formal planning techniques that categorize their divisions. The division managers then must convince their top managers that, despite the dismal projections and warnings of statistically oriented planners, their divisions do face a bright future.

An example illustrates these problems and the ways in which they can be overcome. Consolidated Businesses is a typical diversified company op-

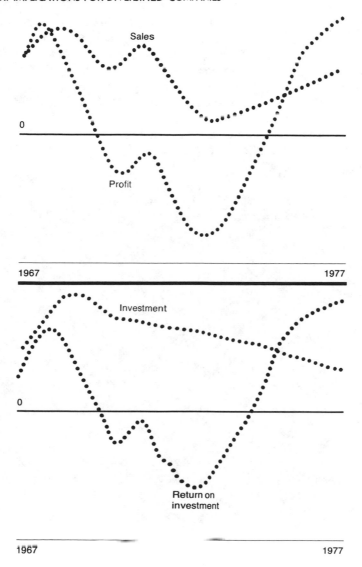

erating in 65 businesses ranging from air conditioners to automobile parts.*
Dedicated to continuous increases in sales and earnings, its semiconductor
division produced a full line of sophisticated devices and had grown quite
rapidly prior to a sudden sharp decline in its sales and profits. After a number
of management changes, a new division team and executives from the group
vice president's staff undertook a complete review of the division and its

*This disguised example was also reported on in Richard Hamermesh's article, "Responding
to Divisional Profit Crises," *HBR*, March-April 1977, p. 124.

industry. They determined that the division could only succeed by concentrating on serving a distinct group of industrial customers.

By doing this, the semiconductor division has recorded the highest ROI in its history; in fact, it enjoys one of the highest ROIs within Consolidated Businesses (see the accompanying table). Even though the division's sales are lower than they were ten years ago and its profits are at about the same level, Consolidated Businesses' top executives understand that the high return it is earning on shareholders' investment more than compensates for these facts. They have also promoted many of the semiconductor division's managers for their performance.

10
How to Compete in Stagnant Industries

RICHARD G. HAMERMESH AND STEVEN B. SILK

As more and more industries decline or increase only modestly, the need for competent managers in stagnant industries will grow. Instead of following the often-heard advice to harvest such businesses, managers should understand the characteristics of their markets and build strategy accordingly. On the basis of their study of a number of declining industries, these authors identify some consistent characteristics in companies that have competed successfully.

From 1950 to 1973, the U.S. economy enjoyed record prosperity. Gross national product and per capita disposable income, measured in real terms, grew at annual rates of 3.7% and 2.4%, respectively. Among the many consequences of this growth has been an attitude among managers that growth is beneficial and will continue and an assumption that the most talented and aggressive managers should lead rapidly growing divisions. Slowly growing or declining divisions have been left to the less aggressive or over-the-hill managers.

Such attitudes and assumptions may have made sense when growth seemed unlimited. Since 1973, however, economic growth has slowed, with real GNP and real per capita disposable income rising very slowly. And the limited supply of natural resources has led most economic observers to forecast a prolonged period of slower growth. Thus, in the future, more industries will experience declines or only modest increases in the demand for their products. This situation will create a tremendous need for managers who can effectively lead businesses that compete in stagnant industries.

Despite the increasing need for competent management in stagnant industries, little research has been conducted on what strategies make the most sense in such industries. Existing theory offers little sound advice. Instead it offers the glib recommendations that companies either divest these businesses or "harvest" them as "cash cows." Unfortunately, harvesting can often become synonymous with abandonment. Moreover, the difficulty of finding a buyer often makes divestment impossible, and liquidation is often impractical. One experienced division manager commented on the problem in the following way:

> Recently our corporate planning people studied our division and determined that we should drop certain product lines because they were in tough, slowly growing markets. But that isn't so easy. Without those sales, we'd no longer be covering our plant overhead and most of our other products would become unprofitable.

In our study of possible approaches to competing in stagnant industries, we first defined stagnant industries as those whose total unit demand over a ten-year period had either declined or increased at less than half the rate of real GNP. After identifying 12 industries which met our criteria, we then looked carefully at those companies that were notably successful or unsuccessful in order to determine what competitive strategies were most likely to succeed or fail in such industries. Finally, through interviews with managers in many of these companies, we were able to gain a better understanding of the administrative problems of managing a stagnant industry.

Our research shows that it is possible to compete successfully and to earn high returns in these industries. More specifically, it reveals some important characteristics of the strategies of the successful businesses. Equally important, our work also indicates that the way top management interacts with and administers its stagnant businesses often has a substantial impact on their performance.

Harsh Realities

Before turning to the most promising strategies, it is necessary to examine the difficult realities of life in a stagnant market. An appreciation of these realities is critical because, as we shall see, strategies that run counter to them nearly always fail, while the successful strategies are consistent with market conditions.

Perhaps the most difficult reality to accept is that rapid growth probably will not return to a stagnant industry. Consider the coffee industry. Between 1960 and 1975, total consumption of coffee fell 3.2%. Admittedly, in certain years demand has increased and in others price increases have led to pronounced declines. But over a long period of time, the overall trend has been a slow decline. The fact that consumption per person has fallen even more rapidly suggests that this trend will continue.

The point is an important one. In a declining or slowly growing industry, there may be some years when demand is buoyant. But it is essential for managers not to let wishful thinking color their views. Instead, they must accurately assess the long-range prospects and face the problems of competing in a stagnant marketplace. Management's acceptance of the reality of a continuing slow demand is a prerequisite for developing successful strategies.

For example, at one company we visited, we were told about the shaky relationship between the corporate office and a division that competed in a declining market. Corporate management was dissatisfied with the division's performance, while the division was upset that none of its capital requests had been approved in the past four years. Closer examination revealed that, although top management did not want to commit additional resources to the division, it was still pressuring the division to grow. The division's response was to develop plans for growth that required additional capital investment.

When both division and corporate management confronted the reality of declining demand in a series of strategy-setting meetings, the problem was eventually resolved. The division then adopted a set of goals consistent with its market opportunities, and corporate management began to measure divisional performance on the basis of cash flow and return on investment.

The next unpleasant reality is that competition is usually more intense in stagnant markets than in those that are growing rapidly.[1] A company can substantially increase its sales in a rapidly growing industry without taking market share from competitors. In fact, often it takes all of a company's managerial and financial resources just to meet growing demand. The major problem is expansion, not competition. When industry growth slows, however, company growth can be achieved only at the expense of others, and competition increases.

As competition intensifies, the number of companies competing in the industry usually declines, and the market shares of the largest companies increase. For example, in the cigar industry, where unit demand has been declining by 5% a year for 15 years, the number of manufacturers declined from 283 in 1958 to 132 in 1972. In the coffee industry, not only has the number of companies declined but the combined market shares of the three largest corporations increased from 47% in 1960 to 67% in 1976.

A final reality, and one that is often overlooked, is that changes in products, technology, production process, and distribution still occur in stagnant industries. In fact, research by William J. Abernathy and James M. Utterback has shown that some innovations, notably in the manufacturing process, tend to occur more frequently as a market matures.[2] For example, improvements in cigar-forming equipment have changed the industry from a "craftsman" business to an automated one. As we shall discuss later, improvements by the Japanese in the manufacturing process of motorcycles made possible the development of the recreational motorcycle market. Stagnant demand, then, does not prevent significant changes.

Failure to recognize these realities can lead to competitive strategies that seem logical but are seldom successful. This is most likely to occur when stagnant sales are viewed as "a marketing problem" instead of as a fact of life. Rather than increasing total demand, typical marketing solutions such as brand proliferation and heavy advertising usually result in higher inventory investment, higher manufacturing costs, and lower profitability. Other research has shown that, although increased advertising tends to benefit businesses in their introduction or growth phases, it is seldom useful for declining businesses.[3]

Strategies for Success

Given these realities, are there any approaches that not only avoid the possibility of extinction but that also offer hope for a reasonable return on investment in stagnant industries? Our research uncovered three common characteristics of the strategies of businesses that have succeeded in stagnant industries: they identify, create, and exploit growth segments within their industries; they emphasize product quality and innovative product improvement; and they systematically and consistently improve the efficiency of their production and distribution systems.

Growth Segments

Perhaps the best way to avoid some of the unpleasant realities in a stagnant industry is to concentrate on growth segments. A classic example is the strategy followed by General Cinema Corporation.

Over the past 30 years, the number of motion picture theaters in the United States has declined by almost 20%. As late as 1946, movie admissions accounted for $1 out of every $5 spent on recreational items versus $1 out of every $40 today. During this extended period of decline and stagnation, one market segment—the shopping center theater—has been growing at an impressive rate. And General Cinema Corporation has been the leader in recognizing this opportunity and in concentrating its resources in this growth segment. Today General Cinema has about 700 shopping center theaters, usually with multiple auditoriums (Cinema I and II theaters). In a declining total industry, General Cinema has been able to maintain average earnings increases of over 20% during the past 10 years and a return on equity of 20%.

Of course, it can be argued that by competing in growth segments a company has merely figured out how to avoid competing in a stagnant industry. And this is precisely the point. Choosing what business to compete in is at the very heart of the strategy formulation problem, and the best strategists spend considerable time analyzing their industries in an effort to identify emerging or growth segments. Admittedly, there are some industries for which it is virtually impossible to identify growth segments, but in most industries opportunities do exist. As the chairman of a $300 million specialty paper and chemical company recently told us, "There is a high-growth segment in every industry you can think of."

Another example illustrates how imaginative thinking can uncover growth opportunities, even within a sluggish capital goods industry. Since the Arab oil embargo in 1973, demand for electrical power in the United States has hardly risen, leading to a major reduction in orders for new power-generating equipment. Westinghouse Electric's Power Systems Company has not been able to avoid this dearth of new orders, but it has compensated for these lost sales by expanding its service business.[4] As customers have postponed or canceled new purchases, demand for repair and maintenance work has surged. Not only is Westinghouse filling this demand, but it is also actively developing new products and concepts that should enable the company to exploit this growth segment.

For example, replacement parts are being developed that improve the efficiency of existing systems, and a portable precision machine shop allows technicians to machine heavy rotors on location. As a result of these efforts, during the past six years service volume has tripled, enabling the Power Systems Company to show steady gains in sales and earnings.

Since the identification of growth segments usually requires considerable insight and creativity, it is difficult to prescribe a set of procedures that will lead to their identification. Nevertheless, there probably is a way to think about an industry that should help identify growth segments. The key is to recognize that, on close examination, most industries are composed of numerous segments and subsegments. And these can be defined along a variety of dimensions: customer group, price, product characteristics, product use, geography, service, and technology.

Merely listing and thinking about segments, however, is not enough, for detailed breakdowns of industry statistics along the relevant dimensions are also required. This information is seldom publicly available and requires a research investment to collect and analyze it. For example, just considering customer grouping, simply to obtain a breakdown by age, sex, geographic location, economic status, and buying motivation may involve considerable effort. In some of the companies we visited, it was not unusual for one or two staff people to work full time at collecting and analyzing such data. Thus a creative management that is willing to view its stagnant industries as being composed of smaller segments and to collect and analyze detailed industry data is much more likely to identify segments with growth potential.

Innovation and Quality

Another characteristic of successful strategies in stagnant industries is the pursuit of high-quality, innovative products. Such products allow the company to avoid some of the price competition that often typifies stagnant markets. Product innovations have the further advantage of being difficult and expensive for competitors to imitate.

An example of a high-quality innovative product is General Foods's freeze-dried instant coffee, which offers better-tasting instant coffee. For almost ten years, it has grown rapidly and achieved the highest margin of all coffee products. The freeze-dry technology is also more expensive than traditional technologies. Most coffee producers—with the notable exception of Nestlé—have been unwilling or unable to invest in either the research or the capital equipment necessary to compete in this segment. Thus this innovation has provided high margins in a segment with few competitors.

Further evidence that high quality and innovation are particularly important in stagnant industries comes from analysis of the 1,000 businesses in the PIMS (profit impact of market strategies) data base.[5] For all these businesses, higher product quality is associated with a larger return on investment, but the relationship appears to be most significant in stagnant markets (see Exhibit 1). Also striking are the relationships among ROI, market growth, and expenditures for research and development (see Exhibit 2). For moderate and rapid-growth markets, the PIMS data indicate no benefits to ROI from increased spending on R&D. However, in the stagnant markets, high rates of R&D spending correlate with higher ROIs.

The association between ROI and R&D spending in stagnant industries may indicate that, in addition to the benefits from a major new product innovation, in many cases there is also a payoff from consistently higher levels of spending on research that produces a steady stream of higher-quality products. The group vice-president in charge of the fastener divisions in a large corporation explained:

> Our business is a mature one, and in some divisions unit demand is actually declining. But because of the nature of our business and our own efforts, each year 20% of our products are new ones designed for the new models in the appliance, clothing, auto industry, and so on. Thus there would be a danger in reducing our spending on R&D. By designing innovative new products we not only maintain our volume but also avoid competing in commodity items.

One result of this strategy was that the fastener group's return on assets was among the highest in the corporation.

Exhibit 1. Return on Investment as a Function of Market Growth and Product Quality (in Percentages)

	Product Quality		
Market Growth	Low	Medium	High
Low	15	14	31
Medium	16	22	29
High	21	23	28

Source: Based on data from PIMS companies in *The Limited Information Report,* distributed by the Strategic Planning Institute (Cambridge, Mass., 1977), p. 16.

Exhibit 2.   Return on Investment as a Function of Market Growth and Research and Development Expenditures (in Percentages)

Market Growth	R&D Sales		
	Low	Medium	High
Low	14	21	19
Medium	22	19	15
High	21	20	12

Source: Based on data from PIMS companies in *The Limited Information Report,* distributed by the Strategic Planning Institute (Cambridge, Mass., 1977), p. 16.

Operating Efficiencies

Another characteristic of the successful stagnant industry businesses we studied was their constant attention to cost reduction. The most common way to achieve lower costs seems to be by improving the manufacturing process. Often these improvements stem from constant and systematic attention to efficiency. For example, Samuel Hollander has shown that more than half of the reduction in rayon costs at Du Pont has resulted from gradual improvements rather than from major investments and programs.[6]

A dramatic example of the power of process innovations is the Japanese approach to the motorcycle industry. During the 1950s, demand for motorcycles declined as fewer people used them as a primary mode of transportation. Rather than exit from this sick industry, the major Japanese manufacturers embarked on an ambitious program to lower their costs and to concentrate on smaller motorcycles (under 750 cc). High degrees of specialization and automation have been the hallmarks of the approach. One Honda plant, for example, makes only engines. Both Suzuki and Yamaha have plants almost entirely dedicated to the manufacture of specialized machine tools. As the Japanese lowered their costs and broke price barriers, they were able to create a new growth segment in the industry—the recreational bike.

Although improvements in the manufacturing process are the most common way of lowering costs, other efficiencies can be achieved. For example, the orderly and planned consolidation of production facilities can have a dramatic impact on ROI. In the previously mentioned fasteners group, one division's ROI was less than 10%. Consolidation of its manufacturing facilities with those of other divisions has helped to lift its ROI to 35%.

The important point, however, is not only that facility consolidations lead to higher rates of return; it is also that by accepting the realities of stagnant demand, management can plan for the orderly consolidation of manufacturing facilities. For example, the division manager of a business that supplies materials to U.S. shoe manufacturers determined that over a three-year period his need for two manufacturing plants would disappear.

He used this time to identify another division in the company that needed manufacturing capacity. The shift from a two- to a one-factory operation has enabled the division to operate at high levels of efficiency, and the changeover was implemented with a minimum of disruption.

A final form of operating efficiency is possible through broad and efficient distribution, which is especially important in stagnant industries requiring high volumes for efficient manufacturing operations. For example, Whirlpool's appliance business is concentrated in the stagnant washer, dryer, and refrigerator segments. To ensure the volume needed to manufacture at efficient scale, Whirlpool has used Sears as the distribution outlet for 60% of its production. Indeed, private labeling is a common way of achieving broad and efficient distribution in stagnant industries.

It should be noted that the three characteristics we have identified of the strategies of the successful businesses often reinforce each other. In both the motorcycle and the appliance industries, attention to operating efficiencies led to concentration on growth segments. And in the motorcycle industry, the smaller, cheaper recreational bikes were high-quality product improvements. Clearly, the successful companies differ in the degree to which they emphasize the three strategies, but most of them exploit elements of each.

Top Management's Role

When we began this study, our objective was to identify the characteristics of successful strategies for competing in stagnant industries. In talking with managers in these businesses, however, it quickly became apparent that the nature of top management's involvement and its choice of general managers for these businesses were also critical determinants of their success.

In most large, diversified corporations, it is beyond the scope of corporate management to set strategy for individual business units. Nevertheless, top managers do influence business unit strategy through the reporting system, compensation system, planning system, organizational arrangements, and personnel selection. Obviously, corporate managers attempt to establish systems and an organizational context that facilitate the business units' efforts to compete successfully. For business units that compete in stagnant industries, corporate-level managers can accomplish this by not labeling the status of these business units, by not mandating "milking" strategies, and by assigning talented general managers to run these businesses.

Avoiding Labels

Throughout this article, we have pointed to the payoffs of accepting and dealing with slowing sales as a reality of life. Although it is essential that top management consider this reality when developing business plans, it is also important not to assign pejorative labels to these businesses.

One label sometimes used for low-growth businesses is "dog." Such a characterization can have a debilitating effect on morale within the division, and it suggests that not much attention needs to be given to these businesses. But, as we have seen, competition in stagnant industries is usually intense, and success is dependent on creative strategies and skilled implementation. A group vice president of a large industrial company explained his experiences as follows:

> Two of the divisions that report to me are in very sluggish industries. In one case, we have been able to develop more original strategies, have the employees all fired up, and are making a good return. But I have had to fight to keep the corporate planners from giving their view of the situation. In the other division, the notion that they have a dog has been allowed to permeate from the top. I feel there are some original things we could do there, but it's impossible to get anyone at the division very excited to try something new. Eventually we'll probably sell or liquidate the division.

The point is a simple one. Top managers do have the responsibility to make sure that the business unit accepts stagnant industry demand as fact. But, as we have shown, stagnation does not mean that successful ways of competing do not exist. Successful strategies are more likely to be adopted when the stagnant condition is accepted as a fact of life rather than labeled as a dreaded condition.

Avoiding Milking

Another inappropriate top management response is to require these businesses to adopt milking, or harvesting, strategies automatically. The overwhelming defect of these strategies is that they are internally oriented, ignoring events in the external environment and assuming a lack of change within the industry. This attitude is often reflected by attempts to milk the businesses for cash and thus to minimize investments in research and engineering. Unfortunately, there is often a thin line between managing a business in this way as a cash cow and abandoning it.

When Alcoa and Reynolds Aluminum developed a process to produce two-piece cans, their intentions reportedly were to make the process available to can manufacturers in order to increase their raw material sales. However, the two largest can producers, American Can and Continental Group, were reluctant to incur the costs involved in line changeovers at a time when they were diversifying into growth businesses and de-emphasizing their slowly growing can operations.

The result was that Alcoa and Reynolds began to build their own can lines and that two smaller producers, National Can and Crown Cork & Seal, also invested heavily in new two-piece can lines. Because the new cans have proved very popular and offer important manufacturing benefits, the companies that were willing to invest in the new process have gained market share at the expense of their larger competitors, who assumed a static situation and were harvesting their can manufacturing businesses.

The penalties for adopting milking strategies that assume a static competitive and technological situation can be severe. The director of corporate planning at one of the widely diversified companies we visited explained:

> If one of our high-growth divisions misses or is late on an innovation, it is not that serious, because in a few months they will have another chance to be first on the next set of innovations. But in slowly growing divisions, change is less frequent. And if you miss a change, the next one may not come for another five to ten years. By that time, you could be out of business.

Admittedly, many successful businesses that compete in stagnant industries do generate more cash than they consume and in this sense could be considered cash cows. But there is an important distinction between generating positive cash flows as the result of strategic actions aimed at improving a business's competitive position and making positive cash flows the major objective of a business.

In the former approach, a business develops its strategy after assessing conditions and changes in the external environment and relates these to internal competence. After management formulates a strategy, it applies financial tests such as ROI, cash flow, or rate of growth and makes a decision whether to adopt the proposed strategy. Conversely, the milking approach leads to a strategy that is consistent with a certain set of cash flows. In our view, this approach is much less likely to produce creative strategies that will be successful over a long period of time.

Choosing Managers

Earlier in this article, we noted the historical tendency of most top managements to assign their most talented and aggressive managers to their rapidly growing divisions while leaving their stagnant divisions to less aggressive and competent managers. Keeping in mind that competition in stagnant industries is usually more intense than in growth situations, it is easy to see the problems that arise when less competent managers are assigned to these businesses.

Choosing appropriate general managers for low-growth businesses, then, is a major challenge. For example, selecting "marketing men" who only focus on increasing sales is likely to lead to strategies that are inappropriate in these industries. Our observation has been that it is crucial for an experienced general manager to be assigned to run one of these businesses and that his or her future promotions be tied to success with these divisions. A group vice president at an industrial company explained:

> I try to assign these [stagnant] businesses to people who are ready for their second or third general management job. These are real good positions to test the flexibility of these people. Also, I think by assigning

talented people we get a leg up on our competitors who may be down-playing these businesses.

Of course, choosing good people becomes a hollow gesture if it is not backed up with bonuses and promotions for outstanding performance. And here it is important to remember that success will usually not manifest itself in high rates of sales growth but rather in high levels of ROI. Nothing signals top management's expectations more clearly than the promotion of general managers who have competed successfully in a stagnant marketplace.

In Summary

We have tried to address one of the most difficult strategic problems that managers face, a problem we think will proliferate in the future. Despite our recommendations regarding successful strategies and management's involve-ment, it should be apparent that competing in these industries will always be difficult. We can then ask: Why bother? Why not diversify into higher-growth businesses and simply divest low-growth businesses?

In answering these questions, it is important to recognize that, from the corporate perspective, diversification is often an effective way to deal with these problems. In fact, one of the major roles of top management in a diversified company is to ensure that growth businesses will be maintained within the corporation. But it is a rare company that competes only in rapidly growing industries. Thus corporations must eventually address problems of competing in slower industries.

There are other reasons why diversification is not a panacea for the problems of competing in stagnant industries. In some companies, these businesses are simply too large to be disposed of or liquidated. For example, even though the coffee industry is declining, General Foods still derives 40% of its sales and one-third of its earnings from its coffee business. It has no choice but to compete vigorously and effectively in the coffee industry.

In other circumstances, divestment is simply impossible. Who would want to buy one of these businesses? So, in many cases, management cannot avoid the problems of competing in stagnant industries. Indeed, as we pointed out earlier, accepting and dealing directly with the problem is usually the first step in adopting and implementing a successful strategy.

The next step is to choose a strategy and stick with it. In several of the situations we studied, divisional management kept wavering among a broad range of strategies. One month management proposed a series of product-line extensions, while the following month simplifying distribution would be the fad. This lack of consistency not only wastes valuable time and fails to produce results for the division but also confuses the corporate managers who are trying to understand and help the divisions.

Competing in stagnant industries requires adoption of clear strategies that emphasize growth segments, innovative products, and production efficiencies. At the same time, top managers must avoid the tendency to label these businesses pejoratively, to require them to implement harvesting strategies, and to assign them to weak managers.

When these guidelines are followed, competing in these industries can be profitable and slow growth can become an ally. As competitors stumble into the ever-present pitfalls, a tremendous opportunity is created for companies that are willing to compete aggressively and imaginatively. For them, competition in these industries is by no means dull; rather, it is exciting and profitable.

Notes

1. See Michael E. Porter, "How Competitive Forces Shape Strategy," *HBR*, March–April 1979, p. 137.

2. See James M. Utterback and William J. Abernathy, "A Dynamic Model of Process and Product Innovation," *Omega*, 3, no. 6 (1975), p. 639.

3. See Paul W. Farris and Robert D. Buzzell, *Relationships Between Changes in Industrial Advertising and Promotion Expenditures and Changes in Market Share*, Marketing Science Institute Working Paper No. 76–119 (Cambridge, Mass, December 1976).

4. See "More Manufacturers Are Selling Services to Increase Returns and Smooth Cycles," *Wall Street Journal*, December 26, 1978, p. 24.

5. For a more complete description of the PIMS project, see Robert D. Buzzell, Bradley T. Gale, and Ralph G.M. Sultan, "Market Share—A Key to Profitability," *HBR*, January–February 1975, p. 97.

6. See William J. Abernathy and James M. Utterback, "Patterns of Industrial Innovation," *Technology Review*, June–July 1978, p. 3.

11
Survival Strategies in a Hostile Environment

WILLIAM K. HALL

How are such domestic manufacturing industries as steel, tire and rubber, auto-motive, heavy-duty truck and construction equipment, home appliance, beer, and cigarette evolving in the face of today's adverse external pressures? Given the lower growth inflationary, regulatory, and competitive impacts, what business strategies are appropriate? Which strategic choices offer the best chances for survival, growth, and ROI in a hostile environment? This author investigates these issues and presents some preliminary findings from an ongoing research project which explores the strategic and structural changes that took place in the 1970s and that are expected to continue into the 1980s.

As economists, managers, and industry analysts pause to look back on the past decade, there remains little doubt that the business environment in the United States grew increasingly hostile during the 1970s. More important, there is now little doubt that this hostile environment will continue (and perhaps even worsen) throughout the 1980s, reflecting the combined effects of:

☐ Slower, erratic growth in domestic and world markets.

☐ Intensified inflationary pressures on manufacturing and distribution costs.

☐ Intensified regulatory pressures on business conduct and investment decisions.

☐ Intensified competition, both from traditional domestic competitors and also from the new wave of foreign competitors entering U.S. markets with different objectives and frequently lower ROI expectations.

As a result of these growing pressures, large U.S. manufacturing corporations are witnessing a major evolution in industry structures and competitive behaviors. Many structures that were stable and highly profitable during the "go-go" decade of the 1960s are now moving toward instability and marginal profitability.

Moreover, the broad range of corporate strategies and business "success formulas" which brought prosperity in those earlier years are no longer working. Instead, these are being replaced with a much narrower range of strategic choices that are becoming essential to survive in the hostile environment ahead.

The purpose of this article is to present some preliminary findings from an ongoing research project that my colleagues and I are conducting to explore these strategic and structural changes in more depth. This project is focusing on two broad questions:

1. How are industry structures in the mature markets evolving in the face of the adverse external pressures of the late 1970s?
2. Given this evolution, what business strategies are appropriate? Which strategic choices give the best chances for survival, growth, and return in the hostile environment ahead?

In-Depth Investigation

To examine these issues, I selected eight major domestic manufacturing industries for comprehensive study because of their importance to national and/or regional economic development and also because the adverse external trends of the 1970s have been especially severe in their impact on them. As a result, during the 1970s, all eight industries underwent a significant structural change which is expected to continue into the 1980s. Within these industries, I examined the strategies and evolving competitive positions of the 64 largest companies by using a combination of public data sources and field interviews.

In examining the impact of external pressures on these companies, I found that the eight industries either matured during the 1970s or will mature in the 1980s, resulting in lower growth records and growth expectations as shown in Exhibit 1. While the industries (on average) exceeded national economic growth rates in the 1950s and 1960s, they grew only slightly faster than the GNP in the 1970s, and they are projected to grow significantly more slowly than the U.S economy in the 1980s.

During this maturation period, these eight industries, which are capital, raw material, and labor intensive, have been subjected to heavy inflationary pressures that cannot easily be price recovered. All are being forced by regulatory agencies to make major investments to comply with new occupational safety and health regulations and with new product safety, performance, and environmental protection standards.

Exhibit 1.   Compound Annual Real Growth Rates in Demand—United States

Eight Basic Industries	1950–1970	1971–1980	1980 Forecast[a]
Industrial goods			
Primary products			
Steel	4.0%	2.2%	1.5%–2.5%
Tire and rubber	4.2	1.4	1.0–1.5
Intermediate products			
Heavy-duty trucks	7.0	2.8	2.5
Construction and materials handling equipment	7.8	3.6	2.3
Consumer goods			
Durable products			
Automotive	4.8	3.5	2.0–3.0
Major home appliances	6.2	2.9	2.3–2.8
Nondurable products			
Beer	3.1	2.5	2.3
Cigarettes	1.6	1.0	0
Average growth rates—eight industries	4.8%	2.4%	1.9%
Average growth rates—U.S. GNP	3.7%	2.3%	2.5%

[a]Based on economic forecasts and industry projections.

In addition to the domestic pressures, foreign competition has been harsh in the eight basic industries selected for study. Foreign competitors have achieved significant market shares in three of the industries—steel, tire and rubber, and automotive; moderate shares in two—heavy-duty trucks and construction and materials handling equipment; and entry positions in the other three—major home appliances, beer, and cigarettes.

Because many of these foreign competitors are either nationalized, quasinationalized, or highly salient in their own countries, they are frequently willing to accept lower returns in U.S. markets, offsetting these lower returns against unemployment, balance of payments, and capital gains at home. While these foreign approaches have been criticized as unfair, the results have altered U.S. domestic industry structures in all eight cases.

Needless to say, the net effect of these adverse trends has made life anything but pleasant for managers and companies in these basic industries. Profitability and sales growth levels have generally fallen to or below the average manufacturing returns in the U.S. economy (Exhibit 2). And industry

Exhibit 2.   Financial Returns and Revenue Growth Rates, 1975–1979

Eight Basic Industries	Return on Equity	Return on Capital	EPS Growth	Revenue Growth
Steel	7.1%	5.7%	5.5%	10.4%
Tire and rubber	7.4	5.9	3.9	9.6
Heavy-duty trucks[a]	15.4	11.6	13.8	13.8
Construction and materials handling equipment	15.4	10.7	16.8	13.0
Automotive[a]	15.4	11.6	13.8	13.8
Major home appliances	10.1	9.0	3.2	6.8
Beer	14.1	10.2	6.2	12.4
Cigarettes	18.2	10.5	8.9	12.2
Average-eight industries	12.9%	9.4%	9.0%	11.5%
Average *Fortune* "1,000" company	15.1%	11.0%	13.1%	13.1%

[a]All vehicle manufacturers.

spokespeople frequently speak out, urging either public assistance or some type of return to the simpler, less painful world of the 1960s.

As one senior executive I interviewed commented: "Maybe I should have accepted that job as an IBM systems engineer after graduation from college. It sure would be fun to look forward to going to work in the morning." Despite the outcries, the adverse external trends haven't gone away, and structural evolution continues at a slow, but inevitable, pace.

The heavy-duty truck manufacturing industry provides an excellent example of this evolution. In the early 1960s, spurred by rapid growth in the economy and by the completion of the U.S. interstate highway system, the industry grew at more than 8% per year. Eight major manufacturers—International Harvester, General Motors, Ford, Mack, White Motor, Diamond Reo, Chrysler, and Paccar—participated fairly equally in this growth, producing 60 truck models to serve the rapidly growing light-heavy and heavy-duty segments (19,000 pounds and greater gross vehicle weight).

However, by the late 1970s, annual growth had slowed to less than 3%. Emission regulations and inflation had raised unit costs. Investments for new truck model development had slowed to the extent that the number of models had dropped from 60 to 35 by 1979.

As a result of this movement toward a hostile environment, Chrysler closed its heavy-duty truck manufacturing operation, Diamond Reo was in bankruptcy, and White lingered near receivership. Both Mack and International Harvester had lost significant market share and were searching for foreign assistance or major cost-cutting programs to maintain their viability. Of the eight healthy domestic competitors in the early 1960s, only three— General Motors, Ford, and Paccar—maintained free-standing, vibrant, competitive positions as they entered the decade of the 1980s.

Similar moves toward lower profitability and consolidation occurred in all eight industries as the hostile environment took its evolutionary toll. In steel, Bethlehem announced in 1977 the largest corporate quarterly loss in U.S. history up to that time (exceeded by Chrysler two years later and U.S. Steel in late 1979), Jones & Laughlin and Youngstown merged under the failing firm provision of U.S. antitrust laws in 1978, and Kaiser tried to sell its steel-making operation to the Japanese in 1979. In rubber, industry analysts waited impatiently for Uniroyal to exit the industry; and in automotive, Chrysler made front-page headlines in its race against time to achieve federal loan assistance. Words like "dinosaur" and "dog" were coined by industry observers to describe the evolving competitive profiles in all eight industries.

However, the profiles of basic industry problems and corporate failures tell only part of the story. These "disaster" tales need to be juxtaposed against some success stories to see how some companies have survived and even prospered in the same hostile environment. The resulting comparisons provide important insights into survival strategies and industry dynamics not only for general managers in the eight industries under study but also for managers in other industries as they lead their companies into the new decade. For example, a careful comparison of success and problem strategies in the eight industries in this study demonstrates that:

- ☐ Great success is possible, even in a hostile environment.
- ☐ Strategies leading to success share common characteristics.
- ☐ Successful strategies come from purposeful moves toward a leadership position.
- ☐ Problems come from failure to gain or defend a leadership position.
- ☐ For a deteriorating position, diversity may not be the proper recovery approach.
- ☐ Structural evolution moves toward a dynamic equilibrium as basic industries face a hostile environment.

I will amplify and discuss each of these insights in subsequent sections of this article.

Great Success is Possible, Even in a Hostile Environment. When one looks at the eight industries in this study, as well as at other basic manufacturing industries facing the hostile environment of the 1980s, it is easy to slip into generalizations by extrapolating from aggregate industry problems to the individual companies within the industry.

Recent articles in the business press, asking, "What Killed the U.S. Steel Industry?," "Is Chrysler the Prototype?," or proclaiming "Tire Industry Goes Flat" or "Last Chances for Cigarette Producers," are typical of those that tend to project adverse trends uniformly onto all competitors in the industry. In fact, however, nothing could be further from the truth. Some of the most vibrant, successful companies in the world reside and prosper in these seemingly hostile industry environments.

If one eliminates from my eight-industry sample of 64 companies all competitors who gain a majority of revenues and profits from diversification efforts outside their basic industry (e.g., Armco Steel and General Tire), then the most profitable remaining competitors (the industry leaders) in terms of corporate return on equity are those shown in Exhibit 3.

While some variation in returns exists among these leading competitors (Goodyear and Inland had significantly lower returns and growth rates than the other six), the corporate average return on equity earned over the last half of the 1970s easily places these companies in the top 20% of the *Fortune* "1,000" industrials and well ahead of the median *Fortune* company on return on capital and annual growth rate.

Moreover, the average returns on both equity and capital in my sample of industry leaders are well ahead of those earned by the leading international oil company (Phillips Petroleum). These average returns are also well ahead of those earned by companies heralded by the business community as tech-

Exhibit 3.   Financial Returns and Growth Rates, 1975–1979:
Leading Companies in Eight Basic Industries[a]

	Average Return on Equity	Average Return on Capital	Annual Revenue Growth Rate
Goodyear	9.2%	7.0%	10.0%
Inland Steel	10.9	7.9	11.4
Paccar	22.8	20.9	14.9
Caterpillar	23.5	17.3	17.2
General Motors	19.8	18.0	13.2
Maytag	27.2	26.5	9.1
G. Heileman Brewing	25.8	18.9	21.4
Philip Morris	22.7	13.5	20.1
Average	20.2%	16.3%	14.7%
Median *Fortune* "1,000" company (same time period)	15.1%	11.0%	13.1%

[a]Excluding those companies which gained a majority of their returns from diversification efforts.

nology leaders (Xerox, Eastman Kodak, Texas Instruments, and Digital Equipment), and these returns are likewise well ahead of those earned by corporations singled out as models of progressive diversification and acquisition planning (General Electric and United Technologies).

In fact, as Exhibit 4 shows, the industry leaders shown in Exhibit 3 outperformed all of the highly touted companies during the most recent five years. In addition, the industry leaders grew faster than premier corporations like 3M and IBM, and they returned only slightly less to their shareholders and capital investors than these same "blue chip" competitors in high-growth industries.

In retrospect, perhaps the much publicized article, "TI Shows U.S. Industry How to Compete in the 1980s,"[1] should have been written about one of the leading companies in my sample instead of about Texas Instruments, because 75% of the leaders in the basic industries I studied outperformed TI during the latter half of the 1970s. Moreover, they outperformed TI in industries that averaged only 2.4% real growth during the past decade, significantly less than the 15% to 20% compound growth rates of the semiconductor industry during this same period.

Exhibit 4. Financial Returns and Growth Rates, 1975–1979:
Leading Companies in Other and More Rapidly Growing Industries

	Average Return on Equity	Average Return on Capital	Annual Revenue Growth Rate
International oil			
Phillips Petroleum	19.5%	14.7%	16.6%
Technology leaders			
Xerox	17.8	14.4	15.5
Eastman Kodak	18.8	17.7	11.8
Texas Instruments	17.2	16.3	14.6
Digital Equipment	17.0	15.5	37.4
Diversification leaders			
General Electric	19.4	16.9	10.5
United Technologies	18.3	12.6	19.0
Average of these "high performance" leaders	18.3%	15.4%	17.9%
Average (leading companies in basic industries from Exhibit III)	20.2%	16.3%	14.7%
"Blue chip" competitors			
IBM	21.9	21.2	13.5
3M	20.7	17.7	13.1

Thus even a cursory analysis of leading companies in the eight basic industries leads to an important observation: survival and prosperity are possible even when the business environment turns hostile and industry trends change from favorable to unfavorable. In this regard, the casual advice frequently offered to competitors in basic industries—that is, diversify, dissolve, or be prepared for below-average returns[2]—seems oversimplified and even erroneous. A hostile environment offers an excellent basic investment opportunity and reinvestment climate, at least for the industry leaders insightful enough to capitalize on their positions.

Strategies Leading to Success Share Common Characteristics. A more detailed, in-depth examination of the business strategies employed by the top two performing (nondiversified) companies in each of the eight industries sampled reveals that these success strategies share strong common characteristics, irrespective of the particular industry. Indeed, throughout their modern history, all 16 of these leading companies have demonstrated a continuous, single-minded determination to achieve one or both of the following competitive positions within their respective industries:

☐ Achieve the lowest delivered cost position relative to competition, coupled with both an acceptable delivered quality and a pricing policy to gain profitable volume and market-share growth.

☐ Achieve the highest product/service/quality differentiated position relative to competition, coupled with both an acceptable delivered cost structure and a pricing policy to gain margins sufficient to fund reinvestment in product/service differentiation.

A rough categorization of the strategies employed by these 16 companies, based on selective field studies and observed behavior over time, is shown in Exhibit 5. In most cases, the industry growth and profit leaders chose only one of the two strategic approaches, on the basis that the skills and resources necessary to invest in a low-cost position are insufficient or incompatible with those needed to simultaneously invest in a strongly differentiated position.

The rudiments of this strategic trade-off can be found as early as the 1920s in Alfred P. Sloan's statements regarding General Motors' selection of a cost-reduced strategy:

> Management should now direct its energies toward increasing earning power through increased effectiveness and reduced expense. . . . Efforts that have been so lavishly expended on expansion and development should now be directed at economy in operation. . . . This policy is valid if our cars are at least equal to the best of our competitors in a grade, so that it is not necessary to lead in design.[3]

However, in at least three cases, the leading companies in my sample chose to combine the two approaches, and each has had spectacular success.

Exhibit 5. Competitive Strategies Employed by Leading Companies

Eight Basic Industries	Achieved Low Delivered Cost Position	Achieved "Meaningful" Differentiation	Simultaneous Employment of Both Strategies
Steel	Inland Steel	National	
Tire and rubber	Goodyear	Michelin (French)	
Heavy-duty trucks	Ford	Paccar	
Construction and materials handling equipment		John Deere	Caterpillar
Automotive	General Motors	Daimler-Benz (German)	
Major home appliances	Whirlpool	Maytag	
Beer	Miller	G. Heileman Brewing	
Cigarettes	R.J. Reynolds		Philip Morris

Caterpillar has combined lowest cost manufacturing with higher cost but truly outstanding distribution and after-market support to differentiate its line of construction equipment. As a result, Caterpillar, ranking as the 24th largest and 39th most profitable company in the United States, is well ahead of its competitors and most of the *Fortune* "500" glamour companies.

Similarly, the U.S. cigarette division of Philip Morris combines the lowest cost, fully automated cigarette manufacturing operation in the world with highest cost, focused branding and promotion to gain industry profit leadership, even without the benefit of either the largest unit volume or segment market share in both domestic and international markets

And finally, Daimler Benz operates with elements of both strategies but in different segments, coupling the lowest cost position in heavy-duty truck manufacturing in Western Europe with an exceptionally high quality, feature differentiated car line for European and North American export markets.

A more complete picture of the strategic and performance profiles of all major competitors in these eight hostile environments can be obtained by positioning on a matrix those businesses whose axes reflect the relative delivered cost position and the relative product/service differentiation with respect to other competition. The result is a conceptual diagram like that shown in Exhibit 6.

While the quantification of competitive profiles in this format is typically inexact—because of the proprietary nature of relevant cost, sector,

Exhibit 6. Strategic Profile Analysis—Basic Mature Industries

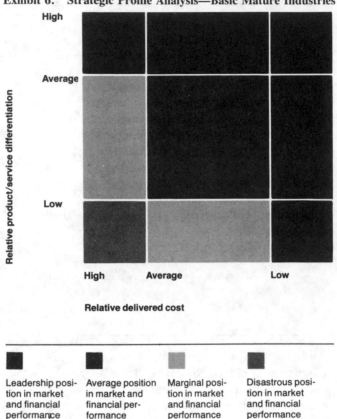

Leadership posi-   Average position   Marginal posi-   Disastrous position in market   in market and   tion in market   tion in market
and financial   financial per-   and financial   and financial
performance   formance   performance   performance

and performance data—a qualitative attempt to perform this analysis for the heavy-duty truck manufacturing industry is presented in Exhibit 7. This representation, based on an analysis of industry interviews and public records, is imprecise, yet it correlates perfectly with the industry performance profiles over time.

For example, from Exhibit 7, it is clear why Ford and Paccar continually lead the heavy-duty truck industry in growth and financial performance. It is equally clear why White lingers near bankruptcy and also why Freightliner and International Harvester are rethinking their strategies for heavy-duty trucks. (Freightliner recently entered into a distribution agreement with Volvo in an attempt to differentiate its distribution system in the light-heavy segment, and International Harvester initiated a major cost-reduction effort in truck design and manufacturing in an attempt to improve its weak relative cost position.)

A similar analysis of business-level returns for all 16 leading competitors in the eight industries (Exhibit 8) indicates some interesting aspects of the respective strategies, as the following comparison reveals:

Exhibit 7.   Strategic Profiles in U.S. Heavy-Duty Truck Manufacturing

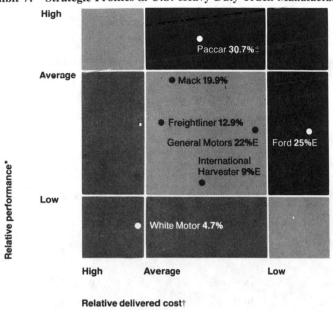

*Based on customer and industry interview data.

†Based on manufacturing and distribution cost analysis, evaluating economies of scale, and vertical integration profiles.

‡ Operating return on assets; E = Estimated from industry sources.

☐ The *lowest delivered cost* leader typically grows more slowly, holding price increases and operating margins down to gain volume, fixed-cost reductions, and improved asset turnover. In addition, this competitor will typically have a lower sales turnover than the differentiated producer, reflecting the higher asset intensity necessary to gain cost reductions in production and distribution.

☐ The *differentiated position* leader typically grows faster, with higher prices and operating margins to cover promotional, research, and other product/service costs. At the same time, this competitor typically operates with lower asset intensity (higher sales turnover), reflecting both higher prices and a lower cost, "flexible" asset base.

Successful Strategies Come from Purposeful Moves toward a Leadership Position.   In examining the business strategies and subsequent performance of the leading competitors, it becomes clear that purposeful movement toward and defense of a "winning" strategic position—either lowest cost and/or superior, price-justified differentiation—has been the fundamental long-term objective of all 16 high performance companies. There is little doubt

Exhibit 8. Business Level Returns and Revenue Growth Rates

	Operating Margins	Sales Turnover	Operating ROA	Revenue Growth Rates, 1975–1979
Leading industrial goods producers[a] 1978				
Steel				
Inland Steel	8.3%	1.3	10.8%	11.4%
National	12.0	1.5	18.0	12.0
Tire and rubber				
Goodyear	8.6	1.5	12.9	10.5
Michelin	10.0 (est.)	N.A.	N.A.	N.A.
Heavy-duty trucks				
Ford	11.0 (est.)	2.3	25.0 (est.)	12.7
Paccar	12.7	2.4	30.5	15.5
Construction and materials handling equipment				
Caterpillar	15.5	1.8	27.9	14.9
John Deere	10.0	1.3	13.0	17.5
Leading consumer goods producers[a] 1978				
Automotive				
General Motors	9.6%	2.0	19.2%	13.2%
Daimler-Benz (automotive)	11.0	2.4	26.4	15.1
Major home appliances				
Whirlpool	8.4	1.0	8.4	5.3
Maytag	21.8	1.8	39.2	9.1
Brewing				
Miller	8.2	1.5	12.3	29.2
G. Heileman	9.5	3.5	33.3	32.2
Brewing				
Cigarettes				
R.J. Reynolds	17.1	2.3	39.3	15.0
Philip Morris	17.7	1.4	24.8	20.1

[a]Lowest delivered cost producer listed first, followed by most differentiated producer.

that consistency and clarity of purpose have helped to mobilize and coordinate internal resources in gaining and defending a leadership position.

It is important to note that the time-phased pattern of investment decisions used to attain and hold these winning positions was based on "doing the right things" to gain leadership in lowest costs and/or differentiation. As a result, all the high performers in my sample used careful strategic analysis to guide their investments, avoiding simplistic adherence to doctrinaire approaches toward strategy formulation which come from the naive application of tools like:

☐ Share/growth matrices—planning models which suggest that mature market segments should be "milked" or "harvested" for cash flows.

☐ Experience curves and PIMS[4]—planning models which suggest that high market share and/or lowest cost, vertically integrated production are keys to success in mature markets.

Instead, based on a case-by-case analysis, the performance leaders made investment decisions which frequently conflicted with these doctrinaire theories:

☐ The leadership positions in mature markets were not being milked by any of the 16 competitors, contrary to the advice of consultants who emphasize the portfolio approach to asset management. In fact, the top managers in two of the leading companies I interviewed laughed when they discussed this concept. They pointed out that their future success and growth opportunities were far greater if they aggressively reinvested in their base business than if they redeployed assets into other (diversified) industries.

☐ Low-cost production is not essential to prosper in mature markets, contrary to the belief of strong proponents of the experience curve. Instead, high sustainable returns also come from reinvesting in an average cost, highly differentiated position, as the data of the previous section and Exhibit 8 demonstrate, and as the ongoing track records of companies like Paccar and Maytag clearly illustrate.

☐ High market share and accumulated experience are not essential for cost leadership in a mature market, as indicated by proponents of the experience curve and some large-sample empirical studies like PIMS. In fact, four of the eight low-cost producers in this study—Inland Steel, Whirlpool, Miller, and Philip Morris—have achieved their lowest cost positions without the benefit of high relative market shares.

Rather, these producers have focused their plants by emphasizing modern, automated process technology, and they have heavily invested in their distribution systems to gain scale economies and other cost reductions in their delivery systems.

☐ Vertical integration is not necessary to exploit cost leadership in mature markets, as suggested by a number of empirical and economic studies. In fact, all of the low-cost producers in the industries under study were less vertically integrated into upstream and downstream activities than at least one other major competitor in their industry.

Instead of emphasizing vertical integration as a policy, all looked for selective integration into high value-added, proprietary componentry, following the type of integration policy first delineated by General Motors in the 1920s of "not investing in general industries of which a comparatively small part of the product is consumed in the manufacture of cars."

Instead of fully integrating, the low-cost leaders invested to have the most efficient process technology in at least one selective stage of the vertical chain. Consider, for example, Ford in truck assembly and Inland in order entry-distribution. The result in all cases is focus—the ability to orient management attention to gain low costs in a partially integrated operation. As one of Ford's major competitors observed:

> Ford is the least integrated of any of the high-volume, heavy-duty truck manufacturers in the world, yet it is still the low-cost producer and gains one of the highest ROIs in the industry. In retrospect, Ford's strategy was brilliant; they let the rest of us learn to manufacture componentry while they learned to manufacture profits.

Problems Come from Failure to Gain or Defend a Leadership Position. A more detailed examination of the marginal or failing competitors in each of the eight basic industries (Exhibit 9) also reveals some interesting observations:

☐ The historical strategies and policies pursued by these companies have placed them in an unstable position. All are the high-cost producers in their segments, and all have a product that not only is largely undifferentiated in any meaningful sense but also in many cases is below average in quality and performance.

☐ The external pressures that these companies complain about— unwarranted regulation and unfair foreign competition—are simply the final blows, sealing a fate that was predestined by improper strategic positioning or repositioning in the 1950s and 1960s, a period when there was still growth and time to maneuver.

☐ Many of these marginal producers held low-cost or differentiated positions in these earlier years, and made strategic errors in their reinvestment decisions which contributed to their marginal or failing positions today, as the following examples show.

International Harvester led the U.S. heavy-duty truck manufacturing industry in 1965 with a market share of 30%. However, over the next decade, IH failed to reduce costs as rapidly as Ford and GM. As a result, the IH truck division is now a high-cost, low-margin producer.

White Motor, a strong number-two truck producer in the mid-1960s, invested in backward integration into cabs, frames, axles, and engine manufacturing, assuming that this would reduce costs. Unfortunately, these in-

Exhibit 9.   Marginal or Failing Companies in U.S. Markets

Steel	J&L—Youngstown
	Kaiser
Tire and rubber	Uniroyal
	Mohawk
	Cooper
Heavy-duty trucks	White Motor
Construction and materials handling equipment	Massey Ferguson
	Allis Chalmers
Automotive	Chrysler
Major home appliances	Tappan
Beer	Most regional breweries
	Schlitz
Cigarettes	Liggett & Myers

vestments, all made at suboptimal capacities for efficient scale economies, resulted in a relative high-cost position, adding momentum to White's deteriorating situation.

Tappan, the technology leader in ranges in the early 1960s, chose to broaden that product line, to diversify, to reduce R&D expenditures, and to outsource certain key engineering activities. As a result, it failed to gain the low-cost position in ranges (today held by GE). And by failing to reinvest in technology, it lost its differentiated position in ranges to Caloric (gas), Jenn-Air (electric), and Raytheon (microwave).

Chrysler, the technology leader in the U.S. automotive market in the early 1950s with a 25% market share, chose to make questionable international expansion decisions while adopting a "me too" participatory strategy in the domestic market. The subsequent decline in Chrysler's position and returns was predictable, and this disaster trajectory was certainly accelerated in the early 1970s when its management team announced a revised (but highly inappropriate) strategy to "try to be a General Motors in whatever segments of the market we choose to compete in."

For a Deteriorating Position, Diversity May Not Be the Proper Recovery Approach.   Over the past several years, it has become fashionable to recommend product/market diversification as a way out of an unstable or failing position for mature companies in hostile environments. Unfortunately, in the 64 companies I examined in this research, diversification has "helped" overcome major competitive/performance problems in only three—B.F. Goodrich, General Tire, and Armco Steel (now Armco Group). These three competitors recognized the tenuous nature of their positions early in the maturity cycle and took steps to resegment their base businesses into more advantageous positions by redeploying assets in carefully chosen diversification moves.

Goodrich moved into high-margin, specialty segments of the tire industry while diversifying to attain a low-cost position in PVC and other basic chemicals.

General shifted into low-cost production of tires for commercial vehicles while diversifying to attain a participatory position in very high-growth, fragmented industries such as communications and aerospace.

Armco proceeded into low-cost steel production in selected regional segments like oil country pipe, while diversifying into high-growth markets like oil-field equipment, oil and gas exploration, and financial services. (A recent public relations release from Armco announced that most of its new capital investment would go toward growing these diversification ventures, while maintaining only current capacity levels in steel making.)

These early efforts to resegment and to gain meaningful diversification have paid off. General and Armco lead all competitors in the rubber and steel industries in return on capital and growth, while Goodrich has moved into a stable third place among the surviving tire and rubber producers.

On the other hand, efforts to gain meaningful economic diversification have eluded most of the other problem competitors in the eight industries. By waiting too long to begin diversification efforts, most lack the capital and managerial skills to enter new markets and/or to grow businesses successfully in these markets. Thus their diversification efforts to date have been too small or have been managed in too conservative a fashion to obtain sustainable performance improvements, as witnessed by the very minor performance contribution of U.S. Steel's diversification program into chemicals and the continuing problems of Liggett & Myers despite a 43% diversification program out of the tobacco industry.

As a result of these modest, participatory efforts, some of the marginal performers in the eight industries have even divested diversified assets to gain capital and "hang on" for a few more years in the base business. Two notable examples are White Motor's recent sale of its construction equipment operation and Uniroyal's sale of its consumer goods division.

On the whole, it would appear that diversification comes too little and too late for most companies caught in a hostile environment. However, for a courageous few, continued managerial commitment and refocus on the base business to provide a steady flow of capital for promoting meaningful positions in diversified businesses may work to ensure ongoing growth and vitality.

Structural Evolution Moves toward a Dynamic Equilibrium as Basic Industries Face a Hostile Environment. A summary of the underlying data in my study suggests that basic industries in mature, hostile environments are moving through a structural evolution, leading ultimately to four industry and performance subgroups (Exhibit 10):

Exhibit 10.   Strategic and Performance Subgroups—Basic Industries

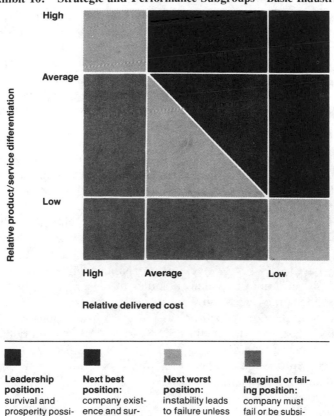

Relative delivered cost

Leadership position: survival and prosperity possible given appropriate strategy for reinvestment.	**Next best position:** company existence and survival possible unless leader aggressive.	**Next worst position:** instability leads to failure unless company resegments and/or diversifies.	**Marginal or failing position:** company must fail or be subsidized in perpetuity.

    1.   *Leadership position.*   Competitors who achieve the lowest delivered cost and/or the highest differentiated position. These positions are gained either on a full product line (Caterpillar) or on an economically viable segment (Whirlpool in washers and dryers). At maturity these competitors will have the highest growth rates and returns in the industry, the best reinvestment prospects, and they should be able to prosper and coexist in dynamic equilibrium even though external pressures continue.

    2.   *Next best position.*   Competitors who attain the second best position in either cost or differentiation (again on either a full or partial line basis). These companies will have moderate but generally acceptable growth rates and returns, and reinvestments can (and will typically) be made at return levels slightly above the cost of capital. For these companies, vulnerability to strategic and performance deterioration occurs mainly when the industry leaders or a set of externally subsidized competitors choose to

aggressively attack. (For example, the recent problems of Ford in the U.S. automotive market can be directly traced to GM's more aggressive market-share strategy, coupled with the European and Japanese attacks on U.S. small car markets.)

   3. *Next worst position.* Competitors who finish in third place as the industry matures. Given a hostile environment, growth rates and return prospects for these companies are bleak unless they resegment into uncovered niches and gain a sustainable leadership position in these segments (AMC in utility vehicles, Goodrich in performance tires), or unless they can make major asset redeployment into meaningful diversified markets (like Armco and General). Without the ability to resegment or diversify, competitors in this class ultimately will move toward a marginal or failing position. (Chrysler in automotive, Uniroyal in tires, and Schlitz in brewing are examples of companies currently going through such a transition.)

   4. *Marginal or failing position.* Competitors who end up last in mature, hostile environments ultimately must fail or be subsidized, either through government ownership or aid (Chrysler) or through cash infusions from a diversified parent (Kaiser in steel, Allis Chalmers in construction equipment). Despite efforts to use such subsidies to resegment and refocus their operations, the survey data show no successful efforts in such turnaround attempts among the 64 competitors in the eight basic industries, raising a fundamental question as to whether there is any real possibility of strategic turnaround. Consequently, a society or a company subsidizing this type of marginal competitor should expect the worst—perpetual subsidies, perhaps slightly offset by infrequent operating returns during high peaks in basic economic cycles.

In Summary

The strategic and performance data from this eight-industry study suggest that both great successes and failures are occurring as basic, mature industries move into a hostile business environment created by slower growth, higher inflation, more regulation, and intensified competition. Uniformly, the successes come to those companies that achieve either the lowest cost or most differentiated position. Simultaneously, survival is possible for those companies that have the foresight to downsize their asset commitments into niches in their basic industry and to use their incremental capital for meaningful diversification moves. For the weaker companies, the inability to achieve a lowest cost or most differentiated position results in high vulnerability and ultimate failure or perpetual subsidy.

   For general managers guiding their companies into the economic environment of the 1980s, the implications of these findings are clear. The laws of the jungle change as maturity comes and hostility intensifies. In such a jungle, the range of strategic options narrows, requiring both an early warning of the coming hostility and an early strategic repositioning for a company to survive and prosper.

Hence, intensified efforts must be made to create internal administrative structures and mechanisms to recognize and efficiently manage this repositioning. (GM's effective organizational restructuring in the early 1970s to respond to the downsizing imperative stands as a brilliant case study in the use of such an administrative effort to create strategic change.)

For public policymakers monitoring and attempting to influence the business environment, these results suggest that failures will be inevitable as industry structures evolve in the face of maturity and hostility. The currently popular attempts at forced consolidation and subsidies are one way of dealing with these failures. However, these actions should be taken with full knowledge that they will not stop the driving market forces.

The question that remains in the decade ahead is whether the short-run employment, balance of payments, and fiscal stability provided by such public policy actions is worth the long-run cost of maintaining an inefficient industry structure that conflicts with the driving market forces created by a hostile environment.

Notes

1. *Business Week,* September 18, 1978, p. 66.

2. See, for example, Theodore Levitt, "Dinosaurs among the Bears and Bulls," *HBR,* January–February 1975, p. 41; also the section on basic industries in Richard P. Rumelt, *Strategy, Structure, and Economic Performance* (Boston, Division of Research, Harvard Business School, 1974), pp. 128–139.

3. Alfred P. Sloan, Jr., *My Years with General Motors* (New York, Doubleday, 1964), pp. 65–66, 172.

4. PIMS (profit impact of market strategies) is a multiple regression model which relates profitability to a number of associative variables. See Sidney Schoeffler, Robert D. Buzzell, and Donald F. Heany, "Impact of Strategic Planning on Profit Performance," *HBR* March–April 1974, p. 137.

12
How Global Companies Win Out

THOMAS M. HOUT, MICHAEL E. PORTER, and EILEEN RUDDEN

International competition. Citizens from most of the older industrialized countries have become obsessed with it since the first Japanese cars started selling well. Vulnerability has replaced invincibility as the adjective many would use to describe once-firmly-established international companies. But this disquiet obscures the steady achievements a number of corporations have made against competition from companies based outside their countries. These companies rely on global strategies to succeed in today's world. That calls on a company to think of the world as one market instead of a collection of national markets and sometimes requires decisions as unconventional as accepting projects with low ROIs because of their competitive payoff. An organization with such a global focus formulates long-term strategy for the company as a whole and then orchestrates the strategies of local subsidiaries accordingly.

The power of global strategies is illustrated here by the histories of three companies (one American, one European, and one Japanese) that have what the authors think it takes to win the new competitive game. These case studies should help managers decide whether a global strategy is appropriate for their companies.

Hold that obituary on American manufacturers. Some not only refuse to die but even dominate their businesses worldwide. At the same time Ford struggles to keep up with Toyota, Caterpillar thrives in competition with another Japanese powerhouse, Komatsu. Though Zenith has been hurt in consumer electronics, Hewlett-Packard and Tektronix together profitably control 50% of the world's industrial test and measurement instrument market. American

Authors' Note: We acknowledge that this article is based in part on a paper coauthored by Eric Vogt.

170

forklift truck producers may retreat under Japanese pressure, but two U.S. chemical companies—Du Pont and Dow—dramatically outperform their competitors.

How do these American producers hold and even increase profitability against international competitors? By forging integrated global strategies to exploit their potential. And by having a long-term outlook, investing aggressively, and managing factories carefully.

Today's international competition in many industries is very different from what it has been. To succeed, an international company may need to change from a multidomestic competitor (which allows individual subsidiaries to compete independently in different domestic markets) to a global organization (which pits its entire worldwide system of product and market position against the competition). (For a more complete discussion of this distinction, see the Appendix.)

The global company—whatever its nationality—tries to control key leverage points, from cross-national production scale economies to the foreign competitors' sources of cash flow. By taking unconventional action, such as lowering prices of a key product or in key markets, the company makes the competitors' response more expensive and difficult. Its main objective is to improve its own effectiveness while eroding that of its competitors.

Not all companies can or should forge a global strategy. While the rewards of competing globally are great, so are the risks. Major policy and operating changes are required. Competing globally demands a number of unconventional approaches to managing a multinational business to sometimes allow:

☐ Major investment projects with zero or even negative ROI.

☐ Financial performance targets that vary widely among foreign subsidiaries.

☐ Product lines deliberately overdesigned or underpriced in some markets.

☐ A view of country-by-country market positions as interdependent and not as independent elements of a worldwide portfolio to be increased or decreased depending on profitability.

☐ Construction of production facilities in both high- and low-labor-cost countries.

Not all international businesses lend themselves to global competition. Many are multidomestic in nature and are likely to remain so, competing on a domestic-market-by-domestic-market basis. Typically, these businesses have products that differ greatly among country markets and have high transportation costs, or their industries lack sufficient scale economies to yield the global competitors a significant edge.

Before entering the global arena, you must decide whether your company's industry has the right characteristics to favor a global competitor. A careful examination of the economies of the business will highlight its ripeness for global competition. Simply put, the potential for global competition is greatest when significant benefits are gained from worldwide volume—in terms of either reduced unit costs or superior reputation or service—and are greater than the additional costs of serving that volume.

Identifying potential economies of scale requires considerable insight. Advantages to increased volume may come not only from larger production plants or runs but also from more efficient logistics networks or higher-volume distribution networks. Worldwide volume is also particularly advantageous in supporting high levels of investment in research and development; many industries requiring high levels of R&D, such as pharmaceuticals or jet aircraft, are global. The level of transport or importing costs will also influence the business's tendency to become global. Transport is a relatively small portion of highly traded optical goods, for example, while it is a barrier in trading steel reinforcing bars.

Many businesses will not be able to take the global step precisely because their industries lack these characteristics. Economies of scale may be too modest or R&D spending too closely tied to particular markets. Products may differ significantly across country boundaries or the industry may emphasize distribution, installation, and other local activities. Lead times may be short, as in fashion-oriented businesses and many service businesses, including printing. Also transportation costs and government barriers to trade may be high, and distribution may be fragmented and hard to penetrate. Many consumer nondurable businesses or low-technology assembly companies fall into this category, as do many heavy raw material processing industries and wholesaling and service businesses.

Our investigation into the strategies of successful global companies leads us to believe that a large group of international companies have global potential, even though they may not know it. Almost every industry that is now global—automobiles and TV sets, for example—was not at one time. A company must see the potential for changing competitive interaction in its favor to trigger a shift from multidomestic to global competition. And because there is no guarantee that the business can become global, the company must be willing to risk the heavy investment that global competition requires.

A company that recognizes its business as potentially global but not yet so must ask itself whether it can innovate effectively and understand its impact on the competition to find the best answers to these three questions:

☐ What kind of strategic innovation might trigger global competition?

☐ Is it in the best position among all competitors to establish and defend the advantages of global strategy?

☐ What kinds of resources over how long a period will be required to establish the leading position against the competition?

The Successful Global Competitor

If your industry profile fits the picture we've drawn, you can better judge your ability to make these kinds of unconventional decisions by looking at the way three global companies have succeeded. These organizations (American, European, and Japanese) exemplify the global competitor. They all perceive competition as global and formulate strategy on an integrated, worldwide basis. Each has developed a strategic innovation to change the rules of the competitive game in its particular industry. The innovation acts as a lever to support the development of an integrated global system but demands a market position strong enough to implement it.

Finally, the three companies have executed their strategies more aggressively and effectively than their competitors. They have built barriers to competitive responses based on careful assessment of competitors' behavior. All three have the financial resources and commitment needed to compete unconventionally and the organizational structure to manage an integrated system.

We will take a careful look at each of these three and how they developed the strategic innovation that led, on the one hand, to the globalization of their industries and, on the other, to their own phenomenal success. The first company's innovation was in manufacturing; the second in technology; and the third in marketing.

The Caterpillar Case: Warring with Komatsu

Caterpillar Tractor Company turned large-scale construction equipment into a global business and achieved world leadership in that business even when faced with an able Japanese competitor. This accomplishment was difficult for a variety of reasons. For one thing, specifications of construction equipment varied widely across countries. Also, machines are expensive to transport, and field distribution—including user financing, spare parts inventories, and repair facilities—is demanding and best managed locally.

Navy Seabees who left their Caterpillar equipment in other countries following World War II planted the seeds of globalization. The company established independent dealerships to service these fleets, and this base of units provided a highly profitable flow of revenue from spare parts, which paid for inventorying new units. The Caterpillar dealers quickly became self-sustaining and to this day are larger, better financed, and do a more profitable parts business than their competitors. This global distribution system is one of Cat's two major barriers against competition.

The company used its worldwide production scale to create its other barrier. Two-thirds of the total product cost of construction equipment is in heavy components—engines, axles, transmissions, and hydraulics—whose manufacturing costs are capital intensive and highly sensitive to economies of scale. Caterpillar turned its network of sales in different countries into a cost advantage by designing product lines that use identical components and investing heavily in a few large-scale, state-of-the-art component manufacturing facilities to fill worldwide demand.

The company then augmented the centralized production with assembly plants in each of its major markets—Europe, Japan, Brazil, Australia, and so on. At these plants Cat added local product features, avoiding the high transportation cost of end products. Most important, Cat became a direct participant in local economies. The company achieved lower costs without sacrificing local product flexibility and became a friend rather than a threat to local governments. No single "world model" was forced on the customer, yet no competitor could match Cat's production and distribution cost.

Not that they haven't tried. The most recent—and greatest—challenge to Caterpillar has come from Komatsu (see Exhibit 1 for a financial comparison). Japan's leading construction equipment producer forged its own global strategy based on exporting high-quality products from centralized facilities with labor and steel cost advantages. Over the last decade Komatsu has gained some 15% of the world construction equipment market, with a significant share of sales in nearly every product line in competition with Cat.

Caterpillar has maintained its position against Komatsu and gained world share. The two companies increasingly dominate the market vis-à-vis their competitors, who compete on a domestic or regional basis.

What makes Caterpillar's strategy so potent? The company has fostered the development of three characteristics essential to defending a leading world position against a determined competitor.

1. *A global strategy of its own.* Caterpillar's integrated global strategy yields a competitive advantage in cost and effectiveness. Komatsu simply plays catch-up ball rather than pulling ahead. Facing a competitor that has consciously devised a global strategy, Komatsu is in a much weaker position than were Japanese television and automobile manufacturers when they took off.

2. *Willingness to invest in manufacturing.* Caterpillar's top management appears committed to the kind of flexible automated manufacturing

Exhibit 1A. Komatsu's Sales Growth Relative to World Market, 1969–1979.

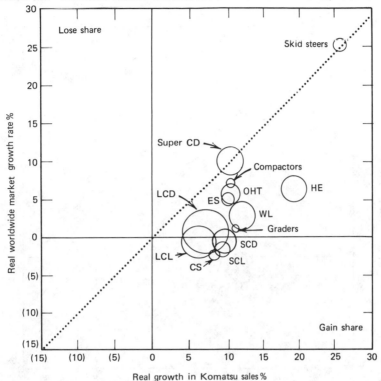

Key: LCD = large crawler dozers; LCL = large crawler loaders; CS = conventional scraper, SCL = small crawler loaders; SCD = small crawler dozers; WL = wheel loaders; ES = elevating scraper; OHT = off-highway trucks; HE = hydraulic excavaters; Super CD = super crawler dozers.

systems that allow full exploitation of the economies of scale from its worldwide sales volume.

3. *Willingness to commit financial resources.* Caterpillar is the only Western company that matches Komatsu in capital spending per employee; in fact, its overall capital spending is more than three times that of the Japanese company. Caterpillar does not divert resources into other businesses or dissipate the financial advantage against Komatsu by paying out excessive dividends. Because Komatsu's profitability is lower than Caterpillar's, it must exhaust debt capacity in trying to match Cat's high investment rates.

4. *Blocking position in the Japanese market.* In 1963, Caterpillar formed a joint venture in Japan with Komatsu's long-standing but weaker competitor, Mitsubishi. Operationally, the venture serves the Japanese mar-

Exhibit 1B.   Caterpillar's Sales Growth Relative to World Market, 1969–1979. See Exhibit 1A for key.

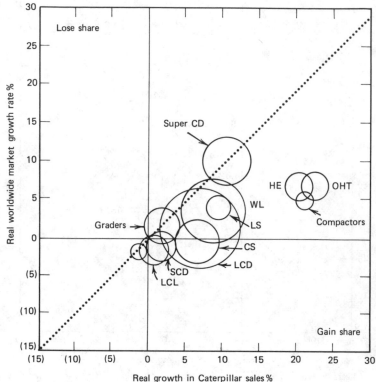

Real growth in Caterpillar sales %

ket. Strategically, it acts as a check on the market share and cash flow of Komatsu. Japan accounts for less than 20% of the world market but yields over 80% of Komatsu's worldwide cash flow. The joint venture is number two in market position, serving to limit Komatsu's profits. Japanese tax records indicate that the Cat-Mitsubishi joint venture has earned only modest profits, but it is of great strategic value to Caterpillar.[1]

L.M. Ericsson: Can Small Be Beautiful?
L.M. Ericsson of Sweden has become a successful global competitor by developing and exploiting a technological niche. Most major international telephone equipment producers operated first in large, protected home markets that allowed the most efficient economies of scale. The additional profits helped underwrite R&D and provided good competitive leverage. Sweden's home market is relatively small, yet Ericsson translated the advent of electronic switching technology into a powerful global lever that befuddled com-

petitors in its international market niche. In the electromechanical era of the 1960s, the telephone switching equipment business was hardly global. Switching systems combine hardware and software. In the electromechanical stage, 70% of total installed costs lay in hardware, and 70% of hardware cost was direct labor, manufacturing overhead, and installation of the equipment.

The design of each country's telephone system was unique, economies of scale were low, and the wage rate was more important than the impact of volume on costs. In the late 1960s, major international companies (including Ericsson) responded by moving electroswitching production to LDCs not only to take advantage of cheaper labor but also to respond to the desire of government telephone companies to source locally.

Eventually, each parent company centrally sourced only the core software and critical components and competed on a domestic-market-by-domestic-market basis. For its part, Ericsson concentrated investment in developing countries without colonial ties to Europe and in smaller European markets that lacked national suppliers and that used the same switching systems as the Swedish market.

The telecommunications industry became global when, in the 1970s, electronic switching technology emerged, radically shifting cost structures and threatening the market position Ericsson had carved for itself. Software is now 60% of total cost; 55% of hardware cost is in sophisticated electronic components whose production is highly scale sensitive. The initial R&D investment required to develop a system has jumped to more than $100 million, which major international companies could have amortized more easily than Ericsson. In addition, the move to electronics promised to destroy the long-standing relationships Ericsson enjoyed with smaller government telephone companies. And it appeared that individual electronic switching systems would require a large fixed-cost software investment for each country, making the new technology too expensive for the smaller telephone systems, on which Ericsson thrived.

Ericsson knew that the electronic technology would eventually be adapted to small systems. In the meantime, it faced the possibility of losing its position in smaller markets because of its inability to meet the ante for the new global competition.

The company responded with a preemptive strategic innovation—a modular technology that introduced electronics to small telephone systems. The company developed a series of modular software packages that could be used in different combinations to meet the needs of diverse telephone systems at an acceptable cost. Moreover, each successive system required fewer new modules. As Exhibit 2 shows, the first system—Södertalje in Sweden—required all new modules, but by the third year, the Åbo system in Finland required none at all. Thus the company rapidly amortized development costs and enjoyed economies of scale that steepened as the num-

Exhibit 2.   Ericsson's Technology Lever: Reduction of Software Cost through Modular Design

Representative Systems	New Modules Required	Existing Modules Used
Year 1: Södertalje, Sweden	57	0
Year 2: Orleans, France	22	57
Year 3: Ābo, Finland	0	77

ber of software systems sold increased. As a result, Ericsson was able to compete globally in small systems.

Ericsson's growth is accelerating as small telephone systems convert to electronics. The company now enjoys an advantage in software cost and variety that continually reinforces itself. Through this technology Ericsson has raised a significant entry barrier against other companies in the small system market.

Honda's Marketing Genius

Before Honda became a global company, two distinct motorcycle industries existed in the world. In Asia and other developing countries, large numbers of people rode small, simple motorcycles to work. In Europe and America, smaller numbers of people drove big, elaborate machines for play. Since the Asian motorcycle was popular as an inexpensive means of transportation, companies competed on the basis of price. In the West, manufacturers used styling and brand image to differentiate their products. No Western market exceeded 100,000 units; wide product lines and small volumes meant slight opportunities for economies of scale. Major motorcycle producers such as Harley-Davidson of the United States, BMW of West Germany, and Triumph and BSA of the United Kingdom traded internationally, but only in modest volumes.

Honda made its industry global by convincing middle-class Americans that riding motorcycles could be fun. Because of the company's marketing innovations, Honda's annual growth rate was greater than 20% from the late 1950s to the late 1960s. The company then turned its attention to Europe, with a similar outcome. Honda invested for seven full years before sustaining profitability in Europe, financing this global effort with cash flows earned from a leading market position at home and in the United States.

Three crucial steps were decisive in Honda's achievement. First, Honda turned market preference around to the characteristics of its own products and away from those of American and European competitors. Honda targeted new consumers and used advertising, promotions, and trade shows to convince them that its motorbikes were inexpensive, reliable, and easy to use. A large investment in the distribution network—2,000 dealerships, retail missionaries, generous warranty and service support, and quick spare parts availability—backed up the marketing message.

Second, Honda sustained growth by enticing customers with the upper levels of its product line. Nearly half of new bike owners purchased larger, more expensive models within 12 months. Brand loyalty proved very high. Honda exploited these trends by expanding from its line of a few small motorcycles to one covering the full range of sizes and features by 1975. The result: self-sustaining growth in dollar volume and a model mix that allowed higher margins. The higher volume reduced marketing and distribution costs and improved the position of Honda and other Japanese producers who invaded the 750cc "super bike" portion of the market traditionally reserved for American and European companies. Here Honda beat the competition with a bike that was better engineered, lower priced, and whose development cost was shared over the company's wide product line.

The third step Honda took was to exploit economies of scale through both centralized manufacturing and logistics. The increasing volume of engines and bike assemblies sold (50,000 units per month and up) enabled the company to use less costly manufacturing techniques unavailable to motorcycle producers with lower volumes (see Exhibit 3). Over a decade, Honda's factory productivity rose at an average annual rate of 13.1%—several times

Exhibit 3. The Effect of Volume on Manufacturing Approaches in Motorcycle Production

Cost Element	Low Volume	High Volume
Machine tools	Manual, general purpose	Numerical control, special purpose
Changeover time	Manual, slow (hours)	Automatic positioning, fast (minutes)
Work-in-process inventory	High (days of production)	Low (hours of production)
Materials handling	Forklift trucks	Automated
Assembly	Bay assembly	Motorized assembly line
Machine tool design	Designed outside the company, available throughout industry	Designed in-house, proprietary
Rework	More	Less

Cost per unit Economic ranges for alternative approaches (Units per month). (Low) 5,000, (High) 50,000

higher than European and American producers. Combined with lower transportation cost, Honda's increased output gave it a landed cost per unit far
lower than the competition's. In turn, the lower production cost helped fund
Honda's heavy marketing and distribution investment. Finally, economies
of scale in marketing and distribution, combined with low production cost,
led to the high profits that financed Honda's move into automobiles.

What Can We Learn?

Each of these successful global players changed the dynamics of its industry
and pulled away from its major competitors. By achieving economies of
scale through commonality of design, Caterpillar exploited both its worldwide sales volume and its existing market for parts revenues. Competitors
could not match its costs or profits and therefore could not make the investment necessary to catch up. Ericsson created a cost advantage by developing a unique modular technology perfectly adapted to its segment of
the market. Its global strategy turned electronics from a threat to Ericsson
into a barrier to its competitors. Honda used marketing to homogenize worldwide demand and unlock the potential for economies of scale in production,
marketing, and distribution. The competition's only refuge was the highly
brand-conscious, small-volume specialty market.

In each case, the industry had the potential for a worldwide system of
products and markets that a company with a global strategy could exploit.
Construction equipment offered large economies of scale in component manufacture, allowing Caterpillar to neutralize high transportation costs and
government barriers through local assembly. Ericsson unlocked scale economies in software development for electronic switches. The modular technology accommodated local product differences and governments' desire to
use local suppliers. Once Honda's marketing techniques raised demand in
major markets for products with similar characteristics, the industry's economies of scale in production combined with low transportation costs and
low tariff barriers to turn it into a global game.

In none of the cases did success result from a "world product." The
companies accommodated local differences without sacrificing production
costs. The global player's position in one major market strengthened its
position in others. Caterpillar's design similarities and central component
facilities allowed each market to contribute to its already favorable cost
structure. Ericsson's shared modules led to falling costs each time a system
was sold in a new country. Honda drew on scale economies from the centralized production of units sold in each market and used its U.S. marketing
and distribution experience to succeed in Europe.

In addition to superior effectiveness and cost advantages, a winning
global strategy always requires abilities in two other dimensions. The first
is timing. The successful global competitor uses a production cost or dis-

tribution advantage as a leverage point to make it more difficult or expensive for the competitor to respond. The second is financial. The global innovator commits itself to major investment before anyone else, whether in technology, facilities, or distribution. If successful it then reaps the benefits from increased cash flows from either higher volume (Honda and Ericsson) or lower costs (all three companies). The longer the competitor takes to respond, the larger the innovator's cash flows. The global company can then deploy funds either to increase investment or lower prices, creating barriers to new market entrants.

A global player should decide against which of its major competitors it must succeed first in order to generate broad-based success in the future. Caterpillar located in the Far East not only to source products locally but also to track Komatsu. (Cat increasingly sources product and manufacturing technology from Japan.) Ericsson's radical departure in technology was aimed squarely at ITT and Siemens, whose large original market shares would ordinarily have given them an advantage in the smaller European and African markets. Honda created new markets in the United States and Europe because its most powerful competitors, Yamaha and Kawasaki, were Japanese. By exploiting the global opportunity first, Honda got a head start, and it remained strong even when competitors' own international ambitions came to light.

Playing the Global Chess Game

Global competition forces top management to change the way it thinks about and operates its businesses. Policies that made sense when the company was multidomestic may now be counterproductive. The most powerful moves are those that improve the company's worldwide cost position or ability to differentiate itself and weaken key worldwide competitors. Let us consider two potential moves.

The first is preempting the leading positions in major newly industrializing countries (NICs). Rapid growth in, for example, Mexico, Brazil, and Indonesia has made them an important part of the worldwide market for many capital goods. If its industry has the potential to become global, the company that takes a leading position in these markets will have made a decisive move to bar its competitors. Trade barriers are often prohibitively high in these places, and a company that tries to penetrate the market through a *self-contained* local subsidiary is likely to fall into a trap.

The astute global competitor will exploit the situation, however, by building a specialized component manufacturing facility in an NIC, which will become an integral part of a global sourcing network. The company exports output of the specialized facility to offset importing complementary components. Final assembly for the domestic and smaller, neighboring markets can be done locally. (Having dual sources for key items can minimize the risk of disruption to the global sourcing network.)

A good illustration of this strategy is Siemens's circuit breaker operation in Brazil. When the company outgrew its West German capacity for some key components, it seized the opportunity presented by Brazilian authorities seeking capital investments in the heavy electrical equipment industry. Siemens now builds a large portion of its common components there, swaps them for other components made in Europe, and is the lower-cost and leading supplier of the finished product in Brazil.

Another move that can be decisive in a global industry is to establish a solid position with your largest customers to block competitors. Many businesses have a few customers that dominate the global market. The global competitor recognizes their importance and prevents current or prospective competitors from generating any sales.

A good example is a British company, BSR, the world's largest producer of automatic record changers. In the 1970s, when Japanese exports of audio equipment were growing rapidly, BSR recognized that it could lose its market base in the United States and Europe if the Japanese began marketing record changers. BSR redesigned its product to Japanese specifications and offered distributors aggressive price discounts and inventory support. The Japanese could not justify expanding their own capacity. BSR not only stalled the entry of the Japanese into the record-changer market, but it also moved ahead of its existing competitor, Garrard.

A global company can apply similar principles to block the competition's access to key distributors or retailers. Many American companies have failed to seize this opportunity in their unwillingness to serve large, private-label customers (e.g., Sears Roebuck) or by neglecting the less expensive end of their product line and effectively allowing competitors access to their distributors. Japanese manufacturers in particular could then establish a toehold in industries like TV sets and farm equipment.

The decision on prices for pivotal customers must not be made solely on considerations of ROI. Equally important in global competition is the impact of these prices on prospective entrants and the cost of failing to protect and expand the business base. One way to control the worldwide chess game in your favor is to differentiate prices among countries.

Manage Interdependently

The successful global competitor manages its business in various countries as a single system, not a portfolio of independent positions. In the view of portfolio planning theory, a market's attractiveness and the strength of a company's position within it determine the extent of corporate resources devoted to it. A company should defend strong positions and try to turn weak ones around or abandon them. It will pursue high-profit and/or high-growth markets more aggressively than lower-profit or lower-growth ones, and it will decide on a stand-alone basis whether to compete in a market.

Accepting this portfolio view of international competition can be disastrous in a global industry. The global competitor focuses instead on its ability to leverage positions in one country market against those in other markets. In the global system, the ability to leverage is as important as market attractiveness; the company need not turn around weak positions for them to be useful.

The most obvious leverage a company obtains from a country market is the volume it contributes to the company's overall cost or effectiveness. Du Pont and Texas Instruments have patiently won a large sales volume in the sophisticated Japanese market, for example, which supports their efforts elsewhere. Winning a share of a market that consistently supports product innovation ahead of other markets—like the United States in long-haul jet aircraft—is another leverage point. The competitor with a high share of such a market can always justify new product investment. Or a market can contribute leverage if it supports an efficient scale manufacturing facility for a region—like Brazil for Siemens. Finally, a market can contribute leverage if a position in it can be used to affect a competitor's cash flow.

Organization: The Achilles Heel

Organizational structure and reporting relationships present subtle problems for a global strategy. Effective strategic control argues for a central product-line organization; effective local responsiveness, for a geographic organization with local autonomy. A global strategy demands that the product-line organization have the *ultimate* authority, because without it the company cannot gain system-wide benefits. Nevertheless, the company still must balance product and area needs. In short, there is no simple solution. But there are some guidelines to help.

No one organizational structure applies to all of a company's international businesses. It may be unnecessarily cumbersome, for example, to impose a matrix structure on all business. Organizational reporting lines should probably differ by country market depending on that market's role. An important market that offers high leverage, as in the foregoing examples, must work closely with the global business-unit managers at headquarters. Coordination is crucial to success. But the manager of a market outside the global system will require only sets of objectives under a regional reporting system.

Another guideline is that organizational reporting lines and structures should change as the nature of the international business changes. When a business becomes global, the emphasis should shift toward centralization.

As countries increase in importance, they must be brought within the global manager's reach. Over time, if the business becomes less global, the company's organization may emphasize local autonomy.

The common tendency to apply one organizational structure to all operations is bound to be a disadvantage to some of them. In some U.S. companies, this approach inhibited development of the global strategy their industries required.

Match Financial Policies to Competitive Realities

If top management is not careful, adherence to conventional financial management and practices may constrain a good competitive response in global businesses. While capital budgeters use such standard financial tools as DCF return analysis or risk profiles to judge investments and creditors and stock analysts prefer stable debt and dividend policies, a global company must chart a different course.

Allocating Capital

In a global strategy, investments are usually a long-term, interdependent series of capital commitments, which are not easily associated with returns or risks. The company has to be aware of the size and timing of the total expenditures because they will greatly influence competitors' new investment response. Most troublesome, however, is that revenues from investments in several countries may have to build up to a certain point before the company earns *any* return on investment.

A global strategy goes against the traditional tests for capital allocation—project-oriented DCF risk-return analysis and the country manager's record of credibility. Global competition requires a less mechanical approach to project evaluation. The successful global competitor develops at least two levels of financial control. One level is a profit-and-cost center for self-contained projects; the other is a strategy center for tracking interdependent efforts and competitors' performance and reactions. Global competitors operate with a short time frame when monitoring the execution of global strategy investments and a long time frame when evaluating such investments and their expected returns.

Debt and Dividends

Debt and dividend policies should vary with the requirements of the integrated investment program of the whole company. In the initial stages, a company with a strong competitive position should retain earnings to build and defend its global position. When the industry has become global and growth slows or the returns exceed the reinvestment needed to retain position, the company should distribute earnings to the rest of the corporation and use debt capacity elsewhere, perhaps in funding another nascent global strategy.

Honda's use of debt over the last 25 years illustrates this logic (see Exhibit 3). In the mid-1950s, when Honda held a distant second place in a rapidly growing Japanese motorcycle industry, the company had to leverage its equity 3.5 times to finance growth. By 1960, the Japanese market had matured and Honda emerged dominant. The debt-equity ratio receded to 0.5 times but rose again with the company's international expansion in motorcycles. In the late 1960s, Honda made a major move to the automobile market, requiring heavy debt. At that time, motorcycle cash flows funded the move.

Which Strategic Road to Take

There is no safe formula for success in international business. Industry structures continuously evolve. The Caterpillar, Ericsson, and Honda approaches will probably not work forever. Competitors will try to push industrial trends away from the strengths of the industry leaders, and technological or political changes may force the leading companies to operate in a multidomestic fashion once again.

Strategy is a powerful force in determining competitive outcomes, whether in international or domestic business. And, although adopting a global strategy is risky, many companies can dramatically improve their positions by fundamentally changing the way they plan, control, and operate their businesses. But a global strategy requires that managers think in new ways. Otherwise the company will not be able to recognize the nature of competition, justify the required investments, or sustain the change in everyday behavior needed.

If the company can successfully execute a global strategy, it may find itself joining the ranks of the truly successful international companies. Whether they be Japanese, American, European, or otherwise, the strategic thread that ties together companies like IBM, Matsushita, K. Hattori (Seiko), Du Pont, and Michelin clearly shows that the rules of the international competitive game have changed.

Note

1. For more on this subject, see Craig M. Watson, "Counter-Competition Abroad to Protect Home Markets," *HBR*, January–February 1982, p. 40.

13

Management Strategies for Small Companies

HERBERT N. WOODWARD

Numerous small businesses suffer from underlying weaknesses which lead to mistakes that can adversely affect their return on investment. These management problems tend to arise when the business is expanded beyond the limits a particular manager can cope with. In this article, the author offers lessons about operating small businesses, drawing from his own successful experience in acquiring and turning around sick companies.

After looking at hundreds of small businesses and working on a number of them, I have seen certain patterns of conduct recur again and again that lead to eventual failure. If a company is in difficulty, it is almost always a management problem, scarcely ever bad luck.

When a company survives for many years but finally comes upon hard times, it usually means (a) that there is a valuable core of talent and expertise somewhere in the corporate structure, yet (b) some persistent management inadequacies have gradually eroded its strengths and left it vulnerable to whatever adverse fortune it encounters.

In a moment, I shall get into those areas that cause management the most trouble, but first permit me to clarify one point. While this article focuses on the lessons I have learned about operating small manufacturing businesses, much of what I discuss is applicable to the practical problems faced by operating units of sizable companies.

In my judgment, there are three principal areas of weakness in small businesses that cause trouble, all of them management centered:

1 Growth of sales is commonly seen as the solution to all problems.
   There is an unawareness that, except in the short run, there is no
   such thing as fixed overhead. Managers, trapped by the concept of
   marginal income accounting, bring out additional products, believing that their overhead will not be affected.
2 Inadequate product-cost analysis blinds managers to the losses incurred by adding new products willy-nilly Usually, there are one
   or more products or product lines that should be dropped.
3 Gearing operations to the income statement, while ignoring the
   balance sheet, is all too common. Lack of concern with cash flow
   and the productivity of capital employed can be fatal. Managers
   tend to seek new funds instead of making better use of those they
   already have.

Growth for Growth's Sake

The most common cause of trouble is the widely held belief that the only
road to success is through growth. Many business people see growth of sales
as the solution to all problems. It seldom is. Growth is not synonymous with
capitalistic success. In fact, shrinking the number of products or product
lines is usually the surest route to better profit and higher return on investment.

The mania for growth is commonly expressed in the battle to increase
sales. Standard methods of accounting tend to encourage the belief that
higher profits automatically follow from higher sales. Several standard accounting techniques tend to mislead those who accept standard cost allocations as gospel.

Marginal Income Accounting

Much has been written about the advantages of marginal income. The theory
is that, for a short period, additional sales can be added to the normal sales
volume profitably even at prices too low to cover a proportionate share of
fixed overhead. Managers often do this because they presume that 100% of
the fixed overhead of the company is borne by their regular business anyway.

However, pricing your product so that it does not cover a full share
of overhead is dangerous. Except for rare and well-controlled exceptions,
marginal business taken to keep the operation going incurs the same overhead
costs as the regular business and, by adding to the complexity of the total
operation, often requires more than normal overhead.

Recently, one company manager proudly mentioned that his leading
accounting firm had advised him to price all products to obtain any profit
margin over his direct material and direct labor costs. He had taken this
advice to heart. No wonder his company was in trouble.

Yet, if the overhead really cannot be cut during a short period of overcapacity, it may make sense to take added business at prices that will pay less than full overhead expenses. Even a modest contribution to paying these expenses for that period may be better than none. However, the danger is that an emergency measure often becomes standard practice. It is a good way to go broke.

Break-Even Accounting

Another management tool that inadvertently encourages growth for growth's sake is break-even accounting. Like marginal income accounting, the theory is that certain elements of overhead cost vary with the volume of operations, while others, which are called "fixed costs," do not. The sale price is set to provide for material and labor costs, plus variable overhead costs, plus an additional increment to allow for fixed overhead costs and profit. When the sales volume is high enough in a given period to absorb all variable costs as well as the lump of fixed overhead costs, you have reached the break-even point. The margin above variable costs on additional sales goes entirely to profit, because all the fixed overhead costs have already been taken care of.

No wonder manufacturers gloat about a high-volume month, because, although they make no money and actually lose until the volume reaches the break-even level, their profit on volume above the break-even point is disproportionately large.

The fallacy of break-even accounting is the assumption that expenses are easily divisible into fixed and variable. Overhead is rarely as fixed as accountants are inclined to think, except for very short periods. In any long-range analysis of a business, there is no such thing as fixed overhead—it is all variable to some degree, even such items as rent, heat, light and power, depreciation and amortization, professional services, and executive salaries. The terms "variable overhead" and "fixed overhead" would be better called "overhead that varies immediately with the level of activity" and "overhead that varies in the long run with the level of activity."

Except in the very short run, there really are few, if any, fixed expenses. If you lease a 100,000 square-foot plant for a ten-year term, cost accountants will normally treat your rent as a fixed expense. But is it really? If you don't have enough space, you can rent more and thus increase that expense. If you have too much space, you can sublet part of the space, or if that is impractical, you can even buy your way out of the lease and move to a smaller building. Thus rent expense can go up or down.

The danger is that some managers tend to pay no attention to so-called fixed expenses. Even worse, they assume that they are stuck with them and see an increase in volume as the only means to pay for them.

One able executive of a large merchandising company recently said: "Our biggest problem is sales. Our industry has high fixed costs, and we have to promote hard to maintain a rate of sales to cover these costs. Securing more sales is far and away our No. 1 problem." This is a typical, mistaken business attitude: assuming that the cost structure is a given and that the company must grow to cover all the overhead.

Variation of Break-Even Costing

Manufacturers often take their profits only at the tail end of a run, absorbing all their fixed overhead before any profit is counted. In airplane manufacture, for instance, it is common to determine how many planes must be sold before the company breaks even. The danger of this variation of break-even accounting is that it may stimulate concern with volume of sales, not with margins.

As such, once the fixed costs have been absorbed, profits on the last increment of volume (either monthly or, if it is a one-shot product, by unit) are big, thus encouraging the attitude that more is automatically better.

It is understandable that accounting practices permit amortization of much of the special costs of a particular project (largely tooling and start-up costs) over the estimated number of units expected to be produced. Also, management may be wise to plan for low sales to avoid the unpleasant possibility of taking a big write-off on unamortized costs should the product not sell well. The result, however, is to put the major emphasis on marketing effectiveness rather than on cost effectiveness. It is not surprising, therefore, that increasing sales is the generally accepted prescription for all corporate ills.

Inadequate Cost Analysis

At best, cost accounting is an inexact study with limited goals. It is a method of looking at the direct costs attributable to a particular product or activity. However, it does a poor job of allocating indirect costs. Old and new product lines are normally charged the same proportionate amounts for overhead, although the more recently added lines cost far more to start up. The new product line that adds one more straw to the management load rarely gets charged as much as it should, while the well-established line that runs itself is expected to carry the load for the new line.

Research and development costs, for instance, are usually charged to current operations—which they don't benefit—rather than to the new lines that the R&D is supposed to develop. It is probably necessary to have the old products subsidize the introduction of the new ones. Many managements are scarcely aware, however, that they are doing this. Therefore, they undervalue the profits on the old line and understate the costs in bringing out the new one. The effect is to encourage costly new projects and downgrade current results.

Advantages of Simplification

Once managers understand how to interpret their cost accounting information, however, they can see that shrinking is a good strategy. If the manager is willing to recognize that all overhead expenses are variable (although a few expenses take time and effort to change), it is easier for him to identify the costs which can be eliminated when his organization is trimmed down in size and complexity.

A few years ago, one of our operating companies disposed of a line of portable positive-displacement pneumatic machines that had an annual sales volume of about $500,000. Although the line was a natural companion to a much larger and long-established line of fan-operated equipment and a prodigious effort had been devoted to get it going, it had not made money and the prospects of success were poor. We finally made the painful decision to sell the line for a nominal amount. The buyer was one of our employees, who set it up as a separate business that later proved modestly successful.

The beneficial effects of that sale on the company's operation were substantial and almost instantaneous. Our balance sheet improved dramatically as we collected the remaining accounts receivable, worked off the inventory, and—by buying no more material—cut our accounts payable. Our earnings improved more than the elimination of this relatively minor line seemed to justify. Only then did top management realize how much this one activity had demanded in attention and effort from almost everyone in the parent company. The product line had had a disproportionately high overhead, but the figures didn't show it.

The advantages of simplification are hard to quantify, but they are real. Despite all that the computer can do to make possible a wide span of control, there is no better road to efficiency than to eliminate complexity entirely, usually by shrinking the business to a smaller and more manageable size.

The manager's job is to maximize the opportunities of the business, not to solve all its problems. He or she can do this best by focusing on a limited number of objectives to the exclusion of all the irrelevancies of much business activity. It is not easy. As E. F. Schumacher says, "Any third-rate engineer or researcher can increase complexity; but it takes a certain flair of real insight to make things simple again."[1]

In simplifying a business, the best place to start is usually with the products. This is where the ball game is really played. Take each product line and analyze it separately. In most companies with more than one product line or group of products, there are some that are contributing to its growth and success and some that are dragging it down; it takes a careful study to tell the difference.

If the company has adequate product-line cost information, so much the better. Learn how the information is developed and analyze whether the cost allocations between product lines are reasonable. Look for the low-margin product lines that represent a substantial part of the volume.

For example, if a line has been a company mainstay for a long time, your people are likely to tell you that, despite its low margins, it is absolutely necessary to keep this line because of the overhead it absorbs. You will probably also be told that it carries more than its share of overhead and that it really does better than the figures say. In my experience, this is usually not true. In fact, such a line may be doing worse than shown on the statement and may have more actual indirect expense than in charged to it on the accounting books.

Often one line is holding a company down. In one of our operating companies, we found a major product line that had been the backbone of the company for almost a generation. The line showed a minor loss year after year, while gradually declining in volume both absolutely and relatively in relation to a newer line marketed through other channels. This old line was being marketed to original equipment manufacturers (OEMs) in an industry where the smaller customer manufacturers were gradually being driven out by a few large survivors, who had become demanding buyers of components. The company's newer line of products, however, was sold to the consumer market through several thousand distributors. And it was growing profitably every year.

We were told that the company could not survive without the old OEM line because the overhead it carried made the profits on the distributor line possible. But that was not true. The OEM line required extensive engineering for annual model changes for each separate customer, had generally more stringent requirements for quality performance, and had a greater variety of more complicated mechanisms. Yet the customers demanded immediate response to up-and-down schedule changes that made production scheduling beyond a few days almost impossible to achieve.

We sold off the OEM line. And, by so doing, we were able (a) to cut the overhead more than proportionately, (b) to free funds tied up in a non-profit program, and (c) to turn the company from a big loss to a big profit in less than a year.

What You Need to Know

In studying product lines, management should ask some basic questions. In this section, I shall discuss seven of them:

1. *Is the sales volume of the product or product line rising or falling?* Most products have a life cycle of from 5 to 20 years (depending on how you define "product"). If sales are on the downtrend, spend little or nothing to keep it from dying a premature death.[2] If it is losing money and it is past its peak, let it die quietly. You should spend money on the product that is on its way up. Indeed, if this product already has a good margin, it probably can be increased even more.

2. *Is the product line making a profit?* If it is not profitable, as shown by the company's existing cost system, don't lightly accept the argument that it is really doing better than the figures show, that it doesn't use as much overhead as is allocated to it, and that, if only such and such were done, it would start making money. Particularly, don't listen to this argument for a product line the company has had for years which once made money. Better than revive it, let it die quietly.

3.   *What are the gross margins of the different product lines?*
There is no fixed rule for a satisfactory gross margin (the difference between net sales price and the total cost of material, direct labor, and applicable factory overhead). One manufacturing company had a material cost alone that represented over 90% of sales price, but the product had a very satisfactory profit. The reasons: the material was expensive but not bulky, and the company made only a slight addition to the product before selling it to a few large users; in addition, operating expense was negligible, and the company didn't pay for the raw material until after it had collected for the modified product from its own customers. Consequently, almost all the gross margin went directly to the owner's salary and profit.

In general, however, in the manufacturing business, if you are to have a profit of at least 10% on sales before federal income taxes, your gross margin should be no less than 35% and preferably well over 45%. If your gross margin is low, unless you can raise selling prices (the first place to look) you face a long struggle to improve operating efficiency. For, while you battle to reduce manufacturing costs, you can be sure that your competitors are plowing that field too. You may find later that your hard-won improvements have only kept you from losing more ground.

4.   *What do your customers think of each product line, its price, its quality, and your company's service?*
Most companies have their own definition of their products' quality and competitiveness, but the customer is the only person who is entitled to judge quality. He or she often has quite different ideas from you about what is important and what is not. Often products that managers or owners think are marvelous fail miserably in the marketplace, for reasons that are entirely unanticipated.

One maker of television sets claims that its product is better because the sets are handcrafted. The company does make a superior product, but handcrafting doesn't impress me. Personally, I trust machine manufacture more. The customer most likely doesn't care how difficult it is to make. If a product is as hard to make as some manufacturers advertise, it probably can't be very reliable. Quality is only what the customer says it is.

5.   *Is the sales department determining the pricing?*
If so, you can bet the prices are too low. Salesmen rarely believe that they can get a higher price for the product until they are told by management that they have no choice. (Overly marketing-oriented officers have the same failing.) It is amazing how often the customer will pay more with little or no complaint, despite all the salesperson's warnings that to raise the price is suicide.

6. *Is your sales department's pitch that "we have to have a full line"?*
Only the "full line" approach justifies continuing to make and sell low-volume items which are expensive to tool and manufacture and which, per unit sold, cost a fortune to catalog and carry in stock. If your competitor carries a full line, your salespeople will insist that they cannot compete unless they have all the items too, because the buyer wants to purchase from one supplier.

One stop purchasing is a good sales gimmick but often is not good business. The Crane Company had the most complete line in the plumbing industry, but its losses mounted until Thomas Mellon Evans acquired it, eliminated the low-margin items, and thus put it back in the black.

7. *Does your sales program offer a wide variety of options, extras, and specials?*
Custom products always cost more and, unless the volume is large enough so that some economies of scale can be realized, they are certain to lose far more money than the books show. Many companies gradually add more and more variations to their line to suit the particular specifications or whims of various customers. These specials are ordered as a matter of habit for years thereafter, even when the customer can do just as well with a standard product. If you rigorously cut out the specials, you can usually convert the customer to a standard item. If you can't, you are probably better off losing his account.

All of the foregoing should aid you in cutting out low-profit or unprofitable product lines. If you are lucky, you can sell off the line to a competitor or someone who wants to get into the business. If you are not able to do this, just stop making it. One way to stop is to put into effect a large, across-the-board price increase. If the line has been grossly underpriced, you may not lose much business and may have turned a bad line into a good one. But even if you lose most of the business, a few of your customers, although they may object noisily to the price, may continue to buy from you—at least for a while—so that you can favorably dispose of your inventory.

When you cut out a line entirely, several things happen. Because your sales volume is reduced, your accounts receivable in that line turn into cash. You stop buying inventory and stop putting in direct labor, and this saves you more cash. You terminate all personnel involved in the line except those necessary for the final salvage operation, saving still more cash. You simplify your total operation which makes even more savings happen. You will probably need less machinery and may be able to sell off the surplus for cash. Finally, even if you can't sell all the inventory, you can scrap the rest, thus freeing up space which you can put to better use or even no use at all.

Closing down a product line is usually recorded on the accounting books as a loss. However, you are merely recognizing losses that were actually incurred sometime ago but don't show on the books yet. You might as well bite the bullet now.

Lack of Balance Sheet Concern

Another common failing is gearing the operations to the income statement and ignoring the balance sheet. The management of one company, International Science Industries, purchased from a large conglomerate, had never seen a balance sheet because the parent supplied all its cash needs automatically on request. Lack of concern with cash flow and the productivity of capital, however, can be fatal to the small company that is on its own. Your best source of capital often is hidden in your balance sheet. I have become particularly aware of this because in most turnarounds the first concern is cash flow.

Accounts Receivable

Look through your assets to see what you can turn into cash. Often, the quickest and best source of cash is your accounts receivable. An intelligent analysis of accounts receivable can be made without knowing much about the details of the business. If the book figure for accounts receivable is higher than the equivalent of 40 to 50 days of company sales, you may be sure that there is work to be done.

Collecting amounts owed you by customers is a boring and unpleasant job. In poorly managed companies, the job is often neglected. If the company has not earned a profit, there has been no income tax incentive to write off uncollectible accounts. As a result, these uncollectibles continue to clutter up the balance sheet, making it harder to identify the accounts you should be working on.

Obtain a report showing all of the accounts by invoice number divided into categories by age of invoice (less than 30 days, 30 to 60 days, 60 to 90 days, over 90 days). Such a report will show you at a glance where the problems are; establish the procedure if you don't already have it. Decide who is to police the accounts receivable and then ensure that they are really worked on.

In many companies, the salespeople are not penalized when their customers have a poor payment record. Salespeople are naturally reluctant to irritate the people on whom they rely for business by insisting that the customer really should pay his bill. The result is that the only customers who make timely payments are those who do so automatically, without the needling that many companies expect before paying any bills. If you find that the salespeople are responsible for collection, reassign the responsibility to someone in the accounting department who has no compunction about being firm with a slow-paying customer. What good is it to make a sale if you don't get paid?

Once the salespersons are freed from the responsibility of collection, they can sympathize with the customer about the demands of that "damn credit department" and spend their time selling, which they do well, instead of collecting, which they do ineffectively—if at all.

Study the accounts receivable records to see whether the financial department is doing a good job. If you find a host of small unpaid balances in the receivables, and, at the same time, many unmatched credit entries, then you know that procedures don't exist or aren't being followed for matching cash receipts with the appropriate invoices in order to straighten out any discrepancies. Examples of the latter are when the customer pays for the product but doesn't pay for the freight, or takes an unauthorized discount, or in any way pays less than what the invoice calls for.

If these discrepancies are ignored for long, it becomes almost impossible to straighten them out without writing off your loss. If an adequate job has been done, such a write-off will never be necessary. I am particularly partial to nit-picking bookkeepers who keep tidy books and work at cleaning up all (and I do mean all) open items within a reasonable period.

If you can find time to be your own credit manager and to do some of the telephoning to delinquent accounts, you will be rewarded with new insights into your business. When you talk to customers who haven't paid their bill, you find out why they aren't paying. Often it is because your own company has made mistakes that no one has done anything to correct.

You also discover which salespeople are doing a poor job in handling difficult product and sales problems. If they aren't solving such problems as they arise, they are not helping to build your company. Instead, they are effectively tearing it down.

Inventory Items

If your company is operating in the black, you have every incentive to write down or write off any inventory that is no longer worth full value. Necessarily, all accountants and auditors have to rely on management judgment as to which inventory is still useful and which is obsolete. Their statistical analyses of inventory aging can be very helpful, but the manager is the one to decide which items are good and which are not.

Even when there are no favorable tax consequences, a physical housecleaning is good. Poor housekeeping generally goes with poor management. Some years ago when a company I ran first took on a turnaround, we trucked out 23 semitrailer loads of scrap inventory in the first three weeks, inventory that the previous management had been afraid to write off the books, although they (and we) knew that it was valueless.

Most of us hate to throw things away. Somehow the right time never seems to come. But never has anything turned up to make me thankful I had not thrown something out or to make me regret that I had. It is good for the soul to roll up your sleeves and to clean house physically. And it is good for the business, too.

Fixed Assets

Managers are likely to neglect looking into their fixed assets for hidden capital. Somehow land, buildings, machinery, and equipment seem sacred. If the company has been in existence many years, these assets are usually deeply depreciated on the books. However, because of inflation, these assets are likely to be worth far more than book value. (Land, although it is not depreciable, usually has inflated in price, too.)

The capital you are actually employing in the business is not measured by the net book value of these assets, but by their current market value. Once you recognize this, you should seriously consider whether you need all of them and whether you are using them effectively. If you have a fully tooled machine shop to support your manufacturing effort, can you justify tying up that much capital in expensive equipment when there are competent subcontractors available to do your work? If not, you can close it down, sell off the equipment for cash, free up some space, and reduce your payroll.

My general rule is to subcontract whenever possible all work for which our company has only an intermittent need. If the work is a follow-up step in the production process that, if not properly done, can damage our products, we may make an exception and invest the money to do it ourselves. Heat treating of critical aerospace parts is a typical example of an exception.

Also, when we manufacture in high volume, it is advantageous to integrate backward as far as possible and to do it ourselves. Only in that way can we keep out unit costs down. But we still let outsiders make our tools.

One important management decision is whether to continue to operate at all in a given location. Years ago, it may have been necessary to have satellite plants in various cities to serve your customers. But is that still true, and, if so, what is it costing you to serve those customers? Several years ago, International Science Industries acquired a manufacturing company with plants in five cities around the country. Within a year, we closed and liquidated two of them. We were able to shift much of the business to the remaining three plants. Thus, while sales volume scarcely declined at all, costs plummeted. More important, this shift released a large chunk of capital for better use.

A Final Reminder

The name of the managerial game is return on investment. ROI is the ratio between the profit of the operation after tax and the assets employed. Management tends to look only at the former, neglecting the latter. In seeking to maximize profits, attention is often focused exclusively on sales. The stockholder, however, has no interest in sales; he or she looks at earnings per share, because they largely determine how much the stock sells for and what dividends are paid.

If assets employed can be sharply reduced, even if profits drop a little, ROI will increase and the stockholder will be better off. Is this a risky strategy? Not if the assets were previously employed inefficiently. Putting the company in a financially sound position is a first step.

Once the company is in a solid position, you can, if you desire, go after renewed growth. Or, if you get hooked on the beauties of simplicity, you may just keep on making money at that level.

Notes

1. E. F. Schumacher, *Small Is Beautiful* (New York, Harper & Row, 1973), p. 146.

2. See Joseph A. Morein, "Shift from Brand to Product Line Marketing," *HBR*, September–October 1975, p. 56.

PART THREE
STRATEGIC PLANNING

AN OVERVIEW

Since the concept of corporate strategy was first articulated in the early 1960s, managers have had to deal with the task of developing planning procedures that facilitate the formulation of meaningful long-range strategies. Despite the difficulty of the task, steady progress has been made. Today, in many companies, strategic planning is the central administrative device that is used to assure that strategic considerations dominate decision making at all levels.

Beginning with "Strategic Planning in Diversified Companies," the articles in this section chronicle both the growth and tools of contemporary strategic planning systems. The lead article describes the steps that most large companies follow in their strategic planning process.

"Balance 'Creativity' and 'Practicality' in Formal Planning" and "Shirt-Sleeve Approach to Long-Range Plans" address some of the major issues in the use of strategic planning systems. The first article warns that formal planning can drive out creative or entrepreneurial thinking. The authors propose ways to achieve a balance between creativity and practicality in strategic planning. The second article considers how companies can develop flexible plans and how smaller companies can engage in strategic planning.

In two of the earliest articles in our collection, Myles L. Mace and Norman Berg discuss some of the original insights that helped move the practice of strategic planning forward. Mace's thesis, that strategic planning will succeed only with the active support of the chief executive, rings as true today as it did in 1965. Berg's discussion of planning as a social and economic process also points to realities that have changed little since the article was first published.

The last two articles of this section chronicle just how far strategic planning has come. The authors of "Strategic Management for Competitive Advantage" describe four phases through which strategic planning efforts typically evolve. They define the fourth phase, strategic management, as "a system of corporate values, planning capabilities, or organizational responsibilities that couple strategic thinking with operational decision making at all levels and across all functional lines of authority in a company." Philippe Haspeslagh's "Portfolio Planning: Uses and Limits" describes another contemporary planning tool, portfolio planning, and considers how it can be used to benefit the development of diversified corporations.

Taken together, the articles in this section deal with both the theory and practice of strategic planning. The authors' suggestions and findings should help all managers forward their current approaches to strategic planning.

14
Strategic Planning in Diversified Companies

RICHARD F. VANCIL and PETER LORANGE

There are two main, but linked, dimensions to consider for the long-range strategic planning effort in diversified corporations, the authors indicate. One is vertical and operates through three organizational levels: headquarters, the divisions, and their functional departments. The other is chronological; as the process moves from level to level it also moves through three cycles: setting corporate objectives at the top, setting consonant business objectives and goals in the divisions, and establishing the required action programs at the functional level. The authors concentrate on the necessarily formal planning procedures in diversified companies, but executives in less complex organizations, where planning is more casual, will also find their insights valuable.

The widely accepted theory of corporate strategic planning is simple: using a time horizon of several years, top management reassesses its current strategy by looking for opportunities and threats in the environment and by analyzing the company's resources to identify its strengths and weaknesses. Management may draw up several alternative strategic scenarios and appraise them against the long-term objectives of the organization. To begin implementing the selected strategy (or continue a revalidated one), management fleshes it out in terms of the actions to be taken in the near future.

In smaller companies, strategic planning is a less formal, almost continuous process. The president and his handful of managers get together frequently to resolve strategic issues and outline their next steps. They need no elaborate, formalized planning system. Even in relatively large but undiversified corporations, the functional structure permits executives to evaluate strategic alternatives and their action implications on an ad hoc basis. The number of key executives involved in such decisions is usually small, and they are located close enough for frequent, casual get-togethers.

Large, diversified corporations, however, offer a different setting for planning. Most of them use the product/market division form of organizational structure to permit decentralized decision making involving many responsibility-center managers. Because many managers must be involved in decisions requiring coordinated action, informal planning is almost impossible.

Our focus in this article is on formal planning processes in such complex organizations. However, the thought processes in undertaking planning (as described in the opening paragraph) are essentially the same whether the organization is large or small. Therefore, even executives whose corporate situation permits informal planning may find that our delineation of the process helps them clarify their thinking. To this end, formalizing the steps in the process requires an explanation of the purpose of each step.

Three Levels of Strategy

All corporate executives use the words *strategy* and *planning* when they talk about the most important parts of their job. The president, obviously, is concerned about strategy; strategic planning is the essence of his job. A division general manager typically thinks of herself as the president of her own enterprise, responsible for its strategy and for the strategic planning needed to keep it vibrant and growing. Even an executive in charge of a functional activity, such as a division marketing manager, recognizes that his strategic planning is crucial; after all, the company's marketing strategy (or manufacturing strategy, or research strategy) is a key to its success.

These quite appropriate uses of strategy and planning have caused considerable confusion about long-range planning. This article attempts to dispel that confusion by differentiating among three types of "strategy" and delineating the interrelated steps involved in doing three types of "strategic planning" in large, diversified corporations. (Admittedly, although we think our definitions of strategy and planning are useful, others give different but reasonable meanings to these words.)

The process of strategy formulation can be thought of as taking place at the three organizational levels indicated in Exhibit 1: headquarters (corporate strategy), division (business strategy), and department (functional strategy). The planning processes leading to the formulation of these strategies can be labeled in parallel fashion as corporate planning, business planning, and functional planning. We have to define these notations briefly before constructing the framework of the planning process:

☐ *Corporate planning and strategy.* Corporate objectives are established at the top levels. Corporate planning, leading to the formulation of corporate strategy, is the process of (a) deciding on the company's objectives and goals, including the determination of which and

Exhibit 1.   Structure of a Divisionalized Corporation

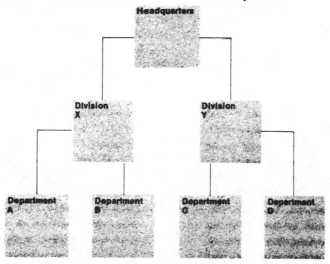

how many lines of business to engage in, (b) acquiring the resources needed to attain those objectives, and (c) allocating resources among the different businesses so that the objectives are achieved. (See the Appendix on page 215 for definitions of *objectives* and *goals* as used in this article.)

☐   *Business planning and strategy.*   Business planning, leading to the formulation of business strategy, is the process of determining the scope of a division's activities that will satisfy a broad consumer need, of deciding on the division's objectives in its defined area of operations, and of establishing the policies adopted to attain those objectives. Strategy formulation involves selecting division objectives and goals and establishing the charter of the business, after delineating the scope of its operations vis-à-vis markets, geographical areas, and/or technology.

Thus, while the scope of business planning covers a quite homogeneous set of activities, corporate planning focuses on the portfolio of the divisions' businesses. Corporate planning addresses matters relevant to the range of activities and evaluates proposed changes in one business in terms of its effects on the composition of the entire portfolio.

☐   *Functional planning and strategy.*   In functional planning, the departments develop a set of feasible action programs to implement division strategy, while the division selects—in the light of its objectives—the subset of programs to be executed and coordinates the action programs of the functional departments. Strategy formulation involves selecting objectives and goals for each functional area (marketing, production, finance, research, and so on) and determining the nature and sequence of actions to be taken by each area to achieve its objectives and goals. Programs are the building blocks of the strategic functional plans.

Obviously, these levels of strategy impinge on each other to some extent—for example, the corporation's choice of business areas overlaps the scope of division charters, and the delineation of the markets by the division can dictate, at the department level, the choice of strategy in the marketing function. But the distinction remains valid and useful.

Three-Cycle System

An important point to note about the planning process is that it requires formal interaction among the managers at different times. The more formal aspects—business planning, functional planning, and budgeting—are a way of organizing the interaction among managers at different levels in the hierarchy; one way of conceptualizing the planning process is as a series of meetings where executives are trying to arrive at decisions about actions to be taken. In each meeting, obviously, the basic question being addressed is the same: "What should we do?"

A detailed answer to that question is best developed by breaking it into a series of more specific questions dealt with in several meetings. These questions include: What are the objectives and goals of our company? What sort of environment can we expect to operate in? What businesses are we in? What alternative strategies could we pursue in those businesses? What other businesses should we enter? Should we make entry through an acquisition or through our research? What is the best combination of existing and new businesses to achieve corporate goals? What programs should the divisions undertake? What should each division's operating budget be?

The series of agreements among individuals in the corporate hierarchy begin on a very broad level and then are framed in progressively more detailed terms. The options are numerous in the early stages of this ordering process but narrow gradually to the final choice: a set of specific goals (budgets) for each responsibility center in the corporation. Initially, only a small group of corporate executives is involved in the process; later, more and more managers at lower levels become involved. The process eventually engages all the managers who must be committed to making the strategy work.

The reason companies adopt a complex planning process such as that shown in Exhibit 2 is made clear by the example of a multibillion-dollar, diversified corporation, headquartered in Europe and multinational, which had a well-established budgeting process but found "negotiating" the final budget in the closing months of each year to be difficult. The company was divisionalized, but it had decentralized very little initiative for examining strategic options.

Top management, increasingly uneasy over its ability to resolve all the strategic issues implicit in the budget, decided to ask the divisions to prepare formal five-year plans for its approval before drawing up the final corporate budget. The controller's department was to coordinate the preparation of the detailed plans. The company moved from a one-cycle planning system to a two-cycle system, as shown in Exhibit 3. The result was a flood of paperwork and very little strategic thinking on the division managers' part.

When top management reviewed the first set of five-year plans—a 20-pound packet of neat notebooks—it decided the results were unacceptable. It made suggestions to the divisions and requested a new set. This process was repeated no fewer than five times during the summer and early fall before all sides reached agreement and the budgeting could proceed.

After this experience, corporate management agreed that the procedure needed much improvement. So in the following year the company installed a three-cycle system. The first step required no comprehensive financial projections; instead, each division manager was asked to identify three or four strategic issues for presentation and discussion at headquarters. Agreement on those issues set the stage for orderly functional planning and budgeting, which had been so cumbersome before.

An important point to note about Exhibit 2 is its demarcation vertically, by cycles, and also horizontally, by activities at the three managerial levels. The degree of involvement at these levels is different in each planning cycle.

In the first cycle, corporate executives and division managers are primarily involved. A division manager draws his or her functional subordinates into discussions about the unit's strategy, but the functional managers' role usually remains informal. At this point the division manager regards the strategy as "his" or "hers," and then, seeking the head office's endorsement, formalizes it for better communication.

Once the division's strategy is set, the second cycle begins; here functional managers play a much more important part. In both that cycle and the budgeting cycle, they have the primary responsibility for developing detailed programs and budgets. The division manager and his or her staff are involved more or less actively in these two cycles, while top management limits itself to a review of division proposals.

Exhibit 2, of course, makes no pretense of depicting the planning process as it is universally practiced; it is only illustrative. Nor is the process as neat and orderly as it appears here. For one reason, the process does not start from scratch each year; the previous year's efforts feed into the first cycle. Moreover, while managers plan, the world keeps turning; so during a cycle events may oblige them to hold many meetings involving two levels.

Exhibit 2. Steps in the Planning Process

Formal planning cycles	Cycle 1					Cycle 2

Line executive responsible for planning

Chief executive

State corporate objectives — Call for division plans — Approve division objectives and strategy — State corporate strategy and tentative corporate and division goals — Call for division programs

Division manager

Define division charter, objectives, and strategy — Propose division goals and resource requirements — State division objectives and strategy — Call for program alternatives — Select best mix of program

Functional department manager

Identify program alternatives — Analyze programs and recommend best ones

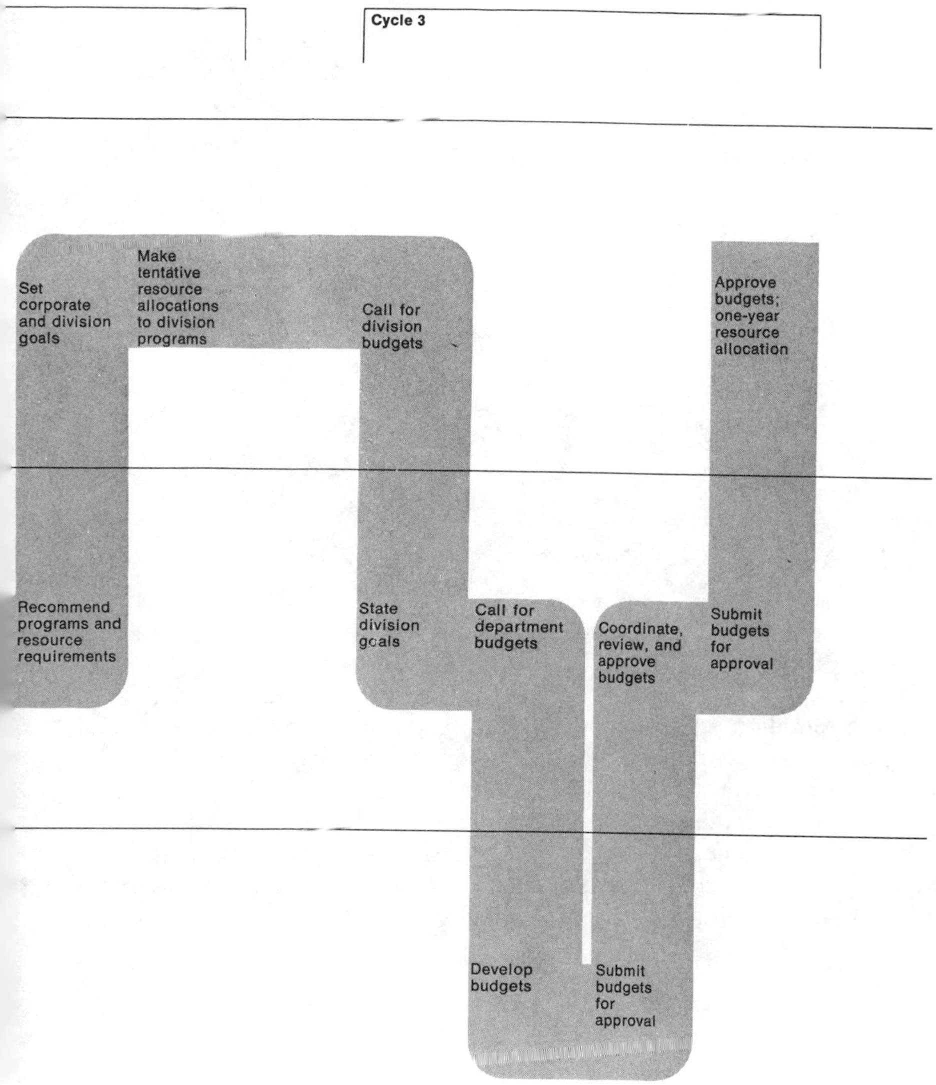

Set corporate and division goals

Make tentative resource allocations to division programs

Call for division budgets

Approve budgets; one-year resource allocation

Recommend programs and resource requirements

State division goals

Call for department budgets

Coordinate, review, and approve budgets

Submit budgets for approval

Develop budgets

Submit budgets for approval

Exhibit 3.   Examples of One-, Two-, and Three-Cycle Planning Processes

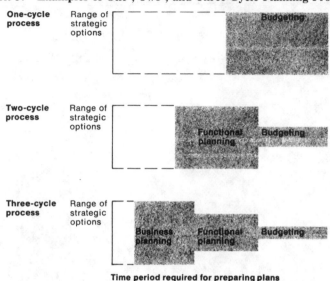

Time period required for preparing plans

First Cycle

The first cycle of a formal planning process serves a dual purpose: (1) to develop a tentative set of agreements between corporate management and the division managers about overall strategy and goals, and thereby (2) to provide focus for the more detailed planning in the next cycle. The process of reaching these initial agreements requires three discrete activities: establishing corporate objectives, drawing up division charters, and setting corporate goals. The ensuing discussion centers on these activities in a hypothetical (but representative) corporation whose fiscal year corresponds with the calendar year.

Establishing Corporate Objectives

In the initial dialogue between corporate and division management—starting in early February—the two groups form a statement of the corporation's purpose and objectives. Naturally, its scope and the degree of detail provided vary greatly from one company to another. Company X prepares a detailed statement, starting this year with the general assertion that it is a "systems-oriented, high-technology, multinational, and socially conscious company."

The principles set out mainly for strategic planning include breakthrough strategies (such as "seek projects, internal or external, waiting for application rather than invention"), resource management (such as "continuous emphasis on market orientation as opposed to product orientation"), financing ("utilization of the borrowing power of subsidiaries to escape the provisions of the debentures and foreign investment regulations"), public relations ("genuine concern for the quality of life, inside, and outside the company"), acquisitions, joint ventures, licensing ("export and import technology in the form of licenses or joint ventures, including third countries"), and so on.

The preparation of such a statement gives division managers guidance as they begin strategic planning for their businesses. So as a minimum the statement must include the intended company policies for allocating resources among the divisions. In effect, such policies constitute a statement of strategy for the entire corporation—although many business people are uncomfortable using the term "strategy" in such an abstract sense. Therefore, the delineation of an explicit statement of corporate strategy is often deferred until the final step in the first cycle.

Whether corporate strategy should be enunciated early or late in the planning process depends primarily on the degree of diversity in the company's businesses. In general, the more diverse the corporation, the less feasible it is to develop an explicit, cohesive strategy for its businesses and, therefore, the more desirable it is to make the resource allocation policies explicit at an early stage. On the other hand, less diversified companies frequently delay preparing a strategy statement until the division heads have developed strategic proposals for their own businesses. Many large corporations are divisionalized, but not so many are highly diversified. The more common practice is to delay the definition (or redefinition) of corporate strategy until it can be stated in fairly explicit terms.

Drawing Up Division Charters

In mid-March headquarters calls on all division managers to (a) write or review the "charter" of their division, specifying the scope of its activities and their objectives for the business as they define it, and (b) propose a strategy for the business and a tentative set of goals for the coming year.

Giving the initiative to the division managers at this step challenges them to think strategically about the scope of their activities and then propose a charter broad enough to permit them to contribute significantly to achieving corporate objectives. Formalizing this step in the planning process is an important device by which corporate management widens the horizons of division heads. An explicit charter also serves two secondary purposes: (1) it increases the likelihood of clear agreement between the top executives and the division manager about the scope of his activities, and (2) it reduces the risk of redundant efforts or competition between divisions.

Establishing a division's charter is not a discrete activity; it is inextricably connected to the task of identification and analysis of alternative strategies that exploit the charter selected. Obviously, the decision based on this analysis is crucial because the long-term performance of any division is a function of the strategy it adopts, and the performance of the company as a whole is likewise a function of the strategies of its particular businesses.

Although the initiative for identifying and analyzing strategic options lies with the division managers, guidelines that headquarters gives them for presentation of their proposals affect the way they pursue the task. Increasingly common is a request by corporate management that when division managers propose a strategy and specify goals, at the time they also present a statement of the alternative strategies which they have evaluated and rejected. The intent is not to permit the head office to second-guess the division managers' thinking, but to ensure that they used strategic thinking in arriving at their recommendations.

In mid-May, four to ten weeks after headquarters presents its request for division proposals, the unit's manager presents his or her recommendations to the corporate management group. The presentation consists at least of an integrated proposal for the division's charter, its objectives, the strategy to be pursued, and tentative goals. The recommendations may also include a general statement of the action programs that would be developed to implement the strategy (developed in more detail in the second cycle) and a crude estimate of the resources that would be required. Detailed financial data are usually not included at this step because such information is not necessary to evaluate the strategy and because the effort of preparing it may go to waste if the recommendations are modified.

In the ensuing discussions, which extend over several meetings in late spring, corporate management and each division chief work toward reaching an agreement about the appropriate division strategy and goals.

Setting Corporate Goals

By the middle of June top management has prepared an explicit statement of corporate strategy and goals. In some companies this document is, in effect, a set of decisions on how resources are to be allocated among the divisions, as well as a forecast of the results expected from each. In most cases, however, the statement is not intended to constitute a final resource allocation decision; rather, it is designed to provide feedback to the division managers about the corporate implications of the agreed-on business strategies. The presentation and discussion of corporate strategy and goals are also commonly used as a device to initiate the second cycle of the planning process.

The sum of the recommended division goals is likely to be inadequate to achieve the goals envisioned by headquarters for the entire organization. In trying to close this "planning gap," corporate management has only three choices:

1   It can improve division performance by pressing, during the review of division recommendations, for more aggressive strategies and more ambitious goals.
2   It can divert company resources into more promising businesses. This move may give rise to an acquisition program.
3   It can decide that the corporate goals are unrealistic and scale them down.

The fact that the corporation's goals normally are more or less the sum of those division goals sought by top management implies that headquarters is concerned with rather minor adjustments of this portfolio of goals. If so, the first cycle of formal planning has the salutary effect of providing an annual "mid-course correction" to the trajectory of the combined businesses. Momentum is a factor in the continued success of a diversified corporation—as with a rocket headed for the moon—and wise chief executives do not dissipate it needlessly. Rather, they nudge the bundle of energies represented by their division managers, trying to make minor adjustments early enough to be nondisruptive and at the same time affect the corporation's position several years ahead.

Occasionally—perhaps inevitably—a major corporate shift is necessary, affecting one of its businesses. Care must be taken to isolate the effect on the remaining businesses. In late spring a couple of years ago, for example, top management of a major diversified corporation went through its usual review of division strategic plans. One operation, created to develop a substantial new business for the corporation, presented its usual story: "Buying market share in this high-technology business is very expensive, breakeven is still two or three years away, and additional investment of several hundred million dollars is required. But the eventual profits will be enormous."

The division's management concluded that it was progressing about as expected and that its strategy was sound, and it recommended continued aggressive investment. With minor modifications, top management approved the proposal. Three months later the company abruptly announced that the business would be discontinued and the investment written off.

Poor planning? Obviously, the decision to enter the business was a mistake. But implementation of that decision, and the planning done to minimize the investment exposure without compromising the chances for success, were probably sound. There are two important lessons here about the process of corporate planning:

1   Strategic decisions—like this divestment—are not made in accordance with some precise timetable. They are made whenever top management reaches the conclusion that interference in a unit's affairs is necessary.

2   Formal planning procedures are *not* intended to facilitate strategic decisions such as this—if only because a division manager rarely recommends the disposal of his or her operation. Rather, formal corporate strategic planning has the more modest, if no less crucial, purpose of seeking to optimize the collective thrust of the continuing businesses.

Approving a division's strategic plan but closing the unit three months later is not hypocrisy or poor planning. The ax is much more merciful than the slow strangulation of providing inadequate resources. In the meantime, until the ax falls, division management must prove the viability of its business. For its part, headquarters must not fail to recognize the difference between a sound plan and a sound business. A sound plan deserves approval, but only top management can decide whether the business is sound enough to continue implementation of that plan.

Second Cycle

The second planning cycle also has two purposes. First, each division head and his functional subordinates should reach tentative agreement on the action programs to be implemented over the next few years. Second, the involvement of functional managers in the long-range planning process should deepen and sharpen the strategic focus of the business and thus provide a better basis for the even more detailed budgeting task to follow.

The division manager in Company X initiates the functional planning process in the middle of June after reaching tentative agreement with top management about his or her organization's charter, objectives, strategy, and goals. In the first planning meeting with subordinates, he or she briefly reviews the corporate/division dialogue that has just concluded and describes the approved division objectives and strategy.

At this time the division manager usually does not make explicit the sales or profit goals, even though tentative agreement on targets has been reached. There are two reasons for dealing in generalities at this point. First, being specific might constrain the thinking of the functional managers, who have the chance in this cycle to make a creative contribution toward achieving the division's objectives. Second, division goals will become final only when corporate management has approved the unit's programs and allocated resources to implement them.

Long-range planning by functional managers is conceptually a simple process, being limited by the tentative agreements reached in the first cycle. It is operationally more complex than the planning activity in the first cycle, however, since it requires substantially more detailed plans and involves many more people. The purpose of such "programming"—so called because the activity focuses on specific programs—is to translate the division's externally oriented business strategy into an internally directed, coordinated set of activities designed to implement it. Inasmuch as the resources available for implementation are always limited, programming must help ensure their optimal use.

Obviously, the scope, magnitude, and duration of a program depend on the nature of the goal. In the broadest sense, a product division of a diversified corporation might be conceived of as a "program." The division managers' goals may be stated in simple financial terms and extend over several years, and their discretion may be constrained only by a charter for their product line and the availability of corporate resources. In such a situation, the division program may be international in scope, almost unlimited in breadth of product line, and may involve hundreds of millions of dollars in expenditures. At the other end of the spectrum, the sales manager for a district in the northeast region of that division may have been charged with improving market penetration by 10% over the next 18 months. His or her actions also fulfill the definition of a program.

Formalized Programming

The need to formalize the programming process grows as functional interdependence in the business increases and as more time is required to evaluate the effectiveness of alternative functional plans. Formalization is designed to improve the specification of programs and the matching of programs and goals.

The charter and strategy for the business and the objectives and goals that top management has set for it limit the functional manager's strategic planning. Within those constraints, however, she may still enjoy very broad discretion concerning the best course to take. Her challenge is to devise more effective ways to combine the available resources in order to achieve her goals. A useful way to look at the specification of programs is in terms of the chronology for involvement of the functional departments. In a typical manufacturing enterprise there are four types of programs to be developed:

1. *Existing revenue programs.* An example is the development of a set of marketing programs for the existing product lines.

2. *New revenue programs.* Planning the development and introduction of new products is an example.

3. *Manufacturing programs.* Typically, sales forecasts by product line are furnished to the manufacturing function, which develops the programs necessary to meet the revenue goals in the marketing programs.

4. *Support programs.* Managers of other functional support activities, such as administration, may also get involved in the development of programs.

The programming process, even when formalized, is inevitably haphazard because it requires repeated interaction among the departments. The intended result is a plan that is integrated like the two sides of a coin. On one side is the set of action programs and on the other a coordinated statement of the resources needed by each functional manager to execute his or her part of the program.

A major purpose of the formal programming process is to review the ongoing programs to see whether they can be expected to fulfill the goals for which they were designed. Or, if more effective programs have been devised, the existing ones must be modified or discontinued. At the same time, some "old" programs may be nearing completion, and new ones will need approval if the goals are to be met. Programming also involves coordination of functional activities to ensure that the selected programs can be implemented efficiently. Each functional department must understand the implications of a set of programs for its own activities, and the department managers must accept the tasks assigned them and the resources to be made available to them.

In our mythical Company X, after much analysis and discussion the division manager and his or her functional subordinates finally agree by the end of August on a set of programs to recommend to headquarters. This time, in contrast to the first, a more elaborate presentation is in order and a large number of managers—corporate and division, line and staff—may attend.

Third Cycle

The third cycle of the formal planning process needs little explanation. Naturally, throughout the planning process top managers and division executives often discuss the allocation of resources among the divisions. But it becomes the focus of attention in the last step of the second cycle, when the divisions have completed their program proposals and sent them to the head office for approval. At this point (mid-September at Company X), decisions on allocation of resources can be made, subject to final approval when the detailed budgets are submitted (in mid-November). These general points are worth making here:

☐ Resource allocation is almost always a very informal, unstructured process, heavily dependent on the skill in advocacy and political weight of the executives concerned. Since it is also a continuous process, by the end of the second cycle the risk of serious mismatch between programs and resources is unlikely—if headquarters/division communications have been good.

☐ Although programs may have an expected life of several years, resources are usually allocated for only one year at a time. Whether top management will make a commitment to meet next year's needs will depend on the scale and timing flexibility of the program in the competition for resources.

☐ Although resource allocation to projects is based on a perception of the desirability of each, corporate planning attempts to ensure that each also fits into a portfolio of undertakings.

Raising the Odds

The formal long-range planning process in large, diversified corporations is both simple and complex. Conceptually, the process is very simple—a progressive narrowing of strategic choices—although it may involve many steps along that path. Operationally, the process is far more complex than the activities we have described because the formal part of the process is only the tip of the iceberg. Good strategic planning can take place only when qualified managers engage in creative thinking—and creativity, by definition, cannot be produced on a schedule.

Yet there is little doubt that formalizing the planning process is worthwhile; it ensures that managers at all levels will devote some time to strategic thinking, and it guarantees each of them an audience for his or her ideas. While formal strategic planning cannot guarantee good ideas, it can increase the odds sufficiently to yield a handsome payoff.

Appendix: Objectives and Goals

It is worth differentiating between *objectives* and *goals*, since these terms are used separately here.

Objectives are general statements describing the size, scope, and style of the enterprise in the long term. They embody the values and aspirations of the managers, based on their assessment of the environment and of the capabilities and health of the corporation. For example, the financial objective of a large, diversified, multinational corporation might be to rank in the top 10% worldwide in compound rate of growth in earnings per share.

Goals are more specific statements of the achievements targeted for certain deadlines. At the corporate level these statements are likely to include such aspects as sales, profits, and EPS targets. Annual budgets constitute goals at all levels in the organization.

15

Balance "Creativity" and "Practicality" in Formal Planning

JOHN K. SHANK, EDWARD G. NIBLOCK,
and WILLIAM T. SANDALLS, JR.

This article contends that to be effective every formal long-range planning system much achieve a compromise between "creativity" and "practicality"—goals for planning that are often in conflict. The authors also argue that the problem of maintaining a satisfactory balance can be directly addressed by varying the design features of the planning/budgeting interface. After specifying the set of design features, they go on to show how six companies have used various combinations of them to achieve an appropriate degree of creativity that is consistent with practicality.

Every company engaged in long-range planning would like its efforts to attain two fundamental but often conflicting goals. On the one hand, management wants the planning function to reflect pragmatic judgments based on what is possible. On the other hand, it wants planning to reflect forward-looking, assertive, and creative thinking.

The primary way of enhancing "realism" is to give the planning function a clear action orientation. Generally, this is done by relating long-range planning closely with short-term budgetary control. And this is where the difficulty lies. While close linkage between planning and budgeting puts the stress on the desired action, it also promotes a focus that can be disastrous to mind-stretching "reach."

We are making the assumption, of course, that for the formal planning system to operate effectively it must achieve a balanced compromise between realism and reach. In this article, we shall argue that these dual objectives need not be mutually exclusive. In fact, our purpose is to illustrate that the long-range planning system can be structured to achieve both an action orientation and a focus on mind stretching. Our discussion will proceed in two steps.

In the first stage, it is important for long-range planners to begin thinking about the realism-reach trade-off as a problem they can do something about. That "something" involves varying those aspects of the long-range planning system which relate to its interface with the short-range budgeting process. In this regard, we shall summarize the general features of the planning system which relate to plan-budget linkage, illustrating both the "tight" and "loose" form of each "linkage device."

Then, in the second step, we shall illustrate some of the most interesting devices actually being used. These reflect the experiences of six companies which we selected because they (a) are successful in terms of compound earnings growth and (b) have long-range planning systems with both action-oriented and mind-stretching characteristics.

In short, we believe that management can control the focus a planning system will exhibit with respect to the realism versus reach problem. It may not always be possible to achieve a totally satisfactory trade-off, but we shall describe the mechanisms being used by a sample of successful companies to achieve what for each of them is a satisfactory compromise.

Plan-Budget Design

On close examination, it quickly becomes apparent that the different aspects of plans and budgets can be linked in three distinct ways:

1 *Content linkage* relates to the correspondence between the data presented in the plan document and that presented in the budget.
2 *Organizational linkage* focuses on the relationship between the units responsible for planning and budgeting.
3 *Timing linkage* concerns the sequencing of the annual planning and budgeting cycles.

Within each of these categories, there are several specific features of the planning system that can be manipulated to influence the extent of plan-budget linkage. Let us take a closer look at each of these linkage devices.

Financial Features

One important feature of content linkage is the amount of detail in the financial statements included in the plan document. The tightest linkage would be to include statements with the same level of detail as in the monthly reporting package which compares budgeted with actual results. The loosest linkage would be not to include financial statements at all.

Another design feature related to the financial content is the level of rounding in the plan document. Although it may not seem particularly significant at first blush, there is evidence that rounding to a much higher level in the plan than in the budget (e.g., millions of dollars in the plan versus thousands in the budget) can foster a kind of mental distinction between plan and budget numbers which reduces the tendency to view the plan as solely a long-range budget. This can in turn facilitate a much more creative planning effort by making it clear that the managers do not have to commit themselves (in a budgetary sense) to delivering the planned financial results.

Still another important content feature is the conformity between plan and budget numbers for those years which are common to both documents. If the numbers differ, planning may face a credibility gap. Many companies, however, feel that allowing such differences is critical to maintaining the aggressive forward thrust of the planning effort.

For example, one conglomerate includes in the first year of its five-year plan the earnings from acquisitions that are projected to be closed during the next twelve months but which are not yet finalized. The company does not include these earnings in the budgeted results for the next year which line managers are asked to commit themselves to deliver.

Several other companies show differences between planned and budgeted profit for the next year because the two documents are prepared at different times. The one prepared later in the year would reflect the latest thinking, and this might differ from projections made earlier in the year.

Situations like these may or may not be desirable, but they certainly reflect loose content linkage. If numerical differences are permitted, one way of moving back toward tightness is to require that some kind of formal reconciliation of them be included in the plan. Many companies which permit differences require such reconciliation.

Related to plan-budget conformity for years common to both documents is the issue of the uniformity of the numbers for any given year as they appear in succeeding annual plan documents. If the planned figures for any one future period change significantly each time a plan is put together, the perceived realism of the planning effort can suffer.

Our evidence suggests, however, that rarely do companies require the numbers for a given year to be "cast in concrete" the very first time that year appears in a plan document. This degree of linkage is probably unrealistically tight.

As we shall illustrate later, a few companies do require formal explanations in the plan for any changes in the projections related to a given future year. This clearly reflects a tighter linkage form of this planning-system variable than would otherwise be reflected by complete freedom to change future years' projections at each iteration of the planning cycle. At least a few companies feel that some tightness at this point is desirable.

A final important design feature is the structure of the content of the plan. In most companies, the budget is structured in terms of the organizational units which will be responsible for carrying it out. Such an approach

is a fundamental part of what is often referred to as "responsibility accounting."

Given this situation, it is possible to restructure the plan to focus on
programs rather than on the organizational units. The total expenditures for
a given year are the same in either case, but there is nevertheless a distinctly
looser impact on the way in which the plan document is interpreted.

Organizational Relationships

The major design feature in this category is the relationship between the
organizational units responsible for the long-range planning and those responsible for the budgetary-control processes. The loosest form is to lodge
planning and budgeting in separate organizational channels reporting to different top-level executives. The tightest form is to have the two functions
combined in one department.

Even in those situations in which planning and budgeting are separated
in terms of formal organizational relationships, there is wide latitude in the
extent to which the controller is formally involved in the long-range planning
effort. Naturally, the loosest linkage situation is to have scant involvement
on the part of the controllers. However, because of their expertise in analyzing and communicating financially oriented data, it is probably neither
possible nor desirable to exclude them completely from the formal planning
effort.

Between this extreme of separate planning and budgeting channels and
the complete integration of these functions lies a very broad middle ground
which can be probed to achieve an appropriate level of involvement for any
given company. Among the relevant questions to ask in this regard are the
following:

☐ Does the controller provide staff support for the preparation of
the financial data in the plan document?

☐ Does the controller review the plan document before it is finalized?

☐ Does the controller have any direct or indirect responsibility for
approving the plan?

☐ Does the controller have any direct or indirect responsibility for
monitoring planned financial results against actual results?

The more questions of this kind that can be answered *yes*, the tighter
the plan-budget linkage, even though the functions may officially be separate.

Timing Considerations

The most important design feature here is concerned with the sequencing
of the annual planning and budgeting cycles. If the two cycles are carried
out sequentially, which one is done first? How much time elapses between
the completion of the first cycle and the beginning of the one which follows

it? If the two cycles are undertaken concurrently, what is the relationship between initiation dates, completion dates, and approval dates?

The loosest timing linkage is to have the planning cycle done before the budgeting cycle and to have several months elapse between the two. One major food products manufacturer, for example, completes the annual planning cycle in February and does not begin the budgeting phase until November. Situations like this are least inhibiting to the achievement of "reach" in the planning effort.

The tightest form of the design feature related to sequencing would be to complete the budgeting cycle first and to have the planning cycle follow it with minimal elapsed time in between. Since the budgeting cycle almost always concludes in the last quarter of the fiscal year, it is rare to find a company in which the planning cycle comes last. There are, however, many companies that undertake the two cycles concurrently.

In general, the more the budget process precedes the plan preparation— in terms of initiation, completion, and approval dates—the tighter the linkage, since the budgeting focus will tend to dominate the joint planning-budgeting effort.

One final timing-related design feature is the time horizon for the long-range planning effort. Usually, the shorter this span, the closer the relationship between the budget and the planning process and thus the tighter the plan-budget linkage. Conversely, the longer the time frame, the easier it becomes to clearly distinquish the process from budgeting and thus the looser the plan-budget linkage.

Nowhere in the whole range of system-design features is the trade-off between realism and reach more clearly defined than in the choice of a planning horizon. The longer the time frame, the wider the range of factors which can be varied and thus the broader the range of strategies which can be considered in moving the company toward its long-range objectives.

At the same time, a longer time span increases the uncertainty regarding environmental assumptions, corporate strengths, and the financial parameters which shape the strategy formulation and evaluation process. At some point, uncertainty overcomes the gain in flexibility.

What constitutes an appropriate time horizon certainly varies from industry to industry. It is probably easier, for example, for most public utilities to do fifteen-year planning than it is for defense-aerospace companies to do five-year planning. Within the reasonable range for any given industry, however, the longer the time considerations, the looser the plan-budget linkage. Furthermore, in our opinion, a planning horizon of three or four years reflects a heavy emphasis on realism at the expense of reach, regardless of the industry.

Linkage Examples

In the preceding section of this article, we concentrated on a general framework for considering the plan-budget problem. Now, we shall turn our attention to some of the interesting devices actually being used by the six manufacturing companies that we selected as a small but representative sample of those which have (a) participated in formal planning studies, (b) earned the reputation for having both action-oriented and creative planning systems, and (c) been highly successful in terms of compound EPS growth. Since we believe it unlikely that their records of sustained performance could have been achieved without the help of good planning, it should be revealing to examine in some detail how these companies cope with the linkage problem.

The six companies we observed were Cincinnati Milacron, General Mills, Quaker Oats, Raytheon, Toro, and Warnaco. In them, we encountered such a large number of different linkage devices that we concluded the variety of specific links is limited only by the imagination of the personnel. We shall use the same categories as in the preceding section in reviewing the most interesting linkage practices in these sample companies.

But, first, a note of caution. It is not our intent to propose *the* right answer to the linkage problem, but only to identify some of the more important factors to be considered in determining *a* right answer for a given company at a specific point in time.

Content-Related Approaches

One of the most innovative attempts to use structure as a mechanism to overcome the creativity-practicality problem is the distinct separation between group and division planning at Warnaco. Each division manager prepares a three-year plan, while each group vice president plans five years out.

Warnaco's objective here is to encourage the group vice presidents to think in more general and longer range terms. They then carry this framework with them to meetings with their division managers. This encourages them to do more creative planning.

It is important to note that the formats of these two plans are much different with the divisional plans being done in much greater detail than the group plans. This serves to focus the group manager's attention on the strategy of the group itself rather than on the specific details of the divisions' operating programs.

A mechanism we mentioned earlier to overcome the problem of loose linkage is the comparison of a plan with its predecessor from a year earlier. Consider, for example, this situation taken from the planning records of a large paper manufacturer. Here are this company's profit projections for 1971 as shown in:

Five-year plan done in 1966	$60 million
Five-year plan done in 1967	$50 million
Five-year plan done in 1969	$36 million
1971 budget prepared in 1970	$16 million

At the very least, a plan-to-plan comparison would have called the company's attention to the increasing lack of realism the further the projections extended into the future. The threat of having to formally justify this ever-receding bonanza might have served as a sobering influence to the planners.

It is also possible to use plan-to-plan comparisons to overcome the problems of overly conservative forecasting. Thus, if the paper company's profit projections had demonstrated an ascending pattern, the happy surprise of realizing more profits than expected might also have been accompanied by the undesirable development of capacity shortages and missed market opportunities. In such a case, a plan-to-plan comparison could serve as an impetus for more expansive projections.

Of the six companies we visited, only General Mills requires the reporting and justification of significant changes from the preceding year's plan. At General Mills, management feels that this checking device is sufficiently useful in preventing blue-sky fantasizing to justify its risk in terms of discouraging open-ended mind stretching.

A third content-related mechanism worth noting is the relationship between the plan and budget formats. As we noted earlier, if the two documents differ in form and style, it is more difficult to directly transpose the plan to the budget. Both Toro and Raytheon approach a program format for planning and a functional format for budgeting, but they also retain the program and project breakout in the budget as well as the functional allocation. In the other companies we sampled, this split is less distinct since the divisions are largely organized by program area or product line. We view this loosening device as a very significant one that has potential applicability in many companies.

Finally, all six of the sample companies vary the level of detail between the plan and the budget. It is interesting to note, however, that the absolute level of detail in the plan also varies significantly among the six companies. Cincinnati Milacron shows only very highly aggregated summary data, whereas Raytheon's plans approach the same level of detail as its budgets. The other four companies fall in between these extreme approaches.

Organization Coordination

At the corporate level, it is important to understand who is coordinating the planning and who is coordinating the budgeting. The basic question here is whether the company wants to split the two processes. The splitting of this coordination function has the effect of loosening the linkage between planning and budgeting. Both Toro and Cincinnati Milacron provide excellent examples of this.

At Toro, planning is coordinated by the corporation planner and budgeting by the controller. No formal attempt is made to ensure that these two functions proceed in a similar fashion. Cincinnati Milacron handles this in much the same way that Toro does.

At General Mills, the end result is the same but the mechanisms are much more complex, with coordination being handled by groups instead of individuals.

Different handling at the division level can also affect the linking process. The basic split here is between strategy formulation and the quantified explication of that strategy. While in almost all instances both are coordinated by the division manager, the degree of delegation of the quantification phase can vary significantly.

It is noteworthy that there is very little divergence in the way quantification of plan results is handled by the six sample companies. All of them largely delegate this phase to the divisional controller. This has a loosening effect by focusing the division manager's attention on policy rather than on detailed profit and loss information.

Although it is not a "device" in the usual sense, a company's informal communication process can function in a way that tightens the linkage between planning and budgeting. A great deal of informal information transfer across the corporate/divisional interface increases top management's cognizance of what is in the plan and how it relates to the budget. The presence of informal channels of communication may make top management appear to have an omniscient awareness of these issues, even if this is not the case.

At Cincinnati Milacron, where the planning and budgeting systems are very closely linked, one division manager stated that he really felt strongly committed to delivering the performance projected in his five-year plan. At Quaker Oats and Toro, where there are loose linkage systems, two division managers reported similar feelings of commitment. It is difficult for us to assess what precise influence the informal communication processes in the foregoing companies had in forging the personal commitments of these three division managers to delivering the planned results. However, the counter-intuitive coincidence of loose systems and strong commitments at least offers circumstantial evidence that this influence does exist and should not be overlooked.

Time Horizons

A separation in time between the end of the planning cycle and the beginning of the budgeting cycle, as we noted earlier, has the effect of loosening the linkage between the two processes. When the time to worry about next year's performance commitment is still several months away, it is easier to be expansive about the future. In addition, since forecast conditions are always changing, the more time that elapses subsequent to submission of the plan, the easier it is to justify a revision in the budget.

Of the six sample companies, only Raytheon pursues its planning and budgeting cycles concurrently. Cincinnati Milacron has a six-month separation between the end of planning and the beginning of budgeting. General Mills, Quaker Oats, Toro, and Warnaco all have at least a two- to three-month separation.

In general, as the number of years in the budget is extended, or the number of years in the plan contracted, the similarity between the plan and the budget increases. Different time horizons for the two processes tend to emphasize the different purposes of each. Five of the six companies we sampled have either a four- or five-year planning range and a one- or two-year budget span. The exception is Warnaco, which we noted previously.

Appropriate Equilibrium

Individual linkage devices impact on the planning system by facilitating an overall planning effort which is either more creative or action oriented. As is evident from the preceding discussion, some devices serve to promote a stronger action orientation in planning while others encourage more creativity.

Since a single planning system will utilize several devices which may have opposing effects on the plan-budget balance, an "algebraic" sum of the devices is needed to determine where the planning system is located on the linkage continuum. This plays a pivotal role in achieving an appropriate equilibrium between divergent requirements for both creative and action-oriented planning.

Whether or not a particular planning balance is appropriate for a given company hinges on the corporate setting. Thus, if the underlying essence of planning is to improve a company's ability to cope with changes, it follows that, as the changes are realized, the need for specific forms of planning will also change. In other words, a dynamic corporate setting may call for heavy emphasis on creativity at one point in time and heavy emphasis on practicality at another. The implication is that, as a company's needs change, devices must be added or subtracted in order to adjust the balance between these planning objectives.

The concept of a dynamic corporate setting seems particularly relevant to the four of the six sample companies which are now diversifying extensively beyond the boundaries of their traditional industries. Consider:

☐ The Toro Company is changing from a manufacturer of lawn mowers and snow blowers to a broad-based participant in the environmental beautification market.

☐ General Mills's Fashion Division, which was established only three years ago, already contributes significantly to the company's sales and earnings and competes in markets dramatically different from those served by Cheerios and other ready-to-eat cereals.

☐ Quaker Oats, in its most recent fiscal year, derived 25% of its sales from nongrocery product sources, including 12% from Fisher-Price Toys. The company has since further diversified in nongrocery areas through acquisition of Louis Marx & Co. Toys and the Needlecraft Corporation of America.

☐ Cincinnati Milacron, the largest manufacturer of machine tools in the world, is seeking points of entry into the minicomputer and semiconductor markets.

A dynamic corporate setting, however, is not necessarily dependent on the diversification activity of a company. For example:

☐ Cincinnati Milacron, with 80% of its sales in the machine tool industry, contends with market cycles which brought machine tool sales volume in 1970 down 50% to 60% below the peak reached two years earlier.

☐ The Raytheon Equipment Division, a defense contractor, faces rapid turnover in electronics technology—a contract bidding process that sometimes makes a ticket in the Irish Sweepstakes look like a sure bet—and concomitant uncertainties and headaches in dealing with mercurial government customers.

☐ Warnaco, competing with 30,000 other companies in the apparel industry, finds that although total sales volume is relatively stable, individual markets are highly volatile as fashions come and go in quick succession.

Whether the result of extensive diversification programs or corporate response to the challenges of traditional markets, all six companies are in a state of perpetual change.

Given this state of flux, it is significant to note that the planning systems in five of the companies have recently been changed, are in the process of being changed, or will be changed in the near future. (The exception is Raytheon Equipment.) To illustrate:

☐ At Toro, David M. Lilly, Chairman and Chief Executive Officer, recently projected the development of looser linkage between the planning and budgeting systems.

☐ At General Mills, the 1971 planning instructions announced a procedure to highlight where the 1971 plan deviated from the 1970 plan; the same instructions reemphasized a year-old procedure which required "new" businesses to be differentiated from "present" businesses.

☐ At Quaker Oats, the corporate planner foresees the emergence of tighter linkage as the company becomes acclimated to its new divisionalized structure.

☐ At Cincinnati Milacron, a new planning system is in its first year of operation; this system is very loosely linked to budgeting and shifts the burden of planning from the division managers to the group managers.

☐ At Warnaco, as we noted earlier, a systems modification has been implemented; this requires group vice presidents to plan five years into the future and their subordinate division managers three years ahead.

In seeking a comprehensive explanation of the planning system changes just described, we find particularly pertinent the observation that management control systems must be consistent with top management's objectives in order to be truly effective. If the same can be said of formal planning systems, then it follows that a change in an effective planning system is usually triggered by a change in top management's objectives.

The implication here is that whether or not a given change improves a planning system may be beside the point. To paraphrase Marshall McLuhan, the planning system and the changes made in it may be "the medium that is the message"—that is, the message from top management.

Criterion of Consistency

In this section, we shall examine more closely two of the planning system changes previously mentioned to see what inferences about top management's objectives we can draw from them.

Since 1971, Cincinnati Milacron has been pulling out of a severe recession that afflicted the entire machine tool industry. Operating management's ordeal during the past two years has been something akin to a day-to-day struggle. As the company has begun to emerge from this traumatic experience, top management has installed a new planning system to allow maximum opportunity for broad-level mind stretching. Furthermore, the burden of planning has been shifted upward to a level of management where there exists the opportunity and authority to implement a diversification program.

The message of Cincinnati Milacron's two planning-system changes appears to be rather straightforward: top management wants aggressive diversification planning.

In his memorandum covering General Mills's 1971 planning instructions, James P. MacFarland, Chairman and Chief Executive Officer, indicated the need for a more aggressive capital investment program in the years ahead to achieve the company's sales and earnings objectives. He also referred to progress in the control of capital use and to a change in the planning procedures which would allow top management to focus easily on the changes made subsequent to the previous planning cycle. His general instructions described this procedural change in more detail and reiterated a year-old procedure which separated the planning for new businesses from that for current businesses.

In our judgment, it is a fair guess that it will be a tougher task to revise estimates upward in order to justify additional capital for a current business than to submit new estimates in order to justify seed capital for a new business. The message of the announcement of both a new procedure and reemphasis on an old one appears to be that the encouragement of heavier investments is intended for new and not for current businesses.

(This message, incidentally, is clearly reflected in the chairman's and president's letter to General Mills's stockholders and employees in the 1971 Annual Report.)

The procedure at General Mills of separating current and new businesses is particularly noteworthy in that it creates an opportunity to differentiate the planning perspectives, and to apply different standards of expectation to each type of business. In this manner, top management can encourage division managers to be creative in planning for their new businesses and action oriented in planning for their current businesses.

Future-oriented businesses will be best suited for loosely linked planning/budgeting systems. As the potential of a business begins to be realized, tighter linkage will be desirable in order to transform promises into results. At that point, a balance between creative planning and action-oriented planning would be especially appropriate. Later, as the business exhausts its growth potential and evolves into a "cash generator," even tighter linkage will be desirable to accommodate the corporation's capital needs for the next generation of new businesses.

In short, recognition of divergent corporate objectives for both the mature and the future-oriented business is manifested in different degrees of linkage in their respective planning/budgeting systems. As evident at Quaker Oats, for example, a divisionalized company can find itself at several points—up and down—on the linkage continuum at the same time. In evaluating whether or not any point on the continuum is "right" or "wrong," the sole criterion must be its consistency with corporate objectives.

Conclusion

To be effective, every formal long-range planning system must achieve a workable compromise between creativity and practicality—twin goals that are often in conflict. This problem of maintaining a satisfactory balance between "reach" and "realism" can be directly addressed by varying those design features of planning which relate to its interface with budgeting. However, in order to put in perspective the importance of loosening the plan/budget linkage, it is important to consider the role of informal communications and the personalities of management.

At the corporate/division interface, companies that have a great deal of informal communication transfer are likely to be constantly aware of what was written in the plan and how that relates to the budget. This has the effect of very tightly linking the plan and the budget, even in structurally loose systems, unless management makes a conscious effort to demonstrate that this is not wanted. Even if this intent is demonstrated at the corporate level, there still may be tight linkage built in at the division level because of the division manager's personality.

Generally speaking, the divisional planning and budgeting are either both done by the division manager herself or at least coordinated by her. As she coordinates the preparation of the budget, she often feels—either consciously or subconsciously—an obligation to justify the value of the plan by reflecting much of it in the budget which represents her short-term game plan for the division.

Briefly, loosening devices have much broader applications than to just those companies which have structurally tight linkage systems. In fact, some of them may be needed in any action-oriented planning system.

We believe that managers should consider these devices as variables they can and should manipulate in the interest of more effective planning. Viewed in this context, the linkage continuum can be considered as a powerful interpreter of the top-management objectives implicit in the planning system.

Although at first this may seem to be counter-intuitive, we believe that it is not the planning system which generates corporate objectives but rather the corporate objectives which dictate the appropriate planning system. We are neither proposing that there is a "correct" form for any of these design features, nor that it is always possible to structure a planning system so that "realistic creativity" is ensured.

We do believe, however, that "realistic reach" in planning is not just an illusory phenomenon which exists independent of management's actions. Rather, it is well within management's control to influence the focus of the efforts by changing the structure of the planning system. That, we feel, is all any manager can ask.

16
Shirt-Sleeve Approach to Long-Range Plans

ROBERT E. LINNEMAN and JOHN D. KENNELL

One bothersome aspect about the future when you're trying to plan is all the un-certainty that surrounds it. In past years forecasters have tried to cope with the problem by coming up with a best guess—a "most probable" scenario—by extrapolating from trends, making a few assumptions, and then suggesting that management plan as if the best guess were the future. More recently this approach has fallen into disfavor as recognition has sunk in that, when you sum up all the variables involved which support such a scenario, the odds are very much against it. And the conse-quences for a company can be monumental. Now forecasters are hedging their bets by developing several widely varying scenarios, and urging management to develop a strategy that may allow an organization to survive and prosper under any of them. But what about the smaller company that doesn't have such resources as a forecasting staff and sophisticated computer hardware and software packages at its disposal? The authors believe that multiple-scenario analysis can be of value to its management as well through a less sophisticated "shirt-sleeve" approach, which they describe in this article.

Forecasting and making long-range plans that are based on forecasts are inevitable. And while the importance of forecasting is recognized, so is its main limitation: too many key variables are just too unpredictable. Listen to the laments in 1974 after two humbling years for forecasters:

Roderick G. Dederick, chief economist for Chicago's Northern Trust Co.: "We did not provide advance warning to our managements of the distressing situation into which the U.S. economy has drifted over the past several years."

Milton W. Hudson, economist for Morgan Guaranty Trust Co.: "We've decided that economic forecasting is so deficient that we're not going to perpetuate any more confusion. There is something misleading about giving people what purport to be accurate numbers when they are really no such thing.''

Perhaps Paul Samuelson isolated a major problem: ''I think that the greatest error in forecasting is not realizing how important are the probabilities of events other than those everyone is agreeing upon.''[1]

Planners usually choose one ''most probable'' future environment as the basis of their thinking. They estimate uncontrollable variables as best they can, and a strategy is then developed to achieve the company's objectives. But what recourse does a company have when, because of faulty forecasting, the assumed values of key variables are wrong and its chosen strategy is inappropriate? Even tactical contingency plans may fail to compensate for a faulty strategy.

As a consequence, many companies now consider a range of plans that cover several possible environments rather than plans with only one outlook for the future. A partial listing of these companies includes: Dow Chemical, Exxon Corporation, Ford Motor Company, Hewlett-Packard, Marine Midland Bank, Olin Corporation, Sun Company, Uniroyal, and Weyerhaeuser. How-to-do-it literature is scanty, however, and the approaches described usually require a large planning staff, a highly structured long-range planning process, and sometimes even computerized routines.

Perhaps the greatest benefits can be gained from a highly sophisticated approach, but we contend that even a ''shirt-sleeve'' method improves appreciation of the possibilities of the future. Consequently, smaller companies—or even larger companies without extensive planning resources—can devise a more adaptive strategy by using a simplified approach in considering several possible environments.[2]

Our purpose in this article is to give a simplified, ten-step approach to developing flexible strategies through what we call multiple-scenario analysis (MSA). Exhibit 1 illustrates the ten steps in MSA. (Although the process is presented in a step-by-step manner, the loop arrows indicate that it is not necessarily sequential. Multiple-scenario analysis involves many experiments that usually necessitate backtracking.)

Simplified Analysis

This ten-step procedure assumes that a person, or perhaps a committee, can devote only part of his (or its) time to long-range planning. After describing each step, we shall use a case example of corporate-level planning at a hypothetical company named ''Quik-Serv'' to show how the step would be carried out.

Step 1. Identify and Make Explicit Your Company's Mission, Basic Objectives, and Policies. At least on the first attempt, assume that your company's mission, objectives, and policies won't change. In order to establish a base for the following steps, you need to state these explicitly.

Exhibit 1. Steps in Multiple-Scenario Analysis

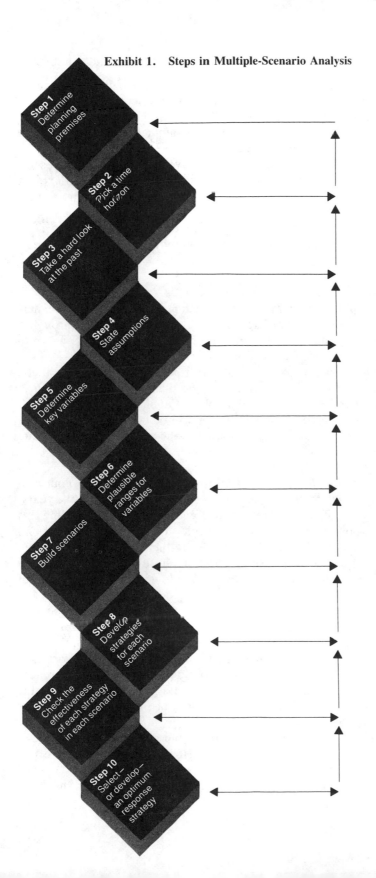

Mission: What is your company's basic reason for being in business? Probably because of existing strengths and commitments, the mission is unlikely to change over the next several years. Consequently, only after present business potential has been carefully examined and found wanting should other possibilities be examined.

Basic objectives: Does your company have long-term objectives for such factors as return on investment, earnings per share, or size? If explicit minimum acceptable standards have not been set, what are common-sense minimums?

Policies: Are there certain limitations, either explicit or implicit, such as "will not expand overseas," or "must provide jobs for existing employees?"

Explicit Planning Premises

Quik-Serv, our hypothetical company, is a small private-brand gasoline marketer. The company retails gasoline under its own brand name through a network of company- and dealer-operated outlets. Quick-Serv is nonintegrated, buying its products from major refiners.

Quik-Serv's mission is to serve consumer needs for automotive fuels. Its objectives are to remain competitive in the marketplace of the future, and to increase aftertax return on stockholders' equity to 12% by 1982. It has two policies: (1) the company's behavior will be both legal and ethical, and (2) new lines of business must be related to the company's mission and support its objectives.

Step 2. Determine How Far into the Future You Wish to Plan. Your current planning horizon is probably one, two, or perhaps as many as five years. Time and planning facility limitations may prevent you from extending this horizon. The purpose of MSA is *not* to enable you to improve detail and precision in planning farther into the future. Rather, it is to give you an improved appreciation of the possible variations in future environments in which you must operate and, subsequently, the long-range implications of today's decisions.

For example, short-range forecasting might indicate a sales decline in the next three years. Given this forecast, one might follow a strategy of across-the-board cutbacks. On the other hand, because of discontinuities, certain scenarios might depict considerably higher sales in ten years (see Exhibit 2). Such long-range forecasts also would probably call for retrenchment, but on a more selective basis to maintain a growth posture. In this respect, consideration of several scenarios makes the implications of present decisions more apparent.

The time length for scenarios is arbitrary, but generally it should be at least five years. The acid test is, of course, "How far in the future are you committing your resources?"

Quik-Serv's planning horizon is five years. While management has little

Exhibit 2. Trend Line for Sales

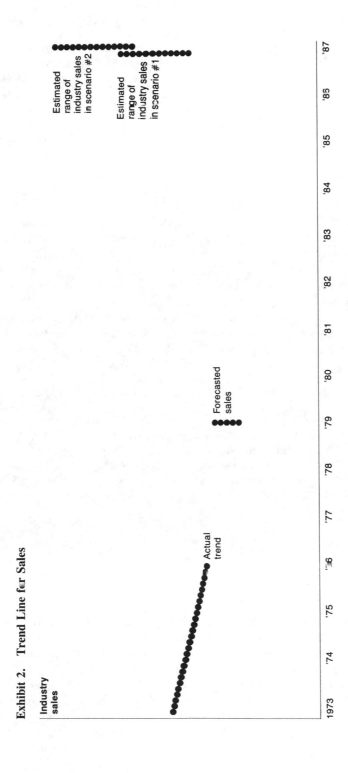

confidence in its ability to plan this far in advance, in some respects a 5-year planning horizon is too short. Quik-Serv's evaluation and depreciation of capital investments, for instance, are based on a 20-year economic life. Therefore, management decides to develop a set of scenarios with a 15- to 20-year horizon.

Step 3. Develop a Good Understanding of Your Company's Points of Leverage and Vulnerability.   First, take a look at your industry. What was it like a decade or two ago? What is it like today? What are the causes for the changes?

Next, examine your own company. Look back over the same time span that you did for your industry. Then, take a look at your company today. Given conditions in the industry, what are the similarities and/or differences between your industry and your company? What are your points of leverage and vulnerability?

Although these analyses should be in writing, they need not be detailed. You are only seeking basic understandings.

Be careful of myths. In any business enterprise there is an abundance of information and opinion; unfortunately, much of it is false. From the history of Sears, Roebuck and Co., Peter Drucker came to the following conclusion:

> The right answers are always obvious in retrospect. The basic lesson of the Sears story is that the right answers are likely to be anything but obvious *before* they have proven themselves. "Everybody knew" around 1900 that to promise "satisfaction guaranteed or your money back" could only bring financial disaster to a retailer. "Everybody knew" around 1925 that the American market was sharply segmented into distinct income groups. . . . "Everybody knew"—as late as 1950—that the American consumer wanted to shop downtown, and so on.[3]

Test for myths. Get data. Summarize past trends. Do they reinforce or oppose what you thought you knew?

Look at Past and Present

A decade ago in Quik-Serv's industry, fuel was cheap and abundant, and demand was growing steadily at approximately 4% a year. The major brand full-service station was the most prevalent type of outlet, and the number was increasing. Volume, not profitability, was the industry-wide criterion of success. Also, a pump-price spread of several cents existed between major and independent brands.

Today, the situation is almost exactly the opposite. Fuel is considerably more expensive, and demand is leveling off, with only a 2% near-term annual growth rate projected. The full-service outlet is still the most prevalent type but is losing ground to gasoline-only and self-service outlets. With profitability as the criterion of success, the outlet population is shrinking as companies close unprofitable units and withdraw from entire geographical areas. Finally, the pump-price spread between majors and independents is becoming blurred as majors increasingly offer self-service islands and gasoline-only outlets.

As for the company itself, ten years ago Quik-Serv was a small regional marketer with just over 100 outlets. Competing on a price basis, Quik-Serv enjoyed a 5% to 6% share of each local market it served. The company's aftertax return on stockholders' equity during this period of severe price competition and low margins averaged 6% to 7%. Quik-Serv's aggressive pricing strategy caused its gasoline volume to grow at about 6% per year, a rate some 50% higher than the industry average. The company's 100-odd outlets were of the gasoline-only type, some having been converted from acquired full-service outlets and others of newer construction without service bays.

After ten years of growth, Quik-Serv today has 165 modern gasoline-only outlets. Industry-wide conditions of a more stable pricing structure and wider margins have raised return on equity to just over 9%. Rapid inflation and a high cost of capital have significantly slowed Quik-Serv's expansion program. Volume at existing outlets is growing at about the same rate as the market.

Quik-Serv's management believes the company has two major competitive advantages: a lean organization with capable, motivated management, and a chain of modern, efficient outlets in good markets and good locations. Management has also identified two points of vulnerability: dependence on other companies for product supply, and the fact that the company serves a highly price-conscious market segment which has little brand loyalty.

Step 4. Determine Factors That You Think Will Definitely Occur within Your Planning Time Frame. Some assumptions might stem from certain factors that can be forecasted with almost complete certainty (in Quik-Serv's case, for example, the number of licensed drivers in 1997), and you might consider some information, such as calculated natural resources, accurate and conclusive. Other projections, such as rate of economic growth, are unpredictable and should be classified as variables.

Assumptions must be accurate and conclusive, not merely variables with a high probability of occurrence. A test: if a "prudent person" could doubt its value, consider it a variable.

Quik-Serv made the following assumptions: (a) by 1997 there will be a 9% increase in licensed drivers; (b) gasoline will remain the major fuel for automobiles; (c) government policies will be protective of small independent companies; (d) there will be less gasoline brand loyalty; (e) mass merchandisers will continue to increase in importance in tires, batteries, accessories (TBA), and repairs; and (f) improved technology will produce autos and TBA requiring less maintenance and repairs, and better gas mileage.

Step 5. Make a List of Key Variables That Will Have Make-or-Break Consequences for Your Company.   Your main consideration at this step is to identify, without going into a lot of detail, the variables that have been crucial to your company in the past and those that will be important to it in the future. Try to use key variables that are commonly predicted and monitored, such as GNP and the rate of inflation. Easily identifiable vital signs facilitate forecasting and simplify control.

If time and resources permit, you may wish to broaden your viewpoint by scanning future-oriented periodicals, such as *Futures* and *The Futurist*, in addition to your normal fare of business and general periodicals. Of course, there are also a number of proprietary services available, such as the Arthur D. Little Impact Service, the National Planning Association Economic Projections Series, Predicasts, the Futures Group Scout Service, and the Stanford Research Institute Business Intelligence Program.

You can keep the planning task on a "shirt-sleeve" basis by limiting key variables to no more than four or five by using the following guidelines:

☐   Delete variables having a low probability of occurrence and a low potential impact. On the other hand, include those with low probabilities but high impact and all those with high probabilities regardless of their impact.

☐   Consider the timeliness of the variable. Because the future is so unpredictable, it is more important to include an event that is likely to happen or have an impact in the next few years than one that may not happen or be insignificant until near the end of the planning horizon.

☐   Delete disaster events. Events that would cause total disaster—such as a major nuclear war—should not be considered seriously.

☐   Aggregate when possible. For example, the factors responsible for economic growth include, to name a few, expenditures on consumer, investment, and government goods. If only the economic growth rate is relevant, just use it as the representative variable for your analysis.

☐   Separate dependent from independent variables. Check for interdependence. Is the value of one variable based upon the value of another? If so, then remove the dependent variable. Keep a separate list of dependent variables for use in building and enriching scenarios.

Quik-Serv thinks that the rate of inflation, GNP (as an indicator of car sales and usage), and gasoline price and availability are the variables that will have the greatest impact on its operations. The company's list of dependent variables are: availability of capital (as affected by rate of inflation and growth rate of GNP), government taxation (taxes to curtail consumption), government restriction (rationing), and the rate of technological change (as affected by growth rate of GNP).

Step 6. Assign Reasonable Values to Each Key Variable.   Now you need to pick a reasonable range over which each variable may vary, and divide the range into two or three sets of values—a "middle ground" and the extremes. Reasonability, of course, can only be determined by common sense. However, two helpful principles are: (1) reject values so extreme that they seem absurd; and (2) if a value lies between the marginal and the absurd, use it. Although it is generally recommended that three sets of values be estimated, in some instances two may suffice for all practical purposes.

To maintain objectivity, you may want to seek the opinions of fellow executives, trade association officials and staff, or, if relationships permit, customers and suppliers. The ranges of values for the key variables that Quik-Serv picked are shown in Exhibit 3.

Step 7. Build Scenarios in Which Your Company May Operate. Scenarios describe possible future operating environments for your organization. A scenario is built by (1) selecting a value for each key variable; (2) estimating the resulting interactions between key variables, dependent variables, and assumptions; and (3) developing a narration describing the future under this set of conditions.

When building scenarios, the following suggestions may be helpful.

☐ Develop at least three, but no more than four, scenarios. Experience has shown that two are too few; the scenarios tend to be classified as good and bad. On the other hand, even four scenarios may be too many unless they have markedly different characteristics.[4] One of the scenarios should be for the most probable case.

☐ Select values of key variables so that each scenario is distinct from the others. Scenarios with small variations have little value since strategies for these scenarios would be almost indentical. In fact, it might be wise to look at a "deadly enemy" scenario.[5]

☐ Keep the scenarios plausible. This is partially accomplished by including only the values that are deemed realistic. But make sure that the combined variable mix in each scenario also makes sense, that it is feasible. For example, low double-digit inflation, rapid economic growth, and severe oil shortage by themselves might seem plausible but their joint occurrence does not. To keep from overlooking plausible combinations of key variables, examine all possibilities.

Exhibit 3. Variable Value Matrix

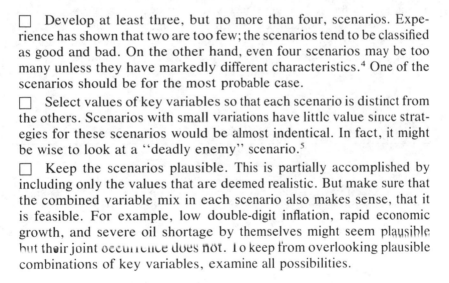

	Value (15 to 20 years in the future)		
Variable	Extreme	Middle	Extreme
Inflation rate	10% to 20%	—	5% to 9%
Price and availability of gasoline	Same as present	—	Tight supply high prices
Growth in GNP	More than 4%	1.5% to 4%	Less than 1.5%

☐   In writing a scenario, first state variables and assumptions in an abbreviated form. Then include the dependent variables and develop the scenario with more description. Write from the viewpoint of someone standing in the future (at the end of your time frame) describing conditions at that time and how they developed. The completed scenario should transmit an appreciation of this hypothesized environment.

☐   Limit the length of each scenario to one or two paragraphs, keeping the length of each scenario the same, and using common language and classifications to allow for point-by-point comparison.

☐   Keep the themes of each scenario neutral. Although you may have scenarios for the "worst," "most probable," and "best" circumstances, avoid labeling them as such to prevent more consideration being given to the "most probable" or "best" scenarios.

Quik-Serv's Scenarios

Exhibit 4 shows the matrix Quik-Serv constructed to test the plausibility of the combined variables. The 12 scenarios listed represent all possible combinations of the three key variables. The company rejected Scenarios 2, 4, 8, and 10 because of inconsistencies among the major variables. Scenarios 3, 6, 9, and 11 were selected for further development. Number 9 was thought to represent the middle of the variables' possible ranges, while numbers 3, 6, and 11 were chosen to represent more extreme possibilities. Scenarios 1, 5, 7, and 12 were not chosen because they were thought to be merely vari-

Exhibit 4.   Matrix for Testing Plausibility

Possible Scenario	Inflation	Variables Gas Price and Availability	GNP	Comments
1	10% to 20%	Present	More than 4%	Plausible
2	10 to 20	Tight supply, high prices	More than 4	Not plausible
3	10 to 20	Present	1.5 to 4	Plausible
4	10 to 20	Tight supply, high prices	1.5 to 4	Not plausible
5	10 to 20	Present	Less than 1.5	Plausible
6	10 to 20	Tight supply, high prices	Less than 1.5	Plausible
7	5 to 9	Present	More than 4	Plausible
8	5 to 9	Tight supply, high prices	More than 4	Not plausible
9	5 to 9	Present	1.5 to 4	Plausible
10	5 to 9	Tight supply, high prices	1.5 to 4	Not plausible
11	5 to 9	Present	Less than 1.5	Plausible
12	5 to 9	Tight supply, high prices	Less than 1.5	Plausible

ations or extreme cases of the general themes of Scenarios 3, 6, 9, and 11, respectively. (For the sake of brevity, we shall only consider Scenarios 3 and 11 further.)

Scenario 3: Advances in technology and design have made the automobile of the early 1990s safer, more reliable, and nearly service-free. From the viewpoint of the gasoline retailer, however, the most significant change in the automobile has been the tremendous increase in fuel efficiency over the past two decades. Better mileage has offset the effects of increases in the number of cars on the road. Overall market demand has grown at an average of only 1% to 1.5% per year.

Because of a low rate of market growth and a high cost of capital, the number of retail gasoline outlets has increased only slightly since the late 1970s. Rapidly escalating labor costs and the "service-free" automobile have been responsible for the demise of the full-service gasoline outlet. The high rate of inflation has made price-conscious consumers extremely receptive to the economies of self-service stations. The price competition between majors and independents is head-on, so there is no pump-price spread.

Scenario 11: The gasoline-powered automobile is still the dominant mode of transportation. Yet, gasoline demand, which peaked in the late 1980s, has been declining slightly each year during this period of prolonged economic stagnation. Gasoline outlets have been decreasing in number since the early 1980s as retailers attempt to cover rising fixed costs in the face of static demand and strong consumer resistance to price increases. Low levels of profitability no longer justify the use of new capital in the retail gasoline business.

One important countertrend has been the growth of the full-service outlet as hard-pressed consumers increasingly choose to repair rather than replace their automobiles. Marketers in a position to do so strive to retain brand identification by building consumer loyalty through the service and repair portions of their operations. The economics of the full-service outlet benefit from the general availability and the relatively low cost of labor. The federal government, concerned with the survival of the small companies in these difficult times, is especially watchful for anticompetitive practices by the larger companies.

Step 8. Develop a Strategy for Each Scenario That Will Most Likely Result in Achieving Your Company's Objectives. The procedure for generating strategies is similar to traditional strategy development. Because of the "unpredictable future," however, a greater emphasis should be placed on flexible strategies that have relatively high payoffs in short and intermediate time spans.

Your "final" strategies, within their respective scenarios, should enable your company to come reasonably close to its objectives. Because of the imprecision inherent in long-term forecasting, avoid the "numbers game." Instead, make common-sense, intuitive judgments.

Constrained Opportunity . . .

The overall theme of Quik-Serv's Scenario 3 is one of constrained opportunity. That is, there is some opportunity for growth in the market segment in which Quik-Serv believes it has competitive advantages (gasoline-only), but this opportunity is constrained by the rather low rate of market growth, the high rate of inflation, the cost of capital, the high cost of labor, and head-on price competition from the majors. With this long-term view of the future, Quik-Serv's management formulates the following selective growth strategy:

☐ *Ownership of outlets.* Strive for ownership of outlets and real estate on a leveraged basis as a hedge against inflation.

☐ *Increased debt posture.* Increase debt/equity ratio as necessary to facilitate buying and building now instead of later during the inflationary period.

☐ *Selective expansion.* Maintain share of market growth through highly selective and carefully timed expansion with new gasoline-only outlets, giving careful consideration to profitability criteria and market supply-demand balances.

☐ *Dealer-operated units.* Minimize the effect of escalating labor costs by increasing emphasis on dealer-operated outlets and decreasing operation of outlets by direct company employees.

☐ *Automated self-service.* Further minimize the effect of escalating labor costs of remaining company-operated outlets by making a shift to automated self-service.

. . . vs. Recessionary Outlook

The message emerging from Scenario 11 is threefold: a decline in the demand for gasoline, consumer resistance to price increases, and a decreasing number of service stations. Quik-Serv's management decides that under this set of conditions, the following strategy is the most feasible course of action:

☐ *Restricted ownership of outlets.* Reduce ownership of low and negative profit outlets where real estate is usable as a gasoline outlet only. Increase ownership of properties which have attractive alternatives for commercial usage.

☐ *Minimize debt.* Avoid new debt and use excess cash to retire existing high-interest obligations.

☐ *Selective divestment.* Identify and divest outlets which make zero or negative contribution to profit and for which turnaround would require large amounts of new capital.

☐ *Company-operated outlets.* Increase profitability by stressing company operations, thus absorbing dealer margins during this period of readily available and relatively low-cost labor.

☐ *Increase labor.* Utilize inexpensive labor rather than automated self-service equipment which is relatively costly.

Step 9. Check the Flexibility of Each Strategy in Each Scenario by Testing Its Effectiveness in the Other Scenarios. Is each strategy adaptable to your other scenarios, or does its effectiveness depend on the values of key variables in the particular scenario for which it was originally developed? The construction of a matrix and subsequent ratings, as shown in Exhibit 5 for Quik-Serv, will help you to visualize each strategy's adaptability.

Step 10. Select—or Develop—an "Optimum Response" Strategy. Now that you have developed a strategy for each scenario, you must choose one of them or form a "compromise" strategy from among them. Because of personal and company attitudes toward risk, there can be no hard-and-fast rules to apply as you make this choice. However, in general, the final strategy should:

☐ Provide maximum adaptability to the conditions of the several scenarios, or conversely, require only a short reaction time for adjustment to the demands of different environments.

☐ Have favorable consequences in scenarios with relatively high probabilities of occurrence.

☐ Be particularly attractive in the near future since the distant future is less predictable.

Exhibit 5. Flexibility of Strategies

Strategies	Fit in Scenario 3	Fit in Scenario 11
Scenario 3		
Ownership of outlets		Poor
Increase debt posture	—	Poor
Selective expansion	—	Poor
Dealer-operated outlets	—	Fair
Automated self-service	—	Fair
Scenario 11		
Restricted ownership	Fair	—
Minimize debt	Poor	—
Selective divestment	Fair	—
Company-operated outlets	Fair	—
Increase labor	Poor	—

☐ Provide for maximum delay of expenditures, taking the impact of possible inflationary price rises into consideration.

Quik-Serv's management believed a future environment similar to Scenario 3 was highly probable, especially over the next five to seven years. It did not totally discount the harsher possibilities of Scenario 11, but felt that if such a condition did materialize it would not be until the latter part of the 15- to 20-year period. Accordingly, it decided to pursue the strategy outlined for Scenario 3, with three modifications to improve its flexibility:

☐ *Go slow on shift to dealer operations,* since, if necessary, it would be easier to shift operations from the company to dealers rather than to shift from dealers back to the company.

☐ *Increase debt/equity ratio slowly* by implementing a more selective expansion program.

☐ *Prepare for a selective divestment strategy* by identifying a list of candidates.

Multiple-scenario analysis gave Quik-Serv management a better appreciation of the long-term outlook, thus providing an improved foundation for its strategic five-year planning.

Pitfalls and Benefits

Of course, there may be a gap between your objectives and common-sense estimates of what you can hope to achieve with the "optimum response" strategy. If so, you should first try to shrink the gap to tolerable limits by developing a better strategy. Perhaps in the planning process some factors have been overlooked or over- or underemphasized. Consider bringing in other viewpoints. Only afterwards should new ventures be investigated to supplement, or possibly replace, the basic mission.

To analyze new ventures, first list potential candidates. Seek those highly compatible with the basic mission. Fast screening of this list is necessary because, as a rule, new ventures will require separate sets of scenarios since some of their key variables will be different from those of the basic mission. Identify and eliminate weak candidates by working through, for each potential new venture, steps four to ten on a cursory basis. Then, perform a more detailed analysis for each of the more plausible ventures.

Although some of the make-or-break variables for venture candidates may be different from those of the basic mission, some will probably be the same (for example, the rate of inflation). Use, when possible, identical values for the same key variables in building scenarios. Then, in selecting the final strategy (for both the basic mission and the new ventures), make sure comparable scenarios are used.

Taking Corrective Action

A major concern is "Will the actual environment, as it unfolds, provide a favorable climate for the implemented strategy?" Consequently, there must be an environmental monitoring system. To develop such a procedure, in general, first establish short-term standards for key variables that will tend to validate the long-range estimates. Although favorable long-range values have been estimated, short-term guidelines are needed to indicate if the scenario is unfolding as hoped. Next, set up criteria to decide when the strategy must be changed. Of course, your decision will depend on the magnitude or the trend (or both) of the deviations.

If the optimum strategy was developed for environmental conditions different from those that actually are occurring, then examine how effective the strategy was judged to be in a scenario closer to the actual conditions, and determine necessary adaptions. In this manner your analysis of different scenarios also can be used to respond to "unforecasted" situations as they develop.

Common Sense

Multiple-scenario analysis does improve the appreciation of the future, and so should enable management to develop strategies with better cognizance of potential risks. At first, however, the procedure may appear to "muddy the water," since it calls for the development of more than one possible environment, and more than one strategy.

Also, you need to be aware of problems that might be caused by misusing MSA. At the beginning of the planning process, for instance, you must carefully avoid favoring what may seem to be *the* right scenario or *the* right strategy. Such prejudice minimizes the value of the process, as it would any type of planning model. Also, be careful of adopting a strategy simply because it fits more scenarios than does any alternative. It might not be the strategy most likely to lead to success.

Finally, in spite of your best laid plans, you may have missed developing a scenario that portrays an environment close to the one that actually occurs. Hence, it is necessary to adopt a systematic method of monitoring the environment and to consider long-range planning as a continuous process.

If you are aware of these pitfalls, the process can help you to focus on the assumptions underlying the scenarios, not on just whether to approve a plan or not. Actually, MSA is simply a matter of common sense. It is essentially a part of a decision-making procedure that we all use daily, although on a highly informal basis. By formalizing the process, however, you facilitate communication, thus improving multiparty participation and comprehension. And there is an important side benefit: a structured approach leads to more rigorous thinking. As a result, multiple-scenario analysis can be a valuable tool in helping to make today's decisions flexible enough for the uncertain future.

Notes

1. "Two Poor Years for the Forecasters," *Business Week,* December 21, 1974, p. 51.

2. Some of the most helpful literature follows: René D. Zentner, "Scenarios: A New Tool for Corporate Planners," *Chemical and Engineering News,* Industrial Edition, October 6, 1975, p. 22; Ian H. Wilson, "Futures Forecasting for Strategic Planning at General Electric," *Long Range Planning,* June 1973, p. 39; Frank L. Moreland, "Dialectic Methods in Forecasting," *The Futurist,* August 1971, p. 169; Peter F. Chapman, "A Method of Exploring the Future," *Long Range Planning,* February 1976, p. 2; and M.J. Creton and Audrey Clayton, "Social Forecasting: A Practical Approach," in *The Next 25 Years: Crisis and Opportunity,* ed. Andrew A. Spekke (Washington, D.C., World Future Society, 1975), p. 267.

3. Peter F. Drucker, *Management: Tasks, Responsibilities, Practices* (New York, Harper & Row, 1974), p. 57.

4. René S. Zentner, "Scenarios: A New Tool."

5. Frank L. Moreland, "Dialectical Methods."

17

The President and Corporate Planning

MYLES L. MACE

The only constant in business is change, and leadership in adapting corporate operations to the changing business world must come from the top. Myles Mace's thesis is that strategic planning will succeed only with the active support of the chief executive.

Throughout the early 1960s, many top executives were concerned about the need for more formalized corporate planning in their respective organizations. Some chief operating executives searched for the "best system" and the "best methods" with the hope that the installation of another company's successful approach would achieve more effective results in their own corporate planning function. This situation was somewhat similar to that of the early 1950s, when many company executives were searching for the best system to provide for the growth and development of key personnel.[1]

As in the 1950s, preoccupation with the forms, procedures, and techniques of a best system produces lip service to an important management function, but accomplishes little toward achievement of real, honest-to-goodness plans for the future direction of corporations. To mechanically adopt the methods and procedures which appear to be useful in the ABC Corporation does not assure fulfillment of the planning function in the XYZ Corporation. Such thinking is analogous to believing that the adoption of a "suggestion system" automatically builds employee morale.

Administrative Focus

Effective corporate planning does not consist simply of a system. Rather, it is an administrative process and a critically important job which should concern the management of every corporation. Forms and procedures may

245

be employed as convenient and useful tools. But the success of corporate planning is not measured by the writing of procedures, the addition of a new box on the organization chart, or the production of an impressive-looking book entitled "Corporate Goals and Plans—1965–1970—Confidential."

Some executives have indicated that corporate planning is required only in large and diverse enterprises and that managements of small and medium-sized companies need not be concerned. Planning as an essential business function is as important to the small company as it is to the large.[2] Indeed, individual planning is important for each person who has aspirations for success in a business organization.

In 1961 and 1962, George G. Montgomery, Jr., now a vice president of White Weld Company in New York, and I made a research study of the problems involved in the acquisition of one company by another.[3] A segment of that study was concerned with planning for growth through acquisition. With this background, which has been augmented by continued interest and experience, especially with regard to the planning function, I shall undertake to deal in this article with what seem to be some of the most important and practical steps involved in the attainment of effective and useful corporate planning.

President's Involvement

Probably the single most important problem in corporate planning derives from the belief of some chief operating executives that corporate planning is not a function with which they should be directly concerned. They regard planning as something to be delegated, which subordinates can do without responsible participation by chief executives. They think the end result of effective planning is the compilation of a "Plans" book. Such volumes get distributed to key executives, who scan the contents briefly, file them away, breathe a sigh of relief, and observe, "Thank goodness that is done—now let's get back to work."

George Montgomery and I found in the course of the acquisition research mentioned above that effective corporate planning is not possible without the personal involvement and leadership of the chief operating executive. Subsequent study confirmed this conclusion. Involvement and leadership mean spending the time and energy to manage the function—to see that something concrete is done. They mean personally putting into action what is too often abrogated by general words and phrases. In specific terms, there are two fundamental functions which absolutely demand the chief executive's active involvement:

1   Leadership in the tough and laborious process of realistically evaluating existing product lines, markets, trends, and competitive positions in the future.
2   Leadership in the establishment of corporate objectives.

After examining each of these critically important leadership functions, I shall discuss the basic elements of a planning program.

Realistic Evaluation

Among many corporate executives, the concept of planning is believed necessary only to find new areas of product opportunity. Planning programs organized to achieve this limited scope completely overlook the possibility of augmenting or strengthening existing product lines or product divisions.

Analysis of the history of sales, margins, and profits by product or product line discloses significant trends which are frequently unnoticed in the course of the day-to-day management of companies. For example:

A five-year history was compiled of the products which comprised 80% of a company's sales. It became clear that some product margins had steadily declined, others had remained stable, and the increase in total company sales and profits was attributable to a few high gross-margin items. The company's success had camouflaged what was happening to products which once had been substantial contributors to profits.

This relatively simple analysis led to further study of market prospects for the less profitable items. It was concluded that an inability to raise market prices or reduce costs required the addition of new, higher margin products if the sales and profits of the corporation were to be maintained or grow in the future.

Some chief operating executives find it difficult to recognize that product lines which have produced generous profits over many years are in jeopardy. Competitive facts of life encroach on markets, but a sentimental attachment to the past leads to a euphoric attitude about the future. Reluctance to face up to the situation is characterized by such statements as, "We have been through tough times before and we can do it again," or, "This business has been mighty good to us in the past and we are going to stick with it," or, "Sooner or later the competitor's prices have got to come back in line, and when that happens, we will be on our way again."

Admittedly it is painful to accept the unpleasant fact that uncontrollable outside competitive forces have depleted long-standing markets and margins. But a chief operating executive who procrastinates in adopting an action-planning program to adjust to changing conditions jeopardizes profits and, in some cases, the company's solvency. For example:

In a situation where competitors had moved in and taken over a certain company's once very profitable market, the chief operating executive of the company recognized the fact that the market was completely gone. However, sentimentally aware of the score of key people whose careers were identified only with that market, he refused to make the hard decision to reduce sharply or eliminate outright the jobs of the people working on the lost cause. The last several years have been characterized by increasing annual deficits, and the inevitable decision remains to be made.

When chief operating executives do not, as an integral part of their planning role, recognize realistically the status of their existing operations and fulfill the leadership role by adapting to changing conditions, they jeopardize current profits as well as the capacity of the organization to prosper in the future.

Corporate Objectives

In some companies a distinction is made between corporate objectives and corporate goals. Here I regard objectives and goals as synonymous, because corporate planning consists of creating the goals and defining in detail the corporate plans to achieve those goals.

I have found that the phrase "creation of corporate objectives" is regarded by some chief operating executives as rather meaningless, academic language—they think creating objectives is something professors talk about, and that such goals have little real value in the management of a business enterprise. Discounting the value of defining corporate objectives probably arises in part from the many published statements which describe the goals in broad general terms—such as increased sales, increased profits, a broader base of operations, a better environment for the growth of personnel, and so forth. Such expressions of objectives are, indeed, neither meaningful nor useful.

Direction Needed

In some companies I have found no explicit or implicit concepts of corporate goals. One consequence of this lack of direction is that product and division managers more often than not create their own goals, and the result is a hodgepodge of unrelated, unintegrated, and expensive internal research and product development programs. Consider this example:

In one company, the division managers were urged by the chief operating executive to "do something about increasing sales and broadening the base of operations." Each of four division managers embarked on independent and uncoordinated product development projects. Later, capital appropriations and operating budgets were approved by headquarters management, and after a four-year period and a loss of $3 million, the four division managers were engaged in liquidating their respective abortive ventures.

A product development program with carefully defined goals certainly is no guarantee that the product produced and marketed will be successful.

But a product development program with goals certainly is financially more economical and less wasteful of management talent at the division level.

Discussions with chief executives about the concept of creating corporate goals indicate that many think there is something mysterious about the process. There is concern about the method or approach to be used in outlining corporate objectives. How does one go about deciding the mission of an organization? Do statements of goals spring full blown from the minds of presidents? Should we hire consultants to tell us what our objectives should be? Or perhaps hire an economist who can forecast the most promising markets of the future? How do we know what business conditions will be like two years or five years from now? How can we plan effectively when our business is so fast moving that the creation of long-range goals means anticipating what we will do next week?

Thinking Required

Some companies neglect corporate planning because the process intrinsically requires thinking about the future and the future is always uncertain. Anticipating all the factors which affect a company's sales and profits means dealing intellectually with mercurial and intangible elements. This is especially difficult for the action-minded, decision-oriented executive who enjoys and derives great satisfaction from "doing things." Also, and this is one of the most common reasons for deferring thinking about the future, day-to-day crises need decisions right now, and there are usually enough crises to occupy most or all of each business day.

One president stated that "the tyranny of the moment prevents me from paying attention to the important future of the company." Another president said:

> Thinking seems to have lost respectability in some companies. If a vice president is caught sitting at his desk without papers, people, or telephone calls and, in response to a query by the president as to what he is doing, says "thinking," the typical reaction of the president is likely to be, "Thinking! If you are going to think, think on your own time."

But despite the obstacles, real and imagined, to corporate planning, many chief executives regard the function as one of their principal duties and are actively engaged in planning the future paths of their organizations.

Simple Process

Yet the process of corporate planning is relatively simple and straightforward. Much of the mystery of planning comes from the many general admonitions provided by students of management who describe planning as a composite of abstract elements made up of strategy, tactics, purpose, specifications, alternatives, and so on. Chief executives who are doing effective planning jobs describe the process in more practical and meaningful terms. From conversations with them, I shall summarize and illustrate briefly the five basic elements of a planning program, including the creation of corporate goals.

Analyzing the Present

Planning for the future starts with an intimate and realistic understanding of existing products, divisions, markets, margins, profits, return on investment, cash flow, availability of capital, research and development abilities, and skills and capacities of personnel. These significant aspects of operations can be looked at in an orderly manner, and there is nothing mysterious about an analysis of the company's strength and weakness in each of these areas. Basic to consideration of a mission for the company in the future is a clear recognition of how well the organization is doing today.

Analysis of present operations can be done effectively be reviewing the past few years' performance as part of the evaluation of the current year's operating and capital budget forecasts. In some cases, top managements ask division or functional managers to submit the proposed annual budgets together with budgets for the next three to five years. The headquarters review of the short-term forecast is thus combined with the long-term forecast, which otherwise would be a separate, second step. This method of reviewing and evaluating both forecasts simultaneously has the apparent advantage of economy of management time and effort.

However, many top executives find that the discussion invariably focuses on the short-term prospect because of its imminence, and that the long-term problems are deferred or given only brief attention. Current operating problems should be distinguished from the longer-term goals and plans. The purposes of evaluating short-term forecasts and long-term projections—both extremely important—are so different that two separate presentations and evaluations need to be made. Short-term budgets require headquarters modification and approval for financial commitments, whereas long-term forecasts are not subject to authority to spend or commit.

Predicting the Future

Forecasts for each of the next three to five years, based on current operations and existing plans for improving operations, are an important element of a sound planning program. If the company continues to do what it is doing and planning to do today, what will be its future sales, profit, market position, and so on?

Many different approaches produce useful forecasts. These vary from elementary dollar results to more detailed and complex breakdowns of business functions. In one company, which is organized on the basis of decentralized, autonomous divisions for which profit and loss are measurable, each of the seven division managers is asked to submit five-year plans based on an eight-point outline. (A detailed breakdown of this type of outline is given in the Appendix for the reader who would like a more concrete picture of such a forecast.)

In another company, as an illustration, division managers are asked to supply the following information for a three-year forecast:

☐ Sales by product line.
☐ Gross profits by product line.
☐ Personnel requirements.
☐ Capital expenditure needs.

Normally, the data prepared by division or functional managers are submitted in writing two or three weeks in advance of a review date so that the president and other headquarters executives can thoroughly examine the forecasts prior to the meeting.

Reviewing the Forecasts

Here again, practices vary among the companies I have observed. In one, for example, eight divisional managers meet for two days at headquarters, and each manager is allowed two hours to make a presentation of his/her present operations and plans for the future. The president and key headquarters executives listen to each presentation and typically ask general, unchallenging questions. It is an essentially meaningless exercise for all concerned.

In contrast, in a certain company where the president regards corporate planning as his most important job, full-day reviews are made of each division manager's report on his goals and his plans to achieve those goals for each of the next three years. Here the president and key headquarters executives study the written portions of the presentation prior to the meeting and are well armed with perceptive and challenging questions about the validity of their managers' forecasts. Several years' experience with this approach has resulted in increasingly effective, realistic forecasts by the division managers and complete recognition by executives in the company that, while the president is the leader in planning, all key personnel have a share in making the planning function real and meaningful.

Critical evaluation of forecasts prepared by division or functional managers is also required to prevent subordinates from regarding the process of preparing forecasts as an exercise and not an integral part of responsible planning. For example:

☐ In some companies managers supply financial forecasts by product line by mechanically projecting 5% increases in sales and profits for each year. Such an approach observes the amenities of corporate procedures but, if unchallenged by top executives, adds little effectiveness to statements of what can be expected in the future.

☐   In other companies managers purposely overstate their expectations with the hope of manifesting to headquarters executives what fine performances can be expected in the future.

☐   Still other managers employ the strategy of understating forecasts for the purpose of establishing financial goals relatively easy to achieve. Thus approbation will come from headquarters if the forecasts are subsequently exceeded. Hopefully, this will be expressed in higher salaries and bonuses.

Careful and thoughtful review, therefore, is required to validate the reasonableness of managers' forecasts and to provide a realistic composite picture of the future achievement of the entire enterprise.

Critical evaluation by top executives of division or functional managers' longer-range goals and plans has another important advantage. A discussion by able, experienced, and interested executives about the operations of a division inevitably results in the disclosure of some new opportunity not thought of previously. The interplay of active minds dedicated to greater growth and success stimulates new avenues of thought which can be enormously helpful to the division and to the company.

When all of the division or functional managers' goals and plans have been reviewed, a composite report representing the totals for the entire company should be prepared. Some companies accept the forecasts of divisions as presented, and the total becomes the program. In others, the chief executive and his key subordinates review again all the separate programs and adjust the division figures according to their previous experience with the respective division managers. History indicates that some managers are unreformed optimists and others are perpetual pessimists. If discussion during the review does not result in adjustment, the chief executive must make appropriate increases or decreases in order to arrive at a realistic overall forecast.

Evaluating the Program

When all managers' forecasts have been reviewed critically and adjusted to represent more appropriately the judgment of the company's top executives, the total program can be evaluated for the purpose of (1) accepting the forecasted performance as reasonable, or (2) deciding that the stated program does not comprise a suitable growth rate for the company.

Dominant Considerations

A significant and controlling determinant in arriving at a conclusion as to the adequacy of proposed division or functional plans is the attitude, personal desire, and aspiration of the chief operating executive. It is frequently assumed that every chief executive aspires to head a growing and increasingly profitable enterprise—that by taking into account the interests of stockholders, employees, customers, and the communities within which the company operates, he will make thoughtful decisions to grow, prosper, and fulfill social and public responsibilities. While this is generally true, some chief executives are motivated by other primary considerations which dominate many major policy decisions. For example:

In a western consumer products company the president and his key subordinates recognized that their major strengths were in the research, development, and manufacturing of potentially profitable new products, but the company's marketing organization had proved to be ineffective in establishing distribution to thousands of outlets in the United States. Several unsuccessful attempts were made to strengthen the marketing group.

Meanwhile, a competitor with a superb marketing staff continued to increase its share of the market. The president of the competing company, in planning the future growth of his enterprise, perceived that continued growth in sales and profits would be possible only with more effective product research, development, and manufacturing facilities. Dissatisfied with the time which would be required to build a stronger development and manufacturing group, he explored the alternative of acquiring another company with the necessary strengths to complement his organization.

A study of possible acquisitions resulted in the identification of the western company described above, and the two presidents initiated negotiations to merge the two companies. Continued discussions disclosed that the fit was even better than originally conceived—stock prices and dividend policies were substantially alike, terms of exchange were agreed on, antitrust laws were not an obstacle—and a plan for the integration of the two organizational structures was evolved which met the desires and aspirations of both groups.

The one snag was: Who would be the chief operating executive of the merged enterprises? It was clear that joining the two companies would substantially benefit the stockholders, the employees, and the communities where the companies had operations. Negotiations continued intensively for several weeks, but were terminated when it was apparent that both presidents wanted to be the chief operating executive of the merged companies. Neither was willing to take the second position, although many possible divisions of authority and responsibility were considered and rejected in turn. The personal desire of each president to retain the position as chief executive prevented the merger, and the two companies continued to operate competitively.

I have found similar examples of dominant personal considerations in other situations, but the real reasons for termination of merger discussions are rarely publicized. The usual explanation is that differences on price or differences on major policies have led both parties to conclude that each company should remain independent and autonomous.

Hidden Motives

In other cases, the chief operating executives disguise their personal desires and goals for their companies. They profess the conviction that their companies should adjust to changed conditions in their respective industries, that new areas of activity should be searched for and entered. But personal, and usually unexpressed, reasons control the decisions not to take the risks involved in moving into promising market opportunities.

At a research seminar conducted at the University of California, Los Angeles, to discuss long-range planning, one of the participants, Rex Land, described his experience with a company which tried to hide its basic objectives, but eventually was found out. Land said:

> I know of a company, very closely held, the executives of which (after a great deal of probing action) finally admitted they were primarily interested in maintaining the prestige of other members of the family. The top executive was not going to take certain risks that would jeopardize his income or that of four or five members of his family. His could have been a growing and healthy company if it had brought in and held executives, but he could not keep people for very long. It took people five years to realize what the real objectives of this company were.[4]

In another company, the president made a review of a five-year forecast of sales and profits based on the continuation of status quo operations. It seemed possible with existing products, he reasoned, to maintain the same flat curve of sales and profits achieved over the last several years. He concluded, therefore, that the company's plan would be to maintain this level of performance and not to try to grow in size or profitability. In a lengthy discussion of his plan and planning process, he conceded that he felt personally comfortable heading the organization at its present size. "If I grow and take on more people, I am not too sure I could do it. And even if I could, I am not willing to pay the price of the extra effort required."

Personal Fears

Other chief operating executives, after reviewing forecasts of gradually declining sales and profits based on present operations and plans, resignedly accept the anticipated results because of personal fears of risking substantial sums of development or capital expenditure money. Consider this example:

The president of a large family corporation in the East regarded his role as that of a conservator. Several members of the family held corporate executive titles, and the value of the company constituted the principal of the family trust created for them by their deceased father, who had founded the company.

Technological changes in the industry resulted in a gradual erosion of the company's sales and profits which, for years, had enjoyed the dominant position in a segment of the industrial instruments business. None of the company's top executives could foresee anything except continued declines in sales, profit, and market position unless the company risked an estimated $3 million investment in product development.

The policy dilemma of whether to risk $3 million of what was regarded as the assets of the family trust or whether to accept the forecasted future of further declines was resolved by the president when he chose to "ride out this temporary decline trend." The company president has continued to reject the alternative risk, and the company sales and profits have continued to deteriorate.

While these foregoing examples illustrate the importance and influence of attitudes, personal desires, and aspirations of chief operating executives, indeed they are not at all typical of the majority of companies.

Typical Executives

Usually presidents are found to be searching for ways to increase the size and profitability of their respective corporations. And if the forecasted performance of existing operations fails to produce expectations of profitable growth, plans are initiated to build on the business of the present. In my studies the more common president is one who is rarely satisfied with nominal growth rates, who stretches the forecasts of divisional or functional managers, and who establishes new and challenging standards of performance for the organization to achieve. Such presidents regard lack of growth as stagnation, an attribute they abhor.

When chief operating executives review and evaluate the forecasted performance for three to five years and conclude that the financial figures are reasonable and plans for their realization feasible, the composite documents constitute the corporate plan for the stated period of years ahead. Sometimes these "working papers" are regarded as "company goals and plans." In other cases the significant elements of them are formalized into "corporate goals," and the various segments of the corporate plans for achievement are spelled out in great detail. The mission and the plan for achievement are thus clearly defined.

However, when the chief operating executives conclude that the anticipated results are not adequate, it becomes imperative to think through and construct a new or modified set of goals and a new plan to fulfill these desired objectives.

Creating the Goals

In my discussions with presidents who are concerned about the anticipated lack of growth in their companies, the query recurs, "Just how do I go about creating a new set of corporate goals?"

While I have found several successful approaches in the many companies studied, my major conclusions will be discouraging to those who are looking for a quick and easy method. There is no mechanical or expert "instant answer method." Rather, defining corporate goals—and modifying those goals as the future becomes the present—is a long, time-consuming and continuous process. Each president in each company must regard the construction and adjustment of goals as an important, absolute, and—in a sense—unique requirement of his or her job.

There are, however, several ways of defining company goals that may suggest a modus operandi to those concerned with this requirement.

Reorganize Work Habits

With the background and essential information resulting from (1) a realistic analysis of existing operations, including opportunities for growth, (2) adjusted forecasts by division or functional managers of their anticipated performance, and (3) an evaluation of the three-, four-, and five-year forecasts, the chief operating executive can embark on the difficult process of creating a structure of corporate goals.

The process is particularly difficult for some chief executives because accepting corporate planning as an important function means not engaging in parts of the satisfying activities which have kept them completely occupied in the past. Planning takes time, and time becomes available for busy men largely through modification of their work habits. The president of a large eastern company stated recently, "The creation and manning of three new group vice presidential positions to cover nine domestic divisions and our international subsidiaries ought to enable me to give more attention to our corporate goals."

Another said:

> In the past I did not take the time as skipper of this corporate ship to plot our course. The absence of direction created a vacuum into which rushed improvisation. The resulting chaos and hodgepodge forced me to recognize that I must take the time to think through where we want to go.

Enlist Key People

While the main responsibility for defining corporate goals rests on the chief executives, they can enlist the minds and imaginations of other key people in their organizations. To do this, some chief operating executives ask the top eight or ten executives to join them in a three- or four-day retreat to help them start thinking through together what the corporate goals should be. Preferably, such a meeting should be held away from "headquarters" to avoid the diversions of telephones, problems, and decisions. Such "think" or "skull" sessions are found to be most effective when tentative drafts of ideas are prepared prior to the meeting to serve as the focus of discussion. Such preliminary drafts can, but need not, delimit the considerations, since thoughtful and imaginative executives usually extrapolate quickly. One president observes that these sessions should also provide for a break of an hour or two in the afternoon for exercise; otherwise everyone gets to thinking in circles.

Some company presidents look for more from such skull sessions than can be reasonably expected. The thinking and planning process, as indicated earlier, is a long, continuing, and tough process. It is long because answers are not easily come by; continuing because the corporate goals are subject to change, adapting to new conditions; and tough because the process of thinking about the future means dealing with intangibles and assumptions. If an organization is formalizing its planning program for the first time, the most that can be expected from such a meeting is the beginning of an understanding of the magnitude of the problems and the start of the process of formulating possible elements of a statement of goals.

Some presidents assign the job of defining corporate goals to a task force made up of three or four key members of the organization. Others ask an experienced line or staff executive to study the problems and recommend a statement of mission for the company. But, irrespective of the approach used, I find that no real and meaningful goals are outlined without the direct involvement of chief operating executives. Without their active leadership in the function, resulting concepts are usually interesting but irrelevant products of an academic exercise. With their leadership, it is possible to analyze, to think through alternatives, and to arrive at a practical, workable, and useful outline of the mission of the enterprise.

Hire Responsible Consultants

Other presidents employ management consultants to advise on what the goals of their corporation should be. Responsible consultants, unbiased and unprejudiced by the way things have been done, can bring to the task the benefit of outside objectivity. Most organizations include undisclosed sacred cows which executives of the company have learned not to molest. Sometimes the unmolested sacred cow is the reason for lack of interest in growth, and the consultant feels a responsibility to report his conclusions objectively. Many times suggestions by consultants on sacrosanct subjects have opened them up for re-examination and, sometimes, even change. New points of view injected by consultants often stimulate corporate top management to audit anew many policies, practices, and other matters which have continued unchallenged over the years. Here is an example:

In one company in the East a substantial part of its sales and profits over the last 20-year period had been derived from one product line in the electronics industry. More recently, competitive Japanese products had entered the United States and pre-empted a large portion of the market. The eastern company sought protection through increased tariffs and intercountry agreements on the amounts to be imported, but neither approach stemmed the increasing market share taken over by the Japanese products. The company management was slow in recognizing the business facts of life and continued to maintain a large and expensive manufacturing facility and a high-salaried marketing group.

A consultant was employed to analyze the company's operations and to recommend a program of remedial action. A few months after she began her analysis of the company, she asked the president and the executive committee, "Why do you stay in that part of the electronics industry when you have been losing money steadily for three years and there are no prospects you can ever make profits there again?"

The directness of the question on a clearly vulnerable point jarred the executives into facing up to a decision not previously even discussed—liquidation of the unprofitable product line with no potential for improvement.

In addition to a hard-nosed look at sacrosanct subjects, the consultant (with wider experience in different companies and industries than corporate executives whose careers may have been limited to one company, one industry, or one geographical area) can often bring to the task new insights. In one company, the president and nine out of ten of the other top executives had devoted their entire careers to the same company. Their understanding of business was limited to a single industry with its small tangential and related activities. Here the consultant—knowing that the world of business is larger than the manufacture and sale of umbrellas, or file cabinets, or maple furniture—was able to suggest possibilities for a broadened base of operations.

No consultants are known, however, who have instantaneous, magic answers as to what goals a particular company might adopt. Surprisingly, some presidents think, "There must be someone, somewhere, who can tell us quickly what we ought to do." Here again, no such consulting sources can be found. The responsible consultant will take the time—and this does take time—to analyze objectively a company's existing operations before he or she is prepared to recommend programs of action and goals.

Adopt a Statement

The form and detail of the actual statements which define company goals vary from very simple to elaborate verbal descriptions. In one company, for example, the corporate goals are briefly stated:

1 To increase the return on investment from 4% to 6% by 1966.
2 To increase earnings from $3 per share in fiscal 1965 to $5 per share in 1967.

Another company's objectives are stated in a more detailed way:

1 To raise aftertax earnings from $12 million to $18 million by 1967 without diluting the equity.

2   To change the proportion of the company's military business from 65% to 40% in two years. (In another company a goal was expressed "to raise the percentage of military business from 40% to 65%.")
3   To liquidate in an orderly manner Division A and those parts of Division B which are unprofitable as soon as possible.
4   To search for and acquire one or more companies in the United States with sales of at least $10 million in the XYZ industry.
5   To establish in the Common Market at least three bases of operations, either by acquisition or by starting our own operations, by 1967.

Design a Plan

The creation of a statement of reasonable goals, in turn, leads to the need for a plan to realize those goals. Here, again, the plan may be a written description or exist only in the minds of top executives, and it may be relatively simple or exceedingly detailed and complex. Many companies of substantial size write descriptions of their goals and an overall company plan to arrive at those goals, and support these with a marketing plan, a technical plan, a manufacturing plan, a personnel plan, and a financial plan which includes a cash-flow plan.

Planning Staff

The importance of involvement by the chief operating executives has been stressed throughout this article to underline my conviction of the need for their participation. But clearly much of the data collection, procedures for the collection of data, and analysis can and should be done by subordinates in the organization or by a corporate planning office. The need for a separate planning staff is determined largely by the capacities, interests, and time of line and staff executives available. Sometimes the vice president of finance is given the responsibility of heading the planning function because the number aspects constitute a common language of plans.

I find, however, that the most effective way of accomplishing corporate planning is to create a new staff group reporting to the president—free from the diversion of day-to-day crises and charged with the responsibility of assisting the president. The assistance includes, among other things, helping the chief operating executive "to crystallize goals in the leadership and direction of the company."

Functions and Qualifications

The functions of a planning group vary, but the vital ones are included in the following statement adopted by a large western company:

1   To assure that divisions and subsidiaries prepare annual and five-year plans for growth.

2   To assist divisions and subsidiaries in the preparation of annual and five-year projections.
3   To identify areas of product opportunity for divisions and subsidiaries, and for corporate investment.
4   To perform market research as requested by divisions and subsidiaries.
5   To coordinate and monitor the preparation of a written, company-wide, five-year plan.
6   To analyze the economic future of existing operations and to recommend programs of growth or divestment.
7   To make analyses of business, economic, and political conditions bearing on existing or prospective areas of operations.
8   To be responsible for all negotiations with possible companies to be acquired.

During the past few years, many company managements have come to recognize the need for more formalized planning activities. This often leads to the creation of new units, ranging in size from one man to a dozen or more. Frequently, the personnel assigned to the function are transferred from existing line or staff activities. In some cases, these people perform admirable jobs. In a New York chemical company, for example, when the need for intensive planning was recognized, a statement was drafted of the ideal personal qualifications and experience for the job. Here are the important elements of that statement:

☐   Technical knowledge of organic and inorganic chemistry.
☐   Ability to manage people.
☐   Ability to inculcate division managers and headquarters staff officers with the importance of planning as an essential part of their jobs.
☐   Analytical capacity.
☐   Knowledge of financial data, including ability to analyze balance sheets, profit and loss statements, cash-flow forecasts, and operating and capital budgets.
☐   Imagination—ability to perceive new applications for corporate competence.

A review of personnel employed within the company disclosed that the manager of the research and development laboratory possessed most of the desired qualities, and he was moved to the new post, "Director of Product Development and Corporate Planning."

Job Requirements

Often, however, chief operating executives do not think through the job requirements of the important role to be performed by the head of planning.

Consequently, they assign somebody who just happens to be available. In some companies, retired, about-to-retire, pseudoretired, or quasi-retired executives are asked to take on this function during their remaining years with the company. The rationale is: "Joe has been with the company for 40 years, and he knows it inside and out. The planning responsibility will keep him busy for three or four years, and, besides, we need a younger man in his important operational job." When the planning group is regarded so lightly that it becomes a dumping ground for the aging or less competent, it is likely to achieve nothing of consequence. Planning today is a critically important function in management, and it requires the best talent, not the infirm of mind or body.

The need for additional personnel is dictated by the magnitude of the corporate tasks and the availability of staff help in the organization. For example:

In one company, the director of budgets had had extensive experience in another company with financial operating forecasts and cash flows, and their analyses. He was able and interested in serving the needs of the director of plans, and it was not necessary to assign a financial analyst to the plans office.

In another company, the market research department, part of the marketing group, regarded assignments from the plans department as an important part of its responsibilities and was equipped to handle them.

Many companies have assigned only a few personnel to the planning task initially and added others only when the job requirements indicated need for additional help.

Planners' Problems

Two critical problems which are sometimes encountered by the director of plans call for special attention and close monitoring by the chief executive to assure the success of the corporate planning function. Let's look at what can be done about each one.

Inculcating Awareness

One difficult problem of a director of plans is to inculcate line managers of divisions, subsidiaries, or other company operations with an awareness of the importance of planning as a vital part of *their* jobs. In some situations, long-range planning means nothing more to a division manager than going through the needless task of preparing an annual operating budget, getting it done, sending it to the vice president of finance, and forgetting about it until the next year.

In one eastern company with five years' experience with formalized corporate planning, the vice president for plans summarized her concepts of what remained to be done on this problem in future planning meetings:

1.   *Create an awareness in division managers of the need for planning beyond the next 12 months into 1966, 1967, and beyond.*   This can be done by directing the questions and discussion away from the current year whenever possible and talking about 1967 and 1968 objectives.

2.   *Assess how well the divisions have integrated all the elements of planning in their programs (including timing) to make sure that programs have been thought through.*   The use of a checklist in this connection may be helpful, of which the key elements should be:

☐   Analysis (e.g., product-line breakdowns).

☐   Potentials—available skills, and available and needed resources.

☐   Problems—deficiencies evident.

☐   Establishment of best alternatives—suggested economic goals.

☐   Coordination-implementation-timing—the results expected, both financial and nonfinancial.

3.   *Create a means of implementing* continued *planning so that the divisions will complete any unfinished plan or revise any inadequate parts of it during 1965.*   As the discussion progresses, it is wise to examine areas in which planning is not complete and ask that a timetable and action plan be set up for putting together the missing elements after the meeting. Such a plan can be worked up between the division and the director of plans. In this instance, it is necessary to cover (a) the need for planning responsibility to be centered in a capable individual, and (b) the importance that management attaches to this function—which might require additional expenditure.

4.   *Determine what standards for measurement, if any, the divisions have in setting goals.*   For example, have the divisions set some overall goal to strive for in sales, profits, investment, and return, as a measuring stick of their own performance? Do they feel that the goals are adequate? What restrictions are holding them back from enlarging these goals?

5.   *Determine whether the divisions have compared the amount of technical effort (either at the division level or at the company's headquarters laboratory) on their long-range projects with the profit potential in these projects.*   In addition, it is important to determine whether they have considered the degree to which they should be investing profits from existing business in technical effort for potential future rewards. (Similar consideration can be given to marketing's planning for future sales by strengthening or adding to the market organization.)

6.   *Get across to the divisions that they should be striving to add more projects to their existing base than they or the corporation can absorb in terms of research and development and capital facilities, so that the most desirable projects can be selected from a wide list.*

7. *Assess the reasonableness of the goals, so as to come up with a consolidated, long-term corporate goal, adjusted to take into account undue optimism or pessimism in the divisions.* The plans should be weighed against past ability to get the job done, how tight a timetable is possible, and how capable the organization is, or can rapidly become, to accomplish the task.

8. *Determine the degree to which the headquarters staff, including marketing, planning, research laboratory, market research, manufacturing, can help implement the division's programs.*

9. *Make sure a program is established to see that the advice given by the headquarters staff is followed up.*

10. *Identify the ways in which the divisions can work together in projects requiring complementary skill.*

Unplanned Plans

Another critical—and frustrating—problem of directors of corporate planning evolves from the actions of the chief operating executive who accepts and approves a carefully worked out set of corporate goals and plans for achievement and then, by his or her arbitrary decisions, moves the company into activities neither related nor contemplated. Indeed, the most carefully thought-out corporate goals and plans must yield to the emergence of some new and previously unthought-of opportunity. Any planning program must be flexible. But, on fundamental plan principles, deviation from agreed-upon programs ought to be restudied before commitments are made. Consider:

In a company where a substantial part of its total investment was subject to the risks of operations abroad, the chief operating executive stated that the ratio of domestic to foreign investment should be increased and that no new money should be exposed to risks from abroad. Shortly after the corporation goals were discussed and adopted by the executive committee, the president learned of a possible acquisition in Italy. He flew to Rome and, within a relatively short time, negotiated and arranged for the purchase of a company. The foreign investment commitment increased by several million dollars, and the stated ratio goals became meaningless standards for the organization.

Concluding Note

Corporate planning is an inseparable part of the job of all chief operating executives; the futures of their companies depend upon the corporate courses prescribed by them. The only constant in the management of business organizations is change. The leadership in adapting corporate operations to the changing business world must come from the chief executives. Unless company presidents who have heretofore shunned the role give hard and fast attention to the future of their enterprises by personal involvement in planning, only the most fortuitous circumstances will enable their companies to avoid declines in sales, profits, and market positions.

Notes

1. See my book, *The Growth and Development of Executives* (Boston, Division of Research, Harvard Business School, 1950).

2. See Roger A. Golde, "Practical Planning for Small Business," *HBR*, September–October 1964, p. 147.

3. *Management Problems of Corporate Acquisitions* (Boston, Division of Research, Harvard Business School, 1962).

4. Reported in *Managerial Long-Range Planning*, edited by George A. Steiner (New York, McGraw-Hill Book Company, 1963), p. 38.

Appendix: Outline of a Five-Year Forecast

I. *Product-Line and Customer-Class Planning*
    A. Reports on major long-term, high-priority product-line or customer-class programs. Each such report should be a 15–30 minute summary giving the highlights of the technical marketing and production aspects of the program with a general timetable and financial projections. These reports should cover the two or three most important programs aimed at any one of these:
        1. Markedly expanding the division's participation in present product lines.
        2. Expanding present customer classes.
        3. Entering a new product area.
    B. A report on the compilation of information needed to do an effective job of long-range planning. Such information might include:
        1. Lists of appropriate product lines in which the division is now making products and product lines which might be considered for the division in the future.
        2. Lists of appropriate customer classes now being served by the division and new ones that might feasibly be served by it in the future.
        3. Market data on:
            a. Size of market—past, present, future.
            b. Rate of growth of market.
            c. Our sales to the market, if any.
            d. Rate of growth of our sales, if any.
        4. Financial data to cover these questions:
            a. In each product line and customer class in which

we now participate, what is our *net* profit, investment, and return on investment?
    b. To the extent that it is possible to say, what are our competitors' profits in the same fields?
    c. In new areas, what level of profitability can be expected?

  5. Analyses of:
    a. Resources (technical, marketing, production) available and required to expand our position.
    b. Competitive situation.

II. *Marketing Planning.* Obviously the previous section has included much of marketing planning, but more general subjects should be discussed under this heading. Possible examples are—

  A. Marketing organization planning, including possible changes in:
    1. Assignment of responsibilities by product line vs. customer class vs. geographical areas.
    2. Greater use of product managers, market managers, or specialists.

  B. Increase or decrease in the use of dealers or distributors to sell the division's products.

  C. Possibility of distributing products manufactured by others.

  D. Statement of pricing policy and pricing practices and discussion of possible changes.

  E. Salesmen's compensation plan—evaluation, expense control, incentives.

III. *Technical Planning.* Insofar as possible give a breakdown of 1964 actual and 1965 estimated expenses of the division's technical program, both in division laboratories and at central research, by the classes of work listed below. Cite the principal projects now being worked on and being considered for the future.

  A. Long-range offensive research—work requiring more than one year to complete that will be aimed at creating new or improved products for markets in which the division either does not participate or has such a small share as to be negligible.

  B. Long-range defensive research—work requiring more than one year to complete that will be aimed at maintaining or expanding the division's business in its present markets.

  C. Offensive development work—work requiring more than a few days, but usually less than a year, to complete that will be aimed at developing products for markets in which the division either does not participate or has a very small position.

     D.   Defensive development work.

     E.   Production service—short-range work aimed at trouble-shooting in plant, routine formulation changes, routine process improvements, and the like.

     F.   Customer service—work required to help the customer use the division's products.

     G.   Quality control—inspection of incoming raw materials, in-process materials, and finished goods.

IV. *Production Planning*

     A.   What major new facilities are being considered?

     B.   What, if any, possibilities are there for major improvements in processing efficiency, and what plans are being made to investigate them?

     C.   Report on status of program to obtain data on the capacity of each plant, preferably by major departments, covering:

          1.   What percent of capacity is now being utilized.

          2.   What further capacity will be required.

          3.   What steps must be taken to provide more capacity where needed or to utilize excess capacity where available.

V. *Export Planning*

     A.   Summary of past export sales by product line.

     B.   Plans, if any, for expanding these sales or adding new product lines.

VI. *Acquisition Suggestions*

     A.   In which geographical areas, product lines, and/or customer classes does the division think that acquisition of allied businesses should be considered as a route toward future growth?

     B.   What specific companies, if any, might be desirable acquisitions?

VII. *Manpower Planning*

     A.   Projection of manpower requirements in 1965, 1966, and 1967 for:

          1.   Key salaried employees.

          2.   Other salaried employees.

          3.   Production (manufacturing) labor.

     B.   In forecasting manpower requirements consider the present number in the group modified by:

          1.   Turnover (including anticipated requirements).

          2.   Needs anticipated for future growth of organization. [An expanded outline must be prepared to assist the divisions in estimating manpower requirements, and mailed to division heads in advance.]

     C.   Brief summary of recruiting and training program.

VIII.   *Financial Statements*
   A.   1963 and 1964 actual; 1965, 1966, 1967 projected.
   B.   Sales by product line.
   C.   Gross profit by product line.
   D.   Sales, administrative, and general expense.
   E.   Profit.
   F.   Investment—working and fixed.
   G.   Return on investment.
   [Sample forms must be provided for these items.]

18

Strategic Planning in Conglomerate Companies

NORMAN BERG

Norman Berg gives particular attention to the problem of how much to spend on development projects. He also presents a thoughtful discussion of planning as a social and economic process.

The art and science of influencing the long-term growth of a company—call it long-range planning, strategic planning, or simply good management—has received much attention of late. There are indications, however, that this outpouring of literature, useful as it has been for a vast variety of planning problems, has as yet provided little practical help to one important group of managers: those concerned with strategic planning for the *large* and *diversified* industrial corporation. In companies of this type, the crucial question that must be answered repeatedly is: "How much should we be spending for the future in each of our divisions?"

My discussions at a number of companies with managers interested in or responsible for long-range planning efforts, extensive field research in one large and highly diversified company, and work experience in the area of long-range planning on the staff of a large electronics company have led me to conclude that answering this deceptively simple question for the highly diversified company poses significantly different problems than does strategic planning in single-business firms, which most of the literature deals with.

These problems deserve top-level attention. Planning in large and diversified organizations is becoming increasingly important in our society, since more and more large companies follow strategies of diversification in their search for greater growth and stability and as an outlet for their retained earnings. The barriers and uncertainties presented by our antitrust laws often contribute to the trend towards diversification by making acquisitions in fields identical or closely related to the present main businesses of a large company seem unattractive.

In this article I shall try to answer the following questions:

☐ Why are the conflicts of interest and viewpoint between division managers and headquarters in diversified companies far more basic than they are in single-business firms?

☐ How do these conflicts produce widely different attitudes toward risk taking, the allocation of funds for development work, the judgment of what is an acceptable profit, and other issues?

☐ Why do top executives at the corporate level typically find that they can make only limited progress toward a solution of these difficulties, even though they strive to comprehend division managements' problems, obtain unbiased information, and use the best possible data about market trends, industry conditions, and so forth?

☐ What kind of view or philosophy of strategic planning will likely subject it to a deadening and uncreative bureaucracy—and what kind of perspective will contribute to a more vital, productive functioning of this important activity?

Conglomerate Companies

What is a "large and diversified" corporation? General Electric and Westinghouse, each with sales of many billions of dollars and with 50 to 100 divisions in significantly different businesses, represent the archetype of the large and diversified corporation as we will discuss it in this article. Enterprises of this sort can appropriately be described as "conglomerate companies." The cutoff point for companies in this range is an organization with perhaps five or six divisions in different businesses and with total sales of a few hundred million dollars. The diversity of the company is far more important than size alone. A large mining company, airline, or integrated steel company is likely to offer significantly different, and in many respects less complex, planning problems than a smaller, but more diversified, corporation.

A conglomerate company, then, consists of a number of product divisions which sell different products principally to their own markets rather than to each other. In terms of a simple diagram, the various divisions of a conglomerate company could be represented as shown in the top part of Exhibit 1. But an integrated company—a steel company, for example—could be represented as shown in the lower diagram. Conglomerate companies will, of course, have some internal sales and transfers, and integrated com-

Exhibit 1. Schematic Representations of Two Types of Companies

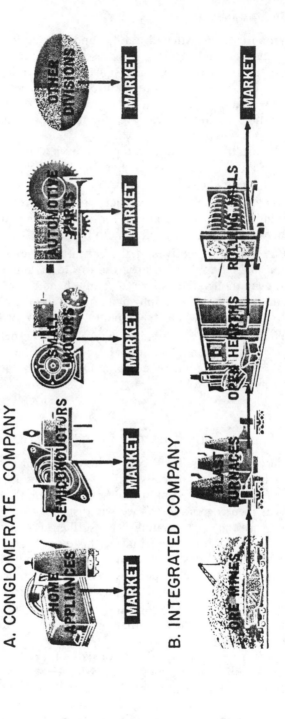

A. CONGLOMERATE COMPANY

B. INTEGRATED COMPANY

panies will have some external sales and purchases at various points in the process. In the main, however, the transfer of products is as shown in the exhibit. The consequences of this difference are twofold:

1   The problems of simply *comprehending* the various technologies and markets the diversified company is engaged in are great—much greater, in fact, than the problems for a single business, even though the latter may be very large in terms of sales and assets.
2   A conglomerate company, unlike an integrated company, has the opportunity to expand its operations in any given area *virtually independently* of its plans for other areas, except that the corporate resources used to promote the expansion of one division cannot be used to promote the expansion of other divisions. An integrated company, by definition, is more constrained by the need to maintain a balance among its various activities.

Both of these factors are a source of considerable difficulty for the conglomerate company with regard to the rational allocation of funds for growth among the many different businesses in which it is engaged. The problem is not the simpler one which the integrated company faces of how to utilize a limited supply of chips in a single poker game. It is the much more difficult one of how to divide a limited supply of chips among perhaps 50 separate but simultaneous poker games in which not only the rules of play and the stakes, but also the experience, ability, resources, and determination of one's own players as well as of their opponents in the many games vary considerably.

Allocation of Funds

How is the top management of a conglomerate company to decide where it should bet its corporate chips? The problem of allocating *capital* funds has been much discussed in the literature, but these funds are only part of a company's investment in the future. Many companies spend at least as much on development in the form in which we are concerned with it in this article— that is, on expense projects intended to enhance the future profits, growth, or stability of the company. These development projects are, to a very considerable extent, discretionary during any given year, and they differ significantly from capital expenditures in that their cost is an expense for the year, and they tend to reduce reported current profits for the unit concerned.

With regard to the authorization of such development projects undertaken by divisions to promote division growth or profits, one highly successful and respected division manager in a conglomerate company claimed that the corporate management should have very little to say about the matter:

If you have good division managers, 80% of the say on spending money on projects for the future should be up to them. I think you have to trust the division managers to a great extent. You pay them well to know and run that part of the business for you, and you should rely on them. Presumably nobody at the corporate level knows as much about the division manager's business as he does. Things have to go from the bottom up, not from the top down; that's what a decentralized business is supposed to do. If the division manager is convinced that his division ought to spend the money for a certain project, and we have the money in the till, that should be the end of it.

We have got to keep in mind what makes the corporation go. It isn't headquarters; I never have seen a headquarters that generated income by itself. The foundation for the whole operation is the divisions; it is in the divisions that the money is spent and the money is earned. That is mainly where we have to worry about selling things for more than they cost to make. Headquarters, of course, has an important role to play, but it is too easy for them to get preoccupied with their own needs.

An offsetting argument to this division viewpoint, however, is that the corporate level is in a position to decide which game offers the best rewards to the corporation, whereas the individual division managers cannot possibly know the other 49 games in any detail. They therefore are not in a position to exercise much judgment as to where the corporation should be risking its money. It was principally for this reason that the company referred to above was engaged in efforts to move the control of the expenditure of funds for these development projects to a higher level in the company. The planning vice president stated his position as follows:

I suppose the simplest explanation of why we are trying to move the control of spending money on expense projects for the future up to higher levels in the corporation is that it is just not possible to set up the rules so that the self-interest of the divisions or the product groups will always coincide with the corporate interest. This presents some severe problems if you permit the divisions a great deal of freedom with regard to determining the amount and the purpose of their expenditures for the future.

Many people, I suppose, will just say that this means the rules or the objectives have not been set correctly or carefully enough, and that they need to be refined or improved. I don't think that this is the case; we simply have to take a larger part in managing the affairs of the divisions so that they come out in the corporate interest. It is more efficient than continually refining the rules and procedures.

It is my contention that such conflicts are not merely another form of the old "top-down vs. bottom-up" planning controversy but instead stem from (1) fundamental differences in interests, and (2) difficulties in comprehending all of the activities of the conglomerate company. Let us explore the nature of, and the reasons for, the differences in interest between the divisions and the corporate level.

Conflicting Interests

If significant amounts of money are spent by divisions on projects originated and evaluated by the divisions, as is likely to be true in any decentralized company, then the issue of the degree to which the interests of the divisions coincide with the interests of the corporation as a whole is crucial. Planning implies the existence of an interest and a purpose or goal; one plans *for* something. A situation in which different organizational units are spending money to attain goals that sometimes conflict with corporate goals would be a clear source of difficulty for those engaged in overall corporate planning.

Much of the writing about business planning assumes either explicitly or implicitly that the goals at various levels and in various subunits within a corporation are for all practical purposes identical or complementary; conflicts, if acknowledged, tend to be treated more as relatively isolated aberrations rather than as evidence of more basic and underlying factors. There are, of course, many respects in which the interests *are* identical; business *is* essentially a cooperative venture. It is also apparent, however, that there are a number of respects in which the interests of various levels and units of a large corporation are in conflict with each other. Furthermore, these differences in interest are a major source of difficulty in corporate attempts to ensure that money spent by divisions on projects for the future is expended in the *corporate* interest.

Origins of Differences

The differences just mentioned stem from two broad conditions. I shall describe each of them briefly.

Everyday Environment

The first condition is definitely the less important of the two. In any large company the everyday environment of the divisions is significantly different from the environment at the corporate level. Managers at the division level are likely to have spent much of their working lives in their present or other divisions. Their "real world" is the people they see and work with every day, the products they manufacture, the physical facilities of the division, and the projects that are underway in the division. Customers and customer complaints are real; the products produced for them are tangible and are probably well understood. How well the product works and how efficiently it is produced are probably the result of innumerable personal challenges, successes, and failures.

The corporation may make a great number of products, and it is somewhat difficult for the personnel in one division to feel much identification with products they do not understand very well and which are made by people they have never met in plants they have never seen. The corporate level itself may also seem to be an abstraction, a sometimes arbitrary and usually remote power which often causes the division managers trouble and worry and extra work—and which assesses a healthy overhead charge against the divisions in return for the harassment!

At the corporate level, in contrast, it is all too easy to feel that the real world consists of "the corporation" and those quantified abstractions which show how the corporation is doing with respect to the outside world—profit and loss statements, balance sheets, the market price of the stock, and so on. *"What does it mean in earnings per share?"* is often the all-important question with regard to division proposals or problems. The real world at the corporate level becomes the external and quantitative measure of corporate performance and health; divisions can all too easily be regarded as suppliers of financial statements which merely fit into the vast corporate totals. Understanding the divisions and their products and businesses in detail, having precise knowledge and independent judgment about the many thousands of divisional development projects throughout the corporation, or being greatly concerned about the effects of decisions regarding projects on *individuals* in the divisions is simply out of the question for the corporate level. As one observer has commented:

> The central staff live in the midst of aggregates, trends, averages, and overall generalization. They are remote from the individual reality behind the words and figures that flow and jumble over their desks. They are dealing with symbols: their input is items on paper, and their output is items on paper. . . .[1]

There is little that can be done about the problems caused by differences in the environments at different levels. Management can be encouraged to become better acquainted with operations and problems at levels other than its own, but this is likely to produce a marginal improvement only. The worlds and problems *are* different, and so the outlooks will remain different.

Compensation and Promotion

The second and by far the most important reason for the existence of different interests at different levels in the organization can be found in the workings of the compensation and promotion procedures in any large organization. Organizational rewards are more likely to come to the manager whose *own* profits and growth are noteworthy; any other contribution any single manager might make to the overall corporate profitability and growth is both minute and obscure by comparison. In addition, it is much easier in any corporation to measure the *current* performance of a manager—whether it be in terms of profits, sales growth, new product introduction, or whatever—than the provision which he or she makes for the future. Hence the latter is likely to be overlooked or minimized. Indeed, the easiest measure of managers' investment in the future is simply their current expenditures for future profits, growth, and stability—expenditures which tend to reduce their current profits. Most corporate managements find it extraordinarily difficult to decide how much any particular manager should be spending for the future and whether or not he or she is spending it wisely.

Executives at headquarters may wish division managers to forgo project expenditures in their own divisions so that other divisions with better opportunities in the future will have more to spend, to sacrifice current profits for possible greater future profits, or to take risks which are desirable from the corporate standpoint but which have a good chance of seriously affecting their own current performance adversely. But such actions are not likely to appear as attractive to the division management as the corporate management might wish. For one thing, division managers have a different viewpoint regarding risk than do executives at the corporate level. This brings us to the next topic.

Attitudes Toward Risk

One of the competitive strengths of a large company is its ability to undertake large and risky projects. If $100 million are to be spent throughout the corporation on various projects for the future, some proportion of these projects can surely be of the type for which the probability of success is very low but for which the rewards of success, if it is achieved, are extremely high.

However, what might be a perfectly acceptable and even desirable level of risk for the *corporation* to undertake on a particular project, because of the averaging effect of a large number of projects undertaken throughout the company, may be much too high a level of risk to appear attractive to the particular division or individual who is striving for the current profits and who must bear responsibility for that particular project. The performance and ability of a given manager are likely to be judged on the *outcome* of the project, not by whether a good job was done even though the project failed and the risk was desirable from the corporate standpoint.

Reactions to Pressure

The following comments from an experienced staff planner in a large corporation point out the possible adverse effects of pressures for current profits on the willingness of people to undertake risky projects:

> We haven't grown because there has been too much emphasis on current profit. We are in effect encouraging the division managers to undertake only low-risk, and as a result low-profit, projects. Consequently we miss out on most of the developments that really pay off, and we seldom get into a market that is growing rapidly early enough. I think we have forgotten that business is inherently risky, and that *we have to make it possible for people at various levels in the organization to take risks*.

It is not only pressures for current profits that can encourage strong aversion to high-risk projects among division personnel. The same effect can be produced when higher-level executives check in detail on the outcome of projects, unless they do so with great care. Witness these comments from a division manager in the same large company referred to above:

If people are going to check up on you, project by project, then it is easy to get into a pattern of looking more favorably at those projects which are more certain to come out. One way we get around this here in this division is to have our own kitty of project funds to work with. Nobody at the group level knows about it—they wouldn't like it, I'm sure—but I feel that we have to operate that way.

Our group planning director is a smart guy, but he would have to have an auditor in here full time to prevent it. Even then I am sure the guys out in the shop could find a way to get around it.

I think this may be one of the dangers for a company as diversified as we are. We end up making things too formalized in our efforts to control the operation, and as a result it is the guy in a garage somewhere that takes on some of the really risky projects that may very well bankrupt him but will pay off handsomely if they work out.

With regard to the danger that such detailed checking on projects will result in the submission of low-risk projects in the future, a vice president in the same company with extensive experience in managing a research laboratory commented as follows:

That's always a problem, but I think we are handling it better by getting it out in the open. The danger with risk is that you won't even get to look at the projects that people turn down because they are too risky unless you have some sort of a system for getting at them. We hope we'll be able to undertake more of the risky projects, rather than fewer, by making the process more explicit.

There are substantial advantages to some form of checking by higher levels of management on the outcome of division projects, of course, and rapid improvements in data-handling techniques are likely to make more checking increasingly common. Such information helps corporate management spot where difficulties are arising so that something can be done about the problem, and also helps it evaluate the claims for money it receives from given divisions during the next planning session. Where the selection criteria are not clear and the information on proposed projects is far from certain, past performance is undeniably useful in assessing the probability of satisfactory future performance. The problem is to find a way for higher management to retain the advantages of checking on the outcome of individual projects without unduly discouraging the undertaking of risky projects. How can this be done?

Project-Failure Allowance

One way to encourage more risk taking at the division level is to establish a norm for project failures. As judged by outcome with respect to plan, *a proportion of the projects should fail*. A record of no failures is no more a sign of good performance or wise choice of projects, from a corporate viewpoint, than is a credit policy that results in no bad-debt losses. Both are unduly conservative from a corporate viewpoint.

The basic difficulty of standards of performance which equate "good performance" with a low failure rate, as is normal in most large organizations, is that such standards may encourage behavior which is clearly not in the corporate interest. A low failure rate may be the result of truly good performance on the projects selected, but it may also be the result of:

1 Selecting only low-risk projects;
2 Expending disproportionate effort on projects which are not turning out well, when this effort might be more profitably expended on projects which are turning out better than expected and are not in trouble; or
3 Showing convincing but misleading figures.

The time pressures on executives and the wide range of technologies encompassed by projects make it unlikely that any form of checking on projects by higher levels of management can amount to much more than seeing how many were successful.

Establishing a norm or standard which allows a manager a certain proportion of failures, then, is likely to encourage him to take on more risky projects. This obviously does not mean that, for any *specific* project, failure is preferable to success; it merely means that success on *every* project should not be weighted so highly by superiors that not enough high-risk projects will be undertaken.

Growth and Profits

The varying attitudes toward risk at different levels in the corporation, which affect the choice of projects on which funds for the future are spent, are important. The influences which affect the *total* amounts of funds available to various units to be spent for the future are also important, however. The problem is not only *what* the money is spent for in each division, but also *how much* each division gets.

The basic assumption underlying the decentralization of management responsibility is that the corporate purposes will thereby be better served than they would be by a different form of organization. Along with decentralization generally goes a system of rewards, both formal and informal, which encourages a manager to seek to enlarge his or her *own* sales and *own* profits. This is all done for the purpose of improving performance with respect to corporate sales and profit goals; the rationale is simply that the overall corporate goals are most likely to be achieved by a system in which the various separate businesses of which the company consists are encouraged to pursue similar goals at their own level.

Such an approach to the management of a large and diversified company has great merit; indeed, it is difficult to imagine how a large and diversified company could operate on a "traditional" centralized basis. There is considerable evidence to show that decentralization and diversification, either product or geographical, tend to go hand in hand.[2] This approach, however, does create some particularly thorny problems with regard to the allocation of resources which are likely to affect the growth of the divisions concerned.

Money for Development

The first of these problems stems from the tendency of people in a large corporation to be primarily concerned with the growth of their own unit rather than with the growth of the corporation as a whole. This is perfectly understandable and is even encouraged by the structure of rewards within the corporation. Since growth is "good," the means by which it can be made more likely become important to the divisions. Funds to support projects intended to enhance future sales and profits are one such resource. The desire of divisions in one large company to compete for money for their own development prompted the following comment from a vice president of planning:

> One complicating factor is that *people always want to spend money for development if they are allowed to*. In our small engine division, for example, we have about 28 engineers working on product development. This is an old field, though, and about all they do is change the appearance a little once in a while and maybe move the accessories from one side to another. *We might do much better from a corporate viewpoint to put this money elsewhere*. I suppose there are lots of products like this. Some people just make dishpans; they make them well for the lowest possible price in an alley shop and don't spend a nickel for R&D. It might be we should run more of our divisions that way.

The tendency for each division to spend as much money as possible in the pursuit of its own growth objectives is tempered by the need to earn at least a minimum level of current profits as well. This immediately leads to conflict, for development projects generally reduce current profits; either can be increased at any time at the price of a reduction in the other. A division manager commented on the relationship between the level of such project expenditures and "acceptable profits" as follows:

> The projects we do are limited by the amount we have available, but you can't separate the two that easily. The amount we have available for our projects is also influenced by the projects we have and by what an acceptable level of profit consists of. The acceptable level of profit is, of course, strongly influenced by our group vice president. If we operate at a loss, then he has to cover it from another of his divisions or else get his profit goal reduced.

Not only, then, are the total project expenses and the level of current profits closely interrelated in any given unit; they may also be related to the profits earned and the projects undertaken at every *other* level in the corporation.

It is possible, of course, for the total corporate profits to be truly "what is left" after "proper provision for the future" is made at every level; it is also possible for any given level to *expand* the total funds available for either development or current profits rather than to increase one by reducing the other. In a conglomerate company studied in some detail, however, current profits and the amount of money available for development projects were felt to be closely related as a practical matter. Executives at each organizational level felt that the *balance* between these development projects and current profits at their level was relatively flexible, but that the *total amount* available to them for both of these categories was relatively fixed, since it tended to be what was left after relatively well-known price, volume, and cost factors were allowed for. In addition, division personnel acknowledged that it followed from simple logic that the corporate profit goals could only be achieved if the divisions contributed their profits.

A reduction in the profit goal for any single division in order to accommodate more of its development projects, then, would result in either (1) the reduction of the total corporate profit goal or (2) an increase in the profit goal of some other division and a likely reduction in the amount of money available for its development work.

Acceptable Performance

Every division in a company is usually under pressure to produce current profits. The controller of a newly formed division in the electronics business stated the pressures quite well:

> Every division *has* to show a profit if it possibly can. That is what we are in business for. The corporation authorized a loss for us for the first two years, but that was all—and because of a cash bind for the corporation, we had to cut back even before we expected. We have been trying to run in the black ever since.

But just what *is* an acceptable profit for a particular division at a particular time? That strong profit pressures exist at all levels in almost every company is common knowledge. But is any company really in business to earn a current profit in *each* division *each* year? Is it in business to earn the same profit in each division, or "as much profit as possible"? Surely most companies are interested in overall company profits for at least a few years into the future—not necessarily maximum individual division profits for one year in any single division at the expense of future profits in other divisions.

Influencing the long-term growth of the corporation through the planning of expenditures for future development is unavoidably related to the question of what an acceptable profit will be for a specific division. To illustrate:

A newly formed electronics division might be judged to have much more favorable opportunities for growth than do many of the existing businesses in which the company is engaged. If this is so, it might be wise for the corporation to permit such a division to spend so much money for various development projects during the next five years that the division would consistently operate at a loss. This loss, of course, would have to be compensated for by the profits from other divisions if the corporate profit level is to be maintained. Presumably this could be accomplished by eliminating some of the *least desirable* projects in other divisions, thus increasing the current profits of these divisions.

To the corporate management, then, falls the role of influencing not only what the balance between current profits and development projects shall be for the *corporation as a whole*, but also what the balance shall be in *each of the divisions* of the corporation. Executives at the corporate level cannot avoid influencing this balance by asking the divisions to act either in their own best interests or in the corporate interests. Division interests are different from the corporate interests in some significant respects, and divisions are likely to spend as much for development as is made available to them. The divisions can no doubt judge what is in their own best interest better than the corporation can, but this ability is of little help to a corporate management interested more in spending the limited resources available to the corporation in *its* interest. In addition, asking the divisions to take a broad corporate viewpoint when striking a balance between their own project expenditures and current profit is asking them to do a job which men at the corporate level themselves find exceedingly difficult to do (and which the divisions are ill-equipped to attempt).

The choice for the corporation is therefore not *whether* management should influence this balance in the various divisions, but *how* it should do it. Funds for such development projects may be allocated explicitly, or, as is much more common, profit goals may be used to influence the level of project spending. Profit goals, though less precise, have the great advantage of being more "socially acceptable;" profit needs are much easier to justify than a more explicit starving of certain divisions.

Deciding on profit goals for various divisions is done in a variety of ways. Management may set corporate-wide profit goals to be used as targets in each of the divisions; it may set goals for improvment in profits each year; it may use profits of competitors of specific divisions as goals for those divisions; it may establish an atmosphere of "the higher the better" for profit performance; it may establish goals arrived at independently of any of the foregoing factors; it may even de-emphasize or ignore current profits. But whatever the method, it affects what the divisions spend on development, which in turn affects the relative opportunities for divisions to shape their own future.

"Administrative" Goals

The setting of profit goals for the various divisions is of course influenced by many factors other than the effect of the goals on project expenditures.

A major factor influencing the *total* amount of profit which must be earned at the division level is the pressure on the company as a whole to earn a satisfactory current profit. Current profits are, to a considerable extent, what the management is evaluated on by the outside world. One of management's most important tasks is to translate these external pressures for satisfactory profits *today* into internal profit goals which will enable the company to earn satisfactory profits in the *future*.

Managements cannot, of course, do very much about the way in which they are evaluated by the external world. If this evaluation is largely in terms of current profits, they will have to learn to live with the fact. For a small company in a single business, pressures from the financial community and the stock market to earn an "acceptable" profit affect management strongly. In a diversified company, however, these external pressures need *not* be translated directly into internal pressures for any specific division. The external profit pressures may be met by means of a variety of administratively determined, internal profit goals.

This potential flexibility in meeting external profit goals provides the large and diversified company with a competitive advantage which it should seek to exploit. There is no reason to suppose that the profit goals or the balance between development and current profits for any specific division at a certain time should bear any close relation to either the external pressures on the company or the profits earned by the competitors of a specific division. To translate such external pressures directly into internal goals is to substitute the judgment of an outside group of hundreds of thousands of investors—the "market"—for the judgment of division and corporate managers. There may well be many cases where, because of unique opportunities to undertake projects to enhance future profits or growth, it would be in the corporate interest to permit and encourage specific divisions to show either higher or lower profits than would be indicated by external measures.

(Such "administratively determined" profit goals have on occasion been criticized as being in violation of either the spirit or the letter of the antitrust laws. The absence of any illegal intent, however, such as to underprice competitors in order to drive them out of business, seems to be sufficient defense against charges of improper use of the financial resources often associated with great size.)

Division profit goals which *are* closely related to external pressures or corporate-wide goals are, of course, very much easier to arrive at and to justify than are administrative profit goals. If the management at the corporate level is to influence the relative growth of the various divisions by means of the funds it makes available to them for projects to enhance future profits and growth, however, the use of administrative profit goals is essential. It is a way to shield some divisions from profit pressures while increasing the profit pressures on others.

Administrative profit goals which allow for each division's opportunities cannot be set in a formal or analytical manner. Peter Drucker, for example, has commented as follows with regard to managed expenditures, which he considers essentially as expenditures to enhance future profits: "There are no formulas for making the decisions on managed expenditures. They must always be based on judgment and are almost always a compromise."[3]

And a planning director, with staff responsibility for about 15 divisions in the large and diversified company studied, commented:

> It's tough to draw the balance between the present and the future. Division managers will always say you are milking the business, not making the proper provision for the long range, and so forth. But the long range has to arrive sometime; you just can't keep spending for the future without the future and the benefits you were supposed to get ever arriving. You have to keep asking where the benefits are from the expenditures you made several years ago. There aren't any easy answers to any of this. If there were, we would have been doing it that way a long time ago.

Can Problems Be Avoided?

There are some things which the corporation can do to make the interests of the divisions correspond more closely with the corporate interests. Efforts can be made to reward the manager who does a good job—but fails—on a risky project which was desirable from a corporate viewpoint (just as the manager who does a good job and succeeds on a less risky project is rewarded). And efforts can be made to reward managers on the basis of their contribution to the long-term growth and development of the company as well as for the growth or current profit performance of their division.

It would be naive, however, to expect that one could eliminate the difficulties caused by the existence of different interests at different levels by simply pointing out how these interests vary. Improvements, of course, are possible, but progress is likely to come slowly. Compensation and promotion practices have evolved over time and depend in part on the formal, quantitative measures of performance which often need to be relied on in large organizations. The time pressures on management personnel, the years of conditioning in a particular organizational environment, and the difficulty of accurately measuring an individual's "good performance" from a *corporate* viewpoint make the problem of different interests a slow one to unravel.

What about moving the responsibility for making decisions which affect the relative long-run growth of the various divisions up to higher levels in the organization? How promising a solution is this? Actually this step does not *avoid* the problems caused by different interests; it merely seeks to *constrain the actions* taken by lower units so that they will be in the corporate interest. It does not, to any significant degree, make the interests of the various levels and units any more identical than they were previously. By moving some of the routine decisions which affect the long-run future of the company up to higher levels in the organization, however, many of the undesirable effects of the existence of different interests within the corporation are minimized. Instead of worrying about decisions made at lower levels because they are sometimes not in the interests of a higher level, the higher levels can make some of the decisions themselves in their own interests.

There are problems and limitations to this approach also, of course. The problems fall into three main categories: (1) comprehending, at the corporate level, the many different businesses the company is in; (2) obtaining unbiased information about projects; and (3) arriving at estimates of the corporate profitability of broad courses of action drawn from broad external data. These will be discussed in turn.

Who Is Smart Enough?

Since many of the allocation decisions at lower levels are based upon a consideration of the specific projects that are competing for the funds, it is natural to consider the problem at the corporate level as being similar. Instead of choosing among projects in a division or even in a group, the problem may seem to be simply that of choosing among projects for the entire corporation. It may appear to be a simple, logical extension of the approach which is widely used at lower levels and which has great theoretical appeal as well.

The trouble is that detailed decisions of this sort are extremely difficult to make at the corporate level in most large and diversified companies. One reason is the impossibility of finding any person or any committee at the corporate level that can comprehend in a significant sense the thousands of projects relating to the company's many different technologies and markets well enough to exercise any independent judgment about the projects. Another reason is the impossibility of obtaining objective and unbiased information at the corporate level about the costs and future benefits of the proposed projects.

The difficulty, then, is not with the manipulation of the data in order to establish a ranking of projects, but with the nature of the inputs to the analysis. Elaborate computational techniques or theories of choice are not likely to be of help, since they do not deal with the principal source of difficulty. Competition for funds to facilitate growth is likely to lead to "optimistic" estimates which make reliance only on the figures submitted unwise; paradoxically, if men at the corporate level could know enough about the individual projects to exercise their own judgment in the matter, this very knowledge would likely result in the submission of more realistic project estimates by the divisions.

These difficulties are expressed in a statement by the vice president of planning in the large diversified company which I studied. He was commenting on the proposal of one of his staff that a corporate approach to the allocation of funds could be based on a consideration of the divisions' individual projects on which funds would be spent—a total of perhaps 10,000 projects throughout the corporation:

> Theoretically, the approach of evaluating the projects and deciding which to back is probably correct. It is based on two assumptions, however, neither of which holds in this case: (1) You need to be assured of objective data. (2) You have to have qualified people to evaluate the projects.

> Those assumptions are not true for us at present, and I doubt that it is possible to make them come true. I agree that if we could get objective information from the divisions on their projects, we could probably do a better job of allocating money by dealing with the specific projects than in any other way. That's impossible, though, so I think we will just have to go from the top down. *We just can't find a common measuring stick that we can apply to all of these projects that will be reliable enough. And I don't see how we can possibly get or develop people for a corporate-level committee who would be qualified to evaluate all of these projects.*

The Rubber Yardstick

This vice president's comments about the lack of a common measuring stick that is reliable enough is a key point which is not very often recognized. To quote Peter Drucker again:

> In human institutions, such as a business enterprise, measurements, strictly speaking, do not and cannot exist. It is the definition of a measurement that it be impersonal and objective, that is, extraneous to the event measured. A child's growth is not dependent on the yardstick or influenced by being recorded. But any measurement in a business enterprise determines action—both on the part of the measurer and the measured—*and thereby directs, limits, and causes the behavior and performance of the enterprise.*[4]

Although in the company I have described executives at the corporate level felt that a project-by-project selection at their level was not feasible, most people at other levels felt that they could take such an approach at *their* level, while agreeing that the corporate level could not. This company was organized into a number of product groups, with each group made up of from five to ten divisions in somewhat related businesses. Several group-level planning personnel claimed to be able to evaluate projects from divisions in their groups, even though total group sales might be several hundred million dollars. A sample comment:

> It would be completely impossible to rank projects for the whole corporation at the corporate level. You can only make such a ranking on the basis of data furnished by divisions, and the only reason we at the group level can do it is that the group vice president that I am working with knows his divisions well enough to be able to go through the budgets project by project, on an individual basis. And I feel at home with it because I have been working with these businesses for five years.

At the division level, however, the feeling was often that moving project control even up to the group level was centralizing things too much. In response to a question whether it would be possible to select projects at the corporate level, for example, a division planning manager commented:

> There would just be too much for any one man or committee to know. That's why we have a group organization—to help corporate management screen and interpret what is going on, and to try to help them make some choice. But I don't think that even the people at the group level can know enough about all of the projects in all their divisions to do much selection or approval of projects in detail. *I think it is a good idea to centralize the control of such projects here at the division level rather than further down in the division; we are better able to spend the funds in the division interest that way.* I also think we will get into trouble if we try to centralize by moving the control much higher. The task gets too complicated; people just can't know enough to do the job as you get to higher levels.

In short, to place control lower in the organization is seen by the higher levels as resulting in inefficiency and waste, either because the goals at the lower levels are different or because the lower levels cannot see the "big picture" and the better opportunities for the corporation to spend money elsewhere. At the same time, moving the control to higher levels is seen by the lower levels as resulting in inefficiency and waste because the higher levels "can't know enough about our problems." Recognizing that such conflicts of opinion are almost certain to be expressed may lead one to avoid the temptation to keep changing the approach to planning merely in response to the comments at the various levels. As Ely Devons has commented so aptly with regard to the centralization-decentralization issue in wartime planning in England:

> This conflict . . . appeared at every stage in the administrative hierarchy. . . . The supreme coordinators struggled for more centralization, the planners in each department for more to be left to their discretion. . . . Given the limitations of the human mind and capacity, this conflict was the greatest obstacle to efficient aircraft planning. If the inevitability of this conflict is not recognized, planning becomes even more inefficient than it need be. For in such circumstances those who influence the planning machinery oscillate between a passion for decentralization, as a result of an exaggerated awareness of the inefficiencies of centralization; and a drive towards central coordination as a result of a terror of the illogicalities which emerge when important decisions are taken at the periphery. . . . The balance between the two is never found, since at each stage the evils of the existing system and the advantages of the alternative always impress most.[5]

Value of External Data?

Finally, management can attempt to evaluate the desirability of spending money in various broad areas by looking at external information: size and

growth of markets, price and profit trends, possible technological developments, probable strength and intentions of competitors, and so on. Reliance
on this approach also has its difficulties. The principal one is simply that
useful and independent estimates of long-term profitability are extremely
difficult for executives at the corporate level to come by, particularly in light
of the many businesses that a conglomerate company is engaged in. The
vice president of planning mentioned earlier commented as follows on the
efforts of his company to use such projections as a basis for determining,
in a rigorous way, levels of spending on development projects or administrative profit goals for the divisions:

> I'm afraid that future profitability is simply too difficult to evaluate when
> dealing with decisions of this type. The most we can do is to list a number
> of factors which we think are indications of future profitability, and
> perhaps gather some information on some of them. We don't have any
> analytical way of taking all of these factors into account or combining
> them with each other—it will simply have to be a matter of discussion
> and judgment. We have a lot of abstract and unquantifiable factors to
> deal with, and someone will just have to decide. I do think that oppor-
> tunities for profits in various fields are likely to depend heavily on growing
> markets and on high and rapidly changing technologies, but I don't think
> we have a good enough way of quantifying and working with these factors
> yet.

Economic and Social Process

A major factor which permeates and complicates all aspects of any planning
process, and any attempts to influence it, is that planning is an economic
and social process. Hence considerations other than purely economic ones
must be taken into account. This observation is inescapable to anyone who
has spent any significant amount of time talking with people at various levels
in a large organization who are actually engaged in planning activities. For
example, take the issue of why the expense funds for development projects
cannot be identified and allocated as explicitly and as formally as capital
funds are administered in most companies. One planning manager, responsible for a number of divisions with total sales of several hundred million
dollars, summed up the general feelings very well:

> This idea of allocating expense funds for development projects more
> explicitly is a tough one. I think it would be unwise at this point to
> attempt to identify these funds explicitly, in effect put them all into a
> corporate kitty, then dole them out again on some basis. It would be
> intolerable to those who are being starved, since it would mean that their
> businesses are probably going to wither. It might look like the most logical
> thing to do, but I'll have to admit that I think a slightly devious approach
> lots of times works best.

What do you suppose such explicit allocation would do to the morale of the division? Also, you put yourself in a tough spot if you take the responsibility for the future away from the division manager. We at the group level would be in a very bad box if we cut many projects from a division and the division did poorly, and the division manager then said, "It is because you cut out those essential projects." If things go bad, he can always blame it on you. The same holds true for the corporate management with respect to the groups and divisions.

I definitely think we have to do this by means of profit pressures rather than by explicit allocations of project funds. We have always been able to accomplish about the same thing in effect in our groups in the past by this means. People don't take exception to this as much. The group vice presidents know the divisions and the businesses well enough so that they can force divisions to spend more or less on development projects by the pressure they exert on profits. The main disadvantage is that you can't very well discriminate between long-range and short-range expenditures that way, but they know the divisions well enough to be able to recognize, and prevent managers from cutting out, projects they think should be kept.

Of course, people kick if the profit goals are too tight, but that isn't the same as saying that someone else is going to grow at your expense. We can always say someone else is having a bad year, the corporation needs profits this year, we have cash flow problems, and so on.

The preference for using "slightly devious" profit pressures to influence the level of project spending in the divisions, rather than explicit allocations which would unfortunately more clearly identify those divisions marked for growth and those likely to decline, is clear evidence of the need to make the planning process socially acceptable as well as economically logical and efficient. Explicit allocations might be more precise and intellectually "neat," but it is much easier to justify difficult profit goals than an equivalent decision to starve certain divisions at the expense of others.

Another important consequence of the fact that the planning process is not just an economic one is that the corporate management can *influence* but not *direct* what happens in the divisions. As corporate executives adopt a strategy to deal with the problems arising from the different interests of the divisions, for example, the divisions will change their own strategy to further their own interests. A corporate staff man with considerable experience in planning commented as follows on the efforts of the corporate level to find some basis for allocating development funds among the divisions:

You know, if we set up some formal and analytical system for splitting up the money among the divisions, we're likely to have trouble with the people trying to beat the system as soon as they figure out how it works. The proposals would probably be inflated a little bit at first anyway, and I suppose if we discount the proposals, they will inflate them even more the next time. *That might make the second year of this more difficult than the first, rather than easier.*

Inescapable Realities

Viewing the process as closed and deterministic and similar to an engineering design problem leads the manager to seek further and further refinements in procedures and in definitions, always hoping that each successive step will lead one closer to the goal of ensuring that all decisions will be made in the corporate interest. A point of diminishing returns is soon reached, not becaude the new procedures do not in fact improve upon specific present shortcomings of the system, but rather because the situation keeps changing as people find some other way to further their own interests, and because the procedures themselves may entail other and more serious costs.

Compensation and promotion policies have a strong and unavoidable effect on how any planning system works. If the organization tends to reward current profit performance, or sales growth, or success on projects, or stability of earnings, or conformance to plan or to corporate-wide "guidelines," any planning system will be hard pressed to direct the attention and efforts of division management to areas in which, from a corporate long-range viewpoint, they "should" be doing more or "should" be acting differently. This is a limitation affecting any planning system. It is an outgrowth of the basic organizational environment in which any planning process operates. Efforts to "tie people down" will all too soon result in a deadening and uncreative bureaucracy, responsive neither to the market nor to competitors.

Conclusion

In perspective, I believe four main ideas stand out in my study of strategic planning in large and diversified companies.

1. *An essential prerequisite to understanding and prescribing for strategic planning in a conglomerate company is to view the process as a multilevel activity.* The corporate level, units at the group level, and units at the division level *each* exist in an environment which is in some respects unique. At each level considerations of stability, profits, or growth *at that particular level* are better understood and of more immediate concern than are similar considerations for other levels. Executives at each level tend to view the process and the problems from the standpoint of their own interests and environment. Planning activities at each level are not simply a part of an overall corporate activity in which each part contributes only to the corporate interests. Each unit is engaged in planning activities which at least partially reflect the unique environment and interests of that particular unit. To the extent that the interests of the divisions and the corporation conflict with each other in significant respects, so will the goals to which each unit directs its planning efforts.

2. *The strategic planning process in a conglomerate company involves noneconomic as well as economic goals at each organizational*

level.   Assuming that the process is not—or asserting that it should not be—influenced by noneconomic goals is unlikely to result in realistic suggestions for the practicing administrator. These noneconomic or social goals of the planning process may include, for example, efforts to ensure the stability, or perhaps promote the growth in size or importance, of any number of social systems or groups within the company, as well as efforts to maintain or create, in these many social systems, an environment satisfactory and rewarding to its members. The opportunity for creative and worthwhile contributions and the degree of responsibility retained at one's *own* level for some of the important and significant decisions and actions affecting one's own future are clearly influenced by the nature and operation of the planning process. As a result, it would be foolish to expect that such non-economic goals will not have an important effect on the planning process.

3.   *Viewing strategic or long-range planning as an activity separate from and independent of short-range planning and current profit goals is both misleading and dangerous.*   Strategic planning does not affect only the future, and current operations are not concerned only with the present. Every company is faced with the problems of surviving and maintaining stability today as well as making provision to ensure survival and stability tomorrow. Providing for the future very often detracts from current performance; for instance, it may mean reducing current profits to undertake development projects which may enhance future profits or stability. It is the planning system which makes possible the continuous balancing of the need to show satisfactory performance this year with the desire to be in a position to show satisfactory performance in the future as well.

4.   *Planning cannot be neatly formularized.*   To quote once more an experienced and able corporate planner: "If there were any easy answers to any of this, we would have been doing it that way a long time ago." Corporate strategy in any conglomerate company is the result of a complex planning process. Executives are not likely to get much help from simple "how-to-do-it" prescriptions based on the assumption that strategic planning is a single, vertical, and largely economic process which can be broken up into distinct divisional tasks, each of which contributes solely to the corporate planning task, and each of which is no different in principle from the corporate planning task. Complex problems seldom have simple solutions.

Notes

1.   Theodore Morgan, "The Theory of Error in Centrally-Directed Economic Systems," *The Quarterly Journal of Economics*, August 1964, p. 398.

2.   See Alfred D. Chandler, Jr., *Strategy and Structure* (Cambridge, Massachusetts Institute of Technology Press, 1962), especially pp. 14–17.

3. *The Practice of Management* (New York, Harper & Brothers, 1960), p. 85.

4. "Long Range Planning Means Risk-Taking," reprinted from *Management Science*, April 1959, in *Long-Range Planning for Management*, edited by David W. Ewing (New York, Harper & Row, 1964), p. 18.

5. *Planning in Practice* (London, Cambridge University Press, 1950), pp. 14–15.

19
Strategic Management for Competitive Advantage

FREDERICK W. GLUCK, STEPHEN P. KAUFMAN, and
A. STEVEN WALLECK

Some companies want to know why others always seem to be out in front; is it just plain luck, or did those organizations really figure out how best to win the market contest? In this article, the authors make a case that the "best" companies, at least as defined by market leadership, plan to win. In fact, they have progressed along a path leading to a new, dynamic form of management, where executives are willing to restructure their companies to generate successful plans, carrying the much overworked term "flexibility" to its logical end.

While the article, and its prescriptions, are logically oriented in the direction of complex enterprises, any executive interested in the future of his or her particular organization can learn from the authors' description of the four phases of corporate planning. Few companies are left that do not engage in some form of planning, and most will find themselves at some time progressing on the path toward the goal of strategic management.

For the better part of a decade, strategy has been a business buzzword. Top executives ponder strategic objectives and missions. Managers down the line rough out product/market strategies. Functional chiefs lay out "strategies" for everything from R&D to raw-materials sourcing and distributor relations. Mere planning has lost its glamor; the planners have all turned into strategists.

All this may have blurred the concept of strategy, but it has also helped to shift the attention of managers from the technicalities of the planning process to substantive issues affecting the long-term well-being of their enterprises. Signs that a real change has been taking place in business's planning focus have been visible for some time in the performance of some large, complex multinational corporations—General Electric, Northern Telecom, Mitsubishi Heavy Industries, and Siemens A.G., to name four.

Instead of behaving like large unwieldy bureaucracies, they have been nimbly leap-frogging smaller competitors with technical or market innovations, in true entrepreneurial style. They have been executing what appear to be well thought-out business strategies coherently, consistently, and often with surprising speed. Repeatedly, they have been winning market shares away from more traditionally managed competitors.

What is the source of these giant companies' remarkable entrepreneurial vigor? Is it the result of their substantial investments in strategic planning which appear to have produced something like a quantum jump in the sophistication of their strategic planning processes? If so, what lessons can be drawn from the steps they have taken and the experience they have gained?

To explore these questions, we embarked on a systematic examination of the relation between formal planning and strategic performance across a broad spectrum of companies (see the Appendix). We looked for common patterns in the development of planning systems over time. In particular, we examined their evolution in those giant companies where formal planning and strategic decision-making appeared to be most closely and effectively interwoven.

Our findings indicate that formal strategic planning does indeed evolve along similar lines in different companies, albeit at varying rates of progress. This progression can be segmented into four sequential phases, each marked by clear advances over its predecessor in terms of explicit formulation of issues and alternatives, quality of preparatory staff work, readiness of top management to participate in and guide the strategic decision process, and effectiveness of implementation (see Exhibit 1).

The four-phase model evolution we shall be describing has already proved useful in evaluating corporate planning systems and processes and for indicating ways of improving their effectiveness.

In this article, we describe each of the four phases, with special emphasis on Phase IV, the stage we have chosen to call strategic management. In order to highlight the differences between the four stages, each will be sketched in somewhat bold strokes. Obviously, not all the companies in our sample fit the pattern precisely, but the generalizations are broadly applicable to all.

Phase I: Basic Financial Planning

Most companies trace the origins of a formal planning system to the annual budgeting process where everything is reduced to a financial problem. Procedures develop to forecast revenue, costs, and capital needs and to identify limits for expense budgets on an annual basis. Information systems report on functional performance as compared with budgetary targets.

Exhibit 1. Four Phases in the Evolution of Formal Strategic Planning

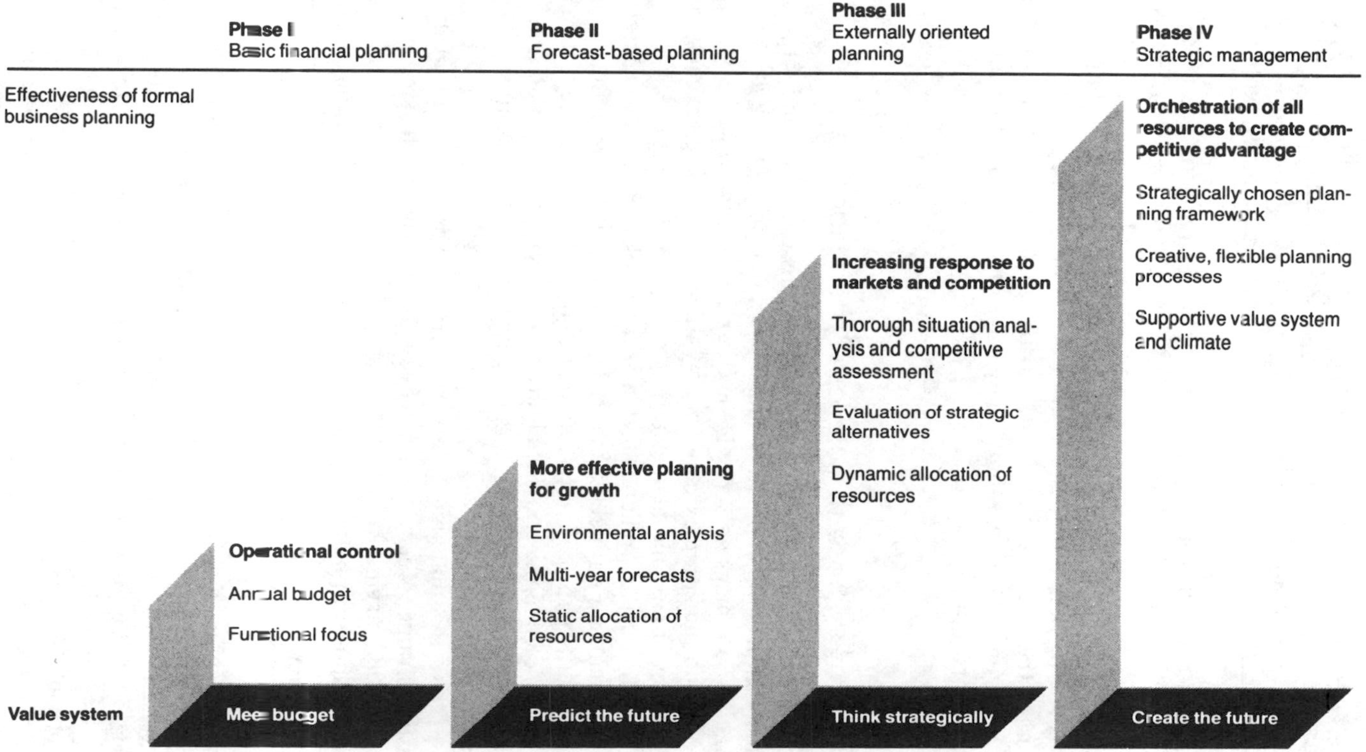

Effectiveness of formal
business planning

	Phase I Basic financial planning	Phase II Forecast-based planning	Phase III Externally oriented planning	Phase IV Strategic management
	Operational control	**More effective planning for growth**	**Increasing response to markets and competition**	**Orchestration of all resources to create competitive advantage**
	Annual budget	Environmental analysis	Thorough situation analysis and competitive assessment	Strategically chosen planning framework
	Functional focus	Multi-year forecasts	Evaluation of strategic alternatives	Creative, flexible planning processes
		Static allocation of resources	Dynamic allocation of resources	Supportive value system and climate

Value system

Meet budget	Predict the future	Think strategically	Create the future

Companies in Phase I often display powerful business strategies, but they are rarely formalized. Instead, they exist. The only concrete indication that a business strategy exists may be a projected earnings growth rate, occasionally qualified by certain debt/equity targets or other explicit financial objectives.

The quality of Phase I strategy depends largely on the CEO and the top team. Do they really know their company's products and markets and have a good sense of what major competitors will do next? Based on their knowledge of their own cost structure, can they estimate what the impact of a product or marketing change will be on their plants, their distribution system, or their sales force? If so, and if they do not plan for the business to grow beyond traditional limits, they may not need to set up an expensive planning apparatus.

Phase II: Forecast-Based Planning

The complexities of most large enterprises, however, demand more explicit documentation of the implicitly understood strategies of Phase I. The number of products and markets served, the degree of technological sophistication required, and the complex economic systems involved far exceed the intellectual grasp of any one manager.

The shoe usually pinches first in financial planning. As treasurers struggle to estimate capital needs and trade off alternative financing plans, they and their staffs extrapolate past trends and try to foresee the future impact of political, economic, and social forces. Thus begins a second phase, forecast-based planning. Most long-range or strategic planning today is a Phase II system.

At first, this planning differs from annual budgeting only in the length of its time frame. Very soon, however, the real world frustrates planners by perversely varying from their forecasts.

In response, planners typically reach for more advanced forecasting tools, including trend analysis and regression models and, eventually, computer simulation models. They achieve some improvement, but not enough. Sooner or later plans based on predictive models fail to signal major environmental shifts that not only appear obvious after the fact, but also have a great and usually negative impact on corporate fortunes.

Nevertheless, Phase II improves the effectiveness of strategic decision-making. It forces management to confront the long-term implications of decisions and to give thought to the potential business impact of discernible current trends, well before the effects are visible in current income statements. The issues that forecast-based plans address   for example, the impact of inflation on future capital needs or the inroads foreign manufacturers may make in domestic markets—often lead to timely business decisions that strengthen the company's long-term competitive position.

One of the most fruitful by-products of Phase II is effective resource allocation. Under the pressure of long-term resource constraints, planners learn how to set up a circulatory flow of capital and other resources among business units. A principal tool is portfolio analysis, a device for graphically arranging a diversified company's businesses along two dimensions: competitive strength and market attractiveness.

As practiced by Phase II companies, however, portfolio analysis tends to be static and focused on current capabilities, rather than on the search for options. Moreover, it is deterministic—that is, the position of a business on the matrix is used to determine the appropriate strategy, according to a generalized formula. And Phase II companies typically regard portfolio positioning as the end product of strategic planning, rather than as a starting point.

Phase II systems also do a good job of analyzing long-term trends and setting objectives (for example, productivity improvement or better capital utilization). But instead of bringing key business issues to the surface, they often bury them under masses of data. Moreover, Phase II systems can motivate managers in the wrong direction; both the incentive compensation program and informal rewards and values are usually focused on short- or medium-term operating performance at the expense of long-term goals. In sum, Phase II planning all too easily becomes a mechanical routine, as managers simply copy last year's plan, make some performance shortfall adjustments, and extend trend lines another 12 months into the future.

Phase III: Externally Oriented Planning

In an environment of rapid change, events can render market forecasts obsolete almost overnight. Having repeatedly experienced such frustrations, planners begin to lose their faith in forecasting and instead try to understand the basic marketplace phenomena driving change. The result is often a new grasp of the key determinants of business success and a new level of planning effectiveness, Phase III.

In this phase, resource allocation is both dynamic and creative. The Phase III planners now look for opportunities to "shift the dot" of a business on a portfolio matrix into a more attractive sector, either by developing new business capabilities or by redefining the market to better fit their companies' strengths. A Japanese conglomerate with an underutilized steel-fabricating capacity in its shipyard and a faltering high-rise concrete smokestack business combined them into a successful pollution control venture.

In the search for new ways to define and satisfy customer needs, Phase III strategists try to look at their companies' product offerings and those of their competitors from the viewpoint of an objective outsider. For example, one heavy equipment manufacturer assigned a strategy team to reverse-engineer the competitor's product, reconstruct its manufacturing facilities on paper, and estimate the manufacturing cost for the competitor's product in the competitor's plant. The team members discovered that design improvements had given the competitor such a commanding advantage in production cost that there was no point in trying to compete on price. But they also found that their own product's lower maintenance and fuel costs offered customers clear savings on a life-cycle cost basis. Accordingly, the sales force was trained to sell life-cycle cost advantages. Over the next three years, the company increased its market share by 30% and doubled its net profit.

Another strategy, derived from an external perspective, was devised by a U.S. industrial commodity manufacturer. When sales in one of its major product lines declined swiftly following the introduction of a new, cheaper competitive product, it decided to find out the reason. Through field interviewing with customers, it discovered that the sales slide was nearly over, something competitors had not realized. Since sales of the product had dropped off to a few core markets where no cost-effective alternative was available, it decided to put more support behind this product line, just as the competition was closing its plants.

The manufacturer trained the sales force to service those distributors who continued to carry the line and revised prices to pick up competitive distribution through master distributor arrangements. It even resisted the move of the trade association to reduce government-mandated safety requirements for handling the newer products. By the time its strategy was obvious to competitors, the manufacturer had firmly established a distribution lead in a small but attractive product/market segment.

The SBU Concept

A distinguishing characteristic of Phase III planning in diversified companies is the formal grouping of related businesses into strategic business units (SBUs) or organizational entities large and homogeneous enough to exercise effective control over most factors affecting their businesses. The SBU concept recognizes two distinct strategic levels: corporate decisions that affect the shape and direction of the enterprise as a whole, and business-unit decisions that affect only the individual SBU operating in its own environment. Strategic planning is thus packaged in pieces relevant to individual decision-makers, and strategy development is linked to strategy implementation as the explicit responsibility of operating management.

There are limitations to the SBU concept. Many enterprises, such as vertically integrated companies in process-oriented industries, cannot be neatly sorted out into discrete business units because their businesses share important corporate resources—sales, manufacturing, and/or R&D. In other situations, strategy may dictate a concerted thrust by several business units to meet the needs of a shared customer group, such as selling to the automotive industry or building a corporate position in Brazil. In still other cases, the combined purchasing power of several SBUs or the freedom to transfer technologies from one business to another can be more valuable than the opportunity to make profit-oriented decisions in discrete business units. For example:

A major chemical company found that several of its competitors, who had grown large enough to integrate backward into feedstock production, were beginning to gnaw at its historic competitive edge as a fully integrated producer. Part of the reason was that by licensing certain technology to the competition, the company had given away a raw-material cost advantage that it could not match with its own older plants. The basic problem, however, was that its product managers were preoccupied with competitive threats in only a handful of the many product/market segments they served. Decisions that seemed to make sense at the individual business-unit level were adding up to deep trouble for the company as a whole.

A major supplier of industrial equipment divided its electric utility business into two SBUs, a power generation business and a power transmission business. Much too late, top management discovered that neither SBU had considered pollution control equipment to be part of its legitimate charter. As a result, the company found itself unable to bid on that business— which accounted for a full quarter of electric utility capital spending.

The most significant way in which Phase III differs from Phase II is that corporate planners are expected to offer a number of alternatives to top management. Each choice is usually characterized by a different risk/reward profile or gives priority to a different objective (for example, greater employment security at some cost to ROI). This change is quite pervasive; in fact, one simple way of determining whether a company has advanced to Phase III is to ask managers whether their boss would regard presenting strategy alternatives as a sign of indecisiveness.

The "alternate strategies" approach becomes both the strength and the weakness of Phase III planning, for it begins to impose a heavy—sometimes unacceptable—burden on top management. As the organizational capability for detailed product/market and business-unit planning spreads through the organization, the number of issues raised, alternatives surfaced and opportunities developed expands alarmingly. Top managers soon recognize that explicit choices are being made by planners and managers deep down in the organization without top-level participation—and that these decisions could significantly affect their company's long-term competitive strength and well-being. This knowledge unsettles top management and pushes it to a heavier involvement in the planning process, Phase IV.

Phase IV: Strategic Management

Phase IV joins strategic planning and management in a single process. Only a few companies that we studied are clearly managed strategically, and all of them are multinational, diversified manufacturing corporations. The challenge of planning for the needs of hundreds of different and rapidly evolving businesses, serving thousands of product/markets in dozens of distinct national environments, has pushed them to generate sophisticated, uniquely effective planning techniques. However, it is not so much planning technique that sets these organizations apart, but rather the thoroughness with which management links strategic planning to operational decision-making. This is largely accomplished by three mechanisms:

1   A *planning framework* that cuts across organizational boundaries and facilitates strategic decision-making about customer groups and resources.
2   A *planning process* that stimulates entrepreneurial thinking.
3   A *corporate values system* that reinforces managers' commitment to the company's strategy.

Planning Framework

As noted previously, many Phase III companies rely on the SBU concept to provide a planning framework—often with disappointing results. However, there are frequently more levels at which strategically important decisions must be made than the two implicit in SBU theory. Moreover, today's organization structure may not be the ideal framework in which to plan for tomorrow's business, and a strategically managed company may arrange its planning process on as many as five distinct planning levels:

1. *Product/market planning.* The lowest level at which strategic planning takes place is the product/market unit, where typically product, price, sales, and service are planned, and competitors identified. Product/market planners often have no control over different sets of manufacturing facilities and so must accept a predetermined set of business economics.

2. *Business-unit planning.* The bulk of the planning effort in most diversified make-and-sell companies is done at a level where largely self-contained businesses control their own market position and cost structure. These individual business-unit plans become the building blocks of the corporate strategic plan.

3. *Shared resource planning.* To achieve economies of scale or to avoid the problem of subcritical mass (e.g., in R&D facilities), resources are shared. In some cases, the assignment of resource priorities to different business units or the development of a plan to manage a corporate resource as a whole is strategically important. In resource-based or process-oriented industries, strategies for shared resource units often determine or constrain business-unit strategy.

4. *Shared concern planning.* In some large companies, a distinct level of planning responsibility is required to devise strategies that meet the unique needs of certain industry or geographic customer groups or to plan for technologies (e.g., microprocessors, fiber optics) used by a number of business units.

5. *Corporate-level planning.* Identifying worldwide technical and market trends not picked up by business-unit planners, setting corporate objectives, and marshaling the financial and human resources to meet those objectives are finally the responsibility of corporate headquarters.

For corporations involved in only a few, closely related product/markets, a two- or three-level planning framework may be entirely adequate. Even when additional planning levels are required, these companies need not insert another level of organizational hierarchy in order to plan shared resources or customer sector problems. Experience suggests, however, that it is important to recognize such issues where they exist and to assign explicit planning responsibility to an appropriate individual or group in the organization.

Otherwise, critical business decisions can slip between the cracks, and the corporation as a whole may find itself unable to capitalize on its strategic opportunities. Because the selection of a framework for planning will tend to influence the range of alternatives proposed, few strategic planning choices are more important. The definition of a strategic planning framework is, therefore, a pivotal responsibility of top management, supported by the corporate planning staff.

Planning Process

While planning as comprehensively and thoroughly as possible, Phase IV companies also try to keep their planning process flexible and creative.

A principal weakness of Phase II and III strategic planning processes is their inescapable entanglement in the formal corporate calendar. Strategic planning easily degenerates into a mind-numbing bureaucratic exercise, punctuated by ritualistic formal planning meetings that neither inform top management nor help business managers to get their jobs done. Division managers have been known to attempt to escape from the burden of "useless" annual planning by proposing that they fold their businesses into other SBUs, at least for planning purposes.

To avoid such problems, one European conglomerate has ordained that each of its SBUs initially study its business thoroughly, lay out a detailed strategy, and then replan as necessary. It has found that well-managed businesses in relatively stable industries can often exist quite comfortably with routine monitoring against strategic goals every quarter and an intensive strategic review every three to five years. The time saved from detailed annual planning sessions for every business is devoted to businesses in fast-changing environments or those not performing according to the corporate blueprint.

Because it is hard to institutionalize a process that can reliably produce creative plans, strategically managed companies challenge and stimulate their managers' thinking by:

Stressing Competitiveness.   The requirement for thorough understanding of competitors' strategies recently has been the planning keynote of a U.S. electrical products company well known for its commitment to planning. Top management comes to the planning meetings prepared by its staff to bore in on a few key issues or events. "If, as you say, our competitors are only three years away from introducing microprocessors in their control units, why are they already talking about it in their annual reports?" the president might ask. "What cost savings could our customers achieve with microprocessor-controlled equipment?" or "Who are our competitors' leading engineers?" It takes only one such grilling session to make division managers aware of gaps in their competitive information.

Focusing on a Theme.   Several major companies periodically reinvigorate their planning processes by asking their managers to key annual plans to a specified theme. International business, new manufacturing process technology, the value of our products to customers, and alternative channels of distribution have all been used successfully. This approach has obvious limitations: it doesn't work with business units in trouble, and it should be avoided until the value of formal planning is well established.

Negotiating Objectives.   Several companies are trying to negotiate strategically consistent objectives between corporate headquarters and business-unit general management. "We want two years and $35 million in additional investment to prove to you we can make this into a 35% gross margin business," said the new general manager of a division in trouble. "During that time we will make zero profit, but we'll strengthen our market share by three points and reduce material waste at our Atlanta plant from 10% to 3%. Alternatively, you can have $4 million per year at the bottom line next year and $6 million the year after that. No investment, and only minimal share loss. But be prepared to sell out the whole division, because after that it's all downhill." Faced with clear options, corporate management could suggest ideas and concessions that would promise them most of their share growth and some profitability for much less cash commitment up front.

Demanding Strategic Insights.   Avoiding competition by an indirect approach is the essence of creative and innovative strategy: a reformulation of a product's function, the development of new manufacturing methods or distribution channels, or the discovery of dimensions of competition to which traditional competitors are blind. One way to generate this kind of thinking is to ask each business manager to describe the specific business advantage he or she intends to achieve. Top management reviews each business plan skeptically. As one CEO tells division heads: "If you can't tell me something about your business I don't already know, you probably aren't going to surprise our competitors either." This technique relies heavily on the corporate planning staff, who are charged with demonstrating to uncreative business-unit planners that there are new ways of looking at old businesses.

Corporate Value System

The value system shared by the company's top and middle managers provides a third, less visible linkage between planning and action. Although the leadership styles and organizational climates of companies that can be called strategically managed vary considerably, and in even one company a great deal of diversity can be found, four common themes emerge from interviews with personnel at all levels in strategically managed companies:

1 The value of teamwork, which leads to task-oriented organizational flexibility.
2 Entrepreneurial drive, or the commitment to making things happen.
3 Open communication, rather than the preservation of confidentiality.
4 A shared belief that the enterprise can largely create its own future, rather than be buffeted into a predetermined corner by the winds of environmental change.

Teamwork on task force projects is the rule rather than the exception in strategically managed companies. Instead of fearing these uniquely dangerous expeditions beyond the security of the organizational thrust, managers learn to live with the ambiguity that teams create in return for the excitement and variety of new challenges.

The resulting continual reorganization can appear bizarre from outside the organization. For example:

Observers trying to make sense of top management personnel changes in one highly successful telecommunications company were left scratching their heads, as first the chairman stepped down to become president and then he was further demoted to become CEO of a major subsidiary. Who was running the company?, observers asked. Which individual was responsible for their brilliantly executed strategy? No one. The whole team at the top was so strong that no single manager deserved sole credit. The changes in title visible to the public were more an indication of the successful execution of phases of the company's strategy than they were signals of the rise or fall of a single individual's career.

Entrepreneurial drive among managers and technical personnel at all levels is a valued form of behavior in strategically managed companies. One organization's top management was eager to get in on the ground floor of a synthetic fuel equipment business. Six levels down from top management, an applications engineer in the specialty metals division was faced with a notice of a substantial cost overrun on an expensive piece of test equipment.

Instead of cancelling the order to source the equipment from a less costly supplier and thereby incur a six-month delay, the engineer went to the boss, and eventually to the boss's boss, to find out whether the delay to execution of the company's strategy was worth the cost savings. As a result, the engineer did overrun the project budget, but the test equipment was available when needed.

Confidentiality about the company's strategy is one of the hardest things for top management to give up. And yet it is impossible for a company to be strategically managed without the involvement of wide niches of relatively junior people in many aspects of the company's strategic plans. It is not necessary for top managers to divulge everything, but as a minimum, junior managers should know the strategic purposes their actions serve.

In retrospect, one chairman confided that he had overestimated the value of confidentiality. "We had a good idea for a strategy for our specialty business. But we couldn't implement it without letting everyone in the company know about it. We took the chance; now I suspect everyone in the industry knows what we're doing. But they can't get their act together to overtake us. We're moving too fast."

A shared commitment to creating their own future is the underlying ethic of strategically managed companies. Instead of marginal improvements—a few more shares of market or a few percentage points of cost reduction—managers set for themselves ambitious goals that if accomplished will lead to a sustainable competitive advantage for their company. For example:

A Japanese television manufacturer, faced with rising material and labor costs, ordered its engineers to reduce the number of component parts in its color TV sets by 30%. Innovative design approaches have since enabled the manufacturer to increase volume substantially while halving the number of workers in its assembly plant.

A machine tool manufacturer has undertaken to change the way a whole industry buys its machinery. Into a sales environment where close personal relations on the plant floor and with the process engineers was formerly the key to success, it is systematically injecting a top-management-oriented, technically and financially argued sales approach.

At the same time, it is radically upgrading its research and development capabilities, adding computer-aided engineering, software development, and systems engineering support. "Very little of our product advantage has patent protection," concedes the CEO. "But if we can persuade the industry to buy on productivity rather than on cost and delivery, the premium we can charge for engineering value will fund enough research to keep us three to four years ahead." Using this approach, the manufacturer has already built one of the five largest machine tool companies in the world.

As the economic system becomes more complex and the integration of single business units into multinational, diverse organizations continues, ways must be found to restore the entrepreneurial vigor of a simpler, more individually oriented company structure. Strategic management, linking the rigor of formal planning to vigorous operational execution, may prove to be the answer.

Appendix: A Quest for Common Patterns

For two years, we and our colleagues studied the development of formal planning systems in 120 companies, mainly industrial goods manufacturers (client and nonclient) in seven countries. To determine how, and to what extent, formal planning actually influenced the major decisions shaping those companies' business strategies, we sifted material ranging from case histories and interview notes to detailed financial analyses. The four phase evolutionary model emerging from this work was further explored by in-depth analysis of 16 representative companies, each with over $500 million in sales, in which the relationship between planning and strategically important action was especially well documented.

For the purposes of the study, "business strategy" was defined as a set of objectives and intergrated set of actions aimed at securing a sustainable competitive advantage. The concept of strategic management described in this article differs somewhat from that of H. Igor Ansoff, who invented and popularized the term.* We define it as a system of corporate values, planning capabilities, or organizational responsibilities that couple strategic thinking with operational decision-making at all levels and across all functional lines of authority in a corporation.

---

*See *From Strategic Planning to Strategic Management*, edited by H. Igor Ansoff, Roger P. Declerch, and Robert L. Hayes (New York, John Wiley & Sons, 1976).

20
Portfolio Planning
Uses and Limits

PHILIPPE HASPESLAGH

Some consultants, academics, and top managers view business in depersonalized, economic terms. There are "rules" in the marketplace that underlie competition; apparent exceptions are simply temporary aberrations. This view has deeply affected the corporate planning process. During the 1970s, theories cropped up, somehow divorced from the real world. A company's future role was dictated more by its structural position than by any subjective managerial judgment.

These approaches often fail in their implementation, however. It is managers, after all, who must ultimately act on the plans a system produces. They have to deal with the real world. And they, and the company, may never be able to fully realize the ideal solution for a particular business problem. The exceptions and discontinuity with which managers are all too familiar may be more important in planning the future of a business than impersonal forces or established industry structures.

How far has a depersonalized planning approach supplanted traditional management? To help discover an answer, the *Harvard Business Review* recently sponsored a survey of *Fortune* "1000" industrials by Philippe Haspeslagh. The subject was strategic portfolio planning, until recently the most popular of planning tools.

Haspeslagh's results show that the approaches do help managers strengthen their planning process and solve the problems of managing diversified industrial companies. But Haspeslagh also found that the secret to success does not lie simply in the analytic techniques that are the cornerstone of portfolio planning theory but rather in meeting the administrative challenges of embodying the theory in the management process. Managers cannot afford the luxury of divorcing theory from practice. For them, the dilemma is a false one; a theory only becomes useful when it meets the light of administrative reality.

Author's Note. I want to thank all the executives who shared their time and concerns by participating in the survey—in particular, Michael Alik at the Mead Corporation, Warren Batts at Dart & Kraft, and Donald Povejsil and William Nesbitt at Westinghouse Electric, where in-depth preliminary research was done. For their comments I want to thank Norman Berg, Joseph Bower, and Richard Meyer of the Harvard Business School, as well as Dominique Heau and Martine van den Poel of INSEAD. All conclusions and shortcomings are mine.

The diversity of large industrial—and mostly multinational—corporations can be at once their greatest source of competitive advantage and the well-spring of their most fundamental difficulties. Diversity provides an opportunity for these companies to use cash flow generated by their mature basic businesses to gain new leadership positions. Internally, however, this same diversity also creates a managerial gap between the corporate level, which has the power to commit resources but often only a superficial knowledge of each business, and the business level, where managers have the substantive knowledge required to make resource allocation decisions but lack the "big corporate picture." Corporate managers may often feel they are too far away to see the trees yet standing too close by to take in the forest.

In the late 1970s, a new generation of strategic planning approaches called portfolio planning spread across a wide range of companies in response to the problems and prospects of managing diversity. On the basis of my survey, I estimate that, as of 1979, 36% of the *Fortune* "1000" and 45% of the *Fortune* "500" industrial companies had introduced the approach to some extent. Each year during the last five years, another 25 to 30 organizations have joined the ranks.

Advocated by consulting firms like the Boston Consulting Group, McKinsey, and Arthur D. Little and touted by organizations like General Electric, Mead, and Olin, portfolio planning has struck the minds of many corporate executives. They speak a new strategic language and set up scores of bubble charts to explain their enthusiasm in corporate boardrooms. Most important, however, portfolio planning seems to have profoundly affected the way executives think about the management of their companies.

But what is all the fuss about? What is portfolio planning—as preached—and as practiced? How widespread is its application? What are the problems with its implementation? Does it really work? Or is it just another set of words that consultants have sold to top management—words that must be learned but that are then easily forgotten?

In 1979, I set out to investigate the impact of portfolio planning and its implications for corporate administration in a survey of *Fortune* "1000" companies sponsored by the *Harvard Business Review* (see the Appendix for an explanation of the methodology). From subsequent conversations and interviews with planners, financial officers, and CEOs, I found that portfolio planning approaches are widespread among large diversified industrial companies and being increasingly introduced.

There seem to be some limits to the practice of portfolio planning as well as tremendous—and sometimes latent—opportunities. Among the more serious limits are that:

☐   The road to portfolio planning is a long one; therefore, companies often get stuck trying to implement it and cannot realize the full potential of the approach.

☐   If a company looks on portfolio planning as merely an analytic planning tool, it will not realize its benefits.

☐ In implementing portfolio planning, companies often write in biases that block its usefulness, including the tendency to focus on capital investment rather than resource allocation—or cost efficiency at the expense of organizational responsiveness.

☐ Portfolio planning seems unable to successfully address the issue of new business generation.

Despite these difficulties, the corporate managers surveyed want to press ahead with portfolio planning, largely because the approach:

☐ Promotes substantial improvement in the quality of strategies developed at both the business and the corporate level.

☐ Produces selective resource allocation.

☐ Provides a framework for adapting their overall management process to the needs of each business.

☐ Furnishes companies with a greatly improved capacity for strategic control when portfolio planning is applied intelligently and with attention to its pitfalls.

Before I explain the findings in detail, I will briefly review the challenge facing diversified companies, the reason behind the widespread application of the portfolio planning approaches, and the characteristics they have in common. Then I will delve closely into the findings before I offer some advice on the introduction of the technique and speculate on its future.

The Challenge: How Best to Manage Diversity

The basic challenge for the modern corporation lies in the sheer number of businesses over which it holds sway. Managers of large companies in the 1980s cannot possibly be familiar with all the relevant strategic aspects of each unit of their organizational structure.

Faced with this challenge, companies react in two ways. They may seek a substantive solution and simplify the problem by limiting their activities to businesses that are easy to comprehend or that share a common strategic logic. Or, to avoid the complexity of managing interrelatedness, they may treat their businesses as stand-alone units.

Usually, however, companies tackle the problem by developing a supra-administrative capability. The typical organization creates intermediate organizational levels (groups or sectors) and uses intermediate managers and administrative systems to measure, evaluate, and reward performance. Yet for all their sophistication, modern companies still experience difficulty in managing diversity.

Often top management is aware only of the short-term financial performance of its businesses (and even that is buried in the fragmentation of profit centers and the aggregation of reporting structures). Senior executives often end up delegating major decisions, which then become based on individual track records and managerial influence and heavily weighted by short-term career risks. Corporate top management becomes actively involved when dramatic across-the-board moves are called for. The uniformity of administrative systems indeed makes it very difficult to escape uniform pressures across all businesses.

As a result, a range of conflicts buffets almost any company. Even supposedly well-run organizations oscillate between periods of uniform emphasis on profits and emphasis on growth—often coinciding with the tenure of a particular CEO. What is needed to counter these problems is a management system that provides (1) corporate-level visibility of performance on both strategic and financial terms, (2) selectivity in resource allocation, and (3) differentiation in administrative attention among businesses.

The Essence of Portfolio Planning: How It Helps

Portfolio planning recognizes that diversified companies are a collection of businesses, each of which makes a distinct contribution to the overall corporate performance and which should be managed accordingly. Putting the portfolio planning philosophy into place takes three steps as the typical company:

1 Redefines businesses for strategic planning purposes as strategic business units (SBUs), which may or may not differ from operating units.
2 Classifies these SBUs on a portfolio grid according to the competitive position and attractiveness of the particular product market.
3 Uses this framework to assign each a "strategic mission" with respect to its growth and financial objectives and allocates resources accordingly.

The approach, then, allows management to see business performance as largely determined by the company's position within the industry. Companies can theoretically assess the strategic position of each of their enterprises and compare these positions using cash flow as the common variable. A verbal and graphic language facilitates communication across organizational levels. Finally, the approach helps build a framework for allocating resources directly and selectively and for differentiating strategic influence.

Focusing Debate on the Real Issues

Given the attractiveness of portfolio planning theory and its rapid acceptance by major companies, it is not surprising that the approach has stirred up much debate. Most of it has been ill focused, however, for proponents and critics alike are more interested in a dialogue about analytic techniques than in solving the practical problems inherent in implementation.

So they argue about which "portfolio grid" technology a company should choose between—the Boston Consulting Group growth/share matrix or the General Electric-McKinsey industry attractiveness/business position grid, the Arthur D. Little industry maturity/competitive position grid or the Shell Directional Policy matrix.

That discussion is sterile; the question of which grid to use and where to place a business on it is least important. The real issue is how a company can best define an SBU and assign a strategic mission to it. In short, what is a company to do with each of its businesses?

The decision on a strategic mission always requires a broad analysis of industry characteristics, competitive positions, expected competitive responses, financial resources, and the opportunities of other businesses in the portfolio. Whatever grid it chooses, a corporation's assessment comes down to a judgment heavily influenced by administrative considerations.

In selling a company on the "what," the consultants sometimes forget the "how." They make it appear that portfolio planning will emerge like a deus ex machina out on the corporate landscape—that its administration will pose no difficulties as long as top management has the will to implement it. A senior partner in a consulting firm explained his position as follows:

> The challenge of portfolio planning really is analytical, not administrative. The way I see implementation is what I call the rule of the prince: once the analysis is done, a strong CEO should see to it that the portfolio strategy gets implemented.

The First Steps

If the experience with previous generations of planning approaches furnishes any lesson, the usefulness of portfolio planning is determined, of course, by the success a company has with its implementation. In formulating the basis for my survey, I made a number of assumptions. The first is most basic— that administrative rather than technical problems create the greatest difficulties for companies implementing any portfolio system.

My assumption was subsequently borne out as respondents reported that administrative problems loomed the largest. In fact, managers found the labels commonly used with the grid technologies to be largely irrelevant and often the source of psychological problems during the introduction of the technique. A lot of the "better" portfolio planning companies avoid their use and focus on what to do with the business.

Another important judgment involves the kinds of categories companies work with. Any theory will mean different things to different practitioners, so I devised categories to help distinguish among the various forms portfolio planning has taken.

My interpretations of the data allowed me to make distinctions among companies (see Exhibit 1 for the various types) with:

Exhibit 1.   **Creating Portfolio Planning Categories**

Sample Section from Questionnaire

11. The following questions seek to determine how far your company has carried portfolio planning.	Yes	No, not yet	No, will not	No, hasn't thought about it
Has your company categorized its businesses on a portfolio grid?	☐	☐	☐	☐
Has your company made a corporate decision to have a strategic mission for each of its businesses?	☐	☐	☐	☐
Does your company explicitly label each of its businesses with a strategic category?	☐	☐	☐	☐
Has your company explicitly assigned each of its businesses a strategic mission?	☐	☐	☐	☐

Evaluating the Responses

Does your company use portfolio planning?	Does it employ a grid analysis?	Has it made a corporate decision about missions?	Does it use labels?	Does it assign each business a mission?	Type of portfolio planning	Companies in sample	Years since intro-duction
Yes	Yes			No	Analytic	13	4.8
Yes	Yes	Yes	Yes	Yes	Process portfolio planning	78	5.5
Yes	Yes	Yes		Not yet	Unassigned portfolio planning	36	4.2
Yes	Yes	Not yet		Not yet	Undecided about portfolio planning	36	3.2
Yes	Not yet	Not yet		Not yet	New portfolio planning	13	1.5
No					No portfolio planning	106ᵃ	

ᵃExcludes 67 respondents whose companies are not diversified.

☐ *No portfolio planning.* No intention to introduce the technique.

☐ *Analytic portfolio planning.* Use confined to a planning tool at the corporate level, no intention to negotiate explicit strategic missions with managers, and business strategies influenced by traditional administrative tools and profit pressures.

☐ *Process portfolio planning.* Portfolio planning as a central part of the ongoing management process, as evidenced by the explicit negotiation of strategic missions with SBU managers.

As could be expected, getting to process portfolio planning is a long road, so I had to develop subcategories to take into account the various stages of introduction, like companies with:

☐ *New portfolio planning.* Having just introduced the approach, the companies are still in the process of constructing the portfolio.

☐ *Undecided portfolio planning.* The initial grid analysis completed, the companies have not yet decided at the corporate level what to do with the businesses or which strategic missions to assign to the SBUs.

☐ *Unassigned portfolio planning.* Corporate-level decisions are reached on the strategic mission for each business unit, but companies hold no explicit negotiations yet with the unit managers.

The Use of Portfolio Planning

Diversified companies, particularly the large ones, widely practice the art of portfolio planning; for most of them, it is indeed much more than an analytic tool. At the corporate level, 75% practice or are implementing process portfolio planning.

Despite the enthusiasm with which companies are jumping onto the bandwagon, I estimate that only 14% of the *Fortune* "1000" have reached the most advanced (the process) stage. The average travel time seems to be at least five years. (See Exhibit 2.) Capital-intensive process industries such as chemicals, petroleum, and paper—and technology-intensive (but industrially mature) industries such as appliances, abrasives, and industrial equipment—are most likely to use some form of this planning process. (See Exhibit 3 for more detail.)

Since they face the greatest challenges, the bigger and more diverse among *Fortune* "1000" companies have introduced the technique. But, among diversified industries, conglomerates rarely use portfolio planning, while diversified industrials often do.

Two-thirds of portfolio planning companies oversee businesses that are related in some way. The majority not only overlap along one dimension (such as technology or market) but also along multiple dimensions (for example, technology, market, and raw materials). Moreover, companies usually attempt to integrate the management of these related businesses through

Exhibit 2. Process Portfolio Planning Stages of Introduction

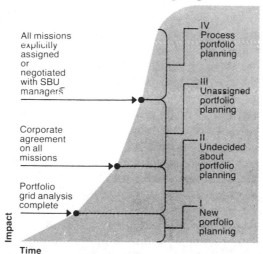

the use of shared resources and staff at the corporate and group levels. (See Exhibit 4.)

It is because of the difficulty they have in assessing the strategic performance of each of their businesses and allocating resources selectively that diversified industrials need a formal tool like portfolio planning. Conglomerates, on the other hand, speak portfolio planning prose like Monsieur

Exhibit 3. Use of Portfolio Planning by Industry

Prevalent Use	Occasional Use	Rare or No Use
Chemicals	Motor vehicles	Aerospace
Industrial farm equipment	Metal products	Musical instruments, toys, and sporting goods
Electronics and appliances	Measuring, scientific, and photographic equipment	Tobacco
Paper and fiber products	Pharmaceuticals	Shipbuilding and railroads
Food	Office equipment, including computers	Soaps and cosmetics
Metal manufacturing	Publishing and printing	Mining and crude oil production
Petroleum refining	Rubber and plastic products	Furniture
Glass, concrete, abrasives, and gypsum	Beverages	Leather
	Textiles and vinyl flooring	Jewelry and silverware
	Apparel	Broadcasting and motion picture production

Exhibit 4. Use of Shared Resources

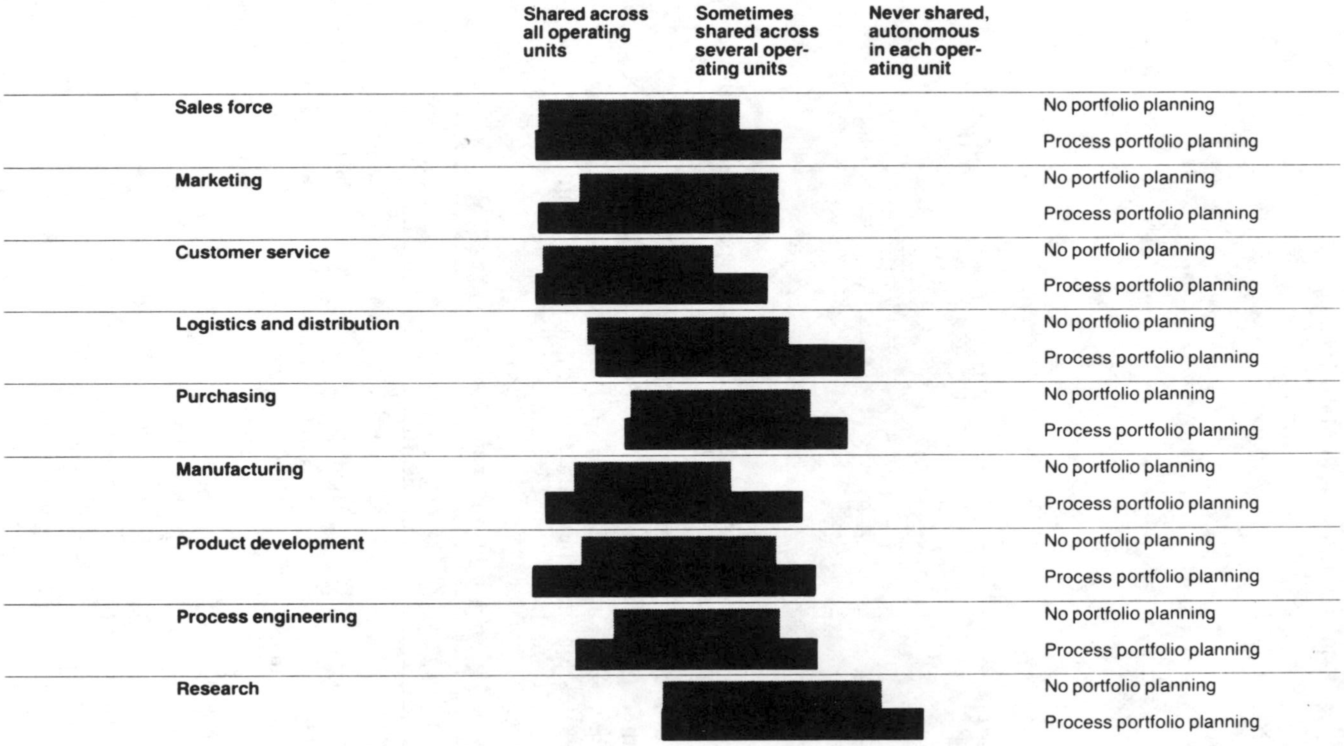
Shared across all operating units
Sometimes shared across several operating units
Never shared, autonomous in each operating unit
Sales force
No portfolio planning
Process portfolio planning
Marketing
No portfolio planning
Process portfolio planning
Customer service
No portfolio planning
Process portfolio planning
Logistics and distribution
No portfolio planning
Process portfolio planning
Purchasing
No portfolio planning
Process portfolio planning
Manufacturing
No portfolio planning
Process portfolio planning
Product development
No portfolio planning
Process portfolio planning
Process engineering
No portfolio planning
Process portfolio planning
Research
No portfolio planning
Process portfolio planning

Jourdain in Molière's *Le Bourgeois Gentilhomme*—sans savoir. How well companies can incorporate these interdependencies in applying portfolio planning will be crucial to the success of the approach.

Portfolio planning companies tend to be international and likely to manage through complex organizational structures. Again, the ease with which the planning approach incorporates both a product and a market dimension will prove crucial to the company's success.

Structuring the Strategic Business Units

Before the introduction of portfolio planning, most companies divide up the corporate whole into organizational units (like divisions) on the basis of operating control considerations. Often these units lack the necessary autonomy appropriate for strategic planning and resource allocation.

Defining what constitutes a business unit is the first step in all strategic—not just portfolio—planning. In the case of portfolio planning, two theoretical principles underlie the definition:

1 An organization must identify its various business units so that they can be regarded as independent for strategic purposes.
2 Companies then should allocate resources directly to these SBUs to support whatever strategies are chosen.

The first principle is an attempt to solve the problem of inappropriate planning units by arriving at a good business definition on the basis of industry economics. Based on the experience curve, this definition sees a business as strategically independent if its value-added structure is such that market leadership in that business alone permits successful performance. To put it another way, a company looks at each market segment to see whether it can survive if it competes only in that segment.

The second principle, tying resource allocation directly to SBU's strategic mission, attempts to solve the problems companies face with typical administrative systems. It hypothesizes that the practice of allocating resources on a project-by-project basis and the step-by-step aggregation of corporate operating results tend to shorten the focus of corporate management and create uniform rather than selective policies. To forge a dynamic strategy throughout the company, the theory states, a company must allocate its resources selectively and directly to strategically independent businesses.

SBUs Without the Theoretical Mask

But that is the theory. It is the application of the theory of portfolio planning to the realities of corporate activities that is most difficult. Anyone simply reading the description of companies employing portfolio planning could list a multitude of obstacles and administrative hurdles; the ordinary manager is dumbfounded by all the possibilities for failure.

In practice, of course, SBUs are not—and cannot be—strategically autonomous units rooted in an industry's structure. A company can only determine the size, shape, and number of SBUs in the light of prior organizational constraints and history, the limits of its managers' intelligence and imagination, and the multiple interdependencies among businesses.

According to my survey results, companies try to apply the theory; 70% of all organizations started off their introduction of portfolio planning by comprehensively reexamining the definition of each of their businesses. In 75% of these organizations, the reevaluation led to the classification of SBUs as sometimes or usually different from operating units. The larger the company, the more likely it is to have SBUs that do not coincide with operating units.

However, let us not assume that the companies started an administrative revolution. Despite the fact that they do not coincide with operating units per se, the resulting SBUs are generally aggregations of existing operating units or segments of single units; they clearly cut across organizational lines in only 7% of the cases. A close examination reveals that careful strategic analysis is rarely followed by an alignment of organizational units; rather, there is strong pressure to define SBUs quickly and good reason, in practice, to put the units clearly within the boundaries of existing organizational structure.

The Administrative Reality

Lest the theoreticians judge too harshly, the degree of diversification of most large companies obviates the possibility of simultaneous consideration of each relevant product/market segment at the corporate level. If the theory were strictly applied, a resulting grid would in most portfolio planning companies have over 100 bubbles and in some over 500. It is no mere coincidence that portfolio planning companies—small and large alike—have ended up with, on the average, only 30 SBUs.

The end result is that, instead of single, homogeneous units, most companies (58% of those in my survey, 72% of those among the *Fortune* "1000") consider each SBU as a portfolio itself — not of different businesses but rather of product/market segments that often may have quite diverse grid positions and strategic missions. In fact, the more experienced companies are with portfolio planning, the more likely they are to treat the exercise as a multilevel operation.

The impact of this redefinition comes alive when you realize the degree to which related businesses of each company share resources along different dimensions. Companies create SBUs at the organizational level, where shared resources can be managed. Top management should therefore see nothing inherently wrong with business units that cut across different market segments and that have widely different positions on the grid or a variety of strategic missions. To the contrary, forcing uniform strategic missions onto the managers of business units leads to either rejection of the mission or buildup of inappropriate strategies.

Those companies most advanced in the art of portfolio planning structure it on two levels. When analyzing the whole corporate portfolio and making trade-offs among businesses, they look at the company in the aggregate. In this larger picture, the companies look at SBUs that are in most cases organizational units and assign them strategic missions that reflect the expected cash flow contribution to the whole company.

During the corporate plan review process, however, companies take a disaggregate view and look within those SBUs at the relevant strategic segments. These strategic segments are more likely to result from an analysis of the industry than from an accommodation to existing organizational structure. Their missions reflect the particular strategy the company wants a business unit manager to follow in each of his competitive arenas.

The definition of SBUs and strategic segments evolves throughout the introduction of the process. As the companies go through more planning cycles, the SBUs become more an organizational reality and the segment definition becomes finer. Often the segments are revised but the original SBU definition stays the same.

The definition of SBUs in each company raises two critical issues: how the company should define SBUs so as to accommodate the interdependencies and how a company can achieve the strategic aggregation and disaggregation that portfolio planning requires.

The question of interdependence, for example, creates nasty problems of the chicken-egg variety. One product/market segment may share manufacturing facilities with a few others, basic technology with an even broader group, and a sales organization with a different set of product/market segments. With all these differing dimensions, trade-offs must always be made. The guiding principle is that a company must define the SBU to incorporate control over those resources that will be the key strategic variables in the future. But how can the company do that before it knows the SBU's strategic mission?

Looking closer at the way in which the surveyed companies make these trade-offs in practice, you detect a bias toward cost efficiency in relation to responsiveness. Indeed, the business economics orientation of portfolio planning pushes cost structure as the only basis for business definition. In most industrial products and consumer durables companies, the market-based part of costs is small. Moreover, things like an SBU's responsiveness to local market conditions or governments are not quantifiable. As a result, these companies define SBUs along technological and manufacturing rather than market lines. Particularly in the international arena, many companies find that their worldwide SBUs are less responsive to local issues and cooler toward international activities than they were under the former international division structure and country plans.

A Hypothetical Case

As seen from the corporate level of a large diversified company, business strategy is the outcome of a process of administrative influence. While no one could expect a solar cell producer and an independent electrical wire manufacturer to perform under a similar set of administrative systems, as divisions of a hypothetical—and of course typical—U.S. diversified industrial company they are subject to fairly uniform sets of pressures and patterns of influence.

A theorist reasonably expects organizations to alter administrative systems to make way for portfolio planning, so planners would encourage this company to change its administrative systems—to be selective, not uniform, in its strategic decision-making. In that way, new patterns of influence arise that correspond to the nature of the business, its competitive position, and strategic mission.

If we assume that the solar cell business is an SBU that our theoretical company has decided to grow while harvesting the electrical wire business, then you might expect the company to put an entrepreneur in charge, make him subject to frequent review and evaluation on the basis of market share and technological development, and encourage him to take some risks. In the case of the electrical wire business, the company gives the reins of that SBU to a penny-pincher and reviews his performance mainly on the numbers. It evaluates return and cash flow and discourages all investment other than cost reduction and maintenance.

In constructing the survey questionnaire, I tried to see if companies altered administrative processes to fit strategic missions. I asked whether they adjusted the financial planning system, the capital investment approval process, the incentive compensation system, or the strategic planning system itself.

Few Formal Administrative Changes

I found that in practice (except for considerations of capital investment and, of course, the strategic planning system itself) companies do not alter formal administrative systems in accordance with the strategic missions of SBUs. (If they did, theorists would see a high level of formal differentiation across businesses.) On one level, this attitude simply reflects the time needed to implement the planning system. For example, one company (acknowledged as a leader in portfolio planning) finally brought its management compensation system into line seven years after it had introduced the portfolio planning process.

In addition, the reluctance to modify administrative systems across businesses is a good indication of the perceived benefits of administrative simplicity. Controllers have excellent arguments for keeping administrative procedures uniform.

More profoundly, however, the basis for this reluctance may lie within the nature of the SBUs themselves. As I've said, diversified industrialists look at SBUs as portfolios of various segments; tying the formal systems to portfolio planning would mean going beyond the business units and would require the company to gear itself to the specific strategic mission of each segment.

The Importance of Informal Systems

Though successful companies did not change administrative systems to accommodate portfolio planning, their managers did informally adapt systems to fit the various businesses. Time and time again in the survey, this informal differentiation seemed to make the difference between portfolio planning as an isolated exercise and as an integral part of the management process. In fact, implementation depends on how well the CEO and other top managers can tailor their attention to each SBU, especially how they monitor strategic plans, how they weight the financial numbers *in light of the planning process*, and how and where they promote managers.

Not all companies are sophisticated about the process. For example, in one company, the CEO had enthusiastically endorsed portfolio planning as the wave of the future. But two years' worth of effort virtually went down the drain when every business manager found a telegram on his desk one morning from that same CEO requesting a 5% across-the-board cut in manpower.

The impact of portfolio planning is most profound on the corporate review process and the capital investment appraisal process. Corporate review of business plans becomes more intense and focuses on different variables than in other companies. Generally, portfolio planning companies separate their strategic plan review from their financial review, so the planning process remains as meaningful as possible. As companies gain experience, the review goes into more and more of the detail of each segment within an SBU. My evidence indicates that the review process does shift from emphasis on short-term profits and sales objectives to long-term profits and sales targets and competitive analysis. (See Exhibit 5.)

Exhibit 5.   Ranking of the Most Important Issues in the Planning Review from 1—Highest in Importance—to 9—Lowest in Importance

	Rank Under No Portfolio Planning	Rank Under Process Portfolio Planning
Next year's profit objectives	1	6
Long-range profit objectives	2	1
Next year's capital investment plan	3	4
Next year's sales objectives	4	8
Long-range sales objectives	5	3
Long-range resource allocation	6	2
Competitive analysis	7	5
Milestones for implementation	8	7
Contingency plans	9	9

Tying Resource Allocation to Strategy

In a diversified company, strategy is essentially about resource allocation across businesses. In most companies, however, formal strategic planning is one thing and the capital investment appraisal process quite another.

My investigations show that companies engaging in process portfolio planning try to correct this inherent contradiction by tying the capital investment process closely to strategic planning. (See Exhibit 6.) Not that many allocate resources primarily on the basis of strategies (only 14% do), but at least the business plan becomes an explicit element in the evaluation process for investment projects. Unfortunately, very few organizations tackle the allocation of strategic expenses (that is, investments that are expensed rather than capitalized, such as R&D, marketing, applications engineering) in the same way.

How Managers Perceive the Benefits

Despite the difficulties associated with the implementation of portfolio planning, almost all the managers surveyed indicated that the process had a positive impact on management. The clearest evidence may be that only one of the 176 respondents that were introducing portfolio planning said it would

Exhibit 6. Link Between Strategic Planning Process and Capital Investment Appraisal

Which statement, in your opinion, best reflects the relation between business plans and capital investment approval in your company?	Percentage of companies in sample that use process portfolio planning	Percentage of companies in sample that do not use portfolio planning
We explicitly allocate capital to our businesses as part of our business plans. Subsequent projects are expected to fall within this allocation guideline.	24%	18%
Fit with the business plan is an important and explicit element in our evaluation of capital investment projects.	57%	22%
The business plan serves primarily as general background information when we are considering capital investment projects on an individual basis.	20%	60%

hold less importance for the organization in the years to come. In fact, managers credit the approach with an array of benefits, with respect to not only the quality of strategy generation but also the commitment of resources and implementation. (See Exhibit 7 for a listing of the benefits.)

In the first place, companies gain a better understanding of each of their businesses. In turn, this allows them to make appropriate strategic decisions. One reason is the approach's emphasis on a company's ability to decipher industry logic and assess its competitive position. Another is the

Exhibit 7.   Managers' Remarks about Benefits

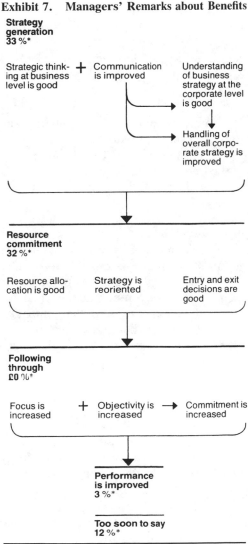

Strategy generation 33 %*

Strategic thinking at business level is good **+** Communication is improved   Understanding of business strategy at the corporate level is good

Handling of overall corporate strategy is improved

Resource commitment 32 %*

Resource allocation is good   Strategy is reoriented   Entry and exit decisions are good

Following through £0 %*

Focus is increased **+** Objectivity is increased **→** Commitment is increased

Performance is improved 3 %*

Too soon to say 12 %*

*Percentage of respondents who thought this benefit was most important.

introduction of verbal and graphic languages that facilitate improved communication in strategic, not just financial, terms.

According to the comments of managers, all of these benefits lead to improving resource commitments, for they improve resource allocation and facilitate strategic reorientation as well as entry and divestment decisions. Managers even credit the approach with improved operations since it encourages focus, objectivity, and commitment.

A Question of Direct Impact

If resource allocation is what strategy is all about, then a fundamental question is whether portfolio planning actually affects the allocation of resources in the companies that adopt it. Since my survey format did not allow me to study the shifts in allotments readily, I measured the impact as perceived by managers. I asked them how serious the following list of common allocation problems were for their companies on a scale from one (no problem) to five (severe problem):

1 We waste resources by continually subsidizing marginal businesses.
2 Our high-return businesses tend to underinvest.
3 Our low-return businesses tend to overinvest.
4 We do not fund our existing growth opportunities adequately.
5 We have a hard time generating new growth opportunities internally.

To reduce subjectivity, I did not ask for an assessment of improvement but rather for separate descriptions of the current situation as well as that before the introduction of portfolio planning. The results, as presented in Exhibit 8, are striking. In general, the introduction of portfolio planning coincides with a perceived improvement in the allocation process. Both process and analytic portfolio planning help the company face the problem of marginal businesses. Changing the investment behavior of basic businesses or their attitudes toward risk that lead to inadequate funding of existing growth opportunities, however, requires a process approach to portfolio planning.

The one problem the approach does not address is the difficulty of generating new internal growth opportunities. I would add that on the basis of interviews I have conducted, the impact—if there is one at all—is rather negative. In theory, portfolio planning is about the allocation of all resources. In practice, however, companies focus on capital investment. The generation of new business requires explicit emphasis on human resource decisions and strategic expenses such as R&D and market research, only later to be followed by capital allocations.

On the most fundamental level, however, it appears that the impact of portfolio planning on resource allocation is a function of the degree and quality of its introduction. We can draw a road map of the potential benefits

Exhibit 8. Improvement of Resource Allocation Through Portfolio Planning

Level of Portfolio Planning in Companies Sampled	Resource Allocation Problems				
	Subsidizing Marginal Businesses	Underinvesting in High ROI Businesses	Overinvesting in Low ROI Businesses	Inadequate Funding of Growth Opportunities	Difficulty in Generating New Growth Opportunities
Analytic portfolio planning	.83	.17	.33	.08	.25
Process portfolio planning	1.09	.70	.61	.83	.19
Unassigned portfolio planning	.53	.47	.68	.56	.32
Undecided about portfolio planning	.56	.36	.25	.19	06
New portfolio planning	.38	(.31)	.67	.38	(.08)
Average level of each problem in all the companies sampled	2.75	2.36	2.87	2.52	2.93

Note: Companies were asked to what extent each of these resource allocation issues was a problem. They answered on a scale of 1 (no problem) to 5 (severe problem).

according to the stages of introduction. First, companies face up to those businesses with untenably weak market positions, make divestments, and inaugurate programs to increase market share. Next, businesses with growth opportunities feel liberated from short-term performance pressure and propose major growth programs from which the corporate level may not yet be ready to select.

In most cases, the investment inclination of base businesses changes slowly and requires the full commitment of top management behind certain power shifts. If a company has been overinvesting, all these resource demands may result in a resource crunch. The way that crunch is handled, in fact, gives a good indication of the degree to which portfolio planning has taken hold. If the company takes into account the various strategic missions of SBUs and counters the resource crunch selectively, then it has firmly established portfolio priorities. If, however, it institutes an across-the-board cut, you have a good sign that nothing has changed from the old days.

Success—or Failure

Some companies in my sample reached the process portfolio planning stage very quickly, while others had not quite gotten there even though they had gone through five planning cycles. The difference between such fast and slow introductions coincided well with how successful or unsuccessful portfolio planning was.

In a set of telephone interviews, I compared the experience of 27 companies that had reached the process portfolio planning stage in three years with the experience of 24 organizations that, after five years or more, were still not negotiating strategic missions explicitly. I found that in these cases five factors determined the ease with which portfolio planning could be implemented. Most are endemic to the corporate situation; planners can do little about them. Yet they allow the corporate planner to gauge the magnitude of challenges that lie ahead.

The Performance Problem: Shock

Portfolio planning reallocates resources and thus implies a redistribution of power. As with all such shifts, a performance crisis—often, according to our data, arising from a profit crunch when fast growth goes out of control—triggers the initial decision to introduce the approach and greatly reduces the resistance. (Exhibit 9 shows how a dip in EPS triggers the institution of portfolio planning.)

CEO Role: Commitment

In all cases, a strong and continuous commitment from the CEO is the key to a fast introduction, even though in many companies the initial force comes

Exhibit 9. How Portfolio Planning Is Triggered

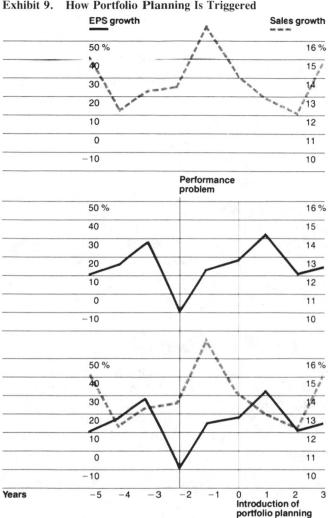

EPS growth   Sales growth

Performance
problem

Years   −5   −4   −3   −2   −1   0   1   2   3
                                              Introduction of
                                              portfolio planning

from someone else—often the corporate planner. He or she signals with more than words; that is, with executive appointments, project approval decisions, and personal time spent on strategic review. Lack of real commitment was the source of major problems that companies in my sample ultimately faced.

Resource Imbalance Level: Low Resistance

Shifts in resource allocation can range anywhere from the improvement of segment strategies in divisions that can "stand on their own two feet" to major shifts across group, and even sector, levels. The degree of inertia and political resistance encountered within the corporate structure is a function of how important (or how high up in the structure) the shifts need to be.

Previous Planning Experience: Capability

Though the approach usually provides a dramatic jump in the quality of strategic analysis, its introduction as an ongoing process is based on the previous planning experience. Outside consultants cannot offer a good substitute for the strategic thinking of line managers and the experience acquired in earlier planning exercises. Skillful corporate planners often elicit support for portfolio planning by avoiding what line managers disliked about previous planning formats (for example, by reducing the amount of paperwork and financial information required).

Previous MBO Experience: Focus

As I've pointed out, good portfolio planning often requires the ability to treat SBUs as portfolios of segments. Companies with a tradition of management by objectives easily introduce the appropriate set of objectives specific to each segment and thereby mold the review process so that it incorporates both an aggregate and a detailed view.

Some Important Advice

Unfortunately, these five factors are largely out of the planner's control. My research turned up some valuable information about other variables which the planner can control and which will help her set the right priorities in introducing portfolio planning.

The following advice deals with the broad issues involved and applies to most companies independent of their specific situations:

1. *Move quickly.* Companies introduce portfolio planning initially on a "wave," the strength of which depends on the extent of CEO support or the existence of a dramatic performance problem. It is important to establish the legitimacy of portfolio planning by pushing through some resource allocation decisions before their immediacy in the corporate atmosphere disappears. Many planners get bogged down because corporate attention shifts elsewhere.

If that happens, advocates may have to carry their selling job "upstairs" as well as "downstairs." The best advice is to demonstrate the strength of the approach through successfully implementing it in one part of the company rather than pushing for across-the-board improvements.

2. *Educate line managers.* Portfolio planning is not a planner's exercise. It depends on improved strategic thinking at all levels of line management. From that perspective, many organizations—even though they invite consultants to analyze myriad divisions—have not taken advantage

of the opportunity presented by the approach to improve the quality of management.

Successful companies usually conceive their planning process as a learning exercise for line management. They also invest heavily in education to allow managers to become familiar with both the basic thinking behind the approach and how best to use its tools.

3. *Redefine strategic business units explicitly.* Defining SBUs is the genesis—and nemesis—of portfolio planning. The units reflect and constrain corporate strategy in the most fundamental way. The period during which the company initially defines their scope gives astute managers the most leverage they will ever have to change strategic focus. This time should not be cut short and will prove to be time well spent if the right questions are asked and the practical problems and organizational biases taken into account.

4. *Avoid labels; focus on missions.* The successful portfolio planning company shuns labels and does not haggle over grids. It focuses on a fundamental discussion of practical strategies for each SBU. Unhappily, many companies still leave fundamental decisions unmade and allocate resources continually by default. If portfolio planning is focused well, it can help by forcing the issue.

5. *Acknowledge SBUs as portfolios to be managed.* In practice, companies often determine what is a manageable number of SBUs around technological or market-based resources. These SBUs consist of many product/market segments. Successful companies, then, tend to accept portfolio planning as a multilevel approach. On the one hand, they develop the capability to take a detailed view of each segment when a strategic issue arises and, on the other, an aggregate view of the SBU when they discuss overall portfolio balance and resource commitments.

6. *Invest corporate management time in the review process.* Portfolio planning is a facilitating framework that allows substantive discussion between the corporate and the business levels. As such, the quality and extent of corporate review are crucial. Successful companies set aside time for reviewing strategic as well as financial plans, but they emphasize strategic planning. When analyzed at the same time, the financial numbers tend to drive out fundamental discussion of the strategic issues. Good companies also maximize the time their top managers spend on strategic plan reviews. Though the theory of portfolio planning would call for reviewing all SBUs simultaneously, many companies spread out their review during the year in order to allow senior executives the most exposure possible.

7. *Avoid across-the-board treatment.* Portfolio planning companies do keep formal administrative systems uniform. However, they rely on a flexible, informal management process to differentiate influence patterns at the SBU level. Every corporate manager should remember an important caveat: have no across-the-board treatment. At a certain point the introduction of portfolio planning is likely to place demands on corporate resources. Those demands should be met squarely without equalizing the pain

through uniform reductions. Any other method will dilute the real impact portfolio planning has.

8. *Tie resource allocation to the business plan.* The approach has no teeth without formal links to the resource allocation system. Forcing congruence between resource allocation, on the one hand, and the nature of the business and its strategic mission, on the other, is vital. In successful companies this link takes the form of setting an asset growth rate objective as well as approving a "quota" for various types of spending. Subsequent requests are evaluated first for their fit within this agreed-on spending pattern.

Such an approach actually alleviates the review burden because it allows decentralization of nonstrategic investments and facilitates approval of those projects that fall within agreed-on strategic priorities.

9. *Consider strategic expenses and human resources as explicitly as, capital investment.* Portfolio planning is about the reallocation of all resources. Many companies subvert the process by focusing solely on the allocation of capital to investment. That can work in industries that are highly capacity oriented, such as paper or steel, especially when the main problem is a deficient selection process between competing investments.

In most industries, however, strategic expenses in R&D, marketing, applications engineering, and recruiting hold the key to portfolio planning, especially if the company's main problem is the creation of growth. Companies that formally attempt to monitor the allocation of these resources tend to be the most successful.

10. *Plan explicitly for new business development.* Though it addresses the resource allocation imbalance in existing businesses, portfolio planning does not address the issue of new business generation. As a matter of fact, the way companies implement the system tends to inhibit innovative behavior at the business level. Companies with excellent track records of internal business development generally introduce some way to focus attention on the issue in their planning formats.

11. *Make a clear strategic commitment to a few selected technologies and/or markets early.* Corporate management can make specific portfolio choices only on the basis of strategy inputs from SBUs. Business unit managers, on the other hand, need guidance from the top to develop specific strategic proposals. When many companies in the survey could not initially decide on strategic missions, for example, business managers felt as if they were in limbo.

The best companies will announce firm commitments to a certain set of technologies and markets as early as possible. Setting up workable frames of reference to guide business level planning allows them to make better product/market decisions later on. Such commitments not only facilitate the introduction of portfolio planning, but in a planning approach that regards essentially interdependent businesses as stand-alone units, they also inject a dimension of commonality in a way that provides leverage for individual business strategies.

Current Fad or Basic Breakthrough?

Does portfolio planning constitute a step forward in the management of diversity, or is it simply a passing phenomenon? Often an administrative change, such as the introduction of a new planning system, is the way a CEO can address an organizational imbalance that might be at the root of a performance problem. Successful introduction may be self-defeating. The new system removes the problem and its own raison d'être.

It is true that in most companies the introduction of portfolio planning is triggered by a performance crisis and the need to allocate resources selectively in a capital-constrained environment.

Also, portfolio planning is not the discovery of the wheel. As I have defined it—the explicit recognition that a diversified company is a portfolio of businesses, each of which should make a distinct contribution to the overall corporate performance and should be managed accordingly—portfolio planning was practiced de facto by many companies before the development of formal "technology."

Yet along with most managers, I feel that, in contrast to previous generations of planning approaches, portfolio planning is here to stay and represents an important improvement in management practice. After the initial portfolio imbalance is redressed, the approach can give companies a permanent added capacity for strategic control because it provides a framework within which the management process can be adapted to the evolving needs of the business. It also helps companies out of the dilemma between stifling centralization and dangerous decentralization. It allows them to reassert the primacy of the center in creating profit potential yet leave their strategic business units maximum operational autonomy in realizing that potential.

Portfolio planning can deliver on three fronts. The first is in the generation of good strategies, by promoting competitive analysis at the business level, more substantive discussion across levels, and strategy that capitalizes on the benefits of diversity at the corporate level. The second contribution is the promotion of more selective resource allocation trade-offs, not by solving the problems or eradicating the power game but by providing a focus for the issues and a vehicle for negotiation.

The third and most important contribution that portfolio planning can add is to the management process. The essence of managing diversity is the creation in each business of a pattern of influence that corresponds to the nature of the business, its competitive position, and its strategic mission. The benefit a company gets out of portfolio planning depends on its ability to create such a differentiated management process. Putting the approach into practice presents the company with some of its greatest challenges.

Success is based more on coping with administrative issues than on developing sophisticated analytic techniques. It requires a real commitment to good management and demands that an elegant theory be stretched to fit a complex reality.

Appendix: The Research Project

The research on which this article is based has three phases. The first is an investigation and a series of interviews at the corporate, group, and business levels of two large diversified industrial companies acknowledged to be among the most advanced in the art of portfolio planning. The second phase, funded by the *Harvard Business Review,* consists of a survey of the use and impact of the approach on *Fortune* "1000" companies. The third phase is an investigation of the problems cited in my earlier research as well as an extension of the original survey to European diversified industrial organizations.

I conducted the *HBR* survey in 1979 by contacting the corporate officers in charge of strategic planning or, in their absence, the CEOs, of *Fortune* "1000" companies. A total of 345 companies responded (see the following table for a list of companies that agreed to be identified as participants). By and large, corporate executives in charge of planning (62%) or finance (15%) and CEOs (11%) responded.

I carried out follow-up telephone interviews with 80% of the respondents to check the initial mail response and to probe specific areas of interest. In addition, I established a data base with performance figures for the five years before and after the introduction of portfolio planning from the Compustat tapes. Finally, I carried out a telephone survey of 9% of those who chose not to respond to the survey to find out why they had done so.

Participating Companies that Agreed to Be Identified as Participants

Out of 57 Participating Companies in *Fortune* "1-100"		Out of 45 Participating Companies in *Fortune* "101-200"		
Exxon	PepsiCo.	Eaton	Scott Paper	
Mobil	Deere	American Cyanamid	Pilsbury	
Gulf Oil	Aluminum Company of	NCR	Levi Strauss	
Atlantic Richfield	America	Celanese	Johns-Manville	
Shell Oil	Weyerhaeuser	American Motors	Koppers	
E.I. du Pont de Nemours	TRW	Texas Instruments	Del Monte	
Union Carbide	Sperry Rand	Crown Zellerbach	Olin	
Phillips Petroleum	Republic Steel	Pfizer	Land O'Lakes	
Dow Chemical	Allied Chemical	Borg-Warner	Studebaker-Worthington	
Westinghouse Electric	Inland Steel	Mead		
United Technologies	General Mills	Fruehauf		
Rockwell International	CPC International	General Tire & Rubber		
Kraft	Dresser Industries	Whirlpool		
Monsanto	FMC	Avon Products		
R.J. Reynolds Industries	Warner-Lambert	Charter		
Firestone Tire & Rubber		Hercules		
Cities Service		Gould		
Armco		Owens-Corning		
Greyhound		Control Data		
Colgate Palmolive		Allis-Chalmers		
W.R. Grace		Martin Marietta		

Participating Companies that Agreed to Be Identified as Participants (continued)

Out of 45 Participating Companies in *Fortune* "201-300"		Out of 30 Participating Companies in *Fortune* "301-400"	
U.S. Industries	Certain-Teed	Consolidated Aluminum	Saxon Industries
International Minerals & Chemical	Blue Bell	General Host	Cluett, Peabody
Emhart	Rexnord	Joy Manufacturing	Bell & Howell
Stauffer Chemical	Avnet	Pitney-Bowes	ConAgra
Rohm and Haas	AMP	Outboard Marine	Fairchild Industries
Corning Glass Works	St. Joe Minerals	Parker-Hannifin	
Armstrong Cork	Potlatch	Newmount Mining	
Murphy Oil		AM International	
Meublein		Hughes Tool	
Lear Siegler		Crown Central Petroleum	
Joseph E. Seagram & Sons		Cincinnati Milacron	
Diamond International		Memorex	
Air Products & Chemicals		Signope	
Baxter Travenol		Hart Schaffner & Marx	
Zenith Radio		Johnson Controls	
Clark Oil & Refining		Norin	
Reliance Electric		General Cinema	
Norton		Southwest Forest Industries	
Black & Decker			
Pennwalt			
Interlake			

Out of 35 Participating Companies in *Fortune* "401-500"	Out of 26 Participating Companies in *Fortune* "501-600"	Out of 29 Participating Companies in *Fortune* "601-700"
GATX	Armstrong Rubber	Shaklee
Dan River	Kohler	Universal Foods
Louisiana Land & Exploration	Barnes Group	Graniteville
Washington Post	Wyman-Gordon	Franklin Mint
Wallace Murray	Keystone Consolidated	Alton Box Board
Ball	Sonoco Products	Prentice-Hall
American Bakeries	Beckman Instruments	Kaiser Cement & Gypsum
Envirotech	Maremont	Mississippi Chemical
New York Times	Houston Oil & Minerals	Sealed Power
Scott & Fetzer	Maytag	Media General
Smith International	Ametek	Mine Safety Appliances
Wm. Wrigley Jr.	Dorsey	Raychem
Bausch & Lomb	Allied Products	Condec
Mattel	American Greetings	Toro
Coca-Cola Bottling Company of New York	Snap-on Tools	Mitchell Energy & Development
	National Cooperative Refinery Assn.	H.B. Guller
Maryland Cup	Nucor	Crompton & Knowles
Arcata	Coachmen Industries	Alaska Interstate
General Refractories	Freeport Minerals	Standard Register
Butler Manufacturing	Robertshaw Controls	
Varian Associates	Storage Technology	
Tyler	Albany International	
Royal Crown Companies	Longview Fibre	

Participating Companies that Agreed to Be Identified as Participants (continued)

Out of 27 Participating Companies in *Fortune* "701-800"	Out of 27 Participating Companies in *Fortune* "801-900"	Out of 24 Participating Companies in *Fortune* "901-1000"
Commercial Shearing	Wolverine Worldwide	Safeguard Industries
Chamberlain Manufacturing	Lenox	Buckeye International
Management Assistance Corp.	Omark Industries	American Business Products
Mark Controls	Richardson	William Carter
Giddings & Lewis	Clow	Conrac
Norlin Industries	Reliance Universal	Cooper Laboratories
Chelsea Industries	Hesston	Marlene Industries
Western Gear	Mesa Petroleum	Imperial Sugar
Stanley Home Products	Datapoint	Roblin Industries
Ludlow	Pope & Talbot	Stride Rite
Scott Foresman	Guilford Mills	Martin Processing
RTE	Affiliated Publications	P.H. Glatfelter
Gould Pumps	Park-Ohio Industries	Courier
Quanex	American Sterilizer	Medalist Industries
Wean United	Wynn's International	Marion Laboratories
Medtronic	Ocean Spray Cranberries	Motch & Merryweather Machinery
Barber-Greene	Combustion Equipment Associates	Facet Enterprises
Commerce Clearing House	Farmer Brothers	Harper & Row
Chesapeake Corp. of Virginia	Mohawk Data Sciences	Clevepak
Atlantic Steel	Bobbie Brooks	Polychrome
Huffy	Union	Multimedia
Texfi Industries	Cubic	
	Russ Togs	
	Elcor	
	Cross	

PART FOUR

IMPLEMENTING STRATEGY

AN OVERVIEW

Once a strategy has been conceived, the job of the general manager is to assure that the strategy is put into practice. The soundest strategic decision will have little impact if it is not implemented effectively.

The major task of implementing strategy is to create a fit between the company's strategic goals and its other activities. Generally, two types of fits need to be created:

1 Fits between the strategy and functional policies.
2 Fits between the strategy and the organization structure, organization processes, information systems, incentive systems, control systems, management selection and development, and leadership style.

In "Coupling Strategy to Operating Plans," John Hobbs and Donald Heany address the first type of fit. Hobbs and Heany show the necessity of adopting functional policies in marketing, manufacturing, engineering, and finance that reinforce and are consistent with the corporate strategy. The authors of "Beyond Theory Y" and "Tailor Incentive Compensation to Strategy" discuss the second type of fit. The authors of the first article argue that the most effective companies are those that adapt their organization structures and climates to fit the needs of their strategies. The second article shows how incentive compensation can be structured to reinforce strategy.

While no two strategies require identical implementation actions, there is a set of recurring implementation situations that general managers face. One of these is discussed by Philip Kotler in "Phasing Out Weak Products."

333

Kotler argues that companies continually need to drop weaker product lines, and he proposes systems and procedures to implement this crucial aspect of strategy. At the same time a company is ridding itself of weak products, new products need to be developed. In "Better Management of Corporate Development," Richard Vancil discusses an ingenious approach of implementing internally generated corporate growth.

The last two articles in this section deal with the individuals most responsible for the implementation of strategy—middle managers. In "General Managers in the Middle," Hugo Uyterhoeven discusses some of the reasons why the number of middle-manager positions has been growing and some of the important differences between middle- and top-level management. Rosabeth Kanter's "The Middle Manager as Innovator" then shows how middle managers can become a positive force in the growth of their companies. Kanter's findings also suggest how middle-level managers can implement change in large corporations.

Coupling Strategy to Operating Plans

JOHN M. HOBBS and DONALD F. HEANY

An imposing literature has been building up around "business policy" and "strategic decision making." Little explicit attention has been devoted to the short-term plans and programs that functional managers must draw up in order to implement such higher level decisions. This article draws attention to the prevalence of a gap between authors of strategic or business plans and those who prepare operating or functional plans. It indicates the reasons for this gap and the penalties paid by businesses that permit such a gap to develop. Finally, it identifies the practical steps a newly appointed manager of a profit center might take to close this gap.

In recent years a growing number of companies have expended considerable amounts of time and money to develop strategic planning skills in their profit centers and at higher organizational levels. We applaud this effort, but as we stand back and observe large and small companies alike apply this new talent and expertise, we are struck by the widespread disappointment with the pace at which new strategies are often implemented. To say the least, it appears to be much easier to conceive a new strategy than to carry it out.

Corporate executives especially are aware that changes in strategic direction do not always occur at the promised tempo. Therefore, they discount the claims advanced by advocates of each new strategy. One executive offered this pithy description of his strategy review procedure: "Halve each earnings projection indicated in the strategic plan. Then double the amount of additional investment sought to implement that strategy." Behind this cynical discounting one can sense a keen appreciation of the problems of maintaining the coupling among the functions as a mature business attempts to change direction.

One barrier to successful implementation is the residue left by strategies formulated by past managers of the business. These strategies have left their

335

imprint on shop procedures, work methods, job descriptions, work measurements, and business lore.

Advocates of bold new strategies have not recognized that they must first "uncouple" the functions from the viselike grip of past strategies *before* they can expect an appropriate response at lower organizational levels. The more that marketing, engineering, and manufacturing perfect their low-cost, efficient systems, the greater the likelihood that their operating plans will fail to discriminate among signals originating above them. They will instinctively resist changes in the way they get things done.

Take, for instance, the time-honored custom in certain segments of the capital goods industry to produce to requisition. Each product is unique. No finished inventory is carried. Each new order calls for individual handling, first by engineering, then by manufacturing, and so many months can elapse between date of order and date of delivery.

The manager in charge of a business that competed in one such segment embarked on a new aggressive strategy. He believed he could increase the business's market share by selling the value of product availability rather than technology alone. The key to his strategy was to release certain models to manufacturing before firm orders were in hand, thereby significantly shortening the delivery cycle.

Months later, this manager began to have second thoughts about this idea. For one thing, the models built in anticipation of demand required costly rework in order to match them to the orders ultimately received. Furthermore, customer complaints made it crystal clear that the publicized reduction in the delivery cycle had not been met. Missed schedules were also creating costly penalties.

An investigation proved the root of these problems to be the measurements used in district sales offices. For years, the bonuses of the sales engineers had been based on the dollar size of orders. Such a system prompted the engineers to give full rein to their customers' normal inclinations to demand tailored products rather than to worry about which model the customers ordered. Allusions to "king customer" were taken quite literally by field personnel. They did not recognize that their general manager's new strategy required a particular response from them.

Why did this happen? To some the answer is simple. The general manager was at fault. Had he communicated his strategy to the district offices, his sales managers would have perceived the need to amend their time-honored bonus system for sales engineers.

We think that a more basic reason can be found in the relentless quest for efficiency that characterized each functional area. Marketing procedures and practices had evolved over the years to control costs and to take full advantage of decentralization and specialization. Unfortunately, this pursuit of efficiency had one unintended result: marketing's operating plans were often independent of higher management's strategic shifts. The authors of these operating plans did not couple functional procedures, practices, or measurements to a given business strategy. In other words, functional momentum dulled marketing's responsiveness to the general manager's imaginative strategic move.

A second factor at work in this case was that the general manager underestimated the impact his new strategy would have on the marketing function. It is no trivial matter to inject a line of standardized products into a business that has been marketing customized products for more than a decade. To make this strategy work, marketing would have to take these steps:

☐ Develop a new measurement system for sales engineers.

☐ Hire salesmen or retrain sales engineers already on the payroll.

☐ Design a promotional campaign that would attract new customers but not divert old customers to the standardized products.

In fact, it is far from obvious that the same district offices can handle both customized and standardized products. As companies that have pioneered in the use of strategic planning can testify, this case is not an isolated instance of a functional failure to support a decision made at a higher level. Their functional managers are not always able to prevent foremen, purchasing agents, stock clerks, warehouse managers, district managers, engineers, and a host of other employees from following a competing strategy.

What Goes Wrong

In short, corporate reviews often fail to detect such weak links, and profit center managers do not always foresee uncoupling problems. We would like to suggest some steps that a profit center manager might take to minimize the risks in uncoupling. But first we shall cite two more actual (though disguised) cases to illustrate how operating plans can become uncoupled from the very strategy they are supposed to support.

Faulty Perspectives

The manager of a consumer durable goods business concluded that, in a climate characterized by recession and rapid inflation, the fastest way to improve profitability was to fill out his product line. Accordingly, he authorized engineering to design a new appliance and asked manufacturing to tool up for an initial production run of 2,000 units. For his part, this manager included in his strategic plan profit targets that reflected the market's (hypothesized) favorable response to this new offering.

Signs that something was amiss soon reached his desk. Performance data revealed that the field failure rate for the new product was significantly higher than that for older models.

An investigation pinpointed what had gone wrong. Engineering had prepared an operating plan that recognized the broad intent of the new strategic plan. Unfortunately, the design engineers had not specified a quantitative quality standard for the initial prototypes. It seemed safer for engineering, if not for the business, to await field results on the initial 2,000 appliances. This low-level decision took little heed of the following facts:

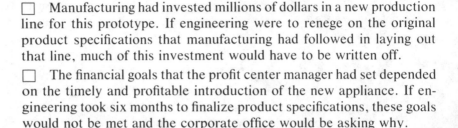

☐ Manufacturing had invested millions of dollars in a new production line for this prototype. If engineering were to renege on the original product specifications that manufacturing had followed in laying out that line, much of this investment would have to be written off.

☐ The financial goals that the profit center manager had set depended on the timely and profitable introduction of the new appliance. If engineering took six months to finalize product specifications, these goals would not be met and the corporate office would be asking why.

When this instance of uncoupling was eventually brought to the attention of the profit center manager, he could not believe his ears. How could such an obvious deficiency in functional planning skills go undetected for so long? He intervened. The linchpin between the strategic plan and engineering's operating plan was reinserted, by edict!

This case illustrates how mismatched perspectives can cause uncoupling. On the one hand, modern businesses strive to achieve low costs via high volume, specialization, and automation. Each step down this road fosters a narrow, inward perspective. The specialists who draw up operating plans focus on the dimensions of their internal world: parts lists, drawings, work standards, shop rules, production schedules, plant layout, and so on. On the other hand, the authors of business plans look outward. Their focus is on the external environment in which the business operates. Thus the profit center manager must match these two perspectives; there is no one to whom he or she can delegate this responsibility.

A related cause of frayed linkages is the existence of a sizable bloc of people at the lower organizational levels who are convinced that stragetic planning is just not practical. In their eyes, strategic planning is a synonym for blue-sky thinking, something undertaken to satisfy the corporate office. They feel little loyalty to a document that reflects few, if any, of their inputs. They are not involved in, nor committed to, the strategic plan.

Incompatible Demands

The announced strategy of a manager running a business that offered a full line of mature, market-tested products was to hold market share in the face of persistent sniping by smaller competitors. His customary response to their pricing moves was to pressure his engineers to squeeze still more efficiency out of their mature technology. For years engineers had obliged, largely by increasing the physical size of their product. The first signal of uncoupling appeared at the final test station of the production line. Costly rework became necessary in order to repair deficiencies discovered so late in the cycle. Naturally, profit margins suffered and delivery schedules slipped.

A corporate study team discovered the problem: Manufacturing could no longer maintain the quality levels specified by engineering. Particles in the air became trapped in the products as they were being assembled. While these particles had always been present, they represented no threat to quality as long as the traditional performance levels were sufficient. Once engineering had escalated these standards to attract new orders, substantial changes in manufacturing processes were mandated. These had never been made because the manpower needed to modify the in-place operating systems was not available.

Operating plans were prepared by people with pressing line responsibilities. These people are not always in a position to monitor the linkages between their operating plan and plans prepared by other functions or by the profit center manager.

For example, the manager of manufacturing was responsible for 2,000 employees, 900 work stations, 75 miles of overhead conveyors, and dealt with more than 300 vendors. He had to contend daily with changes in product specifications, alterations in the production process, unexpected variations in the quality of raw materials, pleas from customers to expedite given orders, and a host of other short-term crises. These realities claimed his allegiance, all day, every day. He was not disposed to search deeply for frayed linkages between his concrete world and a future environment described in the profit center's plan. Invariably, programmed tasks had prior claim on his limited resources over unprogrammed tasks such as the coupling between his operating plan and engineering's new product specifications.

Penalties of Uncoupling
Coupling errors of the type indicated in the three cases we have cited can be quite costly, both in terms of resources as well as people's attitudes.

Wasted Resources.   For instance, it is accepted that the role of raw material inventories and work-in-process inventories is to guard against possible delays at earlier points in the procurement or production process. But what about excessive inventory levels? What about the idle capacity and surplus labor built into operating plans to make doubly sure that operating systems do not halt or falter because of strikes, vendor error, weather, acts of God, or jittery customers? Lower-level supervisors decide what is excessive. Their decisions are not always visible at a distance, nor are they always documented in a form that invites a periodic review by higher management. Once made, these decisions become sanctified by the passage of time. "We always did it that way. . . ."

Bias Toward the Status Quo.   In some companies, the tenure of managers of profit centers averages less than three years. One factor contributing to this rapid turnover is the difficulty of eliciting prompt, integrated, functional responses to a new strategy. New managers commit themselves and their profit center to performance goals far beyond the capability of existing operating systems. The corporate office holds them to these goals. When the announced goals are not attained, a fresh managerial team is brought in and the cycle repeats itself, with one exception: The old strategy is often discredited along with the deposed manager. His replacement feels compelled to differentiate his strategy from that of his predecessor. This launches the functions on still another cycle of operational planning. If the latest manager is in a great hurry to win his spurs, he will not allow his subordinates time to analyze his new strategy or to investigate alternate operating systems. He wants action, now!

When profit center managers observe the risks assumed by colleagues who embark on aggressive moves, they wonder if the rewards reaped by these innovators are adequate. Many conclude that the risk/reward dictates a "hold" strategy. They silently resolve to become efficient administrators of established profit centers rather than midwives of new businesses. In their eyes, the established functional systems are too complex, too deeply rooted to be changed by a manager on his or her own initiative. They judge the turning radius of their profit center to be incompatible with their time horizon and performance measurements. Hence, they disavow any responsibility for nominating strategies that might renew mature businesses or initiate new ones.

In such a company, the de facto strategy is: stand pat. In time, the chief executive is likely to discover that his or her portfolio of businesses is positioned in mature markets and offering commodity-type products. This, of course, is the perfect recipe for low profits. It is a direct consequence of a measurement system that is biased against major strategic moves.

Minimizing Uncoupling Risks

Just how might managers go about forging better linkages between their new strategy and the detailed operating plans, procedures, and measurements prevailing two, three, and even four levels below them? How does the person in the middle cope with this troublesome problem without becoming hopelessly entangled in day-to-day affairs?[1]

Some managers react to evidence of uncoupling just as the Queen of Hearts might have done. "Off with their heads!" An injunction follows in a few hours indicating that all functions are expected to get behind the new strategy.

Another favored reaction is to form a task force to ferret out unnecessary expenditures in each nook and cranny of the company. In other companies, the normal response to flaws in operating plans is to offer a short course in planning to as wide an audience as possible.

We have found the following five steps to be more effective:

Step 1. Before Nominating Ambitious Strategies, Make Certain That a Serious Functional Overload Does Not Exist.   Measures to avoid unnecessary strain on the linkages between a strategic plan and current operating systems are always preferable to after-the-fact remedies. We have no reliable meters for monitoring functional stress and strain. Yet the symptoms are easy to detect

For example, Business X was in trouble. Its return on investment had sunk far below the company average. New competitors had penetrated its market and challenged its product leadership.

A new manager was dispatched to revive this business. Her prescription for a return to a satisfactory level of profitability included the following:

- [ ] Upgrade the old product lines.
- [ ] Retaliate against foreign competitors by entering their traditional markets.
- [ ] Modernize the costing system.
- [ ] Build or acquire a new manufacturing facility.
- [ ] Switch the method of payment for factory workers from piecework to daywork.

She submitted a new strategic plan based on this program. Soon, Operation Rejuvenation was under way. Unfortunately, the profit center did not adhere to the timetable specified in its strategic plan nor deliver on its profit goals. In retrospect, the rejuvenation program was recognized to be overly ambitious. The functional managers could not cope with all these changes simultaneously. Calling for change did not make it happen. Inertia bested the bold new strategy.

The lesson is that a new strategy always sends shock waves throughout a profit center. It is unrealistic to expect that a rebuilt strategy can be executed while some functions are being steered into new markets. Functional overload is unavoidable.

Step 2: Contain Strategic Shock Waves.   If a new strategic course is called for, managers can still avoid some uncoupling problems by insulating parts of the business from strategic shock waves. For example, many chemical companies isolate the coupling problems associated with new product introductions by constructing a new pilot plant for each major addition to a product line. Those who manage these pilot plants have no responsibility for existing products or their operating systems. They run their own experiments and finalize the new process apart from the old. When they judge their new pilot process to be safe and efficient, plans for a full-scale production are drawn up. The existing operating systems are not disturbed by work on the embryonic product/process. This same approach can be taken by most businesses when they make basic changes in their products or their manufacturing processes.

In addition, managers can insist that the advocates of a new strategy spell out the key issues raised by that strategy. For example, if your strategy is based on a new technology, the key strategic issue might be: Can this business successfully reduce to practice its R&D output and at the same time maintain competitive quality levels on its existing products?

Step 3: Give Your Personal Attention to Major Coupling Issues. Profit center managers can personally attend to coupling problems on a selective basis. We suggest that they (a) establish a mechanism for coping with such problems before they arise, and (b) personally monitor the sources of major coupling problems. For example, it is prudent to scrutinize each capital appropriation to make sure that it faithfully supports the thinking in the manager's new strategic plan. It may not. The authors of capital appropriations often have little connection with planning.

We also suggest that a profit center manager lend a hand in linking his center to other organizational components within the company. This is very important in large, diversified companies.

For example, one manager of a profit center that sells complex, high-technology products, each costing over a million dollars, has aimed at building market share for the past five years. With the onslaught of the recession, the market for these products became even more competitive. Customers delayed the receipt of completed orders. Vendors began to increase the prices of components and subsystems. The combined effect brought the center's annual output dangerously close to its breakeven point, and the manager began to question whether he could continue to build market share.

Taking a fresh look at his operations, the manager found a way to salvage his strategy. By amending the specifications his profit center placed on its intracompany vendors, he was able to offset their recent price increases. Specifically, conventional value analysis demonstrated that his product's performance would not suffer if the variety of one type of component purchased from a sister business were reduced from sixteen to four. This single step produced cost savings equivalent to the earnings realized from a 20% increase in his volume.

Encouraged by this result, this manager called for a comprehensive review of the ancient specifications for all his major components. He dug for more profit improvement opportunities by challenging each specification, each work procedure, each method that former functional managers had written when another strategy was in force.

Uprooting these traditional practices required his leadership. Only he could handle the delicate negotiations with managers of other profit centers. Only he could negotiate the terms according to which cost savings were to be shared with vendors.

Step 4: Don't Disband Your Strategic Planning Team Until It Has Identified Follow-Through Actions by the Next Organizational Level. Left to itself, the strategic planning process can become an end in itself, so bureaucratic and so ponderous that all participants in that process yearn to return to more congenial work. They are exhausted before they translate their strategic concept into specific functional support programs. They will say, "It's all in the strategic plan." Often it is not. Only the initial steps are mentioned, only the costs incurred in the next year or so. What profit center managers need is a tool to help them monitor follow-through; they must hold their planning team in place until its members have produced:

☐ A list of the specific tasks each function must perform in its strategy support role.

☐ The specific milestones by which they can assure themselves that the profit center is, in fact, changing to its new course.

☐ The names of the individuals who have accepted responsibility for each major functional program.

If they get less than this, they have been shortchanged. Their new strategy is at risk and will remain at risk until such controls on implementation are in effect.

Why are so many strategic plans lacking in such realism? Sidney Schoeffler, executive secretary of the Strategic Planning Institute, suggests that this lack occurs because planners undergo a subtle but deadly transformation as the strategic planning process unfolds. At the very beginning, business planners are objective and dispassionate analysts. They are ready to examine each and every possibility. At the end of the planning cycle, however, the same individuals have turned into fervent advocates of a single course of action—the one described in their plan. All their energies and political skills are then dedicated to selling that strategy. They are not disposed to seek out or listen to criticism from lower organizational levels.[2]

A general manager can restore a measure of objectivity to the terminal phase of the strategic planning cycle by personally inviting a few key functional specialists to his/her office and asking for their views of the proposed strategy and its impact on their area of work. This would do much to dull the criticism often heard at the functional level that strategic planning is an unimportant, blue-sky activity undertaken merely to please the upper echelons.

Step 5: Communicate Downward, Not Just Upward. Many uncoupling penalties come about because profit center managers are preoccupied with communicating their new strategy to higher organizational levels. As a result, they tend to slight the other, more difficult task, namely, how to reach managers and supervisors at lower echelons. The latter hold the key to their success. Furthermore, they need a deeper insight into proposed changes than managers at higher levels.

After all, the functions are expected to erect a structure of complex, interacting operating systems upon a new strategic foundation. They must dismantle or severely modify the systems in place. Hundreds of specialists have to be retrained and new work procedures documented.

If you think you have already developed an adequate downward communications program, we invite you to put it to the following acid test. Thirty days after you have announced a new strategy, ask a dozen subfunctional managers and specialists to write down what they believe to be the three most important factors that will determine the success or failure of the business and its new plan. If the answers received do not agree or if the functional people do not identify the same key issues you thought you spelled out in your plan, then your new strategy is already in big trouble. You may have given an eloquent speech to your subordinates on the merits of your strategy selection, but your message was not received.

This is your early warning signal that a gap exists between your intent and their understanding, and you may still have time to bridge it. At the outset of this article, we mentioned a business offering customized products. Had the general manager of the business made this test, he might have learned that people in his district sales office were not aligned to his innovative strategy.

Concerted Action

Do these suggestions place too much of a burden on the shoulders of profit center managers? Will they be tempted to take on responsibilities better left with functional subordinates? Will they become hopelessly bogged down in operating work?

Not necessarily. Strategic decisions affect all functional areas of the business. If one area fails to move in concert with the others, the profit center will be swept along on its old strategic course. *All* functional areas must be coupled to the new strategic plan, not just a few. One laggard, one half-hearted functional commitment may endanger the goals established for the center as a whole.

Few planners have the political muscle to oversee the alignment of operating plans to the new strategy. Only profit center managers have the power and the control of resources to make things happen cross-functionally. If they claim the right to chart a strategic course, they must also accept responsibility for monitoring and at times directing its implementation at lower organizational levels.

In conclusion, while companies adhering to a policy of decentralization may find this suggestion hard to swallow—indeed, slightly heretical—we would remind them that integration has always been one of the primary elements of managerial work. It is unrealistic for any company to promote strategic planning as a technique for coping with a fast-changing environment without taking into account how it affects the profit center manager's other duties of organizing, integrating, and measuring.

Notes

1. Hugo E.R. Uyterhoeven, "General Managers in the Middle," *HBR*, March–April, 1974, p. 75.

2. 1976 PIMS Conference, Boston, September 1, 1976.

22
Beyond Theory Y

JOHN J. MORSE and JAY W. LORSCH

The concept of participative management, as symbolized by Douglas McGregor's "Theory Y," was an important insight into improving organizational effectiveness. But many managers assume that Theory Y is the *only* correct approach. In this article, the authors go "beyond Theory Y" to propose that the most productive organization is one that fits the needs of its task and people in any particular situation. In some cases, this may well mean a more directive approach. Even more significant, the proper "fit" among task, organization, and people seems to develop strong "competence motivation" in individuals, regardless of the organizational style.

During the past 30 years, managers have been bombarded with two competing approaches to the problems of human administration and organization. The first, usually called the classical school of organization, emphasizes the need for well-established lines of authority, clearly defined jobs, and authority equal to responsibility. The second, often called the participative approach, focuses on the desirability of involving organization members in decision making so that they will be more highly motivated.

Douglas McGregor, through his well-known "Theory X and Theory Y," drew a distinction between the assumptions about human motivation which underlie these two approaches, to this effect:

☐ Theory X assumes that people dislike work and must be coerced, controlled, and directed toward organizational goals. Furthermore, most people prefer to be treated this way, so they can avoid responsibility.

☐ Theory Y—the integration of goals—emphasizes the average person's intrinsic interest in her work, her desire to be self-directing and to seek responsibility, and her capacity to be creative in solving business problems.

It is McGregor's conclusion, of course, that the latter approach to organization is the more desirable one for managers to follow.[1]

346

McGregor's position causes confusion for the managers who try to choose between these two conflicting approaches. The classical organizational approach that McGregor associated with Theory X does work well in some situations, although, as McGregor himself pointed out, there are also some situations where it does not work effectively. At the same time, the approach based on Theory Y, while it has produced good results in some situations, does not always do so. That is, each approach is effective in some cases but not in others. Why is this? How can managers resolve the confusion?

A New Approach

Recent work by a number of students of management and organization may help to answer such questions.[2] These studies indicate that there is not one best organizational approach; rather, the best approach depends on the nature of the work to be done. Enterprises with highly predictable tasks perform better with organizations characterized by the highly formalized procedures and management hierarchies of the classical approach. With highly uncertain tasks that require more extensive problem solving, on the other hand, organizations that are less formalized and emphasize self-control and member participation in decision making are more effective. In essence, according to these newer studies, managers must design and develop organizations so that the organizational characteristics *fit* the nature of the task to be done.

While the conclusions of this newer approach will make sense to most experienced managers and can alleviate much of the confusion about which approach to choose, there are still two important questions unanswered:

1   How does the more formalized and controlling organization affect the motivation of organization members? (McGregor's most telling criticism of the classical approach was that it did not unleash the potential in an enterprise's human resources.)
2   Equally important, does a less formalized organization always provide a high level of motivation for its members? (This is the implication many managers have drawn from McGregor's work.)

We have recently been involved in a study that provides surprising answers to these questions and, when taken together with other recent work, suggests a new set of basic assumptions which move beyond Theory Y into what we call "Contingency Theory: the fit between task, organization, and people." These theoretical assumptions emphasize that the appropriate pattern of organization is *contingent* on the nature of the work to be done and on the particular needs of the people involved. We should emphasize that we have labeled these assumptions as a step beyond Theory Y because of McGregor's own recognition that the Theory Y assumptions would probably be supplanted by new knowledge within a short time.[3]

The Study Design

Our study was conducted in four organizational units. Two of these performed the relatively certain task of manufacturing standardized containers on high-speed, automated production lines. The other two performed the relatively uncertain work of research and development in communications technology. Each pair of units performing the same kind of task were in the same large company, and each pair had previously been evaluated by that company's management as containing one highly effective unit and a less effective one. The study design is summarized in Exhibit 1.

The objective was to explore more fully how the fit between organization and task was related to successful performance. That is, does a good fit between organizational characteristics and task requirements increase the motivation of individuals and hence produce more effective individual and organizational performance?

An especially useful approach to answering this question is to recognize that an individual has a strong need to master the world around him, including the task that he faces as a member of a work organization.[4] The accumulated feelings of satisfaction that come from successfully mastering one's environment can be called a "sense of competence." We saw this sense of competence in performing a particular task as helpful in understanding how a fit between task and organizational characteristics could motivate people toward successful performance.

Organizational Dimensions

Because the four study sites had already been evaluated by the respective corporate managers as high and low performers of tasks, we expected that such differences in performance would be a preliminary clue to differences in the "fit" of the organizational characteristics to the job to be done. But, first, we had to define what kinds of organizational characteristics would determine how appropriate the organization was to the particular task.

We grouped these organizational characteristics into two sets of factors:

1   Formal characteristics, which could be used to judge the fit between the kind of task being worked on and the formal practices of the organization.

Exhibit 1.   Study Design in "Fit" of Organizational Characteristics

Characteristics	Company I (Predictable Manufacturing Task)	Company II (Unpredictable R&D Task)
Effective performer	Akron containers plant	Stockton research lab
Less effective performer	Hartford containers plant	Carmel research lab

2 Climate characteristics, or the subjective perceptions and orientations that had developed among the individuals about their organizational setting. (These too must fit the task to be performed if the organization is to be effective.)

We measured these attributes through questionnaires and interviews with about 40 managers in each unit to determine the appropriateness of the organization to the kind of task being performed. We also measured the feelings of competence of the people in the organizations so that we could link the appropriateness of the organizational attributes with a sense of competence.

Major Findings

The principal findings of the survey are best highlighted by contrasting the highly successful Akron plant and the high-performing Stockton laboratory. Because each performed very different tasks (the former a relatively certain manufacturing task and the latter a relatively uncertain research task), we expected, as brought out earlier, that there would have to be major differences between them in organizational characteristics if they were to perform effectively. And this is what we did find. But we also found that each of these effective units had a better fit with its particular task than did its less effective counterpart.

While our major purpose in this article is to explore how the fit between task and organizational characteristics is related to motivation, we first want to explore more fully the organizational characteristics of these units, so the reader will better understand what we mean by a fit between task and organization and how it can lead to more effective behavior. To do this, we shall place the major emphasis on the contrast between the high-performing units (the Akron plant and Stockton laboratory), but we shall also compare each of these with its less effective mate (the Hartford plant and Carmel laboratory respectively).

Formal Characteristics

Beginning with differences in formal characteristics, we found that both the Akron and Stockton organizations fit their respective tasks much better than did their less successful counterparts. In the predictable manufacturing task environment, Akron had a pattern of formal relationships and duties that was highly structured and precisely defined. Stockton, with its unpredictable research task, had a low degree of structure and much less precision of definition (see Exhibit 2).

Akron's pattern of formal rules, procedures, and control systems was so specific and comprehensive that it prompted one manager to remark:

"We've got rules here for everything from how much powder to use in cleaning the toilet bowls to how to cart a dead body out of the plant."

In contrast, Stockton's formal rules were so minimal, loose, and flexible that one scientist, when asked whether he felt the rules ought to be tightened, said:

> If a man puts a nut on a screw all day long, you may need more rules and a job definition for him. But we're not novices here. We're professionals and not the kind who need close supervision. People around here *do* produce, and produce under relaxed conditions. Why tamper with success?

These differences in formal organizational characteristics were well suited to the differences in tasks of the two organizations. Thus:

Akron's highly structured formal practices fit its predictable task because behavior had to be rigidly defined and controlled around the automated, high-speed production line. There was really only one way to accomplish the plant's very routine and programmable job; managers defined it precisely and insisted (through the plant's formal practices) that each man do what was expected of him.

On the other hand, Stockton's highly unstructured formal practices made just as much sense because the required activities in the laboratory simply could not be rigidly defined in advance. With such an unpredictable, fast-changing task as communications technology research, there were numerous approaches to getting the job done well. As a consequence, Stockton managers used a less structured pattern of formal practices that left the scientists in the lab free to respond to the changing task situation.

Akron's formal practices were very much geared to *short-term* and

Exhibit 2. Differences in Formal Characteristics in High-Performing Organizations

Characteristics	Akron	Stockton
1. Pattern of formal relationships and duties as signified by organization charts and job manuals	Highly structured, precisely defined	Low degree of structure, less well defined
2. Pattern of formal rules, procedures, control, and measurement systems	Pervasive, specific, uniform, comprehensive	Minimal, loose, flexible
3. Time dimensions incorporated in formal practices	Short-term	Long-term
4. Goal dimensions incorporated in formal practices	Manufacturing	Scientific

manufacturing concerns as its task demanded. For example, formal production reports and operating review sessions were daily occurrences, consistent with the fact that the through-put time for their products was typically only a few hours.

By contrast, Stockton's formal practices were geared to *long-term* and *scientific* concerns, as its task demanded. Formal reports and reviews were made only quarterly, reflecting the fact that research often does not come to fruition for three to five years.

At the two less effective sites (i.e., the Hartford plant and the Carmel laboratory), the formal organizational characteristics did not fit their respective tasks nearly as well. For example, Hartford's formal practices were much less structured and controlling than were Akron's, while Carmel's were more restraining and restricting than were Stockton's. A scientist in Carmel commented:

> There's something here that keeps you from being scientific. It's hard to put your finger on, but I guess I'd call it "Mickey Mouse." There are rules and things here that get in your way regarding doing your job as a researcher.

Climate Characteristics

As with formal practices, the climate in both high-performing Akron and Stockton suited the respective tasks much better than did the climates at the less successful Hartford and Carmel sites.

Perception of Structure. The people in the Akron plant perceived a great deal of structure, with their behavior tightly controlled and defined. One manager in the plant said:

> We can't let the lines run unattended. We lose money whenever they do. So we make sure each man knows his job, knows when he can take a break, knows how to handle a change in shifts, etc. It's all spelled out clearly for him the day he comes to work here.

In contrast, the scientists in the Stockton laboratory perceived very little structure, with their behavior only minimally controlled. Such perceptions encouraged the individualistic and creative behavior that the uncertain, rapidly changing research task needed. Scientists in the less successful Carmel laboratory perceived much more structure in their organization and voiced the feeling that this was "getting in their way" and making it difficult to do effective research.

Distribution of Influence. The Akron plant and the Stockton laboratory also differed substantially in how influence was distributed and on the character of superior-subordinate and colleague relations. Akron personnel felt that they had much less influence over decisions in their plant than Stockton's scientists did in their laboratory. The task at Akron had already been clearly defined and that definition had, in a sense, been incorporated into the automated production flow itself. Therefore, there was less need for individuals to have a say in decisions concerning the work process.

Moreover, in Akron, influence was perceived to be concentrated in the upper levels of the formal structure (a hierarchical or "top-heavy" distribution), while in Stockton influence was perceived to be more evenly spread out among more levels of the formal structure (an egalitarian distribution).

Akron's members perceived themselves to have a low degree of freedom vis-à-vis superiors both in choosing the jobs they work on and in handling these jobs on their own. They also described the type of supervision in the plant as being relatively directive. Stockton's scientists, on the other hand, felt that they had a great deal of freedom vis-à-vis their superiors both in choosing the tasks and projects, and in handling them in the way that they wanted to. They described supervision in the laboratory as being very participatory.

It is interesting to note that the less successful Carmel laboratory had more of its decisions made at the top. Because of this, there was a definite feeling by the scientists that their particular expertise was not being effectively used in choosing projects.

Relations with Others.   The people at Akron perceived a great deal of similarity among themselves in background, prior work experiences, and approaches for tackling job-related problems. They also perceived the degree of coordination of effort among colleagues to be very high. Because Akron's task was so precisely defined and the behavior of its members so rigidly controlled around the automated lines, it is easy to see that this pattern also made sense.

By contrast, Stockton's scientists perceived not only a great many differences among themselves, especially in education and background, but also that the coordination of effort among colleagues was relatively low. This was appropriate for a laboratory in which a great variety of disciplines and skills were present and individual projects were important to solve technological problems.

Time Orientation.   As we would expect, Akron's individuals were highly oriented toward a relatively short time span and manufacturing goals. They responded to quick feedback concerning the quality and service that the plant was providing. This was essential, given the nature of their task.

Stockton's researchers were highly oriented toward a longer time span and scientific goals. These orientations meant that they were willing to wait for long-term feedback from a research project that might take years to complete. A scientist in Stockton said:

> We're not the kind of people here who need a pat on the back every day. We can wait for months if necessary before we get feedback from colleagues and the profession. I've been working on one project now for

three months and I'm still not sure where it's going to take me. I can live with that, though.

This is precisely the kind of behavior and attitude that spells success on this kind of task.

Managerial Style. Finally, the individuals in both Akron and Stockton perceived their chief executive to have a "managerial style" that expressed more of a concern for the task than for people or relationships, but this seemed to fit both tasks.

In Akron, the technology of the task was so dominant that top managerial behavior which was not focused primarily on the task might have reduced the effectiveness of performance. On the other hand, although Stockton's research task called for more individualistic problem-solving behavior, that sort of behavior could have become segmented and uncoordinated, unless the top executive in the lab focused the group's attention on the overall research task. Given the individualistic bent of the scientists, this was an important force in achieving unity of effort.

All these differences in climate characteristics in the two high performers are summarized in Exhibit 3.

As with formal attributes, the less effective Hartford and Carmel sites had organizational climates that showed a perceptibly lower degree of fit with their respective tasks. For example, the Hartford plant had an egalitarian distribution of influence, perceptions of a low degree of structure, and a more participatory type of supervision. The Carmel laboratory had a somewhat top-heavy distribution of influence, perceptions of high structure, and a more directive type of supervision.

Competence Motivation

Because of the difference in organizational characteristics at Akron and Stockton, the two sites were strikingly different places in which to work. But these organizations had two very important things in common. First, each organization fit very well the requirements of its task. Second, although the behavior in the two organizations was different, the result in both cases was effective task performance.

Since, as we indicated earlier, our primary concern in this study was to link the fit between organization and task with individual motivation to perform effectively, we devised a two-part test to measure the sense of competence motivation of the individuals at both sites. Thus:

The *first* part asked a participant to write creative and imaginative stories in response to six ambiguous pictures.

The *second* asked him to write a creative and imaginative story about what he would be doing, thinking, and feeling "tomorrow" on his job. This is called a "projective" test because it is assumed that the respondent projects

Exhibit 3. Differences in "Climate" Characteristics in High-Performing Organizations

Characteristics	Akron	Stockton
1. Structural orientation	Perceptions of tightly controlled behavior and a high degree of structure	Perceptions of a low degree of structure
2. Distribution of influence	Perceptions of low total influence, concentrated at upper levels in the organization	Perceptions of high total influence, more evenly spread out among all levels
3. Character of superior-subordinate relations	Low freedom vis-à-vis superiors to choose and handle jobs, directive type of supervision	High freedom vis-à-vis superiors to choose and handle projects, participatory type of supervision
4. Character of colleague relations	Perceptions of many similarities among colleagues, high degree of coordination of colleague effort	Perceptions of many differences among colleagues, relatively low degree of coordination of colleague effort
5. Time orientation	Short-term	Long-term
6. Goal orientation	Manufacturing	Scientific
7. Top executive's "managerial style"	More concerned with task than people	More concerned with task than people

into her stories her own attitudes, thoughts, feelings, needs, and wants, all of which can be measured from the stories.[5]

The results indicated that the individuals in Akron and Stockton showed significantly more feelings of competence than did their counterparts in the lower-fit Hartford and Carmel organizations.[6] We found that the organization-task fit is simultaneously linked to and interdependent with both individual motivation and effective unit performance. (This interdependency is illustrated in Exhibit 4.)

Putting the conclusions in this form raises the question of cause and effect. Does effective unit performance result from the task-organization fit or from higher motivation, or perhaps from both? Does higher sense of competence motivation result from effective unit performance or from fit?

Exhibit 4.   Basic Contingent Relationships

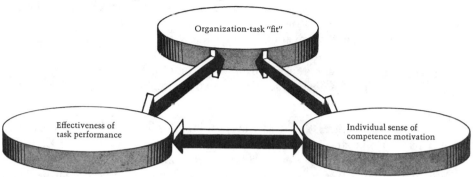

Our answer to these questions is that we do not think there are any single cause-and-effect relationships, but that these factors are mutually interrelated. This has important implications for management theory and practice.

Contingency Theory

Returning to McGregor's Theory X and Theory Y assumptions, we can now question the validity of some of his conclusions. While Theory Y might help to explain the findings in the two laboratories, we clearly need something other than Theory X or Y assumptions to explain the findings in the plants.

For example, the managers at Akron worked in a formalized organizational setting with relatively little participation in decision making, and yet they were highly motivated. According to Theory X, people would work hard in such a setting only because they were coerced to do so. According to Theory Y, they should have been involved in decision making and been self-directed to feel so motivated. Nothing in our data indicates that either set of assumptions was valid at Akron.

Conversely, the managers at Hartford, the low-performing plant, were in a less formalized organization with more participation in decision making, and yet they were not as highly motivated as the Akron managers. The Theory Y assumptions would suggest that they should have been more motivated.

A way out of such paradoxes is to state a new set of assumptions, the Contingency Theory, that seems to explain the findings at all four sites:

1   Human beings bring varying patterns of needs and motives into the work organization, but one central need is to achieve a sense of competence.

2   The sense of competence motive, while it exists in all human beings, may be fulfilled in different ways by different people depending on

how this need interacts with the strengths of the individuals' other needs—such as those for power, independence, structure, achievement, and affiliation.

3 Competence motivation is most likely to be fulfilled when there is a fit between task and organization.

4 Sense of competence continues to motivate even when a competence goal is achieved; once one goal is reached, a new, higher one is set.

While the central thrust of these points is clear from the preceding discussion of the study, some elaboration can be made. First, the idea that different people have different needs is well understood by psychologists. However, all too often, managers assume that all people have similar needs. Lest we be accused of the same error, we are saying only that all people have a need to feel competent; in this *one* way they are similar. But in many other dimensions of personality, individuals differ, and these differences will determine how a particular person achieves a sense of competence.

Thus, for example, the people in the Akron plant seemed to be very different from those in the Stockton laboratory in their underlying attitudes toward uncertainty, authority, and relationships with their peers. And because they had different need patterns along these dimensions, both groups were highly motivated by achieving competence from quite different activities and settings.

While there is a need to further investigate how people who work in different settings differ in their psychological makeup, one important implication of the Contingency Theory is that we must not only seek a fit between organization and task, but also between task and people and between people and organization.

A further point which requires elaboration is that one's sense of competence never really comes to rest. Rather, the real satisfaction of this need is in the successful performance itself, with no diminishing of the motivation as one goal is reached. Since feelings of competence are thus reinforced by successful performance, they can be a more consistent and reliable motivator than salary and benefits.

Implications for Managers

The major managerial implication of the Contingency Theory seems to rest in the task-organization-people fit. Although this interrelationship is complex, the best possibility for managerial action probably is in tailoring the organization to fit the task and the people. If such a fit is achieved, both effective unit performance and a higher sense of competence motivation seem to result.

Managers can start this process by considering how certain the task is, how frequently feedback about task performance is available, and what goals are implicit in the task. The answers to these questions will guide their decisions about the design of the management hierarchy, the specificity of job assignments, and the utilization of rewards and control procedures. Selective use of training programs and a general emphasis on appropriate management styles will move them toward a task-organization fit.

The problem of achieving a fit among task, organization, and people is something we know less about. As we have already suggested, we need further investigation of what personality characteristics fit various tasks and organizations. Even with our limited knowledge, however, there are indications that people will gradually gravitate into organizations that fit their particular personalities. Managers can help this process by becoming more aware of what psychological needs seem to best fit the tasks available and the organizational setting, and by trying to shape personnel selection criteria to take account of these needs.

In arguing for an approach which emphasizes the fit among task, organization, and people, we are putting to rest the question of which organizational approach—the classical or the participative—is best. In its place we are raising a new question: What organizational approach is most appropriate given the task and the people involved?

For many enterprises, given the new needs of younger employees for more autonomy, and the rapid rates of social and technological change, it may well be that the more participative approach is the most appropriate. But there will still be many situations in which the more controlled and formalized organization is desirable. Such an organization need not be coercive or punitive. If it makes sense to the individuals involved, given their needs and their jobs, they will find it rewarding and motivating.

Concluding Note

The reader will recognize that the complexity we have described is not of our own making. The basic deficiency with earlier approaches is that they did not recognize the variability in tasks and people which produces this complexity. The strength of the contingency approach we have outlined is that it begins to provide a way of thinking about this complexity, rather than ignoring it. While our knowledge in this area is still growing, we are certain that any adequate theory of motivation and organization will have to take account of the contingent relationship between task, organization, and people.

Notes

1. Douglas McGregor, *The Human Side of Enterprise* (New York, McGraw-Hill Book Company, 1960), pp. 34–35 and pp. 47–48.

2. See for example Paul R. Lawrence and Jay W. Lorsch, *Organization and Environment* (Boston, Harvard Business School, Division of Research, 1967); Joan Woodward, *Industrial Organization: Theory & Practice* (New York, Oxford University Press, 1965); Tom Burns and G.M. Stalker, *The Management of Innovation* (London, Tavistock Publications, 1961); Harold J. Leavitt, "Unhuman Organizations," *HBR*, July–August 1962, p. 90.

3. McGregor, op. cit., p. 245.

4. See Robert W. White, "Ego and Reality in Psychoanalytic Theory," *Psychological Issues*, Vol. III, No. 3 (New York, International Universities Press, 1963).

5. For a more detailed description of this survey, see John J. Morse, *Internal Organizational Patterning and Sense of Competence Motivation* (Boston, Harvard Business School, unpublished doctoral dissertation, 1969).

6. Differences between the two container plants are significant at .001 and between the research laboratories at .01 (one-tailed probability).

23

Tailor Incentive Compensation to Strategy

MALCOLM S. SALTER

One of the tools top management has to influence policy-level executives' pursuit of corporate goals is the incentive compensation structure. So the structure must be made consistent with strategy. In evaluating whether it is consistent, this article says, top managment should think of it in terms of four aspects of corporate policy: short run versus long run, risk aversion versus risk taking, interdivisional relationships, and company-division relationships. The author considers these in the context of six elements of incentive plans: financial instruments, performance measures, degree of discretion in allocating rewards, size and frequency of awards, degree of uniformity, and funding.

A task of all chief executives is encouraging their policy-level managers to take action that reinforces efforts to achieve corporate goals. Most large companies do not rely solely on personal contact and other informal means to provide that encouragement; they also use formal management appraisal and financial reward systems.

Survey data from 1970 show that of the nation's largest 100 industrials in terms of sales, 81 used cash bonus systems as incentives to executives. Of those 81 companies, 73 also used some other form of incentive to supplement cash payments. The companies that did not pay bonuses typically relied on stock options as the principal reward.[1]

Author's Note. I am indebted to several colleagues and students whose work on executive compensation has formed a stimulus to my research. They include Kenneth R. Andrews, Norman A. Berg, Joseph L. Bower, C. Roland Christensen, Robert A. Pitts, and Bruce R. Scott.

As companies grow and diversify, the character of their executive bonus systems tends to change in three important ways: the range of possible payoffs increases, the variability of bonuses increases over time, and the bonuses become more closely tied to performance than to position in the hierarchy. As top management tries to extend its influence through incentive compensation policy, the important question becomes how to make this policy consistent with the company's overall strategy.

This article attempts to develop a framework to help corporations solve that question. The approach I take is based on my research in single-unit as well as multidivisional companies, ranging in size from $20 million to $600 million in sales.

The first step in evaluating or designing an incentive compensation system for policy-level executives is to identify and analyze company policy with respect to four potential problem areas. I shall identify them briefly and then discuss them in the context of six basic choices that must be made while shaping the program. The four problem areas are:

1 *Short run vs. long run.*   This age-old problem involves the profit trade-offs top management wants its key executives to make in the course of proposing and implementing policy. As the reader will see, this choice can be affected by various kinds of incentive compensation systems.

2 *Risk aversion vs. risk taking.*   In companies or divisions operating in mature industries, managements concentrate on maintaining current market position and improving customer service. Other companies encourage their managers to develop new markets through entrepreneurship and risk taking. These contrasting strategies may call for different approaches to performance rewards.

3 *Interdivisional relationships.*   Incentive compensation can influence the way in which division managers work together. If substantial joint effort or cooperation is required between divisions, the appropriate policy on pay will be quite different from the situation where the units are independent of each other.

4 *Company-division relationships.*   In some multidivisional companies, corporate management plays a direct role in advising managers of divisions or profit centers. In others, the role of headquarters is primarily in resource allocation. Each approach requires a different design of the compensation program for division managers.

Once these potential or existing policy problems have been at least tentatively resolved in the context of a company's goals and strategy, the principal constraints will have been established for answering the difficult questions which I consider in the balance of this article. These questions have to do with financial instruments, performance measures, degree of discretion in allocating rewards, size and frequency of awards, degree of uniformity, and funding.

(Since we are dealing with compensation for those executives responsible for formulating and implementing corporate strategy, the eligibility question is by definition resolved. We must also assume the existence of a competitive and equitable salary structure.[2]

Financial Instruments

Which financial instruments are the best motivators and the most cost-effective for the company?

The available financial instruments are many, of course. They include current cash, current stock, deferred cash, deferred stock, restricted stock, and phantom options. Stock options can be qualified or nonqualified. Some instruments, such as restricted stock and qualified options, have limited appeal nowadays because of the tax laws. But a selection among the alternatives can be made by considering their long-run versus short-run orientation and the degree to which the company wants to stress entrepreneurial activity on the part of its policy-level managers.

The principal alternatives involve choices between current and deferred instruments and between cash and stock. In respect to the first set of choices, the tax status of the persons involved obviously plays a role, but there are policy implications as well. Current awards accent the importance of short-run performance, while deferral of awards tends to minimize the psychological impact of annual bonuses based on annual results.

In addition, use of a deferred instrument risks development of what is commonly called a "gold handcuffs" atmosphere. Many analysts of compensation practices question whether such an atmosphere is consistent with the needs and values of innovative and dynamic managers. On the other hand, deferring rewards is financially attractive from a corporate viewpoint, since the company can invest the conserved cash in operations and share the resulting profits with the executives included in the plan

Despite this argument, the many policy-level executives I have interviewed typically prefer receiving cash bonus awards "when earned"—except in those cases where it pays to defer income so as to minimize current tax liabilities. While some compensation experts have argued that motivation of behavior, rather than satisfying preferences for certain compensation packages, should be the prime goal of executive pay plans, ignoring this apparently widely shared preference can create dissatisfaction with pay at the top levels.

The cash versus stock trade-off raises not only the obvious questions of the balance between short-run and long-run incentives, but also the questions of corporate-divisional relationships. Companies usually justify awards of stock by saying that they link individual interest with the long-term interest of the corporation.

Of the largest 100 U.S. industrials in sales terms surveyed recently by a consulting firm, 65 used stock bonuses and 89 used stock options of some sort.[3] This widespread use of stock-related instruments reflects not only the tax advantages to the recipient but also the degree to which large companies try to tie the interests of their divisions to those of the corporation as a whole. In theory, ownership of stock by profit-center managers reinforces this viewpoint and gives top management leverage in discussing policy with them.

Past a certain point, however, the use of stock awards, whether stock bonuses or stock options, can have negative economic consequences for a company and its shareholders. Some large corporations, such as General Dynamics, have had as much as 15% of their equity out under option. (In comparison, only 3% of Xerox's equity was under option in 1972.) Extensive use of options can seriously dilute stockholders' equity in a company and eventually increase its cost of capital.

This danger, often neglected by companies unable to afford large cash bonuses, can be avoided by limiting stock options to those who are responsible for formulating and implementing policy—that is, top management, divisional and/or subsidiary presidents, and those of their managers who are in charge of major operating units or departments.

Performance Measures

Which measures of executives' performance should be employed as the basis for allocating incentive awards?

The selection of performance measures is one of the most difficult aspects of planning an incentive compensation program. A measure can be total corporate profits, divisional profits, a mix of the two, or some other indicator. Itek Corporation during the 1960s provides an instructive case in point.

Itek was formed in 1957. By the 1960s most of its business was in developing high-altitude cameras and film and ground-based equipment that could interpret the photographic data. Subsequent acquisitions led Itek into the business products area and ophthalmology, but the core technology remained in the photographic and optical fields.

When Franklin A. Lindsay became president in 1962 after a period of severe decline in profits, he restructured the organization and system of measurement and reward while paying particular attention to entrepreneurship, interdivisional relations, and company-division relations. After selling unprofitable segments and regrouping the remaining activities into a new divisional structure, Lindsay developed an approach to performance measurement that centered around the so-called Annual Review Program for division managers and a merit-rating system for every manager from that level down.

Every October the division managers came to corporate headquarters for a two-day meeting. Each made a presentation that included:

☐ A review of reasons for major variances, if any, from the current year's program.

☐ A rough forecast of sales and gross profit by product.

☐ A statement and analysis of division operations, including expenses, operating income, net income, current asset position, return on assets, and number of employees.

☐ A statement of "management objectives" for the coming year.

☐ A review of progress made in accomplishing management objectives for the prior year.

☐ An explanation of any unusual capital expenditures budgeted in the coming year, with the estimated ROI.

After the October meeting, the Annual Review Program took on a more future-oriented format. On the basis of these meetings, a companywide financial forecast and profit plan was established, and in December the financial planning group conducted a second review involving division managers. In this review, a dry run for the directors' meeting in January, the division managers presented their final programs for the coming year.

In their presentations to the board in January, all division managers presented sales and earning forecasts for the new fiscal year, along with their major assumptions, objectives, and a review of their accomplishments in the year past with respect to the goals they had set. These presentations were supplemented, of course, with a review of the companywide financial plan.

During all these review sessions, the performance of each division manager was evaluated with respect to sales, profit as a percentage of sales, return on assets, and achievement of management objectives. The most noteworthy feature of this process, however, was not the objective measures of performance, but the fact that all top-level operating executives had the opportunity to present their judgment of their unit's performance in the broadest possible terms. They knew that this procedure, rather than some summary indicator, formed the basis for evaluating them for the purpose of bonus awards. This policy, Lindsay felt, stimulated individual initiative and a long-run point of view at a time when Itek's fortunes were rebounding from their nadir.

The size of the bonus pool for division executives depended primarily on total profits rather than their own division profits. This feature was very important for a company diversifying from a core technology. Lindsay wanted to minimize any exaggerated divisional self-interest that could threaten the interests of Itek, so he placed a premium on managerial commitment to the welfare of the whole company and stressed interdivisional cooperation. This was particularly important for the divisions doing government contracting; they shared some assets and often performed specialized work for each other on a ''cost plus'' basis.

Textron's Approach

The Itek procedure contrasts with that of Textron in the 1960s, where the key measure of performance in allocating bonus awards to division managers was divisional ROI. While the company also used detailed planning routines and review sessions, the managers' bonuses varied directly with a single measure of division profitability. The absence of transfers and joint work between divisions at Textron helps explain why this performance measure would not have been appropriate for Itek.

While executives of highly diversified companies like Textron often see themselves primarily as allocators of capital among unrelated business units, top executives at Itek viewed themselves as managers and integrators of a complex set of administrative units that shared assets, technologies, and, in some cases, even engineers. This approach was reflected in their incentive compensation plan, which was a mix of subjective measures of individual performance and objective measures of corporate performance.

The selection of performance measures also affects the short-run versus long-run goals problem. In a classic case, a worldwide manufacturer of household products decided in the early 1960s to give profit responsibility to its Brazilian subsidiary and reward its general manager on the basis of return on assets. Much to the chagrin of corporate officers, they discovered that he had sold some of the assets and leased them back so that his year-end figures would show substantial improvement. The long-run implications of this kind of liquidation are obvious; so too is the fallacy of the single performance measure (such as ROI) which has been widely discussed in recent years.[4]

Degree of Discretion

Should the chief executive and the compensation committee of the board of directors have complete discretion in making awards, or should some formula-based method be used?

This question is closely related to that dealing with performance measures. For example, the differences between Itek and Textron were due in large part to the degree of discretion in allocating bonuses. At Itek, the president and board decided that the awards should remain largely discretionary, partly to accent the less quantifiable aspects of a manager's job—

such as strategic planning—and partly to retain their influence over division strategy and policy. At Textron, where top management played only an indirect role in unit operations, the formula procedure allowed for little discretion.

Interdivisional relationships can be influential in the choice between discretionary and formula-based approaches. Where interdivisional transfers are encouraged and joint work by divisions is part of a company's normal operation, fixed-formula bonus plans can hinder the achievement of corporate goals. A problem faced by the Dennison Manufacturing Company is a good case in point.

In 1967 two divisions of Dennison, Industrial Products and Marking Systems, were in disagreement about the introduction and sale of a new product called Secur-A-Tach, a plastic substitute for string or wire in tying items together. The latter division had been split off from the former in 1955, but their markets still overlapped somewhat.

Marking Systems had developed the product. But Industrial Products claimed that it could sell at least as much Secur-A-Tach to its customers, and therefore proposed simultaneous introduction of the product by both divisions. The conflict grew to proportions that threatened to disrupt operations.

This issue had many facets, including transfer pricing and reimbursement of R&D costs. Not the least of the problems was the bonus plan, which was based on divisional profits; the division managers knew that resolution of the dispute would significantly affect their bonus. Predictably, the ultimate decision was passed up to the president. The dispute eventually triggered a review of Dennison's incentive compensation system.

The discretion question also relates to the problem of the proper balance between short-run and long-run points of view. Annual bonuses, for example, usually emphasize the short term, so a manager wants to "look good" at the end of the year. To prevent his concentration on his own immediate rewards, top management should evaluate qualitatively the long-run implications of subordinates' actions and reward them at least in part on that basis.

Fixed Formulas

Bonus plans using fixed formulas have been much criticized for reasons other than their bias toward short-term performances. Arch Patton, for instance, cites a situation in which a company's net income rises 15% and its formula based bonus payments therefore rise sharply too—during a year when industry profits jump 25%. The executives have been rewarded, Patton points out, "when they actually should be penalized for having lost ground to competition."[5]

Nevertheless, the fixed-formula approach is still widely used because it simplifies the administrative process and clearly spells out the company's "rules of the game." Making explicit the relationship between individual performance and rewards helps managers view their personal risks and gains realistically. It is hard to imagine a management team following a high-risk strategy without this awareness. The question that remains is whether a fixed-formula plan is the only way to communicate it.

The choice between a discretionary and a nondiscretionary method depends on many of the same factors that should be considered in selecting appropriate performance measures. Indeed, the cases of Itek, Textron, and Dennison indicate that the two choices should be made in concert.

Size and Frequency

What should be the normal size of incentive payments? Should they have upper limits? With what frequency should awards be made?

Contemporary management theory deemphasizes hard-and-fast rules of management. But one rule worth keeping concerns the so-called risk/ return ratio. Graef Crystal puts it succinctly: "Reward opporutnities [should] be meaningful and commensurate with the risks involved."[6] Examples of this principle in practice abound:

Howard Head spent three years perfecting the first metal ski and put all his savings and more into this venture. The classic entrepreneur, he knew that a successful product innovation would revolutionize both the industry and the sport, and he stood to reap many of the benefits of this revolution.

Lee Iacocca at Ford Motor also put his neck on the line in pushing the Mustang at a time when the painful memories of the Edsel were still lingering in the minds of automotive leaders. The potential payoff for both Ford and Iacocca was substantial.

The men who fought for and then guided the $5-billion investment in developing the third-generation computer at IBM were in a position to gain tremendous payoffs for themselves and their company.

In all three cases, the risk/reward ratio apparently influenced the persons involved to assume considerable personal risk. So far, the principle makes perfect sense. But how much reward should be assumed for what kind of risk? Here the guidelines vanish, and top managers are left to their own devices.

Compensation experts can help by constructing "normal" bonuses for each management position. In addition, they can help by surveying the competition and finding out the going rates for similar positions in companies with comparable sales and rates of profitability. But this is only a beginning, and top management can deal with these questions only by analyzing the

company's own requirements for risk taking and innovation. If these requirements appear to exceed those of the average competitor, the situation
should be reflected in higher rewards for successful managers.

Despite its importance, the principle of the risk/reward ratio tends to
get lost in the current enthusiasm for executive compensation surveys. These
surveys help companies to see whether they are paying their executives
competitively. However, these surveys give little or no attention to the
critical relationship between risk and reward.

The frequency of awards can influence the time horizon of managers.
The annual bonus, for example, encourages a manager to use a twelve-month
time frame for evaluating his progress. But this is not appropriate for every
company. A twelve-month cycle makes sense in the auto industry, but not
necessarily in the real estate development industry. In the latter case, an-
nualizing awards might run counter to the financial structure of projects and
even threaten their success. Distinctions such as these should be carefully
considered before an incentive compensation plan is installed.

Degree of Uniformity

*How much uniformity in performance measures and rewards should exist
among levels of top management and among divisions? Should reward instruments be limited to certain executive positions? Should a "cafeteria"
of compensation packages be offered to top-level managers?*

As was the case with other issues, the degree of uniformity in executive
levels depends on the kind of corporate-divisional relations that characterizes
a company's organizational strategy. If the strategy calls for intimate involvement of corporate-level managers in divisional operations, the incentive
compensation of each level should be structured similarly.

If, however, the corporate-level managers concentrate on supervising
resource generation and allocation among a portfolio of enterprises, they
should be paid on a different basis from the operating managers. In the latter
case, the division managers should be eligible in extremely good years for
total compensation above that of the group-level executives, because of the
much greater operating risks and responsibilities they assume.

The case of the chairman and president is complicated by a conflict of
interest. Both are members of a board of directors which was more likely
than not recruited by them. Thus, determining bonus awards for the chairman
and president can be awkward and even embarrassing for the board. The
most sensible approach is to provide automatic awards to these two top
executives based on overall corporate performance. (Several years without
this bonus would probably oblige the board to consider changing leadership.
At this point, fussing with bonuses is academic.)

Whether the measurement and reward systems should be uniform among the divisions depends on the kind of interdivisional relationships required by a company's strategy. In a profit-centered company like Textron, the need for uniformity is low. Nevertheless, the company may want to deal with division managers in a consistent way in order to evaluate the profit centers on the same terms—not only to make bonus awards but also to determine where the corporation should allocate resources in the future.

The requirements in a company like Itek, whose strategies stress product-related expansion and acquisition, are quite different. Since several Itek divisions operated in the photographic and optical areas in the mid-1960s, the degree of cooperation and interdivisional transfers was high. Different performance appraisal and reward systems would have made division managers subject to unequal stakes and multitudinous rules of the game, and therefore would have inhibited cooperation and complicated transfers.

The uniformity issue has been referred to recently in the business press in discussions of the so-called "cafeteria" approach to compensation.[7] I shall not discuss it in detail here, confining myself to one simple guideline that may be helpful.

Cafeteria methods can be useful only so long as the programs offered are consistent with the requirements of effective control. To take an extreme example, granting a high-level executive the choice of substituting annual cash bonuses for lump-sum option grants every five years would complicate the job of controlling policy formulation and implementation over the short term.

Funding Method

What method should determine the funding required by the incentive compensation plan?

The funding question divides logically into two parts. The first concerns the selection of a formula for determining the total bonus funds available in a given year, and the second concerns corporate versus divisional bonus pools in decentralized companies.

Articulation of economic goals must precede design of a funding formula. The range of choices, of course, is very wide indeed: return on investment, return of capital employed, earnings per share, and so on.

The selection of goals involves choosing the yardstick and the target to be measured by it. Many companies use a minimum threshold rule, such as, "the bonus pool will equal 10% of pretax profits after deducting an amount equal to 16% of invested capital as of the beginning of the year." An alternative approach that avoids the investment valuation problem would be,

"3% of pretax earnings in excess of a 10% improvement over a weighted average of the past three years' earnings."

The question of source of funding also relates to a company's strategy. If companywide measures of performance constitute the principal basis for allocating awards, the bonus pool logically should be directly related to corporate profits. Similarly, divisional bonus pools are used when awards are made according to divisional performance.

Conclusion

There are few easy answers to the questions I have discussed. Rather than suggesting general answers that would be difficult to apply to specific situations, I have tried to demonstrate how incentive compensation policy is intimately related to corporate strategy.

Exhibit 1 summarizes the basic interrelationships among the six key aspects of incentive compensation and the four policy problems considered in this article. It shows that the design of an incentive compensation system for policy-level executives can vary considerably. Making the alternatives explicit and understanding the implications of these alternatives can result in easier design selection.

However useful this framework may be, no rules can replace the judgment needed to arrive at an appropriate measurement and reward system. This judgment should reflect the company's administrative inheritance and the chief executive's concept of how he or she wishes to influence behavior in the organization. An example will make this point clear.

The newly appointed president of a company I visited recently placed his top group-level managers on a formula-based corporate bonus plan in order to eliminate vestigal tendencies of the groups to pursue strategies independent of each other. In addition, he slashed by 50% executive bonuses in a group that had had consistently poor earnings performance.

Both moves, which represented dramatic departures from past practice, reflected the president's commitment to breaking down the company's historical management pattern by altering the rules of the game. Bonuses had been so consistent from year to year that they were considered a salary supplement. The president felt that radical changes in this pattern were necessary for encouraging his top executives to develop a new strategy aimed at employing all the company's resources in its market-exploitation efforts. His changes conveyed his message forcefully throughout the organization.

This president had a very clear concept of his administrative inheritance and how strong a role he should play in changing traditions and practices. He demonstrated his understanding of the need to act boldly at this time in using incentive compensation as an instrument of management control in his company.

Exhibit 1. Key Aspects of Incentive Compensation

Policy Issues	Financial Instruments	Performance Measures	Degree of Discretion in Allocating Bonus Awards	Size and Frequency of Awards	Degree of Uniformity	Funding
Short run vs. long-run	Mix of current bonus awards and stock options should reflect the relevant time horizon for policy-level executives. Deferred instruments are weak reinforcers of short-term performance.	Mix of quantitative measures of performance and more qualitative measures should reflect the relevant time horizon for executives. Qualitative measures usually reflect long-run considerations more effectively than quantitative measures.	Nondiscretionary, formula-based bonuses tend to encourage a short-run point of view.	Frequent bonus awards encourage concentration on short-term performance.		
Risk aversion vs. risk taking	Current bonus awards, in cash or stock, can reinforce risk-taking behavior.	Qualitative measures of performance can reinforce initiative by assuring executives that total performance will be evaluated for purposes of bonus awards.	Completely discretionary, highly personalized bonuses do not clarify the ''rules of the game'' and as a result can discourage risk-taking behavior.	The size of both salary and incentive awards should be commensurate with the business and personal risks involved.		

Interdivisional relationships	Bonus pools can be based on divisional performance, total corporate performance, or some mix of the two. Each arrangement sends different signals in terms of interdivisional cooperation.	Nondiscretionary, formula-based bonuses for division managers are most practical in companies where little cooperation among divisions is required. Discretionary bonuses are practical when top management wants to encourage cooperation among divisions.	Uniformity among divisions in the design of measurement and reward systems facilitates interdivisional cooperation.	The choice between divisional and corporate bonus pools should reflect the reasoning used in selecting appropriate performance measures.
Company-division relationships	Stock options can effectively link the interests of division personnel to the interests of the corporation. Use of objective measures of performance for division managers is more meaningful where the primary role of headquarters is to allocate capital than it is in instances where the head office plays an important role in "managing the business" of the divisions.	Nondiscretionary, formula-based bonuses are most practical in companies where headquarters does not interfere in management of the profit centers. Discretionary bonuses are most useful when top management wants to exert a direct influence on decisions in the divisions.	Uniformity among divisions in the design of measurement and reward systems facilitates the resource allocation process at the corporate level. With respect to uniformity among levels of management, the more decentralized the organization, the more reason there is to differentiate the reward systems of each group.	Bonus pools funded solely from divisional profits tend to limit the ability of corporate headquarters to use financial incentives as an instrument of control. Bonus pools funded solely from corporate profits tend to increase the influence of headquarters over the division and other profit centers.

Notes

1. Mario Leo, "Executive Lures and Incentives in the Nation's Top 100," *Business Management*, March 1971, p. 29.

2. For a discussion of equitable pay, see my article, "What Is 'Fair Pay' for the Executive?" *HBR*, May–June 1972, p. 6.

3. Towers, Perrin, Forster & Crosby, Inc., "Executive Bonus Awards and Stock Options in the Top 100 U.S. Industrial Companies," June 1971.

4. See, for example, John Dearden, "The Case Against ROI Control," *HBR*, May–June 1969, especially pp. 132–133.

5. "Why Incentive Plans Fail," *HBR*, May–June 1972, p. 58.

6. *Financial Motivation for Executives* (New York, American Management Association, 1970), p. 244.

7. See, for example, George W. Hettenhouse, "Compensation Cafeteria for Top Executives," *HBR*, September–October 1971, p. 113.

24
Phasing Out Weak Products

PHILIP KOTLER

The strategies of many companies include plans for dropping weak businesses or products. Yet despite the wisdom of these plans, most managers have great difficulty putting them into action. This article reviews the reasons for dropping weak products and why managers are often reluctant to do so. It then proposes a step-by-step procedure for identifying and phasing out weak products.

Most companies today are multiproduct organizations. Whether large or small, whether in manufacturing, wholesaling, or retailing, a company will generally handle a multitude of products and product varieties. At the present time, the typical supermarket handles 6,800 items, American Optical manufactures 30,000 different items, and General Electric's products and parts number in the hundreds of thousands.

Product Overpopulation

Historically, product lines tend to mushroom over a period of time unless a systematic and regular management effort is made at pruning. Yet management tends to find it easier to add products than to remove them.

The fact is that *as products and product lines increase numerically, the range of management problems seems to grow geometrically.*

Author's Note. I wish to acknowledge the helpful comments of Professor Richard M. Clewett of Northwestern University and the assistance of Hugh Hopkins, a Northwestern University Graduate School of Business Administration student.

Major Headaches

Thus management is stalked by the Malthusian specter of product over-population—of too many product mouths to feed. Its limited productive financial and marketing resources must be spread thinner over a larger number of products. This, in turn, leads to two major headaches:

☐ Management's efforts at sales forecasting and pricing must contend with increasing mutual-*demand* relationships among its products.

☐ Its efforts at production scheduling, costing, and equipment purchasing must contend with increasing mutual-*supply* relationships among its products.

Product overpopulation also poses baffling problems for management in resource allocation and coordination. The antidote lies in top management giving more attention to product simplification than it has in the past. As the pace of competition quickens and as consumer tastes become surfeited, the need for pruning company product lines of casualties becomes as great as that for finding replacements.

Gradual Recognition

This need is gradually being recognized in many companies. Well-known instances of product pruning in recent years include:

☐ American Motors Kelvinator Division's drastic reduction of the number of models in its refrigerator, air-conditioning, and kitchen-range lines.

☐ Seiberling Rubber's cutdown on the number of its passenger-car tire offerings by over one-third.

☐ Champion Papers' elimination of certain lines when a full-scale study showed that 20% of its products were producing 80% of its sales.[1]

These are but a few reflections of the growing concern of corporate management about obsolete lines and slow-moving products and models.

Yet, though these efforts point in the right direction, by their very abruptness and scale they indicate the lack of regular and systematic product-pruning programs. Most executives will see a physician at least once a year to check on their health but will let their product mix go unchecked until a crisis develops. During this time, many products lie infirm in the mix until they fade away or are suddenly massively ejected in a crisis-inspired house-cleaning.

Developing Perspectives

The purpose of this article is to describe a new control system currently under development for conducting efficient and rapid annual product check-ups. I shall try to discuss this new approach in enough detail so that it can be implemented by any company concerned with limiting its product population to the more vigorous contenders. Although this system will be described as designed for a manufacturing company, it can easily be adapted by large retail and wholesale organizations, where the problem of dropping weak products is as, if not more, serious.

Before turning our attention to the elements of the system, however, it is desirable to develop certain perspectives suggested by the following questions:

☐ What is the basis of product obsolescence?
☐ How much does carrying weak products cost a company?
☐ Why does management shy away from dropping these products?
☐ What are current practices on product-line pruning?

Product Life Cycle

No branded product can be expected to hold a permanent franchise in the marketplace. The lifetime sales of many products reveal a typical pattern of development. This pattern, known as the *product life cycle*, consists of four distinguishable stages:

1. *Introduction.* The product is put on the market; awareness and acceptance are minimal.
2. *Growth.* The product begins to make rapid sales gains because of the cumulative effects of introductory promotion, distribution, and word-of-mouth influence.
3. *Maturity.* The rate of sales growth begins to taper off because of the diminishing number of potential customers who either are unaware of the product or are aware but have taken no action.
4. *Decline.* The sales begin to diminish as the product is gradually edged out by newer or better products or substitutes.

Variable Histories

The product life cycle concept represents a useful idealization rather than a rigid description of all product life histories.[2]

In the first place, there is nothing fixed about the length of the cycle, or the length of its various stages. According to Joel Dean, the rate of product degeneration is governed by the rate of technical change, the rate of market acceptance, and the ease of competitive entry.[3] Thus each year some new dress styles are introduced in the knowledge that their whole life cycle may span only a year or a season. On the other hand, new commercial aircraft are introduced in the expectation that they will enjoy good sales for at least a decade.

In the second place, products have been known to begin a new cycle or to revert to some earlier stage as a result of the discovery of new uses, the appearance of new users, or the invention of new features. Thus television sales have exhibited a history of spurts as new sizes of screens were introduced, and color television may well put television sales back into a rapid growth stage.

Important Considerations

Yet, despite these and other difficulties concerning the concept of the product life cycle, the concept remains very useful in that it reminds us of three important phenomena:

1. *Products have a limited life.* They are born at some point, may (or may not) pass through a strong growth phase, and eventually degenerate or disappear.

2. *Product profits tend to follow a predictable course through the life cycle.* Profits are absent in the introductory stage, tend to increase substantially in the growth stage, stabilize and then decline in the maturity stage, and all but disappear in the declining stage.

3. *Products require a different marketing (as well as production and financial) program in each stage.* Management must be prepared to shift the relative levels and emphasis given to price, advertising, product improvement, and so forth during different stages in the product life cycle.

To these must be added a fourth consideration. Under modern conditions of competition, a new product's life span is apt to be shorter than it has ever been in the past.[4] There are too many competitors with fast-moving research laboratories, ingenious marketing techniques, and large budgets who stand ready to woo away the customer. The customers themselves are generally unloyal, fickle in their tastes, and prey to gimmicks.

Dual Problem

Executive conversation is rich with talk of "sick" products, "slow movers," "superannuated" products, "senior citizens," "parasites," "former heavy-weights," "obsolete lines," and "fizzled-out" products. All kinds of products are involved, including those which never quite got off the ground, those whose profit returns were fair for a while and are now vanishing, and those which were huge successes but are now riding a sea of troubles.

The problem is not only one of the health of whole product classes but also one of individual styles, models, and choices within the classes which add so much to cost. We are talking about any product or product variation of dubious value in the scheme of corporate objectives.

Weak-Product Burden

Every weak-selling product which lingers in a company's line constitutes a costly burden. Business people often do not realize the magnitude of this burden because of a fixation with the more direct costs. They are complacent as long as the revenues of the weak product cover at least the direct costs of producing it, relieved if the revenues cover most of the overhead. Their attitude toward the weak product is like that of Damon Runyon's character, Harry the Horse, who said, "I am going to bet on the races today. I hope I break even. I need the money."

Hidden Costs

The cost of sustaining a weak product in the mix is not just the amount of uncovered overhead and profit. No financial accounting can adequately convey all the hidden costs. Thus:

☐ The weak product tends to consume a disproportionate amount of management's time.

☐ It often requires frequent price and inventory adjustments.

☐ It generally involves short production runs in spite of expensive setup times.

☐ It requires both advertising and sales-force attention which might better be diverted to making the "healthy" products more profitable.

☐ Its very unfitness can cause customer misgivings and cast a shadow on the company's image.

Furthermore, as if these hidden costs were not burden enough, the biggest cost imposed by carrying weak products may well be in the future. By not being eliminated at the proper time, these products delay the aggressive search for replacement products; they create a lopsided product mix—long on "yesterday's breadwinners" and short on "tomorrow's breadwinners;"[5] they depress present profitability and weaken the company's foothold on the future.

Potential Savings

The tremendous savings which can be effected by product-pruning programs are dramatized in the following two cases:

Hunt, a medium-sized canner, began to cut its thirty-some-odd lines in 1947. By 1958 it had only three products: fruit cocktail, tomato products, and peaches. Within these lines, Hunt reduced the variety offered. For example, in peaches Hunt packed only one grade (choice) in one type of syrup (thick). This simplification was apparently very successful for Hunt. Its sales increased from $15 million in 1947 to $120 million in 1958. By that time it had the top brand in tomato sauce and tomato paste and was second in peaches and catsup. In addition to cutting down on the number of lines, Hunt also began a diversification program by buying out nonrelated companies, such as a manufacturer of matches.[6]

After a survey one company with annual sales of $40,000,000 eliminated sixteen different products with a total volume of $3,300,000. It also made a number of improvements in methods of handling the products retained.

Over the next three years the company's total sales increased by one-half and its profits by some twenty times. Among the many factors contributing to these spectacular increases, top executives have stated that dropping unsatisfactory products was one of the most important.[7]

Abandonment Aversion

In view of the costs of carrying weak products, why does management typically shy away from product-pruning programs? Certainly sentimentality, as R. S. Alexander suggests, is a part of the aversion to product abandonment:

> But putting products to death—or letting them die—is a drab business, and often engenders much of the sadness of a final parting with old and tired friends. The portable, six-sided pretzel polisher was the first product The Company ever made. Our line will no longer be our line without it.[8]

Retention Rationale

There are, in fact, many reasons for this aversion, logical as well as sentimental.

Sometimes it is expected—or hoped—that product sales will pick up in the course of time when economic or market factors become more propitious. Here management thinks that the poor performance is due to outside factors which will improve.

Sometimes the fault is thought to lie in the marketing program, which the company plans to revitalize. It may be felt that the solution lies in reviving dealer enthusiasm, increasing the advertising budget, changing the advertising theme, or modifying some other marketing factor.

Even when the marketing program is thought to be competent, management may feel that the solution lies in product modification. Specifically, the thinking might be that sales could be stimulated through an upgrading of quality, styling, or features.

When none of these explanations exist, a weak product may nevertheless be retained in the mix because of the alleged contribution it makes to the sales of the company's other products. The weak product may provide the salesman with an entrée to important accounts. It may be used as bait to attract prospect interest in looking at the rest of the line. It may be the sacrificial lamb in full-time merchandising to court those buyers who like to obtain their "nuts and bolts" from the same supplier.

If none of these functions are performed by the weak product, then the retention rationale may be that its sales volume covers more than just actual costs, and the company temporarily has no better way of keeping its fixed resources employed. Any sales receipts above out-of-pocket costs make some contribution to overhead charges. Unless another product is available which could make an even larger contribution to overhead, the weak product ought to be retained in the short run until a decision has to be made on renewing a major fixed resource.

Die-Hard Interests

The foregoing are all logical arguments for retaining weak products in the mix. But there are also situations where the persistence of weak products can only be explained by the presence of vested interests, management or consumer sentiment, or just plain corporate inertia. A lot of people inside and outside an organization grow to depend on a particular product. Among them are the product manager, the employees, and certain customers. Eliminating a product from the mix is organizationally disruptive. Personnel may have to be shifted or, in some extreme instances, released. In such cases sentiment becomes a powerful factor in the decision-making process and often explains the slow decay of many weak products.

Those in the organization whose interests may be adversely affected by a product's elimination may engage in practices designed to conceal its weakness. Through hard selling, the product may be pushed into the dealers' stocks although the consumer "pull" is known to be feeble. The product manager may use some of his or her budget to stimulate sales in artificial ways to postpone the day of judgment. While these and other ruses may conceal the true facts from top management for a period of time, fortunately they cannot work indefinitely.

Abandonment Practices

The vast majority of companies, including some of the most progressive ones in industry, have not established orderly procedures for pruning their products. Such action is usually undertaken either (1) on a *piecemeal* basis, as in instances where the products' money-losing status is incontrovertible, conspicuous, and embarrassing, or (2) on a *crisis* basis, wherein the precipitating event may be a financial setback, a persistent decline in total sales, piling inventories, or rising costs.

But neither piecemeal pruning nor crisis pruning is really a satisfactory practice. Each leaves too many dated products lingering in the lineup for too long. Each leads to hasty "hatchet" jobs under improvised standards. Each is abrupt and possibly traumatic to the morale of certain parties inside and outside the company.

Partial Stride

A somewhat more systematic approach has been described as follows:

> A major manufacturer of consumer durables . . . makes a review every six months of all products whose profitability is less than the corporate average; for each such product, the manager responsible is requested to recommend action for improving earnings or elimination of the product.[9]

Although faults can be found with this approach, it represents a step in the right direction. It provides a standard for appraisal; it communicates a performance objective; it inspires the preparation of plans; and it sets a day of judgment. These features constitute the beginning of a control system for the problem of weak products. However, the system can be improved by developing more comprehensive criteria than profits alone and by involving a management team and the marvelous capacities of a computer. In the balance of this article this more advanced approach will be described.

Product Control System

A company which wishes to maintain a strong product mix must commit itself to the idea of a periodic product review. Such a review can be expected to accomplish two objectives:

1   The *formal* objective of increasing overall company profits through identification of those products which require modification or merit elimination from the mix in the light of changing conditions.
2   The *organizational* objective of providing a periodic incentive for better performance on the part of those executives who share product responsibility.

Awareness of Need

We shall assume, for illustrative purposes, that we are dealing with an established company which produces hundreds of products and models, and whose energies until now have been directed toward further product development. Although several company products produce an exceptionally good return, the overall rate of return on company investment is below that of the industry. The sales of some of the company's mainstay products are slipping, and many models are gathering dust in inventory. The president is concerned with this problem—one that occurs repeatedly in industry—and yet line executives reassure him that the slower moving products are suffering only temporary setbacks.

It is the kind of situation where a reputable management consultant could profitably be brought in. In nine out of ten cases, the consultant would document the case that the high profits on a few good products are being dissipated to support too many has-been products. Such a report would provide an opportunity for the president to accomplish two useful things in one stroke: purge his existing mix of superannuated products and institute a new control system so that the product mix will not become overpopulated again.

An overall view of a practical control system is charted in Exhibit 1. The first two parts are the *creation* stages and take place only when it has been decided that a control system should be installed. The *operational* steps, 1 through 6, represent the system as it is reactivated annually thereafter for product-pruning purposes.

Exhibit 1.   Creation and Operation of Annual Product Review System

CREATION STAGES

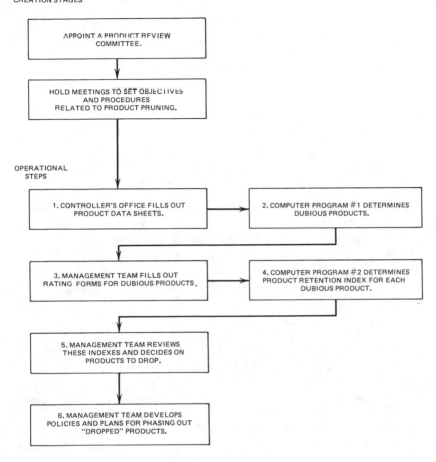

Creation Stages

Product pruning is not a task which can be entrusted to any one man or department in the organization. There are too many parties involved and too many honest differences of opinion on appropriate criteria.

Representative Corporate Team.   Therefore, the first creation stage is the appointment of a management team to assume responsibility for this problem. Because important policy questions are involved, as well as potentially large savings, the product review committee should consist of high-level executives. A representative corporate team, for example, could include executives from the following departments:

☐   Marketing—to provide views on marketing strategy, customer relations, competitive developments, and future sales outlook.

☐   Manufacturing—to describe any scheduling, manufacturing, or inventory problems connected with the products.

☐   Purchasing—to discuss estimates of future costs of materials.

☐   Control (accounting and finance)—to offer data on past sales, costs, and profits and also to develop the implications of product abandonment for cash flow and overall corporate rate of return.

☐   Personnel—to speak about the feasibility of reassignment for company personnel who would be affected by product abandonment decisions.

☐   Research and development—to tell about replacement products being developed which might utilize the physical and human resources affected by abandonment decisions.

Objectives and Procedures.   The second creation stage is for the committee to hold a series of meetings to develop objectives and set up procedures. If the company has used an outside consultant, it might be well to include her in these meetings. She can bring to the company her experience in developing product review procedures for other companies, and she can also be presumed to have more objectivity. At best she will be a moderating influence in the disputations that arise, and at worst a scapegoat for getting things done.

In any event, the purpose of these meetings will be to achieve consensus on the criteria to be applied and the procedures to be used in judging weak products. Because high-level executives are involved, future abandonment decisions are more likely to be carried out without active opposition.

The product control system established by this management team can take numerous forms. The most important thing really is that some system be established in the first place. Nevertheless, control systems differ in their capabilities of leading to optimal abandonment decisions. In the balance of this chapter the six operational steps of the product-pruning control system will be described in detail.

Step 1. Data Sheet

The product review process should be reactivated each year at about the same time, generally following an accounting period. The controller's office takes the first step by preparing a data sheet for every company product and/or model. A sample product data sheet is shown in Exhibit 2. This sheet summarizes key statistics about the product for the last several years. The exact number of years and the particular statistics depend on the nature of the business, the availability of various types of information, and the judgment of the management team as to what data might indicate that the product is of questionable worth.

The purpose of the data sheet is to provide the informational basis for judging whether the product is in a good state of health or merits further

Exhibit 2. Sample Product Data Sheet

PRODUCT NO. _____

MODEL NO. _____

DATE _____

		Past years			
		3	2	1	Current
Industry sales	$				
Company sales	$				
Physical volume					
Unit total cost	$				
Unit variable cost	$				
Price	$				
Cyclical adjustment factor					
Overhead burden					

COMMENTS: _____

---

study for an abandonment decision. *It is not assumed to contain sufficient information for making the abandonment decision.*

Two-Stage Decision. What is the advantage of this two-stage separation of the abandonment decision—first judging which set of products out of the entire set are dubious, and later judging which of these dubious products should actually be eliminated? *The fact is that it takes much less information to detect whether a product is weak than to make a judgment on whether it should be dropped.*

The product data sheet can be easily prepared, and it serves as a quick means for separating the company's products into the weak and the strong. Since the strong are no longer considered in the context of abandonment decisions, the weak can then receive the focused attention of the management group.

Spotting Dubious Products. How does the information on the product data sheet clew the management team that a product should be considered for possible deletion? Signs of product weakness are declining gross margin, declining sales in relation to total company sales, low coverage of its overhead, and so forth. Undoubtedly, experienced executives who studied the product data sheets would be able to spot a weak or faltering product. But herein lies a difficulty: high-level executives on the review committee can ill afford the time to scan the thousands of product sheets for signs of trouble. One recourse is to turn the task over to middle- or lower-management executives. A more efficient, speedy, and inexpensive recourse is to utilize the versatile capacities of a computer to do the job.

Step 2. Determining Candidates

That is the suggested route shown in the second step of the product review program. The challenge is to develop a computer program which can "intelligently" scan the product data sheets (in the form of key-punched cards) for signs of weakness in much the same way the management team would. The best approach is to ask the executives what they look for and to embody these principles in computer decision rules.[10]

A very simple program of decision rules is shown in Exhibit 3, which raises five critical questions—more could be listed—about recent trends in sales, market share, gross margin, and overhead coverage. These trends can be calculated from the product data sheets obtained in Step 2. The questions are hooked in series so that a product must earn a negative answer to all questions to avoid an investigation of its status. Each company sets the

Exhibit 3.   Flow Chart of Computer Program 1 Decision Rules

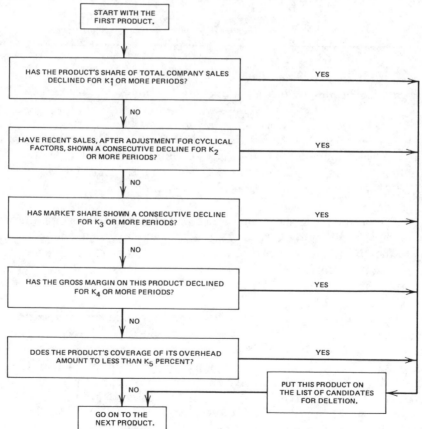

Note: The K's are chosen by the management team. For example, if the team sets $K_1 = 3$, then management thinks that three or more periods of sales decline should put a product on the dubious list.

retention values it regards as critical for placing a product on the dubious list.

Step 3. Rating Form

After the computer has produced a list of the dubious products, the management team meets to review the list. It might seem that now they should decide which products on the list should actually be dropped. But a judgment at this stage would be premature. In the first place, the executives would find themselves lacking vital information bearing on each product. In the second place, they would lack the guidance of formal criteria.

The major purposes of the meeting are for the team members to sense the overall pattern and magnitude of the company's weak-product problem, to remove from the list products which their good sense—as opposed to the computer's intelligence—tells them do not belong there, and to implement a formal product rating device. A formal rating device is quite essential if abandonment decisions are to be guided by consistent and explicit standards.

Developing Comprehensive Criteria.   Without such a device, the committee executives are likely to raise expedient criteria for each product and to vary the importance they attach to different criteria from case to case. But what criteria should the product rating form embody? In this connection there are likely to be sharp differences of opinion, depending on the orientation of the team's members.[11]

Some executives take the view that products which do not cover their full costs (including historical and arbitrarily allocated costs) should be eliminated. Others are less concerned with historical costs and more concerned with present opportunities. Therefore, if a dubious product is covering its direct costs and contributing more to overhead than an alternative use of resources would contribute, they would recommend retention. Still others traditionally prefer to make a judgment on a more intuitive basis. Their prime concern is dollar volume and the full exploitation of sales resources. The only products they care to see abandoned are those which cause a lot of trouble in relation to their volume or to their contribution to the sales of other products.

Each executive's view would lead to quite different sets of criteria for product elimination and therefore would have different long-run sales and profit implications. It is hoped that the meetings held in the creation stage discussed earlier would lead to the development of comprehensive criteria which would blend the more valid aspect of each point of view. A product rating form incorporating a number of important considerations is shown in Exhibit 4.[12]

Rating and Weight Values.   This form calls for a *rating value* for each dubious product against seven different scales. Most of the scales are invariably subjective in this area. Each scale ranges from zero to one, with

Exhibit 4. Seven-Scale Product Rating Form

PRODUCT NO._____

MODEL NO._____

DATE_____

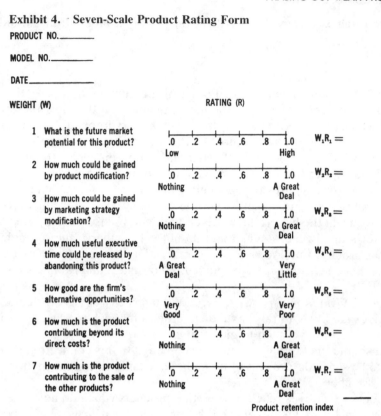

WEIGHT (W)   RATING (R)

Product retention index

Note: Each rating (R) is multiplied by the question's importance or weight (W), resulting in a weighted rating (WR) for that question. All seven weighted ratings are summed and the sum is the Product Retention Index. The higher this index, the greater the arguments in favor of retaining the product.

zero representing strong grounds for eliminating the product and one representing strong grounds for retaining the product.

The first scale, for instance, calls for evaluating the future market potential of the product. A product which is becoming hopelessly obsolescent, such as a detergent which is not able to clean modern synthetic fabrics as well as it cleans cotton and linen, would be rated close to zero on this scale.

Since all scales may not be considered by management to be equally important, each scale is also assigned a *weight value*. These weight values are presumably agreed on earlier in the creation stage and remain constant for all product judgments.

The product rating form serves as a discussion guide for each product case and helps to highlight the informational needs. Ultimately the committee must agree on a rating value for each question for each dubious product.

Sometimes additional meetings may have to be held before the necessary information is available or sufficient consensus develops.

Step 4. Retention Index

When this work is completed, the product rating form can then be processed to yield a single number, the "product retention index," indicating the degree of product desirability. (The fate of some products may already have been decided in the process of the management team's discussion of the ratings in Step 3.) This single number will be the sum of the weighted ratings on the product rating form.

The sum can range from a maximum value of 7, if the product shows superior grounds for being retained on all counts, to a minimum value of 0, if the product shows minimal grounds for retention on all counts. Although the single number can be obtained by using a desk calculator, when many dubious products are involved, it is best to enter the rating values on a mark-sensing card and to use the computer to calculate the index numbers. Thus Computer Program #2 normally consists of a straightforward calculation of products and sums.

Step 5. Abandonment Decisions

When the indexes are ready, the product review committee again convenes to make a final judgment on which products to drop. The committee may have already established a retention index number between 0 and 7 so that any dubious product receiving an index number below it would almost unquestionably be dropped from the line. Any product which scores, for example, less than one out of a possible seven points must be judged as having very little potential, imposing a large burden on executive time, and contributing very little to profits or to the sale of other company products. There is little reason for retaining such a product.

Products whose indexes exceed the established retention value number have more than minimum justification on one or more criteria, but the management team must examine these individual cases carefully. Product retention indexes supply a formal, albeit subjective, basis for ranking the dubious products in order of the strength of the arguments for retention.

Generally speaking, products that have lower indexes will be the weaker ones, and management will want to concentrate on those. At the same time, it is entirely possible that the committee members may decide to drop a product with a higher index value than another which they decide to retain. The indexes serve as a guide rather than as a final verdict. They are designed to aid in the systematic consideration of product intangibles and not to replace judgment.

Product Interactions. Another reason exists for not using this retention index or any other formal device too mechanically. Various products in the line will have joint demands and/or joint cost and manufacturing relationships. If they are judged only in terms of their individual retention indexes, it may seem desirable to drop a set of them. But management must consider the total effect on its business operations of dropping any set of products. The total effect may be more than the sum of the separate effects because of product interactions. The particular set may spell too great a weakening of the company's position in a certain market, may place too great a strain on certain company personnel, or may lead to costly idling of particular facilities. Because of these factors, the savings which the company expects to realize from eliminating a given set of products may be quite different from the sum of the savings calculated individually.

Simulation Hopes.   Is there any tool which can help the management team determine the more global implications of dropping any set of products? Although little work has been done on this problem, computer simulation offers the greatest hope of some breakthrough. Management is interested in what will happen to profits, sales stability, and sales growth as the product mix is changed. A logical approach would be to investigate possible sequences and timings of planned product deletions and additions over some future time period. This approach would require assumptions about the future behavior of sales, costs, and profits for individual products and groups of products.

The computer's contribution would consist of making rapid calculations of profit, stability, and growth characteristics of the many different possible transformations of the product mix through time. By simulating sales and profit patterns of alternative product-mix changes, it would provide management with informative estimates of the expected payoffs and risks of different product-line policies.

Step 6. Phasing Out

There is still one remaining step after management has decided which products to drop, and this is the formulation of the phasing-out policies and plans for the individual products being dropped. (A distinction may be drawn between "dropping" and "milking" a product. In the latter case the company carries the product at a greatly reduced level of promotion and cost, hoping to salvage what it can. Milking amounts to phasing it out very slowly.) For each product, management must determine its obligations to the various parties affected by the decision. Management may want to provide for a stock of replacement parts and service to stretch over the expected life of the most recently sold units. It may want to find a manufacturer willing to take over the discontinued product. Some of the products can be dropped quite easily with little repercussion, while other product eliminations will require an elaborate phasing-out plan.

Influencing Factors.   The criteria for this step are quite general. After a decision has been made to eliminate a product, the actual phasing-out plan has to be custom-tailored to the unique product circumstances. Some of the factors which will influence phasing-out tactics and timing are:

☐ How much finished and semifinished stock remains in our inventory; how much finished goods are in distributors' inventories?

☐ What kinds of guarantees and compensations should be offered to distributors and customers?

☐ How soon could the affected executives and employees be shifted to other useful assignments?

☐ How much salvage value could the company get for its machinery and unfinished stock? Could it gain by waiting?

☐ How much will the discontinuation affect the relations with distributors and customers? Could the company gain by waiting?

Critical Timetables. With the answers to these and other questions, management can prepare timetables for the phasing out of its weak products. Where the product involved is one which has enjoyed major distribution, management should consider preparing a critical path program (such as PERT) to ensure efficiency in its phasing out. The program should show when various parties are to be notified about the decision and when various asset-disposal efforts should be made. The objective is to let the news disseminate in a pattern which does not handicap the company's efforts to dispose of certain products and yet does not lead some parties to feel they were unfairly treated.

Conclusion

In an age of dynamic product competition, product-line pruning must be considered as a problem on a par with product improvement and new-product development. Yet most managements have no systematic procedure for pruning weaker products; these products often linger in the mix until they just fade away. In the meantime, they depress the company's overall level of profitability; they complicate the task of allocating scarce company resources; and they hold the company back from aggressively developing new opportunities.

These things are obvious, and yet corporate managements only rarely rise to the occasion. Their attention is riveted on tomorrow's rather than yesterday's products. There is often sentiment about the former heavyweight products which have passed their prime. There is a valid concern about the effect of dropping products on internal organization morale and external customer and supplier relations. There is uncertainty about whether the product is chronically weak or only pausing before the next sales spurt. There is confusion about the right standards to apply in choosing products for deletion. There is a lack of practicable models and precedents for conducting periodic product reviews.

This article has attempted to define the seriousness of this problem and to describe a practical control system for keeping the product mix relatively free of unprofitable products. The system consists of the appointment of a high-level and broadly representative management team which holds meetings at about the same time each year for the purpose of spotting dubious products, evaluating them, choosing those which must be dropped, and developing the phasing-out program for them. In each of these steps, the executives are guided by explicit standards and information, much of which is processed on the computer to expedite the decision-making.

The proposed control system for product pruning is expensive in executive time, but this cost must be compared to the greater overt and hidden costs of allowing superannuated products to continue in the product mix. Furthermore, in provoking corporate executives to define standards, gather information, and make decisions, the system brings the company much closer to instituting formal long-range product and market planning procedures which would provide the ultimate answer to achieving an optimal product mix.

Notes

1.   See "More Companies Drop Slower-Moving Goods to Improve Earnings," *The Wall Street Journal,* August 9, 1962.

2.   See Arch Patton, "Top Management's Stake in the Product Life Cycle," *The Management Review,* June 1959, pp. 9–14, 67–71, 76–79.

3.   See "Pricing Policies for New Products," *HBR,* November–December 1950, p. 28.

4.   For some interesting examples, see "The Short Happy Life," *Time,* March 29, 1963, p. 83.

5.   See Peter F. Drucker, "Managing for Business Effectiveness," *HBR,* May–June 1963, p. 53.

6.   Ralph Westfall and Harper W. Boyd, Jr., *Cases in Marketing Management* (Homewood, Illinois, Richard D. Irwin, Inc., 1961), p. 181.

7.   Charles H. Kline, "The Strategy of Product Policy," *HBR,* July–August 1955, p. 100.

8.   "The Death and Burial of 'Sick' Products," *Journal of Marketing,* April 1964, p. 1.

9.   See D'Orsay Hurst, "Criteria for Evaluating Existing Products and Product Lines," in *Analyzing and Improving Marketing Performance* (American Management Association, Management Report No. 32, 1959), p. 91.

10.   See R. M. Cyert and J. G. March, *A Behavioral Theory of the Firm* (Englewood Cliffs, N. J., Prentice-Hall, Inc., 1963), Chapters 7 and 8.

11. See Conrad Berenson, "Pruning the Product Line," *Business Horizons*, Summer 1963, p. 63.

12. See, for example, Barry Richman, "A Rating Scale for Product Innovation," *Business Horizons*, Summer 1962, p. 37; and John T. O'Meara, Jr., "Selecting Profitable Products," *HBR*, January-February 1961, p. 83.

25

Better Management of Corporate Development

RICHARD F. VANCIL

In a large number of U.S. corporations, internally generated corporate growth is the most important concern of top management. It is a task far removed from the management of established product lines and businesses. In fact, it demands a whole new way of thinking on the part of executives. This article describes a new way to approach the process of managing internally generated growth, including a new type of planning and control system for executives to use. Only a few companies use an approach like this, the author believes; yet it seems broadly applicable to large, growth-minded companies.

The development of successful new products is a critical element in the strategy of most large business corporations. Acquisitions as a panacea for corporate growth objectives have been largely discredited—they are marvelous when they work, but the odds are long. The odds on new products are long, too, but the individual risks are smaller; the payoffs from a winner are greater; and, perhaps most important, the process of introducing a continuing stream of new products is manageable. How should top executives try to plan and control that process?

Development Costs

To begin, let us consider the kind of corporation commonly referred to as a "growth company." It is likely to be publicly held, to have a good performance record, and to enjoy a high price/earnings multiple. Its primary financial objective is growth in earnings per share, and let us suppose management recognizes that most such growth must be internally generated— that is, acquisitions will not be the prime growth element. The company is organized along divisional lines, reflecting the increasing diversification of its businesses, and the divisions have a fair amount of managerial autonomy.

What permits a company like this to generate continual growth? Or, to state the question in more operational terms, what is the constraint that inhibits even faster growth? In order to manage such growth, management must have a clear fix on the critical controllable resources that produce increases in future sales and profits. The economist's concept of a "scarce resource" is highly relevant here. Identifying and allocating the utilization of that resource is management's primary task.

In many companies, the traditional scarce resource is considered, appropriately, to be capital—whether obtained from internal cash flow, or through borrowing, or from the sale of stock. However, for a growing company with an above-average performance record, capital is not scarce; such a company has expanding debt capacity, and the sale of common stock may cause only a temporary, negligible dilution in earnings per share. In such growth companies, there is a dollar resource far larger and much less well-identified and controlled than capital.

I call this scarce resource "development expenses." I define them as expenditures that are charged against income in the current year but that do not give rise to profits until some subsequent year.

It should be borne in mind that profits are a managed figure in many growth companies. This does not mean that profits are "manipulated" in an accounting sense, but rather that they are the first figures to emerge from the budget-making process, not the last.

Given an objective of steady earnings growth, the profit requirement for next year is a simple extrapolation from the past. To fall short of this requirement is bad and is likely to have an adverse effect on the company's price/earnings multiple. To exceed this requirement is unnecessary and may be almost as bad as falling short, for it both increases the level of profits that must be reported in the following year and raises shareholder expectations (thus making management's task more arduous and the risk of failure higher in the future). As a result, if profits look as though they will be higher than needed, management finds ways to plough pretax dollars back into the development of the business, attempting to insure that future growth can more easily be sustained.

New Accounting Concept

Exhibit 1 illustrates the concept of development expenses. Here we see two versions of the annual profit and loss statements for a growth company that is relying on internally generated funds for capital.

Conventional Statement. The left-hand column in this exhibit is simply a more detailed version of the income statement that is condensed in the annual stockholder's report. It shows that this company spends 5% of sales on research and development and that it has a good technological edge in its field so that its marketing costs are reasonably low at 10% of sales. Its aftertax profit margin is 7.5%, which gives it a respectable return on investment. Retained earnings are large enough both to permit capital expenditures that are 50% larger than current depreciation and to cover the working capital needs arising from growth. In short, the conventional income statement shows a stable, steady growth situation.

New Statement. However, this company is not nearly so placid as these figures might imply. Management is able to generate growth consistently because there are many projects in progress designed to increase sales and profits in future years. These projects all cost money. Where does this money come from?

The middle column in Exhibit 1 shows the same company's income statement presented in an unconventional manner. The only expenses, sales, and profits figures shown are those relating to the "base businesses"—that is, the established, profitable product lines. Expenditures which are not recovered in the current year through higher sales or lower costs are excluded in the middle column. The effect of this procedure is to change every expense item except prime costs and depreciation—reflecting the fact that this corporation, like so many others, charges some items to current expenses that are really an investment for the future.

I am not arguing here for a change in the way accountants calculate net income, but current accounting conventions do obscure, even for management, what is going on in the company.

The difference between the two income statements is, of course, the development expenses. These are shown in the right-hand column of Exhibit 1.

Component Expenses

As can be seen, development expenses break down into *four* broad categories which, in total, amount to $150 million:

1 *R&D Expenses* are fairly obvious. Managers traditionally think of this type of cost as an investment in the future, even though it is charged against current income in most large companies. The mission of R&D is clear: to produce the ideas and technology that permit the company to introduce new or improved products. The activity is critical, but it is only the beginning of the total effort required to provide growth in sales and profits.

2 *Marketing expenses* contain another major segment of corporate development funds. The nature of these outlays varies greatly from one company to another, but every growing corporation incurs sub-

Exhibit 1.   Statement of Annual Corporate Development Expenses (In millions of dollars)

	Conventional Statement	New Statement	
		Base Business	Development Expenses
Sales	$1,000	$1,000	
Less cost of goods sold			
Labor and material	400	400	
Manufacturing overhead	175	150	$ 25
Depreciation	50	50	
Total	$ 625	$ 600	
Manufacturing profit	375	400	
Less other expenses			
Research and development	50		50
Marketing	100	50	50
General administration	75	50	25
Total	$ 225	$ 100	
Profits before tax	150		150
Profits after tax	75		
Dividends	25		
Capital expenditures (including reinvested depreciation)	75		
Increase in working capital	25		

"Column 1 minus Column 2.

stantial current expenses in marketing that have a delayed profit payoff. The two most common examples are the costs of launching a new product and the start-up costs of getting established in new market segments of new geographical areas. Advertising, too, has long-run payoffs.

3 *Manufacturing overhead* has development costs hidden in it. As a percentage of the total overhead, this cost may not be large but the total dollars are still significant. The two main types of development activities at the plant level are (1) the pilot plant operations and debugging costs associated with manufacturing a new product, and (2) the engineering efforts aimed at reducing manufacturing costs for current product lines. Both of these activities trade current expenses for future profits.

4 *General administrative overhead* is traceable in part to the fact that this corporation is trying to grow. The company is intentionally overstaffed; it is doing more than what is required simply to run

the base businesses. The extra people are scattered across a variety of functions, including new products departments, venture teams, market research groups, and others. These people are not employed to produce today's business; their job is to improve profitability in the future and to provide growth.

The numbers in Exhibit 1 are not significant; what is important is looking at the operations of the business in the way described. The size of this pool of funds and the projects for which it is used vary greatly from one company to another, but usually growth companies have a substantial amount of such funds. In terms of order of magnitude, it is probably safe to make two generalizations.

First, if the corporation has a formal R&D effort and costs it out in the conventional manner, this expense is likely to be only a fraction of total development expenditures (one-third in our example).

Second, capital expenditures, which deservedly get a lot of management attention, are also only a fraction of the corporation's total future-oriented expenditure (expense dollars are twice as large in this example).

Realistic Perspective

How do most managements look at capital expenditures and development expenses? Although the purpose of both types of outlay is the same—to lay out money today in the hope of getting it back with a profit in the future—the two categories tend to be managed quite differently.

Most companies have elaborate systems and procedures to guide the decision process for capital investments; they specify careful gradations of spending authority at each hierarchical level, create complex manuals on capital budgeting procedures, and work up elaborate analytical formulas to calculate the probablistic present values of projects. Development expenses, on the other hand, usually get buried in the conventional operating budgets. While the highly visible R&D budget may get management attention (and indeed some companies capitalize these costs), the bulk of the expenses identified in Exhibit 1 are never identified separately, let alone managed as the scarce resource of the company. Why is this so?

One reason is mainly historical and shows the power of accounting conventions to influence thinking. Accountants capitalize the amount of investment in fixed assets while writing off other investment-type expenses primarily because the former are tangible, have some salvage value, and can be recorded easily.

A second reason, as accountants and financial executives point out, is that capital expenditures are irreversible; money put in bricks and mortar is "sunk." Ironically, this is even more true for development expenses. A plant or a machine may be the wrong size or in the wrong place, but it still may have a value to someone else and part of the investment may be recouped. However, development expenses that go awry are not just sunk—they are gone.

And a third reason is that capital investments frequently represent large, separable decisions that deserve the best possible assessment of the risks and rewards. There is some validity to this viewpoint but, in terms of the dollars involved, the expense side of a new product—from research to market acceptance—is frequently much larger than the equipment required to manufacture it. The real difference is in timing. The development program for a new product may take five years or more and require a series of sequential decisions to proceed from one stage to the next. The final decision, to build a new plant after a successful market introduction, is not risky; it is practically a foregone conclusion after the earlier, high-risk money has paid off. Also it is an explicit decision, whereas the series of unrecorded earlier investments are forgotten.

This is not to say that, given their obligations, the accountants' careful distinction between capitalized and written-off expenditures is not defensible or rational. It is to say that the distinction has been given too much importance by managers. Dollars are dollars, and any corporation has too few of them with which to buy growth in future profits.

Economics of Growth

The validity of development expenses as the scarce resource in a growth company is illustrated in Exhibit 2. It shows the profit projection if all development expenses were discontinued. Profits would decline because no new businesses would be added and the franchises of the old businesses

Exhibit 2.   Effect of Development Expenses on Profit Profile

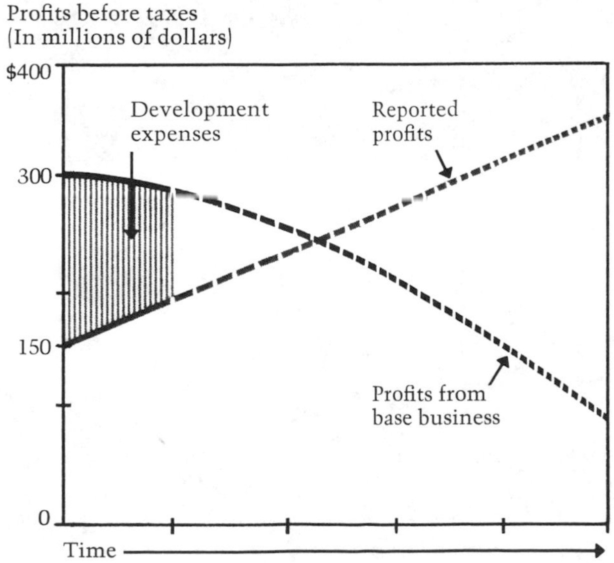

Profits before taxes
(In millions of dollars)

Development expenses

Reported profits

Profits from base business

Time

would eventually wither. Fortunately, the company can meet its growth objectives for the coming year with substantially less profit than that available from the base businesses. Therefore, $150 million can be spent to perpetuate old businesses and develop new ones. If the money is spent wisely, management hopes that the reported profits will continue to grow at a steady rate. Achieving that goal requires the management of many development projects, simultaneously and continuously.

Exhibit 3 shows the profit and cash-flow profiles of a typical development project. For most such projects the curves fall into this well-known pattern, the difference between cash flow and profits being accounted for by expenditures that are capitalized and depreciated (over the life of the project the total amount of profit and cash flow will, of course, be the same). The actual shape of the curve naturally varies substantially from one project to another, particularly with regard to the length of time before profits come in and with regard to the amount of the accumulated deficit up to that time. However, the expected pattern for any successful development project will always have this basic shape.

Exhibit 4 shows the collective effect on the company of a continuing stream of development projects. Each year, if the prior year's development funds have been spent successfully, the residual profit potential in the base businesses is higher than the year before. The result is that the pool of development funds also grows a little, even after allowing for an increase in reported profits.

The fact that the economics of internal development are complex, as illustrated in Exhibits 2-4, is well known. Less well appreciated, perhaps,

Exhibit 3.   Profit and Cash-Flow Effects of a Typical Development Project

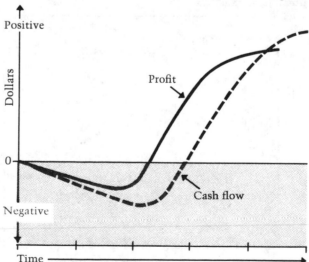

Exhibit 4. Cumulative Profit Profile of Development Projects

Profit before taxes
(In millions of dollars)

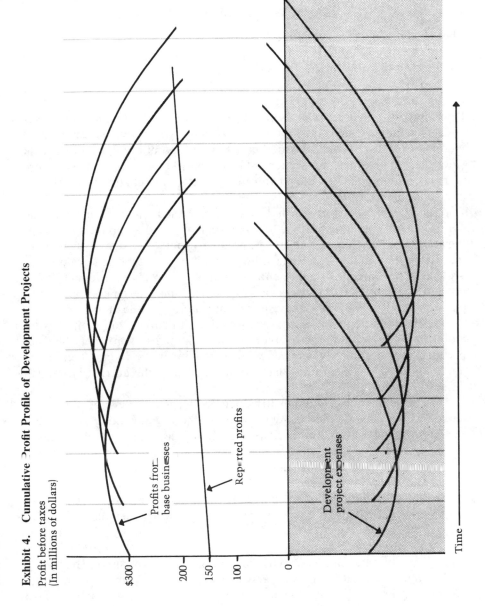

$300

200

150

100

0

Profits from base businesses

Reported profits

Development project expenses

Time

is (a) the complexity of the development process, and (b) the challenges that it poses for management. I shall devote the balance of this article to these two topics.

Complexities of Analysis

There are not many parts of the business which do not incur development expenses of some kind. In order to understand the management task, let us break down the development process into four parts.

1. Identifying Resources

Development resources are essentially people, and development expenses are almost entirely made up of payroll costs. Simply identifying the personnel working on future-profit activities in a large corporation is a difficult task since these individuals are scattered throughout the organization. The more complex the company is, the greater the variety of talents that are deployed in development tasks.

In the situation on which Exhibit 1 is based, determining that the company was spending $150 million per year required a careful analysis of the activities of each department. The company found that personnel in more than 100 departments were engaged either full or part time in development projects. These people were scientists, market researchers, product-development specialists, members of new-product teams, designers, engineers, planners, and others. Moreover, it was not merely a question of pure development departments as such, for throughout the organization there were individuals whose tasks were largely future-oriented—even when their departments were primarily involved with current business. In fact, there were not many organizational units that did not look past the current base businesses in some way.

Management also found that the people engaged in development work tended to be some of the best employees in the organization. A company seeking to grow internally must, as a general rule, employ higher caliber personnel than a similar company must that is content to maintain the status quo. And these people almost inevitably are assigned to development tasks. This makes the management of the development process more difficult because direction and tight control are difficult to combine successfully with the creativity, imagination, and dedication of innovative people.

2. Classifying Activities

The diversity of development activities in a growth company is enormous. In the company used for Exhibit 1, each person engaged in developmental tasks was asked to describe the project or projects he was working on. Two main findings emerged. First, many projects involved the efforts of personnel in more than one department. The bigger the project, the more likely that a half-dozen or more departments, at both the corporate and division levels, were involved. Typically, each individual was aware of some of the related activities of other groups, but no one manager was well informed about the magnitude or rate of progress of the combined efforts. Second, many projects were proceeding simultaneously—nearly 500 in all—so that the management of the entire process was almost impossible without the benefit of specialized planning and control systems.

One helpful way to deal with such complexity is to categorize activities so that they can be dealt with at a summary level by top management as well as at a detailed level by operating people. In the company in question, management classified *new-business* projects as follows:

☐ Research—In the pure exploratory sense, research comprised only about 5% of the total development expenses. These projects were designed to expand the frontiers of technological knowledge in the hope of developing new materials and processes for commercial exploitation.

☐ Product development—Projects in this category were in the early phases of the development cycle shown in Exhibit 3. A project entered this category when the first, crude specifications for the new product were delineated. The project was reclassified into the next category as soon as it began yielding any sales revenue from market tests, even though product development activities continued concurrently with the initial marketing efforts.

☐ Market introduction—This category included all the expenditures concerned with launching a new product. The projects were at the loss-reversal stage in the cycle shown in Exhibit 3; losses tended to increase in the early stages of market introduction, but if successful the product subsequently became profitable. (At the point where a new-product line crossed the profitability threshold, it was reclassified as an existing business—although various kinds of developmental activities would continue over the life of the product, as will be described later.)

Projects for *existing* businesses involved a more diverse and diffuse range of activities, but again some broad subcategories were designated:

☐ Product-modification projects designed to extend the life cycle of existing products by improving and expanding the line (e.g., changes in product design, packaging, or flavors).

☐ Marketing-extension projects aimed at opening new market segments or new geographical areas to existing and modified products (e.g., special promotional campaigns).

☐ Cost-engineering projects designed to improve processes, programs, and other activities.

3. Allocating

A useful analogy for thinking about the allocation process is as an investment portfolio. After deciding on the amount of development funds available, the management of a diversified corporation has to divide the funds among competing projects. A wide range of risks is involved, from very safe cost-reduction projects to high-risk, new-product programs with high payoff. This situation closely parallels the choice facing the manager of an investment portfolio, who has to choose among investments ranging from triple-A bonds to highly speculative common stocks.

The corporate task is more complex than the portfolio manager's. For one thing, the funds to be allocated are less flexible; people resources are mobile only to the extent that they can be reassigned, making major rapid shifts impractical. For another, choices made in one year both constrain and increase opportunities for choices next year.

4. Integrating the System

In order to pull together the identification, organization, and allocation of development resources, management needs to modify the planning and budgeting systems of the corporation. The integrated system that I recommend is illustrated conceptually in Part A of Exhibit 5. This matrix shows a two-step management process involving first planning and then budgeting. Planning, on the horizontal axis, is the process of *deciding* which projects should be funded and what resources (what talents and how much of each) are needed for each project in each organizational unit. Budgeting, on the vertical axis, may be thought of as the process of *obtaining* the necessary resources or ensuring their availability. This means that the budgeting system must identify and separate development personnel and expenses from base-business personnel and expenses.

As Part B of Exhibit 5 indicates, Project X is a proposal to spend $1.2 million to develop an improved product for one of the existing lines of business. The effort required is primarily at the division level, but $140,000 must also be spent by personnel in three different corporate staff groups (research, development, and engineering). The data suggest that the engineering department, which is budgeting $50,000 for Project X, is heavily engaged in current operations; $2,200,000, or slightly more than half, of its total budget is devoted to the base business of the company.

Because the nature of each project changes over time and is never precisely predictable, the integration of needs and resources in this way is no easy task. Moreover, the resources are people whose talents are not interchangeable and who cannot be turned on and off like a tap. Nor can such people—least of all, the dedicated, creative, high-caliber personnel in development work—be moved at random around the organization.

Exhibit 5. Integrated Planning and Budgeting

A. Conceptual scheme

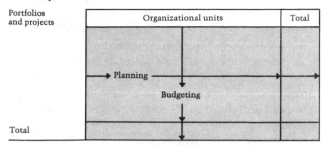

B. Application to one project
(In thousands of dollars)

Types of development projects (use of development expenses)	Types of organizational units (source/location of development expenses)								Total expense
	Corporate level				Division level				
	Research	Development	Engineering	Market research	Development	Market research	Plant engineering	Marketing	
New businesses									

Research
  Development
  Introduction									

Existing businesses									
Product modification									
Project X	$30	$60	-$50		$450	$150	$160	$300	$1,200
Marketing extensions									
Cost engineering									
Total development expense		$1,800							$150,000
Budgeting expenses for base businesses		$2,200							$700,000
Total budget by department		$4,000							$850,000

Critical Issues

We have seen that development expenses, broadly defined, are the critical resources to be managed in a growth company and that the development process is complex. Many of the managerial implications of this discussion are already apparent: major changes in executives' thinking may be required to reconceive the management task along the lines described; and concomitant changes in the corporation's planning, budgeting, and reporting systems will also be required. More specifically, these issues are of pervasive importance to top management.

Strategy and Objectives

The conventional wisdom of corporate planning is that the strategic process begins with a clear and explicit statement by the chief executive officer of his objectives for the corporation and the broad strategy that he proposes to pursue. Such an approach is no doubt appropriate in some situations, but it is not at all clear that it is the right approach for a diversifying growth company like the one discussed earlier. Should a statement of strategy and objectives be issued at the beginning or *the end* of the annual planning effort?

Turning back to Exhibit 2, I suggest that this simple chart is a concise illustration of the objectives and strategy of a company which seeks to grow by internal development. The objective—at least the financially quantifiable one—is expressed by the slope of the growth line. That, in turn, is a function of both the availability of expense dollars for development (the shaded area), and the time-phased payoff of the opportunities available. For a diversified corporation, strategy is best expressed as the choice of which and how many developmental activities to pursue. Viewed in this way, the decisions about *how much* to spend on development and *how* to spend it are the very essence of what most businessmen mean by strategy.

There are advantages in delaying the preparation of a statement of corporate strategy and objectives. A delayed statement can be much more explicit and thus can provide a much better sense of direction and purpose than the typical "motherhood" statements obviously drafted by staff planners. Moreover, the very fact of a delay is, in itself, a statement that the corporate strategy is somewhat opportunistic, as it has to be for a growth corporation. In a statement that is issued as a *wrap-up* of the process of allocating developmental resources instead of as a preamble to that process, the corporate objective can be clear and the available resources can be explicit; yet there can also be an acknowledgment that the biggest elements of change in the equation are the opportunities.

Division Autonomy

Who is responsible for growth in a divisionalized company, corporate management or divisional management? Answers to this question vary greatly in U.S. business today.

At one extreme, the president tells his division managers to run their businesses as if they were independent companies—each responsible for its continuing growth. The attractiveness of this approach is that it creates many centers of initiative, which are each highly motivated to be innovative and to grow. One disadvantage is the problem of communicating corporate objectives to a diverse group of managers. A greater danger is suboptimization; since some divisions have more and better development opportunities than others, they may end up rejecting some projects that are better than the ones accepted by another division.

For a diversified, growing company the answer to this problem does not lie at the other extreme, where the division managers are mere functionaries overseeing today's business while all new-product development is handled at the corporate level. The most promising answer is to institute the same careful sharing of authority for committing development resources as is common in the authorization of capital expenditures. Rather than put dollar limitations on a division manager's authority, however, management can draw a line between development projects for new and for existing businesses. It might proceed as follows:

☐   The primary initiative for development projects in an *existing* business must lie with the divisional personnel; they are the ones who know the most about that business.

☐   But the amount to be spent in each such business should be approved at the corporate level, determined in the context of the opportunities available in other existing or new businesses. (Specific projects connected with the business can then be approved and monitored by the division manager in a way analogous to conventional capital budgeting procedures.)

☐   The divisional personnel, along with their counterparts in the various corporate staff departments, are a major source of ideas for new business developments. Funding such projects, however, is strictly a corporate-level decision because: (a) new businesses tend to be much riskier, if only because they are harder to appraise; (b) in the early stages, a new business or major new-product line may deserve investigation even if it lacks divisional sponsorship or support; (c) while selecting the set of new-business projects—with their complex patterns of risk and reward—can scarcely be an analytically rational process, it can and should reflect the strategic choices of top management.

Implementing this approach, particularly in companies where the divisions have been highly autonomous, is likely to be viewed as a diminution of division managers' responsibility. In fact, in some companies this may be exactly what is needed. If divisional operating budgets include a substantial amount of development expenses, corporate management may have delegated away too much authority over activities that are vital to future corporate growth. For instance, in the company used as an example earlier, roughly two thirds of the total corporate development expenditures were included in divisional budgets until procedures like those described were established.

Measurement and Review

Every project, no matter how small, must have a manager who is responsible for achieving the results that were expected when the project was approved. For most small projects, project management is not a full-time job; it is an addition to the individual's responsibilities in the base business. Most small projects are also related to the existing businesses, thus simplifying the cost-measurement problem to some extent.

In the case of new business development, the management and measurement tasks are complicated by the fact that such projects may stretch out over several years, requiring different kinds of management skills at different points in time. Also, in their latter stages, these projects may be very large, drawing on development resources from many departments.

In order to handle the long development period and the episodic nature of progress, new-business developments should be funded from event to event. Each proposal for an allocation of development funds should specify one or more milestones at which progress will be reviewed and new funds authorized for the next steps. At these review points, official responsibility may be transferred. For example, it might rest first with an engineer in the corporate development lab, then with a senior analyst in the corporate market research department, and finally with a new venture manager or a marketing manager in the division that expects to add the new business to its existing businesses.

To deal with the large, cross-departmental nature of new-business developments, a project accounting system analogous to work-order accounting for capital expenditures may be needed. This approach has the virtue of removing development expenses from the regular departmental operating budgets, thus permitting easier accountability for the manager of each project. (Such a system could also be used for smaller projects but is probably not worth the effort.)

Conclusion

What is the most effective approach to the management of internally generated corporate growth? While no simple set of rules is possible, executives should consider these guidelines:

☐ They should identify and mobilize the developmental resources of the corporation. Most corporate managements do not know, at least not in terms of the broad definition of development expense dollars used here, how much they are spending for the future or where it is spent within the organization. But it is possible to find out, and the result may be a surprise. Many growth companies are engaged in an unbelievable range of developmental projects carried out by people scattered all across the organization chart and representing a vast array of risks, rewards, and time patterns of payoff. Quantifying these activities is a critically important first step.

☐ Top management must focus attention on the use of developmental resources. This set of decisions is *the* critical resource allocation problem and the most tangible expression of corporate strategy. Some sort of formal system to aid in the management of development resources is a necessity, even though it will take a while to work it out.

☐ Top management must reexamine the distribution of authority for committing resources to developmental projects. One thing is certain: the expenses should not be buried in divisional or departmental operating budgets; the amounts involved are too important. Division managers need some discretion, but top management overview is probably more critical here than it is in the case of capital expenditures.

☐ Systems must be devised to monitor the effectiveness of utilization of development funds. This step, too, takes time and may never be done in a completely satisfactory manner, but without some such effort top management will never achieve a sense of control over the destiny of the company.

This approach is not a one-shot analysis of a critical resource; it is a whole new way of thinking about the management of a growth company. Managing change is not a problem that managers solve; it is a problem that they live with. If they decide to devote their efforts to that problem, then they should design the planning, budgeting, and reporting systems to bring the problem into focus. This is a major task, but the potential payoff is enormous.

26

General Managers in the Middle

HUGO E. R. UYTERHOEVEN

Having a boss's responsibility without a boss's authority; functioning as a specialist and a generalist at the same time; meeting the conflicting demands of superiors, subordinates, and peers while still getting the job done—these exacting requirements sound like part of a manager's nightmare. But, according to this author, they are daily facets of general management at middle levels of an organization, where risk and opportunity go hand in hand. While these general management positions are increasingly common in-divisionalized corporations, they are often misunderstood by both middle managers and their superiors. In this article, the author discusses the demanding requirements of the job from a top-management and a middle-management perspective, and shows how it represents an opportunity for individual and corporate growth.

Traditionally, the job of general manager has been equated with that of a company's chief executive. General manager and boss have been thought of synonymously. Yet, increasingly, corporate organizations are providing for general management positions at levels below the chief executive; and, as a result, the number of general managers at the middle level is rising.

The middle-level general manager phenomenon (i.e., a general manager who is responsible for a particular business unit at the intermediate level of the corporate hierarchy) is a direct outgrowth of the movement toward a divisional form of organization. For example, while the *functional* organization requires only one general manager, the *divisional* organization provides for a variety of business units, each requiring a general manager. Often the process of divisionalization extends several levels down into the organization (i.e., group, division, department), further increasing the need for general managers at lower levels.

The shift from functional to divisional organization occurred in the United States largely during the last two decades and is currently taking place in Europe. It is a worldwide phenomenon necessitated by the greater product-line diversity as well as the growing international operations of a vast majority of the larger corporations.

Although the divisional organization is now a familiar phenomenon, little attention has been directed at obtaining a clear understanding of the middle-level general management position. Of course, one approach would be to refer to what is known about the top-level general manager, but this knowledge is not really applicable—the two positions are significantly different. Furthermore, general management at the middle organizational level is, in a number of respects, more difficult.

In this article, I shall attempt to (a) define the characteristics and responsibilities of the middle-level general manager's job and (b) draw the implications for the individual assigned to it (hereafter referred to as "middle manager") as well as for the company that employs her.

Managing Relationships

Middle managers, like most managers, accomplish their goals largely by managing relationships. There are few things which managers can do alone; they must usually rely on the support, cooperation, or approval of a large number of people. As the textbooks say, they "get things done through others."

Managing relationships at their level in the organization, however, is a threefold task, requiring middle managers to act as subordinates, equals, and superiors:

☐ Upward, they relate to their bosses as subordinates; they take orders.

☐ Downward, they relate to their team as superiors; they give orders.

☐ Laterally, they relate to peers in the organization as equals; for example, they may have to secure cooperation from a pooled sales force or solicit assistance from corporate staff services.

Thus middle managers wear three hats in fulfilling their general management role. In contrast, top-level general managers act primarily as superiors—this alone is a significant difference between the two positions.

Managing the triple set of relationships is most demanding; it is analogous to a baseball player having to excel simultaneously in hitting, fielding, and pitching. The middle manager must be able not only to manage all three relationships, but also to shift quickly and frequently from one to another.

In view of these conflicting and changing demands, it is often difficult for middle managers to arrive at a consistent pattern of behavior. Moreover, in the process of satisfying the requirements of one set of relationships they may reduce their effectiveness in managing another. For instance, middle managers who follow orders from headquarters to the letter may thereby, in the eyes of subordinates, either weaken their authority or appear unreasonable and unresponsive. Consider this illustration from an internationally divisionalized company:

Headquarters restricted the freedom of one division manager to purchase from the outside, an order which threatened to undermine his authority as a general manager. He was torn between the dilemma of (a) asserting his authority with his subordinates by ignoring or fighting headquarters' orders, or (b) weakening his image as a superior by following headquarters' orders. Being a good subordinate would have weakened him as a superior; yet, by being a strong superior, he would have been a disloyal subordinate. As it turned out, the general manager held prolonged negotiations with a peer in the pooled sales force to arrive at a mutually satisfactory solution, but this made the general manager appear inconclusive and indecisive to his subordinates.

In order to successfully manage such multiple relationships, and their often conflicting and changing demands, middle managers should recognize the full scope of their job. For instance, they should:

1   Make the network of relationships explicit. To whom do they have to relate? What are the key relationships?
2   Identify, in their specific situation, the triple set of requirements. What is expected of them as good subordinates? What is required to be effective colleagues and equals? And what does it take to provide leadership as superiors? This analysis should force middle managers to focus not only on their own goals and abilities but also on those of their "opposite numbers" at all three levels.
3   Recognize the difficulty of achieving consistent behavior in view of conflicting demands and be willing to wear three hats at the same time. Success will involve the balancing of all three roles. Sometimes it requires trade-offs. Under such complex circumstances, it helps to proceed explicitly.
4   Communicate their understanding of the job to others in the organization with whom they must relate. (These others should bear in mind that, singly, they are part of but one of the multiple relationship sets that they have to manage; their expectations and responses should take this into account.)

A Playing Coach

In some respects, middle managers are the leaders of their unit who delegate, guide, and plan; in other respects, however, they have specific operating responsibilities and must "roll up their sleeves" to achieve output and to meet their targets. Therefore, they are both delegators and doers, both strategists and operators, or, to use another sports analogy, both coaches and players. In contrast, their superiors are usually coaches and their subordinates are normally players.

Continuing the analogy, sports experience indicates that it is easier to excel either as a coach or as a player and that the playing-coach job is clearly the most difficult—the skills of a successful player are different from those of a successful coach, but the playing coach must possess the skills of both. Likewise, the dual role of middle managers combines different skills and actions. On the one hand, they need a broad overview, detachment, and a long-run perspective. On the other hand, they need detailed knowledge and experience, the ability to involve themselves directly and deeply, and a sense of urgency.

Acting both as players and coaches, middle managers must constantly balance the two roles and sometimes make trade-offs. Are they going to be too much of a player, too involved in operating details and in doing things themselves? Or are they becoming too much of a coach by staying aloof, by delegating too much, by not getting sufficiently involved? It is easy to misperceive one's role, especially in regard to the latter. For example:

Top management in a large divisionalized corporation assigned a promising middle manager to a recent acquisition. Charged with enthusiasm for his new position, the manager saw himself as primarily a delegator, an organization builder whose job was to oversee the installation of parent company procedures and guide the acquisition's integration with staff services of the parent. He had not considered becoming directly involved in operating details or concentrating attention on increasing sales, both of which his immediate superior, the former owner/manager, saw as primary responsibilities of the middle-management position.

This question of balance—of asking oneself, "To what extent do I get involved in actual operations and to what extent do I delegate?"—is most delicate. And the balancing of the two roles is, of course, also influenced by the demands, expectations, and abilities of the middle manager's superiors and subordinates. The choice is not entirely free.

The Bilingual Manager

In keeping with their dual roles, middle managers usually receive abstract guidance from their superiors in the form of goals that they must translate into concrete action.

If, for example, a company's chief executive sets the goal of a certain percentage increase in earnings per share (and mentions it to financial analysts, thereby making it an even stronger commitment), how does she go about achieving this goal? She will communicate it to her group vice president, who will salute and pass it on to his divisional general manager, who, in turn, will salute and pass it on to the middle manager. The latter will salute, turn around, and find nobody to pass the goal on to. To use Harry Truman's famous dictum, this is where the buck stops.

The buck stops at the middle manager, who must assume the bilingual role of translating the strategic language of her superiors into the operational language of her subordinates in order to get results. She must turn the abstract guidance of, say, more earnings per share or meeting the budget into the concrete action required to achieve the results.

Often the middle manager is presented these abstract goals carrying the label, "difficult but achievable." While such labels may have a motivating purpose, they are basically a euphemism for the following proposition: top management knows the results it wants to see, has no idea how to achieve them, and assigns the middle manager the twofold duty of figuring out how to perform the task and then getting it done (i.e., bosses tell what they want, not how they want it accomplished).

Strategy Considerations

There are several reasons for the foregoing results-oriented procedure. One explanation is that middle managers are closest to the action; therefore they have most of the data, and hence are in the best position to make the decisions relevant to translating goals into action. A second explanation states that it is a superior's privilege to push decision making down and let his subordinates sweat it out. Why should he stick his neck out when he has a subordinate to do it for him?

The implications of top management's approach, however, are more important than the explanations. First of all, middle-level general managers are provided with much broader *de facto* responsibility than is usually codified in job descriptions or organization charts. Consequently, they must often be more of a strategist than they realize. It is important, therefore, that they go beyond the formal definition of their job, functioning broadly enough so that they deal explicitly with the full scope of their real responsibilities. A narrow understanding of their role, by contrast, may cause them to ignore critical tasks; they cannot assume a responsibility they do not recognize.

But with responsibility goes risk, particularly where the goals are abstract and the charter is unclear. The risk is further compounded by the many constraints, external as well as organizational, within which the middle manager operates. However, along with risk goes opportunity. As Harry Truman put it, "If you can't stand the heat, get out of the kitchen." To be a strategist rather than just an order taker is exciting, even without the job's ceremonial attributes.

Formulating strategy for translating abstract goals into concrete action requires the ability to develop plans. In doing so, middle managers must take into account external factors of an economic, political, marketing, technological, or competitive nature. Moreover, in line with their dual role, they must achieve congruence between the goals of subordinates (whose commitment is essential) and the goals imposed by superiors (whose approval they seek).

This strategic task is both intellectual and administrative in nature, and the communication of plans is as critical as their development. Often, communication is most effectively accomplished not through proclamation but, rather, through "teaching" the general management point of view during day-to-day activities.

Summing up, to translate goals into action middle level general managers must:

☐ Define their job realistically and broadly.

☐ Assume full responsibility for translating the abstract goals into concrete action through strategic decision making and planning, taking into account both external and organizational factors.

☐ Effectively communicate their decisions and plans to both their superiors and subordinates.

From Action to Measurement

Middle managers must be able to translate not only from abstract guidance into concrete action but also from concrete action into abstract measurement. Their superiors measure success in terms of results and are less interested in *how* it has been accomplished. Consequently, the middle manager's performance is most often appraised by matching the abstract results of her actions with the abstract guidance that she has been given.

This fact of organizational life sometimes leads to misunderstanding. In one company, for example, a middle manager was unable to meet his goals, and invoked his actions to show why. Top management, however, perceived the explanations as excuses. Concrete action was not part of its measurement system.

In terms of the total equation, there can be real problems when the signals from abstract measurement contradict those from abstract guidance. Where this occurs, the translation process frequently gets reversed. Instead of starting with the abstract guidance (goals) to develop specific action, middle managers start with the abstract measurement (required results) and translate backward to their plan of action. Here are two illustrations:

In one company, top management emphasized the need for its divisions to have ample productive capacity. In the measurement of performance, however, excess capacity was looked on unfavorably. As a result, division managers added capacity very cautiously, achieving high plant-utilization ratios at the expense of lost sales (which did not show up in the measurement system).

And in another company, top management stressed the need for new product and market development; yet the middle managers were measured on the basis of short-term profitability. With R&D and marketing expenses reducing short-term profitability, pressures to achieve the latter created an obvious reluctance to incur the former.

Translating action into measurement involves the same skills as translating goals into action. One language is operational and involves a variety of dimensions, whereas the other is abstract and is often in terms of a single dimension. The required ability is to relate these two different languages. And when measurement and goals are contradictory, the middle manager must be able to tread a thin line between the two, sometimes making trade-offs.

Furthermore, middle managers must cope with an additional problem: the language of corporate measurement is sometimes inadequate for measuring and guiding the activities of their subordinates. While top management typically measures middle managers on the basis of profit and loss, middle managers have to evaluate their subordinates in terms of different quantitative measures (such as costs, production and sales volume, number of rejects, and so on) as well as qualitative judgments (such as adequacy of the plant layout, effectiveness of the R&D effort, comprehensiveness of the marketing activities). These measures not only are different in kind and more numerous, but also require greater expertise and more intimate knowledge of specifics.

Responsibility/Authority

Middle managers typically assume full responsibility for their unit and are evaluated on the results of the total operation. There is no way to shift the blame as might be done in a functionally organized setup, where marketing could claim that production did not deliver on time or production could point the finger at marketing for not bringing in enough orders.

Like chief executives, middle managers have to account for the performance of others. Unlike chief executives, however, they have only limited authority in the pursuit of their goals. They often need cooperation from equals, say, in a centralized R&D department; and they receive solicited, or unsolicited, guidance from superiors. Thus responsibility and authority do not overlap. The former exceeds the latter.

While textbooks state categorically that such an imbalance is wrong and that responsibility should be backed up with the necessary authority, the responsibility/authority discrepancy is an inevitable fact of life where divisionalization penetrates the organization. To function effectively in this imperfect world, middle managers must meet two requirements:

1 In spite of the limited authority, they must be willing to accept full responsibility and take action accordingly. At the same time, they should recognize that they cannot do everything themselves, that

they must cooperate and coordinate with others. The ability to manage multiple relationships is critical here.

2   While they always have the opportunity to "go to court," to appeal to their superiors when cooperation from equals is not forthcoming, they should rely on this route only as a last resort or when the issue is clear-cut—preventive settlements, even if they involve compromises, may be preferable. By going to court, they are asking somebody higher up to stick his neck out. The fact that this "somebody" has attained a higher position probably means that he is good at *not* sticking his neck out and is unlikely to be receptive unless middle managers pick their fights wisely, carefully, and infrequently.

Inevitable Politics

Discrepancies between responsibility and authority, coupled with all of the previously discussed factors—multiple relationships, the playing-coach role, translation from goals to action and back to results—necessarily result in a structure that requires managers to coexist in a political atmosphere. There are different interests and interest groups, conflicting goals and ambitions, and positions of power and weakness.

Moreover, this coexistence is not necessarily peaceful. Career objectives and prestige, as well as positions of influence, are at stake, and the general manager in the middle is an easy and accessible target—malcontent soldiers do not pick on the general directly; they go for his officers.

The position of middle managers is further exposed by a measurement system requiring direct and frequent responses. To meet their goals, they need cooperation and assistance and are therefore vulnerable to sabotage. In a political sense, they are up for reelection continuously. Thus they must possess a political sensitivity as well as the constitution to stomach pressures and conflicts. They have to be aware of the configuration of the power structure and the direction of political winds. Unfortunately, in this potentially volatile atmosphere, managers often fail to ask an obvious but key question: "Who are my friends and who are my enemies?"

A Major Transition

The middle manager's job is usually an individual's first try at general management. Typically, he has been selected on the basis of outstanding achievement as a functional specialist; hence this previous experience is not transferable to this new terrain. His new position represents a major transition. Fred Borch, General Electric's chairman of the board and chief executive officer, considers the step from functional to general management to be the greatest challenge of a manager's entire career.

Indeed, the skills and activities which led to success in a manager's functional career—whether marketing, manufacturing, engineering, R&D, control, or finance—are usually those of specialization, of deep involvement in a narrow area. The specialist knows more and more about less and less.

In the medical and legal professions, specialization is the usual route to excellence and eminence. Managers, too, during the early phases of their careers, follow this pattern; they establish a track record by excelling in a particular specialty. But unlike doctors and lawyers, their career progression pattern is brutally shifted.

Having earned their spurs as specialists, managers are given a new and drastically different challenge, that of excelling as generalists. Instead of knowing more and more about less and less, they now shift to knowing less and less about more and more.

This transition, in turn, represents a major risk. Previously, each step up the functional specialization ladder led to familiar challenges which required proven skills. Now, the challenges are new and the skills unproven. Not all managers will be able to make this transition; not all will possess the required general management skills; and in spite of earlier successes, not all will successfully meet the new challenge.

Overcoming Resentment

In making their major and risky transition, middle managers, as noted earlier, do not always face a friendly working environment; rather, they may find that their promotion has caused resentment. Some may consider themselves better qualified, because of age or seniority; they may view the new middle manager's capabilities and background as insufficient for the job. Others may resent the promoted individuals because they represent an "educated elite."

Yet the new middle manager needs the support of those very people who may resent his appointment. Their cooperation is essential, and he will face constant obstacles until he has it. In overcoming this possible handicap of resentment, administrative skills and experience are of utmost importance. Unfortunately, however, these skills are typically the new middle manager's short suit; he is more often long on technical abilities and experience, which are obviously less relevant to the task.

Acclimating to New Terrain

Since promotions do not always occur within the same department, middle managers often come from another segment of the organization. As newcomers, they will probably be unfamiliar with their unit's history, opportunities, and problems. And obtaining facts or information to accurately diagnose the situation will not be easy, for the following reasons:

☐ While superiors have assessed the unit's performance in terms of its abstract results, middle managers have to evaluate it in terms of concrete action. The latter is much harder to determine than the former.

☐ Middle managers will have to acquaint themselves not only with the "formal" organization of their unit, but with its "informal" structure as well. While the formal structure can be found in manuals and organization charts, the informal one has to be discovered through daily activities and interpersonal relationships.

☐ Politics may color the facts given. Certain information may be deliberately withheld, while other aspects may be overemphasized.

In summary, the newcomer's fact-finding mission is difficult and hazardous, and he will be required to sift through information that is often contradictory, tough to evaluate, and not always obvious.

Furthermore, he will be dealing with a new set of people, and thus will have to establish new relationships. This is a particularly difficult challenge to the manager who not only is undertaking his first general management job but also is possibly resented as a newcomer. Since relationships cannot be ordered from above, the middle manager will have to earn his own way. He will have to gain the confidence and respect of his counterparts not by virtue of the uniform he wears, but instead by the quality of his daily activities.

Managerial Acrobatics.   Without essential facts and established relationships, it is difficult for middle managers to get off to a fast start. Yet they often walk into a situation that requires quick and decisive action. In this event, they will have to walk a tightrope between (a) an early commitment based on inadequate facts and nonexisting relationships and (b) indecision while they establish their facts and relationships.

This first course of action is often preferred, since it establishes a manager's authority and image. He may also be responding to pressures that are pushing him in this direction. The risks, however, are great. Before he proceeds on such a path, it is worthwhile for him to pause and consider the long-run implications of action that precedes the establishment of facts and relationships. What, for example, are the chances of making major mistakes? While it is often argued that the wrong action is preferable to no action at all, it is important for the middle manager to get off to a good start, not just a fast one. Things that start badly usually get worse.

Experimental Leadership

In making their transition, middle managers often function as agents of change. They may have received their assignment from top management in order to bring about changes in their new unit, or their own ambition may push them to develop new approaches. This implies experimentation and a process of learning through trial and error. Experimentation, however, means vulnerability. The middle manager's unit, for instance, may have been chosen as the experimental laboratory for the entire organization; and, since an experiment is easier to defeat than a long-established policy, the forces of resistance mentioned earlier may be encouraged to mount opposition, or even sabotage. Where the agents of change are inexperienced newcomers, it is particularly easy to shift blame to their shoulders.

Experimental leadership rarely permits one to move ahead at great speed in a single direction. It involves slow testing and occasional backtracking that may be viewed by subordinates as indecision and defeat. Thus, they may interpret experimental leadership as lack of leadership, withholding their support and blaming their leader for inexperience or ignorance.

Under this handicap, success may be difficult to achieve. Top executives, in such circumstances, may not always come to the rescue. They may be watching rather than supporting the experiment. This is their privilege. From their vantage point, why should they stake their reputations, possibly their careers, on the uncertain outcome of an experiment?

Thus it is unrealistic to expect rescue from above. More importantly, to judge the soundness and results of an experimental change, whether initiated from above or by the middle manager himself, an objective and neutral superior is needed. He can also act as a mutually acceptable arbiter where conflicts arise, as in situations of limited authority.

Middle managers may be better served in the long run by having such a neutral arbiter above them rather than a prejudiced ally. In the former instance, cooperation and support can be obtained through candid and open negotiation; the availability of an objective judge encourages reasonable attitudes from all parties concerned. In the latter instance, resistance from others will go "underground," which obviously makes the task of obtaining cooperation and support more difficult. A case from one large company illustrates this point:

One of the divisions had to rely heavily on a centralized R&D department for its custom-made product innovations. Conflicts arose between the market-oriented division and the technology-oriented R&D department, so the division manager took his case to superiors. A new, marketing-oriented group vice president overwhelmingly ruled in favor of the division. Subsequently, the R&D department's contributions declined because of alleged "technical difficulties" and "conflicting demands from other divisions."

Challenge and Opportunity

The preceding description of the characteristics of the middle-management position portrays it as a major challenge, as indeed it is. Why would anyone want to accept such an ill-defined, open-ended, risky assignment? Yet, as I pointed out earlier, with risk goes opportunity; and with open-endedness goes a job of considerably broader scope than what is stated in the formal job description.

Why is it not possible, then, to design this job by including all the positive elements and eliminating all the drawbacks? The answer is that the drawbacks are inherent in a divisional organizational structure—they can be excluded only by eliminating the structure itself.

A divisional structure, however, is essential to the conduct of large-scale operations for a diverse range of products in a variety of countries. It also permits a large number of managers to assume general management responsibilities early in their careers, sometimes in their early or middle thirties after less than 10 years of business experience. In contrast, the functional organization usually offers an individual manager his first attempt at general management only during his middle fifties, after some 25 to 30 years of business experience.

The choice, then, is between having a broad opportunity to assume an imperfect general management job at an early age and having a very limited opportunity to hold a "perfect" general management job late in one's career. To put it in the context of Churchill's famous statement: early in a man's career, the middle-management job is the worst assignment except for all the others. Moreover, the advantages and opportunities are many, both for the company and for the aspiring executives:

☐ The chance to run one's own show at a young age, rather than having to wait for a quarter of a century, should increase the probability of advancement, as well as make a business career more exciting.

☐ The shift from specialist to generalist early in one's career is less perilous, and failure is less painful, than if the shift occurs later. If a manager has spent some 25 years as a specialist, she is apt to be firmly set in her ways and will find it difficult to make a major change. A younger manager, on the other hand, should still be flexible and able to adapt more easily to a different set of job requirements. Failure is also easier to take—and to overcome—early in one's career than it is later on. (Putting a 25-year track record on the line is a major risk and one that might well destory a person's entire career.)

☐ The early shift from specialist to generalist is also less risky from the company's viewpoint. When a manager who has been a specialist for a quarter of a century is selected for the president's job, the total conduct of the company is entrusted to someone with no record in general management. It is not at all certain that a successful engineering, marketing, manufacturing, or finance vice president will turn into a first-rate general manager. In the divisional organization, however, the middle manager typically manages one of several profit centers. Thus risk is greatly reduced by entrusting to an unproven general manager only a small segment of the total enterprise.

☐ A large number of general management slots in an organization enables a corporation to attract and retain many capable managers and avoids an elimination contest for a company's single general management position. This large reservoir of general managers can be transferred and promoted as new opportunities arise. Since the scarcest resource of a company is usually competent management, overcoming this hurdle may eventually constitute a major competitive advantage.

☐   The middle-management phenomenon is conducive to management development and training. Managers can start in a small profit center, establish a track record there, transfer to a larger unit, and so on. Thus both the breadth and the challenge of the general management job can be increased as they move up in the ranks. Their confidence and versatility will also be enhanced, fostering personal career development as well as strengthening corporate competence.

☐   Middle managers are close to the action. Leadership and coordination, therefore, take place on the battlefield rather than from distant headquarters. Decisions are made more quickly by better informed people, who can more closely monitor an action's impact and ensure its proper implementation.

Conclusion

There are some important implications that can be drawn from the characteristics of the middle-level general management job; and they affect not only the person who holds it but his or her superiors as well.

One common pitfall is that superiors tend to judge middle managers in terms of their own jobs. They believe that middle managers have the same opportunities, prerogatives, and power that they do and therefore should shoulder similar responsibility. This same belief is frequently shared by the middle managers themselves.

As I have attempted to show, however, the middle manager's job is quite different from that of the top-level general manager. The job itself is demanding enough. It should not be made more difficult by an incorrect understanding of its scope and characteristics.

Top management often fails to recognize that imperfection is a fact of life in the middle-management job. Furthermore, formal job descriptions frequently reflect sacred dogmas like overlapping authority and responsibility. Such ostrichlike attitudes create unrealistic expectations among all parties involved. Unrealistic expectations inevitably produce disenchantments and failures. Reality, even though it may not correspond to the demands of theoretical elegance, must be faced. If reality imposes imperfection, as it does, then imperfection must be recognized and accepted, rather than swept under the rug.

Need for Ratification

Given their job characteristics, middle managers can govern effectively only with the consent of those being governed. While they are formally promoted or demoted by their superior, the jury usually consists of their subordinates and peers. By giving or withholding their support, they greatly influence the middle manager's career.

This need for ratification is easily overlooked or underestimated by the middle managers. They may approach their job with supreme confidence in their own abilities, viewing their new appointment as evidence of their importance and talents. Where change is required, they may see themselves as the new leaders destined to bring order out of chaos and turn failure into success.

At the same time, they may see their subordinates as old-timers who have failed in the past to meet the challenge. Hence they may doubt their abilities and downgrade their importance. Middle managers who approach their jobs by overestimating their own importance and underestimating that of their subordinates are erecting a self-imposed barrier to ratification. They are creating the conditions for a self-fulfilling prophecy—with themselves as the ultimate victims.

Accommodation and Compromise

Another important implication for middle managers is the necessity of finding their way in a maze of accommodation and compromise. They cannot always make quick decisions, take a straightforward course of action, or follow completely rational and logical solutions. They must bring what they judge as necessary within the realm of what is possible.

Often it is difficult to adjust to such a complex challenge. While they may have made their mark as technical experts whose previous successes were based on purely rational solutions to technical problems, optimization may not be the most successful approach in their new role. Rarely do perfect solutions exist for the middle manager. There are *viable* solutions, however, and they require constant accommodation and compromise.

Job Strategy

Given the difficulty and challenge of general management at middle organizational levels, the job should be approached as explicitly as possible. Middle managers must attempt to define the following:

☐ The scope of their multiple relationships within the organizational structure as well as the specific people to whom they must relate.

☐ The "playing coach" role.

☐ The "bilingual" task of translating goals to action and action to measurement.

☐ The implications of having full responsibility while holding limited authority.

☐ The "political" environment in which they have to survive from a position of limited power and great vulnerability.

Just as companies formulate corporate strategy by matching their resources to their environment, so can middle managers formulate their job strategy—they can identify their total organizational environment and match this with their strengths and weaknesses as well as their personal values.

Looking at their jobs in strategic terms should help them face varied daily challenges, overcome frustrations, and develop a consistent pattern of behavior. Obviously, a job strategy should be not a ceremonial proclamation but, instead, a plan of action which the middle managers "carry in their back pockets" to guide them in their daily actions.

A managerial record, like a judicial one, is established through the cumulative impact of a series of decisions, many of which set precedents. If these decisions can be related not only to the specific demands of each separate issue but also to an overall philosophy and master plan, their internal consistency and cumulative impact will establish a strong and cohesive organizational fabric. This is the landmark of an effective and successful manager.

27

The Middle Manager as Innovator

ROSABETH MOSS KANTER

If there's one thing that most U.S. executives agree on, it's the need for higher productivity in American workplaces. So far most efforts at raising performance have concentrated on factory and office employees—partly, one assumes, because their output is easily measured. However, the increases in productivity at the shop or office level will mean nothing in the long run, if, for instance, new products aren't designed, new structures aren't put in place to accommodate change, or new equipment isn't conceived to improve product quality. In other words, a company's productivity depends to a great degree on how innovative its middle managers are.

In this article, the author describes a study she conducted of 165 middle managers in five companies to determine what managers contribute to innovation and what factors the most innovative companies have in common. She found that, among other things, innovative managers tend to be visionary, comfortable with change, and persistent. Innovation flourishes in companies where territories overlap and people have contact across functions; information flows freely; numbers of people have excesses in their budgets; many managers are in open-ended positions; and reward systems look to the future, not the past.

When Steve Talbot, an operations manager, began a staff job reporting to the general manager of a product group, he had no line responsibility, no subordinates or budget of his own, and only a vague mandate to "explore options to improve performance."

To do this, Talbot set about collecting resources by bargaining with

Author's Note. I'd like to thank the members of the research team who participated in this study, Karen Belinky, Janis Bowersox, Allan Cohen, Ken Farbstein, Henry Foley, William Fonvielle, Karen Handmaker, Irene Schneller, Barry Stein, David Summers and Mary Vogel. Ken Farbstein and David Summers made especially important contributions. All individual and company names in the article are pseudonyms.

423

product-line managers and sales managers. By promising the product-line managers that he would save them having to negotiate with sales to get top priority for their products, he got a budget from them. Then, because he had the money in hand, Talbot got the sales managers to agree to hire one salesperson per product line, with Talbot permitted to do the hiring.

The next area he tackled was field services. Because the people in this area were conservative and tightfisted, Talbot went to his boss to get support for his recommendations about this area.

With the sales and service functions increasing their market share, it was easy for Talbot to get the product-line managers' backing when he pushed for selling a major new product that he had devised. And, to keep his action team functioning and behind him, Talbot made sure that "everyone became a hero" when the senior vice president of engineering asked him to explain his success to corporate officers.

Arthur Drumm, a technical department head of two sections, wanted to develop a new measuring instrument that could dramatically improve the company's product quality. But only Drumm thought this approach would work; those around him were not convinced it was needed or would pay off. After spending months developing data to show that the company needed the instrument, Drumm convinced several of his bosses two levels up to contribute $300,000 to its development. He put together a task force made up of representatives from all the manufacturing sites to advise on the development process and to ensure that the instrument would fit in with operations.

When, early on, one high-level manager opposed the project, Drumm coached two others in preparation for an officer-level meeting at which they were going to present his proposal. And when executives argued about which budget line the money would come from, R&D or engineering, Drumm tried to ease the tension. His persistence netted the company an extremely valuable new technique.

When Doris Randall became the head of a backwater purchasing department, one of three departments in her area, she expected the assignment to advance her career. Understandably, she was disappointed at the poor state of the function she had inherited and looked around for ways to make improvements. She first sought information from users of the department's services and, with this information, got her boss to agree to a first wave of changes. No one in her position had ever had such close contacts with users before, and Randall employed her knowledge to reorganize the unit into a cluster of user-oriented specialists (with each staff member concentrating on a particular need).

Once she had the reorganization in place and her function acknowledged as the best purchasing department in the region, Randall wanted to reorganize the other two purchasing departments. Her boss, perhaps out of concern that he would lose his position to Randall if the proposed changes took place, discouraged her. But her credibility was so strong that her boss's boss—who viewed her changes as a model for improvements in other areas— gave Randall the go-ahead to merge the three purchasing departments into one. Greater efficiency, cost savings, and increased user satisfaction resulted.

These three managers are enterprising, innovative, and entrepreneurial middle managers who are part of a group that can play a key role in the United States' return to economic leadership.

If that seems like an overly grand statement, consider the basis for U.S. companies' success in the past: innovation in products and advances in management techniques. Then consider the pivotal contribution middle managers make to innovation and change in large organizations. Top leaders' general directives to open a new market, improve quality, or cut costs mean nothing without efficient middle managers just below officer level able to design the systems, carry them out, and redirect their staffs' activities accordingly. Furthermore, because middle managers have their fingers on the pulse of operations, they can also conceive, suggest, and set in motion new ideas that top managers may not have thought of.

The middle managers described here are not extraordinary individuals. They do, however, share a number of characteristics:

Comfort with Change. They are confident that uncertainties will be clarified. They also have foresight and see unmet needs as opportunities.

Clarity of Direction. They select projects carefully and, with their long time horizons, view setbacks as temporary blips in an otherwise straight path to a goal.

Thoroughness. They prepare well for meetings and are professional in making their presentations. They have insight into organizational politics and a sense of whose support can help them at various junctures.

Participative Management Style. They encourage subordinates to put in maximum effort and to be part of the team, promise them a share of the rewards, and deliver on their promises.

Persuasiveness, Persistence, and Discretion. They understand that they cannot achieve their ends overnight, so they persevere—using tact—until they do.

What makes it possible for managers to use such skills for the company's benefit? They work in organizations where the culture fosters collaboration and teamwork and where structures encourage people to "do what needs to be done." Moreover, they usually work under top managers who consciously incorporate conditions facilitating innovation and achievement into their companies' structures and operations.

These conclusions come from a study of the major accomplishments of 165 effective middle managers in five leading American corporations (for details on the research, see Appendix A). I undertook this study to determine managers' contributions to a company's overall success as well as the conditions that stimulate innovation and thus push a business beyond a short-term emphasis and allow it to secure a successful future.

Each of the 165 managers studied—all of whom were deemed "effective" by their companies—told the research team about a particular accomplishment; these covered a wide range. Some of the successes, though impressive, clearly were achieved within the boundaries of established company practice. Others, however, involved innovation introduction of new methods, structures, or products that increased the company's capacity. All in all, 99 of the 165 accomplishments fall within the definition of an innovative effort.

Basic accomplishments differ from innovative ones not only in scope and long-run impact but also in what it takes to achieve them. They are part of the assigned job and require only routine and readily available means to carry them out. Managers reporting this kind of accomplishment said they were just doing their jobs. Little was problematic—they had an assignment to tackle; they were told, or they already knew, how to go about it; they used existing budget or staff; they didn't need to gather or share much information outside of their units; and they encountered little or no opposition. Managers performing such activities don't generate innovations for their companies; they merely accomplish things faster or better that they already know how to do.

In contrast, innovative accomplishments are strikingly entrepreneurial. Moreover, they are sometimes highly problematic and generally involve acquiring and using power and influence. (See Appendix B for more details on the study's definitions of *basic* and *innovative* accomplishments.)

In this article, I first explore how managers influence their organizations to achieve goals throughout the various stages of a project's life. Next I discuss the managerial styles of the persons studied and the kinds of innovation they brought about. I look finally at the types of companies these entrepreneurial managers worked in and explore what top officers can do to foster a creative environment.

The Role of Power in Enterprise

Because most innovative achievements cut across organizational lines and threaten to disrupt existing arrangements, enterprising managers need tools beyond those that come with the job. Innovations have implications for other functions and areas, and they require data, agreements, and resources of wider scope than routine operations demand. Even R&D managers, who are expected to produce innovations, need more information, support, and resources for major projects than those built into regular R&D functions. They too may need additional data, more money, or agreement from extra-functional officials that the project is necessary. Only hindsight shows that an innovative project was bound to be successful.

Because of the extra resources they require, entrepreneurial managers need to go beyond the limits of their formal positions. For this, they need power. In large organizations at least, I have observed that powerlessness "corrupts."[1] That is, lack of power (the capacity to mobilize resources and people to get things done) tends to create managers who are more concerned about guarding their territories than about collaborating with others to benefit the organization. At the same time, when managers hoard potential power and don't invest it in productive action, it atrophies and eventually blocks achievements.

Furthermore, when some people have too much unused power and others too little, probems occur. To produce results, power—like money—needs to circulate. To come up with innovations, managers have to be in areas where power circulates, where it can be grabbed and invested. In this sense, organizational power is transactional: it exists as potential until someone makes a bid for it, invests it, and produces results with it.

The overarching condition required for managers to produce innovative achievements is this: they must envision an accomplishment beyond the scope of the job. They cannot alone possess the power to carry their idea out but they must be able to acquire the power they need easily. Thus, creative managers are not empowered simply by a boss or their job; on their own they seek and find the additional strength it takes to carry out major new initiatives. They are the corporate entrepreneurs.

Three commodities are necessary for accumulating productive power—information, resources, and support. Managers might find a portion of these within their purview and pour them into a project; managers with something they believe in will eagerly leverage their own staff and budget and even bootleg resources from their subordinates' budgets. But innovations usually require a manager to search for additional supplies elsewhere in the organization. Depending on how easy the organization makes it to tap sources of power and on how technical the project is, acquiring power can be the most time-consuming and difficult part of the process.

Phases of the Accomplishment

A prototypical innovation goes through three phases: project definition (acquisition and application of information to shape a manageable, salable project), coalition building (development of a network of backers who agree to provide resources and support), and action (application of the resources, information, and support to the project and mobilization of an action team). Let us examine each of these steps in more detail.

Defining the Project.   Before defining a project, managers need to identify the problem. People in an organization may hold many conflicting views about the best method of reaching a goal, and discovering the basis of these conflicting perspectives (while gathering hard data) is critical to a manager's success.

In one case, information circulating freely about the original design of a part was inaccurate. The manager needed to acquire new data to prove that the problem he was about to tackle was not a manufacturing shortcoming but a design flaw. But, as often happens, some people had a stake in the popular view. Even hard-nosed engineers in our study acknowledged that, in the early stages of an entrepreneurial project, managers need political information as much as they do technical data. Without political savvy, say these engineers, no one can get a project beyond the proposal stage.

The culmination of the project definition phase comes when managers sift through the fragments of information from each source and focus on a particular target. Then, despite the fact that managers may initially have been handed a certain area as an assignment, they still have to "sell" the project that evolves. In the innovative efforts I observed, the managers' assignments involved no promises of resources or support required to do anything more than routine activities.

Furthermore, to implement the innovation, a manager has to call on the cooperation of many others besides the boss who assigned the task. Many of these others may be independent actors who are not compelled to cooperate simply because the manager has carved a project out of a general assignment. Even subordinates may not be automatically on board. If they are professionals or managers, they have a number of other tasks and the right to set some of their own priorities; and if they are in a matrix, they may be responsible to other bosses as well.

For example, in her new job as head of a manufacturing planning unit, Heidi Wilson's assignment was to improve the cost efficiency of operations and thereby boost the company's price competitiveness. Her boss told her she could spend six months "saying nothing and just observing, getting to know what's really going on." One of the first things she noticed was that the flow of goods through the company was organized in an overly complicated, time-consuming, and expensive fashion.

The assignment gave Wilson the mandate to seek information but not to carry out any particular activities. Wilson set about to gather organizational, technical, and political information in order to translate her ambiguous task into a concrete project. She followed goods through the company to determine what the process was and how it could be changed. She sought ideas and impressions from manufacturing line managers, at the same time learning the location of vested interests and where other patches of organizational quicksand lurked. She compiled data, refined her approach, and packaged and repackaged her ideas until she believed she could "prove to people that I knew more about the company than they did."

Wilson's next step was "to do a number of punchy presentations with pictures and graphs and charts." At the presentations, she got two kinds of responses: "Gee, we thought there was a problem but we never saw it outlined like this before" and "Aren't there better things to worry about?" To handle the critics, she "simply came back over and over again with information, more information than anyone else had." When she had gathered the data and received the feedback, Wilson was ready to formulate a project and sell it to her boss. Ultimately, her project was approved, and it netted impressive cost savings.

Thus, although innovation may begin with an assignment, it is usually one—like Wilson's—that is couched in general statements of results with the means largely unspecified. Occasionally, managers initiate projects themselves; however, initiation seldom occurs in a vacuum. Creative managers listen to a stream of information from superiors and peers and then identify a perceived need. In the early stages of defining a project, managers may spend more time talking with people outside their own functions than with subordinates or bosses inside.

One R&D manager said he had "hung out" with product designers while trying to get a handle on the best way to formulate a new process-development project. Another R&D manager in our survey got the idea for a new production method from a conversation about problems he had with the head of production. He then convinced his boss to let him determine whether a corrective project could be developed.

Building a Coalition. Next, entrepreneurial managers need to pull in the resources and support to make the project work. For creative accomplishments, these power-related tools do not come through the vertical chain of command but rather from many areas of the organization.

George Putnam's innovation is typical. Putnam was an assistant department manager for product testing in a company that was about to demonstrate a product at a site that attracted a large number of potential buyers. Putnam heard through the grapevine that a decision was imminent about which model to display. The product managers were each lobbying for their own, and the marketing people also had a favorite. Putnam, who was close to the products, thought that the first choice model had grave defects and so decided to demonstrate to the marketing staff both what the problems with the first one were and the superiority of another model.

Building on a long-term relationship with the people in corporate quality control and a good alliance with his boss. Putnam sought the tools he needed: the blessing of the vice president of engineering (his boss's boss), special materials for testing from the materials division, a budget from corporate quality control, and staff from his own units to carry out the tests. As Putnam put it, this was all done through one-on-one "horse trading"—showing each manager how much the others were chipping in. Then Putnam met informally with the key marketing staffer to learn what it would take to convince him.

As the test results emerged, Putnam took them to his peers in marketing engineering and quality control so they could feed them to their superiors. The accumulated support persuaded the decision makers to adopt Putnam's choice of a model; it later became a strong money-maker. In sum, Putnam had completely stepped out of his usual role to build a consensus that shaped a major policy decision.

Thus the most successful innovations derive from situations where a number of people from a number of areas make contributions. They provide a kind of checks-and-balances system to an activity that is otherwise non-routine and, therefore, is not subject to the usual controls. By building a coalition before extensive project activity gets under way, the manager also ensures the availability of enough support to keep momentum going and to guarantee implementation.

In one company, the process of lining up peers and stakeholders as early supporters is called "making cheerleaders;" in another, "preselling." Sometimes managers ask peers for "pledges" of money or staff to be collected later if higher management approves the project and provides overall resources.

After garnering peer support, usually managers seek support at much higher levels. While we found surprisingly few instances of top management directly sponsoring or championing a project, we did find that a general blessing from the top is clearly necessary to convert potential supporters into a solid team. In one case, top officers simply showed up at a meeting where the proposal was being discussed; their presence ensured that other people couldn't use the "pocket veto" power of headquarters as an excuse to table the issue. Also, the very presence of a key executive at such a meeting is often a signal of the proposal's importance to the rest of the organization.

Enterprising managers learn who at the top-executive level has the power to affect their projects (including material resources or vital initial approval power). Then they negotiate for these executives' support, using polished formal presentations. Whereas managers can often sell the project to peers and stakeholders by appealing to these people's self-interests and assuring them they know what they're talking about, managers need to offer top executives more guarantees about both the technical and the political adequacies of projects.

Key executives tend to evaluate a proposal in terms of its salability to *their* constituencies. Sometimes entrepreneurial managers arm top executives with materials or rehearse them for their own presentations to other people (such as members of an executive committee or the board) who have to approve the project.

Most often, since many of the projects that originate at the middle of a company can be supported at that level and will not tap corporate funds, those at high levels in the organization simply provide a general expression of support. However, the attention top management confers on this activity, many of our interviewers told us, makes it possible to sell their own staffs as well as others.

But once in a while, a presentation to top-level officers results in help in obtaining supplies. Sometimes enterprising managers walk away with the promise of a large capital expenditure or assistance getting staff or space. Sometimes a promise of resources is contingent on getting others on board. "If you can raise the money, go ahead with this," is a frequent directive to an enterprising manager.

In one situation, a service manager approached his boss and his boss's boss for a budget for a college recruitment and training program that he had been supporting on his own with funds bootlegged from his staff. The top executives told him they would grant a large budget if he could get his four peers to support the project. Somewhat to their surprise, he came back with this support. He had taken his peers away from the office for three days for a round of negotiation and planning. In cases like this, top management is not so much hedging its bets as using its ability to secure peer support for what might otherwise be risky projects.

With promises of resources and support in hand, enterprising managers can go back to the immediate boss or bosses to make plans for moving ahead. Usually the bosses are simply waiting for this tangible sign of power to continue authorizing the project. But in other cases the bosses are not fully involved and won't be sold until the manager has higher-level support.

Of course, during the coalition-building phase, the network of supporters does not play a passive role; their comments, criticisms, and objectives help shape the project into one that is more likely to succeed. Another result of the coalition-building phase is, then, a set of reality checks that ensures that projects unlikely to succeed will go no farther.

Moving into Action.   The innovating manager's next step is to mobilize key players to carry out the project. Whether the players are nominal subordinates or a special project group such as a task force, managers forge them into a team. Enterprising managers bring the people involved in the project together, give them briefings and assignments, pump them up for the extra effort needed, seek their ideas and suggestions (both as a way to involve them and to further refine the project) and promise them a share of the rewards. As one manager put it, "It takes more selling than telling." In most of the innovations we observed, the manager couldn't just order subordinates to get involved. Doing something beyond routine work that involves creativity and cooperation requires the full commitment of subordinates; otherwise the project will not succeed.

During the action phase, managers have four central organizational tasks. The technical details of the project and the actual work directed toward project goals are now in the hands of the action team. Managers may contribute ideas or even get involved in hands-on experimentation, but their primary functions are still largely external and organizational, centered around maintaining the boundaries and integrity of the project.

The manager's first task is to *handle interference* or opposition that may jeopardize the project. Entrepreneurial managers encounter strikingly little overt opposition—perhaps because their success at coalition building determines whether a project gets started in the first place. Resistance takes a more passive form: criticism of the plan's details, foot-dragging, late responses to requests, or arguments over allocation of time and resources among projects.

Managers are sometimes surprised that critics keep so quiet up to this point. One manufacturing manager who was gearing up for production of a new item had approached many executives in other areas while making cost estimates, and these executives had appeared positive about his efforts. But later, when he began organizing the manufacturing process itself, he heard objections from these very people.

During this phase, therefore, innovative managers may have to spend as much time in meetings, both formal and one-to-one, as they did to get the project launched. Managers need to prepare thoroughly for these meetings so they can counter skepticism and objections with clear facts, persuasion, and reminders of the benefits that can accrue to managers meeting the project's objectives. In most cases, a clear presentation of facts is enough. But not always: one of our respondents, a high-level champion, had to tell an opponent to back down, that the project was going ahead anyway, and that his carping was annoying.

Whereas managers need to directly counter open challenges and criticism that might result in the flow of power or supplies being cut off, they simply keep other interference outside the boundaries of the project. In effect, the manager defines a protected area for the group's work. He or she goes outside this area to head off critics and to keep people or rules imposed by higher management from disrupting project tasks.

While the team itself is sometimes unaware of the manager's contribution, the manager—like Tom West (head of the now-famous computer-design group at Data General)—patrols the boundaries.[2] Acting as interference filters, managers in my study protected innovative projects by bending rules, transferring funds "illicitly" from one budget line to another, developing special reward or incentive systems that offered bonuses above company pay rates, and ensuring that superiors stayed away unless needed.

The second action-phase task is *maintaining momentum* and continuity. Here interference comes from internal rather than external sources. Foot-dragging or inactivity is a constant danger, especially if the creative effort adds to work loads. In our study, enterprising managers as well as team members complained continually about the tendency for routine activities to take precedence over special projects and to consume limited time.

In addition, it is easier for managers to whip up excitement over a vision at start-up than to keep the goal in people's minds when they face the tedium of the work. Thus, managers' team-building skills are essential. So the project doesn't lose momentum, managers must sustain the enthusiasm of all—from supporters to suppliers—by being persistent and keeping the team aware of supportive authorities who are clearly waiting for results.

One manager, who was involved in a full-time project to develop new and more efficient methods of producing a certain ingredient, maintained momentum by holding daily meetings with the core team, getting together often with operations managers and members of a task force he had formed, putting out weekly status reports, and making frequent presentations to top management. When foot-dragging occurs, many entrepreneurial managers pull in high-level supporters—without compromising the autonomy of the project—to get the team back on board. A letter or a visit from the big boss can remind everyone just how important the project is.

A third task of middle managers in the action phase is to engage in whatever *secondary redesign*—other changes made to support the key change—is necessary to keep the project going. For example, a manager whose team was setting up a computerized information bank held weekly team meetings to define tactics. A fallout of these meetings was a set of new awards and a fresh performance appraisal system for team members and their subordinates.

As necessary, managers introduce new arrangements to conjoin with the core tasks. When it seems that a project is bogging down—that is, when everything possible has been done and no more results are on the horizon—managers often change the structure or approach. Such alterations can cause a redoubling of effort and a renewed attack on the problem. They can also bring the company additional unplanned innovations as a side benefit from the main project.

The fourth task of the action phase, *external communication*, brings the accomplishment full circle. The project begins with gathering information; now it is important to send information out. It is vital to (as several managers put it) "manage the press" so that peers and key supporters have an up-to-date impression of the project and its success. Delivering on promises is also important. As much as possible, innovative managers meet deadlines, deliver early benefits to others, and keep supporters supplied with information. Doing so establishes the credibility of both the project and the manager, even before concrete results can be shown.

Information must be shared with the team and the coalition as well. Good managers periodically remind the team of what they stand to gain from the accomplishment, hold meetings to give feedback and to stimulate pride in the project, and make a point of congratulating each staff member individually. After all, as Steve Talbot (of my first example) said, many people gave this middle manager power because of a promise that everyone would be a hero.

A Management Style for Innovation . . .

Clearly there is a strong association between carrying out an innovative accomplishment and employing a participative-collaborative management style. The managers observed reached success by:

☐ Persuading more than ordering, though managers sometimes use pressure as a last resort.

☐ Building a team, which entails among other things frequent staff meetings and considerable sharing of information.

☐ Seeking inputs from others—that is, asking for ideas about users' needs, soliciting suggestions from subordinates, welcoming peer review, and so forth.

☐ Acknowledging others' stake or potential stake in the project—in other words, being politically sensitive.

☐ Sharing rewards and recognition willingly.

A collaborative style is also useful when carrying out basic accomplishments; however, in such endeavors it is not required. Managers can bring off many basic accomplishments using a traditional, more autocratic style. Because they're doing what is assigned, they don't need external support; because they have all the tools to do it, they don't need to get anyone else involved (they simply direct subordinates to do what is required). But for innovative accomplishments—seeking funds, staff, or information (political as well as technical) from outside the work unit; attending long meetings and presentations; and requiring "above and beyond" effort from staff—a style that revolves around participation, collaboration, and persuasion is essential.

The participative-collaborative style also helps creative managers reduce risk because it encourages completion of the assignment. Furthermore, others' involvement serves as a check-and-balance on the project, reshaping it to make it more of a sure thing and putting pressure on people to follow through. The few projects in my study that disintegrated did so because the manager failed to build a coalition of supporters and collaborators.

. . . and Corporate Conditions that Encourage Enterprise

Just as the manager's strategies to develop and implement innovations followed many different patterns, so also the level of enterprise managers achieved varied strongly across the five companies we studied (see Exhibit 1). Managers in newer, high-technology companies have a much higher proportion of innovative accomplishments than managers in other industries. At "CHIPCO," a computer parts manufacturer, 71% of all the things effective managers did were innovative; for "UTICO," a communications utility, the number is 33%; for "FINCO," an insurance company, it is 47%.

This difference in levels of innovative achievement correlates with the extent to which these companies' structures and cultures support middle managers' creativity. Companies producing the most entrepreneurs have cultures that encourage collaboration and teamwork. Moreover, they have complex structures that link people in multiple ways and help them go beyond the confines of their defined jobs to do "what needs to be done."

CHIPCO, which showed the most entrepreneurial activity of any company in our study, is a rapidly growing electronics company with abundant resources. That its culture favors independent action and team effort is communicated quickly and clearly to the newcomer. Sources of support and money are constantly shifting and, as growth occurs, managers rapidly move on to other positions. But even though people frequently express frustration about the shifting approval process, slippage of schedules, and continual entry of new players onto the stage, they don't complain about loss opportunities. For one thing, because coalitions support the various projects, new project managers feel bound to honor their predecessors' financial commitments.

CHIPCO managers have broad job charters to "do the right thing" in a manner of their own choosing. Lateral relationships are more important than vertical ones. Most functions are in a matrix, and some managers have up to four "bosses." Top management expects ideas to bubble up from lower levels. Senior executives then select solutions rather than issue confining directives. In fact, people generally rely on informal face-to-face communication across units to build a consensus. Managers spend a lot of time in meetings; information flows freely, and reputation among peers—instead of formal authority or title—conveys credibility and garners support. Career mobility at CHIPCO is rapid, and people have pride in the company's success.

RADCO, the company with the strongest R&D orientation in the study, has many of CHIPCO's qualities but bears the burden of recent changes. RADCO's once-strong culture and its image as a research institute are in flux and may be eroding. A new top management with new ways of thinking is shifting the orientation of the company, and some people express concern about the lack of clear direction and long-range planning. People's faith in RADCO's strategy of technical superiority has weakened, and its traditional orientation toward innovation is giving way to a concern for routinization and production efficiency. This shift is resulting in conflict and uncertainty. Where once access to the top was easy, now the decentralized matrix structure—with fewer central services—makes it difficult.

As at CHIPCO, lateral relationships are important, though top management's presence is felt more. In the partial matrix, some managers have as many as four "bosses." A middle manager's boss or someone in higher management is likely to give general support to projects as long as peers (within and across functions) get on board. And peers often work decisions up the organization through their own hierarchies.

Exhibit 1. Characteristics of the Five Companies in Order of Most to Least "Entrepreneurial"

	CHIPCO	RADCO	MEDCO	FINCO	UTICO
Percent of effective managers with entrepreneurial accomplishments	71%	69%	67%	47%	33%
Current economic trend	Steadily up	Trend up but currently down	Up	Mixed	Down
Current "change issues"	Change "normal:" constant change in product generations; proliferating staff and units	Change "normal" in products, technologies; recent changeover to second management generation with new focus	Reorganized about 3–4 years ago to install matrix; "normal" product technology changes	Change a "shock;" new top management group from outside reorganizing and trying to add competitive market posture	Change a "shock," undergoing reorganization to install matrix and add competitive market posture while reducing staff
Organization structure	Matrix	Matrix in some areas; product lines act as quasidivisions	Matrix in some areas	Divisional; unitary hierarchy within divisions, some central services	Functional organization; currently overlaying a matrix of regions and markets

	Decentralized / Free / Horizontal	Mixed / Free / Horizontal	Mixed / Moderately free / Horizontal	Centralized / Constricted / Vertical	Centralized / Constricted / Vertical
Information flow / Communication emphasis	(Decentralized, Free, Horizontal)	(Mixed, Free, Horizontal)	(Mixed, Moderately free, Horizontal)	(Centralized, Constricted, Vertical)	(Centralized, Constricted, Vertical)
Culture	Clear consistent; favors individual initiative	Clear, though in transition from emphasis on invention to emphasis on routinization and systems	Clear; pride in company, belief that talent will be rewarded	Idiosyncratic; depends on boss and area	Clear, but top management would like to change it; favors security, maintenance, protection
Current emotional climate	Pride in company, team feeling, some "burnout"	Uncertainty about changes	Pride in company, team feeling	Low trust, high uncertainty	High uncertainty, confusion
Rewards	Abundant. Include visibility, chance to do more challenging work in the future and get bigger budget for projects	Abundant. Include visibility, chance to do more challenging work in future and get bigger budget for projects	Moderately abundant; conventional	Scarce; primarily monetary	Scarce: promotion, salary freeze; recognition by peers grudging

Procedures at RADCO are both informal and formal: much happens at meetings and presentations and through persuasion, plus the company's long-term employment and well-established working relationships encourage lateral communication. But managers also use task forces and steering committees. Projects often last for years, sustained by the company's image as a leader in treating employees well.

MEDCO manufactures and sells advanced medical equipment, often applying ideas developed elsewhere. Although MEDCO produces a high proportion of innovative accomplishments, it has a greater degree of central planning and routinization than either CHIPCO or RADCO. Despite headquarters' strong role, heads of functions and product managers can vary their approaches. Employers believe that MEDCO's complex matrix system allows autonomy and creates opportunities but is also time wasting because clear accountability is lacking.

Teamwork and competition coexist at MEDCO. Although top management officially encourages teamwork and the matrix produces a tendency for trades and selling to go on within the organization, interdepartmental and interproduct rivalries sometimes get in the way. Rewards, especially promotions, are available, but they often come late and even then are not always clear or consistent. Because many employees have been with MEDCO for a long time, both job mobility and job security are high. Finally, managers see the company as a leader in its approach to management and as a technological follower in all areas but one.

The last two companies in the study, FINCO (insurance) and UTICO (communications), show the lowest proportion of innovative achievements. Many of the completed projects seemed to be successful *despite* the system.

Currently FINCO has an idiosyncratic and inconsistent culture: employees don't have a clear image of the company, its style, or its direction. How managers are treated depends very much on one's boss—one-to-one relationships and private deals carry a great deal of weight. Though the atmosphere of uncertainty creates opportunities for a few, it generally limits risk taking. Moreover, reorganizations, a top-management shake-up, and shuffling of personnel have fostered insecurity and suspicion. It is difficult for managers to get commitment from their subordinates because they question the manager's tenure. Managers spend much time and energy coping with change, reassuring subordinates, and orienting new staff instead of developing future-oriented projects. Still, because the uncertainty creates a vacuum, a few managers in powerful positions (many of whom were brought in to initiate change) do benefit.

Unlike the innovation-producing companies, FINCO features vertical relationships. With little encouragement to collaborate, managers seldom make contact across functions or work in teams. Managers often see formal structures and systems as constraints rather than as supports. Rewards are scarce, and occasionally a manager will break a promise about them. Seeing the company as a follower, not a leader, the managers at FINCO sometimes make unfavorable comparisons between it and other companies in the industry. Furthermore, they resent the fact that FINCO's top management brings in so many executives from outside; they see it as an insult.

UTICO is a very good company in many ways; it is well regarded by its employees and is considered progressive for its industry. However, despite the strong need for UTICO to be more creative and thus more competitive and despite movement toward a matrix structure, UTICO's middle ranks aren't very innovative. UTICO's culture is changing—from being based on security and maintenance to being based on flexibility and competition—and the atmosphere of uncertainty frustrates achievers. Moreover, UTICO remains very centralized. Top management largely directs searches for new systems and methods through formal mechanisms whose ponderousness sometimes discourages innovation. Tight budgetary constraints make it difficult for middle managers to tap funds; carefully measured duties discourage risk takers; and a lockstep chain of command makes it dangerous for managers to bypass their bosses.

Information flows vertically and sluggishly. Because of limited cooperation among work units, even technical data can be hard to get. Weak-spot management means that problems, not successes, get attention. Jealousy and competition over turf kill praise from peers and sometimes from bosses. Managers' image of the company is mixed: they see it as leading its type of business but behind more modern companies in rate of change.

Organizational Supports for Creativity

Examination of the differences in organization, culture, and practices in these five companies makes clear the circumstances under which enterprise can flourish. To tackle and solve tricky problems, people need both the opportunities and the incentives to reach beyond their formal jobs and combine organizational resources in new ways.[3] The following create these opportunities:

☐ Multiple reporting relationships and overlapping territories. These force middle managers to carve out their own ideas about appropriate action and to sell peers in neighboring areas or more than one boss.

☐ A free and somewhat random flow of information. Data flow of this kind prods executives to find ideas in unexpected places and pushes them to combine fragments of information.

☐ Many centers of power with some budgetary flexibility. If such centers are easily accessible to middle managers, they will be encouraged to make proposals and acquire resources.

☐ A high proportion of managers in loosely defined positions or with ambiguous assignments. Those without subordinates or line responsibilities who are told to "solve problems" must argue for a budget or develop their own constituency.

☐ Frequent and smooth cross-functional contact, a tradition of working in teams and sharing credit widely, and emphasis on lateral rather than vertical relationships as a source of resources, information, and support. These circumstances require managers to get peer support for their projects before top officers approve.

☐ A reward system that emphasizes investment in people and projects rather than payment for past services. Such a system encourages executives to move into challenging jobs, gives them budgets to tackle projects, and rewards them after their accomplishments with the chance to take on even bigger projects in the future.

Some of these conditions seem to go hand in hand with new companies in not-yet-mature markets. But top decision makers in older, traditional companies can design these conditions into their organizations. They would be wise to do so because, if empowered, innovative middle managers can be one of America's most potent weapons in its battle against foreign competition.

Notes

1. See my book *Men and Women of the Corporation* (New York: Basic Books, 1977); also see my article, "Power Failure in Management Circuits," *HBR*, July–August 1979, p. 65.

2. Tracy Kidder, *The Soul of a New Machine* (Boston: Little, Brown, 1981).

3. My findings about conditions stimulating managerial innovations are generally consistent with those on technical (R&D) innovation. See James Utterback, "Innovation in Industry," *Science*, February 1974, pp. 620–626. John Kimberly, "Managerial Innovation," *Handbook of Organizational Design*, edited by W.H. Starbuck (New York: Oxford, 1981), and Goodmeasure, Inc. "99 Propositions on Innovation from the Research Literature," *Stimulating Innovation in Middle Management* (Cambridge, Mass., 1982).

Appendix A: The Research Project

After a pilot study in which it interviewed 26 effective middle managers from 18 companies, the research team interviewed, in depth, 165 middle managers from five major corporations located across the United States. The 165 were chosen by their companies to participate because of their reputations for effectiveness. We did not want a random sample: we were looking for "the best and the brightest," who could serve as models for others. It turned out, however, that every major function was represented, and roughly in proportion to its importance in the company's success. (For example, there were more innovative sales and marketing managers representing the "market-driven" company and more technical, R&D, and manufacturing managers from the "product-driven" companies.)

During the two-hour interviews, the managers talked about all aspects of a single significant accomplishment, from the glimmering of an idea to the results. We asked the managers to focus on the most significant of a set of four or five of their accomplishments over the previous two years. We also elicited a chronology of the project as well as responses to a set of open-ended questions about the acquisition of power, the handling of roadblocks, and the doling out of rewards. We supplemented the interviews with discussions about current issues in the five companies with our contacts in each company.

The five companies represent a range of types and industries: from rather traditional, slow-moving, mature companies to fast-changing, newer, high-technology companies. We included both service and manufacturing companies that are from different parts of the country and are at different stages in their development. The one thing that all five have in common is an intense interest in the topic of the study. Facing highly competitive markets (for the manufacturing companies a constant since their founding; for the service companies a newer phenomenon), all of these corporations wanted to encourage their middle managers to be more enterprising and innovative.

Our pseudonyms for the companies emphasize a central feature of each:

- [ ] CHIPCO. Manufacturer of computer products
- [ ] FINCO. Insurance and related financial services
- [ ] MEDCO. Manufacturer of large medical equipment
- [ ] RADCO (for "R&D"). Manufacturer of optical products
- [ ] UTICO. Communications utility

Appendix B: What Is an Innovative Accomplishment?

We categorized the 165 managers' accomplishments according to their primary impact on the company. Many accomplishments had multiple results or multiple components, but it was the breadth of scope of the accomplishment and its future utility for the company that defined its category. Immediate dollar results were *not* the central issue; rather, organizational "learning" or increased future capacity was the key. Thus, improving revenues by cutting costs while changing nothing else would be categorized differently from improving revenues by designing a new production method; only the latter leaves a lasting trace.

The accomplishments fall into two clusters:

- [ ] *Basic.* Done solely within the existing framework and not affecting the company's longer-term capacity; 66 of the 165 fall into this category.

☐ *Innovative.* A new way for the company to use or expand its resources that raises long-term capacity; 99 of the 165 are such achievements.

Basic accomplishments include:

☐ *Doing the basic job.* Simply carrying out adequately a defined assignment within the bounds of one's job (e.g., "fulfilled sales objectives during a reorganization").

☐ *Affecting individuals, performance.* Having an impact on individuals (e.g., "found employee a job in original department after failing to retrain him").

☐ *Advancing incrementally.* Achieving a higher level of performance within the basic job (e.g., "met more production schedules in plant than in past").

Innovative accomplishments include:

☐ *Effecting a new policy.* Creating a change of orientation or direction (e.g., "changed price-setting policy in product line with new model showing cost-quality trade-offs").

☐ *Finding a new opportunity.* Developing an entirely new product or opening a new market (e.g., "sold new product program to higher management and developed staffing for it").

☐ *Devising a fresh method.* Introducing a new process, procedure, or technology for continued use (e.g., "designed and implemented new information system for financial results by business sectors").

☐ *Designing a new structure.* Changing the formal structure, reorganizing or introducing a new structure, or forging a different link among units (e.g., "consolidated three offices into one").

While members of the research team occasionally argued about the placement of accomplishments in the subcategories, we were almost unanimous as to whether an accomplishment rated as basic or innovative. Even bringing off a financially significant or flashy increase in performance was considered basic if the accomplishment was well within the managers' assignment and territory, involved no new methods that could be used to repeat the feat elsewhere, opened no opportunities, or had no impact on corporate structure—in other words, reflected little inventiveness. The manager who achieved such a result might have been an excellent manager, but he or she was not an innovative one.

THE ROLE OF
TOP MANAGEMENT

AN OVERVIEW

Strategic management is most commonly defined as a way of managing a company so that strategic purposes dominate decision making at all levels and in all functions of the organization. This deceptively simple definition poses a tremendous challenge to the chief executive who wants to make strategic management a reality. Doing so requires inspired top management leadership; yet there are many who question the ability of top managers to provide this leadership.

In "Managers and Leaders: Are They Different?", Abraham Zaleznik argues that the very nature of large organizations makes it difficult for top managers to exert meaningful leadership:

> Business has established a new power ethic that favors collective over individual leadership, the cult of the group over that of personality. While ensuring the competence, control, and the balance of power relations among groups with the potential for rivalry, managerial leadership unfortunately does not necessarily ensure imagination, creativity, or ethical behavior in guiding the destinies of corporate enterprises.

If Zaleznik is correct, the prospects for strategic management are dim at best.

The articles by Mintzberg and Wrapp are concerned with the behavior patterns of the leaders of large organizations. Mintzberg dispenses with the classical view that managers plan, organize, coordinate, and control and then goes on to describe how top managers actually behave and the important roles they assume. H. Edward Wrapp extends Mintzberg's findings and discusses five ways that top managers can move their organizations forward.

George Albert Smith's "Questions the Business Leader Should Ask Himself" poses thirteen questions for the responsible executive. Smith argues that periodic review and answering of his questions is essential if top managers are to lead their organizations effectively.

The final two articles of this section and this volume are timely and topical. In "Directors' Responsibility for Corporate Strategy," Kenneth Andrews argues that boards of directors should require top management to develop corporate strategy, and that the board should then review and ratify the strategy. Until Andrews' suggestion is implemented, strategic management is not being practiced at all levels of management.

In "Managing Our Way to Economic Decline," Robert Hayes and William Abernathy make perhaps the strongest plea for leadership in the management of large corporations. Hayes and Abernathy contend that it is the application of modern management principles that is responsible for the deteriorating competitive positions of many American companies. Their solution is for more top managers to lead their organizations creatively and innovatively, rather than simply following the latest managerial fad.

28

Managers and Leaders
Are They Different?

ABRAHAM ZALEZNIK

Most societies, and that includes business organizations, are caught between two conflicting needs: one, for managers to maintain the balance of operations, and one for leaders to create new approaches and imagine new areas to explore. One might well ask why there is a conflict. Cannot both managers and leaders exist in the same society, or even better, cannot one person be both a manager and a leader? The author of this article does not say that is impossible but suggests that because leaders and managers are basically different types of people, the conditions favorable to the growth of one may be inimical to the other. Exploring the world views of managers and leaders, the author illustrates, using Alfred P. Sloan and Edwin Land among others as examples, that managers and leaders have different attitudes toward their goals, careers, relations with others, and themselves. And tracing their different lines of development, the author shows how leaders are of a psychologically different type than managers; their development depends on their forming a one-to-one relationship with a mentor.

What is the ideal way to develop leadership? Every society provides its own answer to this question, and each, in groping for answers, defines its deepest concerns about the purposes, distributions, and uses of power. Business has contributed its answer to the leadership question by evolving a new breed called the manager. Simultaneously, business has established a new power ethic that favors collective over individual leadership, the cult of the group over that of personality. While ensuring the competence, control, and the balance of power relations among groups with the potential for rivalry, managerial leadership unfortunately does not necessarily ensure imagination, creativity, or ethical behavior in guiding the destinies of corporate enterprises.

Leadership inevitably requires using power to influence the thoughts and actions of other people. Power in the hands of an individual entails human risks: first, the risk of equating power with the ability to get immediate results; second, the risk of ignoring the many different ways people can legitimately accumulate power; and third, the risk of losing self-control in the desire for power. The need to hedge these risks accounts in part for the development of collective leadership and the managerial ethic. Consequently, an inherent conservatism dominates the culture of large organizations. In *The Second American Revolution,* John D. Rockefeller, 3rd. describes the conservatism of organizations:

> An organization is a system, with a logic of its own, and all the weight of tradition and inertia. The deck is stacked in favor of the tried and proven way of doing things and against the taking of risks and striking out in new directions.[1]

Out of this conservatism and inertia organizations provide succession to power through the development of managers rather than individual leaders. And the irony of the managerial ethic is that it fosters a bureaucratic culture in business, supposedly the last bastion protecting us from the encroachments and controls of bureaucracy in government and education. Perhaps the risks associated with power in the hands of an individual may be necessary ones for business to take if organizations are to break free of their inertia and bureaucratic conservatism.

Manager Versus Leader Personality

Theodore Levitt has described the essential features of a managerial culture with its emphasis on rationality and control:

> Management consists of the rational assessment of a situation and the systematic selection of goals and purposes (what is to be done?); the systematic development of strategies to achieve these goals; the marshalling of the required resources; the rational design, organization, direction, and control of the activities required to attain the selected purposes; and, finally, the motivating and rewarding of people to do the work.[2]

In other words, whether his or her energies are directed toward goals, resources, organization structures, or people, a manager is a problem solver. The manager asks himself, "What problems have to be solved, and what are the best ways to achieve results so that people will continue to contribute to this organization?" In this conception, leadership is a practical effort to direct affairs; and to fulfill his task, a manager requires that many people operate at different levels of status and responsibility. Our democratic society is, in fact, unique in having solved the problem of providing well-trained managers for business. The same solution stands ready to be applied to government, education, health care, and other institutions. It takes neither genius nor heroism to be a manager, but rather persistence, tough-mindedness, hard work, intelligence, analytical ability, and, perhaps most important, tolerance and good will.

Another conception, however, attaches almost mystical beliefs to what leadership is and assumes that only great people are worthy of the drama of power and politics. Here, leadership is a psychodrama in which, as a precondition for control of a political structure, a lonely person must gain control of him or herself. Such an expectation of leadership contrasts sharply with the mundane, practical, and yet important conception that leadership is really managing work that other people do.

Two questions come to mind. Is this mystique of leadership merely a holdover from our collective childhood of dependency and our longing for good and heroic parents? Or, is there a basic truth lurking behind the need for leaders that no matter how competent managers are, their leadership stagnates because of their limitations in visualizing purposes and generating value in work? Without this imaginative capacity and the ability to communicate, managers, driven by their narrow purposes, perpetuate group conflicts instead of reforming them into broader desires and goals.

If indeed problems demand greatness, then, judging by past performance, the selection and development of leaders leave a great deal to chance. There are no known ways to train "great" leaders. Furthermore, beyond what we leave to chance, there is a deeper issue in the relationship between the need for competent managers and the longing for great leaders.

What it takes to ensure the supply of people who will assume practical responsibility may inhibit the development of great leaders. Conversely, the presence of great leaders may undermine the development of managers who become very anxious in the relative disorder that leaders seem to generate. The antagonism in aim (to have many competent managers as well as great leaders) often remains obscure in stable and well-developed societies. But the antagonism surfaces during periods of stress and change, as it did in the Western countries during both the Great Depression and World War II. The tension also appears in the struggle for power between theorists and professional managers in revolutionary societies.

It is easy enough to dismiss the dilemma I pose (of training managers while we may need new leaders, or leaders at the expense of managers) by saying that the need is for people who can be *both* managers and leaders. The truth of the matter as I see it, however, is that just as a managerial culture is different from the entrepreneurial culture that develops when leaders appear in organizations, managers and leaders are very different kinds of people. They differ in motivation, personal history, and in how they think and act.

A technologically oriented and economically successful society tends to depreciate the need for great leaders. Such societies hold a deep and abiding faith in rational methods of solving problems, including problems of value, economics, and justice. Once rational methods of solving problems are broken down into elements, organized, and taught as skills, then society's faith in technique over personal qualities in leadership remains the guiding conception for a democratic society contemplating its leadership require-ments. But there are times when tinkering and trial and error prove inade-quate to the emerging problems of selecting goals, allocating resources, and distributing wealth and opportunity. During such times, the democratic so-ciety needs to find leaders who use themselves as the instruments of learning and acting, instead of managers who use their accumulation of collective experience to get where they are going.

The most impressive spokesperson, as well as exemplar of the man-agerial viewpoint, was Alfred P. Sloan, Jr. who, along with Pierre du Pont, designed the modern corporate structure. Reflecting on what makes one management successful while another fails, Sloan suggested that "good man-agement rests on a reconciliation of centralization and decentralization, or 'decentralization with coordinated control' ."[3]

Sloan's conception of management, as well as his practice, developed by trial and error, and by the accumulation of experience, Sloan wrote:

> There is no hard and fast rule for sorting out the various responsibilities
> and the best way to assign them. The balance which is struck . . . varies
> according to what is being decided, the circumstances of the time, past
> experience, and the temperaments and skills of the executive involved.[4]

In other words, in much the same way that the inventors of the late nineteenth century tried, failed, and fitted until they hit on a product or method, managers who innovate in developing organizations are "tinker-ers." They do not have a grand design or experience the intuitive flash of insight that, borrowing from modern science, we have come to call the "breakthrough."

Managers and leaders differ fundamentally in their world views. The dimensions for assessing these differences include managers' and leaders' orientations toward their goals, their work, their human relations, and their selves.

Attitudes Toward Goals

Managers tend to adopt impersonal, if not passive, attitudes toward goals. Managerial goals arise out of necessities rather than desires, and, therefore, are deeply embedded in the history and culture of the organization.

Frederic G. Donner, chairman and chief executive officer of General Motors from 1958 to 1967, expressed this impersonal and passive attitude toward goals in defining GM's position on product development:

> . . . To meet the challenge of the marketplace, we must recognize changes
> in customer needs and desires far enough ahead to have the right products
> in the right places at the right time and in the right quantity.

> We must balance trends in preference against the many compromises
> that are necessary to make a final product that is both reliable and good
> looking, that performs well and that sells at a competitive price in the
> necessary volume. We must design, not just the cars we would like to
> build, but more importantly, the cars that our customers want to buy.[5]

Nowhere in this formulation of how a product comes into being is there
a notion that consumer tastes and preferences arise in part as a result of
what manufacturers do. In reality, through product design, advertising, and
promotion, consumers learn to like what they then say they need. Few would
argue that people who enjoy taking snapshots *need* a camera that also develops pictures. But in response to novelty, convenience, a shorter interval
between acting (taking the snap) and gaining pleasure (seeing the shot), the
Polaroid camera succeeded in the marketplace. But it is inconceivable that
Edwin Land responded to impressions of consumer need. Instead, he translated a technology (polarization of light) into a product, which proliferated
and stimulated consumers' desires.

The example of Polaroid and Land suggests how leaders think about
goals. They are active instead of reactive, shaping ideas instead of responding
to them. Leaders adopt a personal and active attitude toward goals. The
influence a leader exerts in altering moods, evoking images and expectations,
and in establishing specific desires and objectives determines the direction
a business takes. The net result of this influence is to change the way people
think about what is desirable, possible, and necessary.

Conceptions of Work

What do managers and leaders do? What is the nature of their respective
work?

Leaders and managers differ in their conceptions. Managers tend to
view work as an enabling process involving some combination of people and
ideas interacting to establish strategies and make decisions. Managers help
the process along by a range of skills, including calculating the interests in
opposition, staging and timing the surfacing of controversial issues, and
reducing tensions. In this enabling process, managers appear flexible in the
use of tactics: they negotiate and bargain, on the one hand, and use rewards
and punishments, and other forms of coercion, on the other. Machiavelli
wrote for managers and not necessarily for leaders.

Alfred Sloan illustrated how this enabling process works in situations
of conflict. The time was the early 1920s when the Ford Motor Co. still
dominated the automobile industry using, as did General Motors, the conventional water-cooled engine. With the full backing of Pierre du Pont,
Charles Kettering dedicated himself to the design of an air-cooled engine,
which, if successful, would have been a great technical and market coup for
GM. Kettering believed in his product, but the manufacturing division heads
at GM remained skeptical and later opposed the new design on two grounds:
first, that it was technically unreliable, and second, that the corporation was

putting all its eggs in one basket by investing in a new product instead of attending to the current marketing situation.

In the summer of 1923 after a series of false starts and after its decision to recall the copper-cooled Chevrolets from dealers and customers, GM management reorganized and finally scrapped the project. When it dawned on Kettering that the company had rejected the engine, he was deeply discouraged and wrote to Sloan that without the "organized resistance" against the project it would succeed and that unless the project were saved, he would leave the company.

Alfred Sloan was all too aware of the fact that Kettering was unhappy and indeed intended to leave General Motors. Sloan was also aware of the fact that, while the manufacturing divisions strongly opposed the new engine, Pierre du Pont supported Kettering. Furthermore, Sloan had himself gone on record in a letter to Kettering less than two years earlier expressing full confidence in him. The problem Sloan now had was to make his decision stick, keep Kettering in the organization (he was much too valuable to lose), avoid alienating du Pont, and encourage the division heads to move speedily in developing product lines using conventional water-cooled engines.

The actions that Sloan took in the face of this conflict reveal much about how managers work. First, he tried to reassure Kettering by presenting the problem in a very ambiguous fashion, suggesting that he and the Executive Committee sided with Kettering, but that it would not be practical to force the divisions to do what they were opposed to. He presented the problem as being a question of the people, not the product. Second, he proposed to reorganize around the problem by consolidating all functions in a new division that would be responsible for the design, production, and marketing of the new car. This solution, however, appeared as ambiguous as his efforts to placate and keep Kettering in General Motors. Sloan wrote: "My plan was to create an independent pilot operation under the sole jurisdiction of Mr. Kettering, a kind of copper-cooled-car division. Mr. Kettering would designate his own chief engineer and his production staff to solve the technical problems of manufacture."[6]

While Sloan did not discuss the practical value of this solution, which included saddling an inventor with management responsibility, he in effect used this plan to limit his conflict with Pierre du Pont.

In effect, the managerial solution that Sloan arranged and pressed for adoption limited the options available to others. The structural solution narrowed choices, even limiting emotional reactions to the point where the key people could do nothing but go along, and even allowed Sloan to say in his memorandum to du Pont, "We have discussed the matter with Mr. Kettering at some length this morning and he agrees with us absolutely on every point we made. He appears to receive the suggestion enthusiastically and has every confidence that it can be put across along these lines."[7]

Having placated people who opposed his views by developing a structural solution that appeared to give something but in reality only limited options, Sloan could then authorize the car division's general manger, with whom he basically agreed, to move quickly in designing water-cooled cars for the immediate market demand.

Years later Sloan wrote, evidently with tongue in cheek, "The copper-cooled car never came up again in a big way. It just died out, I don't know why."[8]

In order to get people to accept solutions to problems, managers need to coordinate and balance continually. Interestingly enough, this managerial work has much in common with what diplomats and mediators do, with Henry Kissinger apparently an outstanding practitioner. The manager aims at shifting balances of power toward solutions acceptable as a compromise among conflicting values.

What about leaders, what do they do? Where managers act to limit choices, leaders work in the opposite direction, to develop fresh approaches to long-standing problems and to open issues for new options. Stanley and Inge Hoffmann, political scientists, liken the leader's work to that of the artist. But unlike most artists, the leader himself is an integral part of the aesthetic product. One cannot look at a leader's art without looking at the artist. On Charles de Gaulle as a political artist, they wrote: "And each of his major political acts, however tortuous the means or the details, has been whole, indivisible and unmistakably his own, like an artistic act."[9]

The closest one can get to a product apart from the artist is the ideas that occupy, indeed at times obsess, the leader's mental life. To be effective, however, leaders need to project their ideas into images that excite people, and only then develop choices that give the projected images substance. Consequently, leaders create excitement in work.

John F. Kennedy's brief presidency shows both the strengths and weaknesses connected with the excitement leaders generate in their work. In his inaugural address he said, "Let every nation know, whether it wishes us well or ill, that we shall pay any price, bear any burden, meet any hardship, support any friend, oppose any foe, in order to assure the survival and the success of liberty."

This much-quoted statement forced people to react beyond immediate concerns and to identify with Kennedy and with important shared ideals. But upon closer scrutiny the statement must be seen as absurd because it promises a position which if in fact adopted, as in the Viet Nam War, could produce disastrous results. Yet unless expectations are aroused and mobilized, with all the dangers of frustration inherent in heightened desire, new thinking and new choice can never come to light.

Leaders work from high-risk positions, indeed often are temperamentally disposed to seek out risk and danger, especially where opportunity and reward appear high. From my observations, why one individual seeks risk while another approaches problems conservatively depends more on his or her personality and less on conscious choice. For some, especially those who become managers, the instinct for survival dominates their need for risk, and their ability to tolerate mundane, practical work assists their survival. The same cannot be said for leaders who sometimes react to mundane work as to an affliction.

Relations with Others

Managers prefer to work with people; they avoid solitary activity because it makes them anxious. Several years ago, I directed studies on the psychological aspects of career. The need to seek out others with whom to work and collaborate seemed to stand out as important characteristics of managers. When asked, for example, to write imaginative stories in response to a picture showing a single figure (a boy contemplating a violin, or a man silhouetted in a state of reflection), managers populated their stories with people. The following is an example of a manager's imaginative story about the young boy contemplating a violin:

> Mom and Dad insisted that Junior take music lessons so that someday he can become a concert musician. His instrument was ordered and had just arrived. Junior is weighing the alternatives of playing football with the other kids or playing with the squeak box. He can't understand how his parents could think a violin is better than a touchdown.
>
> After four months of practicing the violin, Junior has had more than enough, Daddy is going out of his mind, and Mommy is willing to give in reluctantly to the men's wishes. Football season is now over, but a good third baseman will take the field next spring.[10]

This story illustrates two themes that clarify managerial attitudes toward human relations. The first, as I have suggested, is to seek out activity with other people (i.e., the football team), and the second is to maintain a low level of emotional involvement in these relationships. The low emotional involvement appears in the writer's use of conventional metaphors, even clichés, and in the depiction of the ready transformation of potential conflict into harmonious decisions. In this case, Junior, Mommy, and Daddy agree to give up the violin for manly sports.

These two themes may seem paradoxical, but their coexistence supports what a manager does, including reconciling differences, seeking compromises, and establishing a balance of power. A further idea demonstrated by how the manager wrote the story is that managers may lack empathy, or the capacity to sense intuitively the thoughts and feelings of others. To illustrate attempts to be empathic, here is another story written to the same stimulus picture by someone considered by his peers to be a leader:

> This little boy has the appearance of being a sincere artist, one who is deeply affected by the violin, and has an intense desire to master the instrument.
>
> He seems to have just completed his normal practice session and appears to be somewhat crestfallen at his inability to produce the sounds which he is sure lie within the violin.

He appears to be in the process of making a vow to himself to expend
the necessary time and effort to play this instrument until he satisfies
himself that he is able to bring forth the qualities of music which he feels
within himself.

With this type of determination and carry through, this boy became one
of the great violinists of his day.[11]

Empathy is not simply a matter of paying attention to other people. It
is also the capacity to take in emotional signals and to make them mean
something in a relationship with an individual. People who describe another
person as "deeply affected" with "intense desire," as capable of feeling
"crestfallen" and as one who can "vow to himself," would seem to have
an inner perceptiveness that they can use in their relationships with others.

Managers relate to people according to the role they play in a sequence
of events or in a decision-making *process*, while leaders, who are concerned
with ideas, relate in more intuitive and empathetic ways. The manager's
orientation to people, as actors in a sequence of events, deflects his or her
attention away from the substance of people's concerns and toward their
roles in a process. The distinction is simply between a manager's attention
to *how* things get done and a leader's attention to *what* the events and
decisions mean to participants.

In recent years, managers have taken over from game theory the notion
that decision-making events can be one of two types: the win-lose situation
(or zero-sum game) or the win-win situation in which everybody in the action
comes out ahead. As part of the process of reconciling differences among
people and maintaining balances of power, managers strive to convert win-
lose into win-win situations.

As an illustration, take the decision of how to allocate capital resources
among operating divisions in a large, decentralized organization. On the face
of it, the dollars available for distribution are limited at any given time.
Presumably, therefore, the more one division gets, the less is available for
other divisions.

Managers tend to view this situation (as it affects human relations) as
a conversion issue: how to make what seems like a win-lose problem into
a win-win problem. Several solutions to this situation come to mind. First,
the manager focuses others' attention on procedure and not on substance.
Here the actors become engrossed in the bigger problem of *how* to make
decisions, not *what* decisions to make. Once committed to the bigger problem, the actors have to support the outcome since they were involved in
formulating decision rules. Because the actors believe in the rules they
formulated, they will accept present losses in the expectation that next time
they will win.

Second, the manager communicates to his or her subordinates indirectly, using "signals" instead of "messages." A signal has a number of
possible implicit positions in it, while a message clearly states a position.
Signals are inconclusive and subject to reinterpretation should people be-

come upset and angry, while messages involve the direct consequence that some people will indeed not like what they hear. The nature of messages heightens emotional response, and, as I have indicated, emotionally makes managers anxious. With signals, the question of who wins and who loses often becomes obscured.

Third, the manager plays for time. Managers seem to recognize that with the passage of time and the delay of major decisions, compromises emerge that take the sting out of win-lose situations; and the original "game" will be superseded by additional ones. Therefore, compromises may mean that one wins and loses simultaneously, depending on which of the games one evaluates.

There are undoubtedly many other tactical moves managers use to change human situations from win-lose to win-win. But the point to be made is that such tactics focus on the decision-making process itself and interest managers rather than leaders. The interest in tactics involves costs as well as benefits, including making organizations fatter in bureaucratic and political intrigue and leaner in direct, hard activity and warm human relationships. Consequently, one often hears subordinates characterize managers as in-scrutable, detached, and manipulative. These adjectives arise from the sub-ordinates' perception that they are linked together in a process whose pur-pose, beyond simply making decisions, is to maintain a controlled as well as rational and equitable structure. These adjectives suggest that managers need order in the face of the potential chaos that many fear in human re-lationships.

In contrast, one often hears leaders referred to in adjectives rich in emotional content. Leaders attract strong feelings of identity and difference, or of love and hate. Human relations in leader-dominated structures often appear turbulent, intense, and at times even disorganzied. Such an atmo-sphere intensifies individual motivation and often produces unanticipated outcomes. Does this intense motivation lead to innovation and high perfor-mance, or does it represent wasted energy?

Senses of Self

In *The Varieties of Religious Experience,* William James describes two basic personality types, "once-born" and "twice-born."[12] People of the former personality type are those for whom adjustments to life have been straight-forward and whose lives have been more or less a peaceful flow from the moment of their births. The twice-borns, on the other hand, have not had an easy time of it. Their lives are marked by a continual struggle to attain some sense of order. Unlike the once-borns they cannot take things for granted. According to James, these personalities have equally different world views. For a once-born personality, the sense of self, as a guide to conduct and attitude, derives from a feeling of being at home and in harmony with one's environment. For a twice-born, the sense of self derives from a feeling of profound separateness.

A sense of belonging or of being separate has a practical significance for the kinds of investments managers and leaders make in their careers. Managers see themselves as conservators and regulators of an existing order of affairs with which they personally identify and from which they gain rewards. Perpetuating and strengthening existing institutions enhance a manager's sense of self-worth: he or she is performing in a role that harmonizes with the ideals of duty and responsibility. William James had this harmony in mind—this sense of self as flowing easily to and from the outer world— in defining a once-born personality. If one feels oneself as a member of institutions, contributing to their well-being, then one fulfills a mission in life and feels rewarded for having measured up to ideals. This reward transcends material gains and answers the more fundamental desire for personal integrity which is achieved by identifying with existing institutions.

Leaders tend to be twice-born personalities, people who feel separate from their environment, including other people. They may work in organizations, but they never belong to them. Their sense of who they are does not depend upon memberships, work roles, or other social indicators of identity. What seems to follow from this idea about separateness is some theoretical basis for explaining why certain individuals search out opportunities for change. The methods to bring about change may be technological, political, or ideological, but the object is the same: to profoundly alter human, economic, and political relationships.

Sociologists refer to the preparation individuals undergo to perform in roles as the socialization process. Where individuals experience themselves as an integral part of the social structure (their self-esteem gains strength through participation and conformity), social standards exert powerful effects in maintaining the individual's personal sense of continuity, even beyond the early years in the family. The line of development from the family to schools, then to career is cumulative and reinforcing. When the line of development is not reinforcing because of significant disruptions in relationships or other problems experienced in the family or other social institutions, the individual turns inward and struggles to establish self-esteem, identity, and order. Here the psychological dynamics center on the experience with loss and the efforts at recovery.

In considering the development of leadership, we have to examine the two different courses of life history: (1) development through socialization, which prepares the individual to guide institutions and to maintain the existing balance of social relations; and (2) development through personal mastery, which impels an individual to struggle for psychological and social change. Society produces its managerial talent through the first line of development, while through the second leaders emerge.

Development of Leadership

The development of every person begins in the family. Each person experiences the traumas associated with separating from his or her parents, as well as the pain that follows such frustration. In the same vein, all individuals face the difficulties of achieving self-regulation and self-control. But for some, perhaps a majority, the fortunes of childhood provide adequate gratifications and sufficient opportunities to find substitutes for rewards no longer available. Such individuals, the "once-borns," make moderate identifications with parents and find a harmony between what they expect and what they are able to realize from life.

But suppose the pains of separation are amplified by a combination of parental demands and the individual's needs to the degree that a sense of isolation, of being special, and of wariness disrupts the bonds that attach children to parents and other authority figures? Under such conditions, and given a special aptitude, the origins of which remain mysterious, the person becomes deeply involved in his or her inner world at the expense of interest in the outer world. For such a person, self-esteem no longer depends solely upon positive attachments and real rewards. A form a self-reliance takes hold along with expectations of performance and achievement, and perhaps even the desire to do great works.

Such self-perceptions can come to nothing if the individual's talents are negligible. Even with strong talents, there are no guarantees that achievement will follow, let alone that the end result will be for good rather than evil. Other factors enter into development. For one thing, leaders are like artists and other gifted people who often struggle with neuroses; their ability to function varies considerably even over the short run, and some potential leaders may lose the struggle altogether. Also, beyond early childhood, the patterns of development that affect managers and leaders involve the selective influence of particular people. Just as they appear flexible and evenly distributed in the types of talents available for development, managers form moderate and widely distributed attachments. Leaders, on the other hand, establish, and also break off, intensive one-to-one relationships.

It is a common observation that people with great talents are often only indifferent students. No one, for example, could have predicted Einstein's great achievements on the basis of his mediocre record in school. The reason for mediocrity is obviously not the absence of ability. It may result, instead, from self-absorption and the inability to pay attention to the ordinary tasks at hand. The only sure way an individual can interrupt reverie-like preoccupation and self-absorption is to form a deep attachment to a great teacher or other benevolent person who understands and has the ability to communicate with the gifted individual.

Whether gifted individuals find what they need in one-to-one relationships depends on the availability of sensitive and intuitive mentors who have a vocation in cultivating talent. Fortunately, when the generations do meet and the self-selections occur, we learn more about how to develop leaders and how talented people of different generations influence each other.

While apparently destined for a mediocre career, people who form important one-to-one relationships are able to accelerate and intensify their development through an apprenticeship. The background for such apprenticeships, or the psychological readiness of an individual to benefit from an intensive relationship, depends upon some experience in life that forces the indivdual to turn inward. A case example will make this point clearer. This example comes from the life of Dwight David Eisenhower, and illustrates the transformation of a career from competent to outstanding.[13]

Dwight Eisenhower's early career in the Army foreshadowed very little about his future development. During World War I, while some of his West Point classmates were already experiencing the war first-hand in France, Eisenhower felt "embedded in the monotony and unsought safety of the Zone of the Interior . . . that was intolerable punishment."[14]

Shortly after World War I, Eisenhower, then a young officer somewhat pessimistic about his career chances, asked for a transfer to Panama to work under General Fox Connor, a senior officer whom Eisenhower admired. The army turned down Eisenhower's request. This setback was very much on Eisenhower's mind when Ikey, his first-born son, succumbed to influenza. By some sense of responsibility for its own, the army transferred Eisenhower to Panama, where he took up his duties under General Connor with the shadow of his lost son very much upon him.

In a relationship with the kind of father he would have wanted to be, Eisenhower reverted to being the son he lost. In this highly charged situation, Eisenhower began to learn from his mentor. General Connor offered, and Eisenhower gladly took, a magnificent tutorial on the military. The effects of this relationship on Eisenhower cannot be measured quantitatively, but, in Eisenhower's own reflections and the unfolding of his career, one cannot overestimate its significance in the reintegration of a person shattered by grief.

As Eisenhower wrote later about Connor,

> Life with General Connor was a sort of graduate school in military affairs and the humanities, leavened by a man who was experienced in his knowledge of men and their conduct. I can never adequately express my gratitude to this one gentleman. . . . In a lifetime of association with great and good men, he is the one more or less invisible figure to whom I owe an incalculable debt.[15]

Some time after his tour of duty with General Connor, Eisenhower's breakthrough occurred. He received orders to attend the Command and General Staff School at Fort Leavenworth, one of the most competitive schools in the army. It was a coveted appointment, and Eisenhower took advantage of the opportunity. Unlike his performance in high school and West Point, his work at the Command School was excellent; he was graduated first in his class.

Psychological biographies of gifted people repeatedly demonstrate the important part a mentor plays in developing an individual. Andrew Carnegie owed much to his senior, Thomas A. Scott. As head of the Western Division of the Pennsylvania Railroad, Scott recognized talent and the desire to learn in the young telegrapher assigned to him. By giving Carnegie increasing responsibility and by providing him with the opportunity to learn through close personal observation, Scott added to Carnegie's self-confidence and sense of achievement. Because of his own personal strength and achievement, Scott did not fear Carnegie's aggressiveness. Rather, he gave it full play in encouraging Carnegie's initiative.

Mentors take risks with people. They bet initially on talent they perceive in younger people. Mentors also risk emotional involvement in working closely with their juniors. The risks do not always pay off, but the willingness to take them appears crucial in developing leaders.

Can Organizations Develop Leaders?

The examples I have given of how leaders develop suggest the importance of personal influence and the one-to-one relationship. For organizations to encourage consciously the development of leaders as compared with managers would mean developing one-to-one relationships between junior and senior executives and, more important, fostering a culture of individualism and possibly elitism. The elitism arises out of the desire to identify talent and other qualities suggestive of the ability to lead and not simply to manage.

The Jewel Companies Inc. enjoy a reputation for developing talented people. The chairman and chief executive officer, Donald S. Perkins, is perhaps a good example of a person brought along through the mentor approach. Franklin J. Lunding, who was Perkins's mentor, expressed the philosophy of taking risks with young people this way: "Young people today want in on the action. They don't want to sit around for six months trimming lettuce."[16]

This statement runs counter to the culture that attaches primary importance to slow progression based on experience and proved competence. It is a high-risk philosophy, one that requires time for the attachment between senior and junior people to grow and be meaningful, and one that is bound to produce more failures than successes.

The elitism is an especially sensitive issue. At Jewel the MBA degree symbolized the elite. Lunding attracted Perkins to Jewel at a time when business school graduates had little interest in retailing in general, and food distribution in particular. Yet the elitism seemed to pay off: not only did Perkins become the president at age 37, but also under the leadership of young executives recruited into Jewel with the promise of opportunity for growth and advancement, Jewel managed to diversify into discount and drug chains and still remain strong in food retailing. By assigning each recruit to a vice president who acted as sponsor, Jewel evidently tried to build a structure around the mentor approach to developing leaders. To counteract the elitism implied in such an approach, the company also introduced an "equalizer" in what Perkins described as "the first assistant philosophy." Perkins stated:

> Being a good first assistant means that each management person thinks of himself not as the order-giving, domineering boss, but as the first assistant to those who "report" to him in a more typical organizational sense. Thus we mentally turn our organizational charts upside-down and challenge ourselves to seek ways in which we can lead . . . by helping . . . by teaching . . . by listening . . . and by managing in the true democratic sense . . . that is, with the consent of the managed. Thus the satisfactions of leadership come from helping others to get things done and changed—and not from getting credit for doing and changing things ourselves.[17]

While this statement would seem to be more egalitarian than elitist, it does reinforce a youth-oriented culture since it defines the senior officer's job as primarily helping the junior person.

A myth about how people learn and develop that seems to have taken hold in the American culture also dominates thinking in business. The myth is that people learn best from their peers. Supposedly, the threat of evaluation and even humiliation recedes in peer relations because of the tendency for mutual identification and the social restraints on authoritarian behavior among equals. Peer training in organizations occurs in various forms. The use, for example, of task forces made up of peers from several interested occupational groups (sales, production, research, and finance) supposedly removes the restraints of authority on the individual's willingness to assert and exchange ideas. As a result, so the theory goes, people interact more freely, listen more objectively to criticism and other points of view and, finally, learn from this healthy interchange.

Another application of peer training exists in some large corporations, such as Philips, N.V. in Holland, where organization structure is built on the principle of joint responsibility of two peers, one representing the commercial end of the business and the other the technical. Formally, both hold equal responsibility for geographic operations or product groups, as the case may be. As a practical matter, it may turn out that one or the other of the peers dominates the management. Nevertheless, the main interaction is between two or more equals.

The principal question I would raise about such arrangements is whether they perpetuate the managerial orientation and preclude the formation of one-to-one relationships between senior people and potential leaders.

Aware of the possible stifling effects of peer relationships on aggressiveness and individual initiative, another company, much smaller than Philips, utilizes joint responsibility of peers for operating units, with one important difference. The chief executive of this company encourages competition and rivalry among peers, ultimately appointing the one who comes out on top for increased responsibility. These hybrid arrangements produce some unintended consequences that can be disastrous. There is no easy way to limit rivalry. Instead, it permeates all levels of the operation and opens the way for the formation of cliques in an atmosphere of intrigue.

A large, integrated oil company has accepted the importance of developing leaders through the direct influence of senior on junior executives. One chairman and chief executive officer regularly selected one talented university graduate whom he appointed his special assistant, and with whom he would work closely for a year. At the end of the year, the junior executive would become available for assignment to one of the operating divisions, where he would be assigned to a responsible post rather than a training position. The mentor relationship had acquainted the junior executive firsthand with the use of power, and with the important antidotes to the power disease called *hubris*—performance and integrity.

Working in one-to-one relationships, where there is a formal and recognized difference in the power of the actors, takes a great deal of tolerance for emotional interchange. This interchange, inevitable in close working arrangements, probably accounts for the reluctance of many executives to become involved in such relationships. *Fortune* carried an interesting story on the departure of a key executive, John W. Hanley, from the top management of Procter & Gamble, for the chief executive officer position at Monsanto.[18] According to this account, the chief executive and chairman of P&G passed over Hanley for appointment to the presidency and named another executive vice president to this post instead.

The chairman evidently felt he could not work well with Hanley who, by his own acknowledgement, was aggressive, eager to experiment and change practices, and constantly challenged his superior. A chief executive officer naturally has the right to select people with whom he or she feels congenial. But I wonder whether a greater capacity on the part of senior officers to tolerate the competitive impulses and behavior of their subordinates might not be healthy for corporations. At least a greater tolerance for interchange would not favor the managerial team player at the expense of the individual who might become a leader.

I am constantly surprised at the frequency with which chief executives feel threatened by open challenges to their ideas, as though the source of their authority, rather than their specific ideas, were at issue. In one case a chief executive officer, who was troubled by the aggressiveness and sometimes outright rudeness of one of his talented vice presidents, used various indirect methods such as group meetings and hints from outside directors to avoid dealing with his subordinate. I advised the executive to deal head-on with what irritated him. I suggested that by direct, face-to-face confrontation, both he and his subordinate would learn to validate the distinction between the authority to be preserved and the issues to be debated.

To confront is also to tolerate aggressive interchange and has the net effect of stripping away the veils of ambiguity and signaling so characteristic of managerial cultures, as well as encouraging the emotional relationship leaders need if they are to survive.

Notes

1. John D. Rockefeller, 3rd., *The Second American Revolution* (New York, Harper & Row, 1973), p. 72.

2. Theodore Levitt, "Management and the Post Industrial Society," *The Public Interest,* Summer 1976, p. 73.

3. Alfred P. Sloan, Jr., *My Years with General Motors* (New York, Doubleday, 1964), p. 429.

4. Ibid., p. 429.

5. Ibid., p. 440.

6. Ibid., p. 91.

7. Ibid., p. 91.

8. Ibid., p. 93.

9. Stanley and Inge Hoffmann, "The Will for Grandeur: de Gaulle as Political Artist," *Daedalus,* Summer 1968, p. 849.

10. Abraham Zaleznik, Gene W. Dalton, and Louis B. Barnes, *Orientation and Conflict in Career* (Boston, Division of Research, Harvard Business School, 1970), p. 316.

11. Ibid., p. 294.

12. William James, *Varieties of Religious Experience* (New York, Mentor Books, 1958).

13. This example is included in Abraham Zaleznik and Manfred F. R. Kets de Vries, *Power and the Corporate Mind* (Boston, Houghton Mifflin, 1975).

14. Dwight D. Eisenhower, *At Ease: Stories I Tell to Friends* (New York, Doubleday, 1967), p. 136.

15. Ibid., p. 187.

16. "Jewel Lets Young Men Make Mistakes," *Business Week,* January 17, 1970, p. 90.

17. "What Makes Jewel Shine so Bright," *Progressive Grocer,* September 1973, p. 76.

18. "Jack Hanley Got There by Selling Harder," *Fortune,* November 1976.

29

The Manager's Job

Folklore and Fact

HENRY MINTZBERG

Just what does the manager do? For years the manager, the heart of the organization, has been assumed to be like an orchestra leader, controlling the various parts of his or her organization with the ease and precision of a Seiji Ozawa. However, when one looks at the few studies that have been done—covering managerial positions from the president of the United States to street gang leaders—the facts show that managers are not reflective, regulated workers, informed by their massive MIS systems, scientific and professional. The evidence suggests that they play a complex, intertwined combination of interpersonal, informational, and decisional roles. The author's message is that if managers want to be more effective, they must recognize what their job really is and then use the resources at hand to support rather than hamper their own nature. Understanding their jobs as well as understanding themselves takes both introspection and objectivity on the managers' part. At the end of the article the author includes a set of self-study questions to help provide that insight.

If you ask managers what they do, they will most likely tell you that they plan, organize, coordinate, and control. Then watch what they do. Don't be surprised if you can't relate what you see to these four words.

When they are called and told that one of their factories has just burned down, and they advise the caller to see whether temporary arrangements can be made to supply customers through a foreign subsidiary, are they planning, organizing, coordinating, or controlling? How about when they present a gold watch to a retiring employee? Or when they attend a conference to meet people in the trade? Or on returning from that conference, when they tell one of their employees about an interesting product idea they picked up there?

The fact is that these four words, which have dominated management vocabulary since the French industrialist Henri Fayol first introduced them

462

in 1916, tell us little about what managers actually do. At best, they indicate some vague objectives managers have when they work.

The field of management, so devoted to progress change, has for more than half a century not seriously addressed *the* basic question: What do managers do? Without a proper answer, how can we teach management? How can we design planning or information systems for managers? How can we improve the practice of management at all?

Our ignorance of the nature of managerial work shows up in various ways in the modern organization—in the boast by the successful manager that he or she never spent a single day in a management training program; in the turnover of corporate planners who never quite understood what it was the manager wanted; in the computer consoles gathering dust in the back room because the managers never used the fancy on-line MIS some analyst thought they needed. Perhaps most important, our ignorance shows up in the inability of our large public organizations to come to grips with some of their most serious policy problems.

Somehow, in the rush to automate production, to use management science in the functional areas of marketing and finance, and to apply the skills of the behavioral scientist to the problem of worker motivation, the manager—that person in charge of the organization or one of its subunits—has been forgotten.

My intention in this article is simple: to break the reader away from Fayol's words and introduce him to a more supportable, and what I believe to be a more useful, description of managerial work. This description derives from my review and synthesis of the available research on how various managers have spent their time.

In some studies, managers were observed intensively ("shadowed" is the term some of them used); in a number of others, they kept detailed diaries of their activities; in a few studies, their records were analyzed. All kinds of managers were studied—foremen, factory supervisors, staff managers, field sales managers, hospital administrators, presidents of companies and nations, and even street gang leaders. These "managers" worked in the United States, Canada, Sweden, and Great Britain. In Appendix A is a brief review of the major studies that I found most useful in developing this description, including my own study of five American chief executive officers.

A synthesis of these findings paints an interesting picture, one as different from Fayol's classical view as a cubist abstract is from a Renaissance painting. In a sense, this picture will be obvious to anyone who has ever spent a day in a manager's office, either in front of the desk or behind it. Yet, at the same time, this picture may turn out to be revolutionary, in that it throws into doubt so much of the folklore that we have accepted about the manager's work.

I first discuss some of this folklore and contrast it with some of the discoveries of systematic research—the hard facts about how managers spend their time. Then I synthesize these research findings in a description of ten roles that seem to describe the essential content of all managers' jobs. In a concluding section, I discuss a number of implications of this synthesis for those trying to achieve more effective management, both in classrooms and in the business world.

Some Folklore and Facts About Managerial Work

There are four myths about the manager's job that do not bear up under careful scrutiny of the facts.

1. *Folklore: The manager is a reflective, systematic planner.* The evidence on this issue is overwhelming, but not a shred of it supports this statement.

Fact: *Study after study has shown that managers work at an unrelenting pace, that their activities are characterized by brevity, variety, and discontinuity, and that they are strongly oriented to action and dislike reflective activities.* Consider this evidence:

☐   Half the activities engaged in by the five chief executives of my study lasted less than nine minutes and only 10% exceeded one hour.[1] A study of 56 U.S. foremen found that they averaged 583 activities per eight-hour shift, an average of 1 every 48 seconds.[2] The work pace for both chief executives and foremen was unrelenting. The chief executives met a steady stream of callers and mail from the moment they arrived in the morning until they left in the evening. Coffee breaks and lunches were inevitably work related, and ever-present subordinates seemed to usurp any free moment.

☐   A diary study of 160 British middle and top managers found that they worked for a half hour or more without interruption only about once every two days.[3]

☐   Of the verbal contacts of the chief executives in my study, 93% were arranged on an ad hoc basis. Only 1% of the executives' time was spent in open-ended observational tours. Only 1 out of 368 verbal contacts was unrelated to a specific issue and could be called general planning. Another researcher finds that "in not *one single case* did a manager report the obtaining of important external information from a general conversation or other undirected personal communication."[4]

☐   No study has found important patterns in the way managers schedule their time. They seem to jump from issue to issue, continually responding to the needs of the moment.

Is this the planner that the classical view describes? Hardly. How, then, can we explain this behavior? The manager is simply responding to the pressures of his or her job. I found that my chief executives terminated many of their own activities, often leaving meetings before the end, and interrupted their desk work to call in subordinates. One president not only placed his desk so that he could look down a long hallway but also left his door open when he was alone—an invitation for subordinates to come in and interrupt him.

Clearly, these managers wanted to encourage the flow of current information. But more significantly, they seemed to be conditioned by their own work loads. They appreciated the opportunity cost of their own time, and they were continually aware of their ever-present obligations—mail to be answered, callers to attend to, and so on. It seems that no matter what they are doing, managers are plagued by the possibilities of what they might do and what they must do.

When managers must plan, they seem to do so implicitly in the context of daily actions, not in some abstract process reserved for two weeks in the organization's mountain retreat. The plans of the chief executives I studied seemed to exist only in their heads—as flexible, but often specific, intentions. The traditional literature notwithstanding, the job of managing does not breed reflective planners; managers are real-time responders to stimuli, individuals who are conditioned by their jobs to prefer live to delayed action.

2. *Folklore: The effective manager has no regular duties to perform.*   Managers are constantly being told to spend more time planning and delegating, and less time seeing customers and engaging in negotiations. These are not, after all, the true tasks of the manager. To use the popular analogy, good managers, like good conductors, carefully orchestrate everything in advance, then sit back to enjoy the fruits of their labor, responding occasionally to an unforeseeable exception.

But here again the pleasant abstraction just does not seem to hold up. We had better take a closer look at those activities managers feel compelled to engage in before we arbitrarily define them away.

Fact: *In addition to handling exceptions, managerial work involves performing a number of regular duties, including ritual and ceremony, negotiations, and processing of soft information that links the organization with its environment.* Consider some evidence from the research studies:

☐ A study of the work of the presidents of small companies found that they engaged in routine activities because their companies could not afford staff specialists and were so thin on operating personnel that a single absence often required the president to substitute.[5]

☐ One study of field sales managers and another of chief executives suggest that it is a natural part of both jobs to see important customers, assuming the managers wish to keep those customers.[6]

☐ Someone, only half in jest, once described the manager as that person who sees visitors so that everyone else can get his work done.

In my study, I found that certain ceremonial duties—meeting visiting dignitaries, giving out gold watches, presiding at Christmas dinners—were an intrinsic part of the chief executive's job.

☐   Studies of managers' information flow suggest that managers play a key role in securing "soft" external information (much of it available only to them because of their status) and in passing it along to their subordinates.

3.   *Folklore: The senior manager needs aggregated information, which a formal management information system best provides.*   Not too long ago, the words *total information system* were everywhere in the management literature. In keeping with the classical view of the manager as that individual perched on the apex of a regulated, hierarchical system, the literature's manager was to receive all his or her important information from a giant, comprehensive MIS.

But lately, as it has become increasingly evident that these giant MIS systems are not working—that managers are simply not using them—the enthusiasm has waned. A look at how managers actually process information makes the reason quite clear. Managers have five media at their command—documents, telephone calls, scheduled and unscheduled meetings, and observational tours.

Fact: *Managers strongly favor the verbal media—namely, telephone calls and meetings.* The evidence comes from every single study of managerial work. Consider the following:

☐   In two British studies, managers spent an average of 66% and 80% of their time in verbal (oral) communication.[7] In my study of five American chief executives, the figure was 78%.

☐   These five chief executives treated mail processing as a burden to be dispensed with. One came in Saturday morning to process 142 pieces of mail in just over three hours, to "get rid of all the stuff." This same manager looked at the first piece of "hard" mail he had received all week, a standard cost report, and put it aside with the comment, "I never look at this."

☐   These same five chief executives responded immediately to 2 of the 40 routine reports they received during the five weeks of my study and to four items in the 104 periodicals. They skimmed most of these periodicals in seconds, almost ritualistically. In all, these chief executives of good-sized organizations initiated on their own—that is, not in response to something else—a grand total of 25 pieces of mail during the 24 days I observed them.

An analysis of the mail the executives received reveals an interesting picture—only 13% was of specific and immediate use. So now we have another piece in the puzzle: not much of the mail provides live, current information—the action of a competitor, the mood of a government legislator, or the rating of last night's television show. Yet this is the information that drove the managers, interrupting their meetings and rescheduling their workdays.

Consider another interesting finding. Managers seem to cherish "soft" information, especially gossip, hearsay, and speculation. Why? The reason is its timeliness; today's gossip may be tomorrow's fact. The manager who is not accessible for the telephone call informing him that his biggest customer was seen golfing with his main competitor may read about a dramatic drop in sales in the next quarterly report. But then it's too late.

To assess the value of historical, aggregated, "hard" MIS information, consider two of the manager's prime uses for his information—to identify problems and opportunities[8] and to build his own mental models of the things around him (e.g., how his organization's budget system works, how his customers buy his product, how changes in the economy affect his organization, and so on). Every bit of evidence suggests that the manager identifies decision situations and builds models not with the aggregated abstractions an MIS provides, but with specific tidbits of data.

Consider the words of Richard Neustadt, who studied the information-collecting habits of Presidents Roosevelt, Truman, and Eisenhower:

> It is not information of a general sort that helps a President see personal stakes; not summaries, not surveys, not the *bland amalgams*. Rather . . . it is the odds and ends of *tangible detail* that pieced together in his mind illuminate the underside of issues put before him. To help himself he must reach out as widely as he can for every scrap of fact, opinion, gossip, bearing on his interests and relationships as President. He must become his own director of his own central intelligence.[9]

The manager's emphasis on the verbal media raises two important points:

First, verbal information is stored in the brains of people. Only when people write this information down can it be stored in the files of the organization—whether in metal cabinets or on magnetic tape—and managers apparently do not write down much of what they hear. Thus the strategic data bank of the organization is not in the memory of its computers but in the minds of its managers.

Second, the manager's extensive use of verbal media helps to explain why he is reluctant to delegate tasks. When we note that most of the manager's important information comes in verbal form and is stored in his head, we can well appreciate his reluctance. It is not as if he can hand a dossier over to someone; he must take the time to "dump memory"—to tell that someone all he knows about the subject. But this could take so long that the manager may find it easier to do the task himself. Thus the manager is damned by his own information system to a "dilemma of delegation"—to do too much himself or to delegate to his subordinates with inadequate briefing.

4. *Folklore: Management is, or at least is quickly becoming, a science and a profession.* By almost any definitions of *science* and *profession,* this statement is false. Brief observation of any manager will quickly lay to rest the notion that managers practice a science. A science involves the enaction of systematic, analytically determined procedures or programs. If we do not even know what procedures managers use, how can we prescribe them by scientific analysis? And how can we call management a profession if we cannot specify what managers are to learn? For after all, a profession involves "knowledge of some department of learning or science" *(Random House Dictionary).*[10]

Fact: *The managers' programs—to schedule time, process information, make decisions, and so on—remain locked deep inside their brains.* Thus, to describe these programs, we rely on words like *judgment* and *intuition,* seldom stopping to realize that they are merely labels for our ignorance.

I was struck during my study by the fact that the executives I was observing—all very competent by any standard—are fundamentally indistinguishable from their counterparts of a hundred years ago (or a thousand years ago, for that matter). The information they need differs, but they seek it in the same way—by word of mouth. Their decisions concern modern technology, but the procedures they use to make them are the same as the procedures of the nineteenth-century manager. Even the computer, so important for the specialized work of the organization, has apparently had no influence on the work procedures of general managers. In fact, the manager is in a kind of loop, with increasingly heavy work pressures but no aid forthcoming from management science.

Considering the facts about managerial work, we can see that the manager's job is enormously complicated and difficult. Managers are overburdened with obligations; yet they cannot easily delegate their tasks. As a result, they are driven to overwork and are forced to do many tasks superficially. Brevity, fragmentation, and verbal communication characterize their work. Yet these are the very characteristics of managerial work that have impeded scientific attempts to improve it. As a result, management scientists have concentrated their efforts on the specialized functions of the organization, where they could more easily analyze the procedures and quantify the relevant information.[11]

But the pressures of the managerial job are becoming worse. Where before managers needed only to respond to owners and directors, now they find that subordinates with democratic norms continually reduce their freedom to issue unexplained orders, and a growing number of outside influences (consumer groups, government agencies, and so on) expect their attention. And managers have had nowhere to turn for help. The first step in providing managers with some help is to find out what their job really is.

Back to a Basic Description of Managerial Work

Now let us try to put some of the pieces of this puzzle together. Earlier, I defined the manager as that person in charge of an organization or one of its subunits. Besides chief executive officers, this definition would include vice presidents, bishops, foremen, hockey coaches, and prime ministers. Can all of these people have anything in common? Indeed they can. For an important starting point, all are vested with formal authority over an organizational unit. From formal authority comes status, which leads to various interpersonal relations, and from these come access to information. Information, in turn, enables managers to make decisions and strategies for their units.

The manager's job can be described in terms of various "roles," or organized sets of behaviors identified with a position. My description, shown in Exhibit 1, comprises ten roles. As we shall see, formal authority gives rise to the three interpersonal roles, which in turn give rise to the three informational roles; these two sets of roles enable the manager to play the four decisional roles.

Interpersonal Roles

Three of the manager's roles arise directly from his or her formal authority and involve basic interpersonal relationships.

1. First is the *figurehead* role. By virtue of his or her position as head of an organizational unit, every manager must perform some duties of a

Exhibit 1.   The Manager's Roles

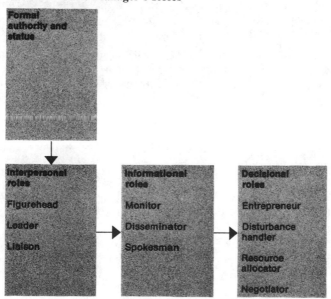

ceremonial nature. The president greets the touring dignitaries, the foreman attends the wedding of a lathe operator, and the sales manager takes an important customer to lunch.

The chief executives of my study spent 12% of their contact time on ceremonial duties; 17% of their incoming mail dealt with acknowledgements and requests related to their status. For example, a letter to a company president requested free merchandise for a crippled schoolchild; diplomas were put on the desk of the school superintendent for his signature.

Duties that involve interpersonal roles may sometimes be routine, involving little serious communication and no important decision making. Nevertheless, they are important to the smooth functioning of an organization and cannot be ignored by the manager.

2.   Because they are in charge of an organizational unit, managers are responsible for the work of the people of that unit. Their actions in this regard constitute the *leader* role. Some of these actions involve leadership directly—for example, in most organizations managers are normally responsible for hiring and training their own staff.

In addition, there is the indirect exercise of the leader role. Every manager must motivate and encourage his employees, somehow reconciling their individual needs with the goals of the organization. In virtually every contact the manager has with his employees, subordinates seeking leadership clues probe his actions: "Does he approve?" "How would he like the report to turn out?" "Is he more interested in market share than high profits?"

The influence of the manager is most clearly seen in the leader role. Formal authority vests him with great potential power; leadership determines in large part how much of it he will realize.

3.   The literature of management has always recognized the leader role, particularly those aspects of it related to motivation. In comparison, until recently it has hardly mentioned the *liaison* role, in which managers make contacts outside their vertical chain of command. This is remarkable in light of the finding of virtually every study of managerial work that managers spend as much time with peers and other people outside their units as they do with their own subordinates—and, surprisingly, very little time with their own superiors.

In Rosemary Stewart's diary study, the 160 British middle and top managers spent 47% of their time with peers, 41% of their time with people outside their unit, and only 12% of their time with their superiors. For Robert H. Guest's study of U.S. foremen, the figures were 44%, 46%, and 10%. The chief executives of my study averaged 44% of their contact time with people outside their organizations, 48% with subordinates, and 7% with directors and trustees.

The contacts the five CEOs made were with an incredibly wide range of people: subordinates; clients, business associates, and suppliers; and peers—managers of similar organizations, government and trade organization officials, fellow directors on outside boards, and independents with no relevant organizational affiliations. The chief executives' time with and mail from these groups is shown in Exhibit 2. Guest's study of foremen shows, likewise, that their contacts were numerous and wide ranging, seldom involving fewer than 25 individuals, and often more than 50.

As we shall see shortly, the manager cultivates such contacts largely to find information. In effect, the liaison role is devoted to building up the manager's own external information system—informal, private, verbal, but, nevertheless, effective.

Informational Roles

By virtue of their interpersonal contacts, both with their subordinates and with their network of contacts, managers emerge as nerve centers of their organizational units. They may not know everything, but they typically know more than any member of their staffs.

Studies have shown this relationship to hold for all managers, from street gang leaders to U.S. presidents. In *The Human Group*, George C. Homans explains how, because they were at the center of the information flow in their own gangs and were also in close touch with other gang leaders, street gang leaders were better informed than any of their followers.[12] And

Exhibit 2.   The Chief Executive's Contacts

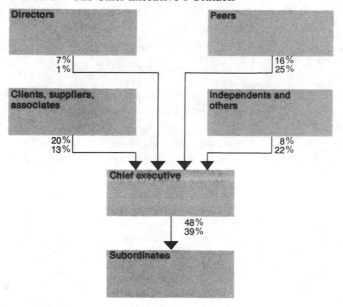

Note: The top figure indicates the proportion of total contact time spent with each group and the bottom figure, the proportion of mail from each group.

Richard Neustadt describes the following account from his study of Franklin D. Roosevelt:

> The essence of Roosevelt's technique for information-gathering was competition. "He would call you in," one of his aides once told me, "and he'd ask you to get the story on some complicated business, and you'd come back after a couple of days of hard labor and present the juicy morsel you'd uncovered under a stone somewhere, and *then* you'd find out he knew all about it, along with something else you *didn't* know. Where he got this information from he wouldn't mention, usually, but after he had done this to you once or twice you got damn careful about *your* information."[13]

We can see where Roosevelt "got this information" when we consider the relationship between the interpersonal and informational roles. As leader, the manager has formal and easy access to every member of her staff. Hence, as noted earlier, she tends to know more about her own unit than anyone else does. In addition, her liaison contacts expose the manager to external information to which her subordinates often lack access. Many of these contacts are with other managers of equal status, who are themselves nerve centers in their organization. In this way, the manager develops a powerful data base of information.

The processing of information is a key part of the manager's job. In my study, the chief executives spent 40% of their contact time on activities devoted exclusively to the transmission of information; 70% of their incoming mail was purely informational (as opposed to requests for action). The manager does not leave meetings or hang up the telephone in order to get back to work. In large part, communication *is* his work. Three roles describe these informational aspects of managerial work.

1 As *monitor,* managers perpetually scan their environment for information, interrogate their liaison contacts and their subordinates, and receive unsolicited information, much of it as a result of the network of personal contacts they have developed. Remember that a good part of the information managers collect in their monitor role arrives in verbal form, often as gossip, hearsay, and speculation. By virtue of their contacts, managers have a natural advantage in collecting this soft information for their organizations.

2 They must share and distribute much of this information. Information they glean from outside personal contacts may be needed within their organizations. In their *disseminator* role, managers pass some of their privileged information directly to their subordinates, who would otherwise have no access to it. When their subordinates lack easy contact with one another, managers will sometimes pass information from one to another.

3 In their *spokesman* role, managers send some of their information

to people outside their unit—a president makes a speech to lobby for an organizational cause, or a foreman suggests a product modification to a supplier. In addition, as part of their role as spokesman, all managers must inform and satisfy the influential people who control their organizational unit. For the foreman, this may simply involve keeping the plant manager informed about the flow of work through the shop.

The president of a large corporation, however, may spend a great amount of his time dealing with a host of influences. Directors and shareholders must be advised about financial performance; consumer groups must be assured that the organization is fulfilling its social responsibilities; and government officials must be satisfied that the organization is abiding by the law.

Decisional Roles

Information is not, of course, an end in itself; it is the basic input to decision making. One thing is clear in the study of managerial work: managers play the major role in their unit's decision-making system. As its formal authority, only they can commit the unit to important new courses of action; and as its nerve center, only they have full and current information to make the set of decisions that determines the unit's strategy. Four roles describe the manager as decision maker.

1. As *entrepreneurs,* managers seek to improve their unit, to adapt it to changing conditions in the environment. In his monitor role, the president is constantly on the lookout for new ideas. When a good one appears, he initiates a development project that he may supervise himself or delegate to an employee (perhaps with the stipulation that he must approve the final proposal).

There are two interesting features about these development projects at the chief executive level.

First, these projects do not involve single decisions or even unified clusters of decisions. Rather, they emerge as a series of small decisions and actions sequenced over time. Apparently, the chief executives prolong each project so that they can fit it bit by bit into their busy, disjointed schedule and so that they can gradually come to comprehend the issue, if it is a complex one.

Second, the chief executives I studied supervised as many as 50 of these projects at the same time. Some projects entailed new products or processes; others involved public relations campaigns, improvement of the cash position, reorganization of a weak department, resolution of a morale problem in a foreign division, integration of computer operations, various acquisitions at different stages of development, and so on.

The chief executives appear to maintain a kind of inventory of the development projects that they themselves supervise—projects that are at various stages of development, some active and some in limbo. Like jugglers, they keep a number of projects in the air; periodically, one comes down, is given a new burst of energy, and is sent back into orbit. At various intervals, they put new projects on-stream and discard old ones.

    2.   While the entrepreneur role describes the manager as the voluntary initiator of change, the *disturbance handler* role depicts the manager involuntarily responding to pressures. Here change is beyond the manager's control. Managers must act because the pressures of the situation are too severe to be ignored: strike looms, a major customer has gone bankrupt, or a supplier reneges on his contract.

    It has been fashionable, I noted earlier, to compare the manager to an orchestra conductor, just as Peter F. Drucker wrote in *The Practice of Management:*

> The manager has the task of creating a true whole that is larger than the sum of its parts, a productive entity that turns out more than the sum of the resources put into it. One analogy is the conductor of a symphony orchestra, through whose effort, vision and leadership individual instrumental parts that are so much noise by themselves become the living whole of music. But the conductor has the composer's score; he is only interpreter. The manager is both composer and conductor.[14]

Now consider the words of Leonard R. Sayles, who has carried out systematic research on the manager's job:

> [The manager] is like a symphony orchestra conductor, endeavouring to maintain a melodious performance in which the contributions of the various instruments are coordinated and sequenced, patterned and paced, while the orchestra members are having various personal difficulties, stage hands are moving music stands, alternating excessive heat and cold are creating audience and instrument problems, and the sponsor of the concert is insisting on irrational changes in the program.[15]

    In effect, every manager must spend a good part of his or her time responding to high-pressure disturbances. No organization can be so well run, so standardized, that it has considered every contingency in the uncertain environment in advance. Disturbances arise not only because poor managers ignore situations until they reach crisis proportions, but also because good managers cannot possibly anticipate all the consequences of the actions they take.

    3.   The third decisional role is that of *resource allocator*. To the managers falls the responsibility of deciding who will get what in their organizational unit. Perhaps the most important resource managers allocate is their own time. Access to the manager constitutes exposure to the unit's nerve center and decision maker. Managers are also charged with designing their unit's structure, that pattern of formal relationships that determines how work is to be divided and coordinated.

Also, in their role as resource allocator, managers authorize the important decisions of their unit before they are implemented. By retaining this power, the manager can ensure that decisions are interrelated; all must pass through a single brain. To fragment this power is to encourage discontinuous decision making and a disjointed strategy.

There are a number of interesting features about the manager's authorizing others' decisions. First, despite the widespread use of capital budgeting procedures—a means of authorizing various capital expenditures at one time—executives in my study made a great many authorization decisions on an ad hoc basis. Apparently, many projects cannot wait or simply do not have the quantifiable costs and benefits that capital budgeting requires.

Second, I found that the chief executives faced incredibly complex choices. They had to consider the impact of each decision on other decisions and on the organization's strategy. They had to ensure that the decision would be acceptable to those who influence the organization, as well as ensure that resources would not be overextended. They had to understand the various costs and benefits as well as the feasiblity of the proposal. They also had to consider questions of timing. All this was necessary for the simple approval of someone else's proposal. At the same time, however, delay could lose time, while quick approval could be ill considered and quick rejection might discourage the subordinate who had spent months developing a pet project.

One common solution to approving projects is to pick the person instead of the proposal. That is, managers authorize those projects presented to them by people whose judgment they trust. But they cannot always use this simple dodge.

4. The final decisional role is that of *negotiator*. Studies of managerial work at all levels indicate that managers spend considerable time in negotiations: the president of the football team is called in to word out a contract with the holdout superstar; the coporation president leads his company's contingent to negotiate a new strike issue; the foreman argues a grievance problem to its conclusion with the shop steward. As Leonard Sayles puts it, negotiations are a "way of life" for the sophisticated manager.

These negotiations are duties of the manager's job: perhaps routine, they are not to be shirked. They are an integral part of his job, for only he has the authority to commit organizational resources in "real time," and only he has the nerve center information that important negotiations require.

The Integrated Job
It should be clear by now that the ten roles I have been describing are not easily separable. In the terminology of the psychologist, they form a gestalt, an integrated whole. No role can be pulled out of the framework and the job be left intact. For example, managers without liaison contacts lack external information. As a result, they can neither disseminate the information

their employees need nor make decisions that adequately reflect external conditions. (In fact, this is a problem for the new person in a managerial position, since she cannot make effective decisions until she has built up her network of contacts.)

Here lies a clue to the problems of team management.[16] Two or three people cannot share a single managerial position unless they can act as one entity. This means that they cannot divide up the ten roles unless they can very carefully reintegrate them. The real difficulty lies with the informational roles. Unless there can be full sharing of managerial information—and, as I pointed out earlier, it is primarily verbal—team management breaks down. A single managerial job cannot be arbitrarily split, for example, into internal and external roles, for information from both sources must be brought to bear on the same decisions.

To say that the ten roles form a gestalt is not to say that all managers give equal attention to each role. In fact, I found in my review of the various research studies that

☐ . . . sales managers seem to spend relatively more of their time in the interpersonal roles, presumably a reflection of the extrovert nature of the marketing activity;

☐ . . . production managers give relatively more attention to the decisional roles, presumably a reflection of their concern with efficient work flow;

☐ . . . staff managers spend the most time in the informational roles, since they are experts who manage departments that advise other parts of the organization.

Nevertheless, in all cases the interpersonal, informational, and decisional roles remain inseparable.

Toward More Effective Management

What are the messages for management in this description? I believe, first and foremost, that this description of managerial work should prove more important to managers than any prescription they might derive from it. That is to say, *the manager's effectiveness is significantly influenced by his insight into his own work.* His performance depends on how well he understands and responds to the pressures and dilemmas of the job. Thus managers who can be introspective about their work are likely to be effective at their jobs. Appendix B, page 482, offers 14 groups of self-study questions for managers. Some may sound rhetorical; none is meant to be. Even though the questions cannot be answered simply, the manager should address them.

Let us take a look at three specific areas of concern. For the most part, the managerial logjams—the dilemma of delegation, the data base centralized in one brain, the problems of working with the management scientist—revolve around the verbal nature of the manager's information. There are great dangers in centralizing the organization's data bank in the minds of its managers. When they leave, they take their memory with them. And when subordinates are out of convenient verbal reach of the manager, they are at an informational disadvantage.

1. *Managers are challenged to find systematic ways to share their privileged information.*   A regular debriefing session with key subordinates, a weekly memory dump on the dictating maching, the maintaining of a diary of important information for limited circulation, or other similar methods may ease the logjam of work considerably. Time spent disseminating this information will be more than regained when decisions must be made. Of course, some will raise the question of confidentiality. But managers would do well to weigh the risks of exposing privileged information against having subordinates who can make effective decisions.

If there is a single theme that runs through this article, it is that the pressures of their job drive managers to be superficial in their actions—to overload themselves with work, encourage interruption, respond quickly to every stimulus, seek the tangible and avoid the abstract, make decisions in small increments, and do everything abruptly.

2. *Here again, managers are challenged to deal consciously with the pressures of superficiality by giving serious attention to the issues that require it, by stepping back from their tangible bits of information in order to see a broad picture, and by making use of analytical inputs.*   Although effective managers have to be adept at responding quickly to numerous and varying problems, the danger in managerial work is that they will respond to every issue equally (and that means abruptly) and that they will never work the tangible bits and pieces of informational input into a comprehensive picture of their world.

As I noted earlier, managers use these bits of information to build models of their world. But managers can also avail themselves of the models of the specialists. Economists describe the functioning of markets, operations researchers simulate financial flow processes, and behavioral scientists explain the needs and goals of people. The best of these models can be searched out and learned.

In dealing with complex issues, senior managers have much to gain from a close relationship with the management scientists of their own organization. Managers have something important that they lack—time to probe complex issues. An effective working relationship hinges on the resolution of what a colleague and I have called "the planning dilemma."[17] Managers have the information and the authority; analysts have the time and the technology. A successful working relationship between the two will be effected when the manager learns to share his or her information and the analyst learns to adapt to the manager's needs. For the analyst, adaptation means worrying less about the elegance of the method and more about its speed and flexibility.

It seems to me that analysts can help the top manager especially to schedule her time, feed in analytical information, monitor projects under her supervision, develop models to aid in making choices, design contingency plans for disturbances that can be anticipated, and conduct "quick-and-dirty" analysis for those that cannot. But there can be no cooperation if the analysts are out of the mainstream of the manager's information flow.

3.   *Managers are challenged to gain control of their own time by turning obligations to their advantage and by turning those things they wish to do into obligations.*   The chief executives of my study initiated only 32% of their own contacts (and another 5% by mutual agreement). And yet to a considerable extent they seemed to control their time. There were two key factors that enabled them to do so.

First, managers have to spend so much time discharging obligations that if they were to view them as just that, they would leave no mark on their organization. Unsuccessful managers blame failure on the obligations; effective managers turn their obligations to their own advantage. A speech is a chance to lobby for a cause; a meeting is a chance to reorganize a weak department; a visit to an important customer is a chance to extract trade information.

Second, managers free some of their time to do those things that they— perhaps no one else—think important by turning them into obligations. Free time is made, not found, in the manager's job; it is forced into the schedule. Hoping to leave some time open for contemplation or general planning is tantamount to hoping that the pressures of the job will go away. Managers who want to innovate initiate projects and obligate others to report back to them; managers who need certain environmental information establish channels that will automatically keep them informed; managers who have to tour facilities commit themselves publicly.

The Educator's Job

Finally, a word about the training of managers. Our management schools have done an admirable job of training the organization's specialists—management scientists, marketing researchers, accountants, and organizational development specialists. But for the most part they have not trained managers.[18]

Management schools will begin the serious training of managers when skill training takes a serious place next to cognitive learning. Cognitive learning is detached and informational, like reading a book or listening to a lecture. No doubt much important cognitive material must be assimilated by the manager-to-be. But cognitive learning no more makes a manager than it does a swimmer. The latter will drown the first time she jumps into the water if her coach never takes her out of the lecture hall, gets her wet, and gives her feedback on her performance.

In other words, we are taught a skill through practice plus feedback, whether in a real or a simulated situation. Our management schools need to identify the skills managers use, select students who show potential in these skills, put the students into situations where these skills can be practiced, and then give them systematic feedback on their performance.

My description of managerial work suggests a number of important managerial skills—developing peer relationships, carrying out negotiations, motivating subordinates, resolving conflicts, establishing information networks and subsequently disseminating information, making decisions in conditions of extreme ambiguity, and allocating resources. Above all, managers need to be introspective about their work so that they may continue to learn on the job.

Many of the manager's skills can, in fact, be practiced, using techniques that range from role playing to videotaping real meetings. And our management schools can enhance the entrepreneurial skills by designing programs that encourage sensible risk taking and innovation.

No job is more vital to our society than that of the manager. It is the manager who determines whether our social institutions serve us well or whether they squander our talents and resources. It is time to strip away the folklore about managerial work, and time to study it realistically so that we can begin the difficult task of making significant improvements in its performance.

Notes

1. All the data from my study can be found in Henry Mintzberg, *The Nature of Managerial Work* (New York, Harper & Row, 1973).

2. Robert H. Guest, "Of Time and the Foreman," *Personnel*, May 1956, p. 478.

3. Rosemary Stewart, *Managers and Their Jobs* (London, Macmillan, 1967); see also Sune Carlson, *Executive Behaviour* (Stockholm, Strömbergs, 1951), the first of the diary studies.

4. Francis J. Aguilar, *Scanning the Business Environment* (New York, Macmillan, 1967), p. 102.

5. Unpublished study by Irving Choran, reported in Mintzberg, *The Nature of Managerial Work.*

6. Robert T. Davis, *Performance and Development of Field Sales Managers* (Boston, Division of Research, Harvard Business School, 1957); George H. Copeman, *The Role of the Managing Director* (London, Business Publications, 1963).

7. Stewart, *Managers and Their Jobs;* Tom Burns, "The Directions of Activity and Communication in a Department Executive Group," *Human Relations* 7, no. 1 (1954): 73.

8. H. Edward Wrapp, "Good Managers Don't Make Policy Decisions," *HBR*, September–October 1967, p. 91; Wrapp refers to this as spotting opportunities and relationships in the stream of operating problems and decisions; in his article Wrapp raises a number of excellent points related to this analysis.

9. Richard E. Neustadt, *Presidential Power* (New York, John Wiley, 1960), pp. 153–154; italics added.

10. For a more thorough, though rather different, discussion of this issue, see Kenneth R. Andrews, "Toward Professionalism in Business Management," *HBR*, March–April 1969, p. 49.

11. C. Jackson Grayson, Jr., in "Management Science and Business Practice," *HBR*, July–August 1973, p. 41, explains in similar terms why, as chairman of the Price Commission, he did not use those very techniques that he himself promoted in his earlier career as a management scientist.

12. George C. Homans, *The Human Group* (New York, Harcourt, Brace & World, 1950), based on the study by William F. Whyte entitled *Street Corner Society*, rev. ed. (Chicago, University of Chicago Press, 1955).

13. Neustadt, *Presidential Power*, p. 157.

14. Peter F. Drucker, *The Practice of Management* (New York, Harper & Row, 1954), pp. 341–342.

15. Leonard R. Sayles, *Managerial Behavior* (New York, McGraw-Hill, 1964), p. 162.

16. See Richard C. Hodgson, Daniel J. Levinson, and Abraham Zaleznik, *The Executive Role Constellation* (Boston, Division of Research, Harvard Business School, 1965), for a discussion of the sharing of roles.

17. James S. Hekimian and Henry Mintzberg, "The Planning Dilemma," *The Management Review*, May 1968, p. 4.

18. See J. Sterling Livingston, "Myth of the Well-Educated Manager," *HBR*, January–February 1971, p. 79.

Appendix A: Research on Managerial Work

Considering its central importance to every aspect of management, there has been surprisingly little research on the manager's work, and virtually no systematic building of knowledge from one group of studies to another. In seeking to describe managerial work, I conducted my own research and also scanned the literature widely to integrate the findings of studies from many diverse sources with my own. These studies focused on two very different aspects of managerial work. Some were concerned with the characteristics of the work—how long managers work, where, at what pace and with what interruptions, with whom they work, and through what media they communicate. Other studies were more concerned with the essential content of the work—what activities the managers actually carry out, and why. Thus, after a meeting, one researcher might note that the manager spent 45 minutes with three government officials in their Washington office, while another might record that he presented his company's stand on some proposed legislation in order to change a regulation.

A few of the studies of managerial work are widely known, but most have remained buried as single journal articles or isolated books. Among the more important ones I cite (with full references in the footnotes) are the following:

Sune Carlson developed the diary method to study the work characteristics of nine Swedish managing directors. Each kept a detailed log of his activities. Carlson's results are reported in his book *Executive Behavior*. A number of British researchers, notably Rosemary Stewart, have subsequently used Carlson's method. In *Managers and Their Jobs*, she describes the study of 160 top and middle managers of British companies during four weeks, with particular attention to the differences in their work.

Leonard Sayles's book *Managerial Behavior* is another important reference. Using a method he refers to as "anthropological," Sayles studied the work content of middle- and lower-level managers in a large U.S. corporation. Sayles moved freely in the company, collecting whatever information struck him as important.

Perhaps the best-known source is *Presidential Power*, in which Richard Neustadt analyzes the power and managerial behavior of Presidents Roosevelt, Truman, and Eisenhower. Neustadt used secondary sources—documents and interviews with other parties—to generate his data.

Robert H. Guest, in *Personnel*, reports on a study of the foreman's working day. Fifty-six U.S. foremen were observed and each of their activities recorded during one eight-hour shift.

Richard C. Hodgson, Daniel J. Levinson, and Abraham Zaleznik studied a team of three top executives of a U.S. hospital. From that study they wrote *The Executive Role Constellation*. These researchers addressed in particular the way in which work and socioemotional roles were divided among the three managers.

William F. Whyte, from his study of a street gang during the Depression, wrote *Street Corner Society*. His findings about the gang's leadership, which George C. Homans analyzed in *The Human Group*, suggest some interesting similarities of job content between the street gang leaders and corporate managers.

My own study involved five American CEOs of middle-to large-sized organizations—a consulting firm, a technology company, a hospital, a consumer goods company, and a school system. Using a method called "structural observation," during one intensive week of observation for each executive I recorded various aspects of every piece of mail and every verbal contact. My method was designed to capture data on both work characteristics and job content. In all, I analyzed 890 pieces of incoming and outgoing mail and 368 verbal contacts.

Appendix B: Self-Study Questions for Managers

1. Where do I get my information, and how? Can I make greater use of my contacts to get information? Can other people do some of my scanning for me? In what areas is my knowledge weakest, and how can I get others to provide me with the information I need? Do I have powerful enough mental models of those things I must understand within the organization and its environment?

2. What information do I disseminate in my organization? How important is it that my subordinates get my information? Do I keep too much information to myself because dissemination of it is time-consuming or inconvenient? How can I get more information to others so they can make better decisions?

3. Do I balance information collecting with action taking? Do I tend to act before information is in? Or do I wait so long for all the information that opportunities pass me by and I become a bottleneck in my organization?

4. What pace of change am I asking my organization to tolerate? Is this change balanced so that our operations are neither excessively static nor overly disrupted? Have we sufficiently analyzed the impact of this change on the future of our organization?

5. Am I sufficiently well informed to pass judgment on the proposals that my subordinates make? Is it possible to leave final authorization for more of the proposals with subordinates? Do we have problems of coordination because subordinates in fact now make too many of these decisions independently?

6. What is my vision of direction for this organization? Are these plans primarily in my own mind in loose form? Should I make them explicit in order to guide the decisions of others in the organization better? Or do I need flexibility to change them at will?

7. How do my subordinates react to my managerial style? Am I sufficiently sensitive to the powerful influence my actions have on them? Do I fully understand their reactions to my actions? Do I find an appropriate balance between encouragement and pressure? Do I stifle their initiative?

8. What kind of external relationships do I maintain, and how? Do I spend too much of my time maintaining these relationships? Are there certain types of people whom I should get to know better?

9. Is there any system to my time scheduling, or am I just reacting to the pressures of the moment? Do I find the appropriate mix of activities, or do I tend to concentrate on one particular function or one type of problem just because I find it interesting? Am I more efficient with particular kinds of work at special times of the day or week? Does my schedule reflect this? Can someone else (in addition to my secretary) take responsibility for much of my scheduling and do it more systematically?

10. Do I overwork? What effect does my work load have on my efficiency? Should I force myself to take breaks or to reduce the pace of my activity?

11.   Am I too superficial in what I do? Can I really shift moods as quickly and frequently as my work patterns require? Should I attempt to decrease the amount of fragmentation and interruption in my work?

12.   Do I orient myself too much toward current, tangible activities? Am I a slave to the action and excitement of my work, so that I am no longer able to concentrate on issues? Do key problems receive the attention they deserve? Should I spend more time reading and probing deeply into certain issues? Could I be more reflective? Should I be?

13.   Do I use the different media appropriately? Do I know how to make the most of written communication? Do I rely excessively on face-to-face communication, thereby putting all but a few of my subordinates at an informational disadvantage? Do I schedule enough of my meetings on a regular basis? Do I spend enough time touring my organization to observe activity at first hand? Am I too detached from the heart of my organization's activities, seeing things only in an abstract way?

14.   How do I blend my personal rights and duties? Do my obligations consume all my time? How can I free myself sufficiently from obligations to ensure that I am taking this organization where I want it to go? How can I turn my obligations to my advantage?

30

Good Managers Don't Make Policy Decisions

H. EDWARD WRAPP

Successful general managers do not spell out detailed objectives for their organizations, the author believes; nor do they make master plans. They seldom make forthright statements of policy. They are opportunists, and they tend to muddle through problems—although they muddle with a purpose. They enmesh themselves in many operating matters and do not limit themselves to "the big picture."

The upper reaches of management are a land of mystery and intrigue. Very few people have ever been there, and the present inhabitants frequently send back messages that are incoherent both to other levels of management and to the world in general. This may account for the myths, illusions, and caricatures that permeate the literature of management—for example, such widely held notions as these:

☐ Life gets less complicated as a manager reaches the top of the pyramid.

☐ The manager at the top level knows everything that's going on in the organization, can command whatever resources he or she may need, and therefore can be more decisive.

☐ The general manager's day is taken up with making broad policy decisions and formualting precise objectives.

☐ The top executive's primary activity is conceptualizing long-range plans.

Author's Note This article is based on a talk delivered at the Executive Program club luncheon in Chicago, April 27, 1967. A similar version of it was published as a Selected Paper in late 1967 by the Graduate School of Business, University of Chicago.

☐ In a large company, the top executive may be seen meditating about the role of his or her organization in society.

I suggest that none of these versions alone, or in combination, is an accurate portrayal of what a general manager does. Perhaps students of the management process have been overly eager to develop a theory and a discipline. As one executive I know puts it, "I guess I do some of the things described in the books and articles, but the descriptions are lifeless, and my job isn't."

What common characteristics, then, do successful executives exhibit *in reality?* I shall identify five skills or talents which, in my experience, seem especially significant. (For details on the method used in reaching these conclusions, see the Appendix.)

Keeping Well Informed

First, each of my heroes has a special talent for keeping himself informed about a wide range of operating decisions being made at different levels in the company. As he moves up the ladder, he develops a network of information sources in many different departments. He cultivates these sources and keeps them open no matter how high he climbs in the organization. When the need arises, he bypasses the lines on the organization chart to seek more than one version of a situation.

In some instances, especially when they suspect he would not be in total agreement with their decision, his subordinates will elect to inform him in advance, before they announce a decision. In these circumstances, he is in a position to defer the decision, or redirect it, or even block further action. However, he does not insist on this procedure. Ordinarily he leaves it up to the members of his organization to decide at what stage they inform him.

Top-level managers are frequently criticized by writers, consultants, and lower levels of management for continuing to enmesh themselves in operating problems, after promotion to the top, rather than withdrawing to the "big picture." Without any doubt, some managers do get lose in a welter of detail and insist on making too many decisions. Superficially, the good manager may seem to make the same mistake — but his purposes are different. He knows that only by keeping well informed about the decisions being made can he avoid the sterility so often found in those who isolate themselves from operations. If he follows the advice to free himself from operations, he may soon find himself subsisting on a diet of abstractions, leaving the choice of what he eats in the hands of his subordinates. As Kenneth Boulding puts it: "The very purpose of a hierarchy is to prevent information from reaching higher layers. It operates as an information filter, and there are little wastebaskets all along the way."[1]

What kind of action do successful executives take to keep their information live and accurate? Here is an example:

One company president that I worked with sensed that his vice presidents were insulating him from some of the vital issues being discussed at lower levels. He accepted a proposal for a formal management development program primarily because it afforded him an opportunity to discuss company problems with middle managers several layers removed from him in the organization. By meeting with small groups of these men in an academic setting, he learned much about their preoccupations, and also about those of his vice presidents. And he accomplished his purposes without undermining the authority of line managers.

Focusing Time and Energy

The second skill of the good manager is that she knows how to save her energy and hours for those few particular issues, decisions, or problems to which she should give her personal attention. She knows the fine and subtle distinction between keeping fully informed about operating decisions and allowing the organization to force her into participating in these decisions or, even worse, making them. Recognizing that she can bring her special talents to bear on only a limited number of matters, she chooses those issues which she believes will have the greatest long-term impact on the company, and on which her special abilities can be most productive. Under ordinary circumstances she will limit herself to three or four major objectives during any single period of sustained activity.

What about the situations she elects *not* to become involved in as a decision maker? She makes sure (using the skill first mentioned) that the organization keeps her informed about them at various stages; she does not want to be accused of indifference to such issues. She trains her subordinates not to bring the matters to her for a decision. The communication to her from below is essentially one of: "Here is our sizeup, and here's what we propose to do." Reserving her hearty encouragement for those projects which hold superior promise of a contribution to total corporate strategy, she simply acknowledges receipt of information on other matters. When she sees a problem where the organization needs her help, she finds a way to transmit her know-how short of giving orders—usually by asking perceptive questions.

Playing the Power Game

To what extent do successful top executives push their ideas and proposals through the organization? The rather common notion that the "prime mover" continually creates and forces through new programs, like a powerful majority leader in a liberal Congress, is in my opinion very misleading.

Successful managers are sensitive to the power structure in the organization. In considering any major current proposal, they can plot the position of the various individuals and units in the organization on a scale ranging from complete, outspoken support down to determined, sometimes bitter, and oftentimes well-cloaked opposition. In the middle of the scale is an area of comparative indifference. Usually, several aspects of a proposal will fall into this area, and *here is where they know they can operate.* They assess the depth and nature of the blocs in the organization. Their perceptions permit them to move through what I call *corridors* of comparative indifference. They seldom challenge when a corridor is blocked, preferring to pause until it has opened up.

Related to this particular skill is their ability to recognize the need for a few trial-balloon launchers in the organization. They know that the organization will tolerate only a certain number of proposals which emanate from the apex of the pyramid. No matter how sorely they may be tempted to stimulate the organization with a flow of their own ideas, they know they must work through idea people in different parts of the organization. As they study the reactions of key individuals and groups to the trial balloons these people send up, they are able to make a better assessment of how to limit the emasculation of the various proposals. For seldom do they find a proposal which is supported by all quarters of the organization. The emergence of strong support in certain quarters is almost sure to evoke strong opposition in others.

Value of Sense of Timing

Circumstances like these mean that a good sense of timing is a priceless asset for a top executive. Let me illustrate:

A vice president had for some time been convinced that his company lacked a sense of direction and needed a formal long-range planning activity to fill the void. Up to the time in question, his soft overtures to other top executives had been rebuffed. And then he spotted an opening.

A management development committee proposed a series of weekend meetings for second-level officers in the company. After extensive debate, but for reasons not announced, the president rejected this proposal. The members of the committee openly resented what seemed to them an arbitrary rejection.

The vice president, sensing a tense situation, suggested to the president that the same officers who were to have attended the weekend management development seminars be organized into a long-range planning committee. The timing of his suggestion was perfect. The president, looking for a bone to toss to the committee, acquiesced immediately, and the management development committee in its next meeting enthusiastically endorsed the idea.

This vice president had been conducting a kind of continuing market research to discover how to sell his long-range planning proposal. His previous probes of the "market" had told him that the president's earlier rejections of his proposal were not so final as to preclude an eventual shift in the corridors of attitude I have mentioned.

The vice president caught the committee in a conciliatory mood, and his proposal rode through with colors flying.

As a good manager stands at a point in time, she can identify a set of goals she is interested in, albeit the outline of them may be pretty hazy. Her timetable, which is also pretty hazy, suggests that some must be accomplished sooner than others, and that some may be safely postponed for several months or years. She has a still hazier notion of how she can reach these goals. She assesses key individuals and groups. She knows that each has its own set of goals, some of which she understands rather thoroughly and others about which she can only speculate. She knows also that these individuals and groups represent blocks to certain programs or projects, and that these points of opposition must be taken into account. As the day-to-day operating decisions are made, and as proposals are responded to both by individuals and by groups, she perceives more clearly where the corridors of comparative indifference are. She takes action accordingly.

The Art of Imprecision

The fourth skill of the successful manager is knowing how to satisfy the organization that it has a sense of direction *without ever actually getting himself committed publicly to a specific set of objectives*. This is not to say that he does not have objectives—personal and corporate, long-term and short-term. They are significant guides to his thinking, and he modifies them continually as he better understands the resources he is working with, the competition, and the changing market demands. But as the organization clamors for statements of objectives, these are samples of what they get back from him:

"Our company aims to be number one in its industry."

"Our objective is growth with profit."

"We seek the maximum return on investment."

"Management's goal is to meet its responsibilities to stockholders, employees, and the public."

In my opinion, statements such as these provide almost no guidance to the various levels of management. Yet they are quite readily accepted as objectives by large numbers of intelligent people.

Maintaining Viability

Why do good managers shy away from precise statements of their objectives for the organization? The main reason is that they find it impossible to set down specific objectives which will be relevant for any reasonable period into the future. Conditions in business change continually and rapidly, and corporate strategy must be revised to take the changes into account. The more explicit the statement of strategy, the more difficult it becomes to persuade the organization to turn to different goals when needs and conditions shift.

The public and the stockholders, to be sure, must perceive the organization as having a well-defined set of objectives and a clear sense of direction. But in reality good top managers are seldom so certain of the direction which should be taken. Better than anyone else, they sense the many, many threats to their company—threats which lie in the economy, in the actions of competitors, and, not least, within their own organization.

They also know that it is impossible to state objectives clearly enough so that everyone in the organization understands what they mean. Objectives get communicated only over time by a consistency or pattern in operating decisions. Such decisions are more meaningful than words. In instances where precise objectives are spelled out, the organization tends to interpret them so they fit its own needs.

Subordinates who keep pressing for more precise objectives are in truth working against their own best interests. Each time the objectives are stated more specifically, a subordinate's range of possibilities for operating are reduced. The narrower field means less room to roam and to accommodate the flow of ideas coming up from his part of the organization.

Avoiding Policy Straitjackets

Successful managers' reluctance to be precise extends into the area of policy decisions. They seldom make a forthright statement of policy. They may be aware that in some companies there are executives who spend more time in arbitrating disputes caused by stated policies than in moving the company forward. The management textbooks contend that well-defined policies are the sine qua non of a well-managed company. My research does not bear out this contention. For example:

The president of one company with which I am familiar deliberately leaves the assignments of his top officers vague and refuses to define policies for them. He passes out new assignments with seemingly no pattern in mind and consciously sets up competitive ventures among his subordinates. His methods, though they would never be sanctioned by a classical organization planner, are deliberate—and, incidentally, quite effective.

Since able managers do not make policy decisions, does this mean that well-managed companies operate without policies? Certainly not. But the policies are those which evolve over time from an indescribable mix of operating decisions. From any single operating decision might have come a very minor dimension of the policy as the organization understands it; from a series of decisions comes a pattern of guidelines for various levels of the organization.

The skillful manager resists the urge to write a company creed or to compile a policy manual. Preoccupation with detailed statements of corporate objectives and departmental goals and with comprehensive organization charts and job descriptions—this is often the first symptom of an organization which is in the early stages of atrophy.

The "management by objectives" school, so widely heralded in recent years, suggests that detailed objectives be spelled out at all levels in the corporation. This method is feasible at lower levels of management, but it becomes unworkable at the upper levels. The top manager must think out objectives in detail, but ordinarily some of the objectives must be withheld, or at least communicated to the organization in modest doses. A conditioning process which may stretch over months or years is necessary in order to prepare the organization for radical departures from what it is currently striving to attain.

Suppose, for example, that a president is convinced his company must phase out of the principal business it has been in for 35 years. Although making this change of course is one of his objectives, he may well feel that he cannot disclose the idea even to his vice presidents, whose total know-how is in the present business. A blunt announcement that the company is changing horses would be too great a shock for most of them to bear. And so he begins moving toward this goal but without a full disclosure to his management group.

A detailed spelling out of objectives may only complicate the task of reaching them. Specific, detailed statements give the opposition an opportunity to organize its defenses.

Muddling with a Purpose

The fifth, and most important, skill I shall describe bears little relation to the doctrine that management is (or should be) a comprehensive, systematic, logical, well-programmed science. Of all the heresies set forth here, this should strike doctrinaires as the rankest of all!

Successful managers, in my observation, recognize the futility of trying to push total packages or programs through the organization. They are willing to take less than total acceptance in order to achieve modest progress toward their goals. Avoiding debates on principles, they try to piece together particles that may appear to be incidentals into a program that moves at least part of the way toward his objectives. Their attitude is based on optimism and persistence. Over and over they say to themselves, "There must be some parts of this proposal on which we can capitalize."

Whenever they identify relationships among the different proposals before them, they know that they present opportunities for combination and restructuring. It follows that they are people of wide-ranging interests and curiosity. The more things they know about, the more opportunities they will have to discover parts which are related. This process does not require great intellectual brilliance or unusual creativity. The wider ranging their interests, the more likely that they will be able to tie together several unrelated proposals. They are skilled as analysts, but even more talented as conceptualizers.

If managers have built or inherited a solid organization, it will be difficult for them to come up with an idea which no one in the company has ever thought of before. Their most significant contribution may be that they can see relationships which no one else has seen. Take this example:

A division manager had set as one of his objectives, at the start of a year, an improvement in product quality. At the end of the year, in reviewing his progress toward this objective, he could identify three significant events which had brought about a perceptible improvement.

First, the head of the quality control group, a veteran manager who was doing only an adequate job, asked early in the year for assignment to a new research group. This opportunity permitted the division manager to install a promising young engineer in this key spot.

A few months later, opportunity number two came long. The personnel department proposed a continuous program of checking the effectiveness of training methods for new employees. The proposal was acceptable to the manufacturing group. The division manager's only contribution was to suggest that the program should include a heavy emphasis on employees' attitudes toward quality.

Then a third opportunity arose when one of the division's best customers discovered that the wrong material had been used for a large lot of parts. The heat generated by this complaint made it possible to institute a completely new system of procedures for inspecting and testing raw materials.

As the division manager reviewed the year's progress on product quality, these were the three most important developments. None of them could have been predicted at the start of the year, but he was quick to see the potential in each as it popped up in the day-to-day operating routines.

Exploitation of Change

The good manager can function effectively only in an environment of continual change. A *Saturday Review* cartoonist has caught the idea as he pictures an executive seated at a massive desk instructing his secretary to "send in a deal; I feel like wheelin'." Only with many changes in the works can the manager discover new combinations of opportunities and open up new corridors of comparative indifference. His stimulation to creativity comes from trying to make something useful of the proposal or idea in front of him. He will try to make strategic change a way of life in the organization and continually review the strategy even though current results are good.

Charles Lindblom has written an article with an engaging title, "The

Science of Muddling Through."[2] In this paper he describes what he calls "the rational comprehensive method" of decision making. The essence of this method is that the decision maker, for each of his problems, proceeds deliberately, one step at a time, to collect complete data; to analyze the data thoroughly; to study a wide range of alternatives, each with its own risks and consequences; and, finally, to formulate a detailed course of action. Lindblom immediately dismisses "the rational comprehensive method" in favor of what he calls "successive limited comparisons." He sees the decision maker as comparing the alternatives which are open to him in order to learn which most clearly meets the objectives he has in mind. Since this is not so much a rational process as an opportunistic one, he sees the manager as a muddler, but a muddler with a purpose.

H. Igor Ansoff, in his book, *Corporate Strategy*,[3] espouses a similar notion as he describes what he calls the "cascade approach." In his view, possible decision rules are formulated in gross terms and are successively refined through several stages as the emergence of a solution proceeds. This process gives the appearance of solving the problem several times over, but with successively more precise results.

Both Lindblom and Ansoff are moving us closer to an understanding of how managers really think. The process is not highly abstract; rather, the manager searches for a means of drawing into a pattern the thousands of incidents which make up the day-to-day life of a growing company.

Contrasting Pictures

It is interesting to note, in the writings of several students of management, the emergence of the concept that, rather than making decisions, the leader's principal task is maintaining operating conditions which permit the various decision-making systems to function effectively. The supporters of this theory, it seems to me, overlook the subtle turns of direction which the leader can provide. She cannot add purpose and structure to the balanced judgments of subordinates if she simply rubberstamps their decisions. She must weigh the issues and reach her own decision.

Richard M. Cyert and James G. March contend that in real life managers do not consider all the possible courses of action, that their search ends once they have found a satisfactory alternative. In my sample, good managers are not guilty of such myopic thinking. Unless they mull over a wide range of possibilities, they cannot come up with the imaginative combinations of ideas which characterize their work.

Many of the articles about successful executives picture them as great thinkers who sit at their desks drafting master blueprints for their companies. The successful top executives I have seen at work do not operate this way. Rather than produce a full-grown decision tree, they start with a twig, help it grow, and ease themselves out on the limbs only after they have tested to see how much weight the limbs can stand.

In my picture, the general manager sits in the midst of a continuous stream of operating problems. His organization presents him with a flow of proposals to deal with the problems. Some of these proposals are contained in voluminous, well-documented, formal reports; some are as fleeting as the walk-in visit from a subordinate whose latest inspiration came during the morning's coffee break. Knowing how meaningless it is to say, "This is a finance problem," or, "That is a communications problem," the manager feels no compulsion to classify his problems. He is, in fact, undismayed by a problem that defies classification. As the late Gary Steiner, in one of his speeches, put it, "He has a high tolerance for ambiguity."

In considering each proposal, the general manager tests it against at least three criteria:

1   Will the total proposal—or, more often, will some part of the proposal—move the organization toward the objectives which he has in mind?

2   How will the whole or parts of the proposal be received by the various groups and subgroups in the organization? Where will the strongest opposition come from, which group will furnish the strongest support, and which group will be neutral or indifferent?

3   How does the proposal relate to programs already in process or currently proposed? Can some parts of the proposal under consideration be added on to a program already under way, or can they be combined with all or parts of other proposals in a package which can be steered through the organization?

The Making of a Decision

As another example of a general manager at work, let me describe the train of events which led to a parent company president's decision to attempt to consolidate two of his divisions:

Let us call the executive Mr. Brown. One day the manager of Division A came to him with a proposal that his division acquire a certain company. That company's founder and president—let us call him Mr. Johansson—had a phenomenal record of inventing new products, but earnings in his company had been less than phenomenal. Johansson's asking price for his company was high when evaluated against the earnings record.

Not until Brown began to speculate on how Johansson might supply fresh vigor for new products in Division A did it appear that perhaps a premium price could be justified. For several years Brown had been unsuccessful in stimulating the manager of that division to see that he must bring in new products to replace those which were losing their place in the market.

The next idea which came to Brown was that Johansson might invent not only for Division A but also for Division B. As Brown analyzed how this might be worked out organizationally, he began to think about the markets being served by divisions A and B. Over the years, several basic but gradual changes in marketing patterns had occurred, with the result that the marketing considerations which had dictated the establishment of separate divisions no longer prevailed. Why should the company continue to support the duplicated overhead expenses in the two divisions?

As Brown weighed the issues, he concluded that by consolidating the two divisions, he could also shift responsibilities in the management groups in ways that would strengthen them overall.

If we were asked to evaluate Brown's capabilities, how would we respond? Putting aside the objection that the information is too sketchy, our tendency might be to criticize Brown. Why did he not identify the changing market patterns in his continuing review of company position? Why did he not force the issue when the division manager failed to do something about new product development? Such criticism would reflect "the rational comprehensive method" of decision making.

But, as I analyze the gyrations in Brown's thinking, one characteristic stands out. He kept searching for the follow-on opportunities which he could fashion out of the original proposal, opportunities which would stand up against the three criteria earlier mentioned. In my book, Brown would rate as an extremely skillful general manager.

Conclusion

To recapitulate, general managers possess five important skills. They know how to:

1   *Keep open many pipelines of information*—No one will quarrel with the desirability of an early warning system which provides varied viewpoints on an issue. However, very few managers know how to practice this skill, and the books on management add precious little to our understanding of the techniques which make it practicable.

2   *Concentrate on a limited number of significant issues*—No matter how skillful managers are in focusing their energies and talents, they are inevitably caught up in a number of inconsequential duties. Active leadership of an organization demands a high level of personal involvement, and personal involvement brings with it many time-consuming activities which have an infinitesimal impact on corporate strategy. Hence this second skill, while perhaps the most logical of the five, is by no means the easiest to apply.

3   *Identify the corridors of comparative indifference*—Are there inferences here that good managers have no ideas of their own, that they stand by until their organization proposes solutions, that they never use their authority to force a proposal through the organi-

zation? Such inferences are not intended. The message is that a good organization will tolerate only so much direction from the top; good managers therefore are adept at sensing how hard they can push.

4 *Give the organization a sense of direction with open-ended objectives*—In assessing this skill, keep in mind that I am talking about top levels of management. At lower levels, managers should be encouraged to write down their objectives, if for no other reason that to ascertain if they are consistent with corporate strategy.

5 *Spot opportunities and relationships in the stream of operating problems and decisions*—Lest it be concluded from the description of this skill that good managers are more improvisers than planners, let me emphasize that they are planners and encourage planning by their subordinates. Interestingly, though, professional planners may be irritated by good general managers. Most of them complain about the manager's lack of vision. They devise a master plan, but the president (or other operating executive) seems to ignore it, or to give it minimum acknowledgement by borrowing bits and pieces for implementation. They seem to feel that the power of a good master plan will be obvious to everyone, and its implementation automatic. But the general manager knows that even if the plan is sound and imaginative, the job has only begun. The long, painful task of implementation will depend on his skill, not that of the planner.

Practical Implications

If this analysis of how skillful general managers think and operate has validity, then it should help us see several problems in a better light.

Investment Analysis. The investment community is giving increasing attention to sizing up the management of a company being appraised. Thus far, the analysts rely mainly on results or performance rather than on a probe of management skills. But current performance can be affected by many variables, both favorably and unfavorably, and is a dangerous base for predicting what the management of a company will produce in the future. Testing the key managers of a company against the five skills described holds promise for evaluating the caliber of a management group.

Incidentally, I believe that managers who are building their own companies and persons who are moving up through the hierarchy of a larger organization require essentially the same capabilities for success.

The Urge to Merge. In today's frenzy of acquisitions and mergers, why does a management usually prefer to acquire a company rather than to develop a new product and build an organization to make and sell it? One of the reasons can be found in the way general managers think and operate.

They find it difficult to sit and speculate theoretically about the future as they and their subordinates fashion a plan to exploit a new product. They are much more at home when taking over a going concern, even though they anticipate they will inherit many things they do not want. In the day-to-day operation of a going concern, they find the milieu to maneuver and conceptualize.

Promotion Practices.   Scarcely any manager in any business can escape the acutely painful responsibility to identify persons with potential for growth in management and to devise methods for developing them for broader responsibilities. Few line managers or staff professionals have genuine confidence in the yardsticks and devices they use now. The five skills offer possibilities for raising an additional set of questions about management appraisal methods, job rotation practices, on-the-job development assignments, and the curricula of formal in-house management development programs.

One group of distinguished executives ignores with alarming regularity the implications of the five skills. These are the presidents of multidivision companies who "promote" successful division managers to the parent company level as staff officers. Does this recurring phenomenon cast doubt on the validity of my theory? I think not. To the contrary, strong supporting evidence for my thesis can be found in the results of such action. What happens is that line managers thus "promoted" often end up on the sidelines, out of the game for the rest of their careers. Removed from the tumult of operations, the environment which I contend is critical for their success, many of them just wither away in their high-status posts as senior counselors and never become effective.

Notes

1. From a speech at a meeting sponsored by the Crowell Collier Institute of Continuing Education in New York, as reported in *Business Week*, February 18, 1967, p. 202.

2. *Readings in Managerial Psychology*, edited by Harold J. Leavitt and Louis R. Pondy (Chicago, University of Chicago Press, 1964), p. 61.

3. New York, McGraw-Hill Book Company, 1965.

Appendix: Basis of Conclusions in This Article

I have reached the conclusions outlined here after working closely with many managers in many different companies. In truth, the managers were not preselected with research in mind. Never did I tell them that they were being studied, nor was I in fact studying their behavior. Research was not the purpose of our relationship. We were collaborating to solve some real problems.

Researching the management process when managers are aware that they are being studied sometimes produces strange results. Rarely are good executives able to think objectively about the management process as it is exemplified in their own methods. When they try to explain to a researcher or writer, they tend to feel compelled to develop rational, systematic explanations of how they do their job—explanations which in my opinion are largely fictional.

Managers cannot be expected to describe their methods even if they understand them. Their methods border on manipulation, and the stigma associated with manipulation can be fatal. If the organization ever identifies them as manipulators, their jobs become more difficult. No one willingly submits to manipulation, and those around them organize to protect themselves. And yet every good manager does have to manipulate.

My definition of a good manager is a simple one: under competitive industry conditions, he is able to move his organization significantly toward the goals he has set, whether measured by higher return on investment, product improvement, development of management talent, faster growth in sales and earnings, or some other standard. Bear in mind that this definition does not refer to the administrator whose principal role is to maintain the status quo in a company or in a department. Keeping the wheels turning in a direction already set is a relatively simple task, compared to that of directing the introduction of a continuing flow of changes and innovations, and preventing the organization from flying apart under the pressure.—*The Author*

31

Questions the Business Leader Should Ask Himself

GEORGE ALBERT SMITH, JR.

In the busy world of top management, it is easy to become so involved in day-to-day problems that little attention is paid to the crucial issues that affect the long-term survival of the company. To combat this, George Albert Smith, Jr., recommends that managers engage in periodic soul-searching about their companies and themselves. Specifically, he recommends careful review of long-range strategy, organizational competence, human relations, and integrity. Although this article was published in 1956, the questions Smith raises are just as relevant for today's managers.

What are some of the basis attitudes, viewpoints, ways of acting and organizing that make it possible for a firm to survive difficult periods of stress, to see and solve problems, to create and exploit opportunities? How do some firms manage to acquire and retain vitality in their operations? Why do others never really achieve that necessary vigor, and still others so quickly lose it?

Some firms last for a long time. They create good opportunities for themselves or exploit opportunities which are created by others. Allowing for the general ups and downs to which all companies are subject, these firms succeed. But others have a less happy experience. They seem unable to cope with the changing events of business life effectively. Some of them, even after lengthy periods of prosperity, gradually sputter and die.

In probing for the reasons behind these successes and failures, I have developed a series of questions which seem to me to be worth asking in regard to executive behavior. (As a matter of fact, the concepts involved apply with almost equal force in nonbusiness organizations and, indeed, to a considerable extent in our own personal lives.) I shall take up the questions one by one, elaborating each to clarify its meaning and intent, and illustrating it with specific case situations. My examples are drawn from the actual experiences of real companies and real people, although in some instances the names used are disguised.

Long-Run Strategy

Does the management distinguish between symptoms and causes?

Though this seems like an obviously important distinction, the failure to make it is one of the most frequent sources of difficulty in business. Many times managers work extremely hard to deal with what they think is a basic problem, when in reality they are dealing only with the symptoms of an ailment which is far more fundamental, and as yet undiagnosed. Perhaps their programs do afford some temporary relief, but if they fail to extirpate the root of the trouble, it will undoubtedly return to plague them again and again—perhaps in more unmanageable form. Here are two illustrations:

Several years ago, a fairly successful dairy company in the western states—we will call it the Mutual Creamery Company—started to have trouble. One of its most noticeable problems was that it continually ran out of money! Behind this, of course, was the fact that profits were not good.

At the same time, the company was unable to borrow from the banks, though some of its competitors could do so; indeed, one competitor, a cooperative, could borrow from the government at a lower interest rate than the banks would charge. Consequently, some directors and officers of Mutual became obsessed with the idea that the source of all their trouble was their inability to borrow at a reasonable rate. In point of fact, however, the real problem was that their competitors, primarily the cooperative, were using better purchasing and production methods, and creating a more uniform product of higher quality. In addition, the competitors were using much better marketing methods. So Mutual was losing both its customers and its sources of supply.

Finally the company failed, and to their dying day, virtually all the Mutual directors never really knew what had caused their trouble. They were so concerned with one symptom that they failed to see their lack of basic competitive strength where it really mattered.

When chain stores were first becoming important in our distribution system, they put many independent grocers out of business. We would all agree that this was most unfortunate for the grocers concerned, but we would also agree that the consumer benefited from the improved methods of distribution that were largely sponsored by the grocery chains.

Most of the independent grocers who were adversely affected by this development—the small ones, in particular—claimed that they were unable to succeed because of the ability of chains to purchase merchandise more cheaply. Initially these small independent grocers failed to realize that the new chains were offering the public a unique form of distribution which was more acceptable to many buyers. They did not see that the chains were developing new purchasing and distribution methods which enabled them to cut the costs of moving food from producres to consumers. Instead of recognizing the important competitive reality, the small grocers tried to blame their troubles exclusively on "unfair competition."

On the other hand, those independents who ultimately survived did so because they saw clearly what methods made for effective grocery operation, and adopted such methods themselves. These independents—and there are more of them than there are chain stores—still have an important role, and those who fill it successfully will prosper.

Before leaving this question, I might add, as a sort of postscript, that a failure to distinguish between symptoms and causes crops up in our thinking on other subjects than business. For example, many American executives never learned to understand why the Republicans were voted out of office in 1932, and why President Roosevelt was elected four times. I believe these businessmen (and they include a high percentage of my friends) have often confused symptoms and causes in their reactions to political affairs.

Does top management frequently ask itself, "In our industry, what are the fundamental tasks we perform?" "What must we do as well as, or better than, someone else in order to compete and to excel?"

Perhaps the significance of these paired questions will become more apparent through these examples:

The railroad, like the truck, the airplane, and the bus, is primarily concerned with moving things and people from one place to another. Yet the failure to recognize this very simple fact has been the cause of many railroad troubles.

Most railroad managers, in earlier decades, instead of regarding themselves as movers, thought that their business was essentially a matter of rolling stock and rails. Consequently, at critical times in the histories of their companies, they concentrated on being expert railroad operators. They had voluminous statistics on railroad operation; they learned a lot about steam engines, grades, and all the other technical aspects of their business. In fact, they became so intent on piling up this sort of information that they failed to recognize the significance of the private automobile, the truck, the bus, the airplane, and the pipeline as these competitive movers came along; they acted as if they thought, "These aren't really competitors of ours."

Needless to say, the people who acted on such assumptions have long since had to recognize the error of their ways.

A friend of mine runs a small manufacturing company. In the earlier years of its existence, it made small gadgets out of metal. Some of these were end products, but most of them were parts which were supplied to other fabricators. Recently, however, this firm changed its raw material from metal to plastic, and my friend has thanked his lucky stars many times that he and his associates did not think of themselves primarily as metalworkers but as manufacturers of small parts. If they had considered themselves metalworkers, then they might never have changed to plastics—a material which served their purposes better and enabled them to hold old customers while adding new ones.

Do the executives watch day-to-day developments in their own industry so closely that they lose track of some big, sweeping, long-range developments in the world, or their part of it, which may affect their business vitally? Do they take time to think about these major trends?

This, it seems to me, is a tremendously important question. There will be few readers that cannot quickly think of many executives who have become victims of their own inaction in this particular respect. Here are two illustrations of situations where this tendency affected a whole industry:

I know of two or three large retail establishments which concentrated with great success on internal store management, and perhaps on merchandising generally, but failed to notice that the urban areas around them were changing, and that the changes would affect their locations adversely. Such stores have ended up with fine buildings, good staffs, and perhaps good merchandise, but in the wrong part of the city. Shopping centers moved away from them, and they did not take this into account.

Similarly, many New England textile companies have gotten themselves into serious trouble by failing to assess the growing business opportunities offered by other parts of the country. Or they failed to see new labor situations and new developments in raw materials.

Does management frequently ask, "What is wrong with our product or our competitors' products which, if corrected, would put us out ahead of the parade?"

I suppose every product has something wrong with it, and in a general way most companies are trying to improve what they sell. But I am referring to conscious, continuous attempts to assess products, or services, with the idea that they can be made still better. Let me cite two examples:

My first illustration is a company with which everyone is acquainted, Cluett-Peabody. This company, which manufactures and sells men's wear, had to make a major decision regarding its product line after World War I. In its earlier years, Cluett-Peabody had been primarily a manufacturer of men's stiff collars, but changes in the public taste had just about put an end to that business. Some of the directors wanted to continue the company as a maker of stiff collars despite the declining market. Others believed that the firm might as well go out of business altogether.

But a third group, headed by C. R. Palmer who was then sales manager and later became president, saw a chance to break into the shirt business by improving the quality of the product currently available to the public. Accordingly, the officers took a very close look at men's shirts and asked in effect, "What is wrong with them?" They came up with these answers: "For one thing, shirts shrink. For another, the buttons come off easily. Finally, they don't fit too well into the trousers." They determined to do something about these defects—and to do it before other shirt manufacturers did.

So the company set Sanford Cluett to work on the problem of shrinkage, and as a result of this deliberate effort he developed the sanforizing process. It is interesting to know that this process was not confined exclusively to Cluett-Peabody products. During the years between its discovery and the expiration of the process patent, Cluett-Peabody probably made more money by leasing the patent to other manufacturers than it did on its own shirt business. In any event, by correcting a major difficulty in the product, the company kept itself in business.

The Polaroid Company has developed several new products as a result of constant search on the part of its president, E. H. Land, for needs that are not being served. One of these is particularly well known, the Land camera.

In this case, Land decided that "one of the things that's wrong with photography is the fact that you have to wait so long after taking a picture before you can see it." So he developed a new kind of camera, which produces a finished picture in less than a minute after the snapshot is taken. Sales developed almost spontaneously.

Organization and Action

Are there people in the organization with commercial sense, who can translate research and new ideas into marketable products?

By this I mean: Is there an individual or a group that has the knack of seeing what items the public would use if they existed, or seeing what developments in the laboratory can be turned into usable, salable products? And are there men or women able to design for manufacture, to manufacture at an appropriately low cost, to advertise and carry on promotional activities so that the public will know of the product and be willing to buy it?

The skill to carry through this whole chain of activities—taking an idea from the laboratory or from a need discovered in the market, and working out this whole series of steps—is important and all too rare. In some few instances one person has all these abilities. More often, they are found only in groups. The important point is that a company must have individuals or groups who possess these complementary characteristics. Thus:

In my mind, one of the outstanding examples in our country of a company that has these abilities in high degree is du Pont. This company has created what have become almost new industries out of discoveries from its laboratories. In the hands of the du Pont people, products which did not amount to very much for the previous owners have become large-volume items. It is one of the tests of real genius in management to know what to develop, how much to spend on it, and when to abandon fruitless avenues of investigation.

Does the management of the company have a good sense of timing?

The history of business is filled with stories of firms that did what might have been the right thing, but did it at the wrong time. A sense of timing has three main components: we have to decide *when* to do something; we have to decide *how long* to allow for something to happen, and, finally, we have to decide *what is the best sequence* of moves. For example:

In the 1930s the Chrysler Corporation introduced what was known as the Air-flow DeSoto, a streamlined car which was not greatly unlike some models that later became quite successful. But apparently the Air-flow DeSoto was a little ahead of its time, and it did not take very well with the public.

By contrast, in 1954 all the models put out by the company, in all it makes, were a little behind the times, for the management was gambling that 1954 would be a year in which automobiles could be sold without much change. But the other auto makers acted on a different assumption and produced cars with more advanced engineering or styling. Chrysler had a very bad year both saleswise and financially.

In recent years the Fairbanks Morse Company has developed a diesel which, I have been told by some friends in the railroad industry, is better than those currently used by most railroads. However, the chances are slim that Fairbanks Morse will sell many, at least in the near future. Why? Because the railroads are already well equipped with other kinds of diesel engines. Their repair facilities are set up to take care of the types they have. Also, they have parts and supply arrangements on hand for maintaining their existing equipment. So it would seem that the Fairbanks Morse Company developed a better product, but did so too late.

But timing is more than a matter of products—it comes into human relations as well. When do you push members of your organization, and when do you leave them alone; when do you needle them, and when is a compliment more effective? One of the arts of management is to do these things at the right time. If you don't push people hard enough, they may become complacent and lazy; if you push them too hard, you may break their spirits, or they may leave their jobs. Pushing at just the right time calls for real genius. To illustrate:

General George S. Patton, Jr., was a strict disciplinarian who had very high standards for himself, and expected other officers to live up to similar standards. He frequently gave his subordinates a severe tongue-lashing if he thought they had fallen down on the job.

During the latter part of World War II when his army was crossing southern Germany, a certain General X allowed his lines to get overextended, so his corps was out ahead of those on his flanks. In this exposed position, he was starting to have trouble and was busily engaged in trying to correct his line so that he would not be cut off or seriously damaged by the enemy.

General X was in his headquarters when an orderly came to the door and said, "Sir, General Patton is arriving. He will be coming in in just a minute." General X said his heart dropped into his stomach as he thought to himself, "Why in hell did the General have to pick this day to call on me?" He did not have a chance to think much more than this before General Patton himself opened the door and walked in.

Patton went straight to General X, put his arm around his shoulders, and said, "My boy, you've got trouble enough today without having a visit from me. If there's anything we can do at headquarters to help you out, let us know." Thereupon he turned and walked out. General X said that if he ever loved a man and respected him, it was at that moment.

Is the organization afraid to make exceptions? Does it recognize them for what they are, and return to a general policy?

In other words, do not be afraid to make exceptions, but avoid making so many of them that basic policies are changed by accident. It is clearly the part of wisdom to have the members of an organization know that they can make exceptions when needed. Nevertheless, safeguards must exist so they will not run away with this right. To illustrate:

A person I know has been in the wholesale business for many years. His company, historically, has been a high-quality house. It never attempted to compete on the basis of price cutting, but relied on good merchandise, good service, and good relations with customers.

Nevertheless, the head of this concern was recently shocked to find that within a period of several months his firm made so many price concessions that it almost became known as a price cutter. Though each of these concessions had been made for what seemed like a good reason at the time, the process had gone so far, and so fast, that customers were beginning to think they should get concessions on everything.

This led to poor relations between the company and some of its customers, and management was faced with a touch uphill job to get the business back into the price brackets where it belonged.

Do the executives work continually at training men? Do they let people make mistakes as part of the cost of growing? Do they find places for them, either inside or outside the company?

Certainly no part of a chief executive's job is more important than the task of finding, attracting, motivating, and rewarding people. This is a time-consuming activity, and it is one which, in my opinion, chief executives themselves must watch closely.

It is emotionally difficult for a boss to let people make mistakes, especially if the chief is also the founder of the firm. Anyone who has been in on the development of a business or at one time has done much of the work oneself often hates to leave decisions to others. Even if the company has grown quite large, such a person finds it hard to accept the mistakes of his or her subordinates, or to see their errors as part of the cost of developing their maturity and wisdom. It may well be that the president could do a job better than one of his assistants, but he has to balance the importance of the immediate task against the importance of developing his people. In other words, allowing people to make some mistakes is part of the price that he has to be paid to insure a future for the company. For example:

Most people know that the elder Henry Ford, as long as he actively managed his business, tried to keep track of a great many details. It was hard for him to delegate. As a young man with a young company, he could and did succeed in running his business on this basis.

In the early years, up to about the time the Model T came to an end, the Ford company was highly profitable. But from then on, until Mr. Ford dropped out of the picture in 1945, in all those years put together, the company probably never added to the earlier earnings. The reasons, of course, were many, but one surely lay in the fact that Mr. Ford did not see fit to build an organization. He did not develop people who were able to do the job which had to be done in view of competition and the size of his company.

But today's top-management group has put together an organization of able subordinates, including a great many young men. Throughout the organization it is understood that young executives will get responsibility—and will make some mistakes as part of the cost of growing. And the Ford company currently is doing very well indeed.

Does the management group contain all the specific abilities it needs?

These do not have to be combined in any one person; indeed, they probably will not be. But are they available in all the personnel, taken together? To answer this question properly, the abilities must be measured against the needs of the particular company and industry, and these will clearly vary from firm to firm. For example:

What kinds of abilities does the management group of Coca-Cola need? I think we could say that the managers probably do not spend much time on the question of developing new products. Moreover, their manufacturing is not a highly complicated process, though they do need people with the best obtainable judgment on price trends to watch the price of sugar, their main ingredient. But what they are betting on, above everything else, is special ability as advertisers and promoters. In this they have achieved great success. Indeed, you can hardly turn around without seeing a Coca-Cola advertisement, and wherever you see one, a bottle of Coke can be bought close by.

In another company, manufacturing various kinds of specialized pumps, the need for abilities has been less clear-cut. For some time the company brought out a brand-new pump every two or three years, based on some substantial difference in engineering principles. Though volume was not large (compared with some of its nationally known competitors), profits were high because the products were well suited to the specialized needs of a great many industries. Then all of a sudden this rate of growth in product development came to an end, and profits began to decline. Why?

During the earlier period, the company was headed by two partners who complemented each other in every way. One of them was an inventor and designer; he had great imagination, but his ideas needed to be curbed and disciplined. The other was a salesman, with tremendous personal drive; moreover, he had the knack of seeing commercial possibilities, both in the plants of his customers and in the ideas of his partner. It was he who steered the course, kept his partner working on new developments which would have good sales possibilities, and also fed in to him suggestions from the field on the kinds of products needed.

These two men together were a great team, but unfortunately they came to a parting of the ways. Since that time, the company has never had people in its management group who had the particular abilities of the two original partners working together as I have described.

Human Relations

Is there good morale, and does management know why?

We all recognize that morale is a very fragile affair. Just a few seemingly minor changes can cause the spirit of a working group to deteriorate very fast. Someone has said that morale is nothing more than the result of a lot of little things put together. It certainly does not come just from fine speeches, nor is it necessarily the result of high wages.

Morale develops out of circumstances which are such that people willingly give themselves to their tasks. To a larger extent it depends on good leadership. People like to follow someone if they believe he is interested in their welfare and able to do something about it. If he is willing but not able, they will not respond to him very long. If he is able but not interested, people will not give their wholehearted support.

But whatever the general truths are in this area, it is important for management to find out the reasons in the particular case. Otherwise, the factors may change without anyone realizing it, and real trouble develops. To illustrate:

In a small New England manufacturing town, there was one company which was by far the largest employer. The officers of the company rather prided themselves on having good morale in their plant. They also prided themselves on the fact that they had this good morale without bothering to do a lot of things to get it that they knew other companies were doing. Then, about two years ago, there was a change of priests in the Catholic Church, which was the main church in the community. Soon the company officers began to notice many disagreements among their employees; the people were less happy with their work and seemed to find more reasons to complain. In sum, morale had deteriorated.

Slowly it dawned on the officers of the company that morale in their plant depended more on the Catholic priest than on anything they had done themselves. Apparently the first priest had been a man who looked favorably on business. He had urged his people to be patient, even if they thought working conditions were not particularly good. He had created an atmosphere in which members of his parish concluded that the circumstances under which they worked were probably as good as they could expect. But the second priest had quite a different point of view. He was a great believer in reform, and let it be known to the members of his parish that they had a right to insist on better working conditions.

Now it is going to be difficult to restore good morale. The managers let slip the opportunity to establish it firmly when circumstances were favorable because they did not realize the true situation.

Does the business maintain an atmosphere in which subordinates and fellow officers feel free to talk to the top officers as well as to each other?

I am including this question in my list, not because it is anything new but because it is so important. Indeed, it has been my experience that here is one of the most crucial factors in keeping a business growing and progressive. If the company atmosphere is such that people do feel free to talk to one another, the chances of success are greatly increased.

I have seen several cases in which the boss told his organization, "Now, I want you people to criticize; I want you to come to me with ideas as you have them." If, however, someone does come only to be ignored or to have his idea laughed at, people will stop trying. It is not what the boss *says* about talking freely that counts; it is the way he *reacts* when people try to give him ideas.

I have often said, and I believe, that outside of every boss's door there is a great pile of good ideas that died right there. They were brought that far by someone who meant to talk them over with the boss, and then for some reason decided, "Oh, it isn't worth the effort." It is one of the skills of management to draw ideas out of the members of an organization. But if people are to contribute, the boss must listen.

Furthermore, this is not just a matter of free talk between subordinate and superior. It is also a matter of free talk between people at the same level. The atmosphere created by the man at the very top of a company tends to be reflected below him. If the head man himself really welcomes suggestions, if he is really willing to listen, the chances are greater that the officers under him will adopt a similar pattern of behavior. To illustrate:

Some students, in the course of working on a report, became well acquainted with a large number of foremen and workers in a manufacturing company of moderate size. They succeeded in winning the confidence of these people, and learned a great many things the managers of the company did not know. A drive for greater productivity and lower costs had been under way for some time, but results were disappointing. Ideas the management sought to introduce bore little fruit.

When asked by the students whether output could not in fact be increased, most of the workers said, "Of course it could, easily." And they had many seemingly good ideas regarding better methods. When asked if they had suggested ideas to the management, they said, "Of course not— they've never asked us."

Do the top executives assume that what they tell people is understood and accepted?

Theoretically, we might suppose that if we talk to someone, he or she will understand us. As a practical matter, this is not necessarily so. Words are the best symbols we have for our ideas; nevertheless, what a word means to me may not be the same as what it means to you. It is therefore necessary that in communication, either oral or written, we take the time and the pains to make sure we are reasonably well understood. Often this may involve asking a person, in some discreet way, to indicate what he or she thinks we have talked about.

Beyond this question of whether or not people understand what we say is the still more important question of whether they accept what we have told them. A person can listen, nod her head or say some words, and seem to be willing to conform. However, if she does not in fact accept our idea, if she does not believe in the reasons behind it, she may not do anything about it at all. Or even if she goes through the motions of doing what we ask, she can do it so badly or with so little heart that the success of the venture is nil. Consequently, we have to take the time to explain things to people. Thus:

A public utility foreman told a crew of men to dig a hole at a particular location. This hole was to be about three feet by five feet and six feet deep. They dug the hole; he went and looked in it and said, "No, fill it up; dig another one over here." With somewhat less enthusiasm, the crew went to work on the second hole. When they finished it, the foreman looked in and again said, "No, fill it up; dig one here." At this point, the crew members were very reluctant, but they went ahead and, swinging their picks and shovels still more slowly, dug the third hole. When they were finished, the foreman once again looked in and said, "No, fill it up; let's dig one over here."

One of the workmen, Tony, said, "Boss, you're crazy. You say, 'Dig a hole, fill it up; dig a hole, fill it up.' I think you're crazy. I'm gonna quit." Not until this moment did it occur to the foreman that the members of the crew had no idea what they were doing, so he said, "Why, what we're doing, boys—we're trying to find a pipe that's buried somewhere around here." At this, Tony shouted, "Why didn't you tell us so? In the second hole we dug, we were right by the side of a pipe."

Does management assume that other people necessarily feel or should feel the same way that it does?

I hasten to suggest that if it does assume this, it is in for some disappointments. It is a common error made by all of us, when judging the reactions of other people, to assume that their responses will be like ours. But actually even those who have more or less the same point of view will differ sharply over some matters. Because this is so, we have to take time to figure out their probable reactions, their assumptions, their feelings. This is the case whether we are dealing with fellow officers, or employees, or the public. To illustrate:

Recently I learned of a manufacturer who has never really recovered from having his feelings hurt when his workers joined a union. He took it as a personal affront. He told his associates, "I can't understand why they believe someone else, a union leader, is more interested in their welfare or can do more for them than I can." Several years have passed since his company was unionized, but his feelings have mended only very slightly. To this day, he cannot understand why his employees would want to join a union, and he still expends a great deal of nervous energy worrying about his situation.

He would be a happier man, and a better executive as well, if he could say to himself, "Apparently my workers do not feel the way I do about this matter." It would help him if he could simply accept this fact and not let it continue to be a major preoccupation.

Basic Integrity

Finally, there is one overall question which is of tremendous importance. It is a simple one, but it touches on something which is vital to the success of individual firms, and vital to the success of business as a part of our civilization.

Do the executives have integrity?

It is very easy to take integrity for granted, to assume that other people recognize its importance and that we ourselves are automatically endowed with it. But integrity is more complex and elusive than we think.

In the first place, integrity concerns our relationships with other people, and involves such simple questions as: Are we honest with them? Do we tell them the truth?

A second aspect of integrity raises the issue: Are we honest with ourselves? It has been my observation that most people, as they grow up and mature, come to realize the unwisdom of being dishonest with others. With greater maturity comes an awareness that we easily are, but certainly should not be, dishonest with ourselves. Do we face up to tough situations if they are unpleasant? Or do we assume, "Well, time will heal this thing," or, "Somebody else will probably take care of it." Do we just close our eyes and pretend the problem does not even exist?

Still a third part of integrity is this: Do we look at all the facts about a situation, or just the facts that support our own hopes and preconceptions? I know a great many people in business—I expect we all do—who are so anxious to succeed in making a point, or in making a sale, or in supporting some pet notion of their own, that they look only for reasons in their favor. Some people regard statistical or factual data as nothing more than a source of arguments which they can use to support their own ideas; they fail to realize that such data should be used as aids in reaching the best conclusions.

There are many areas in which, in my opinion, businesspeople need to guard against temptations to depart from real integrity. Among them are the following:

☐ Making promises to members of your organization which you may or may not be able to fulfill (e.g., holding out hopes of promotion to too many people).

☐ Pretending to act in the public welfare when you are in fact acting chiefly for your own company or, worse still, for yourself personally (e.g., some lobbying tactics).

☐ Abusing expense account privileges.

☐ Using sales promotional tactics which, if not technically dishonest, are at least misleading (e.g., some borderline advertising claims).

☐ Urging people to buy something which you know they do not need and/or cannot afford.

☐ Excusing something of which you disapprove by rationalizing that competition forces you to do it.

These are just a few areas. Businesspeople who read this will think of still others. I think it all boils down to one fact: wise is the person who is thoroughly honest with himself, who has integrity enough to look at all the facts, even though this forces him to change his own view.

It is my opinion that businesspeople do not have substantially more, or less, integrity than people in other occupations. But I think it is important that businesspeople should have a higher sense of integrity than others, and should so conduct themselves that this is recognized by all. We talk sometimes about making business a profession. What does this mean? Certainly a profession is, among other things, a group whose members have adopted high standards of conduct, which they have pledged themselves to observe, and which they do observe.

In our democratic, free-enterprise type of civilization, we have as a basic premise the expectation that people will act responsibly, that we can depend on one another. This certainly assumes self-discipline and integrity.

In sum, it seems to me that, if one is to be truly a business leader, and not just an executive, one must have the persistence to ask oneself about the strengths and weaknesses of one's company and the courage to ask oneself about one's own integrity.

32

Directors' Responsibility for Corporate Strategy

KENNETH R. ANDREWS

A discussion of the board's role in formulating, ratifying, changing, or evaluating corporate strategy. Andrews' intent is to stimulate CEOs and their boards of directors to take a fresh look at this critical issue.

The strengthening of the corporate board of directors has not yet produced a clear or widely accepted conclusion about the board's role in formulating, ratifying, changing, or evaluating corporate strategy. Discussion of this subject among chief executive officers (who are often also board chairmen) does not thrive.

Previous articles in *From the Boardroom*—for instance, Samuel M. Felton's "Case of the Board and the Strategic Process"[1] and William W. Wommack's "The Board's Most Important Function"[2]—produced little response. Not much has been said elsewhere. Audit committees, compensation committees, and social responsibility committees have all become commonplace, yet the pressures bringing them into being have only rarely produced strategy committees.

We do not have to look far to find out why. Many chief executive officers, rejecting the practicality of conscious strategy, preside over unstated, incremental, or intuitive strategies that have never been articulated or analyzed—and therefore could not be deliberated by the board. Others do not believe their outside directors know enough or have time enough to do more than assent to strategic recommendations. Still others may keep

Editor's Note. This article is adapted from a talk given by the author to a *Business Week* conference on corporate strategy and the board of directors in New York City, October 14, 1980.

discussions of strategy within management to prevent board transgression onto management turf and consequent reduction of executives' power to shape by themselves the future of their companies.

Few chairmen whom I have encountered in my experience, research, or correspondence share the wish of Robert A. Charpie. president of Cabot Corporation, to "see a board 100% involved."[3] Able, amiable, and competent as they are, even fewer chairmen want to undertake the work and turmoil required to make such involvement useful.

But even if strategy were not such a sensitive topic, invoking latent tension between CEO and independent directors, it would require more time and sophistication than chairmen or outside directors, however willing, could easily summon to the task. At best, original contribution by outside directors is limited and infrequent. Nonetheless, the forces shaping corporate governance, including restlessness among independent directors, are pressing boards toward greater participation in determining the future direction and character of their companies.

I will make a careful statement now that, however harmless it looks, will certainly not win the commitment of most chief executives for some time:

A responsible and effective board should require of its management a unique and durable corporate strategy, review it periodically for its validity, use it as the reference point for all other board decisions, and share with management the risks associated with its adoption.

What Corporate Strategy Is

Virtually every word of so summary a statement requires definition before the statement can be fully understood. By the fashionable phrase, "corporate strategy," for example, I mean the pattern of company purposes and goals— and the major policies for achieving those goals—that defines the business or businesses the company is to be involved with and the kind of company it is to be.

A statement articulating corporate purpose differentiates the company in some way from all its competitors and stems from a perception of present and future market opportunities, distinctive competence, competitive advantage, available resources, and management's personal aspirations and values.

Corporate strategy reconciles what a company might do in terms of opportunity, what it can do in terms of its strengths, what its management wants it to do, and what it thinks is ethical, legal, and moral.

This concept of strategy thus involves economic, social, and personal purposes—not financial objectives alone. Although it evolves with the development of markets, company strengths, and institutional values, corporate strategy marks out a deliberately chosen direction and governs directly the investment decisions, organization structure, incentive systems, and indeed the essential character of the company. It embodies a disciplined unity of purpose, a purpose which—to be powerful—must be clear and worthy of the commitment of energetic and intelligent people.[4]

Such a concept of strategy makes an important contribution to management. It forces continuous sensitivity to changes taking place in the company's environment and resources. It requires managers to lay conflicting personal agendas on the table and to look beyond immediate opportunities toward long-term growth and development. Such strategy summons up imagination, innovation, and a zest for risk; and it focuses the work of specialists as well.

The concept of corporate strategy has its shortcomings, as well, for it demands tough, high-risk commitment to a choice of direction. Because it means that a company must sometimes forgo immediate profits for long-term superiority, it can seem inconvenient. For instance, an acquisition that raises current earnings per share but has no future fit with either market development or distinctive competence will be ruled out. Corporate strategy demands that companies examine carefully the muted demands of the future and suppress the clamor of the present.

In both business and government, "muddling through" is the classic response to politically confused decisions about purpose. It has its proponents not only among practitioners but also among scholars. The coalition theory of R. M. Cyert and J. G. March substitutes internal bargaining among special interests for corporate strategy—on the assumption that organizations do not have purposes; only people do.[5] David Baybrooke and Charles E. Lindblom, without so much as a smile, call their view of purposeless organization "disjointed incrementalism."[6] And in 1967 H. Edward Wrapp published his beguiling but no less anti-strategic "Good Managers Don't Make Policy Decisions."[7]

If a management group cannot decide on a loftier or more practical purpose than adapting to whatever comes, improvisation becomes its limited strategy and the planning horizon closes in. Should this occur, the board must look for an early breakout—even demanding new leadership if necessary—before its company flunks out of national and international competition.

Why Require a Corporate Strategy?

My argument thus far has been that it is better for corporate management to have a strategy than not. But why should a board concern itself with the strategy's content? I submit four principal reasons:

☐ *First,* the board needs specific evidence that its management has a process for developing, considering, and choosing among strategic alternatives operating within the company.

☐ *Second,* especially if they have no personal experience in the industry, independent directors need to understand the characteristics of their company's business. Knowledge of strategy makes intelligent overview feasible.

☐ *Third,* knowing the company's strategy can give the board a reference point for separate decisions that come before it and insight into what matters should be presented to it. If their approval is to be more than routine assent, board members must be allowed to assess the impact of proposals—whether for capital appropriation, a new R&D facility, or an acquisition in an exchange of stock—on their company's strategy.

If management can answer the directors' questions about the strategic impact of a single proposal, the directors will be reassured not only about the soundness of that proposal but also about the continuing objectivity of management. Through a series of specific questions related to management's stated intentions, the board can prevent the company from straying off its strategic course, without resorting to overcautious conservatism.

☐ The *fourth* reason for directors to insist not only that a company have an explicit strategy but also that it present the strategy to them is that evaluation of corporate strategy and of management's adherence to it allows continuous evaluation of management.

Short-term measures are unsatisfactory for evaluation. The best criterion for appraising the quality of management performance, in the absence of personal failures or unexpected breakdowns, is management's success over time in executing a demanding and approved strategy that is continually tested against opportunity and need. The combination of short-term return and long-term investment can only be evaluated over several years.

How to interpret windfall advantages and undeserved misfortune—and to judge skill against results—becomes straightforward when a board can observe executive performance against a consciously considered and explicitly stated corporate strategy. Discussion of strategic issues in the context of the company reveals executives' quality of mind and depth of judgment and gives directors a foundation for later interpretation of results.

Role in Strategy Development

How should the board participate in the development of strategy? This is a tough question to answer. A board does not formulate strategy; its function is *review*—a word as slippery in meaning as it is soft in sound.

If the review process leads the board to approve corporate actions, the board must stand behind its assent. This support entails sharing with the CEO the risks of the decisions it approves, and the board should not approve decisions until it is fully willing to accept those risks.

The review process, by which a management recommendation wins rather than coerces board approval, begins only after full-scale presentation of strategy to the board. The process resumes, as indicated earlier, whenever a capital appropriation, unexpected shortfall, or other strategically important matter comes before the board.

Review is principally discussion sparked by questions and answers. The rejected alternatives are discussed until the directors are satisfied that the process which produced the recommendation was thorough. Discussion concludes in consensus, either to approve or to support withdrawal of the recommendation. The degree to which the directors are convinced that the recommendation meets the strategic tests applied to it in advance affects their subsequent loyalty to the CEO if and when the project fails.

However, review of strategic recommendations goes beyond establishing the board's satisfaction with the strategic process. For example, a publishing house decided that, because of the progress of information technology, it should expand beyond a solely book-producing orientation. At a board meeting, the president proposed the acquisition of two small supplier companies involved in electronically accessible data bases. The entrepreneurial founders of the data base companies were present at the publisher's board meeting to discuss the synergy that would be made possible by the acquisition. An urbane, high-speed summary of the proposed acquisition, allegedly backed by extensive management inquiry, produced the board's expected affirmative vote—which was apparently justified strategically.

After the meeting, two of the outside directors (who had asked questions and received "answers") met at the elevator. Without speaking, they both shook their heads. Each had formed a negative opinion about the education, breadth, competence, and integrity of the entrepreneurs and about the future of the publishing company if these people became part of management. Subsequent to the acquisition, the two subsidiaries were eventually disbanded for reasons that appeared to justify—at least in the view of these skeptical directors—the wholly unexplored and uncertain distrust they had felt when the board made its original "strategic" decision.

Of course, the outcome might still have been the same, even had the consideration of these small acquisitions been more extensive. Perhaps the judgment, skill, and practice required for such a major decision were lacking among both management and the board.

Nonetheless, hindsight makes clear that the board's discussion should have led to further consideration of the proposal and to more skeptical appraisal of the two data base proprietors. The directors' questions, which could not have been wholly clear in the presence of the visitors, should have led management to realize that it needed better answers and that it needed to withdraw the proposal until it understood the import of the questions and had gotten those answers.

Special Full-Scale Strategy Reviews

A director cannot be incisive and influential unless he or she is familiar with the issues involved. Consideration of new strategies, complex annual reviews, and corporate updates are hard to fit into board meetings of ordinary length. A number of companies have undertaken a special two- or three-day strategy meeting at a location apart from the company, and sometimes with spouses invited for a partially separate program. Senior members of management and planning staff are included.

In such a setting, the systematic presentation of the past year's results compared to the year's plan (with analysis of discrepancies) is accompanied by the presentation of the following one- or two-year plan. The latter plan is then considered against the long-range plan.

More important, in informal sessions at the bar or at meals, the participants' concept of the company and its future is discussed without the usual constraints. Such discussion sometimes includes the board's role and how effectively it contributes to the strategy process.

Assigning more time to the formal consideration of the company's future does not of course guarantee useful contribution from the board, but it does contribute enormously to the board's education. Everyone is exposed to people they might not meet otherwise—directors, managers, staff members, and spouses—and this wider acquaintance leads to (1) greater knowledge of the company and its people, (2) greater trust in individuals' competence and goodwill, (3) understanding of the unevenness of management strength and the opportunity for management development, (4) relaxation of the tension between outside directors and chief executive officers, and (5) keener interest in future opportunities.

To prepare for and schedule a special full-scale strategy review meeting is a formidable undertaking. In fact, the time-consuming nature of the task lends support to Courtney Brown's arguments that the chief executive officer should not be chairman of the board.[8]

Although such a meeting need not culminate in a two- or three-day retreat every year, any effort to prepare a board to understand and play some part in the strategic decisions of a complex company requires more time than a CEO may be able to give it. A separate chairman to look after this and other board functions, or (as William Wommack suggests) a chief strategic officer in management ranks, or a massive delegation of operating responsibilities by the CEO may be necessary to allow time time for strategic leadership.

But no matter how strategy sessions are arranged, good chairmanship—to provoke productive discussions or identification of the more debatable issues—is indispensable. At a minimum, careful reading of well-prepared staff reports, with discussion focused on issues that cannot yet be finally resolved, clarifies insight and informs subsequent judgment.

Corporate Strategy Committee

Especially since the collapse of Penn Central led to the proliferation of audit committees, organization by committee has been the board's means of coping with its increased workload. The audit committee performs the watchdog function by monitoring compliance with SEC regulations and the Foreign Corrupt Practices Act and by investigating problems of ethical conduct. The compensation and nominating committees often not only establish executive compensation and recommend new candidates for election but examine the qualifications and performance of senior management and of the board itself.

Organization by committee economizes the time of directors, puts the most qualified people in charge of given issues, educates directors, and provides a relatively private context for discussion of sensitive subjects.

The arguments against a strategy committee are the same arguments used against any form of board involvement in strategy. These arguments ignore powerful trends in corporate governance, minimize directors' potential contributions, and reduce the possiblity of building a strong and able board. They will almost certainly fall on deaf ears with the onset of a new generation of chief executive officers, the developing awareness of responsibility among independent directors, and the possibility that conventional management practice tends to undermine productivity.

Composition and Function

For a strategy committee to work, it should be composed of carefully chosen outside directors who have shown interest and talent in considering strategic questions brought to the board. New directors can be recruited especially for this function.

In the few companies I know of in which a strategy committee has been established, the committee members started off slowly, hearing from one segment of a business at a time and acquainting themselves with the information as well as the managers presenting it. A second level of sophistication would be to have committee members prepare for meetings by reading staff studies that discuss future risks, possibilities, investments, and projects.

After it had become famliar with current strategy, the committee's function would be to assess the strategy's strengths and weaknesses and to consider what measures might improve the strategy. The committee would also discuss the issues being debated within management and consider key proposals before they reached the board. It would note whether other committees—like finance, investment, or pension management—had interest in a proposal.

One of the principal functions of the committee would be to encourage the strengthening of the strategic planning process within the company—to get to know the key participants and to appraise the context within which capital projects and new product ideas originate.

Character of Discussions

Participation in the strategy formulation process made possible by an active committee could become so intimate as to make CEOs very nervous. Putting information about many possibilities in the hands of outside directors who have become opinionated in their own success and self-esteem can lead to snap-judgment preferences hard to dislodge later.

In some boards where the strategy committee approach has been tried, the unwritten rules constraining discussion have been relaxed to the point that partisanship or bias has been avoided. Individual directors and the CEO challenge each other, and—their relationships strengthened by associations developed in such situations as off-site discussions—they explore things informally as well as more seriously. Directors too quick to substitute their opinions for those of management can be called for interference. Assured that the strategy committee members are not going to take a position prematurely or fault them for indecision, some CEOs have brought to the committee vexing problems, serious threats, and impending choices well before management was ready to make a formal recommendation to the board.

Besides encouraging directors to produce ideas, this strategy committee process could still the restlessness of directors who are uneasy at the yes or no choice given them when a new proposal arrives with a firm recommendation. The basis for saying yes is loyalty to management; the case for the proposal contains little basis for saying no. Prior discussion would let the directors be heard and might make them more understanding and less resentful if they were later overruled. The lines between management and board authority must remain clear, but the more communication across them the better.

The strategy committee would neither create nor dispose of problems of board-management relations. It would simply be a device to make practical the convergence of varied points of view and the dissipation of provincial, functional, or occupational bias. It would do what the board as a whole should but cannot do; it would segregate—like all effective committee structures—the appropriate problems, questions, and recommendations to those most interested and qualified. Like the other committees of the board, it would be shaped by its leadership, composition, and assigned function.

Contribution to Creative Strategy

No discussion of board involvement in strategy formulation, full-board strategy sessions, and corporate strategy committees should conclude without attempting to dispel the solemnity that usually descends on the subject. For individual directors, strategic participation means more work, more time, more thought, and probably at times more uncertainty, frustration, and concern.

Nonetheless, the most common response to exposure to central management issues is stimulation, excitement, satisfaction, greater confidence in being able to contribute, and ideas and knowledge to take back to one's own company. The opportunity to consider someone else's problems is usually exhilarating. The convergence of new points of view on long-standing problems previously viewed between one set of blinders sometimes produces dramatic and satisfying results.

The normal routine of assent to management proposals, based on general confidence in management as justified by past performance, is essentially boring. When participants have reason to wonder whether their confidence in past performance is a sound basis for expecting adequate future performance, they feel frustrated. If in their relationship the CEO is overly forceful and the board overly acquiescent, an unproductive, even dangerous, situation results.

Freer participation by the board in contributing to strategy formation would be of no great importance unless such participation produced better decisions by management. The heart of the strategic process is the generation of alternatives—combining in new ways market opportunity, customer needs and company capabilities. If a company is to stand apart from its competitors with superior returns on its equity (and why not?), then it must nurture the kind of creativity that finds new applications and new definitions of its distinctive competence.

The current erosion of assets under inflation, the decline in productivity, the temporary collapse of our automobile industry, and the lessening of U.S. competitive capabilities all call for more boldness and imagination in the management of innovation and the undertaking of risk. The leaping innovation that is occasionally produced by imagination and creativity cannot be decreed or simulated. It is throttled by the fear of failure, the cracked voice of experience, the tyranny of plans mechanically requiring an arbitrary percentage growth rate quarter by quarter.

Nonetheless, imagination exists in all questing organizations and people; it can be released and encouraged. The articulated goal to be first in a chosen technology or market, supported by money and people focused on bold objectives, can produce a Wang or Intel at the expense of many a pedestrian competitor. Boards of directors do not themselves create or invent, but they can take into their overview the innovative processes of the company and support their strengthening.

Through its concern with its company's strategy, a board could emphasize and contribute to the search for new opportunity. "What's new?" is a question that should have an unending series of answers in the execution as well as formulation of strategy. Every qualified director has some special skill or experience that could be brought to bear without short-circuiting the authority of management.

Creativity can be served, in short, by realizing the potential for board contribution to corporate strategy. The variety of experience, points of view, technical and general knowledge, and quality of judgment present in a well-put-together board can extend management's constrained view of the world and bring stimulation and new ideas to executives grooved by their company's experience to stereotyped policymaking and behavior.

This variety can be made fully effective only by involving boards in the most critical issues facing their chief executive officers—the identity and mission of their companies, the direction they are to maintain in a fast-changing world, and the innovative decisions that will make their strategies successful.

Notes

1. *HBR*, July–August 1979, p. 20.

2. *HBR*, September–October 1979, p. 48.

3. Quoted in *HBR*, July–August 1979, p. 26.

4. For a fuller description, see my book, *The Concept of Corporate Strategy*, revised edition (Homewood, Ill., Dow Jones-Irwin, 1980).

5. R. M. Cyert and J. G. March, *A Behavioral Theory of the Firm* (Englewood Cliffs, N.J., Prentice-Hall, 1963).

6. David Baybrooke and Charles E. Lindblom, *A Strategy of Decision* (New York, The Free Press, 1963).

7. H. Edward Wrapp, "Good Managers Don't Make Policy Decisions," *HBR*, September–October 1967, p. 91.

8. See Courtney C. Brown, *Putting the Corporate Board to Work* and *Beyond the Bottom Line* (New York, Macmillan, 1976 and 1979, respectively).

33

Managing Our Way to Economic Decline

ROBERT H. HAYES and WILLIAM J. ABERNATHY

How are we to fix responsiblity for the current malaise of American business? Most attribute its weakened condition to the virus of inflation, the paralysis brought on by government regulation and tax policy, or the feverish price escalation by OPEC. Not quite right, say the authors. In their judgment, responsibility rests not with general economic foces alone but also with the failure of American managers to keep their companies technologically competitive over the long run. In advancing their controversial diagnosis, the authors draw on their own extensive work in the production field as well as their recent association with Harvard's International Senior Managers Program in Vevey, Switzerland. Having taken a long hard look from abroad at how American managers operate, they propose some strong medicine for improving the health of American business.

During the past several years American business has experienced a marked deterioration of competitive vigor and a growing unease about its overall economic well-being. This decline in both health and confidence has been attributed by economists and business leaders to such factors as the rapacity of OPEC, deficiencies in government tax and monetary policies, and the proliferation of regulation. We find these explanations inadequate.

They do not explain, for example, why the rate of productivity growth in America has declined both absolutely and relative to that in Europe and Japan. Nor do they explain why in many high-technology as well as mature industries America has lost is leadership position. Although a host of readily named forces—government regulation, inflation, monetary policy, tax laws, labor costs and constraints, fear of a capital shortage, the price of imported oil—have taken their toll on American business, pressures of this sort affect the economic climate abroad just as they do here.

A German executive, for example, will not be convinced by these explanations. Germany imports 95% of its oil (we import 50%), its government's share of gross domestic product is about 37% (ours is about 30%), and workers must be consulted on most major decisions. Yet Germany's rate of productivity growth has actually increased since 1970 and recently rose to more than four times ours. In France the situation is similar, yet today that country's productivity growth in manufacturing (despite current crises in steel and textiles) more than triples ours. No modern industrial nation is immune to the problems and pressures besetting U.S. business. Why then do we find a disproportionate loss of competitive vigor by U.S. companies?

Our experience suggests that, to an unprecedented degree, success in most industries today requires an organizational commitment to compete in the marketplace on technological grounds—that is, to compete over the long run by offering superior products. Yet, guided by what they took to be the newest and best principles of management, American managers have increasingly directed their attention elsewhere. These new principles, despite their sophistication and widespread usefulness, encourage a preference for (1) analytic detachment rather than the insight that comes from "hands on" experience and (2) short-term cost reduction rather than long-term development of technological competitiveness. It is this new managerial gospel, we feel, that has played a major role in undermining the vigor of American industry.

American management, especially in the two decades after World War II, was universally admired for its strikingly effective performance. But times change. An approach shaped and refined during stable decades may be ill suited to a world characterized by rapid and unpredictable change, scarce energy, global competition for markets, and a constant need for innovation. This is the world of the 1980s and, probably, the rest of this century.

The time is long overdue for earnest, objective self-analysis. What exactly have American managers been doing wrong? What are the critical weaknesses in the ways that they have managed the technological performance of their companies? What is the matter with the long-unquestioned assumptions on which they have based their managerial policies and practices?

A Failure of Management

In the past, American managers earned worldwide respect for their carefully planned yet highly aggressive action across three different time frames:

☐ *Short term.* Using existing assets as efficiently as possible.

☐ *Medium term.* Replacing labor and other scarce resources with capital equipment.

☐ *Long term.* Developing new products and processes that open new markets or restructure old ones.

The first of these time frames demanded toughness, determination, and close attention to detail; the second, capital and the willingness to take sizable financial risks; the third, imagination and a certain amount of technological daring.

Our managers still earn generally high marks for their skill in improving short-term efficiency, but their counterparts in Europe and Japan have started to question America's entrepreneurial imagination and willingness to make risky long-term competitive investments. As one such observer remarked to us: "The U.S. companies in my industry act like banks. All they are interested in is return on investment and getting their money back. Sometimes they act as though they are more interested in buying other companies than they are in selling products to customers."

In fact, this curt diagnosis represents a growing body of opinion that openly charges American managers with competitive myopia:

> Somehow or other, American business is losing confidence in itself and espeically confidence in its future. Instead of meeting the challenge of the changing world, American business today is making small, short-term adjustments by cutting costs and by turning to the government for temporary relief. . . . Success in trade is the result of patient and meticulous preparations, with a long period of market preparation before the rewards are available. . . . To undertake such commitments is hardly in the interest of a manager who is concerned with his or her next quarterly earnings reports.[1]

More troubling still, American managers themselves often admit the charge with, at most, a rhetorical shrug of their shoulders. In established businesses, notes one senior vice president of research: "We understand how to market, we know the technology, and production problems are not extreme. Why risk money on new businesses when good, profitable low-risk opportunities are on every side?" Says another: "It's much more difficult to come up with a synthetic meat product than a lemon-lime cake mix. But you work on the lemon-lime cake mix because you know exactly what that return is going to be. A synthetic steak is going to take a lot longer, require a much bigger investment, and the risk of failure will be greater."[2]

These managers are not alone; they speak for many. Why, they ask, should they invest dollars that are hard to earn back when it is so easy—and so much less risky—to make money in other ways? Why ignore a ready-made situation in cake mixes for the deferred and far less certain prospects in synthetic steaks? Why shoulder the competitive risks of making better, more innovative products?

In our judgment, the assumptions underlying these questions are prime evidence of a broad managerial failure—a failure of both vision and leadership—that over time has eroded both the inclination and the capacity of U.S. companies to innovate.

Familiar Excuses

About the facts themselves there can be little dispute. Exhibits 1–4 document our sorry decline. But the explanations and excuses commonly offered invite a good deal of comment.

It is important to recognize, first of all, that the problem is not new. It has been going on for at least 15 years. The rate of productivity growth in the private sector peaked in the mid-1960s. Nor is the problem confined to a few sectors of our economy; with a few exceptions, it permeates our entire economy. Expenditures on R&D by both business and government, as measured in constant (noninflated) dollars, also peaked in the mid-1960s— both in absolute terms and as a percentage of GNP. During the same period the expenditures on R&D by West Germany and Japan have been rising. More important, American spending on R&D as a percentage of sales in such critical research-intensive industries as machinery, professional and scientific instruments, chemicals, and aircraft had dropped by the mid-1970s to about half its level in the early 1960s. These are the very industries on which we now depend for the bulk of our manufactured exports.

Investment in plant and equipment in the United States displayed the same disturbing trends. As economist Burton G. Malkiel has pointed out:

> From 1948 to 1973, the [net book value of capital equipment] per unit of labor grew at an annual rate of almost 3%. Since 1973, however, lower rates of private investment have led to a decline in that growth rate to

Exhibit 1.   Growth in Labor Productivity Since 1960 (United States and Abroad)

	Average Annual Percent Change	
	Manufacturing 1960–1978	All industries 1960–1976
United States	2.8%	1.7%
United Kingdom	2.9	2.2
Canada	4.0	2.1
Germany	5.4	4.2
France	5.5	4.3
Italy	5.0	4.9
Belgium	6.9ᵃ	—
Netherlands	6.9ᵃ	—
Sweden	5.2	—
Japan	8.2	7.5

Source: Council on Wage and Price Stability, *Report on Productivity* (Washington, D.C.: Executive Office of the President, July 1979).
1960–1977

Exhibit 2.   Growth of Labor Productivity by Sector, 1948–1978

Time Sector	Growth of Labor Productivity (Annual Average Percent)		
	1948–65	1965–73	1973–78
Private business	3.2%	2.3%	1.1%
Agriculture, forestry, and fisheries	5.5	5.3	2.9
Mining	4.2	2.0	−4.0
Construction	2.9	−2.2	−1.8
Manufacturing	3.1	2.4	1.7
Durable goods	2.8	1.9	1.2
Nondurable goods	3.4	3.2	2.4
Transportation	3.3	2.9	0.9
Communication	5.5	4.8	7.1
Electric, gas, and sanitary services	6.2	4.0	0.1
Trade	2.7	3.0	0.4
Wholesale	3.1	3.9	0.2
Retail	2.4	2.3	0.8
Finance, insurance, and real estate	1.0	−0.3	1.4
Services	1.5	1.9	0.5
Government enterprises	−0.8	0.9	−0.7

Source: Bureau of Labor Statistics.
Note: Productivity data for services, construction, finance, insurance, and real estate are unpublished.

> 1.75%. Moreover, the recent composition of investment [in 1978] has been skewed toward equipment and relatively short-term projects and away from structures and relatively long-lived investments. Thus our industrial plant has tended to age. . . .[3]

Other studies have shown that growth in the incremental capital equipment-to-labor ratio has fallen to about one-third of its value in the early 1960s. By contrast, between 1966 and 1976 capital investment as a percentage of GNP in France and West Germany was more than 20% greater than that in the United States; in Japan the percentage was almost double ours.

To attribute this relative loss of technological vigor to such things as shortage of capital in the United States is not justified. As Malkiel and others have shown, the return on equity of American business (out of which comes the capital necessary for investment) is about the same today as 20 years ago, *even after adjusting for inflation.* However, investment in both new equipment and R&D, as a percentage of GNP, was significantly higher 20 years ago than today.

The conclusion is painful but must be faced. Responsibility for this

Exhibit 3.   National Expenditures for Performance of R&D as a Percentage of GNP by Country, 1961–1978*

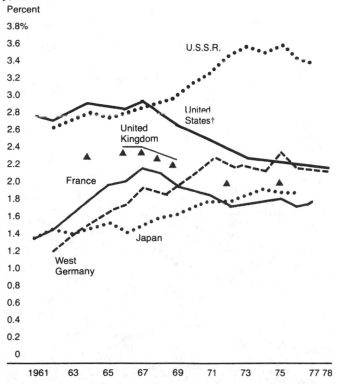

*Gross expenditures for performance of R&D including associated capital expenditures.
†Detailed information on capital expenditures for R&D is not available for the United States. Estimates for the period 1972-1977 show that their inclusion would have an impact of less than one-tenth of 1% for each year.
Source: *Science Indicators – 1978* (Washington, D.C.: National Science Foundation, 1979), p. 6.
Note: The latest data may be preliminary or estimates.

competitive listlessness belongs not just to a set of external conditions but also to the attitudes, preoccupations, and practices of American managers. By their preference for servicing existing markets rather than creating new ones and by their devotion to short-term returns and "management by the numbers," many of them have effectively forsworn long-term technological superiority as a competitive weapon. In consequence, they have abidcated their strategic responsibilities.

The New Management Orthodoxy

We refuse to believe that this managerial failure is the result of a sudden psychological shift among American managers toward a "super-safe, no

Exhibit 4.   Industrial R&D Expenditures for Basic Research, Applied Research, and Development, 1960–1978 (in $ millions)

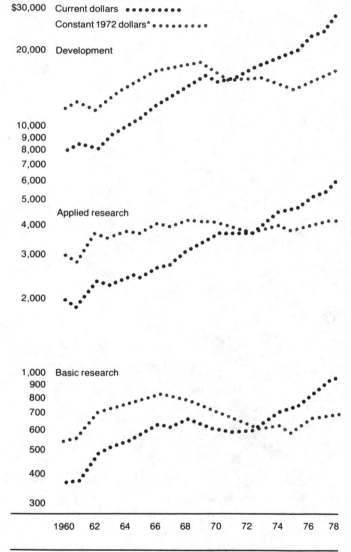

*GNP implicit price deflators used to convert current dollars to constant 1972 dollars.
Source: *Science Indicators – 1978*, p. 87.
Note: Preliminary data are shown for 1977 and estimates for 1978.

risk'' mind set. No profound sea change in the character of thousands of individuals could have occurred in so organized a fashion or have produced so consistent a pattern of behavior. Instead we believe that during the past two decades American managers have increasingly relied on principles which prize analytical detachment and methodological elegance over insight, based on experience, into the subtleties and complexities of strategic decisions.

As a result, maximum short-term financial returns have become the overriding criteria for many companies.

For purposes of discussion, we may divide this *new* management orthodoxy into three general categories: financial control, corporate portfolio management, and market-driven behavior.

Financial Control

As more companies decentralize their organizational structures, they tend to fix on profit centers as the primary unit of managerial responsibility. This development necessitates, in turn, greater dependence on short-term financial measurements like return on investment (ROI) for evaluating the performance of individual managers and management groups. Increasing the structural distance between those entrusted with exploiting actual competitive opportunities and those who must judge the quality of their work virtually guarantees reliance on objectively quantifiable short-term criteria.

Although innovation, the lifeblood of any vital enterprise, is best encouraged by an environment that does not unduly penalize failure, the predictable result of relying too heavily on short-term financial measures—a sort of managerial remote control—is an environment in which no one feels he or she can afford a failure or even a momentary dip in the bottom line.

Corporate Portfolio Management

This preoccupation with control draws support from modern theories of financial portfolio management. Originally developed to help balance the overall risk and return of stock and bond portfolios, these principles have been applied increasingly to the creation and management of corporate portfolios—that is, a cluster of companies and product lines assembled through various modes of diversification under a single corporate umbrella. When applied by a remote group of dispassionate experts primarily concerned with finance and control and lacking hands-on experience, the analytic formulas of portfolio theory push managers even further toward an extreme of caution in allocating resources.

"Especially in large organizations," reports one manager, "we are observing an increase in management behavior which I would regard as excessively cautious, even passive; certainly overanalytical; and, in general, characterized by a studied unwillingness to assume responsibility and even reasonable risk."

Market-Driven Behavior

In the past 20 years, American companies have perhaps learned too well a lesson they had long been inclined to ignore: businesses should be customer oriented rather than product oriented. Henry Ford's famous dictum that the public could have any color automobile it wished as long as the color was black has since given way to its philosophical opposite: "We have got to stop marketing makeable products and learn to make marketable products."

At last, however, the dangers of too much reliance on this philosophy are becoming apparent. As two Canadian researchers have put it:

> Inventors, scientists, engineers, and academics, in the normal pursuit of scientific knowledge, gave the world in recent times the laser, xerography, instant photography, and the transistor. In contrast, worshippers of the marketing concept have bestowed upon mankind such products as new-fangled potato chips, feminine hygiene deodorant, and the pet rock. . . .[4]

The argument that no new product ought to be introduced without managers undertaking a market analysis is common sense. But the argument that consumer analyses and formal market surveys should dominate other considerations when allocating resources to product development is untenable. It may be useful to remember that the initial market estimate for computers in 1945 projected total worldwide sales of only ten units. Similarly, even the most carefully researched analysis of consumer preferences for gas-guzzling cars in an era of gasoline abundance offers little useful guidance to today's automobile manufacturers in making wise product investment decisions. Customers may know what their needs are, but they often define those needs in terms of existing products, processes, markets, and prices.

Deferring to a market-driven strategy without paying attention to its limitations is, quite possibly, opting for customer satisfaction and lower risk in the short run at the expense of superior products in the future. Satisfied customers are critically important, of course, but not if the strategy for creating them is responsible as well for unnecessary product proliferation, inflated costs, unfocused diversification, and a lagging commitment to new technology and new capital equipment.

Three Managerial Decisions

These are serious charges to make. But the unpleasant fact of the matter is that, however useful these new principles may have been initially, if carried too far they are bad for U.S. business. Consider, for example, their effect on three major kinds of choices regularly faced by corporate managers: the decision between imitative and innovative product design, the decision to integrate backward, and the decision to invest in process development.

Imitative Versus Innovative Product Design

A market-driven strategy requires new product ideas to flow from detailed market analysis or, at least, to be extensively tested for consumer reaction before actual introduction. It is no secret that these requirements add significant delays and costs to the introduction of new products. It is less well known that they also predispose managers toward developing products for existing markets and toward product designs of a imitative rather than an innovative nature. There is increasing evidence that market-driven strategies tend, over time, to dampen the general level of innovation in new product decisions.

Confronted with the choice between innovation and imitation, managers typically ask whether the marketplace shows any consistent preference for innovative products. If so, the additional funding they require may be economically justified; if not, those funds can more properly go to advertising, promoting, or reducing the prices of less-advanced products. Though the temptation to allocate resources so as to strengthen performance in existing products and markets is often irresistible, recent studies by J. Hugh Davidson and others confirm the strong market attractiveness of innovative products.[5]

Nonetheless, managers having to decide between innovative and imitative product design face a difficult series of marketing-related trade-offs. Exhibit 5 summarizes these trade-offs.

By its very nature, innovative design is, as Joseph Schumpeter observed a long time ago, initially destructive of capital—whether in the form of labor skills, management systems, technological processes, or capital equipment. It tends to make obsolete existing investments in both marketing and manufacturing organizations. For the managers concerned it represents the choice of uncertainty (about economic returns, timing, etc.) over relative predictability, exchanging the reasonable expectation of current income against

Exhibit 5. Trade-offs Between Imitative and Innovative Design for an Established Product Line

Imitative Design	Innovative Design
Market demand is relatively well known and predictable.	Potentially large but unpredictable demand; the risk of a flop is also large.
Market recognition and acceptance are rapid.	Market acceptance may be slow initially, but the imitative response of competitors may also be slowed.
Readily adaptable to existing market, sales, and distribution policies.	May require unique, tailored marketing distribution and sales policies to educate customers or because of special repair and warranty problems.
Fits with existing market segmentation and product policies.	Demand may cut across traditional marketing segments, disrupting divisional responsibilities and cannibalizing other products.

the promise of high future value. It is the choice of the gambler, the person willing to risk much to gain even more.

Conditioned by a market-driven strategy and held closely to account by a "results now" ROI-oriented control system, American managers have increasingly refused to take the chance on innovative product/market development. As one of them confesses: "In the last year, on the basis of high capital risk, I turned down new products at a rate at least twice what I did a year ago. But in every case I tell my people to go back and bring me some new product ideas."[6] In truth, they have learned caution so well that many are in danger of forgetting that market-driven, follow-the-leader companies usually end up following the rest of the pack as well.

Backward Integration

Sometimes the problem for managers is not their reluctance to take action and make investments but that, when they do so, their action has the unintended result of reinforcing the status quo. In deciding to integrate backward because of apparent short-term rewards, managers often restrict their ability to strike out in innovative directions in the future.

Consider, for example, the case of a manufacturer who purchases a major component from an outside company. Static analysis of production economies may very well show that backward integration offers rather substantial cost benefits. Eliminating certain purchasing and marketing functions, centralizing overhead, pooling R&D efforts and resources, coordinating design and production of both product and component, reducing uncertainty over design changes, allowing for the use of more specialized equipment and labor skills—in all these ways and more, backward integration holds out to management the promise of significant short-term increases in ROI.

These efficiencies may be achieved by companies with commoditylike products. In such industries as ferrous and nonferrous metals or petroleum, backward integration toward raw materials and supplies tends to have a strong, positive effect on profits. However, the situation is markedly different for companies in more technologically active industries. Where there is considerable exposure to rapid technological advances, the promised value of backward integration becomes problematic. It may provide a quick, short-term boost to ROI figures in the next annual report, but it may also paralyze the long-term ability of a company to keep on top of technological change.

The real competitive threats to technologically active companies arise less from changes in ultimate consumer preference than from abrupt shifts in component technologies, raw materials, or production processes. Hence those managers whose attention is too firmly directed toward the marketplace and near-term profits may suddenly discover that their decision to make rather than buy important parts has locked their companies into an outdated technology.

Further, as supply channels and manufacturing operations become more systematized, the benefits from attempts to "rationalize" production may well be accompanied by unanticipated side effects. For instance, a company may find itself shut off from the R&D efforts of various independent suppliers by becoming their competitor. Similarly, the commitment of time and resources needed to master technology back up the channel of supply may distract a company from doing its own job well. Such was the fate of Bowmar, the pocket calculator pioneer, whose attempt to integrate backward into semiconductor production so consumed management attention that final assembly of the calculators, its core business, did not get the required resources.

Long-term contracts and long-term relationships with suppliers can achieve many of the same cost benefits as backward integration without calling into question a company's ability to innovate or respond to innovation. European automobile manufacturers, for example, have typically chosen to rely on their suppliers in this way; American companies have followed the path of backward integration. The resulting trade-offs between production efficiencies and innovative flexibility should offer a stern warning to those American managers too easily beguiled by the lure of short-term ROI improvement. A case in point: the U.S. auto industry's huge investment in automating the manufacture of castiron brake drums probably delayed by more than five years its transition to disc brakes.

Process Development

In an era of management by the numbers, many American managers—especially in mature industries—are reluctant to invest heavily in the development of new manufacturing processes. When asked to explain their reluctance, they tend to respond in fairly predictable ways. "We can't afford to design new capital equipment for just our own manufacturing needs" is one frequent answer. So is: "The capital equipment producers do a much better job, and they can amortize their development costs over sales to many companies." Perhaps most common is: "Let the others experiment in manufacturing; we can learn from their mistakes and do it better."

Each of these comments rests on the assumption that essential advances in process technology can be appropriated more easily through equipment purchase than through in-house equpiment design and development. Our extensive conversations with the managers of European (primarily German) technology-based companies have convinced us that this assumption is not as widely shared abroad as in the United States. Virtually across the board, the European managers impressed us with their strong commitment to increasing market share through internal development of advanced process technology—even when their suppliers were highly responsive to technological advances.

By contrast, American managers tend to restrict investments in process development to only those items likely to reduce costs in the short run. Not all are happy with this. As one disgruntled executive told us: "For too long

U.S. managers have been taught to set low priorities on mechanization projects, so that eventually divestment appears to be the best way out of manufacturing difficulties. Why?

> The drive for short-term success has prevented managers from looking thoroughly into the matter of special manufacturing equipment, which has to be invented, developed, tested, redesigned, reproduced, improved, and so on. That's a long process, which needs experienced, knowledgeable, and dedicated people who stick to their jobs over a considerable period of time. Merely buying new equipment (even if it is possible) does not often give the company any advantage over competitors.

We agree. Most American managers seem to forget that, even if they produce new products with their existing process technology (the same "cookie cutter" everyone else can buy), their competitors will face a relatively short lead time for introducing similar products. And as Eric von Hippel's studies of industrial innovation show, the innovations on which new industrial equipment is based usually originate with the user of the equipment and not with the equipment producer.[7] In other words, companies can make products more profitable by investing in the development of their own process technology. Proprietary processes are every bit as formidable competitive weapons as proprietary products.

The American Managerial Ideal

Two very important questions remain to be asked: (1) Why should so many American managers have shifted so strongly to this new managerial orthodoxy? and (2) Why are they not more deeply bothered by the ill effects of those principles on the long-term technological competitiveness of their companies? To answer the first question, we must take a look at the changing career patterns of American managers during the past quarter century; to answer the second, we must understand the way in which they have come to regard their professional roles and responsibilities as managers.

The Road to the Top

During the past 25 years the American manager's road to the top has changed significantly. No longer does the typical career, threading sinuously up and through a corporation with stops in several functional areas, provide future top executives with intimate hands-on knowledge of the company's technologies, customers, and suppliers.

Exhibit 6 summarizes the currently available data on the shift in functional background of newly appointed presidents of the 100 largest U.S. corporations. The immediate significance of these figures is clear. Since the mid-1950s there has been a rather substantial increase in the percentage of

Exhibit 6.   Changes in the Professional Origins of Corporate Presidents (percentage changes from baseline years, 1948–1952, for top 100 U.S. companies)

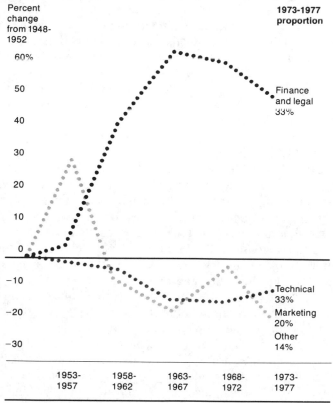

Source: Golightly & Co. International (1978).

new company presidents whose primary interests and expertise lie in the financial and legal areas and not in production. In the view of C. Jackson Grayson, president of the American Productivity Center, American management has for 20 years "coasted off the great R&D gains made during World War II, and constantly rewarded executives from the marketing, financial and legal sides of the business while it ignored the production men. Today [in business schools] courses in the production area are almost nonexistent."[8]

In addition, companies are increasingly choosing to fill new top management posts from outside their own ranks. In the opinion of foreign observers, who are still accustomed to long-term careers in the same company or division, "high-level American executives . . . seem to come and go and switch around as if playing a game of musical chairs at an Alice in Wonderland tea party."

Far more important, however, than any absolute change in numbers is the shift in the general sense of what an aspiring manager has to be "smart about" to make it to the top. More important still is the broad change in attitude such trends both encourage and express. What has developed, in the business community as in academia, is a preoccupation with a false and shallow concept of the professional manager, a "pseudo-professional" really— an individual having no special expertise in any particular industry or technology who nevertheless can step into an unfamiliar company and run it successfully through strict application of financial controls, portfolio concepts, and a market-driven strategy.

The Gospel of Pseudo-Professionalism

In recent years, this idealization of pseudo-professionalism has taken on something of the quality of a corporate religion. Its first doctrine, appropriately enough, is that neither industry experience nor hands-on technological expertise counts for very much. At one level, of course, this doctrine helps to salve the conscience of those who lack them. At another, more disturbing level it encourages the faithful to make decisions about technological matters simply as if they were adjuncts to finance or marketing decisions. We do not believe that the technological issues facing managers today can be meaningfully addressed without taking into account marketing or financial considerations; on the other hand, neither can they be resolved with the same methodologies applied to these other fields.

Complex modern technology has its own inner logic and development imperatives. To treat it as if it were something else—no matter how comfortable one is with that other kind of data—is to base a competitive business on a two-legged stool, which must, no matter how excellent the balancing act, inevitably fall to the ground.

More disturbing still, true believers keep the faith on a day-to-day basis by insisting that as issues rise up the managerial hierarchy for decision, they be progressively distilled into easily quantifiable terms. One European manager, in recounting to us his experiences in a joint venture with an American company, recalled with exasperation that "U.S. managers want everything to be simple. But sometimes business situations are not simple, and they cannot be divided up or looked at in such a way that they become simple. They are messy, and one must try to understand all the facets. This appears to be alien to the American mentality."

The purpose of good organizational design, of course, is to divide responsibilities in such a way that individuals have relatively easy tasks to perform. But then these differentiated responsibilities must be pulled together by sophisticated, broadly gauged integrators at the top of the managerial pyramid. If these individuals are interested in but one or two aspects of the total competitive picture, if their training includes a very narrow exposure to the range of functional specialties, if—worst of all—they are devoted simplifiers themselves, who will do the necessary integration? Who will attempt to resolve complicated issues rather than try to uncomplicate them artificially? At the strategic level there are no such things as pure production problems, pure financial problems, or pure marketing problems.

Merger Mania

When executive suites are dominated by people with financial and legal skills, it is not surprising that top management should increasingly allocate time and energy to such concerns as cash management and the whole process of corporate acquisitions and mergers. This is indeed what has happened. In 1978 alone there were some 80 mergers involving companies with assets in excess of $100 million each; in 1979 there were almost 100. This represents roughly $20 billion in transfers of large companies from one owner to another—two-thirds of the total amount spent on R&D by American industry.

In 1978 *Business Week* ran a cover story on cash management in which it stated that "the 400 largest U.S. companies together have more than $60 billion in cash—almost triple the amount they had at the beginning of the 1970s." The article also described the increasing attention devoted to—and the sophisticated and exotic techniques used for—managing this cash hoard.

There are perfectly good reasons for this flurry of activity. It is entirely natural for financially (or legally) trained managers to concentrate on essentially financial (or legal) activities. It is also natural for managers who subscribe to the portfolio "law of large numbers" to seek to reduce total corporate risk by parceling it out among a sufficiently large number of separate product lines, businesses, or technologies. Under certain conditions it may very well make good economic sense to buy rather than build new plants or modernize existing ones. Mergers are obviously an exciting game; they tend to produce fairly quick and decisive results, and they offer the kind of public recognition that helps careers along. Who can doubt the appeal of the titles awarded by the financial community; being called a "gunslinger," "white knight," or "raider" can quicken anyone's blood.

Unfortunately, the general American penchant for separating and simplifying has tended to encourage a diversification away from core technologies and markets to a much greater degree than is true in Europe or Japan. U.S managers appear to have an inordinate faith in the portfolio law of large numbers—that is, by amassing enough product lines, technologies, and businesses, one will be cushioned against the random setbacks that occur in life. This might be true for portfolios of stocks and bonds, where there is considerable evidence that setbacks *are* random. Businesses, however, are subject not only to random setbacks such as strikes and shortages but also to carefully orchestrated attacks by competitors, who focus all their resources and energies on one set of activities.

Worse, the great bulk of this merger activity appears to have been absolutely wasted in terms of generating economic benefits for stockholders. Acquisition experts do not necessarily make good managers. Nor can they increase the value of their shares by merging two companies any better than their shareholders could do individually by buying shares of the acquired company on the open market (at a price usually below that required for a takeover attempt).

There appears to be a growing recognition of this fact. A number of U.S. companies are now divesting themselves of previously acquired companies; others (for example, W.R. Grace) are proposing to break themselves up into relatively independent entities. The establishment of a strong competitive position through in-house technological superiority is by nature a long, arduous, and often unglamorous task. But it is what keeps a business vigorous and competitive.

The European Example

Gaining competitive success through technological superiority is a skill much valued by the seasoned European (and Japanese) managers with whom we talked. Although we were able to locate few hard statistics on their actual practice, our extensive investigations of more than 200 companies convinced us that European managers do indeed tend to differ significantly from their American counterparts. In fact, we found that many of them were able to articulate these differences quite clearly.

In the first place, European managers think themsleves more pointedly concerned with how to survive over the long run under intensely competitive conditions. Few markets, of course, generate price competition as fierce as in the United States, but European companies face the remorseless necessity of exporting to other national markets or perishing.

The figures here are startling: manufactured product exports represent more than 35% of total manufacturing sales in France and Germany and nearly 60% in the Benelux countries, as against not quite 10% in the United States. In these export markets, moreover, European products must hold their own against "world class" competitiors, lower-priced products from developing countries, and American products selling at attractive devalued dollar prices. To survive this competitive squeeze, European managers feel they must place central emphasis on producing technologically superior products.

Further, the kinds of pressures from European labor unions and national governments virtually force them to take a consistently long-term view in decision-making. German managers, for example, must negotiate major decisions at the plant level with worker-dominated works councils; in turn, these decisions are subject to review by supervisory boards (roughly equivalent to American boards of directors), half of whose membership is worker elected. Together with strict national legislation, the pervasive influence of labor unions makes it extremely difficult to change employment levels or production locations. Not surprisingly, labor costs in Northern Europe have more than doubled in the past decade and are now the highest in the world.

To be successful in this environment of strictly constrained options,

European managers feel they must employ a decision-making apparatus that grinds very fine—and very deliberately. They must simply outthink and outmanage their competitiors. Now, American managers also have their strategic options hedged about by all kinds of restrictions. But those restrictions have not yet made them as conscious as their European counterparts of the long-term implications of their day-to-day decisions.

As a result, the Europeans see themselves as investing more heavily in cutting-edge technology than the Americans. More often than not, this investment is made to create new product opportunities in advance of consumer demand and not merely in response to market-drive strategy. In case after case, we found the Europeans striving to develop the products and process capabilities with which to lead markets and not simply responding to the current demands of the marketplace. Moreover, in doing this they seem less inclined to integrate backward and more likely to see maximum leverage from stable, long-term relationships with suppliers.

Having never lost sight of the need to be technologically competitive over the long run, European and Japanese managers are extremely careful to make the necessary arrangements and investments today. And their daily concern with the rather basic issue of long-term survival adds perspective to such matters as short-term ROI or rate of growth. The time line by which they manage is long, and it has made them painstakingly attentive to the means for keeping their companies technologically competitive. Of course they pay attention to the numbers. Their profit margins are usually lower than ours, their debt ratios higher. Every tenth of a percent is critical to them. But they are also aware that tomorrow will be no better unless they constantly try to develop new processes, enter new markets, and offer superior—even unique—products. As one senior German executive phrased it recently, "We look at rates of return, too, but only after we ask 'Is it a good product?' "[9]

Creating Economic Value

Americans traveling in Europe and Asia soon learn they must often deal with criticism of our country. Being forced to respond to such criticism can be healthy, for it requires rethinking some basic issues of principle and practice.

We have much to be proud about and little to be ashamed of relative to most other countries. But sometimes the criticism of others is uncomfortably close to the mark. The comments of our overseas competitors on American business practices contain enough truth to require our thoughtful consideration. What is behind the decline in competitiveness of U.S. business? Why do U.S. companies have such apparent difficulties competing with foreign producers of established products, many of which originated in the United States?

For example, Japanese televisions dominate some market segments, even though many U.S. producers now enjoy the same low labor cost advantages of offshore production. The German machine tool and automotive producers continue their inroads into U.S. domestic markets, even though their labor rates are now higher than those in the United States and the famed German worker in German factories is almost as likely to be Turkish or Italian as German.

The responsibility for these problems may rest in part on government policies that either overconstrain or undersupport U.S. producers. But if our foreign critics are correct, the long-term solution to America's problems may not be correctable simply by changing our government's tax laws, monetary policies, and regulatory practices. It will also require some fundamental changes in management attitudes and practices.

It would be an oversimplification to assert that the only reason for the decline in competitiveness of U.S. companies is that our managers devote too much attention and energy to using existing resources more efficiently. It would also oversimplify the issue, although possibly to a lesser extent, to say that it is due purely and simply to their tendency to neglect technology as a competitive weapon.

Companies cannot become more innovative simply by increasing R&D investments or by conducting more basic research. Each of the decisions we have described directly affects several functional areas of management, and major conflicts can only be reconciled at senior executive levels. The benefits favoring the more innovative, aggressive option in each case depend more on intangible factors than do their efficiency-oriented alternatives.

Senior managers who are less informed about their industry and its confederation of parts suppliers, equipment suppliers, workers, and customers or who have less time to consider the long-term implications of their interactions are likely to exhibit a noninnovative bias in their choices. Tight financial controls with a short-term emphasis will also bias choices toward the less innovative, less technologically aggressive alternatives.

The key to long-term success—even survival—in business is what it has always been: to invest, to innovate, to lead, to create value where none existed before. Such determination, such striving to excel, requires leaders— not *just* controllers, market analysts, and portfolio managers. In our preoccupation with the braking systems and exterior trim, we may have neglected the drive trains of our corporations.

Notes

1. Ryohei Suzuki, "Worldwide Expansion of U.S. Exports—A Japanese View," *Sloan Management Review*, Spring 1979, p. 1.

2. *Business Week*, February 16, 1976, p. 57.

3. Burton G. Malkiel, "Productivity—The Problem Behind the Headlines," *HBR*, May–June 1979, p. 81.

4. Roger Bennett and Robert Cooper, "Beyond the Marketing Concept," *Business Horizons*, June 1979, p. 76.

5. J. Hugh Davidson, "Why Most New Consumer Brands Fail," *HBR*, March–April 1976, p. 117.

6. *Business Week*, February 16, 1976, p. 57.

7. Eric von Hippel, "The Dominant Role of Users in the Scientific Instrument Innovation Process," MIT Sloan School of Management Working Paper 75–764, January 1975.

8. *Dun's Review*, July 1978, p. 39.

9. *Business Week*, March 3, 1980, p. 76.

About the Authors

William J. Abernathy is the William Harding Professor of Business Administration at the Harvard Business School. He attended the University of Tennessee where he received his BS in electrical engineering in 1955. He later attended the Harvard Business School where he received his MBA (1964) and DBA (1967). After teaching at UCLA he accepted an appointment at Stanford University. In 1972, Mr. Abernathy accepted an appointment at the Harvard Business School, where he now teaches. Mr. Abernathy has published numerous articles as well as several books, including The Productivity Dilemma, *and* Government, Technology and the Future of the Automobile. *He is in* Who's Who in America, *is involved with the National Academy of Science and Engineering as Panel Chairman, and consults for several Fortune 500 companies.*

M. Jack Anderson, Jr. was a marketing manager for IBM when he and J. Elizabeth Harris wrote "Strategies for Low Market-Share Businesses."

Kenneth R. Andrews is the Donald K. David Professor of Business Administration at the Harvard Business School, chairman of the general management faculty, and editor of Harvard Business Review. *He is a director of several corporations, writes in the field of business policy, and is doing research on corporate governance and the management of corporate boards of directors.*

Melvin Anshen is Paul Garrett Professor of Public Policy and Business Responsibility at Columbia University. He is the author of Strategies for Corporate Social Performance *and has published articles in* Harvard Business Review, Management Science, *and* The Journal of Marketing.

Norman A. Berg has been on the faculty of the Harvard Business School since 1963; when he wrote this article, he was much involved in the problems of strategic planning in diversified companies. He teaches in the general management area and has been active as a consultant and as a director of

543

a number of companies. He is co-author of the casebook Policy Formulation and Administration *and author of* General Management: An Analytical Approach.

Robert D. Buzzell *is Sebastian S. Kresge Professor of Business Administration at the Harvard Business School. A member of the HBS faculty since 1961, Mr. Buzzell previously taught at the Ohio State University. In 1967, he was Visiting Professor at the European Institute of Business Administration (INSEAD), Fontainebleau, France. He received his PhD degree from Ohio State in 1957. Mr. Buzzell has written books and articles on a variety of topics related to marketing management, strategic planning, marketing research, international marketing, and public policy issues. Among his recent publications are* Marketing: A Contemporary Analysis, Marketing Research and Information Systems *and* Product Innovation in Food Processing. *Articles by Mr. Buzzell have appeared in* Harvard Business Review, Journal of Marketing, Journal of Marketing Research, *and* Journal of Advertising Research.

E. Raymond Corey *is the Malcolm P. McNair Professor of Marketing at the Harvard Business School. He is currently director of the division of research at the Harvard Business School. His outside professional associations include the American Marketing Association and the Marketing Science Institute, of which he is executive director. He is also a director of Norton Company, Itek Corporation, and Uniroyal, Inc. and has served as a marketing consultant to various companies. Mr. Corey is the author of several books in the field of marketing, including* The Development of Markets for New Materials; Organization Strategy: A Marketing Approach; Procurement Management: Strategy, Organization and Decision-Making; Problems in Marketing *(6th ed., written with Professors Scott Ward of Wharton and Christopher Lovelock of the Harvard Business School); and* Industrial Marketing: Cases and Concepts *(3rd ed.). Mr. Corey received his AB degree from Amherst College, MBA from the Harvard Business School, MA in economics and PhD in business economics from Harvard's Graduate School of Arts and Sciences.*

Peter F. Drucker *is a management consultant, specializing in economic and business policy and in top management organization. He has been consultant to several of the country's largest companies, as well as to leading companies abroad; to agencies of the U.S. government and to the governments of Canada and Japan; to public-service institutions such as universities and hospitals. Mr. Drucker has been Clarke Professor of Social Science and Management at Claremont Graduate School, Claremont, California, since 1971. He is also Professorial Lecturer in Oriental Art at Pomona College, one of The Claremont Colleges. From 1950 to 1972 Mr. Drucker was professor of Management at the Graduate Business School of New York University, where he still serves as Distinguished University Lecturer. Mr.*

Drucker was educated in Vienna and in England. His doctorate in public and international law is from Frankfurt University in Germany.

William E. Fruhan, Jr. *is a Professor of Business Administration at the Harvard Business School. He received his SB degree from Yale University and his MBA and DBA from Harvard University. Mr. Fruhan is the author of* Financial Strategy *and* The Fight for Competitive Advantage. *He is co-editor of* Case Problems in Finance. *In 1980 Mr. Fruhan won the Financial Analysts Federation's Graham and Dodd Award for his feature article entitled "Levitz Furniture: A Case History in the Creation and Destruction of Shareholder Value." Mr. Fruhan served as course head for finance in the first year of Harvard's MBA Program and as faculty chairman for the Corporate Financial Management executive education program.*

Bradley T. Gale *is the Director of Research of the Strategic Planning Institute (SPI) and a member of its Board of Trustees. Mr. Gale holds a BSEE degree from Worcester Polytechnic Institute and a PhD in economics from Rutgers. His recent publications include articles in* Harvard Business Review, Planning Review, *and* The Antitrust Bulletin.

Frederick W. Gluck *is a director and member of the senior management group of McKinsey & Company, Inc. He is responsible for McKinsey's ongoing development of approaches to solving top management problems, bringing together the firm's thinking on issues of strategy, operations, and organization. In addition, his work and interests have focused on the problems of managing international companies, strategic management, and the management of technology. He has published articles on managing technological change in* Harvard Business Review *and* Research Management. *Mr. Gluck holds a bachelors degree in electrical engineering from Manhattan College and a masters in electrical engineering from New York University.*

William K. Hall *is vice president of North American Marketing Operations at the Cummins Engine Company. He is responsible for the areas of parts and service, North American automotive and industrial business, North American field sales, service advertising, and sales promotion, and the Lowest Total Cost Program. Previously he was a professor at the Graduate School of Business, University of Michigan. Mr. Hall has been a consultant on corporate strategy, general management problems, and executive development to a variety of corporations and government agencies. He received his PhD in business administration from the University of Michigan.*

J. Elizabeth Harris *was a consultant for the Southern Agricultural Corporation when she wrote* Strategies for Low Market-Share Businesses *with Richard G. Hamermesh and M. Jack Anderson, Jr.*

Philippe Haspeslagh *is an assistant professor of business policy at INSEAD,* *graduate of the University of Louvain (Belgium). He also holds masters degrees in business administration from the University of Ghent (Belgium) and the Harvard Business School, where he was a Baker scholar. His research and teaching interests are in the area of industry analysis and competitive strategy as well as strategic management in diversified companies. His previous experience includes general management consulting work with PA Management Consultants and McKinsey and Company, as well as a year as attache in the services of the Belgian Prime Minister for the Programmation of Scientific Policy. His latest publications are "Portfolio Planning: Uses and Limits,"* Harvard Business Review *and with W. H. Davidson, "Pitfalls of the Global Product Structure" (both in the* Harvard Business Review).

Robert H. Hayes *is Professor of Business Administration at the Harvard Business School, where he teaches courses in manufacturing strategy and production and operations management. He received his BA from Wesleyan University in 1958, his MS from Stanford University in 1962, and his PhD degree in 1966, also from Stanford. Mr. Hayes' current research is concerned with the facilities investment and productivity improvement activities of manufacturing companies, both here and abroad. He recently completed two years as the faculty chairman for Harvard's International Senior Managers' Program in Vevey, Switzerland, where he studied and worked with a number of European companies.*

Donald F. Heany *is Director–Special Study Program of the Strategic Planning Institute of Cambridge, Massachusetts. He has been consulting on corporate strategy, business strategy, and tactical planning since 1973. Prior to that he was a member of General Electric's corporate planning staff.*

John M. Hobbs *works with General Electric's atomic energy group. Prior to this assignment he was a projects manager for manufacturing consulting with Corporate Consulting Services.*

Thomas M. Hout *is vice president of the Boston Consulting Group. He was educated at Yale, Stanford, and University of Manchester (England). Mr Hout joined BCG in 1969 and has been a president in the firm's London and Tokyo offices. He has published articles in* Foreign Affairs, Wall Street Journal, *and* Harvard Business Review *and is co-author of* Japanese Industrial Policy.

Rosabeth Moss Kanter *is a professor of sociology and organization and management at Yale University, where she conducts research on organization design and change processes. She is the author of* Men and Women of the Corporation. *Her article "Power Failure in Management Circuits" was a 1979 McKinsey Award Winner. Ms. Kanter's most recent book is* The Change Masters: Innovation for Productivity in the American Mode. *She is* *also Chairman of the Board of Goodmeasure, Inc., a Cambridge management consulting firm.*

Stephen P. Kaufman *holds a BS degree in economics and engineering from MIT and an MBA from the Harvard Business School. He was a management consultant with McKinsey & Company, Inc. and a group vice president with the Midland-Ross Corporation in Cleveland, Ohio. He currently is president of the Arrow Electronics Distribution Division and a vice president of the corporate parent, Arrow Electronics.*

John D. Kennell *has been director, planning of the Sun Gas Division of Sun Exploration & Production Co. in Dallas since 1980. Mr. Kennell received a BS in mathematics from Pittsburg (Kansas) State University in 1965 and an MS in computer science from the University of Missouri-Rolla in 1967. He is a member of the Planning Executives Institute and the North AmericanSociety for Corporate Planning.*

Philip Kotler *is the Harold T. Martin Professor of Marketing at the J. L. Kellogg Graduate School of Management of Northwestern University. Mr. Kotler has published extensively in leading business journals and is the author of* Marketing Management: Analysis, Planning and Control *(4th ed.),* Principles of Marketing *(2nd ed.), and* Marketing for Nonprofit Organizations *(2nd ed.). He is a former director of the American Marketing Association and a current director of the Marketing Science Institute. He is listed in* Who's Who in America.

Robert E. Linneman *is on the Faculty at the School of Business Administration, Temple University. Besides his academic work, Mr. Linneman has been in industrial sales, a senior consultant for consulting firms in Philadelphia and New York, a director of marketing for a major bank, and participated in marketing and planning projects at over 40 companies. He has worked with a number of companies—ranging in size from 35 employees to a firm with $700 million in sales—in setting up their corporate planning processes. A frequent speaker at executive development marketing and planning seminars, he has given a series of executive development seminars on a shirtsleeve approach to long-range strategic planning at a number of leading universities, including California Institute of Technology, Southern Methodist University and Vanderbilt. Mr. Linneman is the author of numerous publications which have appeared in various professional journals, including* Harvard Business Review, Long Range Planning, Sloan Management Review, *and the* Journal of Marketing. *He is the author of the book,* A Shirt-Sleeve Approach to Long Range Planning, *which is an expansion of this article. In 1976, Mr. Linneman was a recipient of a Lindback award for distinguished teaching.*

Peter Lorange *is professor of management at the Wharton School, University of Pennsylvania. He is a specialist in strategic planning systems and pro-*

cesses. He has worked extensively with U.S.-based and international corporations. Mr. Lorange has written books and numerous articles on the subject of corporate planning and strategic management. His most recent books are Implementation of Strategic Planning *and* Corporate Planning: An Executive Viewpoint. *He received his undergraduate degree in economics and business administration from the Norwegian School of Economics and Business Administration, an MA degree in administrative science from Yale University, and he holds a PhD in business administration from the Harvard Business School.*

Jay W. Lorsch *is a professor at the Harvard Business School. He is the co-author (with Paul Lawrence) of* Organization and Environment.

Myles L. Mace *is a professor at the Harvard Business School.*

Henry Mintzberg *is Bronfman Professor of Management at McGill University, in Montreal, where he researches and writes on the internal processes of organizations as well as their role in society. His current work involves a study of patterns in strategy formation and a series of books under the general title* The Theory of Management Policy. *His better-known publications include* The Nature of Managerial Work, The Structuring of Organizations *(to appear in condensed form as* Structure in 5's). The Manager's Job: Folklore and Fact *was the winner of the McKinsey prize for 1975. Mr. Mintzberg holds his PhD and MS degrees from the Massachusetts Institute of Technology and his bachelors degree in engineering from McGill. He has lectured widely to management and academic groups in Europe and North and South America, and was elected a Fellow of the Royal Society of Canada in 1980, the first from a faculty of management.*

John J. Morse *is a professor at the UCLA Graduate School of Management.*

Edward G. Niblock *began his career as a financial planner after receiving his MBA from the Harvard Business School. He died suddenly of an aneurysm at age 32.*

Michael E. Porter *is professor at the Harvard Business School and a leading authority in the field of competitive strategy. He received a BSE from Princeton University, an MBA from Harvard where he was a George F. Baker Scholar, and a PhD in business economics from Harvard. Mr. Porter is the author of six books and numerous articles. His award winning* Competitive Strategy: Techniques for Analyzing Industries and Competitors *has been widely recognized as the premier work in its field. Mr. Porter serves as a director or strategic consultant to many U.S. and international companies.*

Eileen Rudden *is a manager with The Boston Consulting Group, which specializes in problems of competitive corporate strategy. Her international assignments have focused on the appropriate strategies for companies and* *countries in Europe, the United States, and Latin America. She holds an MBA from the Harvard Business School and a BA from Brown University.*

Malcolm S. Salter *teaches courses in general management and serves as head of the business policy teaching group at the Harvard Business School. He is an authority on the problems of managing diversified companies and is currently leading a major research project on national strategy and the U.S. auto industry. Mr. Salter is co-author of* New Alliances: The Politics of an American Industry, Policy Formulation and Administration, Diversification Through Acquisition, *and many articles addressing general management issues.*

William T. Sandalls, Jr. *was associated with Arthur Anderson & Company at the time "Balance 'Creativity' and 'Practicality' in Formal Planning" was written.*

John Shank *is the Arthur Young Professor of Accounting at the Ohio State University and chairman of the faculty of accounting. He has also taught at the Amos Tuck School at Dartmouth and the Harvard Business School, and has worked for two international accounting firms and as controller of a small manufacturing firm. He divides his professional efforts among teaching at Ohio State, researching topics in applied management accounting, and working as a consultant and seminar leader for corporations and non-profit institutions around the world.*

Steven B. Silk *is currently a senior product manager at General Foods. Formerly he was with Arthur Young & Company. Mr. Silk has an MBA from the Harvard Business School.*

Ralph G. M. Sultan *is chief economist at the Royal Bank of Canada.*

Seymour Tilles *taught at the Harvard Business School when he wrote* How to Evaluate Corporate Strategy. *He has also been a consultant to the United Nations and to business.*

Hugo E. R. Uyterhoeven *is Timken Professor of Business Administration and Senior Associate Dean for External Relations at the Harvard Business School. He has been active in the areas of executive development, strategic planning, corporate organization, and international business and is a director of several companies.*

Richard F. Vancil *is Lovett-Learned Professor of Business Administration at the Harvard Business School. He received his BS from Northwestern University in 1953 and his MBA (1955) and DBA (1960) from Harvard University. He joined the HBS faculty as an instructor in 1958 and was appointed professor in 1968. Mr. Vancil's professional interests are in the broad field of management systems, focusing particularly on resource allocation sys-*

tems and measurement systems. He is an author, co-author, or editor of more than twenty books and monographs, most recently Strategic Planning Systems *(1977) and* Decentralization: Managerial Ambiguity by Design *(1979). He has also contributed more than a dozen articles to* Harvard Business Review. *Mr. Vancil is active as a management consultant to large industrial corporations. In 1964 he founded Management Analysis Center, Inc., a management consulting firm, and currently serves as chairman of its board of directors. A director of Connecticut General Corporation since 1976, Mr. Vancil became a director of CIGNA Corporation as a result of the merger of CG and INA Corp. He also serves as the chairman of the Financial Resources Committee of CIGNA's board of directors.*

A. Steven Walleck *is a principal with the Cleveland office of McKinsey & Company, Inc. He joined McKinsey in 1971 with degrees from Harvard College and Harvard Business School. He has worked as a consultant in the United States, Europe, and Africa on a broad range of assignments, from corporate strategy and organization to sales force effectiveness. He currently leads McKinsey's manufacturing practice and is preparing several articles for publication on the subject of manufacturing automation, computer-aided engineering, and robotics.*

Herbert N. Woodward *was president of International Science Industries when he wrote "Management Strategies for Small Companies."*

H. Edward Wrapp *is a professor of business policy and a former dean, Graduate School of Business, at the University of Chicago. He was also a professor at the Harvard Business School. Mr. Wrapp is the author of several articles on general management and is the director of several companies. He is also a consultant of corporate strategy and management development.*

Abraham Zaleznik *is the Cahners-Rabb Professor of Social Psychology of Management at the Harvard Business School. He is also a psychoanalyst and an active member of the American Psychoanalytic Association. He is director of several corporations and a consultant to management. Mr. Zaleznik has written extensively on organizations and power. His most recent book, written with Manfred F. R. Kets DeVries, is* Power and the Corporate Mind.

Author Index

Subject Index